Flex Solutions
Essential Techniques for Flex 2 and 3 Developers

Marco Casario

DESIGNER TO DESIGNER™

an Apress® company

Flex Solutions: Essential Techniques for Flex 2 and 3 Developers

ISBN-13 (paperback): 978-1-59059-876-4

ISBN-13 (electronic): 978-1-4302-0424-4

Printed and bound in the United States of America 9 8 7 6 5 4 3 2

Distributed to the book trade worldwide by Springer-Verlag New York, Inc., 233 Spring Street, 6th Floor, New York, NY 10013. Phone 1-800-SPRINGER, fax 201-348-4505, e-mail orders-ny@springer-sbm.com, or visit www.springeronline.com.

For information on translations, please contact Apress directly at 2855 Telegraph Avenue, Suite 600, Berkeley, CA 94705. Phone 510-549-5930, fax 510-549-5939, e-mail info@apress.com, or visit www.apress.com.

The source code for this book is freely available to readers at www.friendsofed.com in the Downloads section.

Credits

Lead Editors Chris Mills, Ben Renow-Clarke	**Associate Production Director** Kari Brooks-Copony
Technical Reviewer David Williamson	**Production Editor** Kelly Winquist
Editorial Board Steve Anglin, Ewan Buckingham, Tony Campbell, Gary Cornell, Jonathan Gennick, Jason Gilmore, Kevin Goff, Jonathan Hassell, Matthew Moodie, Joseph Ottinger, Jeffrey Pepper, Ben Renow-Clarke, Dominic Shakeshaft, Matt Wade, Tom Welsh	**Compositor** Dina Quan **Artist** April Milne **Proofreader** Nancy Riddiough
Project Manager Beth Christmas	**Indexer** Toma Mulligan
Copy Editor Nancy Sixsmith	**Interior and Cover Designer** Kurt Krames
Manufacturing Director Tom Debolski	

To the memory of my grandmother, Maria.

CONTENTS AT A GLANCE

CONTENTS

CONTENTS

CONTENTS

ABOUT THE AUTHOR

Marco Casario is one of the most dynamic developers and consultants in the Adobe world. He has been passionate about Informatics since he was a child. Marco used to program games in Basic for the Commodore 64 before dedicating himself, while still very young, to innovative projects for the Web using Flash and Director (as far back as versions 3 and 5).

In 2001, Marco began to collaborate with Macromedia Italia. Since then he has produced and taken part in a long series of presentations, conferences, and articles, which you can find listed in detail in his blog, "Hands on Adobe World" (http://casario. blogs.com), which is currently receiving several thousand visitors every day.

In 2005, Marco founded Comtaste (www.comtaste.com), a company dedicated to exploring new frontiers in Rich Internet Applications and the convergence of the Web and the world of mobile devices. MobyMobile (www.mobymobile.com) and YouThru (www.youthru.com) are representatives of recent work.

Marco is also the founder of the biggest worldwide Flash Lite User Group (http://groups. yahoo.com/group/FlashLite/) and of www.augitaly.com, a reference point for the Italian community of Adobe users. He is Content Manager for the section dedicated to Flex (www.augitaly.com/flexgala).

Marco is currently busy working on the development (in Flex) of a very ambitious project concerning European bank counters. He is involved in various consulting and Flex and Flash Media Server training activities for the realization of Rich Internet Applications on behalf of buyers such as Capgemini, Engineering, IBM partners, and Adobe Systems Software Ireland Ltd.

Marco often speaks at national and international conferences such as Adobe MAX Conference, O'Reilly Web 2.0 Summit, 360Flex, FromAToWeb, AdobeLive, and many others.

ABOUT THE TECHNICAL REVIEWER

 **Dave Williamson** is a freelance Flash Platform developer with 10 years of industry experience in the production and deployment of rich media web sites and applications. He has worked for clients such as Ford, Intel, Adidas, Microsoft, and Sony.

Dave's work has been focused on the production and integration of Flash and Flash Platform–based technologies since 1997, with a special interest in developing localized application development and (more recently) in applications for cell phones and devices.

Dave has also provided worldwide training and consultancy around Flash Platform technologies for a number of companies, including Adobe and Telefonica.

Dave's mumblings and musing can be found on his blog at http://blog.bittube.com.

ACKNOWLEDGMENTS

Writing a book really is a huge undertaking. During the course of the journey, you often have the feeling that you will never reach the end. Not only because you are working at night after a long day at work and on weekends, but particularly because it is a task that absorbs all your ideas and requires constant and assiduous concentration. You often get to the point of removing yourself from reality and putting personal and working relationships with the people around you to the test. After you finish writing, you realize how much patience your work colleagues, your clients, your partners, and most importantly your family had to have to not turn their backs on you. I therefore want to acknowledge certain people who are particularly important to me and helped me during the writing of this book.

Thank you to my mother, who has always believed in me and pushed me to improve myself and to see beyond the surface of things. Thank you to my father, who finally understands that it is never too late to hang out with his son. Thank you to my brother, who answered my insufferable requests during the writing of this book and who is now in Australia enjoying himself.

Thank you to my beloved honey, Katia, whose patience was really put to the test. Being near me during this period was definitely more difficult than usual, but her unconditional love, support, and help were fundamental for encouraging me to go on. Thanks for inspiring me to do my best. I love you, darling.

Thank you to my partner, Raffaele, and my colleagues Emanuele, Constantine, and Francesco, who were often abandoned by me, but who knew how to take care of their own (and often my own) work commitments. We will do great things together.

Thank you to my friends Fabrizio, Renato, Daniele, Juri, Marmotta, and Alessio, who have not left my side even after all my refusals to their invitations because of this book.

A special thanks to Chris Mills, who gave me the opportunity to write this book and whose ideas and corrections have made it better.

Finally, an enormous thank you to the people who made this book possible and without whose help and tips it could not have been a success: Ben Renow-Clarke, Beth Christmas, and the staff at friends of ED. They are all passionate people whose primary job is to publish the very best.

INTRODUCTION

Adobe Flex has revolutionized the way in which Rich Internet Applications are developed and used. The Flex framework ecosystem has expanded to include Flash Player 9, the declarative MXML language, the new and updated ActionScript 3 language, the SDK, the charting components and the LiveCycle Data Services.

So we can define the Flex framework as a component-based development framework for delivering Rich Internet Applications for the Adobe Flash Player runtime.

I have been using Flex since its inception. As a Flash developer, I quickly understood the power behind Flex because it used the same development approach I used for Java development with Eclipse or Net Beans. No more timelines, poor debugging and code editor tools, or evil movie clips ☺.

Since I first opened Flex Builder and learned the basics of Flex, I've fallen in love with it: a framework to create Flash applications easily. Thank God. The first version of Flex suffered from Macromedia's poor market positioning of the technology (at that time, it was Macromedia, not Adobe). Flex 1 required an expensive server module to compile applications. How could I convince my boss to buy a Flex server just to make my life easier for Flash application development?

Things changed with the release of Flex 2.

Thanks to the new pricing model, the community of developers, the announcement of the release of Flex 3 as open source, and the power of the framework itself, the interest of Flex technology has increased worldwide.

The time was ripe to start thinking of sharing my knowledge and experiences in Flex development. It was almost one year ago when Chris Mills, the editor-in-chief at friends of ED, met me at the Flash On The Beach conference in Brighton, England to discuss writing a book on Flex. My idea of creating a book of built-in, ready-to-use solutions was accepted enthusiastically.

This book was a long journey, not only because of the number of Flex features but also because of the announcement of Flex 3 and Adobe Integrated Runtime (AIR) by Adobe. In fact, after working with the beta of Flex 3 and Adobe AIR, we realized that the new features and capabilities that the framework included should be covered.

So I stopped writing and updated all the solution examples to Flex 3 Beta 2. New solutions that covered Flex 3's new features were added as well as a full chapter dedicated to Adobe AIR.

The Flex framework is huge, so this book consists of the following diverse chapters:

- **Chapter 1**, "Flex Basics." This chapter discusses solutions for basic programming tasks such as data binding and the event model of Flex.

- **Chapter 2**, "Using Flex Components." This chapter discusses extending, customizing, and developing components with ActionScript 3.

- **Chapter 3**, "Working with Data Models and the Value Object." This chapter discusses how Flex manages data, how to work with complex MXML and ActionScript data, and how to convert ActionScript Classes as a data model.

- **Chapter 4**, "Validating and Formatting Data." This chapter discusses using and extending the Validator and Formatter classes to validate and format data.

- **Chapter 5**, "Managing Complex Data." This chapter discusses working with complex data using the new Collection classes, applying sort-and-filter operations to data, and using the Cursor class to move through the collection.

- **Chapter 6**, "Working with Remote Data Using the RPC Classes." This chapter discusses two-way communication with remote data using the HTTP calls to JSP, PHP, and ColdFusion pages; consuming web services; and invoking remote classes with the RemoteObject and AMF3 format.

- **Chapter 7**, "Displaying Data with List-based Components." This chapter discusses displaying data with the list-based controls available within the Flex framework, customizing the content using the item editors and item renderers, and working with the new AdvancedDataGrid components of Flex 3.

- **Chapter 8**, "Compiling and Deploying Flex Applications." This chapter discusses using the Flex command-line compiler to compile application and components, customizing the HTML wrapper to embed the compiled SWF file, and deploying a Flex application.

- **Chapter 9**, "Designing and Programming the Look and Feel of Flex Applications." This chapter discusses changing the look and feel of a Flex application using styles, CSS, skins, and premade Flash components.

- **Chapter 10**, "Flex Security." This chapter discusses the sandbox security of Flash Player and overcoming it with the cross-domain policy file, storing local persistent data with SharedObject, using LocalConnection to communicate between content running in Flash Player, creating a proxy server in PHP and JSP, and securing Flex applications.

- **Chapter 11**, "Advanced Flex Builder Techniques." This chapter discusses improving and customizing the Flex Builder IDE, documenting API language reference with the ASDoc tool, and improving the startup performance of an application.

- **Chapter 12**, "More Flex Framework Libraries and Utilities." This chapter discusses working with charting components, adding multimedia content to a Flex application, printing contents in Flex, and uploading files from clients to servers (and vice versa).

- **Chapter 13**, "User Navigation in Flex Applications." This chapter discusses navigating a Flex application with Navigator containers and using state and transition.

- **Chapter 14**, "Migrating Flex Applications on the Desktop with Adobe AIR." This is an entire chapter dedicated to AIR application development using Flex Builder, taking advantage of file system access, creating occasionally connected applications, and more.

Welcome to the revolution!

Who this book is for

If you want to learn more about Flex, this is the book for you. It is intended for readers who want to take their knowledge further with quick-fire solutions to common problems and best practice techniques to improve their Flex skills for Rich Internet Application development.

Moreover, this book is also aimed at readers who do not know Flex, but want to learn what they can do with Flex by using real-world examples.

Whether you are a Windows, Mac, or Linux developer, this book will work for you. Solutions and examples are intended for all platforms. Throughout the chapters you'll find detailed information that takes into account the differences between these platforms.

What you need

To follow and create the examples shown in this book you'll need the Flex Builder authoring tool. You can download a 30-day trial of Flex Builder here: www.adobe.com/products/flex/. For the solutions that use Flex 3, you can currently download the latest Flex Builder 3 beta from http://labs.adobe.com/technologies/flex/. (Once Flex 3 goes live, it will be available from the first address.)

You can also decide to use your favorite editor and compile the Flex solutions using the totally free Flex SDK that you can download from www.adobe.com/products/flex/sdk/. Or you can download the current beta Flex 3 SDK here: http://labs.adobe.com/technologies/flex/sdk/.

All the solutions and examples used in this book are downloadable from http://flexsolutions.comtaste.com or www.friendsofed.com.

The Flex Solutions site

While I was writing the book, I had one main goal in mind: to create an immortal book that can change according to inevitable updates. My solution was to create a site that will be constantly updated with new and revised content: http://flexsolutions.comtaste.com.

The site (along with www.friendsofed.com) will also be used for tracking the errata page for the book, so make sure to check back frequently for any updates.

Flex resources

Each topic in this book is presented in the context of an applied solution. Although a brief introduction exists for each solution, this book is not intended as a reference or documentation book.

The Flex documentation is huge and very well written. It covers all the aspects of Flex in a comprehensive way. You can download the complete set of Flex documentation for free from www.adobe.com/support/documentation/en/flex/.

Another must-see is the Adobe Flex Documentation Team blog, in which you'll find updates, new content, and other helpful information: http://blogs.adobe.com/flexdoc/.

You'll also find a whole load of dedicated Flex resources at the following sites:

- www.flex.org
- http://weblogs.macromedia.com/mxna/
- www.adobe.com/devnet/flex
- www.adobe.com/devnet/air
- http://onair.adobe.com/blogs/videos/
- http://flexcoders.org/
- www.adobe.com/cfusion/webforums/forum/index.cfm?forumid=60
- www.360conferences.com/360flex/
- http://flexsolutions.comtaste.com

Questions and contacts

Please direct any technical questions or comments about the book to flexsolutions@comtaste.com.

For more information about other Flex books, see our web site: www.friendsofed.com.

Common terminology

Following is a list of terms used throughout the book:

- **Adobe AIR**: The new Adobe Integrated Runtime, a cross-operating system runtime that allows developers to leverage their existing web development skills (Flash, Flex, HTML, JavaScript, Ajax) to build and deploy RIAs to the desktop.
- **Adobe Fireworks**: A bitmap and vector graphics editor.
- **Adobe Flash**: The tool used for authoring SWF files.
- **Adobe Illustrator**: A vector-based drawing program.
- **Adobe LiveCycle Data Services ES**: A server-side J2EE module that has a powerful data services architecture and programming model to synchronize data between client and server in enterprise environments. (This book does not cover this module.)
- **Adobe Photoshop**: A bitmap-based graphics editor.
- **Flash Player**: A Flex application runs within the Flash Player deployment platform.
- **Flex Builder**: The integrated development environment (IDE) for developing and compiling Flex applications.
- **Flex charting components**: This additional set of libraries provides interactive charts and graphs that enable rich data dashboards and interactive data analyses.
- **Flex SDK**: The Software Development Kit used to create Flex applications without the use of Flex Builder.
- **Rich Internet Application (RIA)**: This term, which was created by Macromedia in 2001, indicates an application that runs in a web browser and that has the features of traditional desktop applications.

Layout conventions

To keep this book as clear and easy to follow as possible, the following text conventions are used throughout.

Important words or concepts are normally highlighted on the first appearance in **bold type**.

Code is presented in `fixed-width` font.

New or changed code is normally presented in **`bold fixed-width font`**.

Pseudo-code and variable input are written in *`italic fixed-width font`*.

Menu commands are written in the form Menu ➤ Submenu ➤ Submenu.

Where I want to draw your attention to something, I've highlighted it like this:

> *Ahem, don't say I didn't warn you.*

Sometimes code won't fit on a single line in a book. Where this happens, I use an arrow like this: ➡.

```
This is a very, very long section of code that should be written all ➡
on the same line without a break.
```

1 FLEX BASICS

Flex was created for developers who intend to create Rich Internet Applications, putting together a set of tools and technologies, and supporting standard-based languages to build and deploy scalable web applications.

Flex is based on the functionalities of Flash Player 9 runtime, which takes care of the client-side logic and enables it to also interact with the JavaScript and HTML content of the browser. The penetration rate of the Adobe player and its cross-platform nature enables you to save a lot of time that would otherwise be spent testing and debugging applications on different browser versions and different operating systems.

Flex applications are composed of MXML and ActionScript 3.0 files. The first, MXML, is based on the standard XML (Extensible Markup Language) and defines its layout from user interfaces through the use of tags that correspond to visual elements (containers and controls) and to nonvisual aspects of the application (data-binding and server-side resources.) Every tag has its respective ActionScript class, which then becomes compiled into an SWF file. ActionScript 3.0 is a programming language based on the standard ECMA Script 262 (as is JavaScript), which enables the developer to program the behavior of the application and how the user can interact with the elements of the user interface.

This first chapter introduces the basics of designing Flex applications, illustrating the base elements that make up the Flex Software Development Kit (SDK).

Solution 1-1: Changing the Flex default properties

When an application is developed using Flex, there are a few properties that define its look and feel. The developer can personalize aspects of the application by changing these properties.

Every Flex application defines the default Application container—this is the root element, within which everything else is defined. The Application container has some default layout characteristics and style properties that define the look and feel of an application (which can be modified).

In this solution you'll see how to override the default settings of the Application tag and how to personalize them.

What's involved

For every chapter, a single project is defined in Flex Builder, inside which all the solutions for that chapter are developed. This project will maintain the default settings. You'll create a new folder in the project (named assets), which will contain the eventual external elements (images, fonts, and so on).

The default properties of the Application container that can be personalized are the following:

Property	Description	Default Value
backgroundColor	The background color of the entire area covered by the Flash Player	0x869CA7
backgroundGradientAlphas	The opaque background	[1.0, 1.0]
backgroundGradientColors	The colors that define the gradient	[0x9CB0BA, 0x68808C]
backgroundImage	Defines a background image	No default
backgroundGradientAlphas and backgroundGradientColors styles	Define background alpha values and gradients	mx.skins.halo. ApplicationBackground
backgroundSize	Defines the dimensions of the area of the application	100%
horizontalAlign	Defines the horizontal alignment of the application	Centered
paddingBottom	Defines the amount of bottom padding the application has	24 pixels
paddingLeft	Defines the amount of left padding the application has	24 pixels
paddingRight	Defines the amount of right padding the application has	24 pixels
paddingTop	Defines the amount of top padding the application has	24 pixels

How to build it

You'll start by creating a new Flex project from Flex Builder that you will use throughout the chapter:

1. Open Flex Builder and create a new Flex project by selecting File ➤ New ➤ Flex Project. The New Flex Project Wizard opens. Create a Basic project, as shown in Figure 1-1, click Next, and name the project Chapter_1_Flex_Basics. Click Next again.

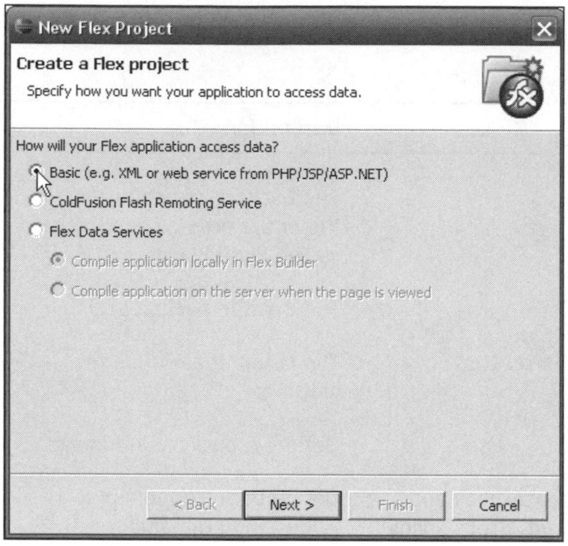

Figure 1-1. The New Flex Project Wizard guides you through the creation of a Flex project.

2. In Step 3 of the wizard, Flex Build Path, change the name of the main application file to Chapter_1_Solution_1.mxml.

3. Click Finish.

The new project will include a main application file with the following code by default:

```
<?xml version="1.0" encoding="utf-8"?>
<mx:Application xmlns:mx="http://www.adobe.com/2006/mxml"
  layout="absolute">
</mx:Application>
```

4. Add the backgroundColor property to define the background of the application, changing the background color:

```
<mx:Application xmlns:mx="http://www.adobe.com/2006/mxml"
layout="absolute"
backgroundColor="#808080">
```

The background color defines a color that will be used to create a gradient effect. With the code written previously, you obtain a faded background color that starts at light gray and gradually changes to a darker tone of gray.

5. To obtain a solid color, avoiding the fading effect, set the backgroundAlpha property to 0:

```
<mx:Application xmlns:mx="http://www.adobe.com/2006/mxml"
  layout="absolute"
  backgroundColor="#808080"
  backgroundAlpha="0">
```

In this way, the background color of the Application assumes a gray color defined by the hexadecimal value in the backgroundColor property (#808080).

Another method used to create a solid color effect is to define the same two values in the backgroundGradientColors property:

```
<mx:Application xmlns:mx="http://www.adobe.com/2006/mxml"
layout="absolute"
backgroundGradientColors="[#808080, #808080]">
```

The backgroundGradientColors property enables you to define the two color values to use for the gradient.

The backgroundImage property is used to add a background image to an application, to which you specify the path and the name of the image to use.

6. In the project, create a new folder called assets. In this folder, insert an image in one of the formats supported by Flex.

> *Flex takes advantage of the new Flash Player 9 runtime environment to display objects on the screen. Flash Player 9 supports a number of file formats that you can make use of in your Flex applications. You can import GIF, PNG, and JPEG files into applications.*

7. Define the path and name of the background image using the backgroundImage attribute of the Application tag, like so:

```
<mx:Application xmlns:mx="http://www.adobe.com/2006/mxml"
  layout="absolute"
  backgroundGradientColors="[#808080, #808080]"
  backgroundImage="assets/bellagio.jpg">
```

Switching to Design mode in Flex Builder should already have loaded and displayed the image, as shown in Figure 1-2.

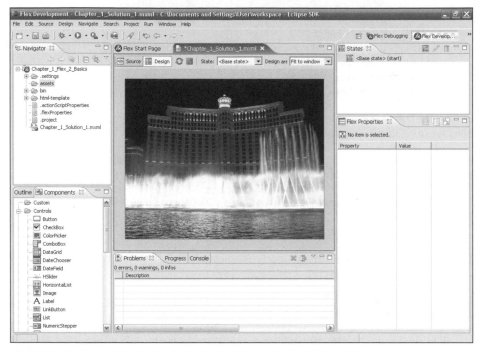

Figure 1-2. The image, imported and visualized in Design mode of Flex Builder

A little flash of color might be seen before the image is loaded, which corresponds to the defined color of the backgroundColor property or backgroundGradientColors property. There is a way to reset all the default setting defined by Flex—by setting the property styleName to plain:

- Sets the padding to 0 pixels
- Removes the default background image
- Sets the background color to white
- Left-aligns the children

It is useful to use this property when you want to overwrite all the default styles and define personalized styles:

```
<mx:Application xmlns:mx="http://www.adobe.com/2006/mxml"
layout="absolute"
styleName="plain">
```

Expert tips

When images are imported and used as a background, the image itself will scale to fit the entire stage dimension. This might cause distortions of the image, so you should define the width and height values for the Application tag as the same dimensions of the image (make sure that you choose an image that is big enough for your application):

```
<mx:Application xmlns:mx="http://www.adobe.com/2006/mxml"
layout="absolute"
backgroundImage="assets/bellagio.jpg"
width="800"
height="600">
```

Solution 1-2: Adding global CSS styles

Cascading Style Sheets (CSS) describe the presentation of a document written in a markup language. The most common application is to control the layout and look of web pages written in (X)HTML. The CSS specification was written by the W3C (www.w3.org/Style/CSS). W3C, which stands for World Wide Web Consortium, is the main standards organization for the World Wide Web.

Through the use of styles you can modify the look and feel of an application or a single component in a Flex application. Many of the styles display an inheritance feature, which enables the developer to define the styles applied to containers of the highest level. They will then be automatically applied to controls and containers contained within the top-level container.

Unfortunately, there are some styles that are not inheritable or supported, so they are not applied to the children of the container. These styles need to be applied individually to a container and control. For example, you can't set styles such as width and height with CSS because they are properties of the UIComponent class. You can use CSS for styling the look and feel of a component, but not for changing its core properties. For a list of styles that you can apply to your Flex controls, refer to Flex online documentation at http://livedocs.adobe.com/flex/2/docs/00000761.html#164917.

Fortunately, global styles exist that apply styles to all controls.

What's involved

Flex enables you to define these styles by using two methods: the CSS global selector and the StyleManager global style. While the first simply becomes defined in the <mx:Style> tag and can be declared as CSS inside or outside of the MXML document, StyleManager uses the ActionScript StyleManager style defined in the mx.styles package.

This solution will use both methods to help you apply global styles to all the noninheritable properties.

How to build it

In Flex, the CSS are used with the same scope as the XHTML web pages and are declared in different ways: inline, external, or embedded. Also, although there are general CSS properties that can be applied to any component, every component has its own unique list of properties.

This solution illustrates how the styles are applied to a document; later you'll see how to resolve the problem of the noninheritable properties using global styles.

1. Open the Flex project created in the previous examples: Chapter_1_Flex_Basics.

2. Create a new MXML document by selecting File ➤ New ➤ MXML Application and call it Chapter_1_Solution_2.mxml.

3. Insert a Panel container; and insert a Label container into it. Insert a short piece of dummy text into the Label control:

```
<mx:Application xmlns:mx="http://www.adobe.com/2006/mxml" >

   <mx:Panel title="Chapter 1 - Solution 1.2"
      width="261" height="178">
   <mx:Label text="This is a dummy text" />
    </mx:Panel>
</mx:Application>
```

4. Insert the <mx:Style> tag in the Application immediately above the declaration of the Panel; your code should now look like this:

```
<mx:Application xmlns:mx="http://www.adobe.com/2006/mxml" >

<mx:Style>

</mx:Style>

   <mx:Panel title="Chapter 1 - Solution 1.2"
      width="261" height="178">
   <mx:Label text="This is a dummy text" />
    </mx:Panel>
</mx:Application>
```

In the <mx:Style> tag, it is possible to insert the property and the respective style values that you want to apply to the application. For example, to add a background color to the Application tag, you can write the following code in the Style declaration:

```
<mx:Style>
Application
{
    backgroundColor: #FFCCFF;
}
</mx:Style>
```

Now you'll see a noninheritable property by adding the textDecoration property to the code listing, as shown here:

```
<mx:Style>
Application
  {
    backgroundColor: #FFCCFF;
    textDecoration: underline;
  }
</mx:Style>
```

The textDecoration property is one of the noninheritable properties mentioned earlier. You might expect that applying the previous rule to the Application element would cause all text contained within it to be underlined. If you run this application, however (by selecting Run ➤ Run As ➤ Flex Application), the text in the label will not be underlined, as demonstrated in Figure 1-3.

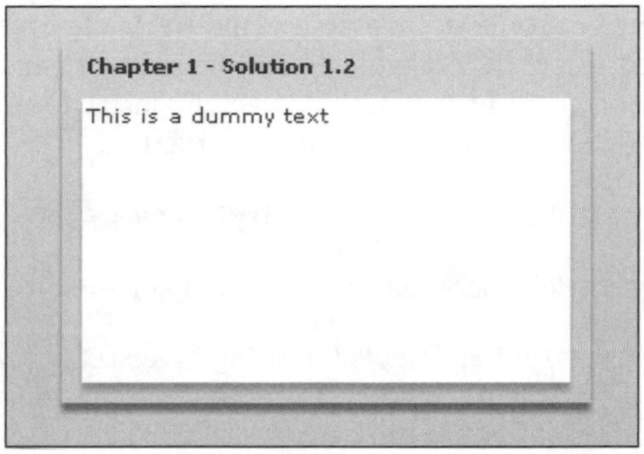

Figure 1-3. textDecoration is a noninheritable property.

To force the inheritance of these properties in the document, you have to use the global selector.

5. Open the Chapter_1_Solution_2.mxml file previously created and add the CSS global selector into the <mx:Style> tag:

```
<mx:Style>

global
  {
    fontFamily:'Arial';
    fontSize:12px;
    textDecoration: underline;
    fontWeight: bold;
    fontStyle: italic;
  }

Application
  {
    textDecoration: underline;
    backgroundColor: #FFCCFF;
  }
```

In the global selector, the font family, the font dimension, the weight, the style, and the textDecoration are defined. All the properties declared in the global—even the noninheritable ones—are applied to the application.

6. Save and run the application. Now all the text, including the Panel title, has the underline applied.

Using ActionScript to apply styles

The global selector can also be defined through the StyleManager class with which you can access a class and type selector using ActionScript. (To be able to use the class, it is necessary to first import the mx.styles.StyleManager package.) The code will be inserted in the <my:Script> tag or in an ActionScript tag that will be instanced.

Through the use of the getStyleDeclaration(selector:Style) method, you define the style parameter that corresponds to a type selector (Panel, Button, and so on), and a CSS class declared in the document or to a global selector. Finally, to select the property and the relative value to set, you can use the setStyle() method.

The following line of code shows the use of the StyleManager class:

```
StyleManager.getStyleDeclaration("global").setStyle("fontSize",12);
```

The method getStyleDeclaration accepts the string "global" as a value, which identifies the global selector. The setStyle() method stores the rules for the specified CSS selector.

In the example, the same properties defined with the CSS global selector will be applied, this time using the ActionScript StyleManager class.

1. Create a new MXML file by selecting File ➤ New ➤ MXML Application, naming it Chapter_1_Solution_2_styleManager.mxml.

2. Define an <mx:Script> block and leave it empty:

```
<mx:Application xmlns:mx="http://www.adobe.com/2006/mxml">

<mx:Script>
  <![CDATA[

  ]]>
</mx:Script>
</mx:Application>
```

3. Insert a Panel container and some random dummy text inside a Label control that's inside it. Your code should resemble this example:

```
<?xml version="1.0" encoding="utf-8"?>
<mx:Application xmlns:mx="http://www.adobe.com/2006/mxml">

<mx:Script>
  <![CDATA[

  ]]>
</mx:Script>
<mx:Panel title="Chapter 1 - Solution 1.2"  width="261" height="178">
  <mx:Label text="This is a dummy text" />
</mx:Panel>

</mx:Application>
```

4. In the `<mx:Script>` block, add the code necessary to apply the global selector with the StyleManager class, as follows:

```
<mx:Script>
  <![CDATA[

    import mx.styles.StyleManager;

    private function initStyle():void
    {
      // Global style: applies to all controls.
      StyleManager.getStyleDeclaration(
      "global").setStyle("fontSize",12);
      StyleManager.getStyleDeclaration(
      "global").setStyle("fontStyle","italic");
      StyleManager.getStyleDeclaration(
      "global").setStyle("fontWeight","bold");
      StyleManager.getStyleDeclaration(
      "global").setStyle("textDecoration", "underline");
      StyleManager.getStyleDeclaration(
      "global").setStyle("fontFamily","Arial");
    }

  ]]>
</mx:Script>
```

You have inserted the definitions of the global selector in the private function called initStyle(). This function now has to be associated with an event. To do this, use the creationComplete event system of the Application tag, which will become the following:

```
<mx:Application xmlns:mx="http://www.adobe.com/2006/mxml"
  creationComplete="initStyle();">
```

5. Save the file and run the application—your example should look like Figure 1-4.

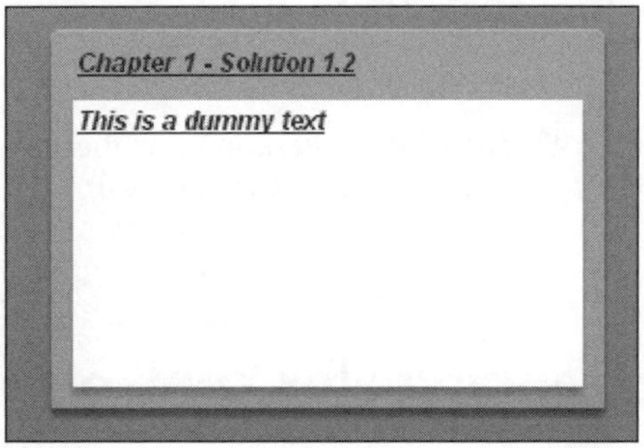

Figure 1-4. The StyleManager class enables the global selector to be applied to the application.

The result is the same as that obtained using the CSS global selector solution, as shown in Figure 1-4. All the texts defined in the application are forced to inherit the defined styles.

Expert tips

Note that even if Flex supports CSS, not all layout components can be formatted by using CSS. The property of the UIComponent class (such as width and height) can't be set through the styles, for example.

Let's now say a little bit about overriding properties. The official term is **specificity**, which refers to rules overriding other rules if they apply to more specific elements. For example, a Panel inside the Application tag is more specific than all elements inside the Application tag. Type selectors and inline styles can even override the global selector. (A good article on specificity can be found at www.htmldog.com/guides/cssadvanced/specificity.)

If you write the following code in the <mx:Style> tag, the background color that will be used by the application will be the one defined at the type selector level (which is declared in Application (backgroundColor: #FFCCFF), not in global (backgroundColor: #FFCCFF;):

```
global
{
  fontFamily:'Arial';
  fontSize:12px;
  textDecoration: underline;
  fontWeight: bold;
  fontStyle: italic;
  backgroundColor: #FFCCFF;
}

Application
{
  textDecoration: underline;
  backgroundColor: #FFCCFF;
}
```

To get a sense of Flex's CSS capabilities, take a look at the Flex Style Explorer online (http://examples.adobe.com/flex2/consulting/styleexplorer/Flex2StyleExplorer.html). We'll cover the Style API and CSS in Chapter 9, Solution 9-3.

Solution 1-3: Extending Flex controls with ActionScript

The Flex Framework puts an ample set of components at your disposal, which can be used in the applications themselves. This model, which is based on the components, is one of the keys to the success of Adobe technology. These components can be extended and customized to answer the needs of the application that you are creating.

The Flex components inherit their properties from the ActionScript UIComponent class. To be able to extend an already existing component, it is enough to create a subclass of the component to be extended and define the methods and properties that will be needed to customize the new object.

In this solution you will see how to create a ComboBox that contains the capitals of the Italian regions.

What's involved

To customize an already existing component, it is necessary to first extend the class of that component. If you have to customize a ComboBox, you create an ActionScript class that extends the ComboBox like so:

```
public class CbRegion extends ComboBox
```

In this class you will write the code to customize the component, and in the main application you will invoke this component, mapping it in a custom namespace and renaming it with its name without the mxml or an extension:

```
<comp:CbRegion
  id="myCB"
  chooseRegion="all" />
```

To access the properties and methods of the class you create, refer to the id of the imported MXML component. Such methods and properties must be declared in the ActionScript class.

A **namespace** is an abstract container providing context for the items. In Flex, each Application tag specifies the mx prefix that maps the ecosystem of Flex components in the mx namespace to its fully qualified class name:

```
<mx:Application
xmlns:mx="http://www.adobe.com/2006/mxml" />
```

You can create customized namespaces to map the custom classes and components.

How to build it

The first step of extending a Flex control is to create an ActionScript class in Flex Builder.

1. Create three new folders in the Flex project, one called com and the others, inside com, called flexsolutions and chapter1 (you can use any name you choose for these folders).

2. Create a new ActionScript class from Flex Builder inside the chapter1 folder by selecting File ➤ New ➤ ActionScript Class. The New ActionScript Class Wizard opens, as shown in Figure 1-5. Name the class CbRegion.as and specify the package com.flexsolutions.chapter1.

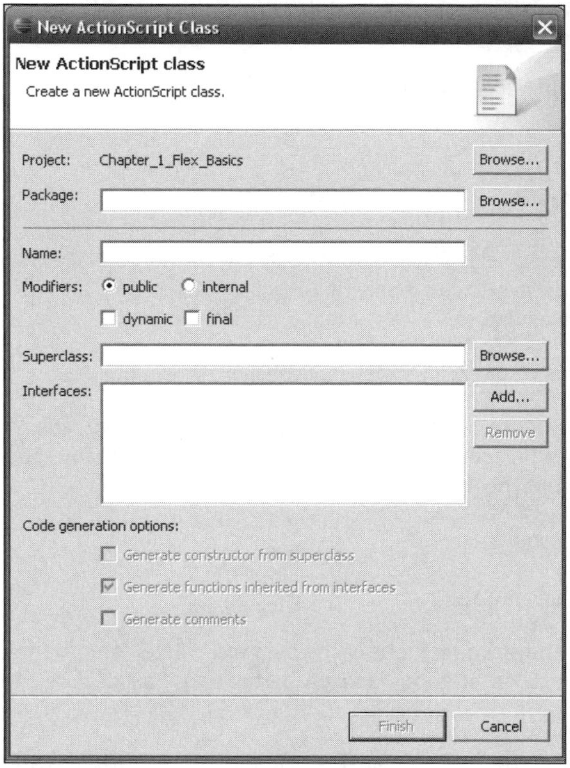

Figure 1-5. The New ActionScript Class Wizard opens and enables you to create your ActionScript class.

3. Import the ComboBox class, which you will extend on the definition of the class; then add an empty constructor. Your code should look like the following:

```
package com.flexsolutions.chapter1
{
  import mx.controls.ComboBox;

  public class CbRegion extends ComboBox
  {
    public function CbRegion():void
    {
    }
  }
}
```

The class is specified as public for you to be able to access it by using an MXML tag.

In object-oriented programming (OOP), a constructor is a method declared in a class that is called when an object is created. It is somewhat different from a standard class method: It has the same name as the declaring class, it never has an explicit return type, it is not inherited, and it usually has different rules for modifiers.

4. The aim is to create a custom ComboBox already populated by a few items. To do this, three properties that contain the regions of Lazio, the regions of Tuscany, and both regions together are defined. These three arrays will function as the data provider for the ComboBox, and in the phase of calling the component, the user can decide which of these values to load. The choice will be carried out by providing a method in the class that performs a check of the choice of the user. Insert the following code in the class:

```
package com.flexsolutions.chapter1
{
  import mx.controls.ComboBox;

  public class CbRegion extends ComboBox
  {
    private var lazio:Array = new Array("Roma","Frosinone",➥
    "Rieti", "Latina", "Viterbo");
    private var tuscany:Array = new Array("Arezzo", "Firenze",➥
    "Grosseto" , "Livorno" , "Lucca","Massa-Carrara" , ➥
    "Pisa" , "Pistoia", "Prato", "Siena");
    // this array contains both lazio and tuscany values
    private var allRegions:Array = lazio.concat(tuscany);

    [Inspectable(defaultValue="all",enumeration="lazio,tuscany,all")]
    private var region:String = "all";

    public function CbRegion():void
    {

    }

    public function set chooseRegion(regionParam:String):void
    {
      region=regionParam;

      if (region == "lazio")
      {
        this.dataProvider = lazio;
      }

      else if (region == "tuscany" )
      {
        this.dataProvider = tuscany;
      }
```

```
      else
      {
        this.dataProvider = allRegions;
      }
    }

    [Bindable]
    public function get chooseRegion():String
    {
      return region;
    }
  }

}
```

The first lines of code create three arrays to which values are assigned. The third array, allRegions, was created by arranging the values of the first with those of the second using the concat() method of the core Array class. It will, in fact, be the array that will contain all the provinces of both regions:

```
private var lazio:Array = new Array("Roma","Frosinone",➥
"Rieti", "Latina", "Viterbo");
private var tuscany:Array = new Array("Arezzo", "Firenze", ➥
"Grosseto" , "Livorno" ,"Lucca","Massa-Carrara" , "Pisa" , ➥
"Pistoia", "Prato", "Siena");
// this array cotains both lazio and tuscany values
private var allRegions:Array = lazio.concat(tuscany);
```

The metadata [Inspectable] is then used, which is needed by Flex Builder to define an attribute of the component and to make it appear in the code hints and in the tag inspector:

```
[Inspectable(defaultValue="all",enumeration="lazio,tuscany,all")]
private var region:String = "all";
```

The metadata [Inspectable] can accept various parameters. You have used the property defaultValue, which sets a default value for the Inspectable property and is necessary when one uses the functions of getter and setter. It is the enumeration property that specifies a comma-delimited list of legal values for the property. In the end, the functions of setter and getter were added to set and remove the value of the ComboBox:

```
public function set chooseRegion(regionParam:String):void
  {

    region=regionParam;

    if (region == "lazio")
    {
      this.dataProvider = lazio;
    }
```

```
    else if (region == "tuscany" )
    {
      this.dataProvider = tuscany;
    }
    else
  {
      this.dataProvider = allRegions;
    }
  }

  [Bindable]
  public function get chooseRegion():String
  {
    return region;
  }
```

> *Getter and setter methods are accessor methods that enable you to change private class properties and make them read-only and write-only. These methods can be invoked outside the class and give you the ability to create properties with sophisticated functionality that you can access like simple properties.*

To the getter function chooseRegion the metadata [Bindable] was added to be able to use it as data binding in the MXML file.

5. Create a new MXML file by selecting File ➤ New ➤ MXML Application and name it Chapter_1_Solution_3.mxml.

6. The file will contain only the native namespace mx. However, to be able to access the ActionScript class, you have to first create a custom namespace on the Application tag. Add the following now:

```
<mx:Application
  xmlns:mx="http://www.adobe.com/2006/mxml"
  xmlns:comp="com.flexsolutions.chapter1.*">

</mx:Application>
```

The custom namespace comp points to the package in which the ActionScript class is contained: com.flexsolutions.chapter1. It is now possible to refer to the class using the MXML tag with the name of the same class (without the .as extension).

7. Insert the component as an MXML tag in a Panel control:

```
<mx:Application
  xmlns:mx="http://www.adobe.com/2006/mxml"
  xmlns:comp="com.flexsolutions.chapter1.*">

<mx:Panel title="Chapter 1 - Solution 1.4"
    width="261" height="178">
```

```
<comp:CbRegion
  id="myCB"
  chooseRegion="all"/>

</mx:Panel>
```

As soon as you type the custom namespace, Flex Builder's code hint feature lists all the components that are found in the comp package (in this case, only the class CbRegion). Figure 1-6 shows the code hint box.

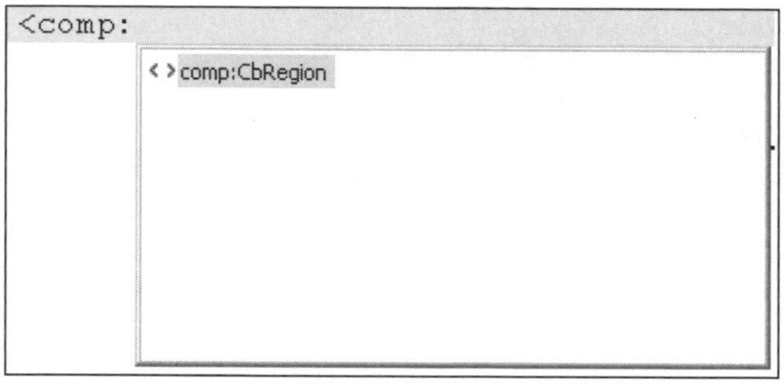

Figure 1-6. The code hints show all the components inserted in the defined package of the custom namespace comp.

In the MXML component <comp:CbRegion>, using the setter function set chooseRegion, the region property with the value "all":

```
<comp:CbRegion
  id="myCB"
  chooseRegion="all"/>
```

In this way you use the Array allRegions as the data provider of the ComboBox. This is the setter method defined in the ActionScript class:

```
public function set chooseRegion(regionParam:String):void
  {
    region = regionParam;

    if (region == "lazio")
    {
      this.dataProvider = lazio;
    }

    else if (region == "tuscany" )
    {
      this.dataProvider = tuscany;
    }
    else
    {
      this.dataProvider = allRegions;
    }
  }
```

8. Save the file and run the application.

You can change the value in the component to see the values in the ComboBox change:

```
<comp:CbRegion
  id="myCB"
  chooseRegion="tuscany"/>
```

In this way you see that only the values relative to the Tuscany array are loaded, as demonstrated in Figure 1-7.

Figure 1-7.
The values of the custom ComboBox when it sends the value Tuscany to the setter function.

Expert tips

There are many things to say about customizing of components in Flex. In this solution you are limited to extending a ComboBox to populate it with default values. The ease in this type of approach is that this class can be used in different applications, enabling you to avoid having to laboriously reinvent the wheel each time.

Another complication has been added to the example. Imagine that you want to trace the changes of the region properties in the class. Begin with the MXML file, in which you add radio buttons to permit the user to select the data provider to use on the ComboBox:

```
<mx:Panel title="Chapter 1 - Solution 1.4"
  width="400" height="208">

<mx:Label
text="The CB runs with {myCB.chooseRegion}
        countries loaded"/>

<comp:CbRegion
  id="myCB"
  chooseRegion="tuscany" />

<mx:Label
  text="Select the region you want to load into the combo box" />

<mx:RadioButtonGroup id="regionType"
itemClick="myCB.changeRegion(
                  event.currentTarget.selectedValue)"/>
<mx:RadioButton groupName="regionType"
id="all" value="all"
```

```
                    label="All" width="150"/>
                <mx:RadioButton groupName="regionType"
                id="lazio" value="lazio"
                  label="Lazio" width="150"/>
                <mx:RadioButton groupName="regionType"
                id="tuscany" value="tuscany"
                  label="Tuscany" width="150"/>

            </mx:Panel>
```

The radio buttons list three possible values to associate with the ComboBox through the value attribute. The mx:RadioButtonGroup in the event itemClick calls the changeRegion event handler of the custom component ComboBox to which it sends as value the selectedValue corresponding to the radio button clicked by the user:

```
            <mx:RadioButtonGroup id="regionType"
            itemClick="myCB.changeRegion(
                            event.currentTarget.selectedValue)"/>
```

It does this by using the currentTarget property of the event object (see Solution 1-6). A Label is also inserted, which will contain the value of the region property of the ActionScript CbRegion class:

```
            <mx:Label
            text="The CB runs with {myCB.chooseRegion}
                  countries loaded"/>
```

You want this value to update every time the user changes it by selecting from the radio buttons. To create this automatic update, you must carry out a dispatch event, which releases the moment in which the value of the region property becomes changed.

Therefore, modify the ActionScript class as follows:

```
            package com.flexsolutions.chapter1
            {
              import mx.controls.ComboBox;
              import flash.events.Event;

              public class CbRegion extends ComboBox
              {

                private var lazio:Array = ["Roma","Frosinone", "Rieti",
                                          "Latina", "Viterbo"];
                private var tuscany:Array = ["Arezzo", "Firenze", "Grosseto" , ➥
                "Livorno" , "Lucca","Massa-Carrara" , "Pisa" , "Pistoia",➥
                "Prato", "Siena" ];
                private var allRegions:Array = lazio.concat(tuscany);

                [Inspectable(defaultValue="all",enumeration="lazio,tuscany,all")]
                private var region:String = "all";
```

```
public function CbRegion():void
{
}

public function set chooseRegion(regionParam:String):void
{
  region = regionParam;
  if (region == "lazio")
  {
     this.dataProvider = lazio;
  }

  else if (region == "tuscany" )
  {
    this.dataProvider = tuscany;
  }
  else
  {
    this.dataProvider = allRegions;
  }

  dispatchEvent(new Event("changeRegionEvt"));

}

[Bindable(event="changeRegionEvt")]
public function get chooseRegion():String
{
  return region;
}

[Bindable(event="changeRegionEvt")]
public function changeRegion (regionParam:String):String
{
  region = regionParam;
  if (region == "lazio")
  {
    this.dataProvider = lazio;
  }

  else if (region == "tuscany" )
  {
    this.dataProvider = tuscany;
  }
  else
  {
    this.dataProvider = allRegions;
  }
  dispatchEvent(new Event("changeRegionEvt"));
```

```
        return region;

    }
}
}
```

The changes are the new changeRegion() method (similar to the setter function chooseRegion()) and the insertion of the dispatchEvent() method, which performs a dispatch of the custom event changeRegionEvt:

```
dispatchEvent(new Event("changeRegionEvt"));
```

With the dispatchEvent() method, it is possible to carry out the dispatch of custom events and existing events with just the click of a button.

In this case, you defined a new custom event and called it changeRegionEvt. This event is registered by the metadata [Bindable], which is declared on the getter functions chooseRegion() and changeRegion():

```
[Bindable(event="changeRegionEvt")]
```

The metadata [Bindable] is required to communicate to Flex to propagate the change of the property to all the data binding that refers to it. Solution 1-4 explains the data binding feature.

If the property value remains the same, Flex does not dispatch the event or update the property.

If you run the file, you'll observe that by changing the value property with the radio button, the values in the ComboBox and the Label change simultaneously, as shown in Figure 1-8.

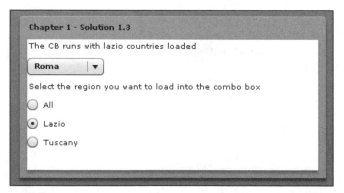

Figure 1-8. By changing the value on the radio buttons, the event will be dispatched, and the region property will be updated where used as the data binding.

Solution 1-4: Using the data binding

One of the features of Flex that you will use frequently during the development phase of an application is **data binding**, which is the process that binds a data object to a component so the latter becomes automatically added when the value to which it is bound changes. In Flex there are three methods to create a data binding:

- Using the curly braces syntax {}
- With the <mx:Binding> tag defined in the MXML code
- By declaring the BindingUtils method with ActionScript

This example uses all three methods that (depending on the context) represent an important point in the development of Flex applications.

What's involved

The first method, which uses the curly braces ({}), is the most simple and also the most commonly used. It enables you to link data to a component, defining the value to bind inside curly braces, as in the following example:

```
<mx:Label id="myLabel" text="Hello World "/>
<mx:Label text="{myLabel.text}" />
```

The second method uses the MXML <mx:Binding> tag, which (as seen following) defines a source property to declare the object to be bound and a destination to specify the component to which it should be associated:

```
<mx:Label id="myLabel" text="Hello World "/>
<mx:Label id="myLabelDest"  text="{myLabel.text}" />
<mx:Binding source=" myLabel.text"
  destination=" myLabelDest.text"/>
```

The last method enables you to create a data binding by using the ActionScript mx.binding.utils.BindingUtils class:

```
BindingUtils.bindProperty(textarea, "text", textinput, "text");
```

The BindingUtils class uses static methods to create a binding to an implemented property as a variable using the bindProperty() method or as a setter method by using the bindSetter() method.

> A **static method** means that it acts at the class level instead of at the instance level.

How to build it

Data binding in Flex is very powerful. Aside from the simple objects, it is also possible to create a binding with functions and ActionScript expressions. This example uses three methods described in the preceding section that demonstrates what you can do with data binding.

1. Create a new MXML file by selecting File ➤ New ➤ MXML Application and name it Chapter_1_Solution_4.mxml.

2. Insert an ArrayCollection tag immediately after the Application, with an id attribute equal to myAC:

```
<mx:Application xmlns:mx="http://www.adobe.com/2006/mxml">

<mx:ArrayCollection id="myAC">
  <mx:source>
    <mx:Object AC_url="http://casario.blogs.com"
      AC_author="Marco Casario"/>
    <mx:Object AC_url="http://www.augitaly.com/flexgala"
      AC_author="Flex User Group"/>
    <mx:Object AC_url="http://weblogs.macromedia.com/downey"
      AC_author="Mike Downey"/>
    <mx:Object AC_url="http://weblogs.macromedia.com/mesh"
      AC_author="Mike Chambers"/>
    <mx:Object AC_url="http://weblogs.macromedia.com/cantrell"
      AC_author="Christian Cantrell"/>
  </mx:source>
</mx:ArrayCollection>
</mx:Application>
```

ArrayCollection makes up part of the Flex collection classes and is used to represent complex data. The myAC ArrayCollection definition contains an object for which the AC_url and AC_author properties have been defined.

3. Create a data binding in the ArrayCollection by using an ActionScript expression that prints out the length of the object on a Label. Insert a Panel container and a Label control:

```
</mx:ArrayCollection>

<mx:Panel title="Chapter 1 - Solution 1.4"
width="261" height="178">
  <mx:Label
    text="This is the lenght of the ArrayCollection:
    {myAC.length}" />
</mx:Panel>
</mx:Application>
```

The tag Label uses the data binding defined with the curly braces in its text property. Aside from a simple string, the length property of the ArrayCollection is also printed on the text of the Label:

```
<mx:Label
text="This is the lenght of the ArrayCollection:
{myAC.length}" />
```

The following text will be displayed in the Label:

```
This is the length of the ArrayCollection: 5
```

The value 5 represents the number of objects defined in the ArrayCollection:

```
<mx:ArrayCollection id="myAC">
  <mx:source>
    <mx:Object AC_url="http://casario.blogs.com"
      AC_author="Marco Casario"/>
    <mx:Object AC_
      url="http://www.augitaly.com/flexgala"
      AC_author="Flex User Group"/>
    <mx:Object AC_
      url="http://weblogs.macromedia.com/downey"
      AC_author="Mike Downey"/>
    <mx:Object AC_
url="http://weblogs.macromedia.com/mesh"
      AC_author="Mike Chambers"/>
    <mx:Object AC_
      url="http://weblogs.macromedia.com/cantrell"
      AC_author="Christian Cantrell"/>
  </mx:source>
</mx:ArrayCollection>
```

4. In the same file you use the second method to create a data binding, defining the <mx:Binding> tag. Modify the code as follows, keeping the first part unchanged:

```
<mx:Panel title="Chapter 1 - Solution 1.4"  width="261" height="178">
  <mx:Label
    text="This is the lenght of the ArrayCollection:
            {myAC.length}" />

<mx:Label id="myLabelDest"  text="test" />

</mx:Panel>

<mx:Binding source="myAC.getItemAt(0).AC_url"
                    destination="myLabelDest.text"/>
</mx:Application>
```

The getItemAt() method enables you to position the index of the collection at a precise point. In the code myAC.getItemAt(0).AC_url, you got the object on the first index of the ArrayCollection (the collection classes are zero index-based).

A new Label control has been inserted, to which you assign the id attribute equal to "myLabelDest". After having closed the Panel container, the <mx:Binding> tag is inserted:

```
<mx:Label id="myLabelDest"  text="test" />
</mx:Panel>
<mx:Binding source="myAC.getItemAt(0).AC_url"
  destination="myLabelDest.text" />
```

In the <mx:Binding> tag, you linked its source property to the AC_url property of the ArrayCollection at index zero, and the destination to the text property of the new Label.

You learned how to create data binding using the <mx:Binding> MXML tag. Only the third method remains, which uses the BindingUtils class.

5. Insert an <mx:Script> block in the code below the Application tag:

```
<mx:Application xmlns:mx="http://www.adobe.com/2006/mxml">

<mx:Script>
  <![CDATA[
    import mx.binding.utils.BindingUtils;

    public function doBinding ():void
    {
        BindingUtils.bindProperty(my_TI, "text",
                                  myAC.getItemAt(0),
                                  "AC_author");
    }
  ]]>
</mx:Script>

<mx:ArrayCollection id="myAC">
```

The doBinding() function uses the bindProperty method of the BindingUtils class (a few lines imported above import mx.binding.utils.*), to which you send the text property of a text input as the destination (which you will now create) and the property AC_author of the ArrayCollection on the index zero as the source. Note that the property AC_author becomes defined in the double apex, not with the dot syntax:

```
BindingUtils.bindProperty(my_TI,

                          "text",
                          myAC.getItemAt(0),
                          "AC_author");
```

6. Modify the block of code in the Panel container by inserting the text input control and the button that releases the doBinding() function on the click event, like so:

```
<mx:Panel title="Chapter 1 - Solution 1.4"  width="261" height="178">
  <mx:Label
    text="This is the lenght of the ArrayCollection:
          {myAC.length}" />
<mx:Label id="myLabelDest"  text="prova" />

  <mx:TextInput id="my_TI" text=""/>
  <mx:Button label="Data Binding with BindingUtils"
    click="doBinding()" />

</mx:Panel>
```

At the click of a button, the doBinding() function is invoked, and the data binding between the ArrayCollection and the text input will be executed.

7. Save the file and run the application.

The application resulting from this code is shown in Figure 1-9.

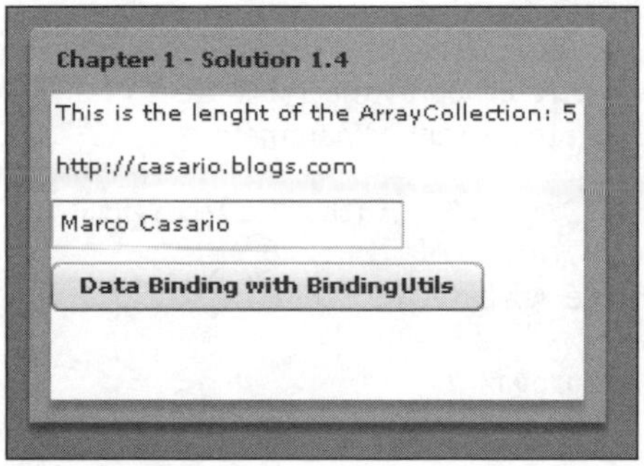

Figure 1-9.
The final result using the three methods
for data binding

Expert tips

Unlike with the curly braces syntax, the use of the <mx:Binding> tag enables you to clearly separate the user interface from the data model and to apply different source properties to the same destination. The use of the BindingUtils class enables you to create and handle the data bindings in a separate ActionScript class that can be applied across different project. The data binding method you choose obviously depends on the situation.

Data binding enables you to define a function as a value. For instance, suppose you inserted this function in the <mx:Script> block:

```
<mx:Script>
  <![CDATA[
    import mx.binding.utils.BindingUtils;
```

```
public function doBinding ():void
    {
        BindingUtils.bindProperty(my_TI, "text",
                                  myAC.getItemAt(0),
                                  "AC_author");
    }

private function isEnabled(item:uint):Boolean
{
  if (item > 0)
  {
    return true;
  } else {
    return false;
  }
}
    ]]>
</mx:Script>
```

This function receives a parameter typed as uint and returns a Boolean according to the value of the parameter sent to it.

You now modify the Button in the previous solution, creating a data binding between the properties enabled by the Button and the value returned by the isEnabled() function, to which the length property of the ArrayCollection is sent as parameter:

```
<mx:Panel title="Chapter 1 - Solution 1.4"  width="261" height="178">
  <mx:Label
    text="This is the length of the ArrayCollection:
          {myAC.length}" />
<mx:Label id="myLabelDest"  text="prova" />

  <mx:TextInput id="my_TI" text=""/>

<mx:Button enabled="{isEnabled(myAC.length)}"
  label="Data Binding with BindingUtils"
click="doBinding()" />
</mx:Panel>
```

Solution 1-5: Understanding the Flex event model

Events enable an application to respond to an occurrence such as a certain variable value being achieved or the user clicking a certain button. They form an essential part of application development.

The Flex event model is based on the Document Object Model (DOM) Level 3 events model, which is a W3C standard defined as a generic platform- and language-neutral event system that enables registration of event handlers, describes event flow through a tree structure, and provides basic contextual information for each event. For more information on this subject, consult the specification at www.w3.org/TR/DOM-Level-3-Events/events.html.

Flex components have a series of built-in events that generate and dispatch events and listen for other events. In a Flex application, the events are managed with ActionScript written in the <mx:Script> block or through classes that are instanced.

All the Flex control and container objects are subclasses of the DisplayObject class and are contained in a hierarchy of visible objects known as a **display list**. The display list contains all the visible elements that the Flash Player will draw on the screen.

The objects in the tree correspond to nodes in the DOM structure. The nodes are navigated by an event object dispatched by Flash Player.

When an event is triggered, there are three phases that Flex uses to determine whether there are event listeners (see Figure 1-10).

- **Capture phase**: Flash Player checks every node from the root of the tree to the direct parent of the target node to see whether it has a listener registered to handle the event.
- **Target phase**: The event is dispatched to the target node.
- **Bubbling phase**: Flash Player carries out a check in a reverse manner with respect to that of the capturing phase (starting from the direct parent of the target node to the root of the tree).

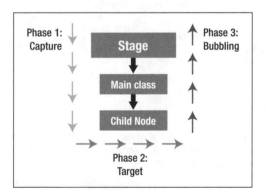

Figure 1-10. Flex event flow schema

What's involved

Two types of events exist in Flex: **System events** are dispatched when the code is executed, and **User events** are dispatched when the user who is using the application interacts with the features of the application itself (for example, buttons and form elements).

In this solution you'll see how to use the event model of Flex to manage the events of both system and user types with the two types of declaration for the event handlers: inline ActionScript and defining ActionScript functions.

How to build it

Managing system events means being able to manage events that are released at the moment in which the code is executed in the application without necessarily waiting for the user to interact with any controls or containers.

The three system events supported by any object that are a subclass of UIObject are creationComplete, initialize, and show.

The following example writes a string of text in a TextArea control every time a system event releases on the Application container and Panel container:

1. Create a new MXML file by selecting File ➤ New ➤ MXML Application and name it Chapter_1_Solution_5_system.mxml.

2. Insert a Panel in the Application for which you set the title property equal to the text "Handling System Events":

```
<mx:Application xmlns:mx="http://www.adobe.com/2006/mxml">
<mx:Panel title="Handling System Events">

</mx:Panel>
</mx:Application>
```

3. Insert a TextArea control and set the following properties:

```
<mx:Panel title="Handling System Events">

<mx:TextArea editable="false"
  height="100%"
  width="100%"
id="event_txt" />

</mx:Panel>
```

4. An event handler is defined for the system events creationComplete and initialized. Use inline ActionScript, writing ActionScript code directly into the declaration of the event on the Application tag:

```
<mx:Application xmlns:mx="http://www.adobe.com/2006/mxml"
  creationComplete="event_txt.text += '\n Application creationComplete
fired'"
  initialize="event_txt.text += '\n Application initialize fired'">
```

This code, written in the event_txt TextArea, creates two strings of text (refer to Step 3). The text "Application creationComplete fired" is inserted in the TextArea when the creationComplete event is executed. It is then released when an object has finished its construction and property processing, and is drawn on the screen. The text "Application initialize fired" is inserted in the TextArea when the event initialize system is executed, which is released when the object has been initialized (has finished its construction and property processing), but is not drawn on the screen.

5. Write the same code for the event management system creationComplete and initialize the Panel container:

```
<mx:Panel title="Handling System Events"
creationComplete="event_txt.text +=
  ('\n Panel creationComplete fired')"
initialize="event_txt.text +=
('\n Panel initialize fired')">
```

6. Save the file and run the application.

The example demonstrates how to manage the system events in Flex, defining them with inline ActionScript. It is also interesting to note the hierarchical order in which the same system events are executed by Flex on the different containers or controls. In fact, if you look at the text inserted in the TextArea, you'll note that the system type events defined for the Application tag are always released last. In particular, the creationComplete event is the last event that is released in the application. For this reason it is often used to set startup settings, as shown in Figure 1-11.

Figure 1-11. Hierarcy of the execution of system events

The following example demonstrates how to manage user type events, defining the event handlers through ActionScript functions, which are called when the user releases an event. In this way, the event handlers, that is the code necessary to respond to the events, is declared in an <mx:Script> block.

1. Create a new MXML file by selecting File ➤ New ➤ MXML Application and name it Chapter_1_Solution_5_user.mxml.

2. In the Application tag, insert a Panel and set its title property equal to the text "Handling User Events".

```
<mx:Application
xmlns:mx="http://www.adobe.com/2006/mxml">

<mx:Panel title="Handling User Events"
width="284" height="179">

</mx:Panel>

</mx:Application>
```

3. Insert a Label, a Button, and a LinkButton control, setting the property as follows:

```
<mx:Panel title="Handling User Events"
width="284" height="179">
  <mx:Label id="myLabel" text="click something please !"/>
    <mx:HBox>
      <mx:Button id="myButton"
        label="Click Me" />
      <mx:LinkButton label="My Link 1" />
    </mx:HBox>
</mx:Panel>
```

4. Insert an <mx:Script> block in which two functions are declared that respond to the click event of the two buttons:

```
<mx:Application
xmlns:mx="http://www.adobe.com/2006/mxml">

<mx:Script>
  <![CDATA[
    private function clickHandler():void
    {
      myLabel.text="The button has been clicked !";
    }

    private function linkHandler():void
    {
      myLabel.text = "The LinkButton has been clicked !";
    }
  ]]>
</mx:Script>
<mx:Panel title="Handling User Events"
width="284" height="179">
```

5. To link these functions to the click event of the buttons, manage the `click` event directly on the MXML tags of the buttons by doing the following:

```
<mx:HBox>

  <mx:Button id="myButton"
    label="Click Me"
    click="clickHandler()"/>

  <mx:LinkButton label="My Link 1"
   click="linkHandler()"/>

  </mx:HBox>
```

6. Save and run the application.

Clicking the two buttons launches one of the two functions, depending on the button clicked. The two functions do nothing other than write a string of text into the Label.

In the functions, you can also write complex actions that must be executed in the application.

Expert tips

Using event handlers linked to ActionScript functions instead of the inline declarations allows you to program more complex responses to the event released. Moreover, the code will be more reusable and maintainable in that it is concentrated in the `<mx:Script>` block and can be enriched with comments from the author. More importantly, it is possible to render the ActionScript code totally external to the document defined in the page using the source property of the `<mx:Script>` tag:

```
<mx:Script source="eventHandlers.as"/>
```

The code in the `eventHandlers.as` document is pure ActionScript, so it does not require the CDATA block (which is instead needed in the MXML document because the code will be sent as an XML block). You can then easily reuse the functions in different applications.

In the preceding example, the file `eventHandlers.as` has the following code:

```
private function clickHandler():void
{
  myLabel.text="The button has been clicked !";
}

private function linkHandler():void
{
  myLabel.text = "The LinkButton has been clicked !";
}
```

In this way you can organize files with `.as` extensions to import into the different applications, creating the crimson library of ActionScript code.

Solution 1-6: Using the event object

The `flash.events.Event` class contains the information related to the event that occurred. Every time that an event is dispatched, the `flash.events.Event` class automatically generates an object event, which is said to be an object implicit class.

To use it in your code, this object must be sent as a parameter in the ActionScript function that manages the event. In this way it is possible to access the property that the event contains. Some of these properties are common to all the objects; others depend on the type of event that has been released.

In this solution you'll see how to send an event object to an event listener and how to use some of its properties.

What's involved

Every event object created from the class contains properties. Some of these properties are common to all the objects; others depend exclusively on the type of event that has occurred. The following table lists the properties of a standard event object.

Property	Type	Description
type	String	Contains the name of the event that has occurred
target	Event	Contains the component instance that broadcasted the event
target.id	String	Contains the instance name of the target

When you send an event object you must assign a data type to it. You can generically use a `flash.events.Event` class as a data type or use one of the subclasses. There are, in fact, many subclasses that extend the `Event` class and that can be used as a stricter data type for the event object. The `MouseEvent` and `DataEvent` classes are two examples.

All subclasses of `flash.events.Event` must be imported with the import command into the ActionScript code before it can be used. The `flash.events.Event` class is implicit to Flex applications, so it doesn't need to be imported.

How to build it

The event becomes automatically created from the `flash.events.Event` class. It already brings with it all its properties. For this reason, the only thing you need to do to use the event object is to pass it as a parameter to the event listener function.

1. Open the Chapter_1_Solution_5_user.mxml file created in the previous solution and rename it as Chapter_1_Solution_6_Event.mxml.

2. Substitute the Label declared in the Panel container with a TextArea, so the text you'll print into it is multiline:

```
<mx:Panel title="Using the Event Object"
width="240" height="282">

<mx:TextArea width="100%" height="100%"
id="myText" text="click something please !"/>

<mx:HBox>
<mx:Button id="myButton"
label="Click Me"
click="clickHandler()"/>
<mx:LinkButton label="My Link 1"
click="linkHandler()"/>
</mx:HBox>
</mx:Panel>
```

3. Modify the code in the two buttons and send the event object to the ActionScript function associated with the click, as follows:

```
<mx:Button id="myButton"
  label="Click Me"
  click="clickHandler(event)"/>
<mx:LinkButton label="My Link 1"
click="linkHandler(event)"/>
```

The only code added is the event parameter itself in the ActionScript function.

4. It is now necessary to intercept this parameter in the ActionScript function. Modify the block of code as follows:

```
<mx:Script>
  <![CDATA[

    private function clickHandler(evt:Event):void
    {
      myText.text="The button has been clicked !";
      myText.text+= "\n\n\t Event type: " + evt.type;
      myText.text+= "\n\n\t Event Target: " + evt.target;
      myText.text+= "\n\n\t Event Target ID: " + evt.target.id;
    }

    private function linkHandler(evt:Event):void
    {
      myText.text = "The LinkButton has been clicked !";
      myText.text+= "\n\n\t Event type: " + evt.type;
      myText.text+= "\n\n\t Event Target: " + evt.target;
```

```
    myText.text+= "\n\n\t Event Target ID: " + evt.target.id;
  }
]]>
</mx:Script>
```

This code uses the `type`, `target`, and `target.id` properties of the event object. These properties are standard and exist for any event object.

Having assigned the `Event` class as the data type for the event object, you haven't imported any class using ActionScript.

5. Save and run the application.

Following the application and clicking (for example) the `Button`, the following test is written in the `TextArea` control:

```
The button has been clicked!
    Event type: click
    Event Target: Chapter_1_Solution_6_Event0.Panel4.HBox10.myButton
    Event Target ID: myButton
```

This demonstrates the contents of the property `type` and `target` of the event object. In particular, while the `target.id` property contains the exact id that you have assigned to the object (myButton in the case of the `Button`), the `target` property contains the entire tree of the display list, starting from the stage (discussed in the preceding solution).

To use a stricter data type to assign to the event object, treating it like a type of event click, you can use the `MouseEvent` class, which is a subclass that extends the `Event` class.

This process allows for further benefits, which are discussed in more detail in the "Expert tips" paragraph of this solution.

1. Open the Chapter_1_Solution_6_Event.mxml file and rename it as Chapter_1_ Solution_6_MouseEvent.mxml.

2. Change the code in the ActionScript block, using it as the data type of the MouseEvent class (see Figure 1-12).

```
<mx:Script>
  <![CDATA[
    import flash.events.MouseEvent;

    private function clickHandler(evt:MouseEvent):void
    {
      myText.text="The button has been clicked !";
      myText.text+= "\n\n\t Event type: " + evt.type;
      myText.text+= "\n\n\t Event Target: " + evt.target;
      myText.text+= "\n\n\t Event Target ID: " + evt.target.id;
    }
```

```
private function linkHandler(evt:MouseEvent):void
{
    myText.text = "The LinkButton has been clicked !";
    myText.text+= "\n\n\t Event type: " + evt.type;
    myText.text+= "\n\n\t Event Target: " + evt.target;
    myText.text+= "\n\n\t Event Target ID: " + evt.target.id;
}

]]>
</mx:Script>
```

3. Save and run the application.

This time, the `MouseEvent` class was used as the data type for the event object, which occurs whenever a mouse event is generated by a user input device.

The result obtained from the application does not change, even if you can access the specific properties of the event by using a stricter data type, as shown in Figure 1-12.

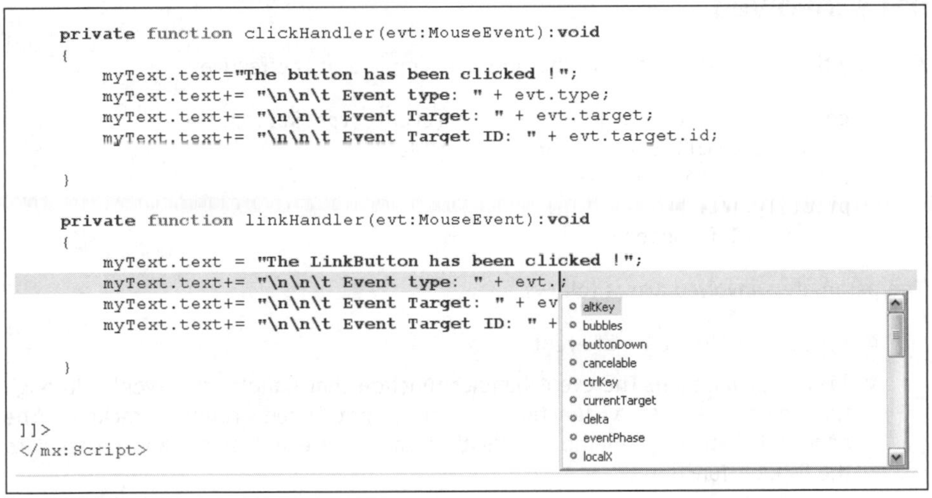

Figure 1-12. You can access the specific properties of the event by using stricter data typing.

Expert tips

Stricter data typing gives you the benefit of having compile-time type checking. If a property that does not support that particular event is used, you immediately get an error message. If a generic Event class is used instead, the compiler can't detect the error, which will be verified at runtime.

Stricter data typing also increases the performance of the application in the runtime phase.

Solution 1-7: Register event handler functions for an object with the addEventListener() method

The preceding solutions illustrated how to manage events through various methods. The event handlers, calls, and event listeners were defined, which are the ActionScript functions launched as soon as the event is dispatched. In ActionScript a way exists to register the event listeners to a specified object using the addEventListener() method, which makes up part of the EventDispatcher class.

Registering an event handler to an object using the addEventListener() method takes advantage of advanced event handling. It enables you, for example, to manage the event handlers registering multiple components with a specified event listener with more flexibility or to add multiple listeners to a single component.

In this solution you'll see how to register an event listener using the addEventListener() method.

What's involved

Creating the addEventListener() method is as simple as it is effective:

```
componentInstance.addEventListener(event_type:String, ➥
event_listener:Function, ➥
use_capture:Boolean, ➥
priority:int, ➥
    weakRef:Boolean)
```

The parameters involved are as follows:

- type:String: The type of event.
- listener:Function: The event handler function that handles the event. Although this parameter is a function, it does not need round brackets. The addEventListener() method implicitly creates the event object and passes it to the listener function.
- useCapture:Boolean: Defines where the event listener should function if in the capture phase or in the target and bubbling phase. The default value is false, so the listener functions only for the target or bubbling phase.
- priority:int: The priority level of the event listener. The default priority is 0.
- useWeakReference:Boolean (default = false): Determines whether the reference to the listener is strong or weak. A strong reference, when the value is set at false (default value), prevents your listener from being garbage-collected. A weak reference does not.

How to build it

Begin by registering an event listener with an addEventListener() method in a MXML file.

1. Create a new MXML file by selecting File ➤ New ➤ MXML Application and name it Chapter_1_Solution_7.mxml.

2. On the Application tag, insert an event listener that launches an ActionScript function:

```
<mx:Application xmlns:mx="http://www.adobe.com/2006/mxml"
  creationComplete ="init()">
```

3. Create a block of <mx:Script> code in which you write the init() function launched from creationComplete of the Application tag:

```
<mx:Application xmlns:mx="http://www.adobe.com/2006/mxml"
  creationComplete ="init()">

<mx:Script>
 <![CDATA[

    import flash.events.MouseEvent;
    private function init():void
    {
      myButton.addEventListener("click",clickHandler);
      myLabel.text = ➡
    "The addEventListener registered the event listener";
    }

    private function clickHandler(event:MouseEvent):void
    {
      myLabel.text="The Button has been clicked";
    }
 ]]>
</mx:Script>
```

The init() function uses the addEventListener() method, which registers the clickHandler event handler on the Application of the myButton component. This component will be a Button control that you define in the application. The first parameter of the addEventListener() method is the event type, which is the type of event for which the object will be registered. The click event was inserted by sending it as a string. It is best practice, however, to use event type static constants because in this way the compiler catches typing mistakes in constants, not in strings. The method becomes the following:

```
private function init():void
{
myButton.addEventListener(➡
            MouseEvent.CLICK, clickHandler);
myLabel.text =
"The addEventListener registered the event listener";
}
```

The <mx:Script> block finishes with the clickHandler() event handler, which does nothing except write a string on a Label:

```
private function clickHandler(event:MouseEvent):void
  {
    myLabel.text="The Button has been clicked";
  }
```

4. Insert the user interface container and controls into the application just below the closure of the Script tag:

```
</mx:Script>

<mx:Panel title="Chapter 1 - Solution 1.7"  ➡
width="450" height="178">
  <mx:Label id="myLabel" text="Watch here"/>
<mx:Button id="myButton"➡
 label="Execute the event handler"/>
</mx:Panel>

</mx:Application>
```

5. Save the file and run the application.

Note that by using the addEventListener() method you have totally separated the view part of the application (represented by the user interface objects) from the controller (which contains the code to respond to the events). In fact, in the MXML tag that defines the controls, no code declaration exists for the management of the events.

> *The view and controller terms refer to the Model-View-Controller (MVC) design pattern. The definition of MVC from Wikipedia (http://en.wikipedia.org/wiki/Model_view_controller) is as follows:*
>
> ***Model-view-controller** (**MVC**) is an architectural pattern used in software engineering. In complex computer applications that present lots of data to the user, one often wishes to separate data (model) and user interface (view) concerns, so that changes to the user interface do not affect the data handling, and that the data can be reorganized without changing the user interface. The model-view-controller solves this problem by decoupling data access and business logic from data presentation and user interaction, by introducing an intermediate component: the controller.*

The way Flex handles data models is based on the MVC design pattern.

It is possible to use an external ActionScript class to define the methods that function as event listeners. Even if the ActionScript classes do not act as event listeners, the methods declared in a class do.

To create an ActionScript class that manages events, it is sufficient to create a simple class with an empty builder, import `flash.events.Event`, and define the methods that you'll then use as event listeners:

1. This step was already done in Solution 1-3. If the com/flexsolutions/chapter1 folders are already present, you can go directly to the creation of the ActionScript class. In case you haven't got those folders handy, here goes. Check if you previously created the three new folders in the Flex project. The first is called com; the second, inside com, is called flexsolutions, and the last one is called chapter1. (You can use whatever name you like for the folders, as long as the code matches them.) In the third folder create a new ActionScript class. By selecting File ➤ New ➤ ActionScript Class, call the class Evt_Listener. Be sure that the package field contains the correct directory you have just created (see Figure 1-13).

2. Add the following code to the class you just created:

```
package com.flexsolutions.chapter1
{
    import flash.events.Event;
    import mx.controls.Alert;

    public class Evt_Listener
    {
        public function Evt_Listener()
        {
            //empty constructor
        }

        public static function fncEvtHandler(event:Event):void
        {
            Alert.show("The button has been clicked");
        }
    }
}
```

The classes in ActionScript 3.0 always begin with the definition of the package, which defines the path of the class.

> In ActionScript 3.0 a **package** is where related classes and interfaces are grouped together.

In this example, the package communicates that the class is found in the com\flexsolutions\chapter1 folder. The constructor has been inserted in the public Evt_Listener class (it is not obligatory to write it because it will be automatically created if it is absent in the compilation phase) and then the fncEvtHandler() method is written.

This public method is declared as static and enables access without having to instantiate the Evt_Listener class.

3. Open the Chapter_1_Solution_7.mxml file and modify the code, adding the following to the <mx:Script> block:

```
<mx:Script>
 <![CDATA[
   import flash.events.MouseEvent;
   import com.flexsolutions.chapter1.*;

   private function init():void
   {
     myButton.addEventListener(
     MouseEvent.CLICK,clickHandler);
     myLabel.text =➡
"The addEventListener registered the event listener";

     myBtn_2.addEventListener(➡
     MouseEvent.CLICK, Evt_Listener.fncEvtHandler);
   }
   private function clickHandler(event:MouseEvent):void
   {
     myLabel.text="The Button has been clicked";
   }
 ]]>
</mx:Script>
```

Only two lines of code are added. The first is found at the beginning and runs an import of the class referring to its package:

```
import com.flexsolutions.chapter1.*;
```

The second is found in the init() function, which was run on the creationComplete of the application. By using an addEventListener() method, it registers the click of the button to the function defined in the ActionScript class:

```
myBtn_2.addEventListener(MouseEvent.CLICK,
Evt_Listener.fncEvtHandler);
```

Having defined the fncEvtHandler() method of the class as static, you can now invoke it without having to apply the class in ActionScript:

```
myBtn_2.addEventListener(MouseEvent.CLICK,

Evt_Listener.fncEvtHandler);
```

4. Insert the Button referred to in the ActionScript block in the MXML code, using the following code:

```
<mx:Panel title="Chapter 1 - Solution 1.7"  width="450" height="178">
  <mx:Label id="myLabel" text="Watch here"/>
  <mx:Button id="myButton" label="Execute the event handler"/>
<mx:Button id="myBtn_2"➡
label="Execute the event listener AS class"/>
</mx:Panel>
```

5. Save the file and run the application.

Running the application and clicking the button loads the Alert pop-up, which demonstrates the execution of the fncEvtHandler() method.

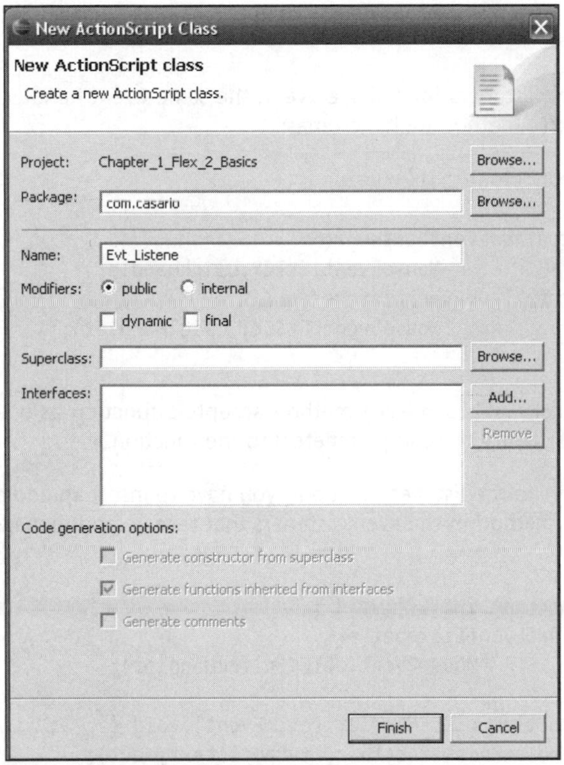

Figure 1-13. The New ActionScript Class dialog box enables you to specify a class name and define a package for the class.

Expert tips

The event listeners can also be registered by using the addEventListener() directly on the MXML component without having to use an event handler function. The definition is called **inline**; to try it, insert a new button in which you run the event click in the example of the solution:

```
<mx:Button id="myButton_3"
label="Execute the event handler inline">
click="this.addEventListener(>
        MouseEvent.CLICK,clickHandler);" />
```

There will be scenarios in which you have to register multiple listeners for a single event or register a single listener with multiple components. To register multiple listeners for a single event, recall the addEventListener() method twice by launching two different event handlers:

```
private function init():void
{
    myButton.addEventListener(➥
                    MouseEvent.CLICK,clickHandler);
    myButton.addEventListener(➥
                    MouseEvent.CLICK,clickAnoterHandler);
}
```

To register multiple listeners for a single event, the same event handler is declared in the addEventListener() method multiple times:

```
private function init():void
{
    myButton.addEventListener(➥
                    MouseEvent.CLICK,clickHandler);
    myButton_2.addEventListener(➥
                    MouseEvent.CLICK, clickHandler);
}
```

Given that the addEventListener() method accepts a function as a second parameter, you'll get errors if you try to send parameters to the function.

To send parameters to the listener functions, you have to insert an additional passage and define an ulterior method in the event listeners that receive and manage these additional parameters:

```
public function init2():void {
myButton.addEventListener(➥
                MouseEvent.CLICK,clickHandler);
}
public function clickHandler (evt:Event):void {
  clickHandlerParameter(this, myLabel.text, evt);
}
public function clickHandlerParameter (me:Object, ➥
enable:Boolean, ➥
evt:Event):void
{
  me.enabled = enable;
}
```

Nevertheless, the unused listeners continue to exist. To optimize the performance of the application, it is best practice to remove any listener that does not get used. The removeEventListener() method enables you to remove the listeners registered with the addEventListener() method:

```
myButton.removeEventListener (➥
                MouseEvent.CLICK,clickHandler);
```

It is not possible, however, to remove the listeners that are declared in the MXML tag.

Solution 1-8: Stop the event propagation

In the capture-target-bubbling event phases Flex checks on all nodes contained in the display list wherever there are event listeners, starting from the root node until it arrives at the object that has unleashed the event. In the bubbling phase it carries out this check in a contrary way, starting from the object that has triggered the event and going backward as far as the root.

If, for example, the application was composed of a Panel in which a Button becomes declared, when the user clicks the button, Flex checks the Application container and the Panel container for event listeners to handle the event (capturing phase).

Not having found anything, it continues as far as the Button, for which it finds an event listener and runs the targeting phase. At this point in the process, it turns back in the reverse order (to that of the capturing phase), again searching for an event listener (the bubbling phase).

There are situations in which a developer wants to prevent an event from further propagation. It is possible to stop this process of propagation by using the stopImmediatePropagation() and stopPropagation() methods.

In this solution you'll see how to use these two methods and learn about the differences between them.

What's involved

The two methods, stopPropagation() and stopImmediatePropagation(), make up part of the flash.events.Event class and are called by the event objects passed to the event listener. Their function is to stop and prevent the event object from moving on to the next node.

The stopPropagation() method prevents any objects beyond the current one from receiving the event. In practice, the method prevents the event object from moving on to the next node.

The stopImmediatePropagation() method prevents the processing of event listeners in both the current node and subsequent nodes. This method prevents the event object from moving on to the next node and does not permit any other event listener to be run.

How to build it

To stop the propagation generated by the event flow of Flex, it is enough to insert one of the two methods—stopPropagation() or stopImmediatePropagation()—in the event listener, from which it will be necessary to stop the propagation.

1. Create a new MXML file by selecting File ➤ New ➤ MXML Application and name it Chapter_1_Solution_8.mxml.

2. Insert one of the event listeners on the Application tag, which will launch an ActionScript function:

```
<mx:Application xmlns:mx="http://www.adobe.com/2006/mxml"
  initialize="init(event)">
```

3. Insert a Panel, a Button, and a TextArea below the Application tag:

```
<mx:Application xmlns:mx="http://www.adobe.com/2006/mxml"
  initialize="init(event)">

<mx:Panel id="myPanel" title="Stop Prapagation">
  <mx:Button id="myBtn_1" label="Enter name"/>
  <mx:TextArea id="myText" width="275" height="171"/>
</mx:Panel>

</mx: Application >
```

4. Create an <mx:Script> block below the Application tag, in which you use the addEventListener() method to handle the events click of the Button and the Panel:

```
<mx:Application xmlns:mx="http://www.adobe.com/2006/mxml"
  initialize="init(event)">

<mx:Script>
 <![CDATA[
   import flash.events.MouseEvent;
   import flash.events.Event;

   public function init(e:Event):void
   {
     myBtn_1.addEventListener(MouseEvent.CLICK,clickBtn_1);
     myBtn_1.addEventListener(MouseEvent.CLICK,clickBtn_2);
     myBtn_1.addEventListener(MouseEvent.CLICK,clickBtn_3);

     myPanel.addEventListener(MouseEvent.CLICK, clickPanel);
   }

   private function clickBtn_1(evt:MouseEvent):void
   {
     myText.text += "\n\nButton 1 clicked !";
   }

   private function clickBtn_2(evt:MouseEvent):void
   {
     myText.text += "\n\nButton 2 clicked !";
   }

   private function clickBtn_3(evt:MouseEvent):void
   {
```

```
      myText.text += "\n\nButton 3 clicked !";
    }

    public function clickPanel(e:Event)
    {
      myText.text += "\n Panel clicked !";
    }

  ]]>
</mx:Script>
```

The functions clickBtn_1, clickBtn_2, clickBtn_3, and clickPanel do nothing but print a string in the TextArea with id attribute equal to myText. The output following the file is as follows:

Button 1 clicked !
Button 2 clicked !
Button 3 clicked !
Panel clicked !

5. Now use the methods to stop the propagation of the events, modifying the clickBtn_2() function like so, and then run the application again:

```
private function clickBtn_2(evt:MouseEvent):void
{
  myText.text += "\n\nButton 2 clicked !";
  evt.stopPropagation();
}
```

The output is as follows:

Button 1 clicked !
Button 2 clicked !
Button 3 clicked !

In this case the propagation is stopped at the event generated by the click of the button. In fact, all three of the functions defined with the addEventListener() for the event click of the mouse are executed:

```
myBtn_1.addEventListener(MouseEvent.CLICK,clickBtn_1);
myBtn_1.addEventListener(MouseEvent.CLICK,clickBtn_2);
myBtn_1.addEventListener(MouseEvent.CLICK,clickBtn_3);
```

While the function that should be released on the click of the Panel is not executed, for the click event of the Panel the event flow has been stopped, and the clickPanel() event handler is not called:

```
myPanel.addEventListener(MouseEvent.CLICK,
                                        clickPanel);
```

6. Change the stopPropagation() method you added in Step 5 to the stopImmediatePropagation() method and run the application again to see what the difference is:

```
private function clickBtn_2(evt:MouseEvent):void
{
  myText.text += "\n\nButton 2 clicked !";
  evt. stopImmediatePropagation ();
}
```

The output obtained is as follows:

Button 1 clicked !
Button 2 clicked !

The difference is that the stopImmediatePropagation() immediately stops the propagation of any other event listener.

Expert tips

The capturing and bubbling phase become executed when the event object moves from one node to another in the display list (navigating in a direct way and then in reverse).

Note that only the objects that are subclasses of the DisplayObject class have all three phases: capturing, targeting, and bubbling.

Solution 1-9: Handling keyboard events

In contrast with traditional web sites, Flex applications are often fitted with keyboard shortcuts because they are often more akin to desktop applications, in which people are used to using the keyboard to quickly activate functions or simply to move more quickly from one part of a document to another.

From the simple closure of a pop-up window, to the activation of a video player or help window, Flash Player enables you to manage keyboard events, and you'll investigate them in this solution.

What's involved

In the operation of the handling of keyboard events, it is necessary to distinguish two types of management: a global one, which takes into consideration the context in which the user is found; and one that is instead linked to the focus of the component on which the user is positioned.

In the example you'll apply both methods by using a listener for the KeyboardEvent to define an event at the global level.

You'll then extend the example to create an ASCII key map using the keyCode and charCode properties to determine which key was pressed by the user.

How to build it

You begin your work with the code handling and global key event. With the use of KeyboardEvent.KEY_DOWN or KeyboardEvent.KEY_UP linked to a listener, you can put the whole application into play with every press of the keyboard.

1. Create a new MXML file by selecting File ➤ New ➤ MXML Application and name it Chapter_1_Solution_9_global.mxml.

2. On the Application tag insert the event listener that launches an ActionScript function:

```
<mx:Application xmlns:mx="http://www.adobe.com/2006/mxml"
  initialize="init()">
```

3. Insert an <mx:Script> block under the Application tag, in which you define the init() function:

```
<mx:Script>
  <![CDATA[
    import flash.events.KeyboardEvent;

    private function init():void
    {
      // set the focus on the canvas.
      myCanvas.setFocus();
      // create the global listener
      //for handling the keyboard event
      this.addEventListener(KeyboardEvent.KEY_DOWN,
                                      keyHandler );
    }

  ]]>
</mx:Script>
```

The listener becomes created and linked to KEY_DOWN, which will release the keyHandler() function. In this function the code that manages or traps the use of the keys is inserted.

Add the following code after the init() function:

```
private function keyHandler (evt:KeyboardEvent):void
{
myText.text += "The key with the keycode" +
                        evt.keyCode +
                     " was pressed \n\n";
}
```

The keyHandler function accepts and uses the event object generated by the KeyboardEvent as a parameter (refer to Solution 1-6). Among the various properties contained in the event object are keyCode and the charCode. This example shows a string written with the keyCode relative to the key pressed by the user in a TextArea control.

4. Complete the file by inserting the TextArea control in a Canvas:

```
</mx:Script>

<mx:Canvas id="myCanvas" width="100%" height="100%">

<mx:TextArea x="225" y="86"
  width="181" height="111"
  id="myText" editable="false"/>

</mx:Canvas>

</mx:Application>
```

5. Save and run the file. Every time a key is pressed, the TextArea adds a string to the control and inserts the relative keyCode.

For example, you can extend the example by creating a mapping system to intercept and print the keyCode and chardCode values.

The difference between the two properties is that although the keyCode property corresponds to the value of a key on the keyboard, the charCode property contains the key in the current character set (the default character set is UTF-8, which supports ASCII).

Continue from the previous example:

1. Open the Chapter_1_Solution_9_global.mxml file and save a copy of it with the name Chapter_1_Solution_9.mxml. Leave the code on the Application tag with the event listener, which launches the unchanged ActionScript function:

```
<mx:Application xmlns:mx="http://www.adobe.com/2006/mxml"
  initialize="init()">
```

2. Modify the block of ActionScript code defined in the <mx:Script> tag as follows:

```
<mx:Script>
  <![CDATA[
    import mx.core.Application ;
    import flash.events.KeyboardEvent;
    import mx.controls.Alert;

    private function init():void
    {
      myCanvas.setFocus();
      this.addEventListener(KeyboardEvent.KEY_DOWN,
```

```
                                         keyHandler );
        }
        private function keyHandler (e:KeyboardEvent):void
        {
          txt_code.text = String(e.keyCode);
          txt_char.text = String(e.charCode);
        }
     ]]>
   </mx:Script>
```

The code is very similar to the previous example. The only difference is that this time you print the keyCode and charCode values in the two text input controls. The keyHandler() function is released every time the user presses a key on the keyboard because the init() function creates a listener:

```
    this.addEventListener(KeyboardEvent.KEY_DOWN,
                                    keyHandler );
```

The init() function is launched on creationComplete of the Application tag.

3. This example is concluded by inserting the following code in the file:

```
   <mx:Canvas id="myCanvas" width="100%" height="100%">
   <mx:Label x="277" y="11"
   text="KeyCode Pressed"/>
   <mx:Label x="10" y="11"
    text="Charcode:"/>
   <mx:TextInput x="84" y="9"
   id="txt_char"/>
   <mx:TextInput x="387" y="9"
   id="txt_code"/>
   </mx:Canvas>
```

4. Save and run the application.

The application is shown in Figure 1-14.

Figure 1-14. Enter the keyCode and charCode values in the two text input controls.

Expert tips

The management of keyboard events enables you to intercept the keys only on the components that have the focus, which might make you wonder whether it is possible to trap keys on a VBox type container or an Application tag.

But even if the Application tag is the container that does not have the focus, it contains children that accept the focus (as in the example, they can be TextInput). Therefore, linking keyboard events to the Application container, it is possible to intercept them by using the bubbling phase of the events. For this reason the following code is executed:

```
Application.application.addEventListener(➥
KeyboardEvent.KEY_UP,keyHandler);
```

If the same function on different containers and controls is linked to the same listener, the rule followed by Flash Player in the execution of the events is that in which the child controls dispatch events before the parents.

If you can follow the example on different operative systems or devices, you'll notice that the values of the keyCode change. In fact, the two properties are operating system–dependent, so you have to pay attention during the programming phase to manage this diversity. The ASCII values are instead common and are available on the ActionScript documentation.

The Flex application remains an application executed in the browser. For this reason, there are keys and combinations of keys that never become intercepted by Flash Player because they are released before the browser. An example of this is the F1 function key or the combination of the Ctrl (Mac) and W keys.

Summary

At its core, the Flex framework comes with many components and a flexible architecture you can customize and extend by using the ActionScript 3 programming language.

This chapter discussed how to customize the surface of the Flex applications by using CSS. Then you made use of one of the coolest Flex features: the data binding process. Flex binds a data object to a component so that the latter becomes automatically added when the value to which it is bound changes (unlike other programming languages, in which you have to write all the code to reproduce this process!). With Flex this feature is built in and ready to use.

To know when something has happened in the application, you need to use the Flex event model. This chapter illustrated how the Flex event model works and how to use the event object to register event listener functions or react to keyboard events.

The solutions in this chapter have just given you a taste for just what's possible with the Flex framework. In Chapter 2 you'll discover the power of Flex components.

2 USING FLEX COMPONENTS

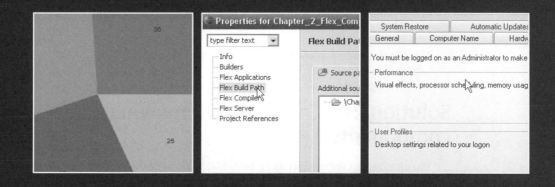

Even though they're based on one page, Flex applications can become very large. If you were to concentrate all the code in the main application file, the resulting application would be difficult to maintain, and it would be impossible to reuse the code and the debugging constructs. Fortunately, Flex supports a component-based development model, which enables the developer to structure the code of the application in a logical way, subdividing it into different files. These external files can be MXML or ActionScript files. When you develop an application with Flex, you use the MXML tag or ActionScript code to declare the objects in the project. These objects are called components, so it is considered to be a **component-based framework**.

You can create custom components in Flex, which enable you to divide the application in a logical way and to structure the functionality on multiple files that can then be maintained separately.

There are many advantages to this approach, including the following:

- **Maintenance**: By subdividing the application into modules, developers can maintain and work on single modules more easily, without having to go through thousands of lines of code to find the portion of code they need.
- **Teamwork**: When working in a team and on a project divided into different files, every developer can dedicate time to specific modules without worrying about overriding the changes made by another developer of the team working on another part of the code.
- **Reusability**: You will often repeat a function or other portion of the code, either in the same or across different projects (a log module that authenticates the user or a data grid listing the responses returned from an HTTP request are common examples). It therefore becomes crucial for a team of developers to be able to reuse already written code.

To create Flex components, you can either extend an existing component in the framework or develop a module from scratch. When you create a component, you extend the Flex class hierarchy by using MXML tags or ActionScript code. Flex is, in fact, implemented with an ActionScript class hierarchy; in the compilation phase, all the objects that you use in the project become compiled in the ActionScript class files before being compiled in a single SWF file.

This chapter covers solutions directly relating to Flex custom components.

Solution 2-1: Creating and invoking MXML components

You can create components using both MXML and ActionScript, and each language brings about the same results—although there are advantages to each approach. While components created using MXML are simpler to develop, they don't offer the control that ActionScript components give.

In this first solution you'll learn how to create an MXML component.

What's involved

Developing MXML components is easy, and there are only a few rules to follow to define a component. The component is defined in a separate MXML file, and instead of using the Application tag as a root tag, a container or control is used (any of them can be used) because only the main application file can contain an Application tag declaration. The MXML components will be invoked and imported in the main application file (where the Application tag is located), so you have to choose which object to base it on (you can use any container or control). At this point, you can insert all the code you require to develop the functionality to be included in the component.

In this solution you'll develop an MXML component to manage a login procedure, with a form to enter user ID and password.

How to build it

Begin by creating a new Flex project from Flex Builder; you will use this same project throughout all of Chapter 2.

1. Open Flex Builder and create a Flex project with the name Chapter_2_Flex_ Components. Click Next.

2. Create an MXML component by selecting File ➤ New ➤ MXML Component. The New MXML Component dialog box that opens is different from the classic dialog box that creates a MXML application (see Figure 2-1).

3. Specify the file name in the Filename field: Chapter_2_Sol_1.mxml, and also set the element that acts as the root tag, choosing from the Based on drop-down menu. Choose a Panel as base component for this example. Set the Width field to 400 and the Height field to 300.

4. Click Finish and open the Chapter_2_Sol_1.mxml file.

The Chapter_2_Sol_1 component contains the following code:

```
<?xml version="1.0" encoding="utf-8"?>
<mx:Panel xmlns:mx="http://www.adobe.com/2006/mxml"
    layout="absolute"
    width="400" height="300">
</mx:Panel>
```

The first line of code specifies the XML document type declaration, followed by the Panel tag, which acts as the root tag for this component. The xmlns:mx namespace is necessary; if this declaration is omitted, the tags used in the code are not recognized as valid.

Now add the user interface elements and the ActionScript functions in the new MXML component.

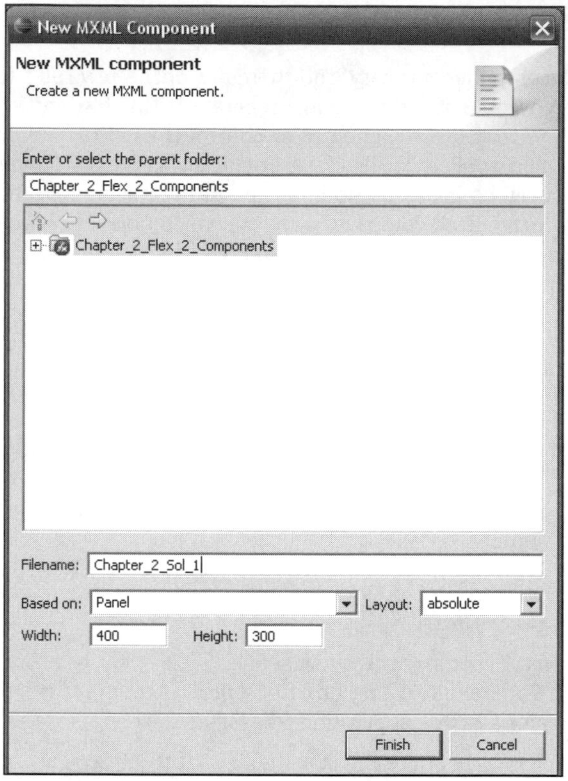

Figure 2-1. The New MXML Component dialog box

5. Add a title to the Panel by setting the property title with the Sign In value. You can use the Flex Property view when your Flex Builder is in Design mode, or you can set the title property of the Panel with this code:

```
<mx:Panel xmlns:mx="http://www.adobe.com/2006/mxml"
    layout="absolute"
    width="400" height="300"
        title="Sign In">
</mx:Panel>
```

6. Insert a Form tag containing the following code into the Panel container:

```
<mx:Form x="10" y="10" width="360" height="240">
  <mx:FormHeading label="Insert your information:"/>
  <mx:FormItem label="User">
    <mx:TextInput/>
  </mx:FormItem>
  <mx:FormItem label="Password">
    <mx:TextInput/>
  </mx:FormItem>
  <mx:FormItem label="Remember me">
    <mx:CheckBox label="Checkbox"/>
  </mx:FormItem>
```

```
<mx:FormItem>
  <mx:Button label="Button"/>
</mx:FormItem>
</mx:Form>
```

The form contains several iterations of TextInput (to insert the user's credentials into), a check box for a Remember me function, and a button to submit the inputted data.

7. Save the MXML component.

Don't run the project yet; to be able to use MXML components, Flex must launch them from the main application file. When you created the Flex project in Flex Builder, a file was automatically created in the main application file to which the name of the project was assigned. If you look in the Navigator in Flex Builder, you will find the Chapter_2_Flex_Components.mxml file, which contains the following code:

```
<?xml version="1.0" encoding="utf-8"?>
<mx:Application
    xmlns:mx="http://www.adobe.com/2006/mxml"
    layout="absolute">

</mx:Application>
```

To invoke an external MXML component in the main application, you need to declare a custom namespace that points to the package containing the MXML component and invoke that component using the custom namespace and its file name (without the .mxml extension).

8. Insert the following new code to invoke the MXML component:

```
<?xml version="1.0" encoding="utf-8"?>
<mx:Application xmlns:mx="http://www.adobe.com/2006/mxml"
layout="absolute"
    xmlns:comp = "*">

<comp:Chapter_2_Sol_1 />

</mx:Application>
```

The declaration of a custom namespace named comp (any value would do) was added into the Application tag. This namespace defines the package that contains the components to import.

Having created an MXML component on the main root of the project, it is enough to use the value "*", which includes all the files located on the root of the project. Using the custom namespace you can invoke the MXML component by referring to the name of the file without the .mxml extension:

```
<comp:Chapter_2_Sol_1 />
```

9. Save the file and run the application. You'll see the component loaded and displayed in the application file.

Expert tips

A Flex project can be made up of many MXML components, and some of them can also be imported from other projects. For this reason, the management of the package is a very important aspect. You should create the MXML components in a separate folder and then create more subfolders to keep custom components conveniently categorized (by function or first letter, for example) and to avoid name duplication. Ensure that the correct custom package is referenced during the creation of the custom namespace in the main application file.

> *Object-oriented programming (OOP) has a convention for generating a unique package name: the reverse domain name. It's an arbitrary convention that uses a specific property to generate a unique name. The general rule is the following:*
>
> *top-level domain names (or organization's name) + project name (or machine's name, author . . .) + name of the class*
>
> *For this example, you could use the following:*
>
> *com.flexsolutions.chapter2.myClass*
>
> *This technique becomes more important when you want to distribute the codes or if you work within a team of developers.*

If all MXML components were saved in the com/flexsolutions/chapter2 folder, the custom namespace should be aimed at this package:

```
<mx:Application xmlns:mx="http://www.adobe.com/2006/mxml"
layout="absolute"
xmlns:comp = " com.flexsolutions.chapter2.* ">
```

Defining a custom namespace also involves the presence of the MXML components defined in that package in the Component view of Flex Builder. This view is found in the Design mode of Flex Builder, when you drag and drop a custom component from the Custom folder into the page area of the file (see Figure 2-2). This ensures that the code necessary to invoke the component is automatically written.

Figure 2-2.
After the custom namespace has been declared, all custom components created in that package are added to the Component view.

Solution 2-2: Defining properties and methods of MXML components

One of the advantages of using external components is that you can divide up the application functionality in a logical way, thereby making it easier to maintain and reuse. To be able to create more reusable MXML components, however, you have to parameterize them by sending properties and defining methods within them. They can then also be used with the component on other projects.

When you create an MXML component, you are, in effect, creating an ActionScript class. When Flex compiles the project at runtime, it converts all the MXML components to ActionScript classes that will then be compiled in the SWF file. To create more reusable and powerful MXML components, you'll add properties and methods to your components. To define properties and methods, you use ActionScript code that you add in an `<mx:Script>` block of your MXML components.

In this solution you'll create properties and methods to parameterize an MXML component.

What's involved

Properties and methods of an MXML component are defined in an `<mx:Script>` block within the MXML component using ActionScript. To define a property in ActionScript you must specify the access modifier (public, private, protected, or internal), use the keyword var, and declare a data type:

```
public var myString:String = "Hello World";
```

ActionScript 3 properties can be declared by using five different access modifiers:

internal: *Makes the property visible to references inside the same package (the default value)*

private: *Makes the property visible to references only in the same class*

protected: *Makes the property visible to references in the same class and derived classes*

public: *Makes the property visible to references everywhere*

static: *Makes the property accessible via the parent class instead of instances of the class*

The previous code creates a public property in the MXML component, which the application can access and reference. A very similar procedure is used to define a method: Specify the access modifier, use the keyword function, indicate the prospective parameters in the brackets (and relative data type), and define the return type (if the function does not return a value, use the keyword void):

```
public function myFunc(param:String):void {}
```

To access the properties of a component from the application file, you have to reference that component by using its id. As with all tags, MXML components that become invoked also put forward an ID attribute that contains the application name. You can add the id directly to the tag that invokes the Chapter_2_Sol_1.mxml component:

```
<?xml version="1.0" encoding="utf-8"?>
<mx:Application xmlns:mx="http://www.adobe.com/2006/mxml"
   layout="absolute"
   xmlns:comp = "*">

<comp:Chapter_2_Sol_1 id="compID" />
<mx:Application>
```

You can now refer directly to every object (control or container), property, or method declared in the MXML component via ActionScript:

```
// invoke the myProp property of the component
compID.myProp
// call the myFunc method of the MXML component

compID.myFunc()
```

How to build it

You'll create a new component that creates a PieChart, taken from the Flex charting components family (the Flex charting components must be installed first).

1. Open the Flex project created in the previous example: Chapter_2_Flex_ Components.

2. Create a new MXML application document by selecting File ➤ New ➤ MXML Application and name it Chapter_2_Sol_2_app.mxml. This will be the main application file that will invoke the MXML component.

3. Insert the following <mx:Script> block into this file:

```
<mx:Application
   xmlns:mx=http://www.adobe.com/2006/mxml
   layout="vertical">
  <mx:Script>
   <![CDATA[
     import mx.collections.ArrayCollection;
     [Bindable]
     public var flashPlayer:ArrayCollection = new ArrayCollection([
       {Penetration: "Market", Value: 36},
       {Penetration: "US / Canada", Value: 40},
       {Penetration: "Europe", Value: 37},
       {Penetration: "Japan", Value: 25},
     ]);
   ]]>
  </mx:Script>
```

This code creates a public variable of type ArrayCollection that contains an array of objects that will function as data providers to compile the MXML component pie chart. This variable uses the metadata [Bindable], which enables the variable to be used with a data binding (refer to Solution 1-4).

4. Create the folder structure com/flexsolutions/chapter2 by selecting File ➤ New ➤ Folder. This will be the directory for housing any external components you create.

5. In the com/flexsolutions/chapter2 folder, create a new MXML component using File ➤ New ➤ MXML Component, name it Chapter_2_Sol_2.mxml, and base it on a Panel. Specify the width, height and title properties with the following values:

- width = "80%"
- height = "80%"
- title = "Solution 2-2: Defining properties and methods of MXML Component"

The code of your MXML component will look like this:

```
<?xml version="1.0" encoding="utf-8"?>
<mx:Panel xmlns:mx="http://www.adobe.com/2006/mxml"
    layout="absolute"
    width="80%"
    height="80%"
    title="Solution 2-2:
    Defining properties and methods of MXML Component" >
</mx:Panel>
```

6. Insert a PieChart component into the component, which displays a data series as a standard pie chart (Flex charting components will be discussed in Chapter 12). Add the following code in the Panel container:

```
<?xml version="1.0" encoding="utf-8"?>
<mx:Panel xmlns:mx="http://www.adobe.com/2006/mxml"
    layout="absolute"
    width="80%"
    height="80%"
    title="Solution 2-2:
    Defining properties and methods of MXML Component" >

    <mx:PieChart id="myPie"
      dataProvider="{myDP}"
      showDataTips="false">
      <mx:series>
        <mx:PieSeries labelPosition="insideWithCallout"
          field="Value" />
      </mx:series>
    </mx:PieChart>

</mx:Panel>
```

The PieChart component displays the data defined in its dataProvider property. In this case, the dataProvider property is populated by myDP, which will be created in the next few steps. It will be sent from the main application to the component and it will contain the data created in the flashPlayer ArrayCollection variable (refer to Step 3). All data in the collection determines the size of each wedge in the pie chart relative to the other wedges:

```
<mx:PieChart id="myPie"
  dataProvider="{myDP}"
  showDataTips="false">
  <mx:series>
    <mx:PieSeries labelPosition="insideWithCallout"
      field="Value" />
  </mx:series>
</mx:PieChart>
```

The PieSeries tag defines a data series for the chart. Within this tag, you specify in the field property the data that will be used to create and design the pie chart. You have linked the field to the Value property of the myDP data provider.

Instead, the labelPosition attribute defines how to render labels in the pie chart (it accepts the following values: none, outside, callout, inside, and insideWithCallout):

```
<mx:PieSeries labelPosition="insideWithCallout"
  field="Value" />
```

You'll learn more about Flex charting components in Chapter 12.

7. Add an <mx:Script> block below the Application tag, in which you will create the myDP property of the MXML component:

```
<mx:Application
xmlns:mx="http://www.adobe.com/2006/mxml"
layout="vertical">

<mx:Script>
<![CDATA[
import mx.collections.ArrayCollection;
[Bindable]
public var myDP:ArrayCollection;
]]>
</mx:Script>
```

The property has only just been declared and is empty at the moment, but it will be populated when the component is invoked from the main application file.

8. You can now invoke the component. Open the Chapter_2_Sol_2_app.mxml file and create a custom namespace in the Application tag:

```
<mx:Application
xmlns:mx="http://www.adobe.com/2006/mxml"
layout="vertical"
xmlns:comp = "com.flexsolutions.chapter2.*">
```

The comp custom namespace defines the package in the com/flexsolutions/chapter2 folder, which is where you created the MXML component.

9. It is now possible to reference and invoke the component. Insert the following code in the body of the application document:

```
<comp:Chapter_2_Sol_2 id="myComp" />
```

You have invoked the component and assigned an id to it.

10. The aim was to access the properties of an MXML component. You will, in fact, pass the myDP property, defined within the MXML component, by creating a binding with the flashPlayer ArrayCollection variable, directly accessing it from the custom component tag:

```
<comp:Chapter_2_Sol_2 id="myComp"
myDP="{flashPlayer}" />
```

11. Save both files and run Chapter_2_Sol_2_app.mxml. You should see the pie chart display, as shown in Figure 2-3.

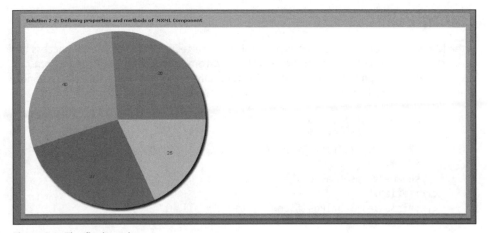

Figure 2-3. The final result

The same procedure can now be applied to create and access a method of the MXML component. Let's do this now.

12. Add an ActionScript method inside the <mx:Script> block of the Chapter_2_Sol_2.mxml file:

```
<mx:Script>
  <![CDATA[
    import mx.collections.ArrayCollection;
    [Bindable]
      public var myDP:ArrayCollection;
```

```
        public function sayHello():String
        {
          return "Hello World from the MXML Component";
        }
      ]]>
    </mx:Script>
```

The sayHello() method returns a string. You will print this returned value in a Label in the application file.

13. Open the Chapter_2_Sol_2_app.mxml file and add a Label control immediately under the declaration of the component:

```
<mx:Label id="myLabel" text="{myComp.sayHello()}" />
```

This Label will write the value returned by the sayHello() method of the myComp component in its text property.

14. Save the file and run the application.

Expert tips

If the MXML component is based on a control such as PieChart, it is possible to access the properties and the methods of that object directly from the invocation of the custom tag. If you base the component directly on a PieChart control instead of starting with a Panel, you can begin directly with the declaration of the PieChart control:

```
<?xml version="1.0" encoding="utf-8"?>

<mx:PieChart xmlns:mx=http://www.adobe.com/2006/mxml
    id="myPie"
    showDataTips="false">
<mx:series>
<mx:PieSeries labelPosition="insideWithCallout"
    field="Value" />
</mx:series>
</mx:PieChart>
```

You can now send the dataProvider property of the PieChart control directly into the declaration of the custom tag in the main application file:

```
<comp:Chapter_2_Sol_2 id="myComp"
dataProvider="{flashPlayer}" />
```

You can do this because the dataProvider is the default property for the PieChart component. This process reduces some lines of ActionScript code.

Solution 2-3: Creating ActionScript components

There is a connection between MXML components and those developed with ActionScript. In the compilation phase, everything is reduced to an ActionScript class. So why does a developer have to create an ActionScript component? This choice obviously depends on the objectives and the requisites of the project, but there are also a few rules for developers to follow:

- If you are creating simple components that modify the behavior of an existing Flex component, it is faster to create an MXML component (for example, if you are just adding functions or custom styles to a ComboBox control).

- If you want to create a visual component to extend the UIComponent class, or create a nonvisual component such as a custom formatter or validator, use an ActionScript component.

In this solution you'll see how to create a simple ActionScript component by creating and working on an ActionScript class.

What's involved

To create an ActionScript component you must first create an ActionScript class that will contain both the visual elements and the logic of the component. All Flex components are implemented in a class hierarchy in ActionScript, which contains all the classes that define the functions of Flex (see Figure 2-4).

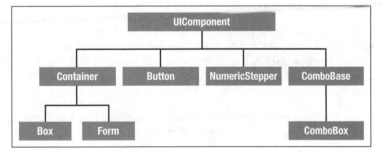

Figure 2-4. Flex class hierarchy

You need to choose which class to extend to create the component. For example, visual components are derived from the UIComponent class. Therefore, to create a custom visual ActionScript component, the ActionScript class extends the UIComponent class or any components that extend the UIComponent class. In this case, all the properties, methods and events become inherited. Although you can create a component from scratch, using the UIComponent class as a base class for a custom component saves you a lot of time because you don't have to create everything from scratch.

To extend a class in ActionScript, all you need is the extend keyword:

```
package com.flexsolutions.chapter2
{
import mx.controls.DataGrid;

public class Chapter_2_Sol_3 extends DataGrid
{
   public function Chapter_2_Sol_3()
{

}

}
 }
```

This class extends the DataGrid control, which extends the UIComponent class, and enables it to inherit all the properties, methods, and events in this component. The ActionScript components are then invoked and referenced in the Flex application as MXML tags.

How to build it

In this solution you extend a ComboBox control by inserting a value in its dataProvider property. As is the case with all data-driven controls, the dataProvider property is a collection of objects that contains data required by a component in order to be populated.

A ComboBox is usually populated with a dataProvider, which can become linked to a data binding (refer to Solution 1-4) and to values received from a remote call. Therefore, in most cases the ComboBox does not display "Select a value..." as the first item, which (according to the norms of usability) helps you understand that you must select one of the values.

You'll create an ActionScript component that will automatically insert this string as the first value to be displayed in the ComboBox. Let's get to work.

1. Open the Flex project created in the previous example: Chapter_2_Flex_ Components.

2. Create a new ActionScript class by selecting File ➤ New ➤ ActionScript Class and save it in the com/flexsolutions/chapter2 folder. In the dialog box that displays, select the following values:

   - Package: com.flexsolutions.chapter2
   - Name: Chapter_2_Sol_3
   - Modifiers: public
   - Superclass: mx.controls.ComboBox

Figure 2-5 shows the settings set in the dialog box.

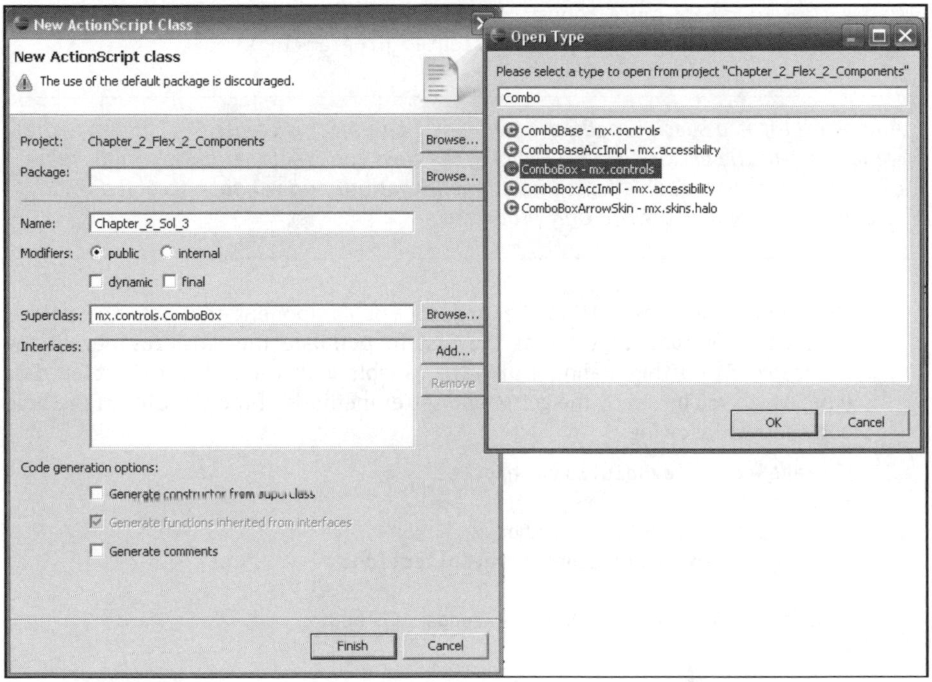

Figure 2-5. Set the superclass and package of the ActionScript class.

You have automatically created an ActionScript class that extends the ComboBox class and therefore inherits all its properties, methods, and events. Moreover, the ActionScript class has been automatically saved in the com/flexsolutions/chapter2 folder, which contains the custom components.

The code for the class should look like this:

```
package  com.flexsolutions.chapter2
{
import mx.controls.ComboBox;

public class Chapter_2_Sol_3 extends  ComboBox
{
   public function Chapter_2_Sol_3()
   {

   }

}
}
```

The Chapter_2_Sol_3() public method is the class constructor. You don't need to worry about putting it there because Flex will look after the process of creating it in the compilation phase. However, it is best practice in OOP not to give direct access to properties

.

within a class to create more robust code (see the encapsulation concept of OOP at http://en.wikipedia.org/wiki/Object_oriented_programming).

> A constructor is a special method called when an object is created. It often has the same name as the declaring class. Defining the class constructor enables you to create class properties with sophisticated functionality, format and validate accepted values, or create read-only and write-only properties.

3. Now you'll add the code to the ActionScript component that sets the default "Select a value..." value as the first to populate the dataProvider of the ComboBox. To do this, define a private variable with the ArrayCollection data type, which will be set by the getter and setter methods of the class. Insert the bold code shown following:

```
package   com.flexsolutions.chapter2
{
      import mx.controls.ComboBox;
      import mx.collections.ArrayCollection;

public class Chapter_2_Sol_3 extends   ComboBox
{

        private var _myDP:ArrayCollection;

        public function set setMyDP(dataP:ArrayCollection):void
        {
          _myDP = dataP;
            myDP.addItemAt("Select a value...", 0);
            this.dataProvider = _myDP;
        }

        public function get setMyDP():ArrayCollection
        {
            return _myDP;
        }

        public function Chapter_2_Sol_3()
        {

        }

    }
}
```

Getter and setter methods are defined accessor methods (they are public interfaces to change private class members). In OOP the direct access to properties within a class is discouraged.

There are other advantages of using getter and setter methods for properties of a class: You can create members with sophisticated functionality, and you can also create read-only and write-only properties.

The setter method assigns the private property _myDP sent as the data provider of the application, which will recall this custom component. Using the addItemAt() method of the ArrayCollection class, you add a string on the zero index (the ArrayCollection class is index zero based), which will appear in the ComboBox in the production of a video phase:

```
public function set setMyDP(dataP:ArrayCollection):void
{
   _myDP = dataP;

   _myDP.addItemAt("Select a value...", 0);

   this.dataProvider = _myDP;

}
```

With the ActionScript component created, you can now reference it in the application.

4. Create a new MXML application document by selecting File ➤ New ➤ MXML Application and give it the name Chapter_2_Sol_3_app.mxml. This will be the main application file that will invoke the ActionScript component.

5. Define a custom namespace on the Application tag with its layout property set to vertical:

```
<?xml version="1.0" encoding-"utf-8"?>
<mx:Application
    xmlns:mx="http://www.adobe.com/2006/mxml"
    layout="vertical"
xmlns:comp = "com.flexsolutions.chapter2.*">

</mx:Application>
```

The xmlns:comp namespace references the com.flexsolutions.chapter2 package, which contains the ActionScript component. To be able to invoke it, as you did with the MXML component, use the tag notation.

6. Reference the ActionScript class using the name of the file (without the .as extension):

```
<?xml version="1.0" encoding="utf-8"?>
<mx:Application
    xmlns:mx="http://www.adobe.com/2006/mxml"
    layout="vertical"
    xmlns:comp = "com.flexsolutions.chapter2.*">

    <comp:Chapter_2_Sol_3 id="myCB" />
</mx:Application>
```

The ActionScript component has been invoked in the application. It now needs to be passed to the data provider.

7. In the <mx:Script> block, you now need to insert a variable with the ArrayCollection data type, containing the values that will populate the custom ComboBox. This variable will be sent to the custom component, which will perform the operations declared in the setMyDP() method. Insert the following code:

```
<mx:Application
    xmlns:mx="http://www.adobe.com/2006/mxml"
    layout="vertical"
    xmlns:comp = "com.flexsolutions.chapter2.*">
  <mx:Script>
   <![CDATA[
      import mx.collections.ArrayCollection;
      [Bindable]
        private var myAC:ArrayCollection =➨
        new ArrayCollection(["First Value", "Second Value",➨
        "Third Value"]);

   ]]>
  </mx:Script>

  <comp:Chapter_2_Sol_3
    id="myCB"
    setMyDP="{myAC}" />

</mx:Application>
```

8. Save and run the application. The final result will be a custom ComboBox populated by the myAC variable (see Figure 2-6).

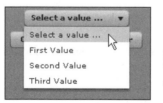

Figure 2-6.
The custom ComboBox defined as an ActionScript component

Expert tips

When developing components that must return data to the main application, it is best practice to dispatch an event from the component using the dispatchEvent(new Event("myEvent")) method. This event contains the return values that will be managed by the event handlers of the main application.

You can insert a Button in the previous example that changes the value of the data provider of the custom ComboBox, setting a new ArrayCollection variable:

```
<mx:Application
  xmlns:mx="http://www.adobe.com/2006/mxml"
  layout="vertical"
  xmlns:comp = "com.flexsolutions.chapter2.*">
  <mx:Script>
    <![CDATA[
      import mx.collections.ArrayCollection;

      [Bindable]
        private var myAC:ArrayCollection = new ArrayCollection(➡
          ["First Value", "Second Value","Third Value"]);

        private var myAC_2:ArrayCollection = new ArrayCollection(➡
          ["Hello", "Goodbye"]);

    ]]>
  </mx:Script>

  <comp:Chapter_2_Sol_3 id="myCB" setMyDP="{myAC}" />

  <mx:Button id="my" label="Change the Data Provider"➡
    click="myCB.setMyDP = myAC_2 ; my.enabled=false " />

</mx:Application>
```

A private variable of ArrayCollection type has been created that contains two strings:

```
private var myAC_2:ArrayCollection =➡
  new ArrayCollection(["Hello", "Goodbye"]);
```

When the Button is clicked, the setter function setMyDP changes the value of the data provider and dispatches the event:

```
<mx:Button id="my" label="Change the Data Provider"➡
  click="myCB.setMyDP = myAC_2; my.enabled=false " />
```

On the click event, the Button is disabled so the user can't click it again.

In the ActionScript component, the dispatch of the custom event with the dispatchEvent() method is carried out like this:

```
dispatchEvent(new Event("changeDP"));
```

This causes the bindable getter function on the custom event to be created:

```
[Bindable(event="changeDP")]
```

This is the completed code for the ActionScript class:

```
package com.flexsolutions.chapter2
{
  import mx.controls.ComboBox;
  import mx.collections.ArrayCollection;
  import flash.events.Event;

  public class Chapter_2_Sol_3 extends  ComboBox
  {

    private var _myDP:ArrayCollection;

    public function set setMyDP(dataP:ArrayCollection):void
    {
      _myDP = dataP;
      _myDP.addItemAt("Select a value...", 0);
      this.dataProvider = _myDP;
      dispatchEvent(new Event("changeDP"));
    }

    [Bindable(event="changeDP")]
    public function get setMyDP():ArrayCollection
    {
      return _myDP;
    }

    public function Chapter_2_Sol_3()
    {

    }

  }
}
```

Solution 2-4: Managing multiple packages for components

A Flex application can make use of many components. Flex gives you the ability to import external projects in the creation phase of a new project or by accessing the Project ➤ Properties menu. From the same panel, it is also possible to import a library of components compiled in the SWC format. These capabilities help optimize the development of applications by reusing the components that were previously developed.

In this scenario, the choice of structure of the packages is of fundamental importance to avoid creating conflicts and to render the code to be clean and easy to read. In this solution you'll see how to apply methods and to follow best practices to avoid these types of errors.

In real-world applications, you might see custom components placed in a package structure that uses a reverse domain name structure (for example, `xmlns:custom="com.adobe. quickstarts.customcomponents.*"`). This convention avoids namespace conflicts between identically named components by different vendors. For example, two component libraries might each have a `Map` component that you use in your application. If one is in the `com.vendorA` package and the other is in the `com.vendorB` package, they don't conflict.

What's involved

To invoke and reference a component in the main application, the first step is to declare a custom namespace that references the package containing the declarations of the components. The namespace is set with the `xmlns` property, followed by the suffix. For MXML files, you use the `mx` suffix, which defines the collection of legal MXML tags you can use throughout your application:

```
<mx:Application xmlns:mx="http://www.adobe.com/2006/mxml">
```

The value given to the namespace, `http://www.adobe.com/2006/mxml`, is a Uniform Resource Identifier (URI), which associates the `mx` prefix with a manifest file in `flex-config.xml`. When you want to create a custom namespace, you aim at a package that represents the folder containing the component declarations:

```
<mx:Application xmlns:mx="http://www.adobe.com/2006/mxml"
    xmlns:myPref=" com.flexsolutions.chapter2.*" >
```

But what if the project uses different packages containing different components? You can reference them all in the following manner:

```
<mx:Application xmlns:mx="http://www.adobe.com/2006/mxml"
        xmlns:myPref=" com.flexsolutions.chapter2.control.*"
        xmlns:myPrefA =" com.flexsolutions.chapter2.utils.*"
    xmlns:myPrefZ =" com.flexsolutions.chapter2.comp.*" >
```

Flex enables you to define the namespaces one after another. In this solution you'll look at a working example.

How to build it

When you invoke a component it usually defines the custom namespace in the Application tag using the `xmlns` attribute. However, when the developer needs to use more namespaces to aim at different pieces of software (in different packages), it is possible to declare them one after the other on the invoked component instead of inserting the declaration in a single tag (the `Application` tag).

1. Download Flex-Ajax Bridge (FABridge) from http://download.macromedia.com/pub/labs/flex/2/FABridge_B3_05-08.zip.

> *FABridge is a small, unobtrusive library of code that you can insert into an Adobe Flex application, a Flex component, or even an empty SWF file to expose it to scripting in the browser. It has been released to the community under an open source license.*

2. Unzip the file and copy the src folder into the com folder of the Flex project. You can also follow the installation instructions in the Readme.txt file in the FABridge unzipped folder.

3. Select your project in the Navigator view, right-click (Apple-click on the Mac), and choose Properties. Select the Flex Build Path section, in which you'll add the src folder to the class path section (see Figure 2-7).

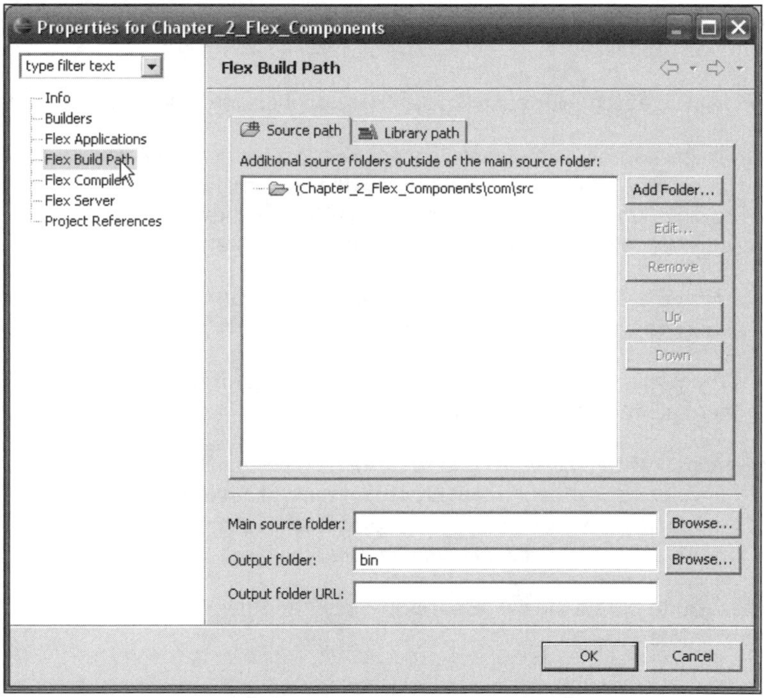

Figure 2-7. Flex Build Path dialog box

4. Create a new MXML application document by selecting File ➤ New ➤ MXML Application and name it Chapter_2_Sol_4.mxml. This will be the main application file that will invoke the component.

5. Invoke the component created in Solution 2.1, first declaring a custom namespace in the Application tag:

```
<mx:Application xmlns:mx="http://www.adobe.com/2006/mxml"
  layout="absolute"
  xmlns:comp = "*">

  <comp:Chapter_2_Sol_1 />
</mx:Application>
```

6. Add the component to use the FABridge class and create the custom namespace in the same tag:

```
<mx:Application xmlns:mx="http://www.adobe.com/2006/mxml"
  layout="absolute"
  xmlns:comp = "*">

  <comp:Chapter_2_Sol_1 />

  <fab:FABridge xmlns:fab="bridge.*" />

</mx:Application>
```

With this method, you can make the code more readable and easier to maintain by referring to just a single invocation of an ActionScript class using the xmlns attribute directly inside that tag's declaration.

Expert tips

FABridge is an alternative to ExternalInterface for writing ActionScript and JavaScript communication. FABridge enables developers to access and control any Flex elements by writing JavaScript on the HTML side.

This solution included FABridge within the Flex application:

```
<mx:Application xmlns:mx="http://www.adobe.com/2006/mxml"
  layout="absolute"
  xmlns:comp = "*">

  <comp:Chapter_2_Sol_1 />

  <fab:FABridge xmlns:fab="bridge.*" />

</mx:Application>
```

To make it work, you'll put the FABridge.js file (hosted in the src/bridge folder of the FABridge archive file) onto the web server folder in which the HTML page resides. Then you can write the JavaScript code to access controls in the Flex application, writing the following code in a JavaScript block within the HTML page:

```
var myFlexRef = FABridge.flash.root;
var flexTextArea = myFlexRef.textAreaID();
```

The TextArea variable contains the instance name given to a TextArea control in the Flex application. You can also access any properties of a control via JavaScript:

```
var myFlexRef = FABridge.flash.root;
var flexText = myFlexRef.textAreaID().text();
```

The flexText variable contains the text value of the Flex TextArea control.

You can learn more about the FABridge library here: http://labs.adobe.com/wiki/index.php/Flex-Ajax_Bridge.

Solution 2-5: Handling events within custom components

Custom components created in either MXML or ActionScript can manage the event listeners they contain. You can define predefined events (those that make up part of the architecture of Flex in the mx.core.UIComponent class) and also manage custom events.

To write an event listener to be managed in the custom component, it must be registered with a addEvent1Listener() method, and the event handler with which you will manage the event must be written.

In this solution, you'll extend the custom component created in Solution 2-3 by creating an event listener in the custom component.

What's involved

The steps involved in managing an event listener within the custom component are few and simple. Using the addEventListener() method, register the event listener that you will write on the release of the event:

```
componentInstance.addEventListener(event_type:String,
    event_listener:Function,
    use_capture:Boolean,
    priority:int,
    weakRef:Boolean)
```

After the event is registered, write the event handler. By invoking the custom component in a main application, you'll see that the event listener defined in the custom component is invoked.

How to build it

Begin by opening the ActionScript component created in the previous solution and saving it under a new name.

1. Create a new ActionScript class in the com/flexsolutions/chapter2 project folder by selecting File ➤ New ➤ ActionScript Class and name it Chapter_2_Sol_5. This class extends the ComboBox class. Insert the following code:

```
package  com.flexsolutions.chapter2
{
  import mx.controls.ComboBox;
  import mx.collections.ArrayCollection;
  import flash.events.Event;

  public class Chapter_2_Sol_5 extends  ComboBox
  {
    private var _myDP:ArrayCollection;

    public function set setMyDP(dataP:ArrayCollection):void
    {
      _myDP = dataP;
      _myDP.addItemAt("Select a value...", 0);
      this.dataProvider = _myDP;
      var myClassesEvent:Event = new Event("changedDP");
      dispatchEvent(myClassesEvent);
    }

    [Bindable(event="changeDP")]
    public function get setMyDP():ArrayCollection
    {
      return _myDP;
    }

    public function Chapter_2_Sol_5()
    {
    }
  }
}
```

The class is very similar to the ActionScript class you created in Solution 2-3 so the comments are skipped this time.

2. Register the event listener using the addEventListener() method in the constructor:

```
public function Chapter_2_Sol_5()
{
    super();
    addEventListener("creationComplete",resize);}
```

In the constructor the super() method is called, which enables you to invoke the parent class' constructor to initialize the inherited items from the super class. Even though this is not obligatory, leaving it out it could mean that the inherited parts of the superclass might not be properly constructed. So you should call the super() method in the constructor.

The addEventListener() method registers the event handler resize() on the creationComplete event, which will be recalled at the moment in which the event is released.

3. Write this event handler as follows (set the width of the custom component to a predefined value and sort on the data provider):

```
public function Chapter_2_Sol_5()
{
  addEventListener("creationComplete",resize);}

private function resize(e:Event):void
{
  addEventListener("focusIn", onFocusIn);
  this.width = 150;
  var sort:Sort = new Sort();
  sort.fields = [new SortField(null, true)];
 _myDP.sort = sort;
  _myDP.refresh();
  super();
}
private function onFocusIn(e:Event):void
{
  this.width = 200;
}
```

The resize() and onFocusIn() functions accept the event object generated by the Event class as a parameter. In reality you won't use it in these functions.

In the resize() function the value of the width property was set at 150px, and a sort on the ArrayCollection class was carried out (this class will be dealt with in more detail in Chapter 5). Take note that the packages making use of the Sort and SortField classes were imported at the beginning of the class:

```
import mx.controls.ComboBox;
import mx.collections.ArrayCollection;
import flash.events.Event;
import mx.collections.Sort;
import mx.collections.SortField;
```

4. To use the custom component, you need to import it into the main application. Create a new application file and name it Chapter_2_Sol_5_app.mxml. Import the custom namespace into the Application tag and insert an <mx:Script> block to define an ArrayCollection variable. It will be passed to the custom component and act as dataProvider for the ComboBox:

```
<mx:Application
  xmlns:mx="http://www.adobe.com/2006/mxml"
  layout="vertical"
  xmlns:comp = "com.flexsolutions.chapter2.*">
  <mx:Script>
```

```
    <![CDATA[
      import mx.collections.ArrayCollection;
      [Bindable]
      private var myAC:ArrayCollection = new ArrayCollection(➥
        ["First Value", "Second Value","Third Value"]);
    ]]>
  </mx:Script>

</mx:Application>
```

5. Insert the custom component in the application file and add a Label control that will print the width property of the custom component:

```
<?xml version="1.0" encoding="utf-8"?>
<mx:Application
  xmlns:mx="http://www.adobe.com/2006/mxml"
  layout="vertical"
  xmlns:comp - "com.flexsolutions.chapter2.*">
  <mx:Script>
    <![CDATA[
      import mx.collections.ArrayCollection;
      [Bindable]
      private var myAC:ArrayCollection = new ArrayCollection(➥
        ["First Value", "Second Value","Third Value"]);
    ]]>
  </mx:Script>

  <comp:Chapter_2_Sol_5 id="myCB" setMyDP-"{myAC}" />

  <mx:Label text="The width of my custom Combo box is: ➥
    {myCB.width}" />
</mx:Application>
```

6. Save the file and run the application. The custom component dispatches the event listener on the creationComplete event, changes its dimension to 150px, and sorts the ArrayCollection. If you open the ComboBox, you'll see that the values inside have been sorted, as shown in Figure 2-8.

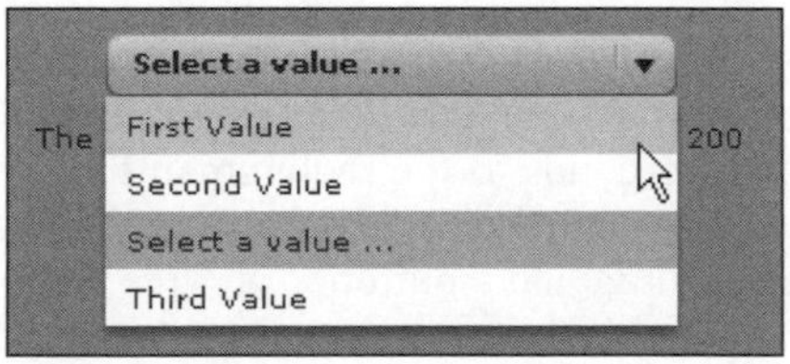

Figure 2-8. The event has been carried out.

Expert tips

In the ActionScript component, the creationComplete event was sent as a string to the addEventHandler():

```
public function Chapter_2_Sol_4()
{
  super();
  addEventListener("creationComplete",resize);
}
```

There is an issue here, however. If you made an error in typing the name of the event, you would not have received any error message at compile time; you would instead have received an error message at runtime.

Best practice dictates that it is necessary to always use the constants of the system and send the event to the addEventListener() method using the name of the event:

```
import mx.events.FlexEvent;

public function Chapter_2_Sol_4()
{
  super();
  addEventListener(FlexEvent.CREATION_COMPLETE,resize);
}
```

The FlexEvent class contains all the system events managed by the Flex framework, which includes CREATION_COMPLETE. If you use this approach, don't worry because if you make a mistake in writing the event, Flex Builder will flag the error at compile time.

One more important point to take on board: To use the FlexEvent class like this, you must import it at the beginning of the code:

```
import mx.events.FlexEvent;
```

Solution 2-6: Creating composite components

Until now you have seen components formatted by only a single element, but you will often come across components that contain other components. For example, if you want to create a component that responds to the requirements of a sign-in procedure for an authenticated login, your component will be formatted by at least three objects: a container, a form with two text inputs, and a button.

A component that contains multiple components for which the definition of the root tag begins with a container is called a **composite component**. When creating a composite component with ActionScript, the components that are used in the class must be instanced as properties of the class. In addition, some of the controls used will have graphical assets, which will be set as default values in the ActionScript class. It isn't possible to access the properties of the single controls in the MXML author's environment because the class that will be extended will be the UIComponent, not that of the single controls (for example, a Button or a Label).

> *The composite name gives you a clue that the composite components use "composition" instead of using the "inheritance" facet of object programming.*

What's involved

In this solution you'll create ActionScript composite components by creating an ActionScript class that extends the UIComponent class:

```
public class MyCompositeComponent extends UIComponent {
```

In this class you'll insert a ComboBox control and a DataGrid control. To use these controls you must import their classes, instance them one at a time as children, and set their properties to represent them on the screen:

```
import mx.controls.ComboBox;
import mx.controls.DataGrid;
// I create the objects which will contain the private var
myDG:DataGrid;
private var myCB:ComboBox;

// Create the istance of a ComboBox class and set
// its  explicitWidth and editable properties
myCB = new ComboBox();
myCB.explicitWidth = 120;
myCB.editable = false;
```

Given that the properties and the methods of the single controls aren't settable from the MXML author's environment (unless the developer has explicitly designed the class to allow access to do this), you'll have to write all the code necessary to visualize, position, and populate the controls to video.

How to build it

The ActionScript composite component you'll create will include a ComboBox control and a DataGrid control, which will be instanced in the ActionScript class.

1. Begin by creating an ActionScript class in the com/flexsolutions/chapter2 folder by selecting File ➤ New ➤ ActionScript Class. Assign the name Chapter_2_Sol_6 to this class.

2. Insert the first parts of the code that are necessary to extend and to instance the objects that you will use in the component. Enter the following into the new class:

```
package  com.flexsolutions.chapter2
{

    import mx.controls.ComboBox;
    import mx.controls.DataGrid;
    import mx.core.UIComponent;
    import mx.controls.TextArea;

    import flash.events.Event;
    import mx.collections.ArrayCollection;
    import mx.events.FlexEvent;
    import mx.controls.Alert;
```

Now you have imported the classes necessary for the component. To instance the ComboBox and DataGrid objects, you have to import their classes (mx.controls.ComboBox and mx.controls.DataGrid) and the UIComponent class necessary to extend the custom ActionScript class.

3. Before the declaration of the class, create the events that will be dispatched from the class, using the [Event] metadata:

```
// The ActionScript Class dispatches a changedDPCombo event when
// the data provider has been setted
[Event(name="changedDPCombo", type="flash.events.Event")]
[Event(name="changedDPDG", type="flash.events.Event")]
[Event(name="change", type="flash.events.Event")]

 public class Chapter_2_Sol_6 {
```

4. You can now pass to the declaration of the class, which must share the same name as the .as file that you have created. The custom class extends the UIComponent class by using the extends keyword. Write the following code below the last [Event] metadata declaration:

```
[Event(name="change", type="flash.events.Event")]

public class Chapter_2_Sol_6 extends UIComponent
{
  private var myDG:DataGrid;
  private var myCB:ComboBox;

    // It contains the data provider for Data Grid
    private var _dataDG:ArrayCollection;
    // It contains the data provider for Combo Box
    private var _dataCB:ArrayCollection;
```

In these first lines of code in the definition of the class, you declared the private variables that will contain the instances of the DataGrid and ComboBox objects. You then created the private variables that contain the data providers that will populate the controls. These properties will use the getter/setter functions (defined following).

5. Add the class constructor Chapter_2_Sol_6() method. You insert the super() method in the class constructor and register an event listener to the INITIALIZE event with the addEventListener() method:

```
public function Chapter_2_Sol_6() {
  super();
  // register an event listener for Initialiaze event
  addEventListener(FlexEvent.INITIALIZE, init);

}
```

> A **constructor** is a special method called when an object is created. It often has the same name as the declaring class.

The INITIALIZE event is sent as a constant of the system instead of a string to have the error immediately flagged in compile time if you have written the event badly. If you declared the event with a string, any typing error would instead only be shown at runtime.

6. The addEventListener() method registers the initialize event to the init() function, which will be responsible for creating, instancing, and designing the visual controls of the component: a ComboBox and a DataGrid. Write the init() function below the class's constructor:

```
private function init(event:FlexEvent):void
{
  // create and set properties for Combo Box control
  myCB = new ComboBox();
  myCB.width = 150;
  myCB.height = 20;
  myCB.editable = false;
  myCB.x = 20;
  myCB.y = 25;
  myCB.addEventListener("change", handleChange);
  addChild(myCB);

  // create and set properties for DataGrid control
  myDG = new DataGrid();
  myDG.width = 400;
  myDG.height = 200;
  myDG.x = 35;
  myDG.y = 80;
  myDG.useHandCursor = true;
  addChild(myDG);
}
```

In the init() function, you inserted the instance of the two controls in the private variables (created at the beginning of the page) and set their properties with a value that will be applied in the rendering phase. You did this because you don't have a way of accessing these properties after the MXML author's environment.

You can now simply use addChild() and removeChild() methods to add or remove the new controls to your component.

The ComboBox control uses the addEventListener() method to register the handleChange() event handler when the change event is triggered:

```
myCB.addEventListener("change", handleChange);
```

7. You now define the event handlers for the change event dispatched by the ComboBox control (myCB.addEventListener("change", handleChange)). This function simply creates an Alert window that prints a string. Then you create the getter/setter methods for the properties _dataDG and _dataCB created in Step 4. Because you defined those variables as private class members to set and get their values outside the class, you need to create the getter and setter accessor methods:

```
private function handleChange(evt:Event):void
{
    mx.controls.Alert.show("Entered");
}

[Bindable(event="changedDPDG")]
public function set dataDG(data:ArrayCollection):void
{
  _dataDG = data;
  myDG.dataProvider = _dataDG;
  var myClassesEvent:Event = new Event("changedDPDG");
  dispatchEvent(myClassesEvent);
}

public function get dataDG():ArrayCollection
{
  return _dataDG;
}

[Bindable(event="changedDPCombo")]
public function set dataCB(data:ArrayCollection):void
{
  _dataCB = data;
  myCB.dataProvider = _dataCB;

  var myClassesEvent:Event = new Event("changedDPCombo");
  dispatchEvent(myClassesEvent);
}
public function get dataCB():ArrayCollection
{
```

```
    return _dataCB;
  }
 }
}
```

> *Getter and setter methods are public methods to change private class members. You use getter and setter methods to get and set the value of a property.*

The two setter methods, dataDG() and dataCB(), set the dataProvider property of the controls to the respective variable and carry out a dispatchEvent(), which causes the release of a custom event. This event is defined as [Bindable] on the getter method, which returns the updated value of the data provider.

8. To use the composite component you have to import it into the main application (as you did for the preceding documents). Open the main application created in the previous solution and rename it Chapter_2_Sol_6_app.mxml.

9. Modify the file by simply changing the name in the invocation of the component on the MXML tag:

```
<?xml version="1.0" encoding="utf-8"?>
<mx:Application
  xmlns:mx="http://www.adobe.com/2006/mxml"
  layout="vertical"
  xmlns:comp = "com.flexsolutions.chapter2.*">
<mx:Script>
  <![CDATA[
    import mx.collections.ArrayCollection;
    [Bindable]
    private var myAC:ArrayCollection = new ArrayCollection(
[{label:"Top 5", data:5}, {label:"Top 10", data:10},
{label:"Top 20", data:20}]);
  ]]>
</mx:Script>

<mx:Panel title="Chapter 2 - Solution 2.6" width="600" height="450" >
  <comp:Chapter_2_Sol_6  dataCB="{myAC}"
    dataDG="{myAC}"  />
</mx:Panel>
</mx:Application>
```

The ActionScript composite component is invoked by referring to itself with the custom namespace, which is directed at the package that contains it (com/flexsolutions/chapter2). In the <mx:Script> block, you have created and populated an ArrayCollection type variable, which will be sent to the composite component through the getter/setter functions.

10. Save the file and run the application. The application carries out the rendering of the two controls and inserts the ArrayCollection variable, which you have already sent as dataProvider.

Expert tips

As a best practice, when you create a control you can use the method createChildren(), overwritten so a subclass can create a different child instead. In the ActionScript class of the custom composite component, carry out an override of the protected createChildren() methods:

```
override protected function createChildren():void {
  super.createChildren();
  if (!myCB) {
    // create and set properties for Combo Box control
    myCB = new ComboBox();
    myCB.width = 150;
    myCB.height = 20;
    myCB.editable = false;
    myCB.x = 20;
    myCB.y = 25;
    myCB.addEventListener("change", handleChange);
    addChild(myCB);
  }

  if (!myDG) {
    // create and set properties for DataGrid control
    myDG = new DataGrid();
    myDG.width = 400;
    myDG.height = 200;
    myDG.x = 35;
    myDG.y = 80;
    myDG.useHandCursor = true;
    addChild(myDG);
  }
}
```

In the method, you check the existence of the children before you create the objects. If the children objects do not exist, the instances of the ComboBox and DataGrid are created:

```
if (!myDG) {
  // create and set properties for DataGrid control
  myDG = new DataGrid();
  myDG.width = 400;
  myDG.height = 200;
  myDG.x = 35;
  myDG.y = 80;
  myDG.useHandCursor = true;
  addChild(myDG);
}
```

Solution 2-7: Building loosely coupled components

To make configurable and reusable components throughout your applications, you might want to create MXML components that accept properties, launch methods, and dispatch events. To achieve it the components must not depend on a specific application (tightly coupled components)—their variable's name or tag instance's name. In this scenario, if the code of the application or the component changes, reliant code won't work, so you'll have to modify the tightly coupled component to reflect that change.

A much cleaner and better approach is to develop a loosely coupled component that dispatches the events to propagate return data to the application and contains property declarations for passing information to it.

This approach enables you to create MXML components as "black boxes" with the following benefits:

- They are easier to reuse and maintain.
- They don't know anything about any other components' inner workings.
- They are independent from the variable's name and tag instance's name.

What's involved

To create a loosely coupled component you need properties to store information and an event model (see Chapter 1 for a discussion of the Model-View-Controller [MVC] design pattern) to dispatch events that contain the return data. Properties are usually defined with ActionScript (although you can define them with MXML) and placed within an <mx:Script> block:

```
<mx:Script>
  <![CDATA[
    import mx.collections.ArrayCollection;
    [Bindable]
    public var lista:ArrayCollection;
  ]]>
</mx:Script>
```

It's the same story for methods of MXML components:

```
<mx:Script>
<![CDATA[
    import mx.collections.ArrayCollection;
    [Bindable]
    public var lista:ArrayCollection;
    public function justWrite():String
    {
      return "This is a method of the component";
    }
  ]]>
</mx:Script>
```

To design a loosely coupled component to handle the dispatching of an event that contains the return data, each MXML custom component dispatches events that can be customized in three simple steps:

- Using the [Event] metadata tag
- Creating an event object
- Dispatching the event and creating the function to handle the event

The [Event] metadata tag defines the events that components can dispatch. It's possible to declare the [Event] metadata tag in an ActionScript class just after the package definition and above the class definition:

```
package com.flexsolutions.chapter2
{
  [Event(name=" changeBlog", type=" flash.events.Event ")]
  public class custComp
{

}
}
```

Or in the <mx:Metadata> tag of an MXML file:

```
<mx:Metadata>
  [Event(name="changeBlog", type=" flash.events.Event ")]
</mx:Metadata>
```

After the [Event] metadata has been created, the component has to dispatch the event using the dispatchEvent() method, which accepts the event object as argument, as shown in the following code:

```
dispatchEvent(new Event("changeBlog"));
```

How to build it

Create an MXML component from DataGrid, which will accept a public property and be sent to it from the main application as data provider. On this component you add an [Event] metadata tag to create a custom event when the user selects an item in the DataGrid.

1. Create a new MXML component in the com/flexsolutions/chapter2 folder by selecting File ➤ New ➤ MXML Component and give it the name Chapter_2_Sol_7. mxml. Make the MXML component based on a VBox container.

2. Enter the following code into the MXML component. The component is based on a VBox container and contains a DataGrid:

```
<?xml version="1.0" encoding="utf-8"?>
<mx:VBox xmlns:mx="http://www.adobe.com/2006/mxml">
```

```
<mx:Script>
  <![CDATA[
    import mx.collections.ArrayCollection;
    [Bindable]
    public var list:ArrayCollection;
  ]]>
</mx:Script>

<mx:DataGrid id="myDG" dataProvider="{list}"  />
</mx:VBox>
```

3. Define an event listener that you manage in the <mx:Script> block on the change event of the DataGrid:

```
<mx:Script>
  <![CDATA[
    import mx.collections.ArrayCollection;
    [Bindable]
    public var list:ArrayCollection;
    private function changeHandler():void
    {
      dispatchEvent(new Event("changeBlog"));
    }
  ]]>
</mx:Script>

<mx:DataGrid id="myDG"
dataProvider="{list}"
change="changeHandler()" />
```

The changeHandler() function simply executes the dispatchEvent() method. This event is released on the change event of the DataGrid when the user selects an item.

4. Adding the [Event] metadata defines a changeBlog event with a generic Event type and makes the event public so the MXML compiler recognizes it. Add the <mx:Metadata> tag after the VBox declaration:

```
<mx:VBox xmlns:mx="http://www.adobe.com/2006/mxml">

<mx:Metadata>
  [Event(name="changeBlog", type="flash.events.Event")]
</mx:Metadata>
```

The use of the [Event] metadata tag needs to define events dispatched by a component so the compiler can recognize them as MXML tag attributes in an MXML file. In this code you defined a changeBlog event typed as flash.events.Event.

5. Now you can create the main application file, which has the job of handling the event triggered by the custom MXML component, with a simple event handler function defined in the <mx:Script> block. Create the new file by selecting File ➤ New ➤ MXML Application and give it the name Chapter_2_Sol_7_app.mxml.

6. On the `Application` tag, create the custom namespace and define the package in which the MXML component has been saved:

```
<?xml version="1.0" encoding="utf-8"?>
<mx:Application
  xmlns:mx="http://www.adobe.com/2006/mxml"
  layout="absolute"
  xmlns:comp="com.flexsolutions.chapter2.*">

</mx:Application>
```

7. Invoke the MXML component and manage the event changeBlog that you created, assigning an event handler to it:

```
<mx:Application
  xmlns:mx="http://www.adobe.com/2006/mxml"
  layout="absolute"
  xmlns:comp="com.flexsolutions.chapter2.*">

<comp:Chapter_2_Sol_7 id="custDG"
  x="258" y="89" lista="{myData}"
  changeBlog="changeBlogHandler(event)"/>
```

You have sent the event object as parameter to the event handler.

8. Now you will add an `<mx:Script>` block, in which you will write the changeBlogHandler event handler and create an ArrayCollection variable that will be sent to the custom component and function as data provider. Add the following below the Application tag:

```
<mx:Application
  xmlns:mx="http://www.adobe.com/2006/mxml"
  layout="absolute"
  xmlns:comp="com.flexsolutions.chapter2.*">

<mx:Script>
  <![CDATA[
    import mx.collections.ArrayCollection;

    [Bindable]
public var myData:ArrayCollection =
new ArrayCollection ([{Values:2000},{Values:3000},
                      {Values:4000},{Values:4000},
                      {Values:3000},{Values:2000},
                      {Values:6000}]);

    private function changeBlogHandler (event:Event):void
    {
      myLabel2.text += "Event fired by Datagrid:"
                        + event.type + "\n" ;
    }
```

```
    ]]>
</mx:Script>
<comp:Chapter_2_Sol_7 id="custDG"
  x="258" y="89" lista="{myData}"
  changeBlog="changeBlogHandler(event)"/>
```

The event handler prints a string, and the event type is contained in the event object in a TextArea. The output will be the following:

```
Event fired by Datagrid:changeBlog
```

9. Insert the TextArea below the custom component declaration, and give it the id of myLabel2.

```
<comp:Chapter_2_Sol_7 id="custDG"
  x="258" y="89" lista="{myData}"
  changeBlog="changeBlogHandler(event)"/>

<mx:TextArea  id="myLabel2"  x="277"
          y="103" height="102" width="273"/>
```

10. Save the file and run the application.

If you click an item on the DataGrid control, you'll see the text in the TextArea. The changeBlog event will be fired, and the changeBlogHandler will be dispatched, as shown in Figure 2-9.

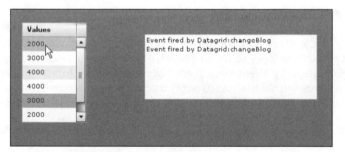

Figure 2-9. The event has been carried out.

Expert tips

The metadata [Event] accepts two parameters:

- eventName: The String that specifies the name of the event
- eventType: A String that declares the class to indicate the data type of the event object

This metadata can be declared both in MXML and ActionScript. The declaration in MXML takes place using the <mx:Metadata> tag, in which you can write the [Event]:

```
<mx:Metadata>
  [Event(name="changeBlog", type="flash.events.Event")]
</mx:Metadata>
```

In ActionScript, however, it is sufficient to define the metadata in the ActionScript class (the [Event] metadata is normally declared above the declaration of the class):

```
[Event(name="changeBlog", type="flash.events.Event")]
public class CustDG extends DataGrid
{
  // your class definition
}
```

The parameter type of the [Event] metadata can be left out when it refers to the flash.events.Event class because Flex uses it for the default:

```
<mx:Metadata>
[Event(name="changeBlog")]
</mx:Metadata>
```

Solution 2-8: Extending the Event class for sending complex data

You saw how simple it is to create a custom event for the loosely coupled component. But with this approach you have some limitations if you want to send data to the custom event. The flash.events.Event class doesn't allow developers to add properties to it. In fact, you use the dispatch event just to notify that something happened in the MXML custom component. But what if you need to send complex data to a custom event?

To solve this problem, you create custom Event classes with ActionScript extending the Event class.

The custom events, therefore, enable you to have more flexibility and to be able to add functionality to respond to the events that are released by the Flex application.

What's involved

With Flex, it is possible to create a custom event that uses an event object of a customized type by developing a subclass that extends the Event class and then adding properties to it. Don't forget that custom components that extend existing Flex classes inherit all the events of the base class.

To develop a subclass you have to create an ActionScript class that usually extends the flash.events.Event class, the base class for all event objects.

In the definition of subclass of the Event class, it is possible to write any type of functionality: adding custom properties, overriding methods, and changing the default values.

After extending the Event class, you call the super() method of the Event class to call the constructor of the superclass and pass the event type to it. You're required to override the clone() method to return a new copy of the event object by setting the type property and any new properties.

To dispatch a new event from your custom component, you can create a new instance of the custom ActionScript class and pass properties to it. In this solution you'll see an example of how to extend the Event class and send complex data to it.

How to build it

You'll develop a simple blog reader that enables users to select from a list of blogs using a ComboBox control. The application is made up of two MXML components that contain the DataGrid to show the blog's post and a ComboBox with the blog's list.

You'll start with the custom Event class:

1. Create a new ActionScript class in the com/flexsolutions/chapter2 folder of the Flex project using File ➤ New ➤ ActionScript Class, name it Chapter_2_Sol_8.as, and save it:

```
package  com.flexsolutions.chapter2
{
  import flash.events.Event;
  public class Chapter_2_Sol_8 extends Event
  {
  }
}
```

2. For now, the class imports the Event class in the flash.events package and extends it. Let's create the property that this custom event can send. Add the following lines:

```
  public class Chapter_2_Sol_8 extends Event
{
        public var evProp:String;
}
```

3. This leaves you with only two more steps to go in creating the class: calling the super() method of the Event class to call the constructor of the superclass and pass the event type to it and then overriding the clone() method. The following code takes care of both these issues. Add it into the ActionScript class:

```
package  com.flexsolutions.chapter2
{
 import flash.events.Event;
```

```
public class Chapter_2_Sol_8 extends Event
{
  public var evProp:String;
  public function Chapter_2_Sol_8(evParam:String,type:String)
  {
    super(type);
    this.evProp = evParam;
  }
   override public function clone():Event
  {
    return new Chapter_2_Sol_8(evProp,type);
  }
 }
}
```

In the constructor, which accepts the custom property and the event type as parameters, you recall the super() method and send the event type to it. You then set the value of the custom property, evProp, with the value sent to the constructor in the creation phase of the custom event.

The override of the clone() method just returns a new copy of the event object by setting the type property and any new properties. You do this to enable the event bubbling to take place.

4. Create the custom component that will use this custom event class. From Flex Builder, select File ➤ New ➤ MXML Component and save it as Chapter_2_Sol_8_CB. mxml. Make the component based on a VBox container.

5. In this component, insert a ComboBox control, which contains an ArrayCollection as data provider, declared as an MXML tag, with URLs pointing to the RSS feeds of a few blogs:

```
<mx:ComboBox id="myCombo" change="changeHandler()">
 <mx:ArrayCollection id="myArray">
    <mx:Object label="Mike Chambers"
      data="http://weblogs.macromedia.com/mesh/index.xml"/>
    <mx:Object label="Matt Chotin"
      data="http://weblogs.macromedia.com/mchotin/index.xml"/>
    <mx:Object label="Mike Downey"
      data="http://weblogs.macromedia.com/mdowney/index.xml"/>
    <mx:Object label="Steven Webster"
      data="http://weblogs.macromedia.com/swebster/index.xml"/>
    <mx:Object label="Alistair McLeod"
      data="http://weblogs.macromedia.com/amcleod/index.xml"/>
 </mx:ArrayCollection>
</mx:ComboBox>
```

When the user selects an item from the ComboBox, the custom event (Chapter_2_Sol_8) will be dispatched, and the item will be passed to the event object of the custom event.

6. The change event of the ComboBox is registered to the event handler changeHandler() (<mx:ComboBox id="myCombo" **change="changeHandler()"** >). This function will create the instance of the custom ActionScript class (Chapter_2_Sol_8.as) and dispatch the custom event. You, therefore, insert an <mx:Script> block below the VBox container tag:

```
<mx:VBox xmlns:mx="http://www.adobe.com/2006/mxml" >
<mx:Script>
 <![CDATA[

    import com.flexsolutions.chapter2.Chapter_2_Sol_8;

     private function changeHandler():void
     {
       var eventObj:Chapter_2_Sol_8 =
        new Chapter_2_Sol_8(myCombo.value as String,"changeBlog");
       dispatchEvent(eventObj);
     }
   ]]>
</mx:Script>
```

Before you could create an instance from the custom ActionScript class, you had to import it, defining its package like this: import com.flexsolutions.chapter2.Chapter_2_Sol_8.

In the creation phase of the object, the value property contained in the ComboBox control (with a casting you have set with a string) was sent to it as the first parameter. The second parameter is the changeBlog event type that you will declare in the [Event] metadata in the next step:

```
var eventObj:Chapter_2_Sol_8 =
        new Chapter_2_Sol_8(myCombo.value as String,"changeBlog");
```

7. Define the [Event] metadata that defines the events that the MXML component can dispatch. The value assigned to the type property is equal to the custom event class (com.flexsolutions.chapter2.Chapter_2_Sol_8). You do this by inserting the <mx:Metadata> MXML tag. The component will have the following code:

```
<?xml version="1.0" encoding="utf-8"?>
<mx:VBox xmlns:mx="http://www.adobe.com/2006/mxml" >

<mx:Metadata>
[Event(name="changeBlog",
  type="com.flexsolutions.chapter2.Chapter_2_Sol_8")]
</mx:Metadata>

<mx:Script>
  <![CDATA[
    import com.flexsolutions.chapter2.Chapter_2_Sol_8;

    private function changeHandler():void
    {
```

```
          var eventObj:evtClass =
       new evtClass(myCombo.value as String,"changeBlog");
          dispatchEvent(eventObj);
        }
     ]]>
  </mx:Script>

  <mx:ComboBox id="myCombo" change="changeHandler()" >
    <mx:ArrayCollection id="myArray">
      <mx:Object label="Mike Chambers"
        data="http://weblogs.macromedia.com/mesh/index.xml"/>
      <mx:Object label="Matt Chotin"
         data="http://weblogs.macromedia.com/mchotin/index.xml"/>
      <mx:Object label="Mike Downey"
        data="http://weblogs.macromedia.com/mdowney/index.xml"/>
      <mx:Object label="Steven Webster"
        data="http://weblogs.macromedia.com/swebster/index.xml"/>
      <mx:Object label="Alistair McLeod"
        data="http://weblogs.macromedia.com/amcleod/index.xml"/>
    </mx:ArrayCollection>
  </mx:ComboBox>

  </mx:VBox>
```

After the user selects a blog under the ComboBox, the change event is fired, and the changeHandler() is called. The event handler's purpose is to create an instance of the custom event class and pass the value selected by the user to the new instance (myCombo.value as String).

8. Create a second MXML component (save it in the com/flexsolutions/chapter2 folder) that contains the DataGrid control and accepts the data provider from the main application by selecting File ➤ New ➤ MXML Component. Name it Chapter_2_ Sol_8_DG.mxml and base it on a VBox container.

9. Add the following code to the file:

```
<?xml version="1.0" encoding="utf-8"?>
<mx:VBox xmlns:mx="http://www.adobe.com/2006/mxml">

  <mx:Script>
    <![CDATA[
      import mx.collections.ArrayCollection;
      import flash.net.*;
      [Bindable]
      public var list:ArrayCollection;
    ]]>
  </mx:Script>

  <mx:DataGrid id="myDG" horizontalCenter="14"
    verticalCenter="18.5" dataProvider="{list}" width="100%"
    change="navigateToURL(new URLRequest➡
```

```
         (myDG.selectedItem.link),'_blank');" >
      <mx:columns>
        <mx:DataGridColumn headerText="Posts" dataField="title" />
        <mx:DataGridColumn headerText="Date"➥
          dataField="pubDate" width="100" />
      </mx:columns>
    </mx:DataGrid>

    </mx:VBox>
```

The DataGrid defines two columns that take data from the RSS feed of the blog selected by the user (from the first component Chapter_2_Sol_8.mxml) and contained in the ArrayCollection variable (list).

On the event change, you used the navigateToURL() method to manage the opening of a new window of the browser sending the value link selected by the user in the choice of an item in the DataGrid as URL:

```
<mx:DataGrid id="myDG"
horizontalCenter="14" verticalCenter="18.5"
dataProvider="{list}" width="100%"
change="navigateToURL(
new URLRequest(myDG.selectedItem.link),'_blank');" >
```

10. The last file you need to create is the main application file, which will invoke the MXML components. Using File ➤ Menu ➤ MXML Application, create a new application file and save it with the name Chapter_2_Sol_8_app.mxml.

11. Add the following code to this file, which defines the HTTPService tag for the remote calls to the feed RSS (the HTTPService class will be discussed in Chapter 6):

```
<?xml version="1.0" encoding="utf-8"?>
<mx:Application xmlns:mx=http://www.adobe.com/2006/mxml
    layout="absolute"
    xmlns:comp="com.flexsolutions.chapter2.*"
    creationComplete="hs.send()" >

  <mx:HTTPService
    id="hs"
    url="{selectedMenu}"
    showBusyCursor="true"
    useProxy="false"/>

</mx:Application>
```

The HTTPService tag is called on the creationComplete of the application and carries out the HTTP remote call at the URL, which is sent to it from the data binding on the selectedMenu variable. The {selectedMenu} value is populated when the changeBlog event of Chapter_2_Sol_8_CB.mxml occurs.

12. Invoke all the components you have created, and send them the properties they expect to receive to populate the DataGrid and the ComboBox:

```
<mx:HTTPService
 id="hs"
 showBusyCursor="true"
 url="{selectedMenu}"
 useProxy="false"/>

<mx:Panel width="70%" height="70%" layout="absolute"
 title="Chapter 2 - Sol 2.8" horizontalCenter="0"
 verticalCenter="-14.5">

<mx:Label text="{hs.lastResult.rss.channel.title}'s Blog"
 id="myLbl"  x="48.5" y="43"   fontWeight="bold"/>

<comp:Chapter_2_Sol_8_CB  x="161" y="10"
 changeBlog="eventFired(event)" />

  <mx:Label x="48.5" y="10" text="Select a Blog" height="25"/>

  <comp:Chapter_2_Sol_8_DG width="80%" x="48.5" y="69"
    list="{hs.lastResult.rss.channel.item}" />

  <mx:ControlBar>
    <mx:Label text="Developed by Marco Casario" />
    <mx:LinkButton label="http://casario.blogs.com"
      click="navigateToURL(newURLRequest(➥
        'http://casario.blogs.com'),'_blank');"/>

  </mx:ControlBar>
</mx:Panel>
```

The Chapter_2_Sol_8_DG component accepts the list variable as its property, which contains the data provider it will use to populate the DataGrid with the values read from the RSS feed:

```
<comp:Chapter_2_Sol_8_DG
  width="80%" x="48.5" y="69"
  list="{hs.lastResult.rss.channel.item}" />
```

The Chapter_2_Sol_8_CB component, which contains the ComboBox control, creates an event handler that links to the eventFired() function:

```
<comp:Chapter_2_Sol_8_CB  x="161" y="10"
  changeBlog="eventFired(event)" />
```

The eventFired() event handler function uses the event object to retrieve the evProp defined in the ActionScript class (Chapter_2_Sol_8.as) that contains myCombo.value. You define the event handler eventFired() inside an <mx:Script> block.

13. Add an `<mx:Script>` block and enter the following code:

```
<mx:Application xmlns:mx=http://www.adobe.com/2006/mxml
  layout="absolute"
  xmlns:comp="com.flexsolutions.chapter2.*"
  creationComplete="hs.send()" >

<mx:Script>
  <![CDATA[
    import com.flexsolutions.chapter2.Chapter_2_Sol_8;

    [Bindable]
    private var selectedMenu:String=
    "http://weblogs.macromedia.com/mesh/index.xml";

    private function eventFired(event:Chapter_2_Sol_8):void
    {
      selectedMenu = event.evProp;
      if (selectedMenu == "null")
      {
        mx.controls.Alert.show("Please Choose a valid Blog");
        return;
      };
    hs.send();
    }
  ]]>
</mx:Script>
```

14. Save and run the application. You'll see the blog reader in action, as shown in Figure 2-10.

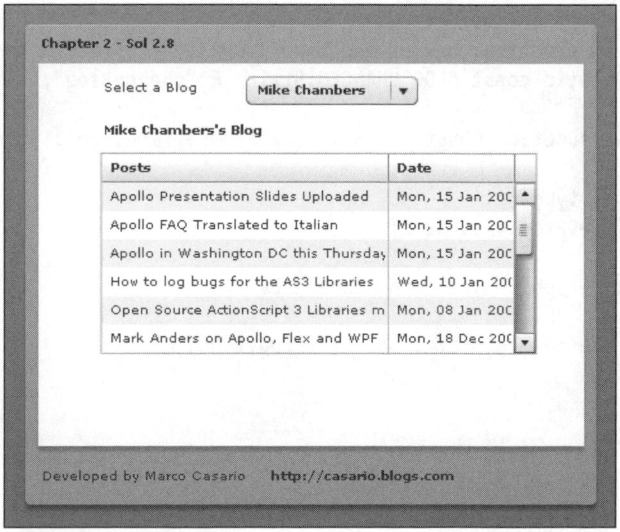

Figure 2-10. The small blog reader in action

101

Expert tips

In the Chapter_2_Sol_8_CB component, you sent the second parameter type as String to the constructor of the class:

```
<mx:Metadata>
  [Event(name="changeBlog", type="
com.flexsolutions.chapter2.Chapter_2_Sol_8")]
</mx:Metadata>

<mx:Script>
  <![CDATA[
    import com.flexsolutions.chapter2.Chapter_2_Sol_8;

    private function changeHandler():void
    {
      var eventObj:Chapter_2_Sol_8 =
      new Chapter_2_Sol_8(myCombo.value as String,"changeBlog");
      dispatchEvent(eventObj);
    }
  ]]>
</mx:Script>
```

The Flex compiler can't examine the data type that is sent to it to determine whether it is a valid parameter. This means that you won't receive a compile-time error; the error will show up only at runtime. This scenario must be avoided. To guarantee that the value of a property type is valid in compile time, you must define it as a static constant in the custom class:

```
public class Chapter_2_Sol_8 extends Event
{
  public var evProp:String;
  // best practice: define the type property as static constants
  public static const BLOG_CHANGED:String = "changeBlog";

  public function Chapter_2_Sol_8(evParam:String,type:String)
  {
    super(type);
    this.evProp = evParam;
  }
  override public function clone():Event
  {
    return new Chapter_2_Sol_8(evProp,type);
  }
}
```

In the creation phase of the instance of Chapter_2_Sol_8, you can use this constant and be confident about not introducing typos into the code (which would result in compile-time errors):

```
private function changeHandler():void
{
var eventObj:Chapter_2_Sol_8 =
new Chapter_2_Sol_8(myCombo.value as
        String,Chapter_2_Sol_8.BLOG_CHANGED);
  dispatchEvent(eventObj);
}
```

Solution 2-9: Creating SWC files to deploy components

In a Flex project, the components created using MXML or ActionScript are usually saved in the same directory of the project or in an appropriate folder (as with the previous solutions). You have learned that a component can be made up of different MXML files, ActionScript, and various assets.

To make the components easier to reuse, and to improve performance and security, you can compile the components in SWC format or as a runtime shared project. In a new Flex project, it would be sufficient to send to and import this single SWC file into the project, without having to pay attention to copying all the files and assets used. However, in a SWC file or SWF file, the code of the components will be obfuscated and protected because it is a compiled file.

In this solution you will see how to create and compile a Flex component in SWC format and how to import it into a Flex project.

What's involved

To create a SWC file for deploying flex components, you must use a compiler and compile all the files involved. When you launch the compiler of Flex Builder in the run phase, all the files, including the components, already become compiled in the final SWF file.

However, creating the SWC file is a separate process from the classic compilation phase that creates the SWF file, so there is a different compiler involved. The Flex SDK (Software Development Kit) has two different compilers: the mxmlc compiler and the compc compiler. To create a SWC file, use the compc compiler (located in the flex_installation/bin directory), which enables you to generate a SWC file compiled from MXML or ActionScript components.

How to build it

The compc compiler accepts more than one component at a time, so you can create a real library to be reused across different projects. In this solution you'll create a SWC file by compiling all the components created up until now and located in the com/flexsolutions/chapter2 folder of the Flex project. However, to better understand the compilation process, you will begin by sending only one component.

1. The first step is to identify the folder containing the component files you want to include in the SWC (in this case, the com/flexsolutions/chapter2 folder). Open the command window of the system and position yourself in the Flex project folder, as shown in Figure 2-11.

Figure 2-11. From this position the compc compiler is launched.

2. To use the compc compiler without having to insert its absolute path every time, you must add it into the environment variables in the variable path.

The **path** to a file is basically its address on the computer. It tells programs how to find a file. To add the path of the compc compiler to your system path (in Windows), you have to perform the following steps to access the environment variables:

A. Select Control Panel ➤ Performance and Maintenance ➤ System.

B. Click the Advanced tab in the dialog box.

C. Click the Environment Variables button.

D. On the System Variables panel, choose the path variable and click Edit (see Figure 2.12).

E. At the end of the Variable value input text, insert the complete path to point to compc.exe compiler (on my computer it was C:\Program Files\Adobe\Flex Builder Plug-in\Flex SDK 2\bin\compc.exe).

You can now launch the compiler from any position by referring to its name: compc.

3. Create the manifest file, which enables you to map a component namespace to a class name. Create an XML file in the Flex project folder with Flex Builder by selecting File ➤ New ➤ File and save the file as manifest.xml.

4. Write the following code inside manifest.xml:

```
<?xml version="1.0"?>
<componentPackage>
  <component id="mySWCcomp" class="
com.flexsolutions.chapter2.Chapter_2_Sol_2"/>
</componentPackage>
```

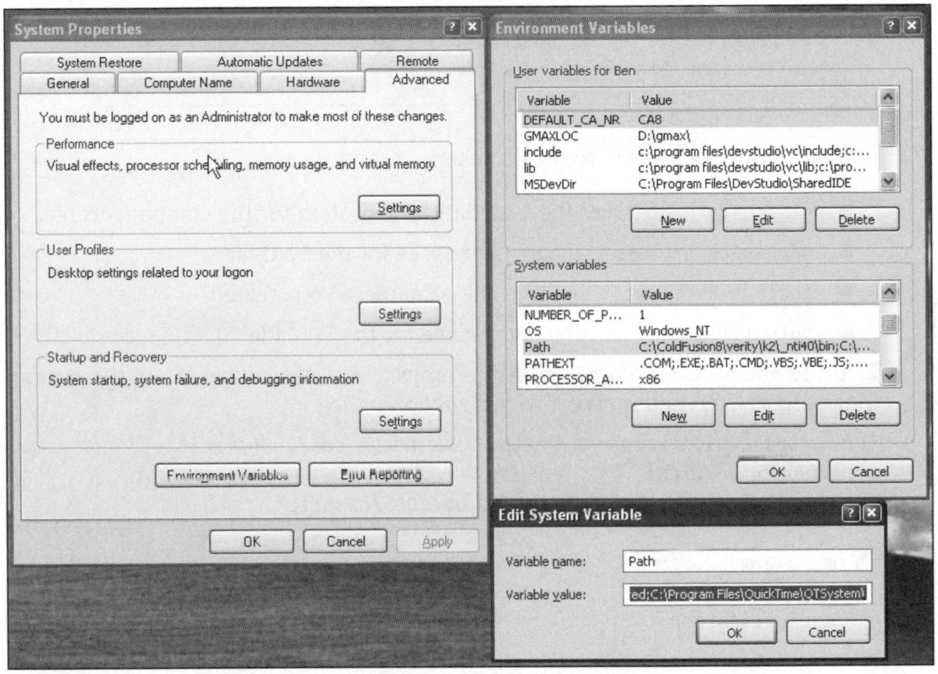

Figure 2-12. Open these windows to add the compc.exe as an environment variable in the variable path.

The manifest file contains the names of the packages and the components used before being compiled into SWC format. You include all the components that you want in the compilation in the root tag <componentPackage>, inserting the declaration in the <component> nodes.

If, for example, you want to add a second component to compile in the SWC file, you can just add it to the manifest file:

```
<?xml version="1.0"?>
<componentPackage>
  <component id="mySWCcomp" class="
com.flexsolutions.chapter2.Chapter_2_Sol_2"/>
  <component id="mySWCcomp_2" class="
com.flexsolutions.chapter2.Chapter_2_Sol_3"/>
</componentPackage>
```

5. From the command line, launch the compc compiler with the following parameters:

```
compc -namespace http://www.adobe.com/2006/casario manifest.xml -
source-path.
-include-namespaces http://www.adobe.com/2006/casario
-include-classes com.flexsolutions.chapter2.Chapter_2_Sol_2
-output=MyComp.swc
```

> *Open the* Chapter_2_Sol_9_compilerScript.txt *file to cut and paste this command line.*

You have sent some parameters to the compiler:

- -source-path: Specifies the base directory location for the components file
- -namespace: Creates a custom namespace for the SWC file
- -include-namespaces: Includes the namespace you created
- -output: Assigns a location and a name for the SWC file

6. To use the SWC file compiled in the project, you can simply insert the custom namespace and then invoke it with the following tag:

```
<mx:Application xmlns:mx="http://www.adobe.com/2006/mxml"
  layout="vertical"
xmlns:myComp="http://www.adobe.com/2006/casario">

<myComp:mySWCcomp / >

</mx:Application>
```

Expert tips

SWC files make life easier because you can reuse the components between different projects. In fact, you can simply import the SWC file as a Library path in a new Flex project to be able to use it.

If the SWC file contains more than one component, Flex Builder automatically detects it and lays out all the components that can be used. If you go to the Design view of Flex Builder modality, in the Components view on the bottom left, you'll find the components imported from the SWC file in the Custom folder.

To include the SWC file in a new project, you must include it in the Library path in the Flex Build Path. In Flex Builder, select Project ➤ Properties ➤ Flex Build Path, click the Add SWC Folder button and select the SWC file that you intend to import and use, as shown in Figure 2-13.

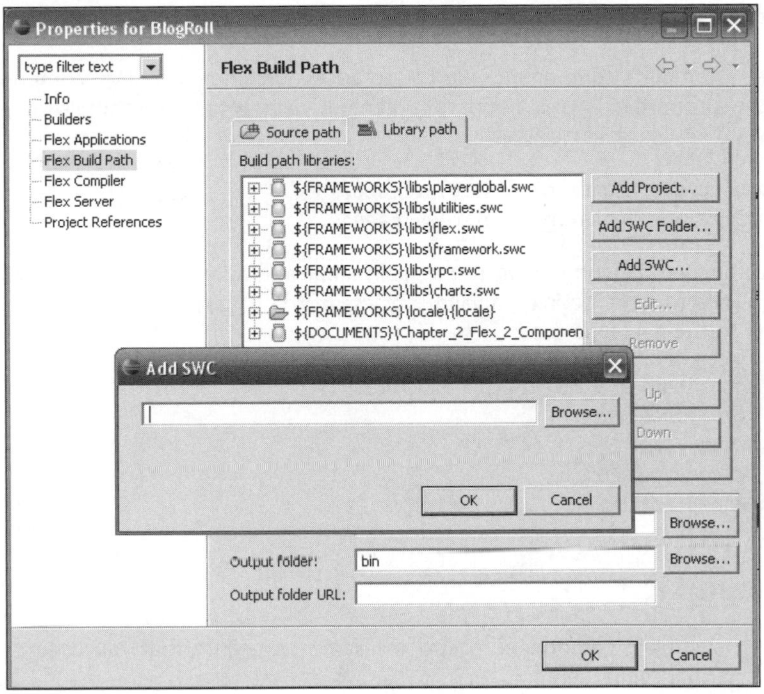

Figure 2-13. Adding a Flex Build Path in Flex Builder

Solution 2-10: Creating reusable components using template components

The template component enables you to define and create properties in the components with a general data type. This means that a template component is equipped to act as a property or as the defined object with the same data type of the property declared in it or a subclass of that data type.

In previous solutions, when you created a property for a component created with MXML or ActionScript, you assigned an ArrayCollection or a String as the data type to these properties. In the invocation phase of the component in a main application, if you try to send another type of value to this property (such as an XMLListCollection data type), you receive an error at compile time.

With template components, the properties that are defined by the developer are the placeholders that wait to be used.

In this way, you can create components that are more reusable. You can also guarantee to everyone who will use this component that you have respected the rules for object creation.

What's involved

To create a template component, you create an ActionScript or MXML component and define the properties linking them to a general data type; for example, one of the UIComponent or Container classes:

```
public var header:mx.controls.Image;
public var footer:mx.controls.Image;
```

When you invoke the component in the main application file, the developer can specify the properties to send, defining a valid subclass of the UIComponent or Container class, according to the data type used:

```
<comp:Chapter_2_Sol_10 id="myTplComp">
  <comp:header>
    <mx:Image source="" />
  </comp:header>
  <comp:bottomRow>
```

How to build it

To create a template component, follow the same procedure that you used when you created a normal component.

1. Create an MXML component in the com/flexsolutions/chapter2 folder by selecting File ➤ New ➤ MXML Component and give it the name Chapter_2_Sol_10.mxml. Base the component on a VBox container:

```
<?xml version="1.0"?>
<mx:VBox xmlns:mx="http://www.adobe.com/2006/mxml" >

</mx:VBox>
```

2. In the MXML component, start a block of ActionScript code in which you define the property of the component with the general data types:

```
<?xml version="1.0"?>
<mx:VBox xmlns:mx="http://www.adobe.com/2006/mxml" >

  <mx:Script>
    <![CDATA[
      import mx.controls.Image;
      import mx.core.UIComponent;

      public var header:Image;
      public var footer:Image;

      // Define an Array of properties for a row of components.
      [ArrayElementType("mx.core.UIComponent")]
      public var content:Array;
```

```
      ]]>
   </mx:Script>
</mx:VBox>
```

You have created three properties: header, footer and content. The first two are properties to which you have assigned a data type of Image, which limits their use to an Image control only (when the developer will send a value to this property, it can be only an Image control). For the third property, content, you used a generic data type of UIComponent type. You can send any value that is a valid subclass of the UIComponent class to this property. To use the UIComponent class you must import it: import mx.core.UIComponent.

The [ArrayElementType] metadata defines the underlying property as an Array of the subclass of UIComponent. This metadata enables you to specify the data type of the elements of the Array.

3. To ensure that these objects become rendered on the screen in the moment of their creation, you must use the addChild() method, which you write in a function launched by the system event initialize:

```xml
<?xml version="1.0"?>
<mx:VBox xmlns:mx="http://www.adobe.com/2006/mxml"
  initialize="draw();">

<mx:Script>
  <![CDATA[
    import mx.controls.Image;
    import mx.core.UIComponent;
    public var header: Image;
    public var footer: Image;

    // Define an Array of properties for a row of components.
    [ArrayElementType("mx.core.UIComponent")]
    public var content:Array;

    private function draw():void {
      addChild(header);
     for (var i:int = 0; i < content.length; i++)
     {
      addChild(content[i]);

     }
       addChild(footer);
}
  ]]>
</mx:Script>
</mx:VBox>
```

To the draw() event handler, you have sent the properties to be added as children to the VBox root tag of the MXML component to the addChild() method.

4. Create the main application file that will import and invoke the template component. Select File ➤ New ➤ MXML Application, name the file Chapter_2_Sol_10_app. mxml, and define a custom namespace within it to import the component:

```
<?xml version="1.0"?>
  <mx:Application xmlns:mx="http://www.adobe.com/2006/mxml"
    xmlns:comp="com.flexsolutions.chapter2.*"
  height="700" width="700">

  <mx:Panel title="Chapter 2 - Solution 2.10">
  </mx:Panel>
</mx:Application>
```

5. Invoke the template component in the Panel container:

```
<?xml version="1.0"?>
<mx:Application xmlns:mx="http://www.adobe.com/2006/mxml"
   xmlns:comp="com.flexsolutions.chapter2.*"
   height="700" width="700">

<mx:Panel title="Chapter 2 - Solution 2.10">

    <comp:Chapter_2_Sol_10 id="myTplComp" />

  </mx:Panel>
</mx:Application>
```

6. You can now send the two properties to the invoked component as child tags of the component. Make the following change to the code:

```
<?xml version="1.0"?>
<mx:Application xmlns:mx="http://www.adobe.com/2006/mxml"
   xmlns:comp="com.flexsolutions.chapter2.*"
   height="700" width="700">

<mx:Panel title="Chapter 2 - Solution 2.10">
   <comp:Chapter_2_Sol_10 id="myTplComp">
     <comp:header>
       <mx:Image source="" />
     </comp:header>
     <comp:content>
       <mx:HBox>
         <mx:Label text="Insert User ID: "/>
         <mx:TextInput />
       </mx:HBox>
       <mx:HBox>
         <mx:Label text="Insert Password:"/>
         <mx:TextInput />
       </mx:HBox>
       <mx:Button label="Send"/>
     </comp:content>
```

```
      <comp:footer>
        <mx:Image source="" />
      </comp:footer>
    </comp:Chapter_2_Sol_10>

  </mx:Panel>
</mx:Application>
```

The comp:header and the comp:footer template tags are the two properties you created in the Chapter_2_Sol_10.mxml component. They contain two Image controls because they were typed as Image classes:

```
<mx:Script>
  <![CDATA[
    import mx.controls.Image;
    import mx.core.UIComponent;

    public var header:mx.controls.Image;
    public var footer:mx.controls.Image;

    // Define an Array of properties for a row of components.
    [ArrayElementType("mx.core.UIComponent")]
    public var content:Array;

    private function draw():void {
      addChild(header);

      for (var i:int = 0; i < content.length; i++)
      {
      addChild(content[i]);
      }

    addChild(footer);
    }
  ]]>
</mx:Script>
```

The preceding code was written in the <mx:Script> block of the Chapter_2_Sol_10.mxml file. For the comp:content template tag, define two Label controls and two Button controls nested to two HBox controls:

```
<comp:content>
    <mx:HBox>
      <mx:Label text="Insert User ID: "/>
      <mx:TextInput />
    </mx:HBox>
    <mx:HBox>
      <mx:Label text="Insert Password:"/>
      <mx:TextInput />
    </mx:HBox>
    <mx:Button label="Send"/>
</comp:content>
```

111

The `comp:content` property can contain any control that is a valid subclass of the UIComponent class, so enter it as an Array of UIComponent types:

```
// Define an Array of properties for a row of components.
[ArrayElementType("mx.core.UIComponent")]
public var content:Array;
```

7. Save and run the application. The final result is shown in Figure 2-14.

Figure 2-14.
The template component and its properties

Expert tips

Template components can also be created by using the deferred creation feature, which enables Flex to load only the controls that initially appear to the user who loads the application. With this approach you can optimize startup performance because Flex loads the components and their properties only when the user requires them.

The `IdeferredInstance` interface defines the `getInstance()` method to initialize the property when it creates an instance of the component. This method returns a value of Object type. The MXML component that you previously created could thus become the following:

```
<?xml version="1.0"?>
<mx:VBox xmlns:mx="http://www.adobe.com/2006/mxml"
  initialize="draw();">

<mx:Script>
  <![CDATA[
    import mx.controls.Image;
    import mx.core.UIComponent;
    import mx.core.IDeferredInstance;
    public var header:IDeferredInstance;
    public var footer:IDeferredInstance;

    // Define an Array of properties for a row of components.
    [ArrayElementType("mx.core.IDeferredInstance")]
    public var content:Array;
```

```
    private function draw():void {
      addChild(UIComponent(header.getInstance()));
      for (var i:int = 0; i < content.length; i++)
    {

    var myHeader:UIComponent =
         UIComponent(content[i].getInstance());

    var myContent:UIComponent =
         UIComponent(header.getInstance());

    addChild(myHeader );
    addChild(myContent );
    }
  ]]>
</mx:Script>
</mx:VBox>
```

When you use the IdeferredInstance interface as a data type, you can send any data type
to the property. In the addChild() method, you have carried out an implicit cast by sending the header, footer, and content properties as arguments of the UIComponent. This
casting is necessary because the addChild() method can add an object that implements
the UIComponent interface to a container.

Summary

As your Flex applications become more complex, it's good practice to break code into
logic modules, which enables you to better maintain and reuse your code.

Flex supports a component-based development model that consists of subdividing the
code into different files. These external files, called components, can be MXML or
ActionScript files.

This chapter discussed and illustrated different ways to develop Flex custom components
using MXML or ActionScript, and how to create and pass properties and methods to and
from components.

You created a custom event class that extended the Flash Event class to develop loosely
coupled components to make them configurable and reusable throughout different Flex
applications.

3 WORKING WITH DATA MODELS AND THE VALUE OBJECT

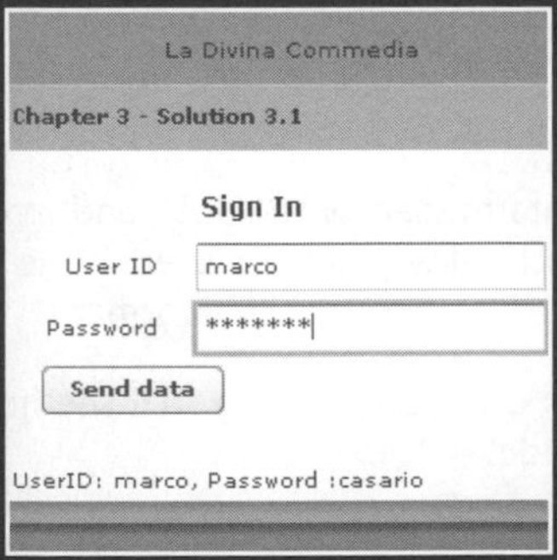

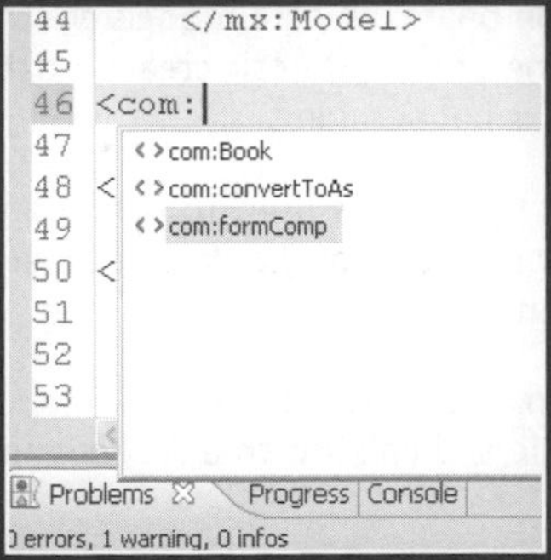

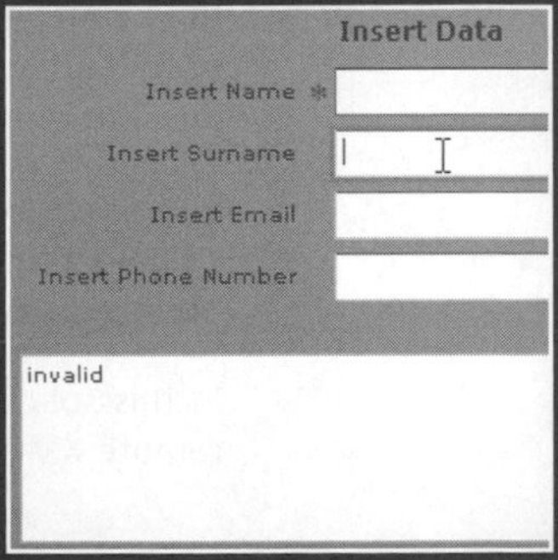

The data modeling method used by Flex is based on the Model-View-Controller (MVC) design pattern. In software development, a **design pattern** is a general repeatable solution to a commonly occurring problem. The MVC design pattern enables you to separate the user interface from the data handling so that you have total independence between the two layers. MVC decouples data access and business logic from data presentation and user interaction by introducing an intermediate component: the controller.

There are three elements that create the MVC: model, view, and controller. The **model** manages the data and its changes during the course of the life cycle of the application. The **view** takes care of displaying the data on the user's screen by defining all the elements of the graphic interface of the application. The **controller** gels these two elements together and manages the events that change the models and the view (you can get more information about this design pattern in Wikipedia: http://en.wikipedia.org/wiki/ Model-view-controller).

The benefits of using this type of design pattern are many, but all have the objective of improving the organization of the code of the application and to maintain the scalability of the project, thereby optimizing reusability and maintainability. It is for these reasons that many frameworks are based on this design pattern—and Flex is one of them.

Flex uses objects that contain the information relative to the data of an application. This information contains the properties that are stored in an ActionScript object, which go under the name *data model*. Data models enable the developer to be able to conserve the data, which can then be sent to a remote server or populate the elements of the Flex application.

Returning to the elements of the MVC design pattern, the data model represents the model element.

Solution 3-1: Using MXML data models

Data models are ActionScript objects that store a series of properties in applications. In the compilation phase, all data models are transformed into an ActionScript class by Flex. In the authoring phase, you can create a data model using MXML tags, particularly if the data structure is not complex.

There are two MXML tags used to define a data model: <mx:Model> and <mx:XML>. Both contain a representation of the data in a hierarchical way and are used in the Flex application to store untyped properties or to load data structures in XML format.

In this solution, you'll create two data models using both tags. You'll see how to load a remote XML file and link it with a Flex data model.

What's involved

To declare the MXML data models, use the following syntax:

```
<mx:Model id="myData">
</mx:Model>
```

In the second case, use this:

```
<mx:XML id="myXMLData">
</mx:XML>
```

The properties are declared as child tags, and the data model must have a root tag and an id declared to enable you to access it:

```
<mx:Model id="myData">
  <rootTag>
    <book>
      <title>La Divina Commedia</title>
      <author>Dante</author>
    </book>
    <book>
      <title>I Promessi Sposi</title>
      <author>Alessandro Manzoni</author>
    </book>
  </rootTag>
</mx:Model>
```

In this solution, you'll learn how to use a data model to store the information inserted in a user form and how to load it from an XML file that is external to the application.

How to build It

Start by creating a new Flex project from Flex Builder, which you'll use throughout the third chapter:

1. Open Flex Builder and create a Flex project with the name Chapter_3_Flex_ DataModel. Click Finish.

2. Create a new MXML application file by selecting File ➤ New ➤ MXML Application and name it Chapter_3_Flex_Sol_1.mxml.

3. Insert an <mx:Model> tag in this file, which will be populated with the static values. You then add a Label onto which you'll print a property of the data model:

```
<?xml version="1.0" encoding="utf-8"?>
<mx:Application xmlns:mx="http://www.adobe.com/2006/mxml"
layout="absolute">

<mx:Model id="myData">
  <rootTag>
    <book>
      <title>La Divina Commedia</title>
      <author>Dante</author>
    </book>
```

```
    <book>
      <title>I Promessi Sposi</title>
      <author>Alessandro Manzoni</author>
    </book>
  </rootTag>
</mx:Model>
<mx:Label text="{myData.book[0].title}" />
</mx:Application>
```

Note the declaration of the rootTag with the <rootTag> tag at the beginning of the data model (you can use any value) that functions as the container of the highest level. If you leave out this declaration, Flex generates a compile-time error. Furthermore, to be able to reference that data, you must specify a name in the id attribute of the model.

The data model being defined with the <mx:Model> MXML tag is a hierarchical representation of data. You can get access to the single values contained in the model referencing its single properties. Using the array syntax and navigating the indexes of the repeating node (the node that contains all the elements of the data model; <book> in this case), you can access the properties directly with the dot syntax:

```
<mx:Label text="{myData.book[0].title}" />
```

You have obviously used a data binding to access the model's data with the curly brackets, omitting the root tag, but working directly from the repeating node. In this case, you'll obtain this text as output on the text of the label: La Divina Commedia.

In Flex Builder, the Problems view (located at the bottom of the Editor view) sends this warning: "Data binding will not be able to detect changes when using the square bracket operator. For Array, please use ArrayCollection.getItemAt() instead".

In fact, you'll learn in Chapter 4 that one of the best practices to access data is to use the getItemAt() method of the ArrayCollection class.

It is also possible to use bindings to populate the properties in a data model:

4. Insert a Panel, as follows (you're defining a form for the user to insert the user id and password into):

```
<mx:Panel title="Chapter 3 - Solution 3.1">
  <mx:Form>
    <mx:FormHeading label="Sign In"/>
    <mx:FormItem label="User ID">
      <mx:TextInput id="userTxt"/>
    </mx:FormItem>
    <mx:FormItem label="Password">
      <mx:TextInput  displayAsPassword="true" id="passTxt"/>
    </mx:FormItem>
    <mx:Button label="Send data"/>
  </mx:Form>
</mx:Panel>
```

5. To populate an `<mx:Model>`, insert a binding between the properties of the model and the values inserted by the user in the Form container, all you need to do is insert the text property of TextInput in the child tags of the model:

```
<mx:Model id="myFormData">
  <signin>
    <user>{userTxt.text}</user>
    <pass>{passTxt.text}</pass>
  </signin>
</mx:Model>
```

The model is formatted by the user and sends the properties that contain the values inserted by the user in TextInput. This association is rendered possible by exploiting Flex data binding. The values inserted between the nodes are, in fact, included between the curly brackets:

```
<user>{userTxt.text}</user>
<pass>{passTxt.text}</pass>
```

6. Before saving and launching the file, insert a Label, to which you'll print the values inserted by the user in the TextInput control directly accessing the data model:

```
<mx:Label text="UserID: {myFormData.user},
        Password :{myFormData.pass}" />
```

In this way, while the user inserts the values in the form fields, the data model becomes populated with these values through the binding, and the Label writes the values inserted in that moment in the data model.

7. Save the file and run the application. If you insert some text into TextInput controls, the result obtained will look like Figure 3-1.

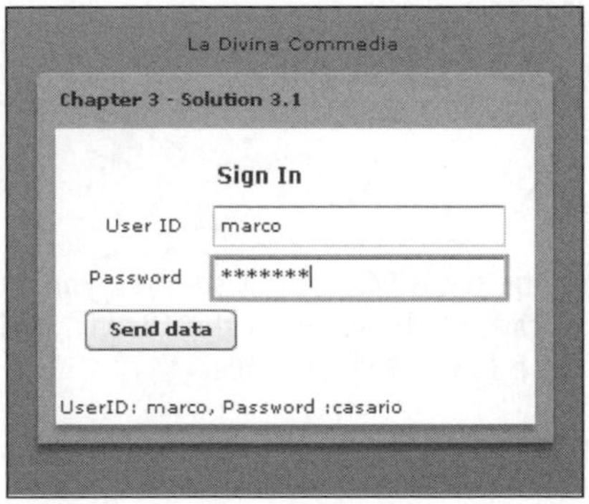

Figure 3-1. The data model becomes populated with the values inserted by the user.

An <mx:XML> variation

The second MXML tag that you can use to define an MXML data model is `<mx:XML>`. The `<mx:Model>` can be used to generate an XML object from a text model and enables you to use the binding to access or set the values of its nodes. In contrast with the <mx:Model>, however, the <mx:XML> tag accepts the format attribute, which enables you to create an XML object based on the powerful and versatile E4X standard.

This standard is a programming language extension that adds native XML support to ECMAScript, the same standard upon which ActionScript and JavaScript are based. It does this by providing access to the XML document in a form that mimics XML syntax. You'll learn about this format and how it can be easily manipulated with ActionScript in Chapter 6; for now you'll concentrate on the XML tag and create a new application file.

1. Create a new MXML application file by selecting File ➤ New ➤ MXML Application and name it Chapter_3_Flex_DataModel_XML.mxml.

2. In this file, create an <mx:XML> tag, to which you assign child nodes as follows:

```
<?xml version="1.0" encoding="utf-8"?>
<mx:Application xmlns:mx="http://www.adobe.com/2006/mxml"
layout="vertical">

<mx:XML format="E4X" id="myMenuModel">
<menu value="Menu">
<items value="Company" data="0">
<item value="History" data="1"/>
<item value="How we work" data="2" />
<item value="Team" data="3" />
</items>
<items value="Services" data="4">
<item value="Adv" data="5"/>
<item value="Web Site" data="6" />
<item value="Rich Internet Application" data="7" />
</items>
<item value="News" data="8" />
<item value="Clients" data="9" />
<item value="Solutions" data="10" />
</menu>
  </mx:XML>
<mx:Application>
```

The default format used by the tag is E4X. In this solution you'll use a simple XML format. To change this format, you can set the value of the format attribute to xml. In this case, you'll obtain an object of type flash.xml.XMLNode.

This data model will be needed by the data provider for one of the list-based controls of Flex, the Tree control.

3. Next, insert a Tree control inside a new Panel inside the MXML application file:

```
<mx:Panel title="Chapter 3 - Solution 3.1"
        width="516" height="402">
<mx:Tree dataProvider="{myMenuModel}" labelField="@value"
        width="248" height="260" id="myTree"/>
</mx:Panel>
```

The Tree control, like all list-based controls, accepts the dataProvider property, which it uses to populate its element structure. You have linked this property with a binding to the data model defined with the <mx:XML> tag. The labelField property specifies the value that must be used as label on the Tree control. In this case, it has been set as value to the value attributes defined in the nodes of the data model. The syntax used with the @ symbol enables you to directly access an attribute in the node tag:

```
<mx:Tree dataProvider="{myMenuModel}" labelField="@value"
        width="248" height="260" id="myTree"/>
```

4. Before saving the file, add an <mx:TextArea> element, as shown following. It writes the value selected by the user in the Tree control into it. To obtain this result, you must again use the E4X language to access the attributes defined in the nodes of the XML data model:

```
<mx:TextArea id="myText"
    text="You selected the
             {myTree.selectedItem.@value.toString()}
              node with the data :
             {myTree.selectedItem.@data.toString()}"
    height="49"/>
```

When the user opens a node of the Tree control, all the data relative to that node will be inserted in the TextArea, as shown in Figure 3-2.

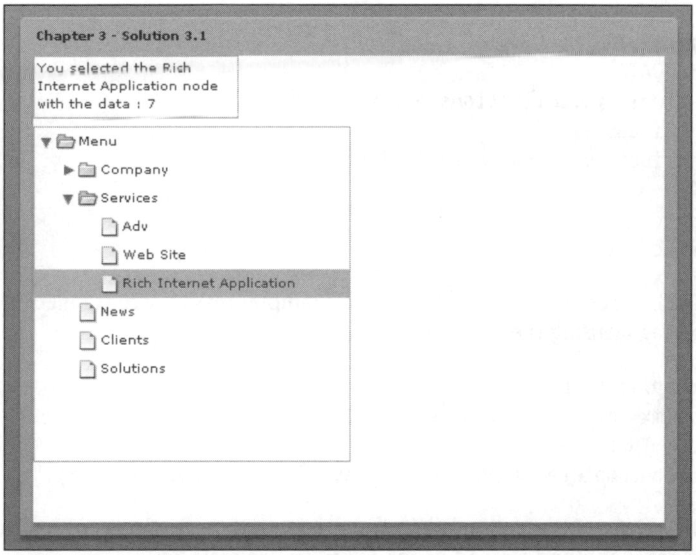

Figure 3-2. The Tree control is populated using the XML data model as data provider.

Expert tips

One of the best practices for using data models is that of always working by converting the data model into a collection class. Flex has two collection classes you can declare: the ArrayCollection class and the XMLListCollection class. Using one of these two objects enables you to access a series of advanced methods and functionalities created specifically for the management of complex data.

In the example, you defined an MXML data model using the `<mx:Model>` tag:

```
<mx:Model id="myData">
  <rootTag>
  <book>
  <title>La Divina Commedia</title>
  <author>Dante</author>
  </book>
  <book>
  <title>I Promessi Sposi</title>
  <author>Alessandro Manzoni</author>
  </book>
  </rootTag>
</mx:Model>
```

You can convert the data to an ArrayCollection by defining a Script block with a private variable:

```
<mx:Script>
  <![CDATA[
    import mx.collections.ArrayCollection;
    [Bindable]
    private var myAC:ArrayCollection;

  ]]>
</mx:Script>
```

The ArrayCollection will be populated, for example, on the creationComplete of the Application tag by using the new operator:

```
<mx:Application
xmlns:mx="http://www.adobe.com/2006/mxml"
layout="vertical"
creationComplete="myAC = new ArrayCollection(myData.book);">
```

To access the values of the data model converted in data type ArrayCollection, you can use the getItemAt method instead of the Array syntax method:

```
<mx:Label text="From ArrayCollection : {myAC.getItemAt(0).title}" />
```

With {myAC.getItemAt(0).title}, you obtain the value on the zero index defined in the title node of the data model.

One of the major benefits of using the collections (ArrayCollection or XMLListCollection) is that these objects enable you to see the changes that the data can undergo in these classes during the life cycle of the application, and consequently change all the controls in which the bindings of the object have been created.

Solution 3-2: Loading external XML data using MXML data models

One of the techniques that improve the separation between user interface and content is the capability to declare the data models externally to the application. In this way, only the presentational tier will be present in the MXML files, whereas the logical tier resides externally. The following approach increases the maintainability and reusability of the application, aside from rendering the code neater and easier to read.

The preceding solution illustrated how to use the two MXML tags to define the data models in Flex (by inserting the data source as a nested tag inside <mx:Model> or <mx:XML>). These two MXML tags also enable you to load an external source, which can be used in the application. In this solution, you'll see how to load external XML files in the data modules defined as MXML tags.

What's involved

To specify an external source and make it load from the <mx:Model> or <mx:XML> MXML tags, you can use their source property, which accepts a valid XML tag resident locally or remotely as value. To do so, the developer can use both the relative and absolute references. The following line of code uses the <mx:Model> tag to load an external XML file locally by using a relative reference:

```
<mx:Model source="data/myfile.xml" id="myModel"/>
```

The following line of code loads an XML file resident on a remote server, aiming at it with an absolute remote path:

```
<mx:XML  source="http://www.domain.com/myfile.xml" id="myModel"/>
```

One of the advantages of using external sources as data models is that you can use this data in more applications and projects, given that it is sufficient to reference them, and also assigning a remote path to them.

How to build it

To avoid reinventing the wheel, you'll open a file created in the preceding solution and modify it, separating the data from the code in the process.

1. Open the Chapter_3_Flex_Sol_1.mxml file created in the preceding example and save it with a different name (Chapter_3_Sol_2.mxml). Find the line of code in which you declared the <mx:Model> tag:

```
<mx:Model id="myData">
  <rootTag>
    <book>
      <title>La Divina Commedia</title>
      <author>Dante</author>
    </book>
    <book>
      <title>I Promessi Sposi</title>
      <author>Alessandro Manzoni</author>
    </book>
  </rootTag>
</mx:Model>
```

2. Cut the content of the <mx:Model id="myData"> to the clipboard (Ctrl/Cmd+X.) The data model, therefore, has the following syntax:

```
<mx:Model id="myData">
</mx:Model>
```

3. Create a new blank XML file by selecting File ➤ New ➤ File and copy the values from the clipboard (Ctrl/Cmd+V). Save the file in the assets folder of the Flex project and call the file data.xml. Add the declaration of the XML document to its first line:

```
<?xml version="1.0"?>

<rootTag>
  <book>
    <title>La Divina Commedia</title>
    <author>Dante</author>
  </book>
  <book>
    <title>I Promessi Sposi</title>
    <author>Alessandro Manzoni</author>
  </book>
</rootTag>
```

> The file was saved in an assets folder, which was created in the Flex project. It is good practice to not leave application assets in the main root of the project.

4. You can't return to the MXML file and add the property source to the <mx:Model> tag to load the data in the external source. You'll use a relative route to aim at the external XML file:

```
<mx:Model id="myData" source="assets/data.xml">
</mx:Model>
```

The source attribute uses the relative address going from the root of the Flex project. This route is, therefore, relative to the project. In fact, the XML file that you have saved is found in the actual assets folder created in the Chapter_3_Flex_DataModel project.

5. To complete the example, add a DataGrid control, which prints all the values contained in the external XML into the Panel. The final MXML file will contain the following code:

```
<?xml version="1.0" encoding="utf-8"?>
<mx:Application
xmlns:mx=http://www.adobe.com/2006/mxml
layout="vertical">

<mx:Model id="myData" source="assets/data.xml">

</mx:Model>

<mx:Panel title="Chapter 3 - Solution 3.2" width="364" height="228">
  <mx:DataGrid dataProvider="{myData.book}" width="95%">
    <mx:columns>
      <mx:DataGridColumn headerText="Title" dataField="title"/>
      <mx:DataGridColumn headerText="Book" dataField="author"/>
    </mx:columns>
  </mx:DataGrid>
</mx:Panel>

</mx:Application>
```

The DataGrid control uses the data model as dataProvider. It aims directly at the repeating node of the XML document:

```
<mx:DataGrid dataProvider="{myData.book}" width="95%">
```

6. Save and run the application, and you'll witness the loading of the external XML data in the DataGrid control.

Expert tips

As stressed many times, it is best practice to use an ArrayCollection variable in the dataProvider property of a DataGrid control. Therefore, in this case, it would be best to bind the data model to an ArrayCollection through an MXML tag:

```
<mx:ArrayCollection source="{myData.book}" id="myAC" />
```

You can also use ActionScript, as seen in the following code. For the latter approach, you have to first declare a variable of ArrayCollection type and then populate it (for example, on the creationComplete event of the Application):

```
<mx:Application
  xmlns:mx="http://www.adobe.com/2006/mxml"
  layout="vertical"
```

```
creationComplete="myAC = new ArrayCollection(myData.book);">
<mx:Script>
  <![CDATA[
    import mx.collections.ArrayCollection;
    [Bindable]
    private var myAC:ArrayCollection;
  ]]>
</mx:Script>
```

At this point, you can send the variable of the DataGrid control to the dataProvider:

```
<mx:DataGrid dataProvider="{myAC}" width="95%">
  <mx:columns>
    <mx:DataGridColumn headerText="Title" dataField="title"/>
    <mx:DataGridColumn headerText="Book" dataField="author"/>
  </mx:columns>
</mx:DataGrid>
```

Be careful not to use both declarations (ActionScript and MXML) for the ArrayCollection of the MXML file. The following code will throw an error because both iterations of ArrayCollection have the same name:

```
<mx:Application
  xmlns:mx="http://www.adobe.com/2006/mxml"
  layout="vertical"
  creationComplete="myAC = new ArrayCollection(myData.book);">
  <mx:Script>
    <![CDATA[
      import mx.collections.ArrayCollection;
      [Bindable]
      private var myAC:ArrayCollection;
    ]]>
  </mx:Script>
  <mx:ArrayCollection source="{myData.book}" id="myAC" />
  <mx:DataGrid dataProvider="{myAC}" width="95%">
    <mx:columns>
      <mx:DataGridColumn headerText="Title" dataField="title"/>
      <mx:DataGridColumn headerText="Book" dataField="author"/>
    </mx:columns>
  </mx:DataGrid>
</mx:Application>
```

Solution 3-3: ActionScript classes as data models

As you saw in Solution 3-2, data models can be defined by using ActionScript instead of MXML tags. Choosing ActionScript makes sense—after all, Flex converts all the code defined in the MXML tags using ActionScript classes in the compilation phase, which then leads to a SWF file being created.

Using MXML is all well and good, but when the data model is formed from a complex architecture, the MXML data models are limited in being able to manage the data, especially when it involves typed properties. In such cases, the use of data models defined with ActionScript classes is a better choice and offers the developer the possibility of managing complex data structures in the application, and also passing as a server-side object.

Creating an ActionScript data model means creating an ActionScript class in which properties and methods representing the structure of the data to be used are defined. This class is instanced in the application through a block of ActionScript code or with a custom MXML tag, and is ready to be used in the project. In this solution, you'll create an ActionScript data model that stores the items selected on a DataGrid.

What's involved

You have already created ActionScript classes in the previous solutions. To create an ActionScript class that functions as a data model, the procedure is the same.

Start the class with the definition of a package. This path is used by the compiler when it has to find a file to compile in the SWF file. The package, defined as follows, represents the physical container (directory structure) of the class:

```
package com.flexsolutions.chapter3
{
}
```

In the package, you define a class by using a class name (you must use the same name as the name of the file that you're creating). If the ActionScript class has been saved with the name myClass.as, the declaration of the class will be as follows:

```
package com.flexsolutions.chapter3 {

public class myClass
{
}

}
```

Even if it is not obligatory to create a class constructor in Flex, it is good practice to define a class constructor in the class. It is not obligatory because if the Flex compiler does not find a constructor, it automatically creates one. But in the object-oriented approach, each class should always have a constructor, even if it is empty. The class constructor is, in all effects, a method that is invoked in the moment of creation of the instance of a class, but it has particular rules:

- It must be a public method.
- It must have the same name as the class.

- It can't specify a return type.

```
package com.flexsolutions.chapter3
{

public class myClass
{

    public function myClass() { }

  }

}
```

It is now possible to begin to define the typed properties in the ActionScript class that functions as the data model:

```
package com.flexsolutions.chapter3 {

  public class myClass {

    public function myClass() { }

    public var name:String;
    public var surname:String;

  }

}
```

After you create the structure of the data inside the class, the ActionScript data model must be instanced in the MXML document for you to be able to use it in the application. To instance an ActionScript class, use the same method that you used to invoke an external MXML component.

To instance an ActionScript data model using MXML, create the custom namespace that defines the package of the class and use it to call the ActionScript class with an MXML tag:

```
<mx:Application
  xmlns:mx=http://www.adobe.com/2006/mxml
  xmlns:cust="com.flexsolutions.chapter3.*">
<cust:myClass id="ASdata" />
```

The class is instantiated using the name of the ActionScript file (myClass.as) as the MXML tag:

```
<cust:myClass id="ASdata" />
```

If you use ActionScript, you instance the class defining the package like so:

```
import com.flexsolutions.chapter3.*;
private var ASdata:myClass = new myClass();
```

How to build it

You begin the example by defining the ActionScript data model. Create an ActionScript class that contains the properties of the data model and contains the methods to add or remove elements on the data model.

1. Create the following directories structure com/flexsolutions/chapter3 by selecting File ➤ New ➤ Folder. In the com/flexsolutions/chapter3 folder, create an ActionScript class by selecting File ➤ New ➤ ActionScript Class, giving it the name Book.as.

2. Immediately after the definition of the package and the class itself, add the constructor and declare the properties, as follows:

```
package com.flexsolutions.chapter3
{

  public class Book
  {
    public function Book()
    {

    }

    private var _books:Array = [];

  }
}
```

The private _books property is an Array that contains all the items you'll add to the DataGrid control. Using the process of encapsulation (see http://en.wikipedia.org/wiki/Object-oriented_programming for a definition) you'll now define the functions of getter and setter to set and get the value of this property.

3. Below the constructor class definition, define the getter/setter methods using the keywords get and set as public methods:

```
public function set books(myBook:Array):void
{
  _books = myBook;
}

public function get books():Array
{
  return _books;
}
```

After the methods are created, add the methods that deal with adding and removing items in the class; they enable you to set and get the value of the private property of the Book ActionScript class. The items are made up of an object containing the properties title and author:

```
{title: book.title,author: book.author}
```

4. At the bottom of the file, add the addBook() method to your code, like so (this accepts an Object containing the properties of the MXML data model as parameter):

```
public function addBook(book:Object):void
    {
        books.push({title: book.title,author: book.author});
    }
```

The Array class has the push() method, which adds the object that specifies the title and author of the book on the last index.

5. Finally, add the method removeItemAt, which looks like so (this removes the last item just inserted):

```
public function removeItemAt():void {

        var index:Number = books.length-1;
        if (index >= 0) {
        books.splice(index, 1);

        }

    }
```

This method carries out a simple check to verify that the items in the array exist to avoid obtaining an error at runtime because of removal of elements that don't exist!

Note that both methods are declared as public to be able to be accessed outside of the application instancing the ActionScript class.

Here is the entire code of the Book.as ActionScript class:

```
package com.flexsolutions.chapter3
{

  public class Book
  {
    public function Book()
    {
    }

    private var _books:Array = [];

    public function addBook(book:Object):void
    {
      books.push({title: book.title,author: book.author});
    }
```

```
public function removeItemAt():void {

  var index:Number = books.length-1;
  if (index >= 0) {
  books.splice(index, 1);

  }
}

[Bindable]
public function set books(myBook:Array):void
{
  _books = myBook;
}

public function get books():Array
{
  return _books;
}
    }
  }
}
```

The ActionScript data model has been created, but now it must be instanced in the application file. To instance an ActionScript class in an MXML, you can use the following ActionScript code:

```
import com.flexsolutions.chapter3.Book;
private var bookClass:Book = new Book();
```

Import the package of the class and then create an instance of the same by using the keyword new.

It is also possible to instance ActionScript classes with MXML by specifying a custom namespace that defines the package of the class and then invokes it with an MXML tag referencing the name of the ActionScript file:

```
<cust:Book id="ASBook"   xmlns:cust="com.*" />
```

6. Now you'll create an MXML application file containing an MXML data model that will function as data provider for a DataGrid. Create a new MXML application file by selecting File ➤ New ➤ MXML Application and save it as Chapter_3_Sol_3.mxml. Write the following code in it:

```
<?xml version="1.0" encoding="utf-8"?>
<mx:Application
  xmlns:mx="http://www.adobe.com/2006/mxml"
  layout="vertical">

  <mx:Model id="myData" source="assets/data.xml" />
```

```
<mx:Panel title="Chapter 3 - Solution 3.3" width="364" height="228">
  <mx:DataGrid id="myDG" dataProvider="{myData.book}" width="95%" >
    <mx:columns>
      <mx:DataGridColumn headerText="Title" dataField="title"/>
      <mx:DataGridColumn headerText="Author" dataField="author"/>
    </mx:columns>
  </mx:DataGrid>
</mx:Panel>

</mx:Application>
```

The MXML data model created with the <mx:Model> tag, seen previously, is the same as the one used in the preceding solution, which loads the data from the data.xml file:

```
<?xml version="1.0"?>
<rootTag>
  <book>
    <title>La Divina Commedia</title>
    <author>Dante</author>
  </book>
  <book>
    <title>I Promessi Sposi</title>
    <author>Alessandro Manzoni</author>
  </book>
</rootTag>
```

The data model will be used as a data provider for the DataGrid, for which you define the Title and Author columns. These columns are bound to the <title> and <author> node values of the XML file with the dataField property of the DataGridColumn tag:

```
<mx:DataGridColumn headerText="Title" dataField="title"/>
<mx:DataGridColumn headerText="Author" dataField="author"/>
```

The data provider aims at the repeating node book of the data model using dot syntax, without having to also define the rootTag:

```
<mx:DataGrid id="myDG" dataProvider="{myData.book}"
  width="95%" change="myBtn.enabled=true">
```

The change event of the DataGrid makes the myBtn button visible (you'll create this button in Step 8).

7. To be able to use the ActionScript class, you have to first instance it in the MXML Application file. Below the <mx:Model> tag definition, add the following line to the code:

```
<cust:Book id="ASBook"
xmlns:cust="com.flexsolutions.chapter3.*" />
```

The custom namespace is created directly on the tag that invokes the class. (This approach was also illustrated in Solution 2-4.) After the reference to the class is created, you can use the two methods to add or remove items from the DataGrid to the class.

8. Insert two buttons, as follows (they recall the methods to add and remove items in the ActionScript class), defined in an HBox right under the DataGrid:

```
<mx:HBox width="100%" height="20">
  <mx:Button id="myBtn" enabled="false"
    click="ASBook.addBook(myDG.selectedItem)"
    label="Add Book" />
  <mx:Button id="myBtn_remove"
    label="Remove"
    click="ASBook.removeItemAt()" />
</mx:HBox>
```

The public method addBook() accepts the item object selected by the user in the DataGrid (which contains the MXML data model as its parameter.) Therefore, on the selectedItem, you have an object with the title and author properties.

The public method removeItemAt() does not accept parameters; it removes the last selectedItem inserted in the property books of the class.

9. Save and run the application file. Select an item in the DataGrid and press the button with the Add Book label. The selected Item will be added on the first index of the array of the Book class.

Expert tips

To avoid a possible error at runtime, the enabled property of the buttons was set as false. In this way, the user cannot click the buttons as the application is being loaded:

```
<mx:Button id="myBtn"
  enabled="false"
  click="ASBook.addBook(myDG.selectedItem) "
  label="Add Book" />
<mx:Button id="myBtn_remove"
  enabled="false"
  label="Remove"
  click="ASBook.removeItemAt()" />
```

You then render the button to add an element as enabled, just as the event change is released on the DataGrid (or when the user selects an item in the component):

```
<mx:DataGrid id="myDG" dataProvider="{myAC}" width="95%"
  change="myBtn.enabled=true">
```

The Remove button, on the other hand is rendered as enabled only after the first click of the Add Book button, as defined by the following code:

```
<mx:Button id="myBtn" enabled="false"
click="ASBook.addBook(myDG.selectedItem);
myBtn_remove.enabled=true" label="Add Book" />
```

Finally, to follow best practices, as discussed in the previous solution, you should convert the MXML data model to ArrayCollection before sending it to the data provider of the DataGrid:

```
<mx:ArrayCollection id="myAC" source="{myData.book}" />
<mx:Panel title="Chapter 3 - Solution 3.3"
width="364" height="228">
    <mx:DataGrid id="myDG"
      dataProvider="{myAC}"
      width="95%"
      change="myBtn.enabled=true">
```

Solution 3-4: Using data binding with data models

Up until now, you have created data models using MXML tags and ActionScript defining static values in them. However, one of the most frequent uses of data models is as data containers that are dynamically generated in the application. In this way, you can insert the values inserted by the user in a form into the structure of the data. It will be possible to, for example, send the data model to the server and process the data by inserting it in a database. This is obviously one of the possible scenarios that use data models as data containers.

To be able to insert data originating from the objects that turn a Flex application into a data model just like the items of a form, you need to create a data binding with these objects.

Data binding is one of the most interesting features of Flex, enabling you to link one object to another. Flex automatically takes note of the changes that happen to the objects during the life cycle of the application and updates the components the data binding is referring to, ensuring that you don't end up with broken references.

This solution shows you how to create and populate a data model with the data entered into a form by a user.

What's involved

To create a data binding in Flex, you can either use the MXML tag `<mx:Binding>` or refer to the property of the object put between the curly brackets (refer to Solution 1-4).

The following shows two objects, one of type `Label` and one of type `TextInput`:

```
<mx:TextInput  id="myTextInput" />
<mx:Label id="myLabel" />
```

You can create a data binding using the MXML Binding tag, as follows:

```
<mx:Binding destination="myLabel.text" source="myTextInput.text"  />
```

Now you can reference the data inside the text attribute of the `Label` tag using the curly brackets:

```
<mx:TextInput  id="myTextInput" />
<mx:Label id="myLabel" text="{myTextInput.text}" />
```

The result is that you'll see the text that the user inserts in the `TextInput` control written out in the `Label`.

The same applies to the data models—here you create a data binding with the visual objects of the application. In fact, when defining the properties that define the structure of the data model, you no longer write a static value; you write a data binding:

```
<mx:Model id="myModel">
  <rootTag>
    <name>{myTextInput.text}</name>
  </rootTag>
</mx:Model>
```

The `TextInput` of the solution is now contained in a `Form` container (which is the container in which you declare all the elements of the form), as follows:

```
<mx:Form width="100%">
  <mx:FormHeading label="Insert Data"/>
  <mx:FormItem label="Name">
  <mx:TextInput id="nameTxt"/>
</mx:FormItem>
```

How to build it

In this solution, you'll create an MXML component that will be invoked in the main application. In the external component you'll include the form, which the data model will declare in the application. The values of the data model will be printed on the `Label` at the click of a button. Figure 3-3 shows the completed user interface for this solution.

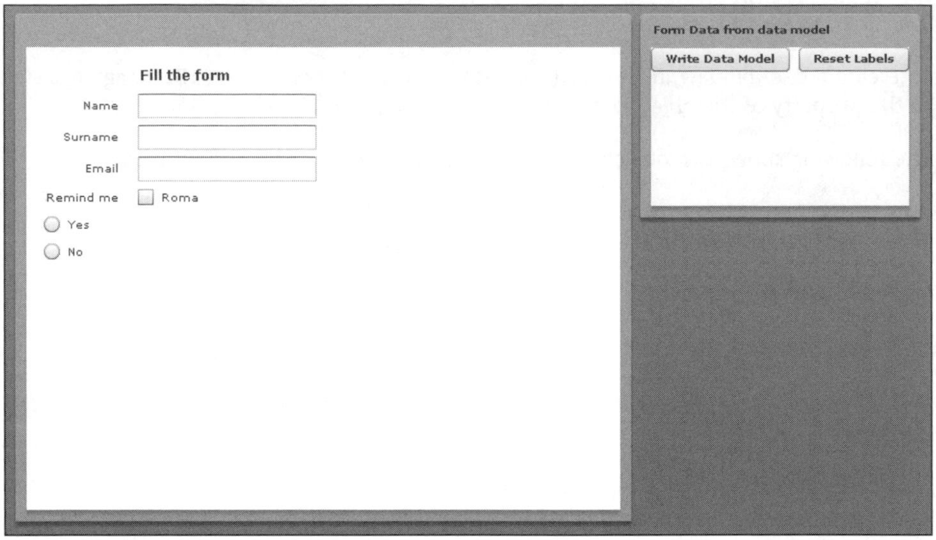

Figure 3-3. The completed file with the form-based MXML component

Begin by creating the MXML component.

1. Create an MXML component based on a Panel by selecting File ➤ New ➤ MXML Component. Save the component file in the com/flexsolutions/chapter3 folder with the name formComp.mxml. Insert the form in this file with the following code:

```
<?xml version="1.0" encoding="utf-8"?>
<mx:Panel xmlns:mx="http://www.adobe.com/2006/mxml"
  layout="vertical" width="550" height="450">

    <mx:Form width="100%">
    <mx:FormHeading label="Fill the form"/>
    <mx:FormItem label="Name">
      <mx:TextInput id="nomeTxt"/>
    </mx:FormItem>
    <mx:FormItem label="Surname">
      <mx:TextInput id="cognomeTxt"/>
    </mx:FormItem>
    <mx:FormItem label="Email">
      <mx:TextInput id="emailTxt"/>
    </mx:FormItem>
    <mx:FormItem label="Remind me">
      <mx:CheckBox id="remindChk" label="Yes"/>
    </mx:FormItem>

    <mx:RadioButtonGroup id="newsletter"/>
    <mx:RadioButton label="Yes" groupName="newsletter"/>
    <mx:RadioButton label="No" groupName="newsletter"/>
```

```
    </mx:Form>
</mx:Panel>
```

Every object inserted in the Form container becomes defined in the FormItem tag, which automatically produces a label for that Item.

In the form, you have declared three TextInput components, two RadioButton components (linked to the id of the RadioButtonGroup through the groupName property), and one Checkbox. These components become bound in the data model of the application.

2. Create an application file by selecting File ➤ New ➤ MXML Application, and save it with the name Chapter_3_Sol_4.mxml.

> *Components were discussed in Chapter 2. Revisit Solutions 2-1 and 2-2 to revise the steps necessary to invoke an MXML component.*

3. Now you'll invoke the MXML component. To do this, you first need to define a custom namespace with the package in which the component is contained. Add the following code to the application file:

```
<?xml version="1.0" encoding="utf-8"?>
<mx:Application xmlns:mx="http://www.adobe.com/2006/mxml"
layout="horizontal" xmlns:com="com.flexsolutions.chapter3.*">

<com:formComp id="myComp" />

</mx:Application>
```

In the definition of the Application tag, you have created the custom namespace com whose package is com.flexsolutions.chapter3.*. You use the namespace to import the component to which you have assigned an id of myComp.

4. You now move on to defining the data model using the <mx:Model> tag. Every property of the data model will have a data binding with the objects of the form in the MXML component. To be able to access them, the dot syntax is used, starting from the id of the component until you arrive at the property text of the TextInput control:

```
<mx:Model id="myModel">

<rootTag>
  <name>{myComp.nomeTxt.text}</name>
  <surname>{myComp.cognomeTxt.text}</ surname >
  <email>{myComp.emailTxt.text}</email>
  <check>{myComp.remindChk.selected}</check>
  <radio>{myComp.newsletter.selectedValue}</radio>
</rootTag>

</mx:Model>
```

The data model not only contains the text inserted by the user in the TextInput but also has the property selected by the CheckBox (it contains true or false depending on which one was selected by the user) and the selectedValue of the RadioButtonGroup (containing the label of the RadioButton selected by the user).

5. Insert a new Panel in a VBox containing two buttons. The first button will launch an event handler, which will write the values contained in the MXML data model into several occurrences of Label. The second button will launch an event handler, which will simply reset the text of the label, emptying it:

```
<mx:VBox>

   <mx:Panel title="Form Data from data model" >

     <mx:HBox>
     <mx:Button id="writeBtn"
        label="Write Data Model"
        click="write(event)" />
     <mx:Button id="resetBtn"
         label="Reset Labels"
         click="reset(event)" />
     </mx:HBox>

     <mx:Label  id="nameLbl" />
     <mx:Label id=" surname Lbl" />
     <mx:Label id="emailLbl" />
     <mx:Label id="checkLbl" />
     <mx:Label id="radioLbl" />

   </mx:Panel>
</mx:VBox>
```

6. You have to write the event handlers launched by the click event of the two buttons. To do this, insert a Script block into the code below the Application tag and define the two functions inside it:

```
<mx:Script>
  <![CDATA[

    private function write(evt:Event):void
    {
      nameLbl.text = myModel.name;
      surname Lbl.text = myModel. surname;
      emailLbl.text = myModel.email;
      checkLbl.text = myModel.check;
      radioLbl.text = myModel.radio;

    }

    private function reset(evt:Event):void
    {
      nomeLbl.text = "";
```

```
          cognomeLbl.text = "";
          emailLbl.text = "";
          checkLbl.text = "";
          radioLbl.text = "";
      }

   ]]>
</mx:Script>
```

In the `write()` function, you populate the text properties of each Label (referencing each id) with the values contained in the model (the model itself has an id of myModel.) The data model does not contain nested tags (although the contents are contained inside a single root tag.) In fact, to access the properties declared in the data model (name, surname, email, radio, check) with ActionScript, it is enough to aim at the data model and the property that you want to remove, without passing the name of the root tag: `myModel.name;`.

7. Save the file and run the application.

As discussed earlier, when you insert values in the form and then click the Write button you'll see the values from the data model (taken from the form) displayed in the panel. You can send the data structure to a server, for example, that inserts the data model in a database with a server-side language.

Expert tips

Importing an external MXML component involves two steps. The first is to define a custom namespace, usually in the Application tag, which references the package containing the components, and the second step directly invokes the external component, referring to the namespace and to the name of the file of the component (notice that the .mxml extension is not included):

```
<mx:Application xmlns:mx="http://www.adobe.com/2006/mxml"
layout="horizontal"
xmlns:com=" com.flexsolutions.chapter3.*">

<com:formComp id="myComp" />
```

This procedure must be nearly completely hand-coded, save for the fact that Flex Builder helps you with its code hints, which list all the MXML components created inside the custom package (xmlns:com="com.flexsolutions.chapter3.*"). If you start to directly invoke the component using the same name of the folder that contains the components as suffix for the namespace without having created the custom namespace in the Application tag, Flex Builder will automatically add the declaration of the namespace to the Application tag.

In the project, you have saved the components in the com/flexsolutions/chapter3 folder. Write the component invocation using com as suffix:

```
<com:formComp id="myComp" />
```

You can coax Flex Builder into automatically adding the custom namespace on the Application tag:

```
<mx:Application xmlns:mx="http://www.adobe.com/2006/mxml"
layout="horizontal"
xmlns:com=" com.flexsolutions.chapter3.*">
```

Flex Builder automatically adds the custom namespace definition in the Application tag. Figure 3-4 shows the code hints served by Flex Builder.

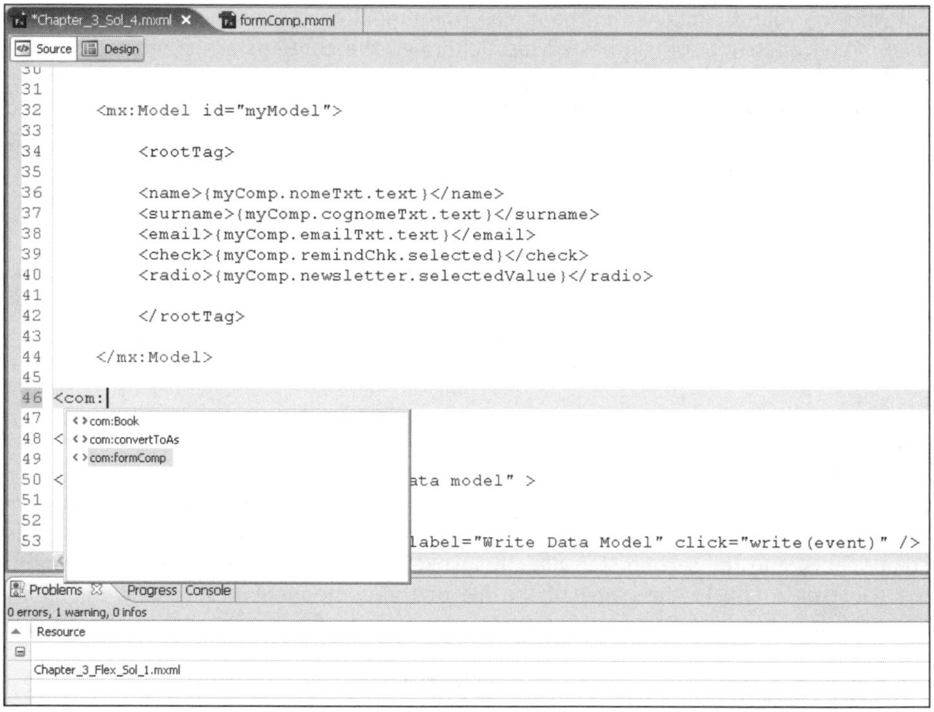

Figure 3-4. Flex Builder code recogniizes that components exist in that folder and automatically declares the custom namespace of the Application tag.

Solution 3-5: Converting an MXML data model into an ActionScript object

Data models are used in many situations as objects for the encapsulation of a set of data, which can be returned by a remote call or by a method originating from an object. This approach makes the management of a data structure easier in a Flex application.

To reduce the number of remote calls and thus keep the associated overhead under control, it is best practice to use value objects that take care of the transport of data from the server to the client. These value objects contain not just individual attributes but also the entire data structure. This model will therefore be managed on the client and linked to the various objects that make up the application. The concept of value objects is not new in programming, particularly in the enterprise Java (J2EE) area. It was, in fact, codified as a design pattern by Sun (you can find out more about it at http://java.sun.com/j2ee/patterns/ValueObject.html).

In Flex, a value object is composed of an ActionScript file in which all the attributes that must be transported are declared. These attributes are the properties of the ActionScript data model.

It is possible to convert a declared data model using MXML, transforming it into an ActionScript object. With this operation you have access to the attributes of the data model as properties of the ActionScript object.

What's involved

So you start off with an MXML data model (declared with the <mx:Model> tag to transform it into an ActionScript object). It will work to send this data model to an ActionScript variable with the data type set as object. To do this, you'll send an MXML data model to a property of an MXML component.

This property is declared in a <mx:Script> block inside the component, typed as Object:

```
<mx:Script>
<![CDATA[

private var _dmOBJ:Object;

[Bindable]
public function set dmOBJ(param:Object):void
{
    _dmOBJ = param;
}

public function get dmOBJ():Object
{
    return _dmOBJ;
}
]]>
</mx:Script>
```

The _dmObject property is of Object type, and is set and returned using getter/setter methods. The values in the data model are automatically inserted in the ActionScript object as properties of that Object. The data model is the same as that created in the preceding solution:

```
<mx:Model id="myModel">
<rootTag>
<name>{myComp.nomeTxt.text}</name>
<surname>{myComp.cognomeTxt.text}</surname>
<email>{myComp.emailTxt.text}</email>
```

```
<check>{myComp.remindChk.selected}</check>
<radio>{myComp.newsletter.selectedValue}</radio>
</rootTag>
</mx:Model>
```

How to build it

This solution uses part of the same code of the main application file created in the preceding solution. In fact, you conserve the elements of the form and the data model declared in the MXML.

In terms of new code, you need to add an external MXML component whose only job will be to accept a property that resides in the data model of the application. This object, which represents the value object, contains the attributes of the model that you print on the text of the Label controls.

1. Create the MXML component by selecting File ➤ New ➤ MXML Component in the com/flexsolutions/chapter3 folder of the project, giving it the name convertToAs.mxml and basing it on a Panel container.

2. To the file you just created, add the following code, which defines the Object:

```
<?xml version="1.0" encoding="utf-8"?>
<mx:Panel
title="AS Data Model converted from MXML Data Model"
  xmlns:mx="http://www.adobe.com/2006/mxml"
  width="400" height="300">
<mx:Script>
  <![CDATA[

    private var _dmOBJ:Object;

    [Bindable]
    public function set dmOBJ(param:Object):void
    {
      _dmOBJ = param;
    }

    public function get dmOBJ():Object
    {
      return _dmOBJ;
    }
  ]]>
</mx:Script>

</mx:Panel>
```

The _dmObject property, typed as Object, uses the getter and setter methods—the setter method is declared as [Bindable] by using the metadata [Bindable] and enables you to use the property in data binding of the component.

The conversion of the data model into an ActionScript Object is carried out automatically, and the attributes of the data model become represented in the object in the form of properties. To access these properties and bind them to Flex controls, use the dot syntax on the ActionScript object created:

```
dmOBJ.property;
```

3. Insert five Label controls in your MXML file and create the data binding with the properties of the data model. Write the code for the binding values in the text properties of the Label controls:

```
<mx:Label text="{dmOBJ.name}" />
<mx:Label text="{dmOBJ.surname}" />
<mx:Label text="{dmOBJ.email}" />
<mx:Label text="{dmOBJ.check}" />
<mx:Label text="{dmOBJ.radio}" />
```

4. Now create an MXML application file and name it Chapter_3_Sol_5.mxml (it will contain the MXML data model that you'll pass to the component).

5. In this file, insert a Form container (the same one used in the previous solution) whose items are used to increase the attributes of the data model. Modify the code in your new file so it looks like the following:

```
<?xml version="1.0" encoding="utf-8"?>
<mx:Application xmlns:mx="http://www.adobe.com/2006/mxml"
layout-"horizontal"
xmlns:com=" com.flexsolutions.chapter3.*">

  <mx:Model id="myModel">
    <rootTag>
      <name>{nameTxt.text}</name>
      <surname>{surnameTxt.text}</surname>
      <email>{emailTxt.text}</email>
      <check>{remindChk.selected}</check>
      <radio>{newsletter.selectedValue}</radio>
    </rootTag>
  </mx:Model>

  <mx:Form width="100%">
  <mx:FormHeading label="Inserisci i tuoi dati"/>
  <mx:FormItem label="Name">
    <mx:TextInput id="nameTxt"/>
  </mx:FormItem>
  <mx:FormItem label="Surname">
    <mx:TextInput id="surnameTxt"/>
  </mx:FormItem>
  <mx:FormItem label="Email">
    <mx:TextInput id="emailTxt"/>
  </mx:FormItem>
  <mx:FormItem label="Remind me">
    <mx:CheckBox id="remindChk" label="Roma"/>
```

3

```
    </mx:FormItem>
    <mx:RadioButtonGroup id="newsletter"/>
      <mx:RadioButton label="Yes"
        groupName="newsletter"/>
      <mx:RadioButton label="No"
        groupName="newsletter"/>
    </mx:Form>

  </mx:Application>
```

6. All that is missing is simply to invoke the MXML component to which you'll send the data model as property of the tag. To invoke MXML components, define the custom namespace and declare the name of the file to call:

```
<com:convertToAs dmOBJ="{myModel.user}" />
```

The _dmObj property was defined as private, so you can't access it from the Application. In fact, to populate the ActionScript object you use the setter dmOBJ method, which is declared as public. You directly send the MXML data model to it.

7. You must not forget to add the custom namespace on the Application tag:

```
<mx:Application xmlns:mx="http://www.adobe.com/2006/mxml"
  layout="horizontal" xmlns:com="com.flexsolutions.chapter3.*">
```

8. Save the file and run the application. The final result, shown in Figure 3-5, displays the values from the data model, printed on the Label controls declared in the MXML component. The difference this time is that the data is coming from the ActionScript Object and is no longer coming directly from the MXML data model.

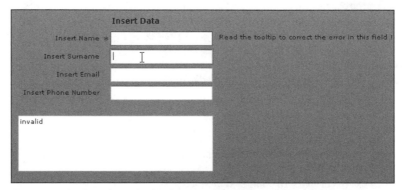

Figure 3-5. The data shown in the right panel is coming from the ActionScript Object and is no longer coming directly from the MXML data model.

Expert tips

To access the attributes of a data model, you reference its id, skipping the rootTag of the model:

```
<mx:Model id="myModel">
  <rootTag>
    <name>Marco</name>
    <surname>Casario</surname>
    <email>m.casario@comtaste.com</email>
    <check>True</check>
    <radio>Yes</radio>
  </rootTag>
</mx:Model>

<mx:Label text="{myModel.name}" />
<mx:Label text="{myModel.surname}" />
<mx:Label text="{myModel.email}" />
<mx:Label text="{myModel.check}" />
<mx:Label text="{myModel.radio}" />
```

This is an example of a flat data model without nested values. If the data model does not have a flat structure, but is more nested, you must access the nested values through the repeating node. A good example is when the data model is composed of nested nodes:

```
<mx:Model id="myModel">
  <rootTag>

    <user>
      <name>Marco</name>
      <surname>Casario</surname>
      <email>m.casario@comtaste.com</email>
    </user>

    <user>
      <name>Katia</name>
      <surname>Casario</surname>
      <email>k.casario@comtaste.com</email>
    </user>

    <user>
      <name>Alex</name>
      <surname>Casario</surname>
      <email>a.casario@comtaste.com</email>
    </user>

  </rootTag>
</mx:Model>
```

To send all the values defined in all the <user> nodes to the ActionScript object, you would have had to reference not only the id of the data model but also its repeating node:

```
<com:convertToAs dmOBJ="{myModel.user}" />
```

You have to edit and modify the convertToAs MXML component by adding the following code:

```
<?xml version="1.0" encoding="utf-8"?>
<mx:Panel  title="Actionscript Data Model converted from MXML Data
Model"
xmlns:mx="http://www.adobe.com/2006/mxml"
width="400" height="300">


<mx:Script>
<![CDATA[
import mx.controls.Alert;

private var _dmOBJ:Object;

[Bindable]
public function set dmOBJ(param:Object):void
{
_dmOBJ = param;
}

public function get dmOBJ():Object
{
return _dmOBJ;
}

private function init():void
{
for (var i:String in dmOBJ)
{
    objTxt.text += i + ": " + dmOBJ[i].name + "\n" +
    dmOBJ[i].surname + "\n" +
    dmOBJ[i].email + "\n";
}
}
]]>
</mx:Script>


<mx:Label text="{dmOBJ.name}" />
<mx:Label text="{dmOBJ.surname}" />
<mx:Label text="{dmOBJ.email}" />
<mx:Label text="{dmOBJ.check}" />
<mx:Label text="{dmOBJ.radio}" />

<mx:TextArea id="objTxt"  width="217" height="91"/>
<mx:Button click="init()"
label="See the Object's Structure" />

</mx:Panel>
```

The init() function, which is called by the click event of the button, executes a for loop to navigate through the dmOBJ and print its properties into the TextArea control.

In this case, the data model is a complex structure formed from an Array containing the objects with the relative properties on various indexes, as shown in Figure 3-6.

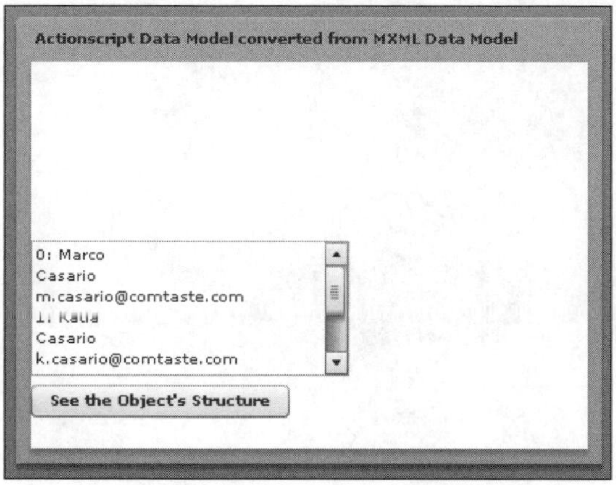

Figure 3-6. The structure of the data model with a repeating node

Summary

The data modeling method used by Flex is based on the MVC design pattern. The data models are ActionScript objects, which store a series of properties in the applications. They're used as data binding in Flex controls or to store the information relative to the users.

This chapter looked at the benefits of using data models and how to create them inside a Flex application. You created MXML data components by using the two MXML tags (<mx:Model> and <mx:XML>) and ActionScript.

Although MXML data models contain a representation of the data in a hierarchical manner and are used in the Flex application (particularly to store untyped properties or to load data structures in XML format), ActionScript data models can be formed by complex data structures and offer the possibility to work with typed properties.

MXML data models can load data from external files. One of the techniques that improve the separation between user interface and content is the capability to declare the data models externally to the application.

The last solution showed a technique to convert an MXML data model into an ActionScript object and introduced the concept of ActionScript value objects, which take care of the transport of data from the server to the client. These value objects contain not just individual attributes but also entire data structures.

4 VALIDATING AND FORMATTING
DATA

Insert Data

me *

me

nail

ber

New ActionScript Class

New ActionScript class

⚠ By convention, ActionScript type names start
letter.

Project: Chapter_4_Flex_2_Validators_Forma

Package: com

Name: socialValidator

Modifiers: ◉ public   ○ internal
            ☐ dynamic ☐ final

Percentage's Calc

t your price: 1000

ercentage :   20

Calculate

ue: €200,00

Flex offers a powerful built-in system to validate and format data. In the development of an application, the data validation process is a very delicate and important aspect. It facilitates effective cooperation between the data models and the objects that make up the user interface of the project. In fact, one of the most common uses of validation is actually with data models (refer to Chapter 3 for more information).

The Flex Software Development Kit (SDK) provides a series of specific validator classes that extend the main Validator class:

- CreditCardValidator
- CurrencyValidator
- DateValidator
- EmailValidator
- NumberValidator
- PhoneNumberValidator
- RegExpValidator
- SocialSecurityValidator
- StringValidator
- ZipCodeValidator

All these classes can be extended and customized to meet the requirements of an application. For example, you might want to change the criteria used to verify the validity of a credit card number that a user inserts in a TextInput control.

It is the same story with the formatter classes in Flex, which enable you to format raw data. You can, for example, create a union between two fields of a data model to obtain both the name and surname of the user as a single string. Or you can format the telephone number inserted into a TextInput field using a determined pattern.

> *All the formatter classes included in Flex extend the* mx.formatters.Formatter *class.*

The use of these ready-made objects saves a lot of time that you would otherwise have to spend if you created them from scratch.

In this chapter you'll work on data using the validator and formatter classes.

Solution 4-1: MXML validator classes

The Flex validator classes work in a similar way to client-side JavaScript validation. Because Flex validation occurs on the client, users receive feedback about the validity of the data they're writing without having to wait until the server has processed the data. It is also good for developers because they can be more confident that the data sent to the server will be correct.

Flex provides a series of ready-made validator classes that can be declared by using MXML or ActionScript. Both methods require the definition of a few properties needed by the class to intercept the object or the data to be validated, and a definition of the moment in which these validation checks must be performed.

In this solution you'll declare the validator classes using MXML and see how to validate the data inserted in a TextInput control (in which you want to accept only numbers as valid values).

What's involved

To use a validator class in Flex using MXML, you need to refer to the relative tag of the class:

- CreditCardValidator class: <mx: CreditCardValidator />
- CurrencyValidator class: <mx:CurrencyValidator />
- DateValidator class: <mx:DateValidator />
- EmailValidator class: <mx:EmailValidator />
- NumberValidator class: <mx:NumberValidator />
- PhoneNumberValidator class: <mx:PhoneNumberValidator />
- RegExpValidator class: <mx:RegExpValidator />
- SocialSecurityValidator class: <mx:SocialSecurityValidator />
- StringValidator class: <mx:StringValidator />
- ZipCodeValidator class: <mx:ZipCodeValidator />

As with all MXML tags, you must declare the id attribute to be able to refer to its instance and access its properties. Besides the id, there are at least two other essential properties that are required by each validator class to be able to carry out validation operations:

- source: Contains the object to be validated
- property: Contains the property on which the validation will be carried out

How to build it

Start by creating a new Flex project that you'll use for all the solutions throughout this chapter.

1. Open Flex Builder and create a Flex project with the name Chapter_4_Flex_ Validators_Formatters. Step through, leaving everything else at the default values; then click Finish.

2. Create a new MXML application file by selecting File ➤ New ➤ MXML Application and name it Chapter_4_Flex_Sol_1.mxml.

3. Create the Form container and the FormItem objects below the Application tag declaration, like so:

```
<mx:Form id="myForm">
  <mx:FormHeading label="Insert Data">
  </mx:FormHeading>
  <mx:FormItem label="Insert Name" >
    <mx:TextInput id="nameTxt" />
  </mx:FormItem>
  <mx:FormItem label="Insert Surname">
    <mx:TextInput id="surnameTxt" />
</mx:FormItem>
<mx:FormItem label="Insert your Salary">
    <mx:TextInput id="salaryTxt" />
  </mx:FormItem>
</mx:Form>
```

4. Add the following code to the MXML file above the Form container—you'll use the built-in class mx:NumberValidator, declaring it with MXML, to validate the TextInput controls as numbers:

```
<mx:NumberValidator id="salaryV"
    source="{salaryTxt }"
    property="text" />
```

The NumberValidator class uses its source attribute to reference the TextInput (which has an id equal to salaryTxt). This sole declaration is not enough for the validator to be able to carry out the validation checks on the field. In fact, the data that the user inserts in the TextInput is contained in the text property. For this reason, the property attribute of the NumberValidator references the property text.

> *Make sure that the property of the* TextInput *sent to the* property *attribute of the* NumberValidator *is text. This property is sent as a String, which means that you won't receive an error at compile time. In that case, if you make a typing error, the* NumberValidator *will not be applied.*

5. Save the file, run the application, and enter some text into the input fields. If you enter non-numeric characters and then take the focus away from the TextInput as soon as it loses focus, the validator will be run and the error message will be displayed, as shown in Figure 4.1.

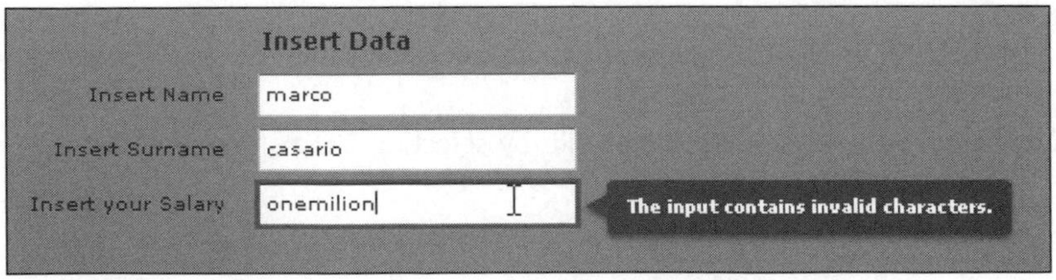

Figure 4-1. The validator is run when the TextInput control loses focus.

Expert tips

When associated with a `TextInput` control, the `NumberValidator`, like all other built-in validators, uses the `valueCommit` event. In a `TextInput` control, Flex dispatches the `valueCommit` event whenever the text value changes.

Sometimes you'll want the validation to be triggered on other events. To do this, the validator classes expose two other properties:

- `trigger`: Contains the object that will cause the event to be triggered
- `triggerEvent`: Contains the name of the event

In code, the two properties look like this:

```
<mx:NumberValidator id="salaryV"
  source="{salaryTxt }"
  property="text"
  trigger="{salaryTxt }"
  triggerEvent="change" />
```

In this example, the validation will occur with the change event of the `TextInput` control or as soon as the user types a value into the control.

You'll see in the next solution how to program the validators so they will be applied at the click of a button.

Solution 4-2: Creating mandatory FormItems

You might want to make a few items mandatory in a form. If so, you'll want to set up the form so users can't send the data to the server if they haven't inserted values into these fields. Flex enables you to display a visual clue to make users understand that the field is obligatory and to carry out the check and the validation of that field through the validator classes.

In this solution you'll see how to implement mandatory form fields.

What's involved

To create a mandatory form field, use a property of the `FormItem` class, which has a Boolean `required` property that denotes a form field as being required. Another nice touch is that when `required="true"` is added to as form field, the asterisk symbol is automatically added to the left of the item (see Figure 4-2).

```
<mx:FormItem label="Insert Name" required="true">
  <mx:TextInput id="nameTxt"  />
</mx:FormItem>
```

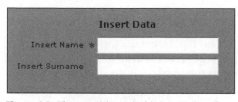

Figure 4-2. The asterisk symbol is inserted to the left of the TextInput control.

> *The asterisk is the universally recognized symbol to show that an item in a form is mandatory.*

After visual indication has been provided to the user, you can proceed with the validation of that field, which simply should never be left empty, so you can use the generic Validator tag to carry out the validation (notice that it requires a required property with a value of true):

```
<mx:Validator id="surnameV"  required="true" />
```

So the required property of the FormItem tag gives you the visual clue on the TextInput control, the asterisk symbol, while the required property of the Validator class carries out the validation on that field.

How to build it

You'll use the same form created in the preceding solution, but you'll insert a required field on one of the two FormItems.

1. Create a new MXML application file by selecting File ➤ New ➤ MXML Application and name it Chapter_4_Flex_Sol_2.mxml.

2. As in Solution 4-1, you'll add a Form container with a FormItem field. Insert the following:

```
<?xml version="1.0" encoding="utf-8"?>
<mx:Application xmlns:mx="http://www.adobe.com/2006/mxml"
layout="absolute">

  <mx:NumberValidator id="nameV"
    source="{nameTxt}"
    property="text" />

  <mx:Form id="myForm">
    <mx:FormHeading label="Insert Data">
    </mx:FormHeading>
    <mx:FormItem label="Insert Name">
```

```
    <mx:TextInput id="nameTxt"  />
  </mx:FormItem>
  <mx:FormItem label="Insert Surname">
    <mx:TextInput id="surnameTxt" />
  </mx:FormItem>
</mx:Form>
</mx:Application>
```

3. Render the FormItem as required by setting its required property as true:

```
<mx:FormItem label="Insert Surname" required="true">
  <mx:TextInput id="surnameTxt" />
</mx:FormItem>
```

4. You now need to declare a Validator to carry out the check on this required text field. Below the Application tag, write the <mx:Validator> tag, setting its source, property, and required properties:

```
<mx:Validator id="surnameV"
  required="true"
  source="{surnameTxt}"
  property="text" />
```

The source attribute references the object on which the validation will be carried out. The property attribute contains the property of that object on which the validation will be applied, and finally the required property dictates that the form field should be mandatory in the first place.

5. Save the file and run the application.

Try entering and exiting from the mandatory TextInput; you'll see the error message shown in Figure 4-3.

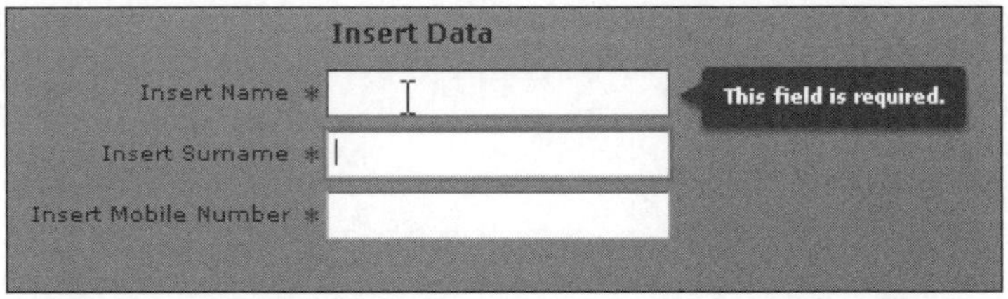

Figure 4-3. The alert that appears if you leave the required TextInput blank.

Expert tips

If you use the generic Validator class, you can't take advantage of any other type of built-in validation. If you know the data type to validate in the fields, you can use one of the set of Flex validators, choosing from the following: e-mail address, date, ZIP code, phone number, and credit card number.

For example, to validate a field so that it can accept only strings, you can use the StringValidator class. Thus you also carry out the validation of a mandatory input by using a StringValidator tag:

```
<mx:StringValidator id="nameV"
  source="{nameTxt}"
  property="text"
  required="true" />
```

This way, you'll obtain a double validation check:

- The first one checks the existence of data in the TextInput nameTxt
- The second is a validation of its value type, which should be String

The required property is present in all the other validator classes.

Solution 4-3: Customizing error messages in Validator classes

Error messages enable you to give users feedback to help them better understand any errors that can occur when performing actions such as filling out forms. This is all well and good, but the default error messages provided by application frameworks can be very confusing to users, who more than likely won't understand the technology the site is written in. Such cryptic messages can be more of a hindrance than a help.

By default, Flex validators automatically send an error message to users. Every validator class puts forward different properties to carry out the validation, based on determined criteria. The StringValidator class, for example, has the maxLength and minLength properties that check on the validity of maximum and minimum lengths of a field string. All these properties also come with a relative error message with its own default text. For example, the two properties of the StringValidator class have the following two error messages:

- This string is longer than the maximum allowed length.
- This string is shorter than the minimum allowed length.

These messages, like all error messages, can be personalized with text. In fact, each property that sets a validation criterion has its own property that manages the text of the error message.

In this solution you'll learn how to personalize the error messages of a few validator classes.

What's involved

In the `StringValidator` class the `maxLength` and `minLength` properties enable the validator to carry out a validity check on the maximum and minimum length of a field string, tapping into the error messages contained in the `tooLongError` and `tooShortError` property:

- This default property contains the values:
- This string is longer than the maximum allowed length.
- This string is shorter than the minimum allowed length.

If you open the `StringValidator` class (the package of the class is mx.validators. StringValidator), these values are declared as follows:

```
private var _tooShortError:String;

[Inspectable(category="Errors", defaultValue=
"This string is shorter than the minimum allowed length.
This must be at least {0} characters long.")]

private var _tooLongError:String;

[Inspectable(category="Errors", defaultValue=
"This string is longer than the maximum allowed length.
This must be less than {0} characters long.")]
```

To modify this text, you need to reference the property by using attributes of the `StringValidator` tag in the MXML or ActionScript declaration:

```
<mx:StringValidator id="nameV"
  source="{nameTxt}"
  property="text"
  required="true"
  maxLength="10"
  minLength="2"
  tooLongError="This field contains 10 chars"
  tooShortError="You have to insert 2 chars at least" />
```

Let's apply this theory to a real example.

How to build it

To save time, you'll modify the main application of the preceding solution, inserting a `TextInput` into which users will insert their mobile telephone numbers.

1. Create a new MXML application by selecting File ➤ New ➤ MXML Application and name it Chapter_4_Flex_Sol_3.mxml.

2. Insert a `Form` container containing three `FormItems`, as shown here:

```
<mx:Application xmlns:mx="http://www.adobe.com/2006/mxml"
layout="absolute">

  <mx:Form id="myForm">
    <mx:FormHeading label="Insert Data">
    </mx:FormHeading>
    <mx:FormItem label="Insert Name" required="true">
      <mx:TextInput id="nameTxt" />
    </mx:FormItem>
    <mx:FormItem label="Insert Surname" required="true">
      <mx:TextInput id="surnameTxt" />
    </mx:FormItem>
    <mx:FormItem label="Insert Phone Number" required="true">
      <mx:TextInput id="phoneTxt" />
    </mx:FormItem>
  </mx:Form>

</mx:Application>
```

3. Now you'll add three validators, one for each `TextInput`. Three different validators were used to make you more familiar with the various classes available. Insert the following code, just above the opening `Form` tag:

```
<mx:Application xmlns:mx="http://www.adobe.com/2006/mxml"
layout="absolute">

<mx:PhoneNumberValidator id="phoneV"
  source="{phoneTxt}"
  property="text"
  required="true"
  allowedFormatChars="+-" />

<mx:StringValidator id="nameV"
  source="{nameTxt}"
  property="text"
  required="true"
  maxLength="10"
  minLength="2" />

<mx:Validator id="surnameV"
  required="true"
  source="{surnameTxt}"
  property="text" />

<mx:Form id="myForm">
```

In the `PhoneNumberValidator` class the `allowedFormatChars` property is set, which defines the characters to be accepted in the `TextInput` defined in the source. It specifies that the characters + and − are allowed, as well as numbers, of course. (People often insert the symbol + in front of the international code, and use the symbol – to separate different parts of their phone numbers.) Note that the PhoneNumberValidator checks that the input entry is at least 10 digits long.

In the StringValidator class the properties maxLength and minLength were inserted—values inserted into the nameTxt TextInput therefore have to be between two and ten characters long.

For the Validator class, all you have done is set the property required as true, meaning that the TextInput surnameTxt is a mandatory data field.

4. You'll now add personalized error messages to manage the errors that arise when this form fails validation. Add the following code to the three validator tags:

```
<mx:PhoneNumberValidator id="phoneV"
    source="{phoneTxt}"
    property="text"
    required="true"
    allowedFormatChars="+-"
invalidCharError=➡
"You inserted an invalid char. ➡
Only numbers and + and - characters will be valid "
requiredFieldError=➡
"This field is required. It can't be empty."
wrongLengthError=➡
"The phone number has not a valid format" />

<mx:StringValidator id="nameV"
    source="{nameTxt}"
    property="text"
    required="true"
    maxLength="10"
    minLength="2"
tooLongError=➡
" This field can contain a maximum of 10 characters "
tooShortError=➡
" This field can contain a minimum of 2 characters " />

<mx:Validator id="surnameV"
    required="true"
    source="{surnameTxt}"
    property="text"
requiredFieldError="This field is required. ➡
You can't leave this field empty." />
```

These error messages are fairly self-explanatory: PhoneNumberValidator has error messages to display if the text is too short or too long, contains invalid characters, or is left empty. StringValidator has error messages to display if the entered text is too long or too short. Finally, on the Validator tag you have provided an error message to display if no text is entered—it is a mandatory field.

In this solution you have seen the simplicity with which Flex enables you to customize the validator classes, which become powerful instruments in the data inputted into the applications under control.

Expert tips

To open any class that corresponds to an MXML tag, it is enough to Ctrl/Cmd+click the tag in Flex Builder. From here, you can personalize the validators in many other ways, such as changing the look of various aspects (for example, a tool tip appears when one of the error criteria is met and its message appears in red).

You can personalize this color by changing the Cascading Style Sheet (CSS) class .errorTip:

```
<mx:Style>
  .errorTip {
    borderColor: #0000FF;
  }
</mx:Style>
```

With this declaration you changed the background color of the tool tip of your validation error messages.

> You'll deal with CSS in Flex in a lot more detail in Chapter 9.

Solution 4-4: Validating data using ActionScript 3.0

As with all other types of components provided by Flex, the validator classes can be declared using MXML tags, but they can also be declared using ActionScript code. Don't forget that in the compilation phase, the MXML code becomes converted into ActionScript classes before being transformed into a SWF file.

It can be useful to declare the validators using ActionScript code to use these powerful objects in the class definition instead of in the MXML inside of the application.

When you use a validator through ActionScript code, you have to insert the code in a function that will be associated with a user or system event. An advantage is that you can run the validations at the click of a button instead of on the creationComplete event of the Application.

In this solution you'll see how to declare a validator using ActionScript.

What's involved

To create an instance of a validator class in ActionScript you have to refer to its package, so you have to import the validator class you want to use before creating the instance:

```
import mx.validators.PhoneNumberValidator;
private var phoneV:PhoneNumberValidator;
```

Or you can use a fully qualified class name anywhere you reference the class:

```
private var phoneV:mx.validators.PhoneNumberValidator;
```

Both methods can be used, but I recommend using the import method because you can reuse the class wherever you want without having to refer to the fully qualified class name every time, thus writing much less code in the process.

After the variable containing the instance of the validator class is created, you begin to set the properties that enable you to link the validation to an object:

- source: Contains the reference to the object you want to validate
- property: Specifies the property of the control that contains the data to be validated (for a TextInput control, the data to be validated is the text property)
- trigger: Contains the reference to the object that causes the event trigger to take place

```
phoneV.source = phoneTxt;
phoneV.property = "text";
phoneV.trigger = phoneTxt;
```

With ActionScript you can customize the error message properties that set the validation criteria of the class:

```
phoneV.required = true;
phoneV.allowedFormatChars = "+-";
phoneV.invalidCharError = ➡
"You inserted an invalid char. ➡
Only numbers and + and - characters will be valid ";
phoneV.wrongLengthError = ➡
"The phone number has not a valid format";
phoneV.requiredFieldError = ➡
"This field is required. It can't be empty.";
```

How to build it

You'll work on the same file as the one you used in the preceding solution, but you'll delete the PhoneNumberValidator you declared as an MXML tag to rewrite it using ActionScript.

1. Open the file Chapter_4_Flex_Sol_3.mxml and save a copy of it with the name Chapter_4_Flex_Sol_4.mxml.

2. Delete the declaration of the PhoneNumberValidator tag, leaving the following code:

```
<?xml version="1.0" encoding="utf-8"?>
<mx:Application xmlns:mx="http://www.adobe.com/2006/mxml"
layout="absolute">

  <mx:StringValidator id="nameV"
    source="{nameTxt}"
    property="text"
    required="true"
    maxLength="10"
    minLength="2"
  tooLongError=➥
" This field can contain a maximum of 10 characters "
      tooShortError=➥
"This field can contain a minimum of 2 characters " />

  <mx:Validator id="surnameV"
    required="true"
    source="{surnameTxt}"
    property="text"
    requiredFieldError=➥
  "Your Surname is a required field. You can't leave it blank" />

  <mx:Form id="myForm">
    <mx:FormHeading label="Insert Data">
    </mx:FormHeading>
    <mx:FormItem label="Insert Name" required="true">
      <mx:TextInput id="nameTxt" />
    </mx:FormItem>
    <mx:FormItem label="Insert Surname">
      <mx:TextInput id="surnameTxt" />
    </mx:FormItem>
    <mx:FormItem label="Insert Phone Number">
      <mx:TextInput id="phoneTxt" />
    </mx:FormItem>
  </mx:Form>

</mx:Application>
```

3. Add the ActionScript code necessary to apply a PhoneNumberValidation class to the phoneTxt TextInput control. In the <mx:Script> block, you begin by importing the class you intend to use and then declare a private variable that contains the instance of the class. Insert the following <mx:Script> block below the Application tag:

```
<mx:Application xmlns:mx="http://www.adobe.com/2006/mxml"
layout="absolute">
```

```
<mx:Script>
  <![CDATA[
    import mx.validators.*;

    private var phoneV:PhoneNumberValidator;
  ]]>
</mx:Script>
  <mx:StringValidator id="nameV"
    source="{nameTxt}"
    property="text"
    required="true"
    maxLength="10"
    minLength="2"
    tooLongError="This field contains 10 chars"
    tooShortError="You have to insert 2 chars at least" />
```

4. You can now create a function in which you define the property of the PhoneNumberValidator by accessing it as a property of the object. Insert this function as follows:

```
<mx:Script>
  <![CDATA[
    import mx.validators.*;

    private var phoneV:PhoneNumberValidator;
    private function doValidate():void
    {
      phoneV = new PhoneNumberValidator();
      phoneV.source = phoneTxt;
      phoneV.property = "text";
      phoneV.required = true;
      phoneV.allowedFormatChars = "+-";
      phoneV.invalidCharError = ➡
    "You inserted an invalid char. ➡
      Only numbers and + and - characters will be valid ";
      phoneV.wrongLengthError = ➡
      "The phone number has not a valid format";
      phoneV.requiredFieldError = ➡
      "This field is required. It can't be empty.";

      phoneV.trigger = phoneTxt;
    }
  ]]>
</mx:Script>
```

In the private doValidate() function you have set the properties necessary to apply the validation to the phoneTxt TextInput control using the text property:

```
phoneV = new PhoneNumberValidator();
phoneV.source = phoneTxt;
phoneV.property = "text";
```

Declare the required and allowedFormatChars properties to render the TextInput control mandatory and define the symbols + and – as valid characters (as well as numbers):

```
phoneV.required = true;
phoneV.allowedFormatChars = "+-";
```

Finally, customized error messages that appear to the user on the insertion of invalid characters (invalidCharError) are defined on the insertion of a string that is too long or too short (wrongLengthError) and when the field is left blank (requiredFieldError).

To make the validator work, it is necessary to explicitly declare the trigger property. It accepts as an input the object that causes the event trigger to take place:

```
phoneV.trigger = phoneTxt;
```

The triggerEvent isn't defined because, by default, the event that causes the TextInput check to be carried out is valueCommit. Before running the application, you must launch the doValidate() function at the occurrence of a determined event.

5. Add the event handler doValidate() on creationComplete of the Application tag, as follows:

```
<mx:Application xmlns:mx="http://www.adobe.com/2006/mxml"
layout="absolute"
  creationComplete="doValidate()">
```

6. Save the file and run the application. The final result will be that you have a validator associated with the phoneTxt TextInput control, which will carry out the validation of the phone numbers inserted in that TextInput. It should work just as it did in the preceding solution, except that this time you have declared it using ActionScript, not MXML.

Expert tips

You have seen that the event on which the validation occurs by default is valueCommit (for TextInput controls). In ActionScript you can associate the validation with another event by defining it in the triggerEvent property:

```
private function doValidate():void
{
  phoneV = new PhoneNumberValidator();
  phoneV.source = phoneTxt;
  phoneV.property = "text";
  phoneV.required = true;
  phoneV.allowedFormatChars = "+,-";
  phoneV.invalidCharError = "Insert valid chars";
  phoneV.wrongLengthError = "The number is too short or too long";
  phoneV.requiredFieldError = "This input is required";
  phoneV.trigger = phoneTxt;
  phoneV.triggerEvent = "change";
}
```

The doValidate() function will now carry out the validation check when the change event appears on the TextInput.

The ActionScript function doValidate() creates the instance of the PhoneNumberValidator class and sets the properties of the object. In the solution this function becomes launched on the creationComplete user event of the Application tag.

It is possible to link the event handler to any event of any object. For example, you can launch the function on a click of a Button event:

```
<mx:Button click="doValidate()" label="Validate" />
```

Solution 4-5: Triggering validation with Events

When a validation fails, sometimes you want to do more than send a message to the user to show the error that occurred. And in the case of a successful validation you usually want to submit the data contained in the form to the server.

In both cases, you need to define event handlers that are triggered as a result of the validation succeeding or failing. Flex enables you to manage the validation events by using valid and invalid events of the components, or by intercepting the validation events dispatched by the validators.

With these approaches you can see whether the process of validation has been successful and assign an appropriate function afterward. In this solution you'll use both methods for triggering validations with events.

What's involved

Flex components dispatch two events according to the results returned from the validation: valid and invalid. The event object generated by these two events, which comes from the ValidationResultEvent class, carries a type property containing the result of the validation:

```
eventObject.type==ValidationResultEvent.VALID
```

And this:

```
eventObject.type==ValidationResultEvent.INVALID
```

To create an event handler to link to these events, you declare them directly in the TextInput control to which the validators are associated, declaring them as attributes:

```
<mx:FormItem label="Insert Name" required="true">
  <mx:TextInput id="nameTxt"
    valid="isValid(event)"
    invalid="notValid(event)" />
</mx:FormItem>
```

You created two event handlers for the valid and invalid event of the TextInput control. You passed as a parameter of the event handler functions the event object generated by the Event class (refer to Solution 1-6).

Write the necessary functions and operations in an <mx:Script> block, as follows:

```
<mx:Script>
  private function isValid(evt:Event):void
  {
    Alert.show(evt.type);
  }

  private function notValid(evt:Event):void
  {
    Alert.show(evt.type);
  }
</mx:Script>
```

The property type in the event object (evt.type) returns a valid or invalid string according to the result produced by the validation.

Now look at using the second method to trigger the validation events. In this case, you use the event object of the ValidationResultEvent class, which contains two constants of the system in its property type: ValidationResultEvent.VALID and ValidationResultEvent. INVALID.

From the point of view of the code, the only change is that the data type of the event object is transported by the valid and invalid methods of the validator classes.

In this solution you'll use both methods to add a visual message to the form to follow the results produced by the validation operations.

How to build it

Again you'll use the example from the preceding solutions as a starting point. You'll leave the validators in the file and add the valid and invalid events, which will launch an event handler to the TextInput controls.

1. Open the file Chapter_4_Flex_Sol_4.mxml and save a copy of it as Chapter_4_Flex_ Sol_5.mxml. The code, unaltered so far from the last example, should look like this:

```
<?xml version="1.0" encoding="utf-8"?>
<mx:Application xmlns:mx=http://www.adobe.com/2006/mxml
  layout="absolute"
  creationComplete="doValidate()">

  <mx:Script>
    <![CDATA[
      Import mx.controls.Alert;
      Import mx.validators.*;
```

```
        private var phoneV:PhoneNumberValidator;

        private function doValidate():void
        {
          phoneV=new PhoneNumberValidator();
          phoneV.source=phoneTxt;
          phoneV.property="text";
          phoneV.required=true;
          phoneV.allowedFormatChars="+,-";
          phoneV.invalidCharError = ➥
          "You inserted an invalid char. ➥
          Only numbers and + and - characters will be valid";
           phoneV.wrongLengthError = ➥
          "The phone number has not a valid format";
           phoneV.requiredFieldError = ➥
          "This field is required. It can't be empty.";
          phoneV.trigger=phoneTxt;
          phoneV.triggerEvent="change";
        }
    ]]>
  </mx:Script>

  <mx:StringValidator id="nameV"
    source="{nameTxt}"
    property="text"
    required="true"
    maxLength="10"
    minLength="2"
  tooLongError=➥
" This field can contain a maximum of 10 characters "
        tooShortError=➥
"This field can contain a minimum of 2 characters " />

  <mx:Validator id="surnameV"
    required="true"
    source="{surnameTxt}"
    property="text"
    requiredFieldError=➥
  "Your Surname is a required field. You can't leave it blank" />


  <mx:Form id="myForm">
    <mx:FormHeading label="InsertData">
    </mx:FormHeading>
    <mx:FormItem label="InsertName" required="true">
      <mx:TextInput id="nameTxt"/>
    </mx:FormItem>
    <mx:FormItem label="InsertSurname">
      <mx:TextInput id="surnameTxt"/>
```

```
    </mx:FormItem>
    <mx:FormItem label="InsertPhoneNumber">
      <mx:TextInput id="phoneTxt"/>
    </mx:FormItem>
  </mx:Form>

</mx:Application>
```

2. Add an event handler on the valid and invalid events to the nameTxt TextInput control and insert an HBox container and a Label between the opening and closing FormItem tags. Make the following changes:

```
<mx:FormItem label="Insert Name" required="true">
<mx:HBox>

<mx:TextInput id="nameTxt"
valid="isValid(event)"
invalid="notValid(event)" />
<mx:Label id="myLbl" text="" visible="false" />
</mx:HBox>
```

The Label, positioned on the right of the TextInput, is initially invisible. You'll render it visible by using the functions isValid() and notValid(), which cause it to appear and add an appropriate message to it in each case, telling the user what is going on.

3. Now insert a block of code in the <mx:Script> block above the doValidate() function, in which you define the two event handlers. These functions will be responsible for rendering the Label visible, inserting a text message in the text property, and printing the value contained in the type property of the event object in an alert window. Add the code in bold:

```
<mx:Script>
<![CDATA[
import mx.controls.Alert;
import mx.validators.*;

private var phoneV:PhoneNumberValidator;

private function isValid(evt:Event):void
{
  Alert.show(evt.type);  // it contains a valid string value
  myLbl.visible=true;
  myLbl.text="This field has been validated! Congrats!"
}

private function notValid(evt:Event):void
{
  Alert.show(evt.type);  // it contains an invalid string value
  myLbl.visible=true;
  myLbl.text="Read the tool tip to correct the error in this field!"
}
```

```
private function doValidate():void
{
        phoneV=new PhoneNumberValidator();
        phoneV.source=phoneTxt;
        phoneV.property="text";
        phoneV.required=true;
        phoneV.allowedFormatChars="+,-";
        phoneV.invalidCharError = ➡
        "You inserted an invalid char. ➡
        Only numbers and + and - characters will be valid";
         phoneV.wrongLengthError = ➡
        "The phone number has not a valid format";
         phoneV.requiredFieldError = ➡
        "This field is required. It can't be empty.";
        phoneV.trigger=phoneTxt;
        phoneV.triggerEvent="change";
   }
```

If you want to use the event object generated by the valid and invalid events of the validator classes instead, you could insert event handlers in these events defined as attributes on the Validator tag.

4. You now need to make a change to the Validator MXML tag. In this tag, you write the valid and invalid events and associate them to the same function, handleResultEvent, bringing the automatically generated event object with you. Make the following change to the Validator tag:

```
<mx:Validator id="surnameV"
  required="true"
    source="{surnameTxt}"
    property="text"
    requiredFieldError=➡
  "Your Surname is a required field. You can't leave it blank"
  valid="handleResultEvent(event)"
  invalid="handleResultEvent(event)" />
```

5. The handleResultEvent() function carries out a check of the value contained in the type property of the event object and makes an appropriate message appear in a TextArea control that you'll add to the code, depending on the result of the check. Add the handleResultEvent() function below the notValid() function and import the ValidationResultEvent class:

```
import mx.events.ValidationResultEvent;
```

```
private function notValid(evt:Event):void
{
  Alert.show(evt.type); // it contains invalid string value
  myLbl.visible=true;
  myLbl.text="Read the tool tip to correct the error in this field!"
}
 private function handleResultEvent(evt:ValidationResultEvent):void
```

```
  {
    if(evt.type==ValidationResultEvent.VALID)
    {
      validationTxt.text  = "The FormItem has succesfully
validated!";
    }

    else if(evt.type==ValidationResultEvent.VALID)
    {
      validationTxt.text  = "The FormItem has NOT been validated!";
    }
  }
  private function doValidate():void
  {
          phoneV=new PhoneNumberValidator();
          phoneV.source=phoneTxt;
          phoneV.property="text";
          phoneV.required=true;
          phoneV.allowedFormatChars="+,-";
          phoneV.invalidCharError = ➥
          "You inserted an invalid char. ➥
          Only numbers and + and - characters will be valid";
           phoneV.wrongLengthError = ➥
          "The phone number has not a valid format";
           phoneV.requiredFieldError = ➥
          "This field is required. It can't be empty.";
          phoneV.trigger=phoneTxt;
          phoneV.triggerEvent="change";
  }
```

The type property of the event object contains the ValidationResultEvent.VALID or ValidationResultEvent.INVALID constants. With a simple if() condition, you check the value returned and act accordingly.

Note that to be able to use the event object of the ValidationResultEvent class you have to first import it with import mx.events.ValidationResultEvent;.

6. Add the TextArea control that contains the messages of the valid and invalid events:

```
</mx:Form>

<mx:TextArea x="10" y="172"
width="305" height="87"
id="validationTxt"/>

</mx:Application>
```

7. Save and run the application.

Expert tips

You have already seen in previous solutions how it is possible to use Cascading Style Sheets (CSS) to style some elements of the objects in the application.

In the example that you created, you can change the color of the text that is written into the Label according to the result of the validation. If the validation is successful, you can make the message green; if an error occurs in the validation, you could make the message red.

To create this effect, you need to create two CSS classes as follows, declared in the <mx:Style> block after the Script tag closure:

```
</mx:Script>
 <mx:Style>
.invalid {
 color:#FF0000;
}
.valid {
color:#004000;
}
 </mx:Style>

 <mx:StringValidator id="nameV"
     source="{nameTxt}"
     property="text"
     required="true"
     maxLength="10"
     minLength="2"
tooLongError=" This field can contain a maximum of 10 characters " />
```

Note that the CSS classes have a dot in front of their names, which denotes that you are selecting containers to styles based on their class names. To apply these styles to each Label, use the styleName property of the validation functions, as follows:

```
private function isValid(evt:Event):void
{
  validationTxt.text  = evt.type as String;
  myLbl.visible = true;
  myLbl.text = "This field has been validated ! Congrats!"
  myLbl.styleName = "valid";
}

private function notValid(evt:Event):void
{
  validationTxt.text  = evt.type as String;
  myLbl.visible = true;
  myLbl.text = "Read the tooltip to correct the error in this field!"
  myLbl.styleName = "invalid";
}
```

4

The styleName property accepts a string equivalent to the name of the class defined in the `<mx:Style>` block. This was anticipated, so the CSS classes have the same name returned from the type property of the event object. You could also write it like this:

```
private function isValid(evt:Event):void
{
  Alert.show(evt.type);
  myLbl.visible = true;
  myLbl.text = "This field has been validated ! Congrats !"
  myLbl.styleName = evt.type;
}

private function notValid(evt:Event):void
{
  myLbl.visible = true;
  myLbl.text = "Read the tooltip to correct the error in this field !"
  myLbl.styleName = evt.type;
}
```

If you make these changes and run the example again, you'll see the result shown in Figure 4-4.

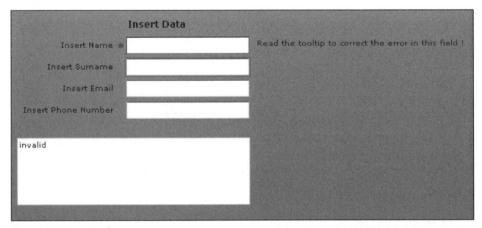

Figure 4-4. The Label assumes a text color depending on the value contained in the type property of the event object.

Solution 4-6: Validating a data model using the validate() method

The preceding chapter talked about Flex data models, and you saw their use in storing data in an application. The validations you have looked at up to now in this chapter have validated values inserted in TextInput controls by users. However, it is also possible to apply the validator classes to data models.

In this solution you'll see how to validate the data transported into a data model using the validate() method. This method is generated by all validator classes and deals with applying the rules for the validation of data. To use this method you'll use ActionScript code to manage programmatic validations and the result returned by the validation.

What's involved

To be able to apply a validation with ActionScript and use the validate() method you do not need to set the trigger and triggerEvent properties in the validator class. It will, therefore, be sufficient to define the value of the source and text properties, like so:

```
<mx:StringValidator id="nameV"
    source="{nameTxt}"
    property="text"
    required="true"
    maxLength="10"
    minLength="2"
    tooLongError="This field can contain a maximum of 10 characters "
    tooShortError="This field can contain a minimum of 2 characters "
/>
```

By not setting the validator's trigger or triggerEvent, you can carry out the validation in the moment in which you'll make an explicit call to the validate() method. To have more control over the validation phase and decide the exact moment when to validate fields, you need to use the validate() method.

The validate() method has the following syntax:

```
validate(value:Object = null, ➡
supressEvents:Boolean = false):ValidationResultEvent
```

When the value parameter is null, it uses the object inserted in the source and property properties; otherwise it specifies a field of an object in the scope of the document. The parameter supressEvents is a Boolean that dispatches both the valid and invalid events if false; it does not dispatch any event if true.

The validate() method returns an event object with a type defined by the ValidationResult class. This class transports the property type containing the ValidationResultEvent.VALID and ValidationResultEvent.INVALID values. These properties can be used to intercept the result of the validation:

```
if (vResult.type == ValidationResultEvent.INVALID)
{
  mx.controls.Alert.show("Error");
}
else if (vResult.type == ValidationResultEvent.VALID)
{
  mx.controls.Alert.show("Congrats");
}
```

In this solution you'll programmatically trigger validation on a data model.

How to build it

Instead of carrying out validation on values input into a form, you'll carry out validation on a data model. Therefore, in the main application you create a dynamic data model that contains the values inserted by the user.

1. Create a new MXML application file by selecting File ➤ New ➤ MXML Application and name it Chapter_4_Flex_Sol_6.mxml.

2. Define a form inside the Application tag, as follows (this is the same as in the preceding solution with two more TextInput controls):

```
<mx:Form id="myForm">
  <mx:FormHeading label="Insert Data">
  </mx:FormHeading>
  <mx:FormItem label="Insert Name" required="true">
    <mx:HBox>
      <mx:TextInput id="nameTxt"  />
      <mx:Label id="myLbl" text="" visible="false" />
    </mx:HBox>
  </mx:FormItem>
  <mx:FormItem label="Insert Surname">
    <mx:TextInput id="surnameTxt" />
  </mx:FormItem>
  <mx:FormItem label="Insert Email">
    <mx:TextInput id="emailTxt" />
  </mx:FormItem>
  <mx:FormItem label="Insert Phone Number">
    <mx:TextInput id="phoneTxt" />
  </mx:FormItem>
</mx:Form>
```

3. Insert an MXML data model containing the values inserted by the user in the TextInput controls. Add this code above the Form container:

```
<mx:Model id="myModel">
  <root>
  <name>{nameTxt.text}</name>
  <surname>{surnameTxt.text}</surname>
  <phone>{phoneTxt.text}</phone>
  </root>
</mx:Model>
<mx:Form id="myForm">
```

4. Write an <mx:Script> block in which you declare a validator to perform the valuation on the properties of the data model. Add this now:

```
<mx:Application xmlns:mx="http://www.adobe.com/2006/mxml"
layout="absolute">
<mx:Script>
  <![CDATA[
```

```
    import mx.controls.Alert;
    import mx.events.ValidationResultEvent;
    import mx.validators.PhoneNumberValidator;

    private var phoneV:PhoneNumberValidator;
    private var phoneVResult:ValidationResultEvent;

    private function doValidate():void
    {
      phoneV = new PhoneNumberValidator();
      phoneV.source = myModel;
      phoneV.property = "phone";
      phoneV.listener=phoneTxt;
      phoneV.required = true;
      phoneV.allowedFormatChars = "+,-";
      phoneV.invalidCharError = "Insert valid chars";
      phoneV.wrongLengthError = "The number is too short or too long";
      phoneV.requiredFieldError = "This input is required";
      phoneVResult = phoneV.validate();
      if(phoneVResult.type==ValidationResultEvent.VALID)
      {
        Alert.show("The FormItem has been succesfully validated!", ➡
"Validation Message", 4);
      }
      else if(phoneVResult.type==ValidationResultEvent.VALID)
      {
        Alert.show("The FormItem has NOT been validated!", ➡
"Validation Message", 4);
      }
    }
  ]]>
</mx:Script>
```

The first few lines of this code perform an import of the classes you'll make use of (ValidationResultEvent and PhoneNumberValidator in particular) and create the private variables you'll use:

```
    import mx.controls.Alert;
    import mx.events.ValidationResultEvent;
    import mx.validators.PhoneNumberValidator;

    private var phoneV:PhoneNumberValidator;
    private var phoneVResult:ValidationResultEvent;
```

In the doValidate() method you create an instance of the PhoneNumberValidator() class contained in the phoneV variable and you define its properties. Take note that you have also set the listener property of the validator. Because you'll validate a data model (which is not a visual component of the Flex application) to give visual feedback to the user where an error has been generated, you must set the listener property and link it to the object on which the validation has been performed. In this case it is the id assigned at the TextInput:

```
phoneV = new PhoneNumberValidator();
phoneV.source = myModel;
phoneV.property = "phone";
phoneV.listener=phoneTxt;

phoneV.required = true;
phoneV.allowedFormatChars = "+,-";
phoneV.invalidCharError = "Insert valid chars";
phoneV.wrongLengthError = "The number is too short or too long";
phoneV.requiredFieldError = "This input is required";
```

At this point you have set the validate() method. Considering that this method returns the event object of the ValidationResultEvent class, you assign the result to the phoneVResult variable that will therefore contain the property type with the ValidationResultEvent.VALID and ValidationResultEvent.INVALID constants:

```
phoneVResult = phoneV.validate();
```

Finally, all you have to do is create an if structure to check the result of the validation by checking the value that the event object brings with it in its type property:

```
if(phoneVResult.type==ValidationResultEvent.VALID)
{
  Alert.show("The FormItem has succesfully validated !",
"Validation Message", 4);
}
else if(phoneVResult.type==ValidationResultEvent.VALID)
{
  Alert.show("The FormItem has NOT been validated !", "Validation
Message", 4);
}
```

5. The last step triggers the validate() method. To do this you'll insert a button that, when clicked, executes the doValidate() function. Add the following tag after the closure of the Form container:

```
</mx:Form>
<mx:Button label="Validate" click="doValidate();"
x="284" y="172"/>
```

6. Save the file and run the application. You should now be able to insert values into the TextInput controls and have them validated as before by using ActionScript with the validate() method, but this time you are validating a data model, not the TextInput controls directly.

The benefit of using the validate() method is that you can invoke a validator directly, instead of triggering the validator automatically using an event. Then you can call a validator programmatically, associating it with a system or user event.

Expert tips

The validate() method can also be used with a validator declared using MXML. Open the Chapter_4_Flex_Sol_6.mxml file and add a StringValidator tag:

```
<mx:StringValidator id="nameV"
source="{myModel}"
property="surname"
required="true"
maxLength="10"
minLength="2"
tooLongError="This field contains 10 chars"
tooShortError="You have to insert 2 chars at least"
/>
```

Modify the StringValidator of the example by inserting the listener property:

```
<mx:StringValidator id="nameV"
source="{myModel}"
property="surname"
required="true"
maxLength="10"
minLength="2"
tooLongError="This field contains 10 chars"
tooShortError="You have to insert 2 chars at least"
listener="{surnameTxt}"
/>
```

Take note that the validator aims at the source and property properties on the data model by using its surname node. Furthermore, there is a listener property present, which points to the surnameTxt object (the id of the TextInput being validated).

In the block of ActionScript code you can manage the doValidate() method and its results by first declaring the variable that will contain the results of the validation:

```
<mx:Script>
<![CDATA[
import mx.controls.Alert;
import mx.events.ValidationResultEvent;
import mx.validators.PhoneNumberValidator;

private var phoneV:PhoneNumberValidator;
private var phoneVResult:ValidationResultEvent;
private var nameVResult:ValidationResultEvent;

private function doValidate():void
```

You then invoke the doValidate() method and check the value returned by the validation using an if() construct. Add the following code to the function:

177

```
private function doValidate():void
{
phoneV = new PhoneNumberValidator();
phoneV.source = myModel;
phoneV.property = "phone";
phoneV.listener=phoneTxt;
phoneV.required = true;
phoneV.allowedFormatChars = "+,-";
phoneV.invalidCharError = "Insert valid chars";
phoneV.wrongLengthError = "The number is too short or too long";
phoneV.requiredFieldError = "This input is required";
phoneVResult = phoneV.validate();
 if(phoneVResult.type==ValidationResultEvent.VALID)
{
Alert.show("The FormItem has succesfully validated !", ➡
"Validation Message", 4);

} else if(phoneVResult.type==ValidationResultEvent.INVALID)
{
Alert.show("The FormItem has NOT been validated !", "Validation
Message", 4);
}

nameVResult = nameV.validate();

 if(nameVResult.type==ValidationResultEvent.VALID)
{
Alert.show("The FormItem has been succesfully validated !", ➡
"Validation Message", 4);

} else if(nameVResult.type==ValidationResultEvent.INVALID)
{
Alert.show("The FormItem has NOT been validated !", "Validation
Message", 4);
}
}
```

In the previous example the MXML data model had a plain structure without nested nodes. But if the data model has a nested structure (as in the following example), it is sufficient to point at the repeating node in the property property:

```
<mx:Model id="myModel">
  <root>
    <user>
      <name>{nameTxt.text}</name>
      <surname>{surnameTxt.text}</surname>
      <phone>{phoneTxt.text}</phone>
    <user>
  </root>
</mx:Model>
```

```
phoneV = new PhoneNumberValidator();
phoneV.source = myModel;
phoneV.property = "user.phone";
```

Solution 4-7: Extending the RegExpValidator class

Regular expressions were introduced in ActionScript 3.0. As the Wikipedia definition (http://en.wikipedia.org/wiki/Regular_expression) states, a regular expression (abbreviated as regexp or regex, with plural forms regexps, regexes, or regexen) is a string that describes or matches a set of strings according to certain syntax rules.

Regular expressions can basically be used to validate input by matching specific patterns, such as e-mail addresses, phone numbers, or credit card numbers. Flex provides the RegExpValidator class, which enables you to use and define regular expressions for the validation of data. The validation returns a positive value when the validator can find a match of the regular expression in the data being validated.

This RegExpValidator validator class accepts properties different from those of other validators. The public properties this class accepts are as follows:

- expression: Contains the regular expression that the RegExpValidator will use to validate data.
- flags: The flags to use when matching.
- noExpressionError: Defines the error message when the regular expression is not specified.
- noMatchError: Contains the error message when no matches were found to the regular expression.

The RegExpValidator dispatches the valid and invalid events. The invalid event generates an event object that is an instance of the ValidationResult class and that contains an Array of the ValidationResult object. The valid event, on the other hand, generates an object that is an instance of the ValidationResult class, but contains an Array of RegExpValidationResult objects.

The RegExpValidationResult class contains other properties specific to regular expressions:

- matchedIndex: An integer that contains the starting index in the input string of the match
- matchedString: A string that contains the substring of the input string that matches the regular expression
- matchedSubStrings: An array of strings that contains parenthesized substring matches, if any

In this solution you'll see how to extend the RegExpValidator class to carry out a validation check on Social Security numbers in Italy.

What's involved

To use the RegExpValidator in MXML, the syntax is the same as that of the other validators:

```
<mx:RegExpValidator
    expression="No default"
    flags="No default"
    noExpressionError="You missed the expression"
    noMatchError="There is an error on the field" />
```

In this solution you'll extend this class to create a personalized class that directly carries out a check on the Social Security numbers using a regular expression that you send to it. To extend any class in Flex, you need to create an ActionScript class that extends the class from which you want to inherit the properties:

```
public class socialValidator extends RegExpValidator
```

At this point you write the methods and the properties of the new class. In this case you want to give the expression and flags properties of the RegExpValidator class the default values. In this way, in the moment in which you instance the class by using either ActionScript or MXML, the criteria of the validation will be automatically applied to the field. To set the properties of a parent class (the RegExpValidator in this example), use the super() method in the constructors of the class. In this way you invoke the constructor of the parent class and access its properties:

```
public function socialValidator()
{
    super();
    super.expression = "myExpression";
    super.flags = "myFlag";
}
```

Finally, you can use the custom class in the main application file by simply defining a custom namespace and adding the corresponding MXML tag to the name of the ActionScript class:

```
<mx:Application xmlns:mx="http://www.adobe.com/2006/mxml"
layout="absolute"
  xmlns:class="com.*">
  <class:socialValidator  id="myValidator"
    source="{socialTxt}"
    property="text"
    trigger="{socialTxt}" />
```

This is the same way you invoked a custom MXML component in Chapter 2 (refer to Solution 2-1).

How to build it

The operation of extending a class always begins with the creation of an ActionScript class.

1. Create a new folder in the project by selecting File ➤ New ➤ Folder, in which you'll save the custom ActionScript class—call it com.

2. Create a new ActionScript class by selecting File ➤ New ➤ ActionScript Class. Before you click Finish, set the following values in the dialog box:

   - Package: com
   - Name: socialValidator
   - Modifiers: public
   - Superclass: mx.validators.RegExpValidator
   - Check the Generate constructor from superclass option

3. Your dialog box should look like Figure 4-5. Click Finish.

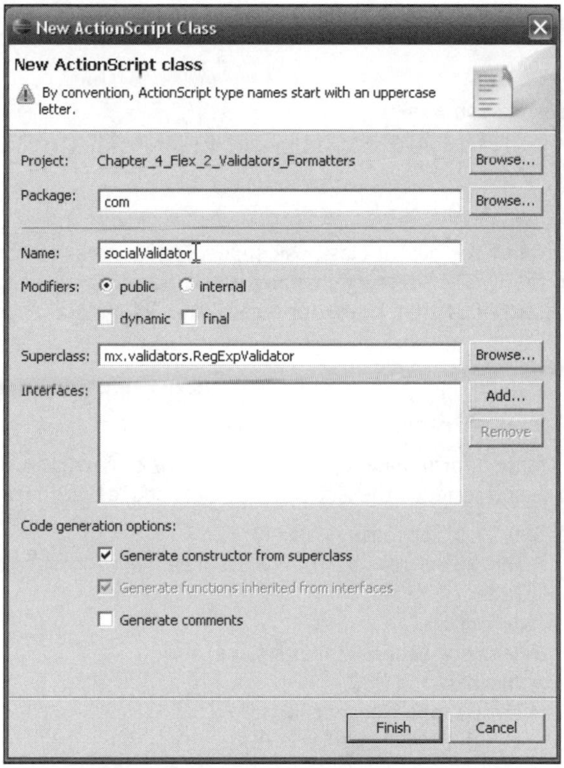

4

Figure 4-5. The dialog box for a custom ActionScript class

The code that will be generated is as follows:

```
package com
{
  import mx.validators.RegExpValidator;

  public class SocialValidator  extends RegExpValidator
  {
```

```
public function SocialValidator()
{
  super();
}
}
}
```

The class extends and inherits all the functions of the RegExpValidator class. In addition, the super() method is run in the constructor to invoke the constructor of the parent class.

4. You can now set the properties of the custom class, which have to be applied to enable validation of the fields to which the class will be linked. In the constructor you set the following values for the expression and flags properties:

```
public function SocialValidator()
{
  super();
  super.expression = ➥
"[A-Z]{6}[0-9]{2}[A-Z][0-9]{2}[A-Z][0-9]{3}[A-Z]";
  super.flags = "i";
}
```

To recall the property of the parent class, use super. The expression property contains a regular expression that will validate against any Italian Social Security number. The flags property, set as i, specifies that both uppercase and lowercase characters should be counted as valid.

5. Save the ActionScript class and create a new application file by selecting File ➤ New ➤ MXML Application; name it Chapter_4_Flex_Sol_7.mxml.

6. In this file, create a form made up of two iterations of Formitem, as shown following (you'll invoke and instance the ActionScript class socialValidator.as later on):

```
<?xml version="1.0" encoding="utf-8"?>
<mx:Application xmlns:mx="http://www.adobe.com/2006/mxml"
layout="absolute">
  <mx:Form id="myForm">
    <mx:FormHeading label="Insert Data">
    </mx:FormHeading>
    <mx:FormItem label="Insert Name">
      <mx:TextInput id="nameTxt" />
    </mx:FormItem>
    <mx:FormItem label="Insert Social Security code">
      <mx:TextInput id="socialTxt" />
    </mx:FormItem>
  </mx:Form>
</mx:Application>
```

7. To be able to invoke the ActionScript class you must create a custom namespace in which you specify the package in which the class is contained. Make the following change to the opening Application tag:

```
<mx:Application xmlns:mx="http://www.adobe.com/2006/mxml"
  layout="absolute"
  xmlns:class="com.*">
```

You have created the class suffix, which aims at the "com" package (the folder containing the ActionScript class).

8. You can now instance the class; add an MXML tag corresponding to it—it has the same name as the class, but without the .as extension. Add the following code to your file now:

```
<mx:Application xmlns:mx="http://www.adobe.com/2006/mxml"
  layout="absolute"
xmlns:class="com.*">

<class:SocialValidator  id="myValidator"
  source="{socialTxt}"
  property="text"
  trigger="{socialTxt}" />
```

The class inherits and uses the same properties as the RegExpValidator class to aim at the object on which the validation should be carried out. For this, you have set the source property to the socialTxt object, the TextInput property to the text property of the object, and the trigger to the socialTxt object. These properties are the same as the properties used for the validator in the previous solution.

9. Save the file and run the application. Test the validation by inserting the following value, which is a valid Italian Social Security number: CSRMRC77L29I501E.

Expert tips

If you want to customize the result messages of the validation you can simply extend the doValidation() method of the parent class. In fact, the RegExpValidator class has the doValidation() method declared as protected, but you can override it to validate a regular expression. This method accepts the Object to be validated as a parameter.

To do this, add the following code into the SocialValidator.as ActionScript class:

```
public function SocialValidator()
{
  super();
super.expression = ➡
"[A-Z]{6}[0-9]{2}[A-Z][0-9]{2}[A-Z][0-9]{3}[A-Z]";
  super.flags = "i";
}

protected override function doValidation(input:Object):Array
{
}
```

This method returns an array containing the properties of potential errors that occurred. In fact, in the example, you'll add two custom error messages that warn the user if the field is not filled in (it is mandatory) and if the value inserted is not a valid Social Security number. This is achieved with the following code:

```
protected override function doValidation(input:Object):Array
{
  var results:Array = [];
  var inputString:String = input.toString();
  results = super.doValidation(input);
  if(results.length > 0)
  {
    if(super.required == true && inputString.length == 0)
    {
      results[0].errorMessage = "This is a required field";
    }
    else
    {
      results[0].errorMessage = "It's not a valid italian social
number";
    }
    return results;
  }
}
```

The first lines of code in the function create two variables:

- results: Has the data type Array and contains the event object
- inputString: Contains the object passed to the method, returned as a String (using the toString() function)

You then launch the validate() method, which you dealt with in the preceding solution. This method returns the event object (which contains the results of the validation as properties) to the ValidationResultEvent class:

```
results = super.doValidation(input);
```

You then have an if construct that does nothing more than check that the length of the inserted data is more than zero, ensuring that something has been inserted in the field, and if the validation has sent back errors. The error messages are inserted in the errorMessage property of the Array result on the zero index:

```
results[0].errorMessage
```

Solution 4-8: Formatting data with the formatter classes

Formatting complex data in a more legible format is something your users will thank you for, and the good news is that Flex makes this very easy using the formatter classes. The formatter classes are built-in objects that format data in strings.

Flex provides the following formatter classes:

- `CurrencyFormatter`
- `DateFormatter`
- `NumberFormatter`
- `PhoneFormatter`
- `ZipCodeFormatter`

All these classes extend the `mx.formatters.Formatter` class, which uses the `format()` method to take the value that is to be formatted and returns the formatted string.

In this solution you'll see how to format data using a formatter class declared with MXML.

What's involved

The formatter classes can be declared using both ActionScript and MXML. Depending on the formatter class used, it is possible to set different properties that will be applied by the `format()` method to return the formatted data.

As an example, to carry out a formatting operation on a currency field, the CurrencyFormatter class is used:

```
<mx:CurrencyFormatter id="totalF" />
```

This formatter is similar to the NumberFormatter, but it provides specific properties for the formatting of currency, such as currency symbols and their alignment (currencySymbol and alignSymbol) and the separators for decimals and thousands:

```
currencySymbol="€"
precision="2"
decimalSeparatorFrom=","
decimalSeparatorTo=","
 thousandsSeparatorFrom="."
 thousandsSeparatorTo="."
 useThousandsSeparator="true"
```

The format() method accepts the value to be formatted and returns the result as a string. This method can be used for data binding in the field in which you want to visualize the data:

```
<mx:Label  text=" {totalF.format(myPrice)}."/>
```

Or you can use it in an event handler in the `<mx:Script>` block:

```
<mx:Script>
  <![CDATA[
    private function calculate(event:Event):void
    {
      var result:Number = Number(priceTxt.text) * ➡
        (Number(ivaTxt.text) / 100);
      totalTxt.text = totalF.format(result.toString());
    }
]]>
</mx:Script>
```

In this solution you'll apply a CurrencyFormatter to a calculated field.

How to build it

In this solution the aim is to create an automatic percentage calculator that formats the data using the currencyFormatter class. The formatting is applied at the click of a button, which launches an event handler in which the format() method is executed. The value returned by this method will be written into a Label.

Begin by creating all the controls you'll need.

1. Create a new MXML application file by selecting File ➤ New ➤ MXML Application; name it Chapter_4_Flex_Sol_8.mxml.

2. Define a Panel and a Form container with some TextInput controls inside this file, as follows:

```
<?xml version="1.0" encoding="utf-8"?>
<mx:Application xmlns:mx="http://www.adobe.com/2006/mxml"
layout="vertical">
  <mx:Panel title="Formatter" width="347" height="252">
    <mx:Form>
      <mx:FormHeading label="Percentage's Calculator"/>
      <mx:FormItem label="Insert your price: ">
        <mx:TextInput id="priceTxt"/>
      </mx:FormItem>
      <mx:FormItem label="Insert your percentage: ">
        <mx:TextInput id="valTxt"/>
      </mx:FormItem>
      <mx:FormItem label="">
        <mx:Button label="Calculate"
            click="calculate(event)"
            id="submitButton " />
      </mx:FormItem>
    </mx:Form>
    <mx:ControlBar>
    <mx:Label text="This is your value: " />
```

```
    <mx:TextInput id="totalTxt" editable="false"/>

    </mx:ControlBar>
  </mx:Panel>
</mx:Application>
```

The Form simply contains two TextInput controls and a Button that launches the ActionScript function calculate(event) to which the event object (not used in this example) is also sent:

```
<mx:Button label="Calculate" click="calculate(event)" />
```

3. Add the currencyFormatter class, instanced with an MXML tag, as follows. Here you specify the currencySymbol and the decimal and thousands separator. Add this tag now:

```
<mx:Application xmlns:mx="http://www.adobe.com/2006/mxml"
layout="vertical">

<mx:CurrencyFormatter id="totalF"
  currencySymbol="€"
  precision="2"
  decimalSeparatorFrom=","
  decimalSeparatorTo=","
  thousandsSeparatorFrom="."
  thousandsSeparatorTo=","
useThousandsSeparator="true" />

<mx:Panel title="Formatter"
 width="477" height="252">
<mx:Form>
```

The formatter to which you have assigned the totalF id will use the Euro as the symbol for the currency and will have two numbers after the decimal point (precision = "2"). You set the decimal separator as a decimal point and the thousands separator as a comma.

The formatter is not applied until the format() method is launched, which happens automatically. This method will return the formatted data with the properties defined in the tag of the CurrencyFormatter class.

4. Insert a block of ActionScript code to manage the function launched on the click of the button below the Application tag:

```
<mx:Script>
  <![CDATA[
    private function calculate(event:Event):void
    {
      var result:Number = Number(priceTxt.text) * ➡
      (Number(valTxt.text) / 100);
      totalTxt.text = totalF.format(result.toString());
    }
  ]]>
</mx:Script>
```

The function creates a temporary variable of Number type, which contains the percentage value calculated based on the data inserted by the user. The value of this variable is sent as parameter to the format() function of the CurrencyFormatter, which returns the string in the text property of the TextInput.

5. Save the file and run the application. Test it by inserting some values in the text fields:

- priceTxt: 1000
- valTxt: 20

When you click the button, the formatted value you should obtain in the totalTxt field is €200,00, as shown in Figure 4-6.

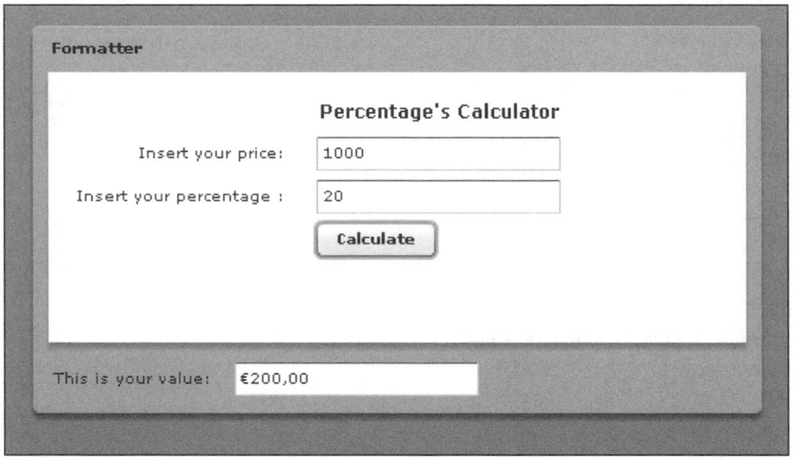

Figure 4-6. The CurrencyFormatter is applied to the calculated field.

Expert tips

For the CurrencyFormatter to be correctly applied to the data, you must ensure that the values inserted in the fields by the user are numbers. You have seen in the preceding solutions that by using the validators you can validate the data in the insertion phase.

To make the application more robust, add two NumberValidators to the code, which validates the data that the user enters, making sure that only numbers are passed:

```
<mx:NumberValidator id="amountV"
  source="{priceTxt}" property="text"
  trigger="{ priceTxt }"
  minValue="1"
  requiredFieldError="Amount is required"/>

<mx:NumberValidator id="percentV"
  source="{valTxt}" property="text"
  trigger="{ valTxt }"
```

```
        requiredFieldError="Enter a percentage"
        maxValue="100"
        exceedsMaxError="Percentage can't exceed 100%"
        domain="int"
        integerError="Enter percent as a whole number"/>
```

When a formatter class detects an error, a string is returned in the error property of the formatter. You can write an error handler function by checking the value of the error property by using an if construct:

```
    if (totalF.error != null )
    {
        if (myFormatter.error == "Invalid value")
        {
            totalTxt.text = " The value is not valid.";
        }
        else
        {
            totalTxt.text = "The formatString is not valid.";
        }
    }
```

This condition verifies that the property error of the CurrencyFormatter is empty: totalF.error != null.

If it is not, an error has occurred, in which case you write a message for the user in the text field:

```
    totalTxt.text = " The value is not valid.";
```

Solution 4-9: Formatting list-based controls with the labelFunction property

One of the most common uses of the formatter classes is associated with Flex list-based controls: DataGrid, Tree, List, TileList, ComboBox, and so on. These controls enable you to visualize complex data. You often need to visualize data in a DataGrid or ComboBox, but you have to format it first.

You have already seen that formatter classes exist to enable you to format data. In the specific case of the list-based controls, the labelFunction property exists, which enables you to determine the text that will be visualized by the control.

This property accepts a function as its parameter and automatically propagates an Object that contains the list of items in the list-based control. The labelFunction returns a String, which is the value to be displayed in the control.

You can, therefore, use the labelFunction to specify the format() method of the formatter class to be applied to the data coming in. In this solution you'll see how to use the DateFormatter to format data to display in a ComboBox.

What's involved

The labelFunction is a property provided by the list-based controls, which accepts a function as value. This function brings with it the list of items contained by the data provider of the list-based control and returns the string to be inserted in the control:

```
<mx:ComboBox id="myCombo" dataProvider="{myAC}"
labelFunction="formatData" />

private function formatData(item:Object):String {}
```

In this function you'll apply formatting to the data that you want to be displayed in the component. To apply the format() method, which returns the formatted value to you, you must first instantiate a formatter class:

```
<mx:DateFormatter id="dateF" ➥
formatString="EEE, DD/MMM/YYYY" />
```

After this is done, you can use the format() method in the labelFunction:

```
public function formatData(item:Object):String {
  return dateF.format(item.data);
}
```

In this solution you'll use the DateFormatter class, which returns data of Date type, formatted as a date. The data becomes formatted based on a pattern that the user can customize through the formatString property. The pattern uses repeated letters to represent how the data should be formatted. The following table lists the values that can be used in the formatString property:

Pattern Letter	Usage
Y	Represents the year. Examples: YY = 07, YYYY = 2007.
M	Represents the months. Examples: M = 1, MM = 01, MMM = Jan, MMMM = January.
D	Represents the days. Examples: D = 5, DD = 05.
E	Represents the days of the week. Examples: E = 2, EE = 02, EEE = Tue, EEEE = Tuesday.
A	Indicates the AM/PM indicator.
J	Represents the hour of the day in European format. Example: 15 (3PM in US format).
H	Represents the hour of the day in European format and is non–zero based. Example: 1- 24.

Pattern Letter	Usage
K	Represents the hour of the day using the AM/PM format.
L	Represents the hour of the day using the AM/PM and is non–zero based. Example: 1 -12.
N	Represents the minute in an hour. Examples: N = 1, NN = 01.
S	Represents the seconds in a minute. Example: SS = 10.

So the value EEE, DD/MMM/YYYY, which you saw in the code before the table, would produce a date formatted as Tue, 01/May/2007.

How to build it

The solution uses a ComboBox, which contains data formatted according to the pattern that you send to the DateFormatter class.

The data is created statically in an ArrayCollection, which defines the label property and data in an Object. Using ActionScript, you create Date variables that you format in the labelFunction of the ComboBox control.

1. Create a new MXML application file by selecting File ➤ New ➤ MXML Application and name it Chapter_4_Flex_Sol_9.mxml.

2. Begin by defining the ComboBox and ArrayCollection to be used as dataProvider:

```
<?xml version="1.0"?>
<mx:Application xmlns:mx="http://www.adobe.com/2006/mxml" >

  <mx:ArrayCollection id="myAC">
    <mx:source>
      <mx:Object label="{new Date()}" data="{new Date()}"/>
      <mx:Object label="{new Date(2007,1,2)}" ➥
          data="{new Date(2007,1,2)}"/>
      <mx:Object label="{new Date()}" data="{new Date()}"/>
    </mx:source>
  </mx:ArrayCollection>

<mx:ComboBox id="myCombo" ➥
    dataProvider="{myAC}" ➥
labelFunction="formatData" />
</mx:Application>
```

The ArrayCollection is created with the MXML tag and takes, as its source, an Object in which you declare the label and data properties. The list-based controls use the labelFunction property to format values to be rendered and shown in the ComboBox control.

The values of label and data properties are declared by creating instances of the ActionScript Date object. The Date object, when declared without parameters and sent to the new Date() constructor, returns the current date of the system.

The ComboBox control uses the ArrayCollection as its data provider and defines the formatData() function.

3. Insert the DateFormatter to define the pattern to be used to format the data:

```
  </mx:ArrayCollection>
<mx:DateFormatter id="dateF" ➥
formatString="EEE, DD/MMM/YYYY" />
```

To be able to apply this pattern, you must launch the format() method of the class and have it return the formatted string. The method will be executed in the label function.

4. Insert a block of </mx:Script> code to declare the format() label function. This function brings (with the item parameter) an Object that contains the data sent to the dataProvider and returns the formatted string:

```
<mx:Application xmlns:mx="http://www.adobe.com/2006/mxml" >
<mx:Script>
  <![CDATA[
    public function formatData(item:Object):String
    {
      return dateF.format(item.data);
    }
  ]]>
</mx:Script>
```

The data property contained in the item object, which contains the data to be formatted according to the pattern defined in the DataFormatter class, is sent to the format() method.

5. Save and run the application. You'll see the data formatted according to the custom format and displayed in the ComboBox control.

Expert tips

The advantage of having a formatter class declared in the Flex application is that it enables you to use it as many times as you want and on different objects. In fact, the formatter classes define only the properties to apply for the formatting of data; they do not become linked to any single object. This again enables you to write less code, instead reusing the same formatter classes and applying them as many times as you like.

Taking the solution you just created, you can create a function that writes the value of a formatted date (formatted according to the pattern defined in the DateFormatter) from a ComboBox into a TextInput; when the date selected in the ComboBox is changed, the date in the TextInput automatically updates.

To do this, add an event handler that will execute the `format()` method on the data selected by the user when the change event of the `ComboBox` occurs. Insert a `TextInput` control in which you'll insert the formatted value:

```
<mx:TextInput id="dateTxt" editable="false"  />

<mx:ComboBox id="myCombo" dataProvider="{myAC}"
   labelFunction="formatData"
   change="changeData(myCombo.selectedItem)" />
```

You can now write the `changeData()` function to apply a `DateFormatter` and bind the formatted value into the `TextInput` control:

```
private function changeData(obj:Object):void
{
   dateTxt.text =  dateF.format(obj.data);
}
```

Try making this change and testing the application again. You should get the result seen in Figure 4-7.

Figure 4-7. The DateFormatter can be used more times in the application and can receive different values to format.

Summary

Flex validator and formatter classes are powerful built-in systems to validate and format data.

One of the benefits of these classes is that the code to validate and format data executes on the client, which enables you to validate input data before transmitting it to the server. This reduces the bandwidth of the server and improves the user experience of the application.

In this chapter you learned how to use some of the validator classes to validate fields, forms, and data models. Flex validator classes dispatch valid and invalid events. Each control automatically handles these events, but you can customize the default behavior by intercepting and modifying the validation events dispatched by the validators. With these approaches you can see whether the process of validation has been successful and assigned an appropriate function afterward.

Being ActionScript classes, the validators can be extended and customized. You created your own custom validator with a custom ActionScript class that extended the `RegExpValidator` class, which enabled you to carry out a validation check on Social Security numbers in Italy.

The formatter classes enable developers to format complex data in a more legible format (this is something that users—and your server—will thank you for). You used the formatter's built-in classes to format data and you saw how to use the `labelFunction` property of the list-based controls to apply formatting.

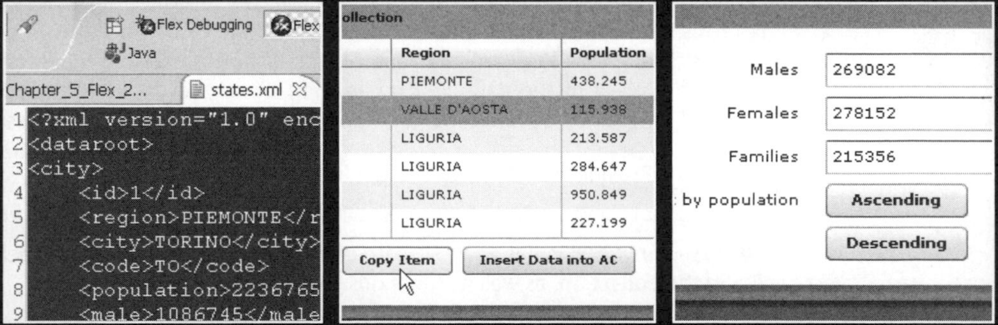
Flex Debugging
Flex
Java
Chapter_5_Flex_2...
states.xml
<?xml version="1.0" enc
<dataroot>
<city>
<id>1</id>
<region>PIEMONTE</r
<city>TORINO</city>
<code>TO</code>
<population>2236765
<male>1086745</male
ollection
Region
Population
PIEMONTE
438.245
VALLE D'AOSTA
115.938
LIGURIA
213.587
LIGURIA
284.647
LIGURIA
950.849
LIGURIA
227.199
Copy Item
Insert Data into AC
Males
269082
Females
278152
Families
215356
by population
Ascending
Descending

Data management represents one of the fundamental operations in the development of any application. Flex provides very powerful classes for accessing and managing complex data, which then becomes visualized through the multiple components put at your disposal.

These classes, which are called **collections**, enable you to access and represent data. These representations are then used as data providers for the components. Data providers, common to all Flex components that have the property to display and visualize data, are objects that contain the data requested by the component.

The standard Flex collection classes you'll meet are ArrayCollection and XMLListCollection. The former represents data in an array-based format; the latter is XML-based. This is all well and good, but you can take it further—these collections, besides being powerful and valid solutions for containing complex data, also provide very useful methods for any developer who wants to carry out diverse data-management operations.

But before moving on to a further discussion of these collections, you should know about an interesting potential usage of the collection classes. If you were to use a raw data object such as an Array or an Object as a data provider in a Flex application, you would be greatly limited because the control data bound to it is not updated when changes are carried out on that object. In practical terms, this means that if the structure of the raw data object (typed as Array or Object) changes, the component bound to that object could not visually display the changes.

The collection classes guarantee that the component is updated the moment a change is carried out on the data. Therefore, by using a data collection that is modified at runtime, the changes are propagated on all components that use that data provider.

This is only one of the advantages of using the collection classes to access and manage complex data. Other advantages include the ability to inherit a powerful mechanism to manage paged data and the existence of a set of operations that can be performed on data and methods to apply different views of the data.

The collection classes implement the ICollectionView interface. Interfaces, in programming terms, contain a list of the methods and declarations of constants implemented by the classes through the keyword interface. The collection classes use the interfaces to provide a specific view of the data, which can then be sorted or filtered according to the determined criteria. Three interfaces are implemented by the collection classes:

- IList: Provides functions to set, get, and remove data
- ICollectionView: Provides more complex functions for sorting and filtering data
- IViewCursor: Enables you to create cursors in the data to find and seek bookmarks in the collection, as well as functions to insert and remove items

Both ArrayCollection and XMLListCollection implement the ICollectionView and IList interface. XMLListCollection also implements a subset of XMLList methods.

In this chapter you'll use the collection classes and their methods to execute operations on collection data.

> *Flex 3 implements the following collection classes:*
>
> - IGroupingCollection: *allows the creation of grouped data from flat data.*
> - IHierarchicalCollectionView: *provides functions to work with hierarchical or grouped data.*
> - IHierarchicalCollectionViewCursor: *provides the interface for bidirectionally enumerating a hierarchical collection*
> - IHierarchicalData: *provides the functions to represent hierarchical data as the data provider for a Flex component*
>
> *We will present some solutions that use the new Flex 3 collection classes in Chapter 7.*

Solution 5-1: Using ArrayCollection to handle complex data

ArrayCollection is often used as a data provider with the list-based controls. List-based controls are those controls that receive input from a data provider to visualize the data:

- List control
- HorizontalList control
- TileList control
- ComboBox control
- DataGrid and AdvancedDataGrid (Flex 3) control
- Tree control

The DataProvider property is the default property of these controls, so it is possible to specify a collection object to these controls in a direct way. In this solution you'll see how to use an ArrayCollection class, declaring it both in MXML and ActionScript, and assign it as data provider to list-based controls.

What's involved

An ArrayCollection class accepts an Array as input; to populate the ArrayCollection class, you'll use an Array that you can declare using MXML as well as ActionScript. First, let's look at an MXML array:

```
<mx:ArrayCollection id="myAC">
<mx:Object label="{new Date()}" data="{new Date()}"/>
<mx:Object label="{new Date(2007,1,2)}" data="{new Date(2007,1,2)}"/>
<mx:Object label="{new Date()}" data="{new Date()}"/>
</mx:ArrayCollection>
```

In this code, the ArrayCollection is populated with an array of Objects, each with a label and field property. Now let's look at the same thing declared with ActionScript:

```
<mx:Script>
<![CDATA[
  import mx.collections.*;
  [Bindable]
  private  var myAC_AS:ArrayCollection;

  public function createAC():void
  {
    // Define an array of data that we will use in our Collection
    var myDataArray:Array = new Array({label:"Marco", ➥
      data:"Casario"},{label:"Katia", data:"Casario"}➥
      {label:"Alessio", data:"Casario"});

    // create a new ArrayCollection object using myDataArray as its data.
   myAC_AS = new ArrayCollection(myDataArray);

  }
]]>
</mx:Script>
```

Note that the private myAC_AS variable (which is declared as [Bindable]) was created first because to use the data binding between the dataProvider property and the collection class you must use the ArrayCollection class as the dataProvider of a list-based control. The createAC() function populates the ArrayCollection, sending it an array of objects as data.

In this solution you'll see how to visualize the data container in an ArrayCollection, declared with both MXML and ActionScript.

How to build it

Begin by creating a new Flex project that will be used throughout Chapter 5.

1. Open Flex Builder and create a new Flex project called Chapter_5_Flex_Collections. Accept the default values in the wizard and click Finish.

2. Create a new MXML application file by selecting File ➤ New ➤ MXML Application and give it the name Chapter_5_Flex_Sol_1.mxml.

3. Declare two ArrayCollection variables: the first using the MXML ArrayCollection tag, and the second using ActionScript. Add the <mx:Script> block below the Application tag:

```
<mx:Script>
  <![CDATA[
    import mx.collections.ArrayCollection;

    [Bindable]
    public var myAC_AS:ArrayCollection;
```

```
    ]]>
  </mx:Script>

  <mx:ArrayCollection id="myAC">
   <mx:Object label="{new Date()}"
   data="{new Date()}"/>
   <mx:Object label="{new Date(2007,1,2)}"
   data="{new Date(2007,1,2)}"/>
   <mx:Object label="{new Date()}" data="{new Date()}"/>
  </mx:ArrayCollection>
```

To be able to use the ArrayCollection class, you must first import the class by using the import keyword. The collection classes are found in the mx.collections package. In the preceding ActionScript code, the myAC_AS variable has been declared as Bindable by using the metadata [Bindable]. You must now populate this collection.

4. Define a function that populates the ArrayCollection and that is launched on the creationComplete event of the Application tag:

```
public function createAC():void {
  myAC_AS = new ArrayCollection(➡
    [{label:"Marco", data:"Casario"},➡
    {label:"Katia", data:"Casario"},➡
    {label:"Alessio", data:"Casario"}]);➡
  }
```

```
<mx:Application xmlns:mx="http://www.adobe.com/2006/mxml"
  layout="vertical"
  creationComplete="createAC()">
```

As soon as the application is loaded and drawn, both the created ArrayCollection and populated ArrayCollection have the values that were sent.

Because ArrayCollection is an array of objects, you can use the Array notation to be able to access its internal data. Try to make it print one of the values contained on an index of the collection on a Label.

5. Now you'll insert a Label control and create a data binding between it and the ArrayCollection on its text property by pointing to the property data container on the second index of the object. Add the following to the MXML file, above the <mx:ArrayCollection> tag:

```
<mx:Label text="{myAC[1].data}" />
```

The value you'll see written into the Label is Fri Feb 2 00:00:00 GMT+0100 2007, which corresponds exactly to the value on the second index (the ArrayCollections are zero index based like each Array) of the object.

A warning icon appears next to the code, which is related to the Problems view of Flex Builder IDE, with the following sentence:

"Data Binding will not be able to detect changes when using square bracket operator. For Array, please use ArrayCollection.getItemAt() instead." (See Figure 5-1.)

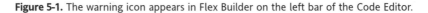

```
22
23
24        <mx:Label text="{myAC[1].label}" />
25
26        <mx:ArrayCollection id="myAC">
27
28              <mx:Object label="{new Date()}" data="{new Date()}"/>
29              <mx:Object label="{new Date(2007,1,2)}" data="{new Date(2007,1,2)}"/>
30              <mx:Object label="{new Date()}" data="{new Date()}"/>
31
32        </mx:ArrayCollection>
33
```

Problems 🔎 Progress Console   ✖ 🔌 ▽ ▭ ▢
0 errors, 1 warning, 0 infos

Description	Resource	In Folder	Locat
⚠ Data binding will not be able to detect changes when using square bracket operator. For Array, please use ArrayCollection.getItemAt(...	Chapter_5_Flex_2_Sol_1...	Chapter_5_Flex_2_Collec...	line 2-

Figure 5-1. The warning icon appears in Flex Builder on the left bar of the Code Editor.

> *In the next solution, you'll see how to use the* ArrayCollection.getItemAt() *method to access the data in an* ArrayCollection.

6. You can now declare the list-based controls and send the collection that you want to make them visualize in their dataProvider property. Insert two controls after the closing ArrayCollection tag: a List and a ComboBox:

```
<mx:List id="myList" dataProvider="{myAC}" />
<mx:ComboBox id="myCombo" dataProvider="{myAC_AS}" />
```

To use the ArrayCollection as the dataProvider, you must create a data binding on that object. In the List control you use the ArrayCollection declared with MXML as the input, while for the ComboBox you use the ArrayCollection declared with ActionScript. These two controls automatically take their data from the Label property of the ArrayCollection and render it to the screen.

7. Save and run the application. You should see the final result of the solution, as shown in Figure 5-2.

```
Fri Feb 2 00:00:00 GMT+0100 2007

Tue Mar 6 11:02:17 GMT+0100 2007

Fri Feb 2 00:00:00 GMT+0100 2007

Tue Mar 6 11:02:17 GMT+0100 2007




          Marco    ▼
          Marco
          Katia
          Alessio
```

Figure 5-2.
The two list-based controls show the ArrayCollection that was sent to their dataProvider.

Expert tips

Because the dataProvider is the default property for the list-based controls, the ArrayCollection could be written as a nested tag of the control, like so:

```
<mx:List>
  <mx:ArrayCollection id="myAC">
    <mx:Object label="{new Date()}" data="{new Date()}"/>
    <mx:Object label="{new Date(2007,1,2)}"
   data="{new Date(2007,1,2)}"/>
    <mx:Object label="{new Date()}" data="{new Date()}"/>
  </mx:ArrayCollection>
</mx:List>
```

The result would be the same. You would still see the values of the collection inserted in the List control.

If you want to return the value selected by the user in one of the two controls, you can use the selectedItem property containing the items of the ArrayCollection on the index the user has selected. To do this, create a TextInput control and make it return the item selected by the user on the change event of the ComboBox using the following ActionScript code:

```
<mx:ComboBox id="myCombo"
dataProvider="{myAC_AS}"
change="myTxt.text =➡
 myCombo.selectedItem.label" />

<mx:TextInput id="myTxt" />
```

The selectedItem property contains an Object that represents the data on the index selected by the user in the ComboBox. To avoid having [object Object] returned to you in the TextInput, you must point exactly to a property contained in the selectedItem:

```
myTxt.text = myCombo.selectedItem.data;
```

In this case, the data property will be returned.

Solution 5-2: Converting an MXML data model into an ArrayCollection

Data models are excellent tools that function as containers for the data information of an application (refer to Chapter 3). This information contains properties that become stored in an ActionScript object.

While the data models are useful, versatile, and easy to use (especially those declared using the MXML language), they don't make the life of the developer any easier when operations are required to be carried out on the data. It is therefore extremely useful to convert the MXML data model into an ArrayCollection. This conversion operation is extremely simple because a data model has an XML-based structure and therefore contains a repeating node that can be sent as an array of Objects to an ArrayCollection.

In this solution you'll see how to go from a simple MXML data model to an ArrayCollection.

What's involved

An MXML data model is declared by using the `<mx:Model>` tag or the `<mx:XML>` tag (refer to Chapter 3 for a refresher on MXML data models). It can be declared by defining its properties as child tags:

```
<mx:Model id="myData">
  <rootTag>
    <book>
      <title>La Divina Commedia</title>
      <author>Dante</author>
    </book>
    <book>
      <title>I Promessi Sposi</title>
      <author>Alessandro Manzoni</author>
    </book>
  </rootTag>
</mx:Model>
```

You can also choose to load it from an external XML file using the source property of the Model:

```
<mx:Model id="myData" source="myFile.xml" />
```

In the previous solution you created an ArrayCollection by using the MXML tag `<mx:ArrayCollection>` and then using ActionScript. To convert an MXML data model you can use either mode of declaration; for MXML you use the source property to which you associate the input data to be converted:

```
<mx:ArrayCollection source="{myData }" id="myAC" />
```

With ActionScript you send the data model to the constructor of the class at the moment in which it is instanced:

```
private var myAC:ArrayCollection;
myAC = new ArrayCollection(myData.book);
```

In this solution you'll see how to use both methods to convert an MXML data model in an ArrayCollection.

How to build it

The steps necessary to go from an MXML data model to an ArrayCollection are really simple, so get to it!

1. Create a new MXML application file with the name Chapter_5_Flex_Sol_2.mxml.

2. Below the Application tag, insert an MXML data model to this file as follows (as you did in Solution 3-1):

```
<mx:Model id="myData">
  <rootTag>
    <book>
      <title>La Divina Commedia</title>
      <author>Dante</author>
    </book>
    <book>
      <title>I Promessi Sposi</title>
      <author>Alessandro Manzoni</author>
    </book>
  </rootTag>
</mx:Model>
```

3. Immediately convert this data model into an ArrayCollection by using the relative MXML tag. Insert the following line below the data model:

```
<mx:ArrayCollection source="{myData.book}" id="myACC" />
```

The repeating node of the data model is sent (the book node in this case) to the source property of the ArrayCollection. Note that you do not send it the root tag (<rootTag>); instead you directly access the repeating node, which contains the array of objects.

4. Insert a List control below the ArrayCollection line, as follows. This code outputs the data contained in the ArrayCollection, which you send to it from the dataProvider:

```
<mx:List id="myList" dataProvider="{myACC}"
labelFunction="formatData" />
```

The labelFunction launches the formatData() function, which takes care of formatting the data shown in the List control. In this solution the List control will print both the value of the title and the author of the book.

5. Below the <mx:Model> tag, insert the following <mx:Script> block into the application file (here the formatted label function is defined):

```
<mx:Script>
  <![CDATA[
    private function formatData(item:Object):String
    {
      // declare the variable that will hold the
      // formatted return string
      var returnString:String;
```

```
            // format our values and store them for return
            returnString = "Title: "+ item.title + ➥
            ", Author: " + item.author;

            //return the formatted string
            return "Title: "+ item.title + ", Author: " + item.author;

          }
        ]]>
      </mx:Script>
```

The `labelFunction` brings with it an `item` object, which contains the properties of the underlying data and returns the formatted `String` value to be displayed in the `List` control.

6. Save the file and run the application. The result should look like Figure 5-3.

Figure 5-3. The MXML data model converted into an ArrayCollection and used as data provider in the List control

Expert tips

To convert an MXML data model using an `ArrayCollection` declared with ActionScript, you must be sure that the population of the collection class takes place after the creation of the data model. In fact, if you were to write the following ActionScript code, the code would become compiled without generating an error, but the application would not load any data into the `ArrayCollection` and the `List` control:

```
<mx:Script>
  <![CDATA[
    import mx.collections.ArrayCollection;
    [Bindable]
    private var myAC:ArrayCollection = ➥
    new ArrayCollection(myData.book);
  ]]>
</mx:Script>
```

The data model has not yet been initialized. You must, therefore, create an instance of the ArrayCollection class and link it to a User or to a System event.

In the <mx:Script> block you should create only the variable:

```
<mx:Script>
  <![CDATA[
    import mx.collections.ArrayCollection;

    [Bindable]
    private var myAC:ArrayCollection;

  ]]>
</mx:Script>
```

The ArrayCollection will be populated, for example, on the creationComplete event of the Application, like so:

```
<mx:Application xmlns:mx="http://www.adobe.com/2006/mxml"➥
  layout="vertical"
  creationComplete="myAC = new ArrayCollection(myData.book)">
```

You now have a populated ArrayCollection at your disposal, ready to be correctly sent to the List control with a line such as the following:

```
<mx:List id="myList" dataProvider="{myACC}"
  labelFunction="formatData" />
```

Solution 5-3: Setting and getting items in an ArrayCollection

The first operations necessary to be able to access and work with a collection class are the methods and the properties that the IList interface provides. This interface enables you to complete the get, set, add, and remove operations of an item in the collection, but it also provides methods to determine the index of the collection on which the operation is carried out.

You can, for example, add an item at the end or at the beginning of the collection or substitute a value positioned at a precise index.

The methods of the IList interface can be applied to all the collection classes, both of ArrayCollection type and XMLListCollection type, and also to the dataProvider properties put forward by the list-based controls.

In this solution you'll learn how to carry out operations put forward by the IList interface of an ArrayCollection.

What's involved

To immediately have a complete picture of all the methods and properties put forward by the IList interface, all you need to do is open it and look at the code in it. The IList is a collection of items organized in an ordinal manner and provides the methods for accessing and manipulating items.

To open a Flex class from Flex Builder, write it in the editor, hold down the Ctrl key (or Apple on the Mac), and click it with the mouse. Note that the class becomes an underlined hyperlink. You can also open the class from its package: mx.collections.IList.

> Take care here: Make sure that you don't edit and save the ActionScript class.

On opening the IList interface (http://livedocs.adobe.com/labs/flex/3/langref/mx/collections/IList.html) you'll see the following methods and properties declared:

Properties and Methods	Description
length	Returns the length or the number of items in the collection.
addItem(item:Object)	Adds an item at the end of the collection.
addItemAt(item:Object, index:int)	Adds an item on the index that is sent as parameter.
getItemAt(index:int, ➥ prefetch:int = 0):Object;	Gets an item at the specified index. The prefetch parameter indicates the direction and the number of items to fetch.
itemUpdated(item:Object, ➥ property:Object = null	Advises when an item has been updated in the collection.
removeAll()	Removes all the items in the collection.
removeItemAt(index:int):Object	Removes an element on the index that has been specified.
setItemAt(item:Object, ➥ index:int):Object	Inserts an item at the specified index, substituting the item already present on that index.
toArray()	Returns an Array that contains the same items as the collection and in the same order.

In this solution you'll use some common methods to carry out a few operations on the collection.

How to build it

You'll begin with the creation of an MXML data model, which will constitute the base of the structure of the data. This model will take the data from an external XML file.

1. Create a new folder in the Flex project called data, create a file called states.xml inside it, and add the following code to that file:

```xml
<?xml version="1.0" encoding="UTF-8"?>
<dataroot>
  <city>
    <id>1</id>
    <region>PIEMONTE</region>
    <city>TORINO</city>
    <code>TO</code>
    <population>2236765</population>
    <male>1086745</male>
    <female>1150020</female>
    <family>886053</family>
  </city>
  <city>
    <id>2</id>
    <region>PIEMONTE</region>
    <city>VERCELLI</city>
    <code>VC</code>
    <population>183869</population>
    <male>88304</male>
    <female>95565</female>
    <family>75317</family>
  </city>

    ...

</dataroot>
```

The root tag is <dataroot>; the repeating node (the one you'll point to when you convert the data model into an ArrayCollection) is the <city> node.

2. Refresh the project by right-clicking/Ctrl-clicking the Flex project in Navigator view and clicking the Refresh option on the context menu, as shown in Figure 5-4.

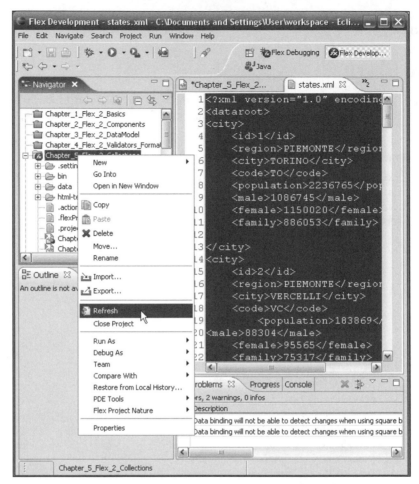

Figure 5-4. The Refresh option from the context menu of the Flex project

3. Create a new MXML application file and name it Chapter_5_Flex_Sol_3.mxml.

4. Insert an MXML data model into this file and convert it into an ArrayCollection:

```
<mx:Application xmlns:mx="http://www.adobe.com/2006/mxml"
    layout="horizontal" >

<mx:Model id="myRegion" source="data/states.xml" />

<mx:ArrayCollection id="myAC" source="{myRegion.city}" />
```

The data model loads the states.xml file. The id of the model is then sent to the ArrayCollection referenced in the source property, which points directly at the repeating node of the XML file. In this way the collection class contains all the items contained in the data model within various indexes.

5. Insert controls capable of visualizing the complex structure of the ArrayCollection in video. You'll use a DataGrid, but you'll be able to see only some of the properties contained in the collection. To do this, define three DataGridColumns tags and link them to the id, region, and population properties:

```
<mx:Panel width="70%"
  title="Show me ArrayCollection"
 layout="vertical" id="myPanel1">

<mx:DataGrid id="myDG"
   dataProvider="{myAC}" width="100%" >

  <mx:columns>
    <mx:DataGridColumn headerText="ID" dataField="id"/>

    <mx:DataGridColumn headerText="Region"
      dataField="region"/>

    <mx:DataGridColumn headerText="Population"
      dataField="population" />

  </mx:columns>

</mx:DataGrid>
```

The ArrayCollection is sent to the DataGrid as the dataProvider, and the data of the collection is shown through the dataField properties of the DataGridColumn.

6. Add two Button controls, with which you'll execute the methods of the IList interface to access and work with the data of the ArrayCollection. Insert a Label control that you'll use to write the data. Add the following code to the application file below the closing of the DataGrid tag:

```
<mx:HBox >

 <mx:Button label="Get Item 1"
 click="myLbl.text = ➥
 myAC.getItemAt(myDG.selectedIndex).population" />

 <mx:Button label="Copy Item" click="copyIntoList()" />
 <mx:Button label="Insert Data into AC" click="addData()" />

</mx:HBox>

<mx:Label id="myLbl" />

</mx:Panel>
```

Each Button is positioned horizontally using the HBox container. Clicking the first Button causes it to write the value selected by the user on the DataGrid into the text of the Label control through the following ActionScript:

```
myLbl.text = myAC.getItemAt(myDG.selectedIndex).population
```

The getItemAt() method of the ArrayCollection was used to get the population data at the index selected by the user on the DataGrid (myDG.selectedIndex). The getItemAt() method returns an object containing all the items on the specified index, so it is necessary to specify the name of the property you want to be printed on the Label (in this case, the population property):

```
myLbl.text = myAC.getItemAt(myDG.selectedIndex).population
```

7. For the other two Button controls, you'll instead call the event handlers, which will be invoked upon the click event. Add the following code in a <mx:Script> block declared below the Application tag:

```
<mx:Script>
  <![CDATA[

    [Bindable]
    private var myAC_AS:ArrayCollection;

    private function addData():void
    {
      // create a new data object to add to the ArrayCollection
      var newDataObject:Object = {
      id:0,
      region:'lazio',
      city:'Roma',
      code:'RM',
      population:3738685,
      male:1799138,
      female:1939547,
      family:1423856};

      // Add the new data Object to
      // the ArrayCollection at Index zero (0)
      myAC.addItemAt newDataObject, 0);

      myAC.getItemIndex(0);
    }

    private function copyIntoList():void
    {
      myAC_AS  = new ArrayCollection()
      myAC_AS.addItem(myDG.selectedItem);
    }
  ]]>
</mx:Script>
```

The first function, addData(), adds an item to the ArrayCollection by using the addItemAt() method. This method, besides accepting the item to be inserted, also accepts the index on which it must position the new item. In this case, insert the data at the beginning of the collection, or on the index 0 (like arrays, the collection classes are zero index based):

Instead, the second function, copyIntoList(), uses the addItem() method to add an item to a new ArrayCollection you declared at the beginning of the block of code:

```
[Bindable]
private var myAC_AS:ArrayCollection;
```

The myAC_AS collection has just been created, so it is empty. The copyIntoList() function then instances and populates the ArrayCollection with the item selected by the user on the DataGrid:

```
myAC_AS  = new ArrayCollection()
myAC_AS.addItem(myDG.selectedItem);
```

This new ArrayCollection is, for now, not bound to any other visual component. In the next step you'll create a List control into which the items added by the user will be added.

8. In a new Panel, create a List control to which you send the ArrayCollection created by the copyIntoList() function as its dataProvider. The List control, unlike the DataGrid, can't show all the items contained in the data provider. It can, in fact, display data only in a single column, so you have to specify which data you want to visualize by sending it to the labelField property:

```
<mx:Panel title="List control" width="30%"
  height="{myPanel1.height}" >

 <mx:List id="myList" dataProvider="{myAC_AS}"
  width="80%" labelField="region" />

</mx:Panel>
```

9. Save and run the application. By clicking the various Button controls you'll see how the data in the ArrayCollection undergoes the modifications you have specified using the methods of the IList interface (see Figure 5-5).

Figure 5-5. The get and add operations are carried out on the ArrayCollection.

Expert tips

You can complete the example by adding other Button controls to carry out the other methods of the IList interface. removeItemAt() and removeAll() are used to remove one or all of the items in an ArrayCollection:

```
<mx:Button label="Remove me"
  click="myAC.removeItemAt(myDG.selectedIndex)" />
<mx:Button label="Remove All" click="myAC.removeAll()" />
```

You can also use a Formatter class to format the data visualized in the DataGrid. In this example, the Population column contains the numerical value, which becomes formatted by default as a String. You can create a NumberFormatter tag that you apply to the data with the format() method:

```
<mx:NumberFormatter id="numberF"
  useThousandsSeparator="true"
  decimalSeparatorTo=","
  thousandsSeparatorTo="." />
```

On the column of the DataGrid to which you intend to apply the NumberFormatter, you can link a label function that will launch the format() method of the Formatter, which is necessary so that the properties defined in the NumberFormatter are applied:

```
<mx:columns>
  <mx:DataGridColumn headerText="ID" dataField="id"/>
  <mx:DataGridColumn headerText="Region" dataField="region"/>
  <mx:DataGridColumn headerText="Population"
  dataField="population" labelFunction="formatPopulation"/>
</mx:columns>
```

The formatPopulation() function, defined as a label function, does nothing other than return the formatted item:

```
private function formatPopulation(item:Object, ➡
column:DataGridColumn):String
{
  return numberF.format(item.population);
}
```

Solution 5-4: Filtering data

The filtering- and data-sorting functionalities of an ArrayCollection are provided by the ICollectionView interface. This interface represents the data as a collection of items and enables you to work with the ArrayCollection class, XMLListCollection class, and dataProvider property (although not in the ButtonBar, LinkBar, TabBar, and ToggleButtonBar components).

In this solution you'll use the filterFunction of the ICollectionView to filter on an ArrayCollection, returning a subset of the data source with the specified filter criteria applied.

What's involved

To apply a filter to the data, a filter function of the ArrayCollection is used, limiting it to the subset of data. The filter function is sent to the filterFunction property put forward by the collection class (in this case, the ArrayCollection), and it automatically brings with it an item typed as Object and returns a Boolean:

```
public function myFilterFunction(item:Object):Boolean { }
```

The Object represents the collection item, whereas the returned Boolean value specifies whether the criteria for the filter on the data must include the item in the filtered collection:

```
private function myFilterFunction(item:Object):Boolean
   {
     if (myCombo.selectedItem == "All regions")
   {
     return true
   }
     else
   {
     return item.id_region == myCombo.selectedItem.id ;
   }
}
```

In this filter function, if the value selected on a ComboBox corresponds to the "All regions" label, the filter function returns true, and no filter is applied to the collection. If the id_region value of the collection (item.id_region) is equal to the id value selected by the user in the ComboBox (myCombo.selectedItem.id) instead, the item that verifies that equation will be returned.

The filter function is assigned to the filterFunction property of the ArrayCollection, to which you want to apply the filtering:

```
private function filterData():void
{
   cityAC.filterFunction = applyFilter;
   cityAC.refresh();
}
```

In this solution you'll see how to filter data visualized in a DataGrid by applying a filter on the selection of data in a ComboBox.

How to build it

Two different models of data are used: the first functions as data provider for the ComboBox; the second visualizes the data in the DataGrid. The filtering will be applied to the second model of data, an ArrayCollection, which then filters the data in the DataGrid according to what the user has selected in the ComboBox.

The data will be loaded with two MXML data models that will take the values from external XML files. The data models will be converted in more than one ArrayCollection to avail the ICollectionView interface.

1. Create a new application file by selecting File ➤ New ➤ MXML Application and call it Chapter_5_Flex_Sol_4.mxml.

2. Add the following code below the Application tag, which loads data from the XML file using the <mx:Model> tag and is then transformed into an ArrayCollection using the MXML tag, and the source property points at the repeating node of the data model, omitting the root tag:

```
<mx:Model id="myRegions" source="data/regions.xml" />
<mx:Model id="myCities" source="data/states.xml" />

<mx:ArrayCollection id="regionAC" source="{myRegions.region}" />
<mx:ArrayCollection id="cityAC" source="{myCities.city}" />
```

The XML files are contained in the data folder, which was created in the Flex project in the previous solution. The structure of the states.xml file is the same as that illustrated and created in Solution 5-3, whereas the second XML file contains the following data:

```
<?xml version="1.0" encoding="UTF-8"?>
<dataroot>
  <region>
    <id>1</id>
    <region>PIEMONTE</region>
  </region>
  <region>
    <id>2</id>
    <region>VALLE D'AOSTA</region>
  </region>
  <region>
    <id>3</id>
    <region>LOMBARDIA</region>
  </region>
</dataroot>
```

3. Create a new XML file by selecting File ➤ New ➤ File. Copy the preceding code and save it as regions.xml. The file must be saved in the data folder of the Flex project. This XML file will be used as a model to populate the ComboBox.

4. Add two controls that define the user interface of the application and load the data in them: a ComboBox and a DataGrid. Add the following code after the second ArrayCollection tag:

```
<mx:ComboBox id="myCombo"
  dataProvider="{regionAC}"
  labelField="region"
  change="filterData()"
 creationComplete="regionAC.addItemAt('All regions',0); ➡
  myCombo.selectedIndex = 0;"/>

<mx:DataGrid id="myDG" dataProvider="{cityAC}">
  <mx:columns>
    <mx:DataGridColumn headerText="Region" dataField="region"/>
    <mx:DataGridColumn headerText="City" dataField="city"/>
    <mx:DataGridColumn headerText="Population"
      dataField="population"/>
  </mx:columns>
</mx:DataGrid>
```

The ComboBox uses the ArrayCollection regionAC as its dataProvider. An ArrayCollection is complex data, whereas the ComboBox control can show linear data, so you must specify the item to be visualized with the labelField property. Obviously, this item must be present in the ArrayCollection. In this case you insert the region value in the control, which contains the name of the region in that node (refer to the structure of the regions.xml file).

In the creationComplete event of the control, you have added an item on the first index of the ArrayCollection with the addItemAt() method.

This item is a String containing the text "All regions", which is useful for users when they don't want to filter data for a single region and just want an option to select so they can see all the data. It also needs to be the initial value displayed in the ComboBox, so the second instruction on creationComplete ensures that the index 0 of the control is selected:

```
creationComplete="regionAC.addItemAt('All regions',0); ➡
  myCombo.selectedIndex = 0;"
```

On the change event of the ComboBox an event handler is called that will execute the operations for the filtering of the data.

Instead, DataGrid uses the ArrayCollection cityAC as its dataProvider, but shows only some of the data loaded in the collection. In fact, you have declared only three columns that are linked to the item in the ArrayCollection with the dataField property:

```
<mx:DataGridColumn headerText="Region" dataField="region"/>
<mx:DataGridColumn headerText="City" dataField="city"/>
<mx:DataGridColumn headerText="Population"
  dataField="population"/>
```

When the application starts up, no filters will be initially applied to the data displayed by the DataGrid, as shown in Figure 5-6.

Figure 5-6. On application activation the data has not yet been filtered.

5. You can now write the function launched on the change event of the ComboBox that will execute the filter on the data. Insert the following <mx:Script> block at the beginning of the MXML file, below the Application tag:

```
<mx:Script>
  <![CDATA[
    private function filterData():void
    {
      cityAC.filterFunction = applyFilter;
      cityAC.refresh();
    }

    private function applyFilter(item:Object):Boolean
    {
      if (myCombo.selectedItem == "All regions")
      {
        return true
      }
      else
      {
        return item.id_region == myCombo.selectedItem.id ;
      }
    }
  ]]>
</mx:Script>
```

The code is very simple, which is one of the principal advantages for developers using collection classes and their interfaces. The first filterData() function (the event handler of the change event of the ComboBox) performs only two operations:

- The first operation links the applyFilter() to the filterFunction property of the ArrayCollection—this function applies the filter and returns the updated ArrayCollection.

- The second instruction performs a refresh of the ArrayCollection to update it with the new subset of the filtered data:

```
cityAC.filterFunction = applyFilter;
cityAC.refresh();
```

The applyFilter() filter function returns a Boolean specifying whether to include the item in the collection view. There are only two conditions to be verified: the one in which the user selects the "All regions" item in the ComboBox and the one in which the id_region in the cityAC ArrayCollection (sent to this function by the item Object parameter) is equal to the id of the selected item of the ComboBox:

```
if (myCombo.selectedItem == "All regions")
{
  return true
}
  else
{
  return item.id_region == myCombo.selectedItem.id ;
}
```

When these two conditions are both met by a portion of the data, an ArrayCollection will be returned to you that contains only the data that meets those conditions.

6. Save and run the application. Try to select one of the regions in the ComboBox and you'll see the updated values displayed in the ArrayCollection, as shown in Figure 5-7.

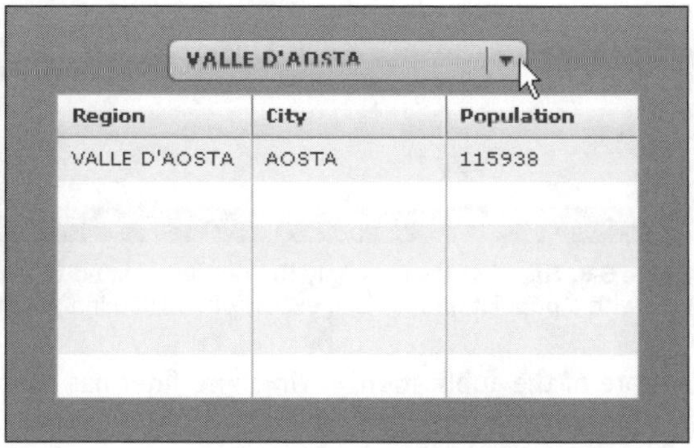

Figure 5-7. By selecting an item in the ComboBox, the data becomes filtered and updated in the DataGrid.

Expert tips

In this solution you have applied a simple filter that verifies whether the user has selected the "All regions" item from the ComboBox; if not, the filter is applied based on the user's selection.

You can, however, also create more complex filters, which are applied on more restrictive conditions. For example, you could filter only the regions selected from the ComboBox that have a population of more than 200,000 inhabitants. In this case, the filter function would become the following:

```
private function applyFilter(item:Object):Boolean
{
  if (myCombo.selectedItem == "All regions")
{
  return true
}
  if (item.population > 200000)
  return item.id_region == myCombo.selectedItem.id;

  return false;
}
```

The second condition verifies that the population value of the item:Object (to be more precise, the ArrayCollection used by the DataGrid) has a value in excess of 200,000. Only in this case will the filtered data of the regions be returned. You would now be filtering based on both region and population, as shown in Figure 5-8.

Region	City	Population ▲
LIGURIA	IMPERIA	213587
LIGURIA	LA SPEZIA	227199
LIGURIA	SAVONA	284647
LIGURIA	GENOVA	950849

(Combo box selection: LIGURIA ▼)

Figure 5-8. The filter displays only the region selected by the user with a population that is in excess of 200,000 inhabitants.

To restore the initial state of the application, in which no filter has been applied, it is necessary to empty the filter function (this is an obvious bit of functionality to include).

To do this, create a function that sets the value of the filterFunction property of the ArrayCollection to null and loses the reference to the filter function; following this you carry out a refresh of the collection:

```
 private function killFilter():void
{
  cityAC.filterFunction = null;
  cityAC.refresh();
}
```

Solution 5-5: Sorting data

The ICollectionView interface enables the developer to apply sorting to collection classes or on data providers. It contains a view of the data source represented as a collection of items.

Using the methods of the ICollectionView interface, developers can sort and filter the data in the data provider so that the view represented by the collection is a reordered subset of the data.

By using the Sort class you can sort the data or find items in a collection, while in the SortField class you specify the fields to be used in the sort. The data sort requires that the resulting entries be unique and enable you to specify a comparison function for sorting the output.

These data operations are very useful for changing the order of visualization of data inside Flex controls because only a few components have this feature included (see the DataGrid). Furthermore, they can also be linked to filtering operations.

In this solution you'll see how to add a method for sorting data visualized in a DataGrid.

What's involved

To perform the sorting operations on data you must use the Sort and SortField classes. The Sort class takes care of the information and the methods necessary for the sorting in ICollectionView and provides the fields property to which you send the instances of the SortField class:

```
var mySort:Sort = new Sort();
```

You can send the fields by directly declaring them in the fields property:

```
mySort.fields = [new SortField("population"), new SortField("region")]
```

You can also send fields by instancing the class and sending the instance to the property:

```
var myFieldA:SortField = new SortField("population");
var myFieldB:SortField = new SortField("region");
mySort.fields = [myFieldA, myFieldB];
```

The SortField class takes care of specifying which fields must be applied for the sorting and how it will be done. The class has the following syntax:

```
SortField(name:String = null, caseInsensitive:Boolean = false,➥
    descending:Boolean = false, numeric:Boolean = false);
```

The parameters are as follows:

- name: Contains the name of the field on which the sorting has to be applied
- caseInsensitive: Specifies whether the ordering must take uppercase or lowercase letters into account

- descending: Specifies the direction of the order
- numeric: Specifies whether the ordering is carried out on numerical fields

The only mandatory parameter of the SortField class is name; the others are all optional. It's easy to create a sort:

1. Create an instance of the Sort class: var mySort:Sort = new Sort().
2. Assign an Array of SortField object to the fields property: mySort.fields = [new SortField("population"), new SortField("region")].
3. Apply the Sort object to the ArrayCollection using its sort property: myAC.sort = mySort.
4. Perform a refresh method of ArrayCollection: myAc.refresh().

In this solution you'll extend the example created in Solution 5-3 by adding sorting functions to create a Master/Detail view.

> *Master/Detail view or page means creating two views: one to show a summary of all the information available (Master) and another to display expanded information on each of the summary details shown in the master (Detail).*

How to build it

For this solution you begin by taking the file created in Solution 5-3, Chapter_5_Flex_ Sol_4.mxml, and add a Panel right under the DataGrid containing the controls necessary to display the other information contained in the ArrayCollection.

In the file you specify two ArrayCollections: regionAC, which populates the ComboBox and contains the regions; and cityAC, which is sent to the data provider of the DataGrid and contains all the information relative to the individual cities. Here is the structure of the cityAC ArrayCollection, which takes data from an external XML file:

```
<city>
  <id>1</id>
  <region>PIEMONTE</region>
  <city>TORINO</city>
  <code>TO</code>
  <population>2236765</population>
  <male>1086745</male>
  <female>1150020</female>
  <family>886053</family>
</city>
<city>
  <id>2</id>
  <region>PIEMONTE</region>
  <city>VERCELLI</city>
```

```
        <code>VC</code>
        <population>183869</population>
        <male>88304</male>
        <female>95565</female>
        <family>75317</family>
    </city>
```

1. Open Chapter_5_Flex_Sol_4.mxml (created in Solution 5-3) and save a copy of it as Chapter_5_Flex_Sol_5.mxml.

2. Below the end of the DataGrid add a Panel, a List, and a Form container with three TextInput and two Button controls:

```
<mx:Panel title="Details View" layout="horizontal">

    <mx:List dataProvider="{cityAC}" labelField="population"
      change="addDetail(event.target.selectedItem)"
      labelFunction="formatList" width="152">
    </mx:List>

    <mx:Form width="100%">
      <mx:FormItem label="Males">
        <mx:TextInput enabled="true" id="maleTxt" editable="false"/>
      </mx:FormItem>
      <mx:FormItem label="Females">
        <mx:TextInput enabled="true" id="femaleTxt" editable="false"/>
      </mx:FormItem>
      <mx:FormItem label="Families">
        <mx:TextInput enabled="true" id="familyTxt" editable="false"/>
      </mx:FormItem>
      <mx:FormItem label="Sort by population">
        <mx:Button label="Ascending" click="sortData(true)"/>
        <mx:Button label="Descending" click="sortData(false)"/>
      </mx:FormItem>
    </mx:Form>
</mx:Panel>
```

The List control uses the ArrayCollection of the DataGrid as its data provider, but visualizes only the population data sent to the labelField property. In addition, it launches an event handler on the change event, addDetail(), to which it sends the item selected by the user:

```
<mx:List dataProvider="{cityAC}" labelField="population"
  change="addDetail(event.target.selectedItem)"
  width="152">
</mx:List>
```

In the addDetail() event handler write the data containing the number of males, females, and families for the data selected by the user on the List control in the TextInput.

In the Form container, besides the TextInput there are also two Button controls. Clicking either of them launches the sortData() event handler to which the Boolean is sent. The Boolean parameter will be used to inform the sortData() function whether to apply the sorting in ascending or descending order, depending on which Button control you clicked:

```
<mx:Button label="Ascending" click="sortData(true)"/>
<mx:Button label="Descending" click="sortData(false)"/>
```

3. Insert a `<mx:Script>` block below the Application tag and add two ActionScript functions:

```
private function addDetail(sel:Object):void
{
  maleTxt.text = sel.male;
  femaleTxt.text = sel.female;
  familyTxt.text = sel.family;
}

/*
 * The sortData function applies
 * the sort filter to the cityAC ArrayCollection
 * using the direction specified in the direction parameter
 * @param direction Boolean value
 *     specifying the direction the sorting should be applied
 *
 */
import mx.collections.Sort;
import mx.collections.SortField;

public function sortData(direction:Boolean):void
{
  // declare the sort object
  var mySort:Sort = new Sort();

  //declare and define the new sortField Object
  var mySortField:SortField = ➡
  new SortField("population", true, direction,true);

// Assign the new sort field object to the fields
// property of the Sort Object
  mySort.fields=[mySortField];

// sort the Array collection using the
// newly defined sort object
  cityAC.sort=mySort;

  // refresh the display
  cityAC.refresh();

}
```

The first addDetail() function brings as its parameter the item object created when the user makes a selection from the List component and writes the other data contained in the ArrayCollection into Detail view.

The second function, which takes care of the sorting, executes when either Button control is clicked. It accepts a Boolean as its parameter, which will be sent to the SortField class to establish whether the order should be ascending or descending.

The population field is specified in the fields property of the Sort object. Here, you also set the properties caseInsensitive to false, descending to Boolean (this is sent to the function) and numeric to true.

At the end of the function, the refresh() method of the ArrayCollection is invoked to reload the sorted data in the collection class.

4. Save and run the application.

When the application is started, the population for the various provinces becomes visualized in the List component. The ArrayCollection used by the List control is the same used by the DataGrid; in fact, the values of the latter in the population field are the same as those reported in the list.

When you select an item from the List control, more information displays in the TextInput on the right, as shown in Figure 5-9.

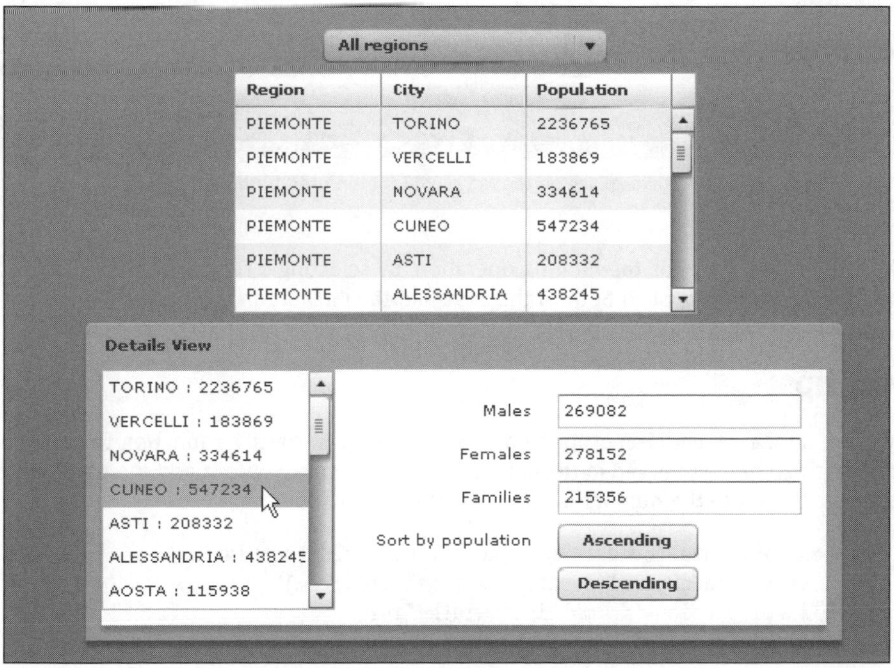

Figure 5-9. The List control contains the values of the population of the various cities. By selecting a value, the detailed information is displayed in the TextInput on the right.

By pressing one of the two Button controls that launch the sorting function, sending the value to establish the order direction, you'll see the order of the items change in the List and the DataGrid controls. The sorting function acts on the ArrayCollection that (because it is being bound by both controls) propagates the modification in visualization both on the List and on the DataGrid control, as shown in Figure 5-10.

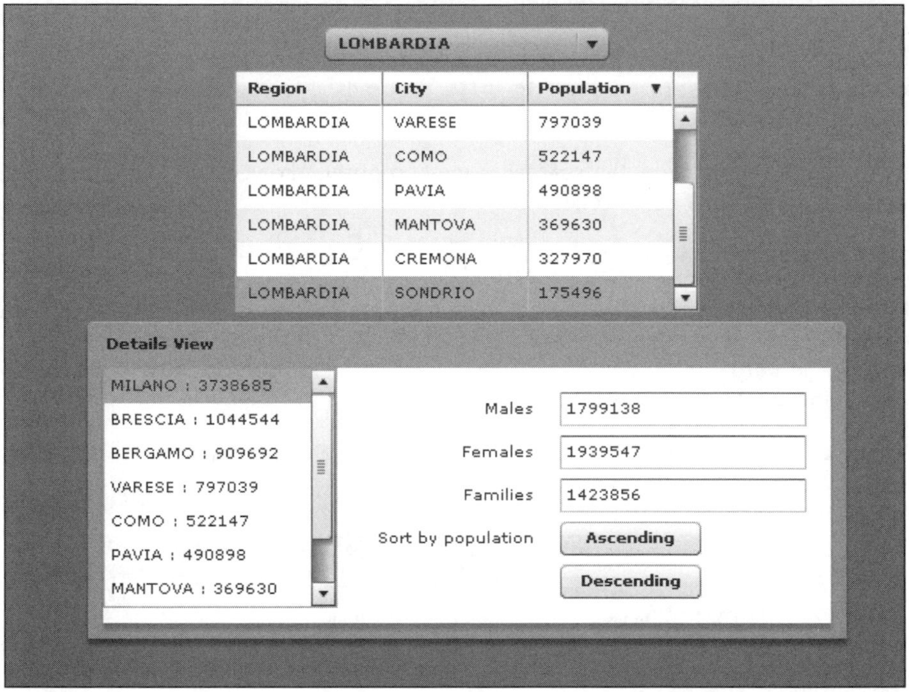

Figure 5-10. The sorting takes place on the ArrayCollection used both by the List and the DataGrid.

The story is the same for the filtering operation. By selecting a region from the ComboBox the filter function is applied both to the List and the DataGrid.

Expert tips

By using the labelFunction property of the List you can specify a function to apply formatting to an item visualized in the control. In this example, you can add the name of the relative city next to the number of the population:

```
<mx:List dataProvider="{cityAC}" labelField="population"
  change="addDetail(event.target.selectedItem)"
  labelFunction="formatList" width="152">
</mx:List>
```

The relative ActionScript function will return the formatted String to be visualized in the List:

```
private function formatList(item:Object):String
{
  return item.city + " : " + item.population
}
```

You can apply a sort to multiple fields by declaring the Sort class, creating the SortField objects and assigning them to the fields property of the Sort class.

You can, for example, carry out a sort on the population and number of men by simply modifying the relevant line of code relative to the fields property and adding an instance of the SortField class:

```
public function sortData(direction:Boolean):void
{
  var mySort:Sort = new Sort();
  var citySortField:SortField = ➡
      new SortField("city", true, direction,false);
  var populationSortField:SortField = ➡
      new SortField("population", true, direction,true);

  mySort.fields=[ populationSortField , citySortField ];
  cityAC.sort=mySort;
  cityAC.refresh();
}
```

Solution 5-6: Using cursors with the ArrayCollection

The third interface used by the collection classes is the IViewCursor. The IViewCursor objects are created by the createCursor() method of the ICollectionView class and enable you to create a cursor to navigate within the data and modify it.

> *These cursors, known in the Java world as* Iterators, *put forward the properties and methods to traverse the items in the data moving forward and backward, positioning on a precise item and adding and removing items.*

In this solution you'll see how to create a cursor to navigate within an ArrayCollection, progressing through its items.

What's involved

To create a cursor you'll use the createCursor() method of the ICollectionView interface, launching it from an ArrayCollection class:

```
myCursor = cityAC.createCursor();
```

After the cursor is created, you can use the methods that the object exposes. In the solution you'll see how to move through the collection of data using the moveNext() and movePrevious() methods:

```
myCursor.moveNext();
myCursor.movePrevious();
```

You'll also use the current, afterLast, and beforeFirst properties of the cursor object:

- current: The property that contains the current item on which the cursor is positioned
- afterLast: Returns a Boolean to determine whether the cursor object has arrived on the last item of the view
- beforeFirst: Returns a Boolean to determine whether the cursor object is at the beginning of the view

```
if (! myCursor.afterLast) {
  myCursor.moveNext();
}
```

How to build it

In this solution you'll manage the navigation of all the items that make up an ArrayCollection through the use of two Button controls. You'll create a Form container to visualize the data in the TextInput controls. You'll use a data model that reads the values from an XML file and converts it into an ArrayCollection.

The structure of the cityAC ArrayCollection is the same as the one used in Solution 5-5:

```
<city>
  <id>1</id>
  <region>PIEMONTE</region>
  <city>TORINO</city>
  <code>TO</code>
  <population>2236765</population>
  <male>1086745</male>
  <female>1150020</female>
  <family>886053</family>
</city>
```

The city node is the repeating node containing the properties that will be visualized in the Form container.

1. Create a new application MXML file by selecting New ➤ File ➤ MXML Application and give it the name Chapter_5_Flex_Sol_6.mxml.

2. Create a data model by adding the following code into your application file (it loads the data from the states.xml file in the data directory of the Flex project):

```
<mx:Model id="myCities" source="data/states.xml" />
<mx:ArrayCollection id="cityAC" source="{myCities.city}" />
```

3. Insert a `Form` container under the last bit of code with five `TextInput` controls, as shown here:

```
<mx:Form width="100%">
  <mx:FormItem label="Region">
    <mx:TextInput enabled="true" id="regionTxt" editable="false"/>
  </mx:FormItem>
  <mx:FormItem label="City">
    <mx:TextInput enabled="true" id="cityTxt" editable="false"/>
  </mx:FormItem>
  <mx:FormItem label="Males">
    <mx:TextInput enabled="true" id="maleTxt" editable="false"/>
  </mx:FormItem>
  <mx:FormItem label="Females">
    <mx:TextInput enabled="true" id="femaleTxt" editable="false"/>
  </mx:FormItem>
  <mx:FormItem label="Families">
    <mx:TextInput enabled="true" id="familyTxt" editable="false"/>
  </mx:FormItem>
</mx:Form>
```

Each `TextInput` acts as a container for the data to be visualized. Every control will contain an item from the `ArrayCollection`:

- `regionTxt.text`: Contains the region value
- `cityTxt.text`: Contains the city value
- `maleTxt.text`: Contains the number of male values
- `femaleTxt.text`: Contains the number of female values
- `familyTxt.text`: Contains the number of family values

4. Insert the following code, which will create two `Button` controls to navigate through the items in the `ArrayCollection` by using the `moveNext()` and `movePrevious()` method of the cursor object immediately below the end of the `Form` container:

```
<mx:HBox width="100%">
  <mx:Button label="Previous" click="goPrevious()"/>
  <mx:Button label="Next" click="goNext()"/>
</mx:HBox>
```

The two `Button` controls are responsible for moving forward and backward within the data. They launch two functions on the click event that use the cursor object to move (you'll see this in Step 6).

5. Create an instance of the cursor object by using the `createCursor()` method of the `ArrayCollection`. Insert the following `<mx:Script>` block; the `handleCursor()` function is invoked on the `creationComplete` event of the Application:

```
<mx:Application xmlns:mx="http://www.adobe.com/2006/mxml"➥
  layout="vertical" creationComplete="handleCursor()">
```

```
<mx:Script>
 <![CDATA[
 import mx.collections.IViewCursor;
 [Bindable]
 private var myCursor:IViewCursor;

 private function handleCursor():void
 {
   myCursor = cityAC.createCursor();
 }

 ]]>
</mx:Script>
```

The handleCursor() function creates an instance of the cursor object on the creationComplete event of the Application. To be able to instance the object, you have already imported the IViewCursor class and created a private variable data typed as IViewCursor.

6. You can now write the functions that fire when the Button controls are clicked—they use the methods discussed previously to move the cursor backward or forward. Add the following ActionScript function to the <mx:Script> block under the handleCursor() function:

```
private function goNext():void
{
  myCursor.moveNext();
  addDetail();
}

private function goPrevious():void
{
  myCursor.movePrevious();
  addDetail();
}
```

After the moveNext() and movePrevious() methods of the cursor object have executed, launch the addDetail() function. Up until now no operation has been written to display the data within the TextInput controls. This function will link the text properties of the TextInput controls to the current item on which the cursor is positioned.

7. You'll now write the addDetail() function that will use the current property of the cursor object. This property contains the current item on which the cursor is positioned. In the current property there is an object that contains the same structure of the ArrayCollection. To access the properties of this object, use the dot syntax. Add the following into the <mx:Script> block after the goPrevious() function:

```
private function addDetail():void
{
  regionTxt.text = myCursor.current.region;
```

```
    cityTxt.text = myCursor.current.city;
    maleTxt.text = myCursor.current.male;
    femaleTxt.text = myCursor.current.female;
    familyTxt.text = myCursor.current.family;
}
```

The addDetail() function is launched every time the moveNext() method or movePrevious() methods are executed. These methods change the item contained; that is, they move the position of the cursor forward or backward.

8. Save and run the application. When the application first executes, no data displays in the TextInput. If you click the Next button, you'll see the item on the first index with all its properties in the controls.

Expert tips

There are a few improvements you can make in this solution. The first is to add functionality to visualize information on the position of the cursor in the ArrayCollection. All you need to do is add some iterations of Label between the two Button controls that write the id property found in the cursor object:

```
<mx:HBox width="100%">
  <mx:Button label="Previous" click="goPrevious()"/>
  <mx:Label text="{myCursor.current.id}" id="a" />
  <mx:Label text=" / " id="s" />
  <mx:Label text="{cityAC.length}" />
  <mx:Button label="Next" click="goNext()"/>
</mx:HBox>
```

This code allows you to give the user the information relative to the position in which you are with respect to the total length of the ArrayCollection.

As mentioned before, no data is displayed in each TextInput when you first launch the application. But you should change it so that the first data item is immediately displayed upon launch.

To do this simply launch the addDetail()function on creationComplete:

```
<mx:Application xmlns:mx="http://www.adobe.com/2006/mxml"➥
  layout="vertical"
  creationComplete="handleCursor();addDetail();">
```

Try clicking the Move Next button until you arrive at the last value and then beyond; you'll notice that after the last value, the button will go ahead without displaying any more data because you have gone beyond and exceeded the length of the total items contained in the ArrayCollection. The same situation occurs when you click the Move Previous button when the cursor object is positioned on the first item.

To control these two situations, the IViewCursor interface puts forward two methods: beforeFirst and afterLast. These two methods return a Boolean that gives you the possibility of controlling situations in which you don't want to stray outside of your data set.

Now you can add the following conditions to the functions (which are invoked when the user clicks either button):

```
private function goNext():void
{
  if (!myCursor.afterLast)
  {
    myCursor.moveNext();
    addDetail();
  }
}

private function goPrevious():void
{
  if (!myCursor.beforeFirst)
  {
    myCursor.movePrevious();
    addDetail();
  }
}
```

If you get to the beginning or the end of the ArrayCollection data, the addDetail() function will no longer launch if you try to go any farther. So you'll no longer get an empty value in the TextInput controls.

Solution 5-7: Moving to the last or first item in the view with bookmarks

Bookmarks enable you to save a specific position of a cursor object—you can move a cursor to a specific location by saving that position and then recalling it later. They are extremely useful tools that enable you to create functions to work with data in a much simpler and more efficient manner.

In addition, bookmarks have the FIRST and LAST properties built in, which enable you to move the cursor to the first or last item in the view. In this solution you'll see how to add functionality by moving the cursor straight to the first and last positions of the ArrayCollection.

What's involved

Bookmarks are instances of the CursorBookmark class, which puts forward just three properties, as you can see in the LiveDocs Language Reference (http://livedocs.adobe.com/flex/2/langref/mx/collections/CursorBookmark.html):

```
CursorBookmark.CURRENT
CursorBookmark.LAST
CursorBookmark.FIRST
```

These are static variables that you can use without creating an instance of the CursorBookmark class.

> *Refer to the* CursorBookmark *class documentation (*http://livedocs.adobe.com/
> flex/2/langref/mx/collections/CursorBookmark.html) *to find the* public *properties you can use for the class.*

To create and use a bookmark you have to assign the value of the Bookmark property of the collection to a variable:

```
var myBookmark:CursorBookmark=myCursor.bookmark;
```

At this point a bookmark has been saved for that current value. To go back to that saved item in the myBookmark variable, use the seek() method of the collection:

```
myCursor.seek(myBookmark);
```

If you want to use the FIRST and LAST properties to position the cursor at the beginning or end of the collection, write the following:

```
myCursor.seek(myBookmark.FIRST);
myCursor.seek(myBookmark.LAST);
```

All three properties are static properties, so you don't have to import the CursorBookmark class and create an instance of it to use the properties. You can write this:

```
myCursor.seek(CursorBookmark.FIRST);
myCursor.seek(CursorBookmark.LAST);
```

How to build it

For this solution you'll take the example created in the preceding solution and add two Button controls and two ActionScript functions to it.

1. Begin by opening the Chapter_5_Flex_Sol_6.mxml and saving a copy of it under the name Chapter_5_Flex_Sol_7.mxml.

2. Below the Application tag, add the two Button controls as follows:

```
<mx:HBox>
  <mx:Button label="Move First" click="moveFirst()" />
  <mx:Button label="Move Previous" click="goPrev()" />
  <mx:Label text="{myCursor.current.id}" id="a" />
  <mx:Label text=" / " id="s" />
  <mx:Label text="{myAC.length}" />
```

```
<mx:Button label="Move Next" click="goNext()" />
<mx:Button label="Move Last" click="moveLast()"/>
</mx:HBox>
```

As you can see, the Button controls launch two functions upon being clicked, so you have to manage these event handlers.

3. Write the following ActionScript code into the `<mx:Script>` block defined above the HBox container:

```
private function moveLast():void
{
  myCursor.seek(CursorBookmark.LAST);
  addDetail();
}

private function moveFirst():void
{
  myCursor.seek(CursorBookmark.FIRST);
  addDetail();
}
```

These two functions do nothing more than use the static FIRST and LAST properties to move the cursor, so the items displayed in the TextInput controls at the beginning or end of the ArrayCollection.

4. Save and run the application. You'll see the two buttons you just added; ensure that they work as expected.

Expert tips

The bookmarks can also be saved and then loaded afterward. By linking the current position of the cursor to a bookmark, its position becomes saved and can be recalled through the seek() method. Let's see how to implement this functionality.

Add the following HBox container under the first HBox container you added previously:

```
<mx:HBox>
<mx:List height="98" id="myList" dataProvider="{bookmarkAC}"➥
labelField="label"></mx:List>
  <mx:Button label="Add Bookmark" click="addBookmark()"/>
  <mx:Button label="Load Bookmark" click="gotoBookmark()"/>
</mx:HBox>
```

The HBox container has a List component that becomes linked to an ArrayCollection called bookmarkAC and two buttons that perform the saving and loading operations of the bookmark.

The ActionScript functions associated to the click event take care of adding the bookmarks into the ArrayCollection, visualizing them in the List control, and positioning the cursor object on the position saved by the bookmark:

```
    private var bookmarkAC:ArrayCollection = new ArrayCollection();

    private function addBookmark():void
    {
      var myBookmark:CursorBookmark=myCursor.bookmark;
    bookmarkAC.addItem({label:'ID ' + myCursor.current.id + ➥
      ' bookmarked',data:myBookmark});
    }

    private function gotoBookmark():void
    {
      myCursor.seek(myList.selectedItem.data as CursorBookmark);
      addDetail();
    }
```

In this code an empty ArrayCollection class is created. The addBookmark() class then inserts the current position of the cursor object (saved in a CursorBookmark object), adding it as an element to the empty ArrayCollection with the addItem() method:

```
    bookmarkAC.addItem({label:'ID ' + myCursor.current.id +➥
      ' bookmarked',data:myBookmark});
```

The gotoBookmark() function, on the other hand, uses the seek() method of the cursor object to position itself on the position of the saved cursor. The seek() function accepts a CursorBookmark object as a parameter. You passed the selectedItem property of the List object to the seek() method. The selectedItem property contains a String, whereas the seek() method accepts a CursorBookmark object. So you need to cast the selectedItem property as a CursorBookmark type:

```
    myCursor.seek(myList.selectedItem.data as CursorBookmark);
```

Finally, you launch the addDetail() method to change the values in the TextInput, which are linked to the current position of the cursor.

Solution 5-8: Adding and removing data with the cursor

The IViewCursor interface also enables you to use methods to change data in the view. It provides two methods, insert() and remove(), which respectively insert an item before the current cursor location and remove an item at the current cursor location.

With these two methods you can modify, update, remove, and add data to the base data set. In this solution you'll see how to add and remove items in the collection class—you'll insert two Button controls to the example that add the insert() and remove() functionality to the application.

What's involved

The two insert() and remove() methods make up part of the IViewCursor interface, which means that they make up part of the cursor object:

```
myCursor.insert(item);
myCursor.remove();
```

These methods can be used together with the moveNext() and movePrevious() methods to move the location of the cursor object and decide which one should be modified. They can also be used with the methods find(), findAny(), findFirst(), and findLast() to move the cursor to an item that matches the parameters:

```
myCursor.findFirst({id:1});
```

In this case the cursor will be moved to find the first object containing the id 1 property. To use the find() method, a sort is needed on the ICollectionView.

How to build it

1. Open the Chapter_5_Flex_Sol_6.mxml file and save a copy of it with the name Chapter_5_Flex_Sol_8.mxml.

2. Add two Button controls under the Application tag:

```
<mx:Button label="Insert New Item" click="insertItem()"/>
<mx:Button label="Remove Item" click="myCursor.remove()"/>
```

The first Button looks after the execution of the event handler insertItem(), which will add an item to the collection, whereas the second Button executes the remove() method on the cursor object to remove the item at the current location of the cursor.

3. Add the following ActionScript function to the <mx:Script> block. This takes care of inserting a new item in the collection:

```
<mx:Script>
<![CDATA[
private function  insertItem():void
{
  myCursor.insert({id:myCursor.current.id-1,
  id_region:1,
  region:regionTxt.text,
  city:cityTxt.text,
  code:cityTxt.text.toUpperCase(),
  population:Number(maleTxt.text)+ ➡
  Number(femaleTxt.text)+ ➡
  Number(familyTxt.text),➡
  male:maleTxt.text,female:femaleTxt.text, ➡
  family:Number(maleTxt.text)+Number(femaleTxt.text)});
}
]]>
</mx:Script>
```

The insert() method of the IViewCursor interface enables you to add an item before the current cursor location. The structure of the cursor object created with the createCursor() method of the ArrayCollection (myCursor = cityAC.createCursor();) is as follows:

```
[{id:1,id:region:1,region:"PIEMONTE",city:"TORINO",code:"TO", ➥
population:1200000,male:55000,female:50000,family:10000}, ➥
{etc. etc.}]
```

To look at it another way, the insert() method adds an object whose properties are taken from the TextInput controls in the Form container of the application:

```xml
<mx:Form width="100%">
  <mx:FormItem label="Region">
    <mx:TextInput enabled="true" id="regionTxt" editable="true"/>
  </mx:FormItem>
  <mx:FormItem label="City">
    <mx:TextInput enabled="true" id="cityTxt" editable="true"/>
  </mx:FormItem>
  <mx:FormItem label="Males">
    <mx:TextInput enabled="true" id="maleTxt" editable="true"/>
  </mx:FormItem>
  <mx:FormItem label="Females">
    <mx:TextInput enabled="true" id="femaleTxt" editable="true"/>
  </mx:FormItem>
  <mx:FormItem label="Families">
    <mx:TextInput enabled="true" id="familyTxt" editable="true"/>
  </mx:FormItem>
</mx:Form>
```

4. Save and run the application. The new functionality should be added as expected, but you should test the new buttons to ensure they work.

By modifying the TextInput control and clicking the button with the Insert New Item label, you'll add an item with those values to the collection.

If you click the Remove Item button instead, you'll delete the item on which the cursor is currently located.

Expert tips

The application currently inserts an item before the current cursor location. If you want to substitute an item with the new data inserted in the form and simulate an update, you can cancel the item at that cursor and then insert the new values with code:

```
myCursor.remove();
myCursor.insert({id:myCursor.current.id-1,
id_region:1,
region:regionTxt.text,
city:cityTxt.text,
```

```
code:cityTxt.text.toUpperCase(),
population:Number(maleTxt.text)+Number(femaleTxt.text)+➡
  Number(familyTxt.text), male:maleTxt.text,female:femaleTxt.text,
family:Number(maleTxt.text)+Number(femaleTxt.text)});
```

If you want to insert the new item at the end of the collection, you have to position the cursor at the end of the collection with the LAST property of the CursorBookmark class and then carry out the insert():

```
myCursor.seek(CursorBookmark.LAST, 1);
myCursor.insert({id:myCursor.current.id-1,
id_region:1,
region:regionTxt.text,
city:cityTxt.text,
code:cityTxt.text.toUpperCase(),
population:Number(maleTxt.text)+Number(femaleTxt.text)+➡
  Number(familyTxt.text), male:maleTxt.text,female:femaleTxt.text,
family:Number(maleTxt.text)+Number(femaleTxt.text)});
```

Summary

Some of the best features of Flex are collection classes, which provide very powerful methods for accessing and managing complex data. Flex has two collection classes, ArrayCollection and the XMLListCollection, which are usually used as data providers for list-based controls.

In this chapter you learned how to create and use collection classes in list-based controls. You used techniques to convert a data model into an ArrayCollection class.

The collection classes provide methods to easily work with data to enable you to complete the get, set, add, and remove operations of an item in the collection.

You used methods to filter and sort data, and you created cursors to navigate through the collection.

6 WORKING WITH REMOTE DATA USING THE RPC CLASSES

☑ Enable strict type checking
☑ Enable warnings

Additional compiler arguments:

-locale en_US -use-network=false

─ HTML wrapper
☑ Generate HTML wrapper file
☑ Detect Flash Player version: 9 . 0
　　☑ Use Express Install
☑ Enable history management (browser Back bu

Region	City
PIEMONTE	TORINO
PIEMONTE	VERCELLI
PIEMONTE	NOVARA
PIEMONTE	CUNEO
PIEMONTE	ASTI
PIEMONTE	ALESSANDRIA

Show Liguria Population

⬅ New Flex Project

Create a Flex project

Specify how you want your application to acces

How will your Flex application access data?
○ Basic (e.g. XML or web service from PHP/JSP
○ ColdFusion Flash Remoting Service
○ Flex Data Services
　　◉ Compile application locally in Flex Builder
　　○ Compile application on the server when

Up to this point in the book, you have familiarized yourself with the basic methods of Flex: you learned how to use some of the elements that allow you to define the user interface of an application, how to load external data using data models, and how to convert these data models into collection classes.

The next logical topic for discussion is **remote data sources**. Flex takes care of the presentation part of the application, but it does not have native access to any databases. Remote data sources allow you to take advantage of the RPC classes to perform calls to business logic built using ColdFusion, Java, or any other server-side technology to send and receive remote data. RPC, which stands for **remote procedure call**, allows you to execute a subroutine or procedure either locally or on another computer without having to code specific procedures for the remote interaction. (For more details on RPC, check out the Wikipedia article at http://en.wikipedia.org/wiki/Remote_procedure_call.)

In Flex, the RPC services provide a call-and-response model to access remote data and expose the components based on service-oriented architecture (SOA). There are three RPC classes in Flex: the HTTPService class, the WebService class (compliant with Simple Object Access Protocol, or SOAP), and the RemoteObject class.

The HTTPService class allows you to carry out HTTP requests in GET or POST to specific URLs, as well as to use both the HTTP and the HTTPS protocols to call XML data in a static and dynamic manner. Static XML is physically placed on the server, while dynamic XML is generated by a server-side language. In this chapter, you will learn to use both types of XML.

The url property of the HTTPService class specifies an address for the call:

```
<mx:HTTPService id="myHS"
  url="http://www.mydomain.com/myFile.php"
 result="resultHandler(event)"
 fault="faultHandler(event)"
 showBusyCursor="true"
 method="GET">
```

The call, carried out using the send() method, will return the data received in the result event in the result property of the ResultEvent class or in the lastResult property of the object.

The WebService class allows you to access web services, or to be more precise, software modules that set remote operations. Web services are a W3C specification—see www.w3.org/2002/ws/ for more information.

A Flex application can interact with a web service if its interface is defined using Web Services Description Language (WSDL version 1.1) and if the requests and the results are formatted as SOAP messages:

```
<mx:WebService
wsdl="http://www.myDomain.com/myWS.cfc?wsdl"
useProxy="false"
id="myWS"
showBusyCursor="true"
fault="faultHandler(event)" >
```

240

```
<mx:operation
name="getDataByCognome"
result="getbyNameresult(event)">
<mx:request xmlns="">
<strSurname>{nameTxt.text}</strSurname>
</mx:request>
</mx:operation>
</mx:WebService>
```

The W3C web services definition can encompass many different systems, but in common usage the term refers to clients and servers that communicate using XML messages that follow the SOAP standard. However, there are alternatives to the SOAP standard that unfortunately are not supported by the Flex WebService tag:

- JSON-RPC
- XINS
- GXA
- Hessian
- REST
- XML-RPC
- BEEP

The RemoteObject class allows access to public methods of remote classes. To use the RemoteObject component, you have to install Flex Data Services or Macromedia ColdFusion MX 7.0.2 with the Remoting Update.

The RemoteObject uses a binary format to transfer data between the client and the server, Action Message Format (AMF), the latest version being AMF3. This is a native format used by the Flash Player. You'll see how to deal with the AMF3 format in Solution 6-9.

All the calls that Flex performs with the RPC are asynchronous requests. This means that after having launched one or more remote calls, the data that is returned from the request does not respect any order, and the response time (the interval between user request and server response) could cause problems in the application, in terms of both usability and functionality.

Your job as developer, therefore, is to carefully check the status of every single remote request and make the application respond accordingly.

Solution 6-1: Using the HTTPService class

The HTTPService class is used in MXML with the HTTPService tag, while in ActionScript it is used by creating an instance of the aforementioned class. When an HTTPService object is declared, no request is made. You have to use the send() method of the RPC object to launch the call to the specified URL.

Once the call to the remote object has been performed, the response data is returned to the lastResult property of the HTTPService service or managed with an event handler on the event result. To visualize the returned data on the request, you use a list-based control.

In this solution, you will see how to load remote data from an XML file on another domain. Remember that the Flash Player security sandbox does not permit an application to receive data from a domain other than the one in which the SWF is located. For this reason, if you want to make your application function and return the data, you must put the crossdomain.xml file on the web server. This procedure is illustrated in the "Expert tips" section of this solution.

What's involved

The HTTPService class makes up part of the RPC classes of Flex. These classes are found in the mx.rpc package, and the HTTPService service is located in the mx.rpc.http. HTTPService package. You can declare an HTTPService object in MXML using the <mx:HTTPService> tag or using ActionScript. The creation of the object does not cause the dispatch of an HTTP call to the remote server until the send() method is executed.

```
<mx:HTTPService id="myHS" method="POST"
  url="http://localhost/states.xml"  />
```

Depending on the moment in which you want to launch the call, the send() method can be associated with a system or a user event. First, here's how you call the send() method on a system event:

```
<mx:Application xmlns:mx="http://www.adobe.com/2006/mxml"
  layout="absolute"
  creationComplete="myHS.send()">
```

And here's how you call the send() method on a user event:

```
<mx:Button label="Send HTTP"
  click="myHS.send()"
  x="132" y="10"/>
```

The url property of the HTTPService object can also contain a path relative to the position of the SWF file (or MXML in authoring time):

```
<mx:HTTPService id="myHS" method="POST"
url="data/states.xml"  />
```

After having carried out the HTTP request, the response data is returned to the lastResult property, which contains the entire object returned by the web server. At this point, you can decide to use this property in data binding on a list-based control such as a DataGrid or convert the result into an ArrayCollection.

In this solution, you will carry out your first HTTP call with the HTTPService service and display the results in a DataGrid.

How to build it

Begin by creating a new Flex project from Flex Builder that you will use during the course of this chapter:

1. Open Flex Builder and create a Flex project with the name Chapter_6_Flex_RPC.

2. Create a new MXML application file by selecting File ➤ New ➤ MXML Application and name it Chapter_6_Flex_Sol_1.mxml.

3. Your application will carry out an HTTP call to the external XML file, sending it a relative path (subsequently, you will also use an absolute reference), and will display the response data in a DataGrid. To start, declare the HTTPService service in your file using an MXML tag. Add this now below the Application tag:

```
<mx:HTTPService id="myHS" url="data/states.xml" />
```

The service will execute the call to the states.xml file, which is found in the data folder (or you can create it on your own by selecting File ➤ New ➤ File). In the deployment phase of this project, you will give your attention to carrying out the upload of this folder and its contents, ensuring the path is persisted. The structure of the states.xml file is as follows:

```xml
<?xml version="1.0" encoding="UTF-8"?>
<dataroot>
  <city>
    <id>1</id>
    <id_region>1</id_region>
    <region>PIEMONTE</region>
    <cityName>TORINO</cityName>
    <code>TO</code>
    <population>2236765</population>
    <male>1086745</male>
    <female>1150020</female>
    <family>886053</family>
  </city>
  <city>
    <id>2</id>
    <id_region>1</id_region>
    <region>PIEMONTE</region>
    <cityName>VERCELLI</cityName>
    <code>VC</code>
    <population>183869</population>
    <male>88304</male>
    <female>95565</female>
    <family>75317</family>
  </city>
</dataroot>
```

The repeating node you will aim at is the tag <city>, while the root tag is <dataroot>.

4. Define the graphical user interface (GUI) of the application by inserting a DataGrid control after the closure of the HTTPService tag as follows:

```
<mx:DataGrid id="myDG"
  dataProvider="{myHS.lastResult.dataroot.city}" x="92" y="49">
  <mx:columns>
    <mx:DataGridColumn headerText="Region" dataField="region" />
    <mx:DataGridColumn headerText="City" dataField="cityName" />
    <mx:DataGridColumn headerText="Population"
      dataField="population" />
  </mx:columns>
</mx:DataGrid>
```

The dataProvider of the list-based control becomes linked to the lastResult property, which contains the exact structure of the XML file returned by the remote call.

Unlike the MXML data models in which you directly access the repeating node without passing the root tag, in the lastResult property the whole XML structure, including the root tag, is returned. If you try to run the application now, no data will be displayed in the DataGrid. This is because, as mentioned previously, the HTTP service does not become executed until the send() method is launched.

5. Launch the send() method on the creationComplete event of the application, which then invokes the remote call by adding the following to the Application tag:

```
<mx:Application xmlns:mx="http://www.adobe.com/2006/mxml"
  layout="absolute"
  creationComplete="myHS.send()">
```

At this point, you can run the application and see the values returned as a result of the call printed in the DataGrid, but before running the application, you need to convert the response data into an ArrayCollection. Recapping briefly the advantages of using the collection classes of which ArrayCollection is a part: The first major advantage is having the data contained in an object that automatically notifies all the controls to which it is bound. If, for example, your ArrayCollection is updated, you do not need to worry about having to update the data providers of the list-based controls, as the process takes place automatically. Aside from this feature, the collection classes provide methods to complete operations on data such as edit, add, remove, and update, in a simple and effective manner.

To convert the response data in the lastResult property of the HTTPService into an ArrayCollection, you must associate this cast to an event. If you try to write the ArrayCollection as follows:

```
<mx:ArrayCollection id="myAC" ➥
source="{myHS.lastResult.dataroot.city}" />
```

you will not obtain any values written in the collection. This is because the remote service has not yet carried out the call, and so has not yet obtained the response data when the ArrayCollection is initialized. For your ArrayCollection to become initialized, you must make sure that the remote call has returned the value.

6. To ensure the HTTPService object dispatches the result event at the moment the remote call has been successfully completed and the values have been returned, add the following Script block:

```
<mx:Script>
  <![CDATA[
    import mx.collections.ArrayCollection;
    [Bindable]
    private var myAC:ArrayCollection;
  ]]>
</mx:Script>

<mx:HTTPService id="myHS" url="data/states.xml"
    result="myAC = myHS.lastResult.dataroot.city as ArrayCollection" />
```

In the Script block, you simply declare a private variable typed as ArrayCollection. The Flex Builder automatically writes the necessary code for importing the collection class. The variable is declared as Bindable, in that it will subsequently be used in data binding on the DataGrid control.

In the HTTPService tag, you instead set the ArrayCollection at the moment when you are sure the values have been returned by the call. You write the ActionScript code at the trigger of the event result:

```
result="myAC = myHS.lastResult.dataroot.city as ArrayCollection"
```

Note that in the code you carry out a casting to transform the data contained in the lastResult property into an ArrayCollection. In programming, a **type casting**, also called **type conversion**, refers to changing an entity of one data type into another.

7. Now you only need to change the dataProvider of the DataGrid and create a data binding with the ArrayCollection. To do so, add the following:

```
<mx:DataGrid id="myDG"
  dataProvider="{myAC}" x="92" y="49">
```

8. Save and run the application—you should see the finished result of the solution, as shown in Figure 6-1.

Region	City	Population
PIEMONTE	TORINO	2236765
PIEMONTE	VERCELLI	183869
PIEMONTE	NOVARA	334614
PIEMONTE	CUNEO	547234
PIEMONTE	ASTI	208332
PIEMONTE	ALESSANDRIA	438245

Figure 6-1. The HTTP call is executed on the creationComplete event of the application.

Expert tips

In this solution, you have begun to work with the HTTPService object. There is still much to explore with this service. The HTTPService service, as with all the RPC classes, is very powerful and provides many properties.

For example, when you launch the call with the send() method of the service, the user receives no feedback or visual message. This is, of course, a bad practice in the development of the application. The calls are asynchronous and therefore invisible to the end user, but the downside is that no response will be given to let him know the application is working unless you explicitly add some kind of feedback mechanism.

In the Solution 6-2, you will learn how to manage this information with the event handlers on the fault event, but for now, you can employ a very useful property of HTTPService, showBusyCursor, to give a visual clue to the user to indicate that the remote call is waiting for a response. This changes the cursor of the mouse into an animated egg timer for the whole duration of the call, until the response data is returned.

To manage this property, it is enough to specify it in the HTTPService tag and set it as true:

```
<mx:HTTPService id="myHS" url="data/states.xml"
  result="myAC = myHS.lastResult.dataroot.city as ArrayCollection"
  showBusyCursor="true"/>
```

In your solution, you have sent a relative path that points to an XML file (the url of the HTTPService). If you now run the application, the data may not be displayed because you are referring to local files rather than files on a network. To resolve the problem, you must insert an additional parameter to the compiler. Go to Project ➤ Properties ➤ Flex Compiler and insert the following parameter in the Additional compiler arguments text field: -use-network=false. The Properties dialog box should now look like Figure 6-2.

At this point, run the application, and it will load all of the data in your DataGrid.

Solution 6-2: Handling result and fault events

The HTTPService class dispatches two events that allow the developer to check the reception of data against the calls made and to manage the errors that can happen during the HTTP request. As calls made by Flex are asynchronous, it becomes even more important to ensure an operation has been successfully completed and particularly that no errors have occurred before carrying out additional operations.

In many fields of programming, such an operation is carried out through complex procedures; in Flex you simply make use of two attributes of the HTTPservice class: result and fault.

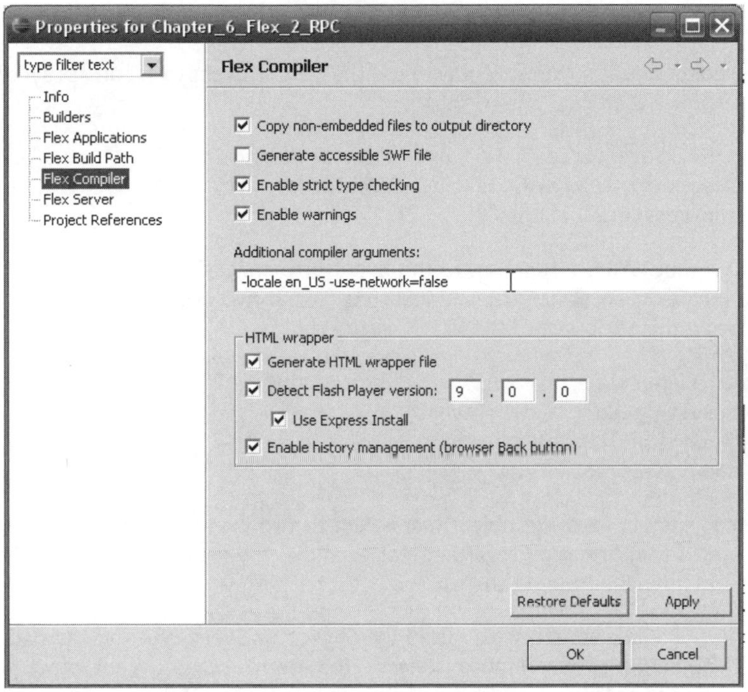

Figure 6-2. Add parameters to the compiler using this dialog box.

These two attributes are events that can be linked to event handlers. In the preceding solution, you used the `result` event to populate a variable of `ArrayCollection` type with the response data. Although convenient, this approach does not permit you to carry out different operations on the data (for example, validation or formatting checks on received data) before a data binding is created on some controls.

If something in the remote call goes wrong, the Flash Player displays an error message. This is not a good scenario for a well-developed application.

By instead linking an event handler to the `fault` event, you can give appropriate feedback messages to the users of the application to show them the error that has occurred and to make them understand the reason the remote connection has not been successfully completed.

In this solution, you will see how to create event handlers to manage the `result` and `fault` events on an `HTTPService` remote call.

What's involved

In the preceding solution, you saw how to use the result event to set an ArrayCollection with the response data:

```
<mx:HTTPService id="myHS" url="data/states.xml"
  result="myAC = myHS.lastResult.dataroot.city as ArrayCollection"
  showBusyCursor="true"/>
```

But you have not linked a function to this event or managed the occurrence of possible errors. To create an event handler and associate it with two events, it is sufficient to send it as a value to the attributes of the HTTPService class:

```
<mx:HTTPService id="myHS" url="data/states.xml"
  result="resultHandler(event)"
  fault="faultHandler(event)"
  showBusyCursor="true"/>
```

Both events generate an event object that is sent to two event handlers. The event object contains precious information regarding, for example, the values returned or the type of error that has happened during the call.

Although in preceding solutions you used the Object or Event types as the data type for the event object, for the remote services the event objects generated have type ResultEvent and FaultEvent. These two classes indicate an RPC operation that has successfully returned a result (ResultEvent) or has a fault (FaultEvent). The event objects generated by these classes contain the information about the remote procedure call (HTTPService) other than the standard target and type properties.

To handle this data, two classes must be imported with the mx.rpc.events.* package at the beginning of your ActionScript code:

```
<mx:Script>
  <![CDATA[
    import mx.rpc.events.*;

    private function resultHandler(evt:ResultEvent):void
    {

    }

    private function faultHandler(evt:FaultEvent):void
    {

    }

  ]]>
</mx:Script>
```

Flex Builder will help you in importing and data typing the event classes you need to handle, showing you the code hints that appear in Figure 6-3.

```
<mx:Script>
    <![CDATA[
        import mx.collections.ArrayCollection;
        import mx.rpc.events.*;

        [Bindable]
        private var myAC:ArrayCollection;

        private function resultHandler(evt:ResultEvent):void
        {

        }

        private function faultHandler(evt:faultE
                                    ⊕ FaultEvent

    ]]>
</mx:Script>

    <mx:HTTPService id="myHS" url="data/st
        result="myAC = myHS.lastResult.da
        showBusyCursor="true"/>
```

Figure 6-3. Flex Builder code hints suggest you write the data type for the event object and the import statement.

Now, in the two event handlers you can complete the operations necessary to better manage the HTTP call. You will use the event object generated from the class to set the ArrayCollection with the response data. In case any errors occur, the fault event will show a message in a TextArea control.

The event object generated by the result event contains the result property of the data returned from the data connection:

```
private function resultHandler(evt:ResultEvent):void
{
    myAC = evt.result.dataroot.city;
}
```

Therefore, you can use this property instead of lastResult (this was a property of the HTTPService):

```
<mx:HTTPService id="myHS" url="data/states.xml"
    result="myAC = myHS.lastResult.dataroot.city as ArrayCollection"
    showBusyCursor="true"/>
```

Error handling is a very simple operation using the HTTPService tag, because it's handled by the fault properties of that class:

```
<mx:HTTPService id="myHS" url="data/states.xml"
    result="resultHandler(event)"
    fault="faultHandler(event)"
    showBusyCursor="true"/>
```

Now you need to write the fault event handler and use the event object generated by the fault event:

```
private function faultHandler(evt:FaultEvent):void
{
var errors:String = "Some errors occurred \n";
errors += "\n Fault Code is :  \n" + evt.fault.faultCode;
errors += "\n Fault Detail is : \n" + evt.fault.faultDetail;
errors += "\n Fault String is : \n" + evt.fault.faultString;
mx.controls.Alert.show(errors);
}
```

The event object of the fault event instead contains the fault property, which in turn allows you to retrieve the code of the error that has occurred, the details, and the string in the following properties:

- fault.faultCode: Describes the fault with a code number
- fault.faultDetail: Contains the details of the error
- fault.faultString: Contains the text description of the error
- fault.name: Contains the name of the Error object
- fault.message: Contains the message of the Error object
- fault.errorID: Contains the number associated with the error message

In this solution, you will see how to manage the event handlers for the result and fault events of an HTTPService.

How to build it

You will begin with the file from Solution 6-1 and modify the management of the result and fault events. You will also add a TextArea, which will contain information relative to the errors that have occurred during the remote call.

1. Open the file Chapter_6_Flex_Sol_1.mxml from your Flex project and save a copy of it with the name Chapter_6_Flex_Sol_2.mxml.

2. Modify the HTTPService tag by linking two functions to the result and fault events by passing the event objects to the events:

```
<mx:HTTPService id="myHS" url="data/states.xml"
  result="resultHandler(event)"
  fault="faultHandler(event)"
  showBusyCursor="true"/>
```

To the event handlers called by the result and fault events a parameter is passed: event. This parameter passes an event object to the event listener. The word event is not a reserved word, but it's a common convention used by developers.

3. Add a VDividedBox to manage the presence of a DataGrid and a TextArea aligned vertically as follows:

```
<mx:VDividedBox x="10" y="10" width="345" height="100%">
  <mx:DataGrid id="myDG"
    dataProvider="{myAC}" width="344">
    <mx:columns>
      <mx:DataGridColumn headerText="Region" dataField="region" />
      <mx:DataGridColumn headerText="City" dataField="cityName" />
      <mx:DataGridColumn headerText="Population" dataField=
        "population" />
    </mx:columns>
  </mx:DataGrid>
  <mx:TextArea width="345" id="errorTxt" height="166"/>
</mx:VDividedBox>
```

The data provider of the DataGrid is bound to an ArrayCollection variable, which for now is empty, but you will set it in the resultHandler() function linked to the result event. The TextArea will contain a String with the error messages that have occurred, using the properties contained in the event object of the faultHandler function.

4. In the Script block, you will now write the two event handlers. As you now know, the event objects generated by the remote service have ResultEvent and FaultEvent as data types. These two classes must therefore be imported with the mx.rpc.events.* package. To do so, add the following code below the Application tag:

```
<mx:Application xmlns:mx-"http://www.adobe.com/2006/mxml"
layout="absolute" >

<mx:Script>
  <![CDATA[
    import mx.collections.ArrayCollection;
    import mx.rpc.events.*;

    [Bindable]
    private var myAC:ArrayCollection;

    private function resultHandler(evt:ResultEvent):void
    {
    }
    private function faultHandler(evt:FaultEvent):void
    {
    }
  ]]>
</mx:Script>
```

The parameter that accepts the two functions is the corresponding event object, which for the resultHandler is ResultEvent and for the faultHandler is FaultEvent. You now write the code in these two event handlers.

6

5. The function of the resultHandler sets the ArrayCollection used as the data provider for the DataGrid. You will use the result property contained in the event object, which contains the structure of the data returned from the data connection. Add the following code to the resultHandler:

```
private function resultHandler(evt:ResultEvent):void
{
  myAC = evt.result.dataroot.city;
  errorTxt.text = "No errors found";
}
```

You also print a text message in the TextArea with an id equal to errorTxt to communicate to the user that errors have not occurred. The fault event handler you'll create in the next step will handle any errors that might occur with the HTTP call.

6. In the faultHandler event handler, use the fault property of the event object to print the error messages that have occurred. In particular, you write the code of the error that has occurred in the TextArea (evt.fault.faultCode), the details of the error (evt.fault.faultDetail), and the string (evt.fault.faultString). Add the following code to the faultHandler:

```
private function faultHandler(evt:FaultEvent):void
{
  var errors:String = "Some errors occurred \n";
  errors += "\n Fault Code is :  \n" + evt.fault.faultCode;
  errors += "\n Fault Detail is : \n" + evt.fault.faultDetail;
  errors += "\n Fault String is : \n" + evt.fault.faultString;

  errorTxt.text = errors;
}
```

You populate a temporary variable with strings and send it to the text property of the TextArea. You can now save and run the file. To be able to check the functioning of the event handler, you must force an error in the call. It will be enough to try calling an XML file that does not exist or aim at a nonexistent domain.

7. Save the file and run the application. If no error occurs during the remote call to the XML file, you will see the data loaded in the DataGrid control as shown in Figure 6-4. If instead you force an error, the error messages will be displayed in the TextArea, as shown in Figure 6-5.

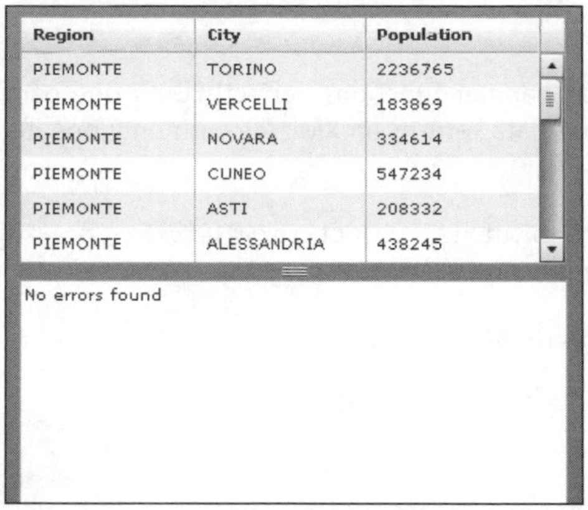

Region	City	Population	
PIEMONTE	TORINO	2236765	▲
PIEMONTE	VERCELLI	183869	▤
PIEMONTE	NOVARA	334614	
PIEMONTE	CUNEO	547234	
PIEMONTE	ASTI	208332	
PIEMONTE	ALESSANDRIA	438245	▼

No errors found

Figure 6-4. The response data is added to the DataGrid control.

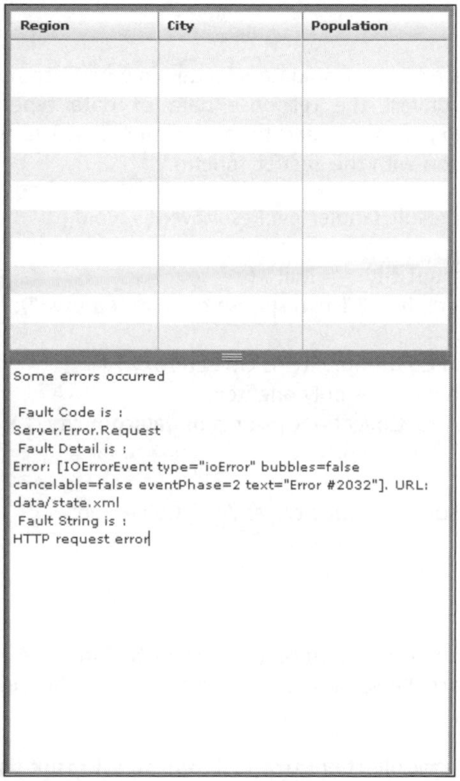

Region	City	Population

Some errors occurred

 Fault Code is :
Server.Error.Request
 Fault Detail is :
Error: [IOErrorEvent type="ioError" bubbles=false
cancelable=false eventPhase=2 text="Error #2032"]. URL:
data/state.xml
 Fault String is :
HTTP request error

Figure 6-5. The error messages are shown in the TextArea control.

Expert tips

The code in the result handler functions perfectly until one particular case occurs. For example, if the response data returns an XML file with only one item, an error is received as follows:

```
cannot convert mx.utils::ObjectProxy@36fbf81 to
mx.collections.ArrayCollection
```

This is the sample response XML data:

```
<dataroot>
  <city>
  <id>22</id>
  <region>TRENTINOALTOADIGE</region>
  <city>TRENTO</city>
  <population>449852</population>
  </city>
</dataroot>
```

The final result of this error is that no data is loaded in your DataGrid. This occurs because Flex is not able to convert the response data of data type ObjectProxy into an ArrayCollection, which instead expects to receive an Array. The solution to this problem is to manage this situation with the result function:

```
private function resultHandler(evt:ResultEvent ) :void {

if(evt.result.dataroot.city  == null ) {
  mx.controls.Alert.show("The response data are empty !");
  }
  else if ( evt.result.dataroot.city  is ObjectProxy ) {
  // the response date has only one item
  myAC =  new ArrayCollection( [evt.result.dataroot.city  ] );
  }
  else {
  myAC = evt.result.dataroot.city   as ArrayCollection;

  }
}
```

You can also use the ArrayUtil.toArray() method to force the type conversion. In this case, you need to import the mx.utils.ArrayUtil class at the beginning of your Script block:

```
myAC  = new ArrayCollection(ArrayUtil.toArray(evt.result.dataroot.city));
```

In this way, you make your code more robust and you guarantee the correct functioning of the application even in situations in which the response data is null (and therefore nothing is returned) or in the case in which there is only one node in the XML.

Solution 6-3: Loading dynamically generated XML using PHP and ActionScript

In the preceding solution, you carried out a call to an HTTPService that aims at a static local XML file.

But the HTTPService can also recall XML data dynamically generated by middleware. Suppose you carried out an HTTP call that implements a file written in a server-side language (such as PHP, ColdFusion, JSP, or Ruby on Rails) that performs operations on a database. It runs the queries and is ready to return the data to the application that has made the request.

The HTTPService is capable of receiving the response data in XML format. In this solution, you will see how to call some XML data generated by a PHP file.

What's involved

For the HTTPService class, very little changes if the call is changed so that it targets a remote file, compared to a local file as in the last solution. What is important is that the response data is in XML format. From the point of view of the code, therefore, you will always have your declaration of the class with the properties necessary to render the call valid:

```
<mx:HTTPService id="myHS"
    url="http://www.comtaste.com/xmloutput/index_xml.php"
    showBusyCursor="true"/>
```

This time you have inserted a URI that aims at a PHP file in the url property.

To differentiate this exercise from the preceding one, you will use ActionScript to declare and manage the HTTPService. In ActionScript, to be able to create an instance of the HTTPService object, you must first import its package and those relative to the ResultEvent and FaultEvent classes for the management of the result and fault methods:

```
import mx.rpc.http.HTTPService;
import mx.rpc.events.ResultEvent;
import mx.rpc.events.FaultEvent;
```

At this point, you can create an instance of the HTTPService class and set the url property to which you send the URI of the remote service and execute the send() method to launch the service:

```
myHTTP = new HTTPService();
myHTTP.url = "http://www.comtaste.com/xmloutput/index_xml.php";
myHTTP.send();
```

With ActionScript, you must also handle the result and fault events by registering them to an event handler through the addEventListener() method:

```
myHTTP.addEventListener(ResultEvent.RESULT, resultHandler)
myHTTP.addEventListener(FaultEvent.FAULT, faultHandler)
```

In this solution, you will see how to invoke a remote service that targets a PHP file, which in turn returns dynamically generated XML.

How to build it

Before you can create your MXML application, you must create the PHP script, which you call with the HTTPService class. Installing and setting up PHP and a web server is out of the scope of this book. On the Web, you can find tons of tutorials and instructions on how to do this. Following are links to just a few of the resources you can use in case you don't have the requirements for this solution (a web server with installed support for PHP scripting):

- "Installing Apache and PHP" (www.php-mysql-tutorial.com/install-apache-php-mysql.php)
- "Setting up PHP, Apache, and MySQL on a Mac OS X machine" (www.adobe.com/devnet/dreamweaver/articles/php_macintosh.html)
- Flex and PHP Adobe Developer Center (www.adobe.com/devnet/flex/flex_php.html)

Moreover, there are many great books out there on this topic, including the following:

- *Beginning PHP and MySQL 5: From Novice to Professional, Second Edition* by W. Jason Gilmore (Apress, 2006)
- *PHP 5 Recipes: A Problem-Solution Approach* by Lee Babin et al. (Apress, 2005)

Another great resource to quickly install all the programs you need to develop with PHP is WAMP5 (called MAMP for Mac). WAMP5 installs automatically Apache 1.3.31, PHP 5, MySQL, phpMyAdmin, and SQLiteManager on your computer. Its principal aim is to allow you to easily install the environment you need to use PHP. You can download WAMP5 at www.wampserver.com/en/download.php or MAMP at www.mamp.info/en/home/.

In this solution, you will use two PHP files that have the simple job of returning XML data. For creating the PHP files, you can use your favorite PHP editor (I've used Adobe Dreamweaver for years). Flex Builder will allow you to create a PHP file using File ➤ New ➤ File and save it with the .php extension. Do so now, and name your file index_xml.php. Add the following PHP code to the new file:

```php
<?php
  require_once('classes/xmlGenerator.Class.php');

  $xml = new xmlGenerator();

  $xml->openTag('root');
```

```php
$xml->openTag('user');
$xml->newItem('name', 'marco');
$xml->newItem('surname', 'casario');
$xml->closeTag('user');
$xml->openTag('user');
$xml->newItem('name', 'raffaele');
$xml->newItem('surname', 'mannella');
$xml->closeTag('user');

$xml->closeTag('root');

?>
```

The PHP file uses and includes a class found in the classes folder. This class defines the openTag(), newItem(), and closeTag() methods, which you still use to write your XML file. The PHP code creates an instance of the xmlGenerator object, which, in the constructor, immediately prints the heading of the XMI file.

After this, you create the root tag of your dynamically generated XML file and create its structure using the methods of the xmlGenerator object:

- openTag(): Opens a tag node of your data structure.
- newItem(): Creates an item in the repeating node. This method accepts two parameters: the name of the node and its value.
- closeTag(): Closes a tag.

In this case, the XML file that is generated by this call will be the following:

```xml
<?xml version="1.0" encoding="ISO-8859-1" ?>
<root>
  <user>
    <name>marco</name>
    <surname>casario</surname>
  </user>
  <user>
    <name>raffaele</name>
    <surname>mannella</surname>
  </user>
</root>
```

The code in the PHP xmlGenerator class is the following:

```php
<?php
class xmlGenerator
{
  var $opened = 0;

  function xmlGenerator($charset = "ISO-8859-1") {
    // Inside the constructor write the declaration of the XML file
    echo '<?xml version="1.0" encoding="'.$charset.'" ?>';
```

```php
      echo "\n";
    }

  // This method opens and closes a tag,
  // passing to it the name of  the node
  // and its value
  function newItem($tag, $value) {

  // Bear in mind how many tags
  //are opened at the time of printing
  // N \t to have indented XML
    for($i = 0; $i < $this->opened; $i++) {
      echo "\t";
    }
    echo "\t";
    // I open the tag
    echo '<'.$tag.'>';
    // I print the value
    echo $value;
    // I close tag
    echo '</'.$tag.'>';
    echo "\n";
  }

  // With this method, I open a generic tag without
  // sending the value (it will probably contain other tags)
  // The only thing that I do here is to increase the
  // counter opened to have a correct indentation
  // I must remember to close the tag
  function openTag($tag) {
    for($i = 0; $i <= $this->opened; $i++) {
      echo "\t";
    }
    echo '<'.$tag.'>';
    echo "\n";
    $this->opened++;
  }

  // This method closes the tag
  function closeTag($tag) {
    $this->opened--;
    for($i = 0; $i <= $this->opened; $i++) {
      echo "\t";
    }

echo '</'.$tag.'>';
echo "\n";
  }
}

?>
```

In this solution, assume that your server supports PHP and that all files with the .php extension are handled by PHP. You can ask your server administrator to determine whether the server gives you PHP support. Otherwise, you can develop locally having a web server installed on your machine (Apache, at www.apache.org, is an example web server). You can follow the instructions on the PHP installation on this page: www.php.net/manual/en/install.php.

In order to make the solution work, you have to put the PHP file on your web server. If you have Apache installed locally, by default the document root is set to the htdocs directory (the document root is where you put all your PHP or HTML files so it will be processed by Apache). Within the htdocs directory, create a new directory called flexsolutions. Put the two PHP files into this directory. You can access these files using the following URL in your web browser: http://localhost/flexsolutions/.

> *Be sure your Apache server is started. If it isn't, select* Start ➤ Programs ➤ Apache HTTP Server ➤ Control Apache Server ➤ Start.

You can already test the correct functioning of the two scripts by launching them from your web server or by trying to insert this URL in a common browser:

> www.comtaste.com/xmloutput/index_xml.php

The browser is capable of interpreting the value returned—it deals with XML and will write out an XML output of the final result, which is shown in Figure 6-6.

```
<?xml version="1.0" encoding="ISO-8859-1" ?>
- <root>
  - <user>
      <name>marco</name>
      <surname>casario</surname>
    </user>
  - <user>
      <name>giovanni</name>
      <surname>lenoci</surname>
    </user>
  </root>
```

Figure 6-6. The browser interprets the data returned from the PHP file in an XML parser.

You are now able to create your Flex application, which will launch the HTTP call invoking the PHP file and then insert the response data in a DataGrid control.

1. Create a new MXML application file (File ➤ New ➤ MXML Application) and name it Chapter_6_Flex_Sol_3.mxml.

2. Create the HTTPService object by simply using ActionScript declarations. Create a Script block after the Application tag, as follows—here you define a private function that will be launched on the creationComplete event of the Application tag:

```
<mx:Script>
<![CDATA[
import mx.controls.Alert;
import mx.rpc.events.ResultEvent;
import mx.rpc.events.FaultEvent;
import mx.collections.ArrayCollection;
import mx.rpc.http.HTTPService;
import mx.managers.CursorManager;


[Bindable]
private var myAC:ArrayCollection;

private var myHTTP:HTTPService;

private function init():void
{
myHTTP = new HTTPService();
myHTTP.url = "http://www.comtaste.com/xmloutput/index_xml.php";
myHTTP.send();
myHTTP.addEventListener(ResultEvent.RESULT, resultHandler);
myHTTP.addEventListener(FaultEvent.FAULT, faultHandler)
}
]]>
</mx:Script>
```

The ActionScript code starts with importing of some classes you'll use throughout the application. Then you create two variables: myAC and myHTPP. The first is the ArrayCollection variable used as a dataProvider bound to the DataGrid control, and the latter contains the reference to the HTTPService class.

The init() function creates the instance of the HTTPService class and sets up its url property. It specifies the URL address of the PHP file to be invoked by the remote class:

```
myHTTP = new HTTPService();
myHTTP.url = "http://www.comtaste.com/xmloutput/index_xml.php";
```

Then the send() method of the HTTPService class is called and the remote service is launched. Using the addEventListener() method, you register two event handlers for handling the ResultEvent.RESULT and FaultEvent.FAULT event:

```
myHTTP.send();
myHTTP.addEventListener(ResultEvent.RESULT, resultHandler);
myHTTP.addEventListener(FaultEvent.FAULT, faultHandler)
```

3. Call the init() function on the creationComplete event of the Application tag:

```
<mx:Application xmlns:mx="http://www.adobe.com/2006/mxml"
layout="absolute"
  creationComplete="init();">
```

4. The HTTPService call dispatches the result and fault events. You associate these two events with two event handlers. Add within the Script block the two handlers:

```
private function init():void
{
myHTTP = new HTTPService();
myHTTP.url = "http://www.comtaste.com/xmloutput/index_xml.php";
CursorManager.setBusyCursor();

myHTTP.send();
myHTTP.addEventListener(ResultEvent.RESULT, resultHandler);
myHTTP.addEventListener(FaultEvent.FAULT, faultHandler)
}

private function resultHandler(event:ResultEvent):void
{
myAC = event.result.root.user;

}

private function faultHandler(evt:FaultEvent):void
{
var errors:String = "Some errors occurred \n";
errors += "\n Fault Code is :  \n" + evt.fault.faultCode;
errors += "\n Fault Detail is : \n" + evt.fault.faultDetail;
errors += "\n Fault String is : \n" + evt.fault.faultString;
mx.controls.Alert.show(errors);
}
```

The resultHandler() function populates the myAC variable with the response data of the HTTPService call. The data is contained in the result property of the event object:

```
myAC = event.result.root.user;
```

The faultHandler() intercepts any errors due to the HTTPService call and outputs it in an Alert window. It uses the properties within the event object of the FaultEvent class (fault.faultCode, fault.faultDetail, fault.faultString).

5. Insert the DataGrid control to show response data contained in the myAC ArrayCollection variable:

```
</mx:Script>

<mx:DataGrid id="myDG"
dataProvider="{myAC}"
x="92" y="49"/>

</mx:Application>
```

6. Save the file and run the application.

6

When the application starts up, the HTTPService call is invoked and the PHP file hosted in the URL www.comtaste.com/xmloutput/index_xml.php returns the response data to the application. The DataGrid control displays the data, as shown the Figure 6-7.

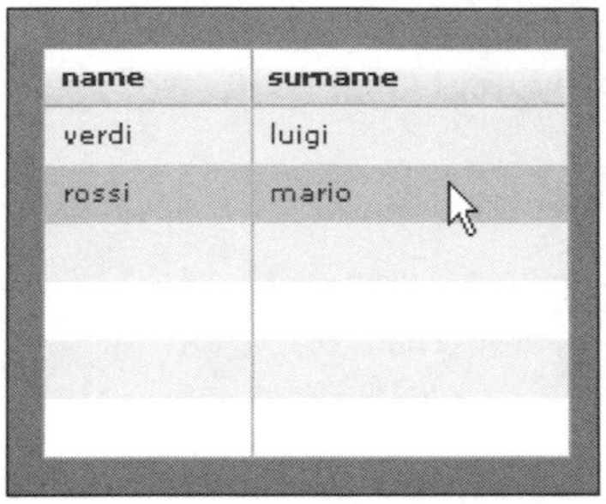

Figure 6-7.
The response data passed from the PHP server-side file is shown in the DataGrid control.

Expert tips

In this solution, you used ActionScript to define and execute the remote call with the HTTPService class. Then you displayed the response data in a DataGrid declared by using the MXML tag, without specifying any DataGridColumn tags. Doing this, the DataGrid automatically creates a column for each item contained in the dataProvider property. But you can use ActionScript to filter the column to display and the data to use. The DataGridColumn class in the mx.controls.dataGridClasses package allows you to specify the number of columns to be shown in the DataGrid and which data to be loaded. The instances of DataGridColumn will be passed to the columns property of the DataGrid.

1. Within the Script block of this solution, insert a new function named initColumn(), which will be called by the initialize event of the DataGrid control. This function will define the DataGridColumn classes used by the columns property of the DataGrid control (myDG):

```
<mx:Script>
<![CDATA[
import mx.controls.dataGridClasses.DataGridColumn;
import mx.controls.Alert;
import mx.rpc.events.ResultEvent;
import mx.rpc.events.FaultEvent;
import mx.collections.ArrayCollection;
import mx.rpc.http.HTTPService;
import mx.managers.CursorManager;

import mx.controls.dataGridClasses.DataGridColumn;

[Bindable]
private var myAC:ArrayCollection;

private var myHTTP:HTTPService;
```

```
private function init():void
{
myHTTP = new HTTPService();

//myHTTP.url="http://www.comtaste.com/xmloutput/index_xml.php";
myHTTP.url = "http://88.149.156.198/develop/xmloutput/index_xml.php";
CursorManager.setBusyCursor();
myHTTP.send();
myHTTP.addEventListener(ResultEvent.RESULT, resultHandler);
myHTTP.addEventListener(FaultEvent.FAULT, faultHandler);
}

private function initColumn():void
{

var dgColumn:DataGridColumn = new DataGridColumn("surname");

myDG.columns = [new DataGridColumn("name"),dgColumn];

}

private function resultHandler(event:ResultEvent):void
{
myAC = event.result.root.user;
CursorManager.removeBusyCursor();
}

private function faultHandler(evt:FaultEvent):void
{
var errors:String = "Some errors occurred \n";
errors += "\n Fault Code is :  \n" + evt.fault.faultCode;
errors += "\n Fault Detail is : \n" + evt.fault.faultDetail;
errors += "\n Fault String is : \n" + evt.fault.faultString;
mx.controls.Alert.show(errors);
CursorManager.removeBusyCursor();
}

]]>
</mx:Script>
```

In order to use the DataGridColumn class, you must import the mx.controls.
dataGridClasses.DataGridColumn package. In the initColumn() function, you pass to
the columns property an Array of DataGridColumn classes. Each index of the Array creates
a column in the DataGrid control:

```
var dgColumn:DataGridColumn = new DataGridColumn("surname");
myDG.columns = [new DataGridColumn("name"),dgColumn];
```

6

With this code, you create two columns and you use two different declarations of DataGridColumn for the columns property. The first index of the Array creates an instance of a DataGridColumn on the fly, whereas the second index uses the dgColumn variable that contains an instance of the DataGridColumn class.

2. Within the `<mx:DataGrid>` tag, launch the initColumn() function when the initialize system event is dispatched:

```
<mx:DataGrid id="myDG"
dataProvider="{myAC}" x="92" y="49"
initialize="initColumn()">
```

3. Save the file and run the application to see the DataGrid control and its columns.

If you want to show only one column in the DataGrid, delete one index in the Array of columns:

```
private function initColumn():void
{

var dgColumn:DataGridColumn = new DataGridColumn("surname");

myDG.columns = [new DataGridColumn("name")];

}
```

The preceding code will display only the column with the name data in the DataGrid control.

Flex does not permit you to connect directly to the data source by performing connections and operations with the database. It does, however, allow you to make calls to HTTP or web services. On the surface, this seems limiting, but it is actually a huge advantage, because it completely ignores the server-side technology that is used. Flex permits you to make calls to files composed in languages capable of returning data in XML format, such as PHP, ColdFusion, JSP, and Ruby on Rails.

For example, you can quickly carry out the same HTTP call on a JSP file that performs the same operations as the PHP file. You can create the following JSP file, which returns the same XML as the PHP script did, using the method out.println():

```
<%
  out.println("<?xml version=\"1.0\" encoding=\"UTF-8\"?><root><user>➥
    <name>marco</name><surname>casario</surname></user><user><name>➥
    raffaele</name><surname>mannella</surname></user></root>");
%>
```

This file needs to be deployed using a servlet container such as Tomcat (http://tomcat.apache.org/).

Having declared the HTTPService class using ActionScript, to be able to change the cursor of the mouse from the moment in which the call is launched until the data is received, you must use the CursorManager class.

The CursorManager class, which makes up part of the mx.managers.CursorManager package, provides two static methods for changing the cursor of the mouse: setBusyCursor() and removeBusyCursor(). The first method changes the icon of the cursor using the egg timer; the following code inserts it in the same portion of code in which you launched the remote service with the send() method:

```
import mx.managers.CursorManager;
private function init():void
{
  myHTTP = new HTTPService();
  myHTTP.url = "http://www.comtaste.com/xmloutput/index_xml.php";
  myHTTP.send();
  myHTTP.addEventListener(ResultEvent.RESULT, resultHandler);
  myHTTP.addEventListener(FaultEvent.FAULT, faultHandler)
  CursorManager.setBusyCursor();
}
```

While in the event handler of the result event, when you are sure that the data has been correctly loaded, you can remove the cursor using the static removeBusyCursor() method of the CursorManager class:

```
private function resultHandler(event:ResultEvent):void
{
  myAC = event.result.root.utente;
  CursorManager.removeBusyCursor();
}
```

You must remove the cursor in the busy state even if an error occurs; therefore, you must use the same method in the faultHandler:

```
private function faultHandler(evt:FaultEvent):void
{
  var errors:String = "Some errors occurred \n";
  errors += "\n Fault Code is :  \n" + evt.fault.faultCode;
  errors += "\n Fault Detail is : \n" + evt.fault.faultDetail;
  errors += "\n Fault String is : \n" + evt.fault.faultString;
  mx.controls.Alert.show(errors);

  CursorManager.removeBusyCursor();
}
```

Solution 6-4: Using the E4X format with the resultFormat property

One of the new additions of ActionScript 3.0 is the introduction of the E4X format for the management of XML files. The E4X format (ECMAScript for XML) is a subset of the subset of the standard ECMA 262 on which the ActionScript language is based. The E4X is a set of programming language extensions that add native XML support to ECMAScript. You can find other information on this format and download the entire specification at this address: www.ecma-international.org/publications/standards/Ecma-357.htm.

With the RPC services of HTTPService and WebService types, it is possible to set the data type that the lastResult object contains. Through the resultFormat property, you can therefore change from its default value of Object to the new E4X format.

This property also accepts other values as shown in the code hints of the Figure 6-8:

- object: Returns an XML file. This is the default value.
- array: Returns an XML file, too, the difference being that if the top-level object is not an Array, a new Array is created, and the result is set as the first item.
- xml: Returns a literal XML in an ActionScript XMLnode object.
- flashvars: Returns values in the format of name=value pairs separated by ampersands.
- text: Returns simple raw text.

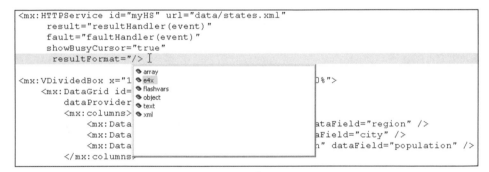

```
<mx:HTTPService id="myHS" url="data/states.xml"
    result="resultHandler(event)"
    fault="faultHandler(event)"
    showBusyCursor="true"
    resultFormat="/>

<mx:VDividedBox x="1                                   ]%">
    <mx:DataGrid id=
        dataProvider
        <mx:columns>
            <mx:Data                        ataField="region" />
            <mx:Data                        aField="city" />
            <mx:Data                     " dataField="population" />
        </mx:columns>
```

array
e4x
flashvars
object
text
xml

Figure 6-8. The values that can be given to the resultFormat property

The E4X format often turns out to be the best choice because it offers simple and logical access to data using the dot syntax to navigate between the nodes of the XML.

Using this format as resultFormat of an HTTPService call, you must also change the data type of the variable containing the response data. In the preceding solutions, you dealt with an ArrayCollection, but this can't be used here, as Flex does not convert the XML object with this data type. You must therefore use the data type XMLList or XML with the E4X format.

In this solution, you will carry out an HTTPService request by setting the resultFormat property to the e4x value, and you will learn a few of the potential benefits to using the E4X standard to quickly parse XML data.

What's involved

E4X format renders the life of the developer much easier. There are, however, a few solutions to which attention should be paid, in contrast to the default format that is returned from a call made with the HTTPService.

The first change needed is the data type of the variable that you use as data binding for your controls. In fact, the E4X format does not function with ArrayCollections, but needs XMLList or XML as its data type. For this, you need to change the ActionScript code in which you assign the data type to the variable from

```
private var myAC:ArrayCollection;
```

to

```
private var myAC:XMLList;
```

Furthermore, E4X has a different way of parsing the XML data. Take for example the following XML file:

```
<?xml version="1.0" encoding="UTF-8"?>
<dataroot>
  <city>
   <id>1</id>
   <region>PIEMONTE</region>
   <cityName>TORINO</cityName>
   <population>2236765</population>
  </city>
  <city>
   <id>2</id>
   <region>PIEMONTE</region>
   <cityName>VERCELLI</cityName>
   <population>183869</population>
  </city>
</dataroot>
```

To make a call with HTTPService, you have up until now used the following syntax to populate an ArrayCollection:

```
var myAC:ArrayCollection  = myHTTPService.lastResult.dataroot.city;
```

In this case, E4X expressions do not reference the root (topmost) tag of the XML, so you must change the code as follows:

```
var myAC:XMLList = myHTTPService.lastResult.city;
```

It is also possible to use the following syntax to skip to a child node:

```
var myAC:XMLList = myHTTPService.lastResult..region;
```

6

The myAC variable, in this case, contains all the <region> nodes included in your XML. In fact, the syntax with the two dots allows you to skip to a child node. Furthermore, E4X also allows you to filter the values container in the XML using research criteria:

```
var myAC:XMLList = myAC.(cityName=='TORINO').population
```

This returns all the <population> nodes that have the <cityName> node equal to the string TORINO.

This is only a taste of what ActionScript 3.0 can do with the support of E4X format. Let's create a working example.

How to build it

The solution you will create will execute a call with HTTPService, but you will use the resultFormat property to change the format of the received data.

1. Create a new MXML application file by selecting File ➤ New ➤ MXML Application and name it Chapter_6_Flex_Sol_4.mxml.

2. Begin by inserting the HTTPService tag and all of the user interface, or to be more precise, a vertical divided box with a DataGrid and a TextArea:

```
<mx:HTTPService id="myHS" url="data/states.xml"
  result="resultHandler(event)"
  fault="faultHandler(event)"
  showBusyCursor="true"
  resultFormat="e4x"/>

<mx:VDividedBox x="10" y="10" width="345" height="100%">
  <mx:DataGrid id="myDG" dataProvider="{myAC}" width="344">
    <mx:columns>
      <mx:DataGridColumn headerText="Region" dataField="region" />
      <mx:DataGridColumn headerText="City" dataField="cityName" />
      <mx:DataGridColumn headerText="Population"
        dataField="population" />
    </mx:columns>
  </mx:DataGrid>
  <mx:TextArea width="345" id="errorTxt" height="80"/>
</mx:VDividedBox>
```

The HTTPService class loads a file locally (in this case from your data folder). It is the same file that you have used in the preceding solutions. Then you link two event handlers to manage the result and fault events and finally set the value of the property resultFormat to e4x. The DataGrid has a binding with a myAC variable, which is sent to its data provider. You will use the TextArea as an error message container; if the remote connection does not successfully complete, the resulting error messages will be printed there.

3. Write the ActionScript code to manage the event handler for the result and fault. On the resultHandler you will set the variable that will contain the response data, while the fault will print the potential errors in the TextArea:

```
<mx:Script>

  <![CDATA[
    import mx.rpc.events.*;

    [Bindable]
    private var myAC:XMLList;

    private function resultHandler(evt:ResultEvent):void
    {
        myAC = evt.result.city;
      errorTxt.text = "No errors found";
    }
    private function faultHandler(evt:FaultEvent):void
    {
      var errors:String = "Some errors occurred \n";
      errors += "\n Fault Code is :  \n" + evt.fault.faultCode;
      errors += "\n Fault Detail is : \n" + evt.fault.faultDetail;
      errors += "\n Fault String is : \n" + evt.fault.faultString;

      errorTxt.text = errors;
    }

  ]]>
</mx:Script>
```

The first lines of code import the classes you will use, which in this case are only those that define the event object (ResultEvent and FaultEvent).

You then declare the myAC variable with data type XMLList. This is the variable that will contain the response data in E4X format.

Finally, in the resultHandler, you populate the XMLList variable without reference to the root (topmost) tag using the result property of the event object automatically generated by the event result of the HTTPService:

```
myAC = evt.result.city;
```

The faultHandler function manages the potential errors that could occur, printing the faultCode, the faultDetail, and the faultString in the TextArea errorTxt.

4. All you need to do now is execute the send() method to launch the remote service. You call the method on the creationComplete event of the Application tag. Add the following to the creationComplete property of the Application tag:

```
<mx:Application xmlns:mx="http://www.adobe.com/2006/mxml"
  layout="absolute"
  creationComplete="myHS.send();">
```

5. Save and run the application.

The final result will display the data loaded in the DataGrid. In the "Expert tips" section, you will see other interesting ways of accessing the XML data that E4X permits.

Expert tips

The E4X format allows you to search for a string in the XML file and to filter data based on set criteria. You can, for example, have only the values of a node that match determined parameters returned to you.

Take your example code and add a Vbox containing a Button and a List control immediately under the closure of the DataGrid.

You want to launch a function when the button is clicked, which filters the data contained in the myAC variable typed as XMLList and displays the <population> node in the List control.

To do this, you can use the parentheses operator in which you define the name of the node and the value for which you carry out the search. After this, still using the dot syntax, you declare the node to which the filter is to be applied. The following syntax returns the XML data of the population that has a PIEMONTE value in the region node:

```
myAC.(region=='PIEMONTE').population;
```

1. Open the file Chapter_6_Flex_Sol_4.mxml and add the following declaration after the closure of the DataGrid tag:

```
<mx:VBox width="344">
<mx:Button label="Show Liguria Population"
 id="regionBtn" click="filterButton()"  width="164"/>

<mx:List width="223" id="myList"></mx:List>

</mx:VBox>
```

2. Now write the filterButton() function in the Script block:

```
private function filterButton():void
{
    myList.dataProvider = myAC.(region=='PIEMONTE').population;
}
```

Take note that you are using the E4X syntax directly on the myAC variable typed as XMLList. The result obtained from this filtering becomes used as data provider for the List control.

3. Save the file, run your application, and click the button; you should obtain the result shown in Figure 6-9.

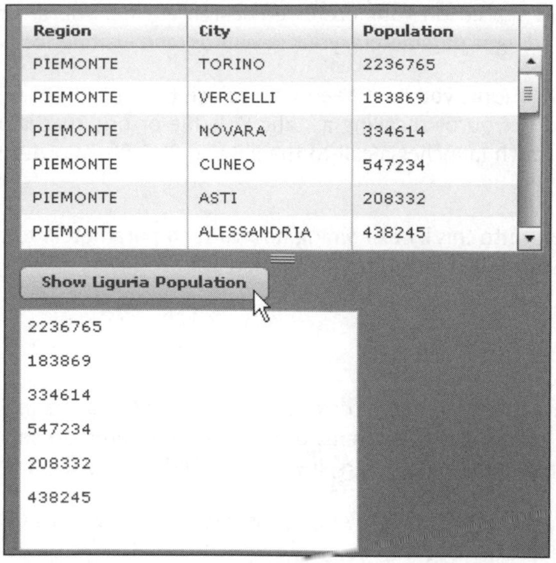

Figure 6-9. The E4X language also permits you to carry out searches in the XML data to filter data.

With E4X, it is also possible to access attributes in the XML data with the dot syntax. Imagine if you had the city node with a defined attribute:

```
<city country="Italy" >
  <id>1</id>
  <region>PIEMONTE</region>
  <cityName>TORINO</cityName>
  <population>2236765</population>
</city>
```

The following E4X code returns a list of all country attribute nodes of all of those <cityName> elements:

```
var myXL:XMLList = myHTPPService.lastResult.city;
myList.dataProvider = myXL.@country;
```

Solution 6-5: Sending parameters to a PHP and a JSP file

The RPC classes allow you to communicate with the remote services in a bidirectional manner, receiving data and sending parameters. In any web application, interactivity with the user generates requests. These requests are the result of how the user uses applications and what he wants to obtain in response to his request.

When you launch a search on your preferred search engine, you are making a call to a remote service, sending it parameters, your keywords, and waiting for a response.

In the preceding solutions, you have seen how to use the RPC HTTPService class to have XML data returned to you by recalling a static XML file or one that is dynamically generated. This last approach launches a call to the JSP and PHP file in order to have the values returned to it.

You can look deeper into this by examining how to send parameters to the remote service and consequently printing a response in your application.

What's involved

Sending parameters to the HTTPService call is a very simple process in Flex. Web developers, who are used to the classic methods of sending parameters to server-side languages, might consider sending the parameters, invoking an URL with URL parameters:

```
<mx:HTTPService url="http://www.dominio.com/file.cfm?id=1&name=marco"
   id="myHTTPData" method="GET">
```

However, this code instead generates the following error: "HTTPService Fault: Parameters are not allowed in the url, use the request object".

The approach for sending parameters within the HTTPService call involves using the <mx:request> object and defining the parameters as child items of this object:

```
<mx:HTTPService
   id="saveHS"
   url="http://www.mydomain.com/savenews.php"
   method="POST"
   result="linkHandler(event)"
   fault="faultHandler(event)">

   <mx:request>
     <name>Marco</name>
   </mx:request>
</mx:HTTPService>
```

The <mx:request> object becomes defined in the declaration of the HTTPService class, and the parameters are the nodes of this object. Furthermore, the HTTPService can send parameters both in POST and in GET by changing this value in the property method. In the example code, the HTTP call will send the value defined in the parameter named (the string Marco) in POST modality.

The server-side file, savenews.php, should simply receive this parameter and execute resulting operations with the data received. In the <mx:request> object, you can use data bindings as valued for the parameters or send an ActionScript variable:

```
<mx:Script>
  <![CDATA[
    var name:String="Marco";
    var surname:String="Casario";
  ]]>
</mx:Script>
<mx:HTTPService
  id="saveHS"
  url="http://www.mydomain.com/savenews.php"
  method="GET"
  result="linkHandler(event)"
  fault="faultHandler(event)">

  <mx:request>
    <name>{name}</name>
    <surname>{surname}</surname>
    <link>{myDataGrid.selectedItem.link}</link>
  </mx:request>
</mx:HTTPService>
```

In this second portion of code, two variables of String with ActionScript type have been created. These two variables have been sent as parameters to the <mx:request> object together with a third parameter, <surname>, which instead contains the link property of the selectedItem of a DataGrid:

```
<mx:request>
  <name>{name}</name>
  <surname>{surname}</surname>
  <link>{myDataGrid.selectedItem.link}</link>
</mx:request>
```

In this solution, you will see how to send parameters to a server-side JSP file and a PHP file by making an HTTP call.

How to build it

You will first see the server-side code in PHP, which will accept the parameters sent to it by the Flex application through an HTTPService call. The file is very simple and uses the xmlGenerator PHP class already discussed in Solution 6-3.

The index_get.php file creates an instance of the xmlGenerator class and executes the openTag() method of this class to create the root node of the XML file that will be returned. In fact, the same PHP file looks after receiving the call, accepting the parameters in GET, and returning the XML data that contains, as values, the same parameters that you have sent:

```
<?php
  require_once('classes/xmlGenerator.Class.php');
  $xml = new xmlGenerator();
```

```
$xml->openTag('root');
foreach($_GET as $key => $val) {
  $xml->newItem($key, $val);
}

$xml->closeTag('root');
?>
```

The for() loop launches the newItem() method, as they are the parameters in GET that you send with the HTTPService call. The newItem() method creates a child node using the name/value pair as the name and value of the node. The PHP file terminates with the closure of the root tag using the closeTag() method.

You are now ready to create the Flex application that executes the HTTP call, sends the parameters to this file, and receives the response data that is then visualized in two TextInputs.

1. Create a new MXML application file using File ➤ New ➤ MXML Application and name it Chapter_6_Flex_Sol_5.mxml.

2. Begin by inserting the HTTPService tag into it as follows:

```
<mx:HTTPService id="myHS"
  url="http://88.149.156.198/develop/xmloutput/index_get.php"
  result="resultHandler(event)"
  fault="faultHandler(event)"
  showBusyCursor="true"
  method="GET">

  <mx:request xmlns="">
    <name>Marco</name>
    <surname>Casario</surname>
  </mx:request>
</mx:HTTPService>
```

The HTTPService aims at the get.php file index and sends it the parameters using the GET method. The <mx:request> object has two parameters, <name> and <surname>, to which you send two strings. Your PHP file is parameterized in such a way that it accepts an indefinite number of parameters. In this example, you send two parameters to the PHP file that will generate the following XML code in response:

```
<?xml version="1.0" encoding="UTF-8"?>
<root>
  <name>Marco</name>
  <surname>Casario</surname>
</root>
```

3. Before writing the event handlers to manage the result and fault events, you need to add two TextInputs in which you print the response data of the remote call. Add this after the HTTPService tag:

```
    </mx:HTTPService>

    <mx:VDividedBox x="10" y="10" width="345">
      <mx:HBox>
        <mx:TextInput  id="nameTxt" />
        <mx:TextInput  id="surnameTxt" />
      </mx:HBox>
      <mx:TextArea width="345" id="errorTxt" height="50"/>
    </mx:VDividedBox>
```

You immediately write this declaration under the closure of the DataGrid. You need the TextArea to debug in case errors occur in the call.

4. The Script block must manage the functions for the result and fault events. In the resultHandler(), you use the result property of the event object of the ResultEvent class to populate the two TextInputs with the response data. Open a Script block and add the code to it shown here:

```
<mx:Script>
  <![CDATA[

  import mx.rpc.events.*;

  private function resultHandler(evt:ResultEvent):void
{
  nameTxt.text = evt.result.root.name;
  surnameTxt.text = evt.result.root.surname;

  errorTxt.text = "No errors found";
}
```

5. The faultHandler() function only manages the possible errors that can occur and prints the relative messages in the TextArea. Add the following to complete the Script block:

```
  private function faultHandler(evt:FaultEvent):void
  {
    var errors:String = "Some errors occurred \n";
    errors += "\n Fault Code is :  \n" + evt.fault.faultCode;
    errors += "\n Fault Detail is : \n" + evt.fault.faultDetail;
    errors += "\n Fault String is : \n" + evt.fault.faultString;

    errorTxt.text = errors;
  }
  ]]>
</mx:Script>
```

6. All that is left for you to do is execute the send() method to launch the HTTPService. The HTTP call to the remote PHP file is automatically made, and the parameters defined in the <mx:request> are sent to it. You launch the send() method on the creationComplete of the application:

```
<mx:Application xmlns:mx="http://www.adobe.com/2006/mxml"
  layout="absolute"
  creationComplete="myHS.send();">
```

7. Save the file and run the application. Your results should be similar to what you see in Figure 6-10.

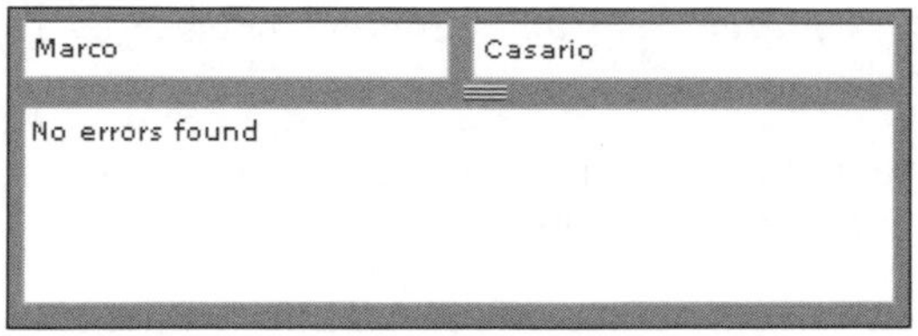

Figure 6-10. The parameters sent to the HTTPService are the same as those returned by the remote call.

One of the powerful features of Flex is that it is totally independent of the server-side language used for the application. This means that you as developer can spend your time in creating cool and rich features for Flex applications without worrying about the language used. In order to connect the view layer (the controls that define the user interface) with the business logic, the only thing you have to do is to send the response data from your server in an XML format and launch an HTTPService call.

In this solution, you use PHP as the server-side scripting language. Now I'll show you how easy it is to switch to another server-side language such as JSP to send parameters from the application to the server layer.

You have seen in this solution how to send parameters to an HTTP call using the <mx:request> object. But there is also another method for sending parameters to a remote service: using the send() method. The send() method invokes the remote call. You can use this method to pass parameters to the remote service:

```
myHS.send(myParams)
```

You'll now look at how to send parameters from a Flex page to a JSP file that resides on the server, this time using the send() method.

1. Add a Form container within the VDividedBox container to the preceding example with two simple TextInputs:

```
<mx:VDividedBox x="10" y="10"
width="100%" height="100%">

  <mx:VBox>
    <mx:TextInput  id="nameTxt" />
    <mx:TextInput  id="surnameTxt" />


  <mx:Form width="100%">
    <mx:FormItem label="Region">
```

```
    <mx:TextInput enabled="true" id="regionTxt" editable="true"/>
  </mx:FormItem>
  <mx:FormItem label="City">
    <mx:TextInput enabled="true" id="cityTxt" editable="true"/>
  </mx:FormItem>
</mx:Form>

  </mx:VBox>
<mx:TextArea width="345" id="errorTxt" height="50"/>
</mx:VDividedBox>
```

You also change the first child of the VDividedBox switching from an HBox to a VBox container.

2. Create an MXML data model, declaring it above the VDividedBox tag, that contains data bindings with values inserted in the TextInput by the user. Also add a new HTTPService tag to make a new call to the JSP file:

```
<mx:HTTPService id="myHSjsp"
 url="http://localhost/flexsolutions/incomingData.jsp"
method="POST" useProxy="false" />


<mx:Model id="myModel">
  <root>
    <region>{regionTxt.text}</region>
    <city>{cityTxt.text}</city>
  </root>
</mx:Model>
```

3. You are now ready to send these parameters with the send() method of the HTTPService. In fact, you can directly send the data model as a parameter to the send() method using its precise id. Add a Button control with the following code:

```
<mx:VDividedBox x="10" y="10"
width="100%" height="100%">

  <mx:VBox>
    <mx:TextInput   id="nameTxt" />
    <mx:TextInput   id="surnameTxt" />

<mx:Form width="100%">
  <mx:FormItem label="Region">
    <mx:TextInput enabled="true" id="regionTxt" editable="true"/>
  </mx:FormItem>
  <mx:FormItem label="City">
    <mx:TextInput enabled="true" id="cityTxt" editable="true"/>
  </mx:FormItem>
</mx:Form>
```

```
<mx:Button label="Send Data to JSP PAge" ➥
click=" myHSjsp.send(myModel)" />


    </mx:VBox>
    <mx:TextArea width="345" id="errorTxt" height="50"/>
    </mx:VDividedBox>
```

At the click of the Button, the send() method is launched and the myModel object is sent as a parameter to the JSP remote file.

4. Create the JSP file by selecting File ➤ New ➤ File and save it with the name incomingData.jsp. The JSP file will receive these two parameters through the getParameter() method of the object request and will return the XML file with the values that it has received as parameters:

```
<%
  String region= request.getParameter("region");
  String city = request.getParameter("city");
 String newRegion = "<myRoot><region>" + region +➥
 "</region><city>" + city + "</city></myRoot>"
  out.println(newRegion);
%>
```

If your web hosting supports JSP files, it's enough to put the incomingData.jsp file into the server. Just remember to change the url property of the HTTPService tag with your address:

```
<mx:HTTPService id="myHS"
 url="http://www.mydomain.com/flexsolutions/incomingData.jsp"
method="POST" useProxy="false" />
```

If you want to develop locally, you need a web server installed on your machine with a servlet engine. In my solution, I used Tomcat as the servlet engine.

> *Apache server does not run JSP by itself, but it requires a servlet engine to be plugged in. A well-known and much-used servlet engine is the Jakarta-Tomcat engine, also supported by Apache (http://jakarta.apache.org).*

For installing and setting up Tomcat, you can follow the instructions published on the Tomcat site: http://tomcat.apache.org/tomcat-5.0-doc/setup.html.

By default, Tomcat's document root is the webapps directory. This is where your JSP and HTML files should go.

5. Create a flexsolutions folder within the webapps directory of your Tomcat and put the incomingData.jsp into that folder.

6. Save and run the application. Figure 6-11 shows the final result.

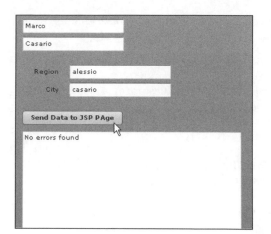

Figure 6-11. The parameters inserted into the Region and City TextInput controls are sent to the HTTPService using its send() method.

Expert tips

In your solution, the parameters have been sent to the remote service with the GET method. With very few changes, you can use the POST method to send the parameters. It is sufficient to set the method property of the HTTPService to POST and change the PHP file:

```
<mx:HTTPService id="myHS"
  url="http://88.149.156.198/develop/xmloutput/index_get.php"
  result="resultHandler(event)"
  fault="faultHandler(event)"
  showBusyCursor="true"
  method="POST">

  <mx:request xmlns="">
    <name>Marco</name>
    <surname>Casario</surname>
  </mx:request>
</mx:HTTPService>
```

HTTP receives information in one of two ways: GET *or* POST. *The difference between* GET *and* POST *is primarily defined in terms of form data encoding. The* GET *method appends name/value pairs to the URL. Unfortunately, the length of a URL is limited, so this method only works if there are only a few parameters. The* POST *method packages the name/value pairs inside the body of the HTTP request, which makes for a cleaner URL and imposes no size limitations on the form's output. It is also more secure.*

6

The only change made to the code on the HTTPService tag is the method property. The PHP file must instead receive the data through the keyword $_POST used in the foreach() loop:

```php
<?php
  require_once('classes/xmlGenerator.Class.php');

  $xml = new xmlGenerator();
  $xml->openTag('root');

  foreach($_POST as $key => $val) {
    $xml->newItem($key, $val);
  }
  $xml->closeTag('root');

?>
```

If you run the application with these changes, you will obtain the same result.

Solution 6-6: Consuming a web service

In addition to the HTTPService class, with Flex you can carry out calls to web services.

The W3C defines a web service as a software system designed to support interoperable machine-to-machine interaction over a network. Web services are frequently just web APIs that can be accessed over a network, such as the Internet, and executed on a remote system hosting the requested services. See www.w3.org/TR/ws-arch/ for more information.

Flex can use any web services that define a WSDL 1.1 document and whose requests and results are formatted as SOAP messages. WSDL is an XML format that allows service interfaces to be described, along with the details of their bindings, to specific protocols. SOAP is an XML-based, extendible message envelope format for exchanging information between a client and a web service.

To invoke a web service in Flex applications, you can use the MXML WebService tag or declare the class in ActionScript. While in HTTPService, the url property defines the path of the remote file to call; for web services, you have to set the wsdl property of the WebService class. This property contains the path to the file that allows you to access the web service.

A web service can be made up of different operations or methods. For example, take the MXNA 2.0 web service, which allows read-only access to the Macromedia XML News Aggregator (http://weblogs.macromedia.com/mxna/webservices/mxna2.html). If you connect to this address, you will see that by accessing the WSDL file at http://weblogs.macromedia.com/mxna/webservices/mxna2.cfc?wsdl, you can invoke different methods to obtain different responses. The getAggregateLanguageData method returns a query with aggregated language data, including the total number of feeds MXNA is aggregating in each language and the total number of posts as well. Or, the getCategories method returns a query with all MXNA 2.0 categories.

To communicate with the WebService class and determine which operation (or method) to invoke, you can use the <mx:operation> object, which accepts this value in the name property. In this solution, you will see how to use the WebService class to consume a web service.

What's involved

To make a call to web service, you must use the WebService class, which is one of the three RPC classes of Flex. You can create an instance of the WebService class by using the relative MXML tag or via ActionScript. In both cases, the following are the steps required to complete the call:

1. Create the WebService object and assign the WSDL file:

```
<mx:WebService
 wsdl="http://api.domain.com/WebSearchService/myService?WSDL"
id="myWS">
</mx:WebService>
```

2. Manage the event handlers for the result and fault events:

```
<mx:WebService
wsdl="http://api.domain.com/WebSearchService/myService?WSDL"
id="myWS"
result="resultHandler(event)"
fault="faultHandler(event)">
</mx:WebService>
```

3. Call a method of the web service through the <mx:operation> compiler tag:

```
<mx:WebService
wsdl="http://api.domain.com/WebSearchService/myService?WSDL"
id="myWS"
result="resultHandler(event)"
fault="faultHandler(event)">
  <mx:operation name="webSearch">
  </mx:operation>
</mx:WebService>
```

4. Send the possible parameters to the invoked method:

```
<mx:WebService
wsdl="http://api.domain.com/WebSearchService/myService?WSDL"
id="myWS"
result="resultHandler(event)"
fault="faultHandler(event)">
  <mx:operation name="webSearch">
  <mx:request xmlns="">
    <appid>1</appid>
    <query>finances</query>
    <format>pdf</format>
  </mx:request>
</mx:WebService>
```

6

281

5. Launch the call to the remote web service using the send() method:

```
<mx:Application xmlns:mx="http://www.adobe.com/2006/mxml"
layout="absolute"
 creationComplete="myWS.webSearch.send()">
```

These are the steps that allow you to use a web service, to send it parameters, and to manage the response data. To be able to intercept the response data of the calls, I use the lastResult property of the method that has been invoked:

```
myWS.getCategories.lastResult
```

In this solution, you will see how to use the MXNA web services created by Adobe to access the feed and get the posts aggregated by Adobe.

How to build it

At http://weblogs.macromedia.com/mxna/webservices/mxna2.html, you can see all the methods made available by the MXNA web service. The ones you will use in your solution are getCategories, getFeedsByCategory, and getMostRecentPosts. While the first method does not require parameters, the other two do require parameters. Following is a brief list of the methods:

Method	Parameters	Return Data
getCategories	None	Returns categoryId and categoryName columns
getFeedsByCategory	categoryId (Number)	Returns feedId, feedName, feedDescription, feedCategories, feedUrl, languageId, lastUpdated, siteName, siteUrl, and siteDescription columns
getMostRecentPosts	limit (Number) offset (Number) languageIds (String)	Returns postTitle, postExcerpt, postLink, and clicks Returns ranking (1–11), uniqueId, and dateTimeAggregated Returns feedId columns

You can find further information on the methods at the URL given at the beginning of this section.

The WSDL for the web service is available at http://weblogs.macromedia.com/mxna/webservices/mxna2.cfc?wsdl; therefore, this will be the parameter to send to the WSDL property of the WebService tag. Create your application now by following these steps:

1. Create a new MXML application file using File ➤ New ➤ MXML Application and name it Chapter_6_Flex_Sol_6.mxml. Add a Panel container below the Application tag:

```
<mx:Panel x="10" y="10" width="475" height="400" layout="absolute"
title="Solution 6-6: Consuming Web Services">

</mx:Panel>
```

2. You will make use of the WebService class by declaring it with MXML. Add this code before the Panel container declaration:

```
<mx:WebService
 wsdl="http://weblogs.macromedia.com/mxna/webservices/mxna2.cfc?wsdl"
useProxy="false" id="wsBlogAggr" showBusyCursor="true" />

<mx:Panel x="10" y="10" width="475" height="400" layout="absolute"
title="Solution 6-6: Consuming Web Services">
```

In the tag, you insert the WSDL file that aims at the remote address where the web service is resident and you set the useProxy value, which specifies whether to use the Flex proxy service as false. Finally, you set the showBusyCursor property, which changes the icon of the mouse during the call phase until a response is returned, as true.

3. Next you choose the method that you want to invoke, declaring it with the operation object in the declaration of the WebService tag. The <mx:operation> tag is a compiler tag, or to be more precise, a tag that does not correspond to ActionScript objects or properties. Add the following:

```
<mx:WebService➡
  wsdl="http://weblogs.macromedia.com/mxna/webservices/mxna2.cfc➡
  ?wsdl" useProxy-"false" id="wsBlogAggr" showBusyCursor="true">
<mx:operation name="getCategories">
</mx:operation>
</mx:WebService>
```

Note that the operation tag cannot contain an id, and the getCategories method returns a query with all MXNA 2.0 categories. The web service has now been created, but no call to that remote method has been made. To invoke the getCategories method, it is necessary to launch the send() method.

4. On the creationComplete of the Application, you make a call by launching the send() method. Add the following property to the Application tag:

```
<mx:Application xmlns:mx="http://www.adobe.com/2006/mxml"➡
  layout="vertical"➡
  creationComplete="wsBlogAggr.getCategories.send()" />
```

Unlike the HTTPService, the send() method is carried on the method of the WebService you want to invoke.

The categoryId and categoryName columns are returned to you by the getCategories operation. This last data, which contains the names of all the categories that were used by the MXNA aggregator, will be put in a ComboBox and will give the user the option of selecting a feed category among those listed.

5. Add a ComboBox control in the Panel container, as in the following code. This will use the response data of the remote call as data provider. The ComboBox, unlike the DataGrid, does not permit you to visualize a structure of complex data. If in fact the data provider contains an object, the ComboBox will attempt to visualize the label property of this object. In the case in which it does not find it, it is necessary to set the labelField property to specify the name of the property to visualize, which in this case is categoryName:

```
<mx:ComboBox x="30" y="25" id="categoryCbx"
dataProvider="{wsBlogAggr.getCategories.lastResult}"
  labelField="categoryName">
</mx:ComboBox>
```

6. Save the file and run the application; you will see how the ComboBox becomes populated with all the categories defined in the web service MXNA, as shown in Figure 6-12.

Figure 6-12. The ComboBox is populated with a list of the categories.

In the same definition of WebService, you can invoke multiple methods. Imagine that you want to load all the relative feeds to this criteria, depending on the selection of the user in the category.

Another method, the getFeedsByCategory method, returns all the feeds depending on the categoryId parameter that is sent. You go and insert the list of feeds that are returned to you by this remote method in a DataGrid.

You will now see how to call multiple methods of a web service and send parameters to one of them.

7. To the declaration of the WebService, you now add a new <mx:operation> object, which invokes the getFeedsByCategory method. Considering, however, that this operation expects to receive a parameter, you must specify the categoryId value as child of the <mx:request> object by adding the following code:

```
<mx:WebService
  wsdl="http://weblogs.macromedia.com/mxna/webservices/mxna2.cfc→
  ?wsdl" useProxy="false" id="wsBlogAggr" showBusyCursor="true">

  <mx:operation name="getCategories">
  </mx:operation>
  <mx:operation name="getFeedsByCategory">
    <mx:request xmlns="">
      <categoryId>{categoryCbx.selectedItem.categoryId}</categoryId>
    </mx:request>
  </mx:operation>
</mx:WebService>
```

The getFeedsByCategory operation requires the categoryId parameter, which corresponds to the item the user has selected in the ComboBox (written in ActionScript, this corresponds to categoryCbx.selectedItem.categoryId).

8. This operation has been declared, but the method has not yet been invoked because send() has not yet been launched. The invocation of the web service must take place in the moment in which the user has selected an item in the ComboBox. To do this, execute the send() method of the operation on the change event, as follows:

```
<mx:ComboBox x="30" y="25" id="categoryCbx"
  change="wsBlogAggr.getFeedsByCategory.send()"
  dataProvider="{wsBlogAggr.getCategories.lastResult}"
  labelField="categoryName">
</mx:ComboBox>
```

The response data that you obtain from the call is as follows: feedId, feedName, feedDescription, feedCategories, feedUrl, languageId, lastUpdated, siteName, siteUrl, and siteDescription. A DataGrid will visualize a few of these fields.

9. After the closure of the ComboBox control, you insert the DataGrid that accepts the lastResult property of the remote call as dataProvider (wsBlogAggr. getFeedsByCategory.lastResult), and you specify the columns with the DataGridColumn tag to visualize only the feedName and siteName property by adding the following code:

6

```
<mx:DataGrid x="30" y="75" id="dgFeed" width="400"
  dataProvider="{wsBlogAggr.getFeedsByCategory.lastResult}">
  <mx:columns>
    <mx:DataGridColumn headerText="Feed Name" dataField="feedName"/>
    <mx:DataGridColumn headerText="Site Name" dataField="siteName"
      width="75"/>
  </mx:columns>
</mx:DataGrid>
```

The dataProvider of the DataGrid is bound to the lastResult property, which contains the data returned by the call of the getFeedsByCategory method of the WebService.

10. Save the file and run the application.

As soon as the application is loaded, it will launch the send() method of the getCategories operation of the WebService. The data returned is loaded in the ComboBox, which displays all the categories put forward by the method (see Figure 6-13). In the moment in which the user selects an item from the menu, the getFeedsByCategory method is invoked, to which the categoryId parameter contained in the categoryId property of the selectedItem of the ComboBox is sent. The response data is bound to the data provider of the DataGrid, which visualizes only the two columns feedName and siteName.

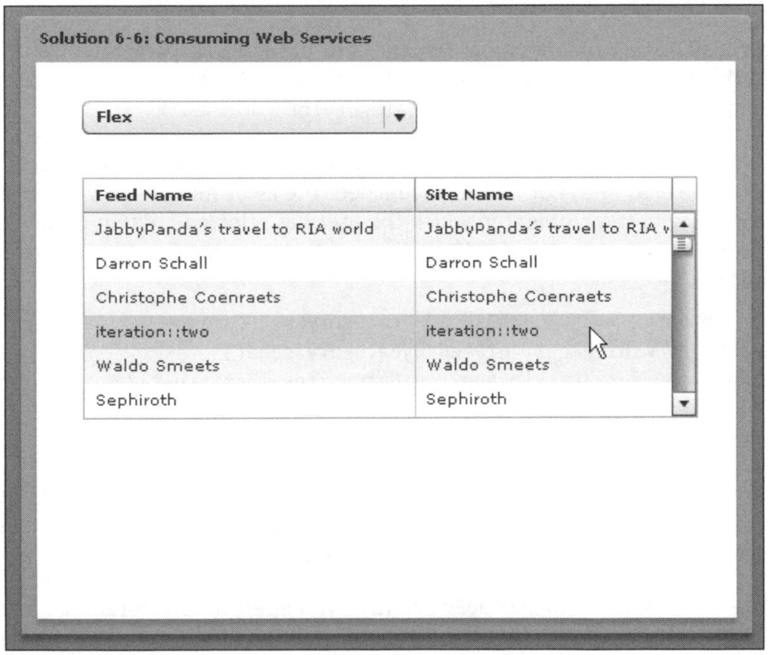

Figure 6-13. By selecting a category from the ComboBox, the call to the getFeedsByCategory method of the web service is carried out, and the response data becomes visualized in the DataGrid.

Expert tips

In your solution, you used two methods of the same web service. For this call, you have not managed event handlers for the result and fault event. This is a bad practice, because you are not able to check any possible errors that can occur or perform operations in the exact moment in which the data is returned by the call.

By offering the possibility of declaring multiple methods for the same WebService class, you must be able to individually check every result event according to the methods that you have launched. The fault event is instead declared on the WebService.

You will make a little addition to the preceding example by including a LinkButton control that opens the web page of the feed that the user selects in the DataGrid. In this way, you can see how to manage event handlers for multiple methods.

The LinkButton is a single-line hypertext link and is generally used with a ViewStack or to open a web page.

1. Insert a LinkButton below the DataGrid control, as shown here, which will manage the click event that will set off the opening of the page:

```
<mx:DataGrid x="30" y="75" id="dgFeed" width="400"
dataProvider="{wsBlogAggr.getFeedsByCategory.lastResult}">
<mx:columns>
<mx:DataGridColumn headerText="Feed Name" dataField="feedName"/>
<mx:DataGridColumn headerText="Site Name" dataField="siteName"
width="75"/>
</mx:columns>
</mx:DataGrid>

<mx:LinkButton label="Open this site" id="urlBtn"  visible="false"
click="navigateToURL(new URLRequest(➥
          dgFeed.selectedItem.siteUrl),'_blank')"
 x="30" y="254"/>

</mx:Panel>
```

The navigateToURL() method loads a document in a window of the web browser and accepts an instance of the URLRequest class as parameter. This class wraps all the information in a single HTTP request. In your code, you in fact create an instance of the URLRequest class to which you send the siteUrl property of the relative item selected by the user in the DataGrid:

```
navigateToURL(new URLRequest(dgFeed.selectedItem.siteUrl),'_blank')
```

Finally, you send the blank string, which specifies to the method to open a new instance of the web browser, as a second parameter of the navigateToURL() method.

However, this button must be invisible as soon as the application is loaded in that it will be capable of launching the site only after the user has selected a category in the ComboBox and, therefore, the second method has been launched. In the moment in which the data is returned from the second call, the button must become visible.

6

2. The LinkButton needs to be set to visible initially. To do so, make the following change:

```
<mx:LinkButton label="Open this site" id="urlBtn" visible="false"
 click="navigateToURL(new URLRequest(➡
          dgFeed.selectedItem.siteUrl),'_blank')"➡
 x="30" y="254"/>
```

It is enough to set the visible property to false, rendering it invisible initially. It will, however, have to become active and visible when the data linked to the DataGrid is loaded.

3. On the result event of the getFeedsByCategory method, you need to set the visible property of the LinkButton as true, so make the following changes:

```
<mx:WebService➡
wsdl="http://weblogs.macromedia.com/mxna/webservices/mxna2.cfc?wsdl"➡
 useProxy="false" id="wsBlogAggr" showBusyCursor="true"➡
 fault="faultHandler(event)" >

  <mx:operation name="getCategories">
  </mx:operation>
 <mx:operation name="getFeedsByCategory"
   result="{urlBtn.visible=true}">
    <mx:request xmlns="">
      <categoryId>{categoryCbx.selectedItem.categoryId}</categoryId>
    </mx:request>
  </mx:operation>
</mx:WebService>
```

4. Aside from having added the ActionScript code to the result, you have also inserted an event handler on the fault event of the web service. Therefore, you must add a Script block, after the Application tag, to write the function:

```
<mx:Script>
  <![CDATA[
    import mx.rpc.events.FaultEvent;

    private function faultHandler(evt:FaultEvent):void
    {
      var errors:String = "Some errors occurred \n";
      errors += "\n Fault Code is :  \n" + evt.fault.faultCode;
      errors += "\n Fault Detail is : \n" + evt.fault.faultDetail;
      errors += "\n Fault String is : \n" + evt.fault.faultString;
      mx.controls.Alert.show(errors);
    }
  ]]>
</mx:Script>
```

5. Save the file and run the application.

When the application starts, the LinkButton won't be visible, but when the user changes the value inside the ComboBox for choosing a blog category, the WebService call will be invoked and the LinkButton will be visible when the result event is dispatched.

Clicking the button, a new browser window will be launched, using the navigateToURL() method, and the selected URL feed will be loaded (dgFeed.selectedItem.siteUrl), as shown in Figure 6-14.

```
<mx:LinkButton label="Open this site" id="urlBtn" visible="false"
  click="navigateToURL(new URLRequest(➡
         dgFeed.selectedItem.siteUrl),'_blank')"
  x="30" y="254"/>
```

Figure 6-14. By selecting a category from the ComboBox, the call to the getFeedsByCategory method of the web service is carried out, and the response data appears in the DataGrid.

Solution 6-7: Using the RemoteObject with ColdFusion Flash Remoting

ColdFusion introduces a new version of Flash Remoting that supports the latest version of the Action Message Format, AMF3, to communicate with Flex applications. Using Flash Remoting makes the communication between Flex and ColdFusion very simple. In fact, AMF3 translates native data types between ActionScript and ColdFusion automatically.

To access ColdFusion via Flash Remoting, you use Flex's RemoteObject, which is another class that comes from Flex's RPC classes. It accesses classes on a remote application server and takes care of the serialization/deserialization process using the AMF3 format.

On the ColdFusion side, you'll develop a CFC, which is a ColdFusion component file. This is the remote class that the Flex application will access for data.

The CFC represents a first step toward the programming of objects with ColdFusion. In fact, CFCs enable you to create methods and constructs, allowing the easy reuse of code across different projects.

In this solution, you will see how to create a CFC file in ColdFusion with a pair of methods that accept parameters. You will then create a Flex application capable of using this remote class via Flash Remoting and using the RemoteObject.

A detailed explanation of ColdFusion server and CFML language is out of the scope of this book, but if you are interested in learning more, you can check out the CFML Language Reference at http://livedocs.macromedia.com/cfmxdocs/CFML_Reference/contents.htm.

> *You can download a free copy of ColdFusion Developer Edition from this URL:* https://www.adobe.com/cfusion/tdrc/index.cfm?product=coldfusion&loc=en%5Fus.

What's involved

The RemoteObject class allows you to access a remote service for getting data. When you use ColdFusion via Flash Remoting, your remote service is represented by a CFC file, or to be more precise, a common text file saved with a .cfc extension. A CFC file begins with the declaration of the <cfcomponent> tag, which is the topmost container in which you will create your methods.

```
<cfcomponent displayname="flex remote service"➥
   hint="The remote service to be consumed by Flex application">
```

The displayname attribute contains the name of the components that will be displayed when the developer launches the automatically generated file, while the hint attribute contains the text that describes the CFC.

You can add comments in a CFC just like in any HTML file:

```
<!---This is a comment in the  CFC --->
```

The methods are specified in a CFC with the <cffunction> tag; in this tag, you also specify the following properties:

- name: Specifies the name with which the method will be recalled
- access: Specifies the type of access to your remote case
- returntype: Specifies the data type of the response data

The final tag looks like this:

```
<cffunction name="queryData" access="remote" returntype="numeric">
```

The returntypes you can use are as follows:

- Any
- Array
- Binary
- Boolean
- Numeric
- Date
- Guid
- Query
- String
- Struct
- Uuid
- Variablename
- Void

In the declaration of the function, you will specify all the operations that you intend to carry out.

From the point of view of Flex, using CFC is equivalent to using a web service. It will, in fact, be enough to use the WebService or the RemoteObject tag and invoke the methods with the <mx:operation> or <mx:method> tag, sending them the parameters that they expect and managing the response data.

In this solution, you will see how to use a remote service created in ColdFusion that accesses a database and carries out queries using the values that are sent to it by the Flex application as search parameters.

How to build it

When you create a Flex project with Flex Builder and use ColdFusion as your back-end solution, you need to select the right project type. The New Flex Project dialog box allows you to choose from three different Flex project types: Basic, ColdFusion Flash Remoting Service, and Flex Data Services (see Figure 6-15). To create a Flex project that will use ColdFusion via Flash Remoting, you have to select the second option: ColdFusion Flash Remoting Service.

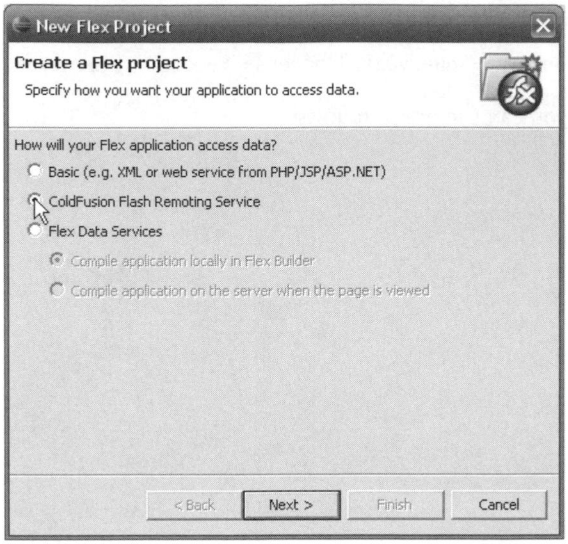

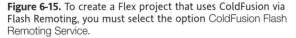

Figure 6-15. To create a Flex project that uses ColdFusion via Flash Remoting, you must select the option ColdFusion Flash Remoting Service.

Make sure to have ColdFusion 8 (or ColdFusion 7.0.2) installed on your machine (see the instructions at http://livedocs.adobe.com/coldfusion/8/) and know where your ColdFusion server is installed. During the installation of the ColdFusion server, if you select the built-in web server, your web root directory will be drive:/ ColdFusion8/wwwroot by default. This web server runs on the 8500 port. To display a page, append 8500 to the end of the host name or IP address as follows: http:// localhost:8500/coldFusionPage.cfm.

1. Start by creating a new Flex project in Flex Builder that uses ColdFusion Flash Remoting by selecting the appropriate option on the first screen of the wizard, as shown in Figure 6-15.

2. Click the Next button and specify the following settings on the screen that appears, as shown Figure 6-16:

   - Use Local ColdFusion Server: Make sure this option, which specifies that the local installation of ColdFusion be used by the project, is not selected.

   - Root Folder: This option specifies the ColdFusion root folder.

   - Root URL: Enter the root URL in this text field (for example, http://localhost: 8500/).

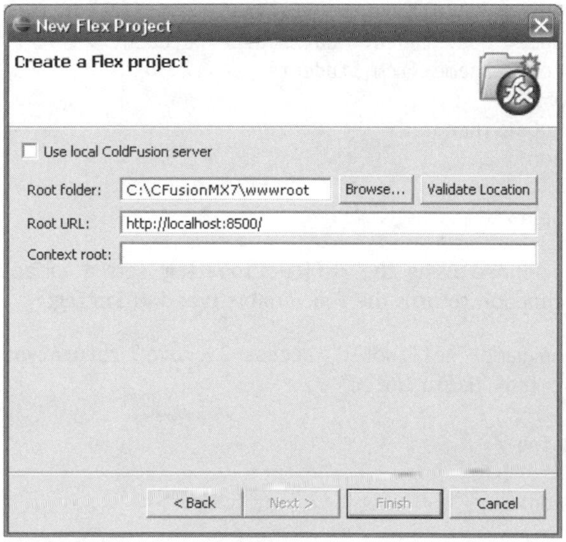

Figure 6-16. You have to specify the root folder and the root URL of the ColdFusion server.

3. Click the Next button, give the Flex project the name Chapter_6_Flex_ColdFusion, and specify a project location. Click the Finish button.

When you create a ColdFusion Flash Remoting project, an additional option will be added to the compiler. You can see it using Project ➤ Properties ➤ Flex Compiler. In the Additional compiler arguments text field, you'll see the following new argument: -services "C:\ColdFusion8\wwwroot\WEB-INF\flex\services-config.xml". The services-config.xml file is needed to specify the configuration of the remote services that the Flex application will have to use.

4. Create the ColdFusion component file that will allow you to communicate with the Flex application. You can use your favorite editor for writing ColdFusion code, but you can also decide to use Flex Builder. From File ➤ New ➤ File, create a new file named remoteService.cfc. This file will be located in the server web root: C:/ColdFusion8/wwwroot/components/flexsolutions/. The path of the remote CFC file is important because it's passed to the source property of the RemoteObject class.

5. The CFC will have two simple methods: one that returns a simple Hello World string, and another that connects to a database, selects some records in a table, and returns the response data back. Insert the following code in the CFC file:

```
<cfcomponent name="FlexFlashRemoting"
hint="This is a remote CFC service that ➥
        uses a Coldfusion Flash Remoting Flex project">

<cffunction name="helloWorld" access="remote" returntype="string">
<cfset var foo="Hello World" />
<cfreturn foo />
</cffunction>
```

```
<cffunction name="helloQuery" access="remote" returntype="query">
<cfquery name="qGetStudent" datasource="student">
SELECT name, surname from students
</cfquery>
<cfreturn qGetStudent />
</cffunction>

</cfcomponent>
```

The first method, defined using the <cffunction> tag, sets a variable with the Hello World string. This function returns the foo variable typed as String:

```
<cffunction name="helloWorld" access="remote" returntype="string">
<cfset var foo="Hello World" />

<cfreturn foo />

</cffunction>
```

The second method, helloQuery, accesses a data source named student and makes a query to select the name and surname field of the records in the students table:

```
<cffunction name="helloQuery" access="remote" returntype="query">
<cfquery name="qGetStudent" datasource="student">
SELECT name, surname from students
</cfquery>
<cfreturn qGetStudent />
</cffunction>
```

The function embeds the returned data into the qGetStudent query variable.

> In ColdFusion, a **data source** is a complete database configuration that uses a JDBC driver to communicate with a specific database. You must configure a data source for each database that you want to use. In your solution, you create the student data source. You can learn how to create a data source using the ColdFusion Administrator console following the instructions here: http://livedocs.adobe.com/coldfusion/8/htmldocs/datasources_ADV_MJS_01.html.

Now you can access this remote CFC file and consume these two methods in the Flex application using the RemoteObject tag.

6. Create a new MXML application file by selecting File ➤ New ➤ MXML Application and name it Chapter_6_Flex_Sol_7.mxml. Below the Application tag, insert a DataGrid control and a Label control bound to the response data of the RemoteObject:

```
<mx:Label text="{myFoo}" />
<mx:DataGrid id="myDG" dataProvider="{myAC}"  visible="false"/>
```

The Label control uses the content of the myFoo variable in its text property, while the DataGrid control uses the myAC variable as dataProvider. This control is not visible at the startup of the application (visible="false"). It will become visible only when the remote method dispatches the result event.

7. Add the RemoteObject tag above the Label control:

```
<mx:RemoteObject
id="myRO"
destination="ColdFusion"
source="components.flexsolutions.remoteService"
showBusyCursor="true">
</mx:RemoteObject>

<mx:Label text="{myFoo}" />
```

The RemoteObject uses some important properties: destination and source. The destination property is set to ColdFusion, and the source property contains the location of the CFC file you're accessing. You point to the CFC file using its fully qualified path (components.flexsolutions.remoteService) assuming that the file resides on the web root folder of the ColdFusion server.

The destination property is referenced in the identifier specified in the <destination> tag of the services-config.xml file. If you open this configuration file, you'll see that node with its id attribute set to ColdFusion:

```
<destination id="ColdFusion">
    <channels>
        <channel ref="my-cfamf"/>
    </channels>
    <properties>
        <source>*</source>
        <!-- define the resolution rules and
            access level of the cfc being invoked -->
        <access>
            <!-- Use the ColdFusion mappings to find CFCs,
                by default only CFC files under your webroot
                can be found. -->
            <use-mappings>false</use-mappings>
            <!-- allow "public and remote" or just "remote"
             methods to be invoked -->
            <method-access-level>remote</method-access-level>
        </access>

        <property-case>
            <!-- cfc property names -->
            <force-cfc-lowercase>false</force-cfc-lowercase>
            <!-- Query column names -->
            <force-query-lowercase>false</force-query-lowercase>
            <!-- struct keys -->
```

6

```
      <force-struct-lowercase>false</force-struct-lowercase>
    </property-case>
  </properties>
</destination>
```

8. The RemoteObject, such as the WebService class, supports the call of multiple methods. The CFC file you create has two methods. Using the <mx:method> tag, you can declare the methods you want to access:

```
<mx:RemoteObject
id="myRO"
destination="ColdFusion"
source="components.flexsolutions.remoteService"
showBusyCursor="true">
<mx:method name="helloWorld"
result="helloResultHandler(event)"
fault="faultHandler(event)"/>

<mx:method name="helloQuery"
result="queryResultHandler(event)"
fault="faultHandler(event)"/>

</mx:RemoteObject>
```

Each method tag selects the remote method it wants to access using the name attribute. For the two <mx:method> tags, you create the event handlers for their result and fault events.

9. Insert a Script block below the Application tag, where you'll create the event handlers that are called by the result and fault event of the RemoteObject methods:

```
<mx:Script>
<![CDATA[
import mx.collections.ArrayCollection;
import mx.rpc.events.FaultEvent;
import mx.rpc.events.ResultEvent;
import mx.controls.Alert;

[Bindable]
private var myFoo:String;

[Bindable]
private var myAC:ArrayCollection;

private function helloResultHandler(evt:ResultEvent):void{
    myFoo = evt.result as String;
}
```

```
    private function queryResultHandler(evt:ResultEvent):void
    {
      myAC =evt.result as ArrayCollection;
      myDG.visible = true;
    }

    private function faultHandler(evt:FaultEvent):void
    {
      mx.controls.Alert.show("The following error(s) occurred: ➡
        " + evt.fault.faultDetail)
    }

  ]]>
  </mx:Script>
```

You declared two variables that will contain the response data of the remote call. The first event handler, helloResultHandler(), called by the result event of the helloWorld method, inserts the foo string returned by the CFC method into the myFoo variable:

```
    private function helloResultHandler(evt:ResultEvent):void{
      myFoo = evt.result as String;
    }
```

The event handler called by the result event of the helloQuery method populates the ArrayCollection variable using the response data. Therefore, it makes the DataGrid visible. In your CFC file, the helloQuery cffunction returns a variable typed as query:

```
    private function queryResultHandler(evt:ResultEvent):void
    {
      myAC =evt.result as ArrayCollection;
      myDG.visible = true;
    }
```

It's Flash Remoting with the support of AMF3 that takes care of the serialization/deserialization process between ActionScript and ColdFusion data types.

10. As with the HTTPService and the WebService classes, no remote call is made until the RPC class has been invoked. The HTTPService and WebService classes use the send() method; otherwise, the RemoteObject launches the name of the remote methods to invoke it. Add the following code on the creationComplete event of the Application tag:

    ```
    <mx:Application xmlns:mx="http://www.adobe.com/2006/mxml"
    layout="vertical"
    creationComplete="myRO.helloWorld();myRO.helloQuery()" >
    ```

11. Save the file and run the application to see the ColdFusion Flash Remoting connection in action.

Expert tips

One of the cool features of ColdFusion 8 is the event gateway, which allows the ColdFusion server to communicate with the Short Message Service (SMS), interact with Java Messaging Services, and as far as Flex is concerned, send and receive messages with the Flex Data Services.

The recent update of ColdFusion to version 8, released in conjunction with the release of Flex, introduces the Flex Messaging event gateway and a new version of the Action Message Format, AMF3, compatible with the new ActionScript 3.0 data types. AMF is used by Flash Remoting and allows Flex applications to communicate directly with the RemoteObject of ColdFusion.

Therefore, another system for using CFC files with Flex is to use the RemoteObject class and define the path of the CFC as the destination of the remote service by configuring it in the file services-config.xml.

Another great integration between ColdFusion and Flex is the ColdFusion Extensions for Adobe Flex Builder. The extension is an Eclipse plug-in, and it adds the Application Generation Wizard, a Flex Builder–specific dialog box that makes communication with Flex easy. Moreover, it installs RDS panels, the Services Browser panel, the CF Log Viewer, RDS support, help, wizards, and the interactive debugger.

To install the ColdFusion extensions for Adobe Flex Builder, do the following:

1. Start up Flex Builder and select Help ➤ Software Updates ➤ Find and Install.

2. Select Search for New Features to Install **and click the** New Archived Site **button.**

3. Browse to select the extension's ZIP file that you downloaded.

4. Finish the installation and restart Flex Builder.

You can learn more about the ColdFusion extensions for Adobe Flex Builder in the video tutorials at the following site: www.adobe.com/devnet/coldfusion/articles/wizards.html.

Solution 6-8: Remote communication with the Flash Player URLLoader class

The RPC classes are not the only system for remote data communication with Flex. There also exists the URLLoader class, part of the flash.net package, which permits the downloading of data as text, binary data, or URL-encoded variables.

With this class, the same results can be obtained as with the RPC class. You can, in fact, send requests with parameters to any server-side languages using the load() method of the class.

Furthermore, you can manage the response data, given that URLLoader sends notifications on the progress of the download process (which you can access through the bytesLoaded and bytesTotal properties) and also on the occurrence of the receipt of data.

The events in this class are usually recorded with the addEventListener method of the event handlers:

```
myURLService.addEventListener(Event.COMPLETE, completeHandler);
```

In this solution, you will see how to load an XML file using the URLLoader class.

What's involved

In order to begin, you must first create an instance of the URLLoader class:

```
private var myURLService:URLLoader;
```

At this point, you can call the load() method of the class, which expects to receive a URLRequest object as a parameter. The URLRequest class specifies that all the information is wrapped in a single HTTP request:

```
myURLService.load( new URLRequest("data/states.xml"));
```

The XML file of this example is local, but the URLRequest class can also load remote files or recall server-side files.

The moment in which the data is returned by the call, the COMPLETE event is dispatched. This event makes up part of the flash.events.Event class, and you usually record it with the addEventListener method:

```
myURLService.addEventListener(Event.COMPLETE, completeHandler);
```

You will see in this solution how to load the response data of a URLLoader class in a ComboBox.

How to build it

1. Create a new MXML application file by selecting File ➤ New ➤ MXML Application and name it Chapter_6_Flex_Sol_8.mxml.

2. On the creationComplete event of the application, you launch an init() method, which will bring the event object with it and initialize your URLLoader class. Update the Application tag as follows:

```
<mx:Application
xmlns:mx="http://www.adobe.com/2006/mxml" layout="vertical"
creationComplete="init(event)">
```

3. Write the init() function in a Script block, and then create the private variable with which you will work in this exercise:

```
<mx:Script>
  <![CDATA[
    private var myURLService:URLLoader = new URLLoader();
    private var myURL:URLRequest =  new URLRequest("data/states.xml");
    [Bindable]private var myData:XMLList;
```

```
      private function init(event:Event):void {
        myURLService.addEventListener(Event.COMPLETE, completeHandler);
        XML.ignoreWhitespace = true;
      }
    ]]>
  </mx:Script>
```

You declare three private variables:

- myURLService contains an instance of the URLLoader class and carries out the call to the XML file.
- myURL contains the URL in which the XML file is located.
- myData is an XMLList that will contain the response data of the call.

The init() method records the event handler completeHandler() for the COMPLETE event, which will take care of loading the data into the XMLList variable and using it as data provider for a ComboBox.

4. Add the event handler that dispatches on the completion of the call and when the data has been received by including this code below the init() function:

```
      private function init(event:Event):void {
        myURLService.addEventListener(Event.COMPLETE, completeHandler);
        XML.ignoreWhitespace = true;
      }

      private function completeHandler(event:Event):void {
      myData = new XMLList(myURLService.data);
      myCBX.dataProvider = myData.children();
      }
```

The data returned by the call is contained in the data property of the URLLoader object. The myData variable is used as data provider for your ComboBox.

Up until now, no call has yet been made. In fact, until the load() method is launched from the URLLoader, no call will be carried out.

5. Add the elements of the user interface of your example—insert a ComboBox and a List control, as shown in the following code. The latter will contain the data of the population contained in the myData variable but will be loaded only after the user has selected a city in the ComboBox. You must launch the load() of the class that you will trigger on the click event of a Button event:

```
<mx:ComboBox id="myCBX" labelField="city" change="filterData(event)" />
<mx:List id="myList"  />
<mx:Button label="Send Remote Call" click="myURLService.load(myURL);"/>
```

The structure of the XML file is the same as what you have already seen in preceding solutions:

```
<?xml version="1.0" encoding="UTF-8"?>
<dataroot>
<city>
<id>1</id>
<id_region>1</id_region>
<region>PIEMONTE</region>
<cityName>TORINO</cityName>
<code>TO</code>
<population>2236765</population>
<male>1086745</male>
<female>1150020</female>
<family>886053</family>
</city>
```

This is why the ComboBox uses the city property to load in label: labelField="city". The ComboBox, on the event change, specifies the filterData() function, which will have the job of loading the data in the List control.

The Button simply makes the call to the load() method on the click. The myURL variable typed as URLRequest, which contains the local path of the XML file, is sent to the load() method:

```
private var myURL:URLRequest = new URLRequest("data/states.xml");
```

6. Before running the application, you need do nothing more than add the following filterData function in the Script block, which will have the job of loading the data of the population in the list control:

```
private function filterData(evt:Event):void
{
  myList.dataProvider = myData.city.population;
}
```

7. Save the file and run the application. You should see the result shown in Figure 6-17.

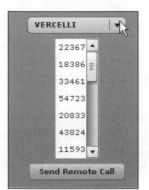

Figure 6-17.
The URLLoader class allows you to make remote calls through the load() method.

Expert tips

The URLLoader also allows you to send parameters to the remote call that is being made. To send parameters, it is necessary to add the values appended to the data property of the URLRequest object, which can send binary data or string data:

```
private var myURLService:URLLoader = new URLLoader();
private var myURL:URLRequest = ➡
           new URLRequest("http://localhost/myfile.php");

private var myValues:URLVariables = new URLVariables();
myValues.id = myData.city.id;
myValues.city = myCBX.value;
myURL.data = myValues;

myURLService.load(myURL)
```

In this example, you created the myValues variable of URLVariables() type and inserted the id and city property in it. This object has been inserted in the data property of the URLRequest object.

Finally, when you launch the load() method, you send it the entire myURL object as a parameter.

Your remote PHP file is capable of intercepting the single properties that are sent to it by the call.

It is possible to also set the modality with which the data is launched through the method property, which accepts the values flash.net.URLRequestMethod.POST and flash.net. URLRequestMethod.GET.

Solution 6-9: Using the RemoteObject with AMFPHP

The latest version of AMFPHP (www.amf-php.org/), the 1.9 beta2, includes support for the AMF3 format. This means that you can use the open source AMFPHP with the RemoteObject of Flex. You can read about the latest release of the kit here: www.5etdemi. com/blog/archives/2007/01/amfphp-19-beta-2-ridiculously-faster/.

> *AMF is a proprietary data format created by Adobe. It's a binary format for data seri-alization/deserialization and remote method invocation, and it's used by Flash Remoting,* NetConnection, NetStream, LocalConnection, *and* SharedObject. *AMF3 in Flex is used with* RemoteObject's *components.*

The AMFPHP project, headed by Patrick Mineault (www.5etdemi.com/blog), has added support for AMF3, the newest AMF format that is used by Adobe Flex 2 (or above) and ActionScript 3.0.

Using the RemoteObject class, PHP developers are able to write applications that can translate PHP objects directly into ActionScript objects in their Flex projects. This means there is a more powerful way to transfer data than using XML-based data.

In this tutorial, you will use the RemoteObject together with the AMFPHP toolkit to transfer data from the server to the client using PHP.

What's involved

To be able to use AMFPHP 1.9, you must first of all download it. From www.5etdemi.com/uploads/amfphp-1.9.beta.zip, you can download the ZIP file containing AMFPHP, which you can then unzip in the root folder of your application server. The kit will therefore be recallable from the local address: http://localhost/amfphp1_9.

To be able to use AMFPHP in the Flex project, you must add the file services-config.xml to the compiler. This file is needed to specify the configuration of the services that the Flex application will have to use. The content of the file will be the following:

```
<?xml version="1.0" encoding="UTF-8"?>
<services-config>
<services>
<service id="amfphp-flashremoting-service"
class="flex.messaging.services.RemotingService"
messageTypes="flex.messaging.messages.RemotingMessage">
<destination id="amfphp">
<channels>
<channel ref="my-amfphp"/>
</channels>
<properties>
<source>*</source>
</properties>
</destination>
</service>
</services>
<channels>
<channel-definition id="my-amfphp"
class="mx.messaging.channels.AMFChannel">
<endpoint uri="http://localhost/amfphp1_9/gateway.php"
class="flex.messaging.endpoints.AMFEndpoint"/>
</channel-definition>
</channels>
</services-config>
```

6

To add this file to the compiler, send the path of the file to the parameter services:

```
-services "services-config.xml"
```

Once this is done, you can use the RemoteObject, which is the class that gives you the access to the methods of remote objects (Java, ColdFusion, PHP) using AMF encoding.

The RemoteObject points to the service to which you must connect through the destination properties. In this case, as it has been specified in the services-config.xml file, the destination property points to the service AMFPHP:

```
<mx:RemoteObject id="myservice"
showBusyCursor="true"
source="flexsolutions.HelloWorld"
 destination="amfphp">
<mx:method name="myMethod"
result="resultHandler(event)"
fault="faultHandler(event)" />
</mx:RemoteObject>
```

As for the WebService tag, you can invoke different methods on the same remote object. Therefore, with the method tag, you access the remote method that you intend to recall, myMethod in the example code.

In this solution, you will see how to invoke a remote method written in PHP using AMFPHP 1.9.

How to build it

Start with the download of the AMFPHP 1.9 kit from www.5etdemi.com/uploads/amfphp-1.9.beta.zip. Create a folder in your web root server named /amfphp1_9 and unzip the amfphp-1.9.beta.zip file in this folder. This way you can access the AMFPHP services from this location: http://localhost/amfphp1_9.

> If you want to test the file you'll create in this solution on your local machine, you need to have an application server with the support of PHP installed on your machine. Read the "How to build" section of Solution 6-3 for references to help you install a web server.

1. In the amfphp1_9 folder you just created, create a folder that you will call flexsolutions (http://localhost/amfphp1_9/flexsolutions/).

2. Open Flex Builder and create a new file by selecting File ➤ New ➤ File and save it as remoteObject.php. Your PHP file will have only one method, remoteMethod(), which will return the string Hello World. Insert the following code in the file:

```php
<?php
class remoteObject
{
    function remoteMethod()
    {
        return "Hello World";
    }
}
?>
```

3. Save the file and put it in the folder that you have created in the web root of the server: http://localhost/amfphp1_9/flexsolutions/. You can use the AMFPHP Browser, which you access from the folder http://localhost/amfphp1_9/browser, to navigate all the remote services you have created in the folder.

4. Create another file by selecting File ➤ New ➤ File and save it as services-config.xml. This file must be located in the root of the project (If you change the path, you must then send it to the compiler). In this file, copy the following code:

```xml
<?xml version="1.0" encoding="UTF-8"?>
<services-config>
<services>
<service id="amfphp-flashremoting-service"
class="flex.messaging.services.RemotingService"
messageTypes="flex.messaging.messages.RemotingMessage">
<destination id="amfphp">
<channels>
<channel ref="my-amfphp"/>
</channels>
<properties>
<source>*</source>
</properties>
</destination>
</service>
</services>
<channels>
<channel-definition id="my-amfphp"
class="mx.messaging.channels.AMFChannel">
<endpoint uri="http://localhost/amfphp1_9/gateway.php"
class="flex.messaging.endpoints.AMFEndpoint"/>
</channel-definition>
</channels>
</services-config>
```

This is the file that configures the services for the RemoteObject, which must, however, be added as additional settings to the compiler of Flex Builder (or also to the compc command-line compiler).

5. Go to the Project menu and select the Properties option. Click Flex Compiler Category and, in the Additional compiler arguments text field, add the following option: -services "services-config.xml".

6. Create a new MXML application file by selecting File ➤ New ➤ MXML Application and name it Chapter_6_Flex_Sol_9.mxml. Add a Button control, which will have the task of launching the RemoteObject and invoking the method, and a TextArea control that instead visualizes the response data (the string Hello World):

```
<?xml version="1.0" encoding="utf-8"?>
<mx:Application xmlns:mx="http://www.adobe.com/2006/mxml"
layout="vertical">

<mx:Button label="Invoke the remote Method" />

<mx:TextArea width="200" height="100"
id="myResult"/>

</mx:Application>
```

7. Insert the RemoteObject tag and set its source and destination properties. The first contains the package of the remote object to call, while the second contains the service to use and corresponds to the id of the destination node in the service-config.xml file:

```
<mx:Application xmlns:mx="http://www.adobe.com/2006/mxml"
layout="vertical">

<mx:RemoteObject id="myRO"
showBusyCursor="true"
source="flexsolutions.remoteObject"
destination="amfphp">

<mx:method name="sayHello"
result="resultHandler(event)" />
</mx:RemoteObject>
```

The method to invoke is instead recalled in the <mx:method> tag and specified in the name property. Also, you link an event handler, which will have the job of printing the response data in the TextArea control, to the result event.

As for the other RPC services (HTTPService and WebService), no invocation occurs until the send() method of the RPC class is invoked. For this reason, you'll now add the send() method to the click event of the Button.

8. On the Button tag, write the following ActionScript code for the click event:

```
<mx:Button label="Invoke the remote Method"
click="myRO.getOperation('remoteMethod').send();"/>
```

When the user clicks the Button control, the remoteMethod function is called by using the getOperation() method of the RemoteObject, myRO. The remoteMethod() is the function defined in the remoteObject.php file.

9. Now you only need to write the event handler for the result event of the RemoteObject. Add a Script block immediately under the declaration of the RemoteObject tag with the following function:

```
<mx:Script>
<![CDATA[
private function resultHandler(evt:ResultEvent):void
{
myResult.text = evt.result.toString();
}
]]>
</mx:Script>
```

10. Save the file and run the application

By clicking the Button, you invoke the remote method. The remote service is invoked and the remoteMethod() method run. This method simply returns a string that will be printed in the TextArea when the result event of the operation is invoked.

In your solution, your method is very simple. But you can see how the PHP involved allows you to do practically anything you like on the server side: integrate tables of a database, write to and read files from the disk, and so forth.

Furthermore, you can also use the reflection to automatically send the properties of a PHP class to an ActionScript class and vice versa.

By using the variable $explicitType in the PHP class, you declare the class mapping options. Then, in the ActionScript class, you can reference the PHP class by using the [RemoteClass] metadata:

```
[RemoteClass(alias="mypackage.myPHPClass")]
```

11. Create a value object in PHP that will then be mapped to the ActionScript value object class (Solution 3-3 deals with value objects). Create a new PHP file named StudentVO.php and save it in the folder that you have created in the web root of the server: http://localhost/amfphp1_9/flexsolutions/. Copy the following PHP code into it:

```php
<?php
class StudentVO
{
   var $stuId;
   var $firstName;
   var $lastName;
  var $email;
  // explicit actionscript package
   var $_explicitType = "com.flexsolutions.chapter6.Student";
}
?>
```

6

12. Create a new ActionScript class in Flex Builder and save it as StudentVO.as in the folder com/flexsolutions/chapter6. Insert the following code:

```
package com.flexsolutions.chapter6
{
   [RemoteClass(alias="flexsolutions.StudentVO")]
   [Bindable]
   public class StudentVO
   {
      public var stuId:int;
      public var firstName:String;
      public var lastName:String;
      public var email:String;

   }
}
```

As for the PHP class, the ActionScript class that functions as the value object (or DataTransferObject if you prefer) defines only the properties that your object will transport and that will be mapped with those of the remote PHP class.

At this point, in your Flex application, you can use the ActionScript value object and the properties that it transports:

```
import com.flexsolutions.chapter6.StudentVO
 [Bindable]
private var myStudentVO:StudentVO = newStudentVO();
```

Through the RemoteObject, you can invoke a remote PHP method that saves the ActionScript class with all its values that are taken, for example, from TextInputs of a form. The function that sends the parameters to the RemoteObject takes the values from the text inputs and sends them with the send() method to the remote method:

```
private function saveStudentVO():void
{
        var myStudentVO:StudentVO = new StudentVO();

        myStudentVO.empId = idTxt.text;
        myStudentVO.firstName = nameTxt_name.text;
        myStudentVO.lastName = lastTxt.text;
        myStudentVO.email = emailTxt.text;

        myRO.saveMethod.send(myStudentVO);

}
```

AMFPHP represents an excellent alternative for creating Flex applications and optimizing the performance of the application on the exchange of remote data from the server to the client. In fact, the AMF3 format performs best of all other methods that are instead XML based and therefore affected by the slowness of the management of this type of file.

Expert tips

The AMFPHP toolkit is not the only one that enables you to work with the AMF format in Flex. Other projects exist that offer support for AMF3:

- **SabreAMF** (www.osflash.org/sabreamf): An AMF client and server for PHP5. The goal of the project is to create a lean AMF library that is fully PHP5 E_STRICT-compliant.
- **WebOrb for PHP** (www.themidnightcoders.com/weborb/php/index.htm): A server-side technology enabling connectivity between Flex and Flash Remoting clients and PHP applications.
- **RubyAMF** (http://wiki.rubyamf.org/): An open source gateway for Flash Remoting. As the name suggests, the exposed services are written with the wonderful language of Ruby.

Summary

6

Remote data communication is essential to every web application. It allows you to send and receive data between the client and the server.

Because Flex does not have native access to databases, you need to use remote data sources to take advantage of the RPC classes to perform calls to business logic built using whichever server-side solution you choose to send and receive remote data.

As you now know, the RPC services in Flex provide a call-and-response model to access remote data and expose the components based on SOA via the three RPC classes of Flex: HTTPService, WebService, RemoteObject.

In this chapter, you've learned how to use the HTTPService to load remote data from an XML file on another domain and put the response data in Flex controls such as the DataGrid, the ComboBox, or the TextInput.

As calls made by Flex are asynchronous, it becomes even more important to carry out operations only after you are certain that the operation has been successfully completed and particularly that no errors have occurred. In order to handle the response of the remote calls in Flex, you've learned to use two events: result and fault. You wrote the code for handling and displaying the response data contained in the result property of the ResultEvent event object. Then you gave the appropriate feedback messages to users of the application to show them any errors that occurred and to make them understand the reason the remote connection was not completed successfully.

Other than loading static XML data, you used the HTTPService to call XML data dynamically generated by middleware. The HTTPService is capable of receiving response data generated by any server-side language in XML format. So you explored scripts written using PHP and JSP to send and receive data to and from the Flex application.

Flex can use a new scripting language, E4X, to handle the XML response data. With the RPC services of type HTTPService and WebService, it is possible to set the data type that the lastResult object contains. As you saw, you can use the resultFormat property to change from its default value, Object, to the new E4X format.

In addition to the HTTPService class, with Flex you saw how to carry out calls to web services using the WebService class. To reinforce what you learned about web services, you created an application that can load different methods of the same web services performing different operations.

You created a solution that took advantage of the URLLoader class, which permits the downloading of data as text, binary data, or URL-encoded variables. In the example solution, in fact, you saw how to call a remote service passing parameters to it using the load() method of the URLLoader class.

At the end of the chapter, you were introduced to the latest version of the AMFPHP kit, 1.9 beta 2, which adds support for the AMF3 format, allowing PHP developers to write applications that can translate PHP objects directly into ActionScript objects in their Flex projects and thus providing a more powerful way to transfer XML data.

In the next chapter, you'll learn how response data has to be displayed in the application and linked to the components that make up the user interface. You'll use a set of specific controls for this type of operation, which facilitate the work of the developer to show the user the data. These components are known as the list-based controls.

7 DISPLAYING DATA WITH LIST-BASED COMPONENTS

Item renderer and editor example

title	header
Flex 2 and EJB 3	How to integrate Fle
Apollo and the HTMl	Swf files and Javasc
Adobe LiveCycle PDl	How to automate th

```
<article>
  <title>Flex 2 and EJB 3</title>
  <header>How to integrate Flex with J2EE
```

One to many relationship

► YouThru.com
► Acme spa
▼ Comtaste Corp.
   Marco
   Raffele
   Liviu

Flex Compiler

Flex SDK version
○ Use default SDK (currently "Flex 3 M3 (Beta
● Use a specific SDK: Flex 3 M3 (Beta 2)
  Flex 2.0.1 Hotfix 3
  Flex 3 M3 (Beta 2)

Compiler options
☑ Copy non-embedded files to output directo
☐ Generate accessible SWF file
☑ Enable strict type checking
☑ Enable warnings

Additional compiler arguments:

Rich Internet Applications (RIAs) developed with Flex differ considerably from classic web applications developed with XHTML and server-side languages (such as ColdFusion, PHP, JSP, or Ruby on Rails) because they can reload small amounts of data without having to reload the entire page (for example, if a user adds an item to a shopping basket and a price update is required). The same approach is used by Ajax applications.

> *Ajax (shorthand for Asynchronous JavaScript and XML) is asynchronous in that loading does not interfere with normal page loading. JavaScript is the programming language in which Ajax function calls are made. Data retrieved using the technique is commonly formatted using XML, as reflected in the naming of the* XMLHttpRequest *object from which Ajax is derived. For more information see "Ajax" on wikipedia:* http://en. wikipedia.org/wiki/Ajax_(programming).

In Flex, things are very different: The model program of Flex is based on an event model. For every interaction the user has with the application's user interface, you can include operations that make remote calls to change the state of the application or load external elements.

In the preceding chapter, you saw how to use remote calls to invoke remote data. More often than not, this data has to be displayed in the application and linked to the components that make up the user interface. Flex provides a set of specific components for this type of operation that facilitates the work of the developer to show the end user the data (which you'll explore in this chapter). These components are said to be list-based and use the ListBase component (http://livedocs.adobe.com/labs/flex3/langref/mx/controls/listClasses/ListBase.html) as their base class and put forward the dataProvider property, an object that contains the data to be shown. For example, the List control, which you'll see in Solution 7-1, enables you to show a vertical list of items, while the Tree control enables you to represent hierarchical data under the form of an expandable tree.

The following controls make up part of the category of components defined as list-based:

- List
- HorizontalList
- DataGrid, AdvancedDataGrid
- Menu
- PrintDataGrid, PrintAdvancedDataGrid
- TileList
- Tree

Another important characteristic of these Flex controls is that they support the common operations of drag and drop. In web applications that use HTML or DHTML, adding functions to move items from one place on the page to another is not a simple operation. It requires some fairly complex JavaScript, which is prone to cross-browser compatibility issues.

In Flex, drag and drop is rendered easily with the Drag and Drop Manager, which enables you to create functions for moving data from one place to another. For example, you can trace an item of a DataGrid control to a List control by setting only a few properties (dragEnabled, dropEnabled, dragMoveEnabled, and so on). This chapter also illustrates techniques for managing drag-and-drop operations.

Solution 7-1: Display data using list-based controls

The first of the list-based controls for representing data is the List control, which represents data in a vertical list. This is probably the most common list-based control you'll use because you often need to show ordered data to the user, be it the products of a shopping cart or the list of employees of a company.

The components covered in this chapter can be easily modified and adapted to fit your needs. By using features such as data binding it is easy to manipulate the data exactly how you want it. Flex's data binding lets you bind data to a component and link its value for the entire life cycle of the application. In Flex there are three ways to create a data binding:

- Use the curly braces syntax
- Use the <mx:Binding> tag defined in the MXML code
- Declare the BindingUtils method with ActionScript

7

> If you want to review these techniques, refer to Chapters 1 and 6.

This first solution displays some data with List and DataGrid components and then shows how to modify them to customize data visualization.

What's involved

Access the MXML tag <mx:List> to use the List control. As for all the other list-based controls, you must specify a data provider that will link the data to be visualized to this control.

You can define the dataProvider property both as an attribute of the <mx:List> tag and as a nested node, as shown in the following code:

```
<mx:List id= "myList" dataProvider="{myData}">
```

Or use the following:

```
<mx:List id= "myList">
  <mx:dataProvider>
    <mx:String>Marco</mx:String>
```

```
        <mx:String>Francesco</mx:String>
        <mx:String>Emanuele</mx:String>
      </mx:dataProvider>
    </mx:List>
```

In this simple example, the List control would be populated with all the items defined as String in the <mx:dataProvider> tag. If the data to be linked to the List control with a data provider was not linear but complex, you would have to use the labelField property. You'll consider a collection of complex data now.

This solution uses XML data, which will be passed to the Flex application via an HTTPService request. Remember that Flex treats XML data structures as objects, so you can easily work with these types of data. The XML file will have the following structure:

```
<root>
  <person>
    <name>Francesco</name>
    <surname>Rapana</surname>
    <phone>00391234567</phone>
    <age>23</age>
  </person>
</root>
```

This is an example of complex data, not linear data. In fact, if you were to use this structure of data in a dataProvider of the List control, you would obtain the result shown in Figure 7-1.

```
<person>
  <name>Constantin</name>
  <surname>Moldovanu</surname>
  <phone>5551234</phone>
  <age>24</age>
</person>

<person>
  <name>Emanuele</name>
  <surname>Tatti</surname>
  <phone>5552341</phone>
  <age>23</age>
</person>

<person>
  <name>Francesco</name>
  <surname>Rapanà</surname>
  <phone>5553412</phone>
  <age>23</age>
</person>
```

Figure 7-1. The List control represents simple data and can't visualize complex structures without specifying the labelField property.

In practice, the content of every repeating node of the XML file has been displayed in every index of the List control.

To correctly display the data, you must specify which item must be visualized to the component by using the labelField property. This enables you to link a single field to a particular value within a complex data structure:

```
    <mx:List id="myList"
      dataProvider="{myXMLData}"
      labelField="name" />
```

In this solution you'll see how to load and consume a remote XML file, treating the response data as E4X format and as an Object. Furthermore, you'll learn that if you send a collection of objects to the DataGrid, it can automatically generate the columns starting from the data structure.

How to build it

Begin by creating a new Flex project, which will be used throughout the chapter.

1. Open Flex Builder and create a Flex project with the name Chapter_7_Flex_ Solution_List. Create a new folder by selecting File ➤ New ➤ Folder and then name it assets.

2. Create a new MXML application file by selecting File ➤ New ➤ MXML Application and name it Chapter_7_Flex_Sol_1.mxml. The application file will contain two remote calls through the HTTPService class (discussed in Chapter 6). The HTTPService calls will load an XML file locally (data.xml), saved in the assets folder of the project. You can use the completed XML file or write your own. Select File ➤ New ➤ File, save the new file with the name data.xml, and insert the following structure in the XML file:

```
<?xml version="1.0" encoding="utf-8"?>
<root>
  <person>
    <name>Constantin</name>
    <surname>Moldovanu</surname>
    <phone>5551234</phone>
    <age>24</age>
  </person>
  <person>
    <name>Emanuele</name>
    <surname>Tatti</surname>
    <phone>5552341</phone>
    <age>23</age>
  </person>
  <person>
    <name>Francesco</name>
    <surname>Rapana</surname>
    <phone>5553412</phone>
    <age>23</age>
  </person>
</root>
```

3. Add an event handler for the creationComplete event of the <mx:Application> tag. This function will have the job of launching the send() method of the two HTTPService classes and carrying out the calls to the XML file:

```
<mx:Application xmlns:mx="http://www.adobe.com/2006/mxml"
  layout="vertical"
  creationComplete="onCreationComplete()">
```

7

4. Create two HTTPService instances, which will load the same XML file present in the assets folder specified in the url property, but will present different modes for access to that data. Insert this code below the <mx:Application> tag:

```
<mx:Application xmlns:mx="http://www.adobe.com/2006/mxml"
  layout="vertical"
creationComplete="onCreationComplete()">

<mx:HTTPService id="myHTTPxml"
  url="assets/data.xml"
  resultFormat="e4x"
  result="handleResultXML(event)" />

<mx:HTTPService id="myHTTPobj"
  url="assets/data.xml"
  resultFormat="object"
  result="handleResultObj(event)" />
```

The first HTTPService instance uses the E4X format for the data—Flex treats E4X data as native objects. The E4X format comes from the ECMAScript for XML and it is a subset of the standard ECMA 262 (the same one on which the ActionScript language is based). E4X is a set of programming language extensions that add native XML support to ECMAScript (refer to Solution 6-4).

The second HTTPService instance (with the id equal to myHTTPobj) instead returns data as a Flex Object, specifically an instance of ObjectProxy (http://livedocs.adobe.com/flex/2/langref/mx/utils/ObjectProxy.html.) Both HTTPService instances defined as such will call a specific method that takes the remote data and uses it as a collection of XML objects. The first is a collection of Flex objects, and the second links an event handler through the event result that will manage the data result.

5. Add an <mx:Script> block. Define two data structures inside the block, in which you'll put the results of the two remote calls, as follows:

```
<mx:Application xmlns:mx="http://www.adobe.com/2006/mxml"
  layout="vertical"
creationComplete="onCreationComplete()">

<mx:Script>
  <![CDATA[
    import mx.collections.ArrayCollection;
    import mx.collections.XMLListCollection;
    import mx.rpc.events.ResultEvent;

    [Bindable]
    private var resultColl:XMLListCollection;
    [Bindable]
    private var resultArr:ArrayCollection;
```

The two private variables are data typed as XMLListCollection and ArrayCollection and have the job of containing the response data. Furthermore, these variables will be used as data binding for the dataProvider property of the List control.

6. In the <mx:Script> block and below the variable declaration, add the event handler called on the creationComplete event of the Application, as follows:

```
private function onCreationComplete():void
    {
      myHTTPxml.send();
      myHTTPobj.send();
    }
```

This function runs the HTTPService calls, launching their send() method. Without running the send() method of an HTTPService, no remote call can be launched.

7. Every HTTPService call manages a function that links the response data to two variables declared in Step 5 on the result event. Add the following two event handlers to handle it:

```
private function onCreationComplete():void
{
  myHTTPxml.send();
  myHTTPobj.send();
}

private function handleResultXML(event:ResultEvent):void
{
  resultColl = new XMLListCollection(event.result.person);
}
private function handleResultObj(event:ResultEvent):void
{
  resultArr = event.result.root.person as ArrayCollection;
}

]]>
</mx:Script>
```

The handleResultXML() function can easily create a collection of XML objects (in this case, all <person> type data) because the HTTPService has been declared with the resultFormat property equal to e4x. Note that, by using E4X as the result type, the event.result object returned is an XML object. Therefore, event.result.person will be an XMLList or a list of XML objects of <person> type.

In the same way, it is possible to browse the structure of the object received in the handleResultObj() event handler (to which a remote service that returns an object is linked). You can access its root property and list all the underproperties of <person> type.

In this case, you have a collection of Flex objects with properties identical to the XML objects.

7

319

8. Create the List control to display the response data obtained by the HTTPService call. Add the following MXML code below the two <mx:HTTPService> tags:

```
<mx:HTTPService id="myHTTPobj"
  url="assets/data.xml"
  resultFormat="object"
  result="handleResultObj(event)" />

<mx:List id="myList"
  dataProvider="{resultColl}"
  labelField="name" />
```

The List control has declared a data binding with the resultColl variable, typed as XMLListCollection. Furthermore, the name property of the resultColl has been used as a labelField variable of the control.

9. Before running the application, insert two DataGrid controls, one that will use the data taken from the XML data collection (resultColl), and another that will use the data collection of object type (resultArr). Add this code below the List control:

```
<mx:DataGrid id="dgXML"
  dataProvider="{resultColl}" />

<mx:DataGrid id="dgObj"
  dataProvider="{resultArr}" />
```

10. Save the file and run the application.

Figure 7-2.
The name values become shown in the List control.

Constantin
Emanuele
Francesco

In the List control you'll see the name nodes of the loaded XML file as items, as shown in Figure 7-2.

Note that the first DataGrid, dgXML, does not show any information, while the second creates a column for every property and correctly displays the data. This happens because the second DataGrid uses a collection of objects and can obtain the property.

To correctly display the data in the first DataGrid (remember that it uses XML data as dataProvider), you have to define the relevant columns one by one by using the <mx:DataGridColumn> tag.

This is also useful in the case of the second DataGrid because you can use it to specify which columns to display, how to present the information, and so on (giving you more control).

11. Substitute the line that defines the first DataGrid with this code:

```
<mx:DataGrid id="dgXML" dataProvider="{resultColl}">
  <mx:columns>
    <mx:DataGridColumn headerText="Name" dataField="name" />
    <mx:DataGridColumn headerText="Surname" dataField="surname" />
    <mx:DataGridColumn headerText="Phone" dataField="phone" />
  </mx:columns>
</mx:DataGrid>
```

12. Save the file and run the application again. Now you'll see the data displayed in both the DataGrid controls.

You see how easy it is to start working directly with the columns of the DataGrid, defining the title with the headerText property and indicating the property you want to visualize in the column using the dataField property.

In this way, you can also control the order and number of columns you want to display, and then edit and format them.

Expert tips

It is assumed that the XML data also contains attributes linked to names. Remember that an XML attribute is defined in a tag as follows:

```
<person code="1">
  [...]
</person >
```

If you try to modify the assets/data.xml file to add attributes to every node of <person> type and then run the example, you'll not see them reflected in the first DataGrid. The second DataGrid, which displays data transformed into a Flex Object, shows an additional code column, which becomes attributed by the data structure.

To add a column to the first DataGrid displaying the information contained in the attribute just added, you must insert the following column among the other columns of the DataGrid:

```
<mx:DataGrid id="dgXML" dataProvider="{resultColl}">
<mx:columns>

    <mx:DataGridColumn headerText="Name" dataField="name" />
    <mx:DataGridColumn headerText="Surname" dataField="surname" />
    <mx:DataGridColumn headerText="Phone" dataField="phone" />

    <mx:DataGridColumn headerText="Code" dataField="@code" />

</mx:columns>
</mx:DataGrid>
```

To access an XML attribute, you must use its name, preceded by the @ character. The attribute will be dealt with just like every other property of the XML data.

It's always important to decide which components would be best to represent the data you want to display. A List component can display data simply, but it can also be used to represent subsets of complex data effectively. A DataGrid component can represent data in the form of a table and give a quick overview and representation of complex data. Finally, a Tree component is useful for representing data organized in a hierarchy.

7

All these list-based components provide ample scope to personalize the display of data, including ad hoc rendering, filters, and a data editor that even enables you to modify the data beneath.

Solution 7-2: Getting the selected item

After displaying the data in a list-based control, the next step is to enable the user to interact with this data by changing options in the user interface (UI). Any type of interaction involving the selection of data in a List control dispatches a change event that requires an event handler to manage user interaction.

In this solution you'll display a collection of data representing people, with names, surnames, ages, and so on. Initially just the names will display, but you'll enable the user to click those names to display more details on each person—in effect, a master/detail page.

> A **master page** is a page that lists database records and corresponding links for each record. When the user clicks a link, a **detail page** opens and displays more information about the record.

What's involved

As in Solution 7-1, for the data collection you'll use XML data that will arrive to the Flex application through an HTTPService request. The XML file is found in the assets folder of the Flex project. You can use the completed XML file or write it on your own. Open Flex Builder by selecting File ➤ New ➤ File, save it with the name data.xml, and insert the following XML structure:

```
<?xml version="1.0" encoding="utf-8"?>
<root>
  <person>
    <name>Francesco</name>
    <surname>Rapana</surname>
    <phone>0039</phone>
    <age>23</age>
  </person>
</root>
```

You'll use the List control to display the data to which you'll link an event handler to the change event. This event is released when the user selects an item in the list. Because it is a nonlinear data structure, you must use the labelField property of the List control and link it to the name of the property you want to display:

```
<mx:List id="myList"
  dataProvider="{data}"
  labelField="name"
  change="changeHandler(event)" />
```

When an item is selected, the List control puts forward two properties: selectedItem and selectedIndex:

- The selectedItem property returns an object, which is a reference to the selected item in the data provider.
- The selectedIndex property returns the index in the data provider of the selected item. In this case, the data provider is the XML file loaded by the HTTPService call.

During development, these properties are often used for data binding with other controls of the application. When the user clicks a person's name in the List control, the entire object represented by that item is selected, and three fields of text are bound, which will display the other information associated with that person taken from the XML List object.

To obtain the selected item or better, the data object present in the collection sent to the dataProvider, you also need the selectedIndex property, which in List and list-based components recognizes the index of the object selected in the collection of data sent to the data provider.

Writing the data binding is simple:

```
<mx:Label text="Last Name: {myList.selectedItem.surname }" />
```

If no item on the List is selected, selectedItem property is null, and selectedIndex is -1.

How to build it

You'll begin by creating a new application file on which to work.

1. Use the same Flex project that you created in the first solution: Chapter_7_Flex_ListBased. Within it, open a new MXML application file by selecting File ➤ New ➤ MXML Application and name it Chapter_7_Flex_Sol_2.mxml.

2. Add an event handler for the creationComplete event of the <mx:Application> tag:

```
<mx:Application xmlns:mx="http://www.adobe.com/2006/mxml"
  layout="vertical"
  creationComplete="onCreationComplete()">
```

This event handler has the single purpose of launching the send() method of HTTPService to make the call to the XML file to be loaded and make it return the data.

3. Create an <mx:HTTPService> tag as follows; it loads the data from the XML file:

```
<mx:Application xmlns:mx="http://www.adobe.com/2006/mxml"
  layout="vertical"
creationComplete="onCreationComplete()">
<mx:HTTPService id="myHTTP"
  url="assets/data.xml"
  resultFormat="e4x"
  result="onResult(event)" />
```

This remote service can connect to the XML file specified (assets/data.xml) by using the E4X result format to manage the XML data and will invoke the onResult() method after the XML file loads (on the result event).

4. Add an <mx:Script> block below the <mx:Application> tag, as shown following. Here you are managing the event handlers for the creationComplete event and the result event of the HTTPService. When the application starts up, the onCreationComplete() event handler will send the HTTPService request to obtain the XML data. After they are returned, you'll put them in an XMLListCollection object:

```
<mx:Script>
  <![CDATA[
    import mx.collections.XMLListCollection;
    import mx.rpc.events.ResultEvent;

    private function onCreationComplete():void
    {
      myHTTP.send();
    }

    private function onResult(event:ResultEvent):void
    {
      data = new XMLListCollection(event.result.person);
    }

  ]]>
</mx:Script>
```

The data variable is populated with the response data of the remote call and typed using the XMLListCollection class.

5. Insert the <mx:XMLListCollection> tag and assign it an id equal to data:

```
</mx:Script>
<mx:XMLListCollection id="data" />
```

6. Declare the elements of the user interface of the application by inserting the following code below the <mx:XMLListCollection> tag, which creates a List control and three Label controls:

```
<mx:Panel width="50%" height="80%" title="Contacts"
  layout="vertical"
  horizontalAlign="center">
  <mx:Label text="Select a name: " />

  <mx:List id="myList"
    dataProvider="{data}"
    labelField="name"
    width="50%"
    change="changeHandler(event)" />
```

```
<mx:Label text="Name: {myList.selectedItem.name}" />
<mx:Label text="Last Name: {myList.selectedItem.surname}" />
<mx:Label text="Age: {myList.selectedItem.age}" />
</mx:Panel>
```

The List control uses the collection of XML data defined previously (data) as dataProvider and the selectedItem property to the three Label controls underneath through the data binding links. In this way, when the user selects an item, the data binding notifies the Label controls, which update their contents. In addition to this binding, the event handler changeHandler() will be invoked by the change event of the List control. In fact, the List control dispatches a change event when the value of the control changes and automatically creates an event object. This object is sent as a parameter to the event handler: change="changeHandler(event)".

7. In the <mx:Script> block add the changeHandler() event handler shown following, which is called when the change event of the List control is dispatched:

```
<mx:Script>
  <![CDATA[
    import mx.collections.XMLListCollection;
    import mx.rpc.events.ResultEvent;

    private function onCreationComplete():void
    {
      myHTTP.send();
    }

    private function onResult(event:ResultEvent):void
    {
      data = new XMLListCollection(event.result.person);
    }

    private function changeHandler(evt:Event):void
    {
      var selectedItem:String = evt.currentTarget.selectedItem.toString();
      var selectedIndex:String =
      evt.currentTarget.selectedIndex.toString();
      var myText:String = " You've selected: " + selectedItem;
      myText += "\n" + "at the index: " + selectedIndex;
      mx.controls.Alert.show(myText);
    }
  ]]>
</mx:Script>
```

This event handler populates the variable myText (typed as String.) This variable uses the event object created by the change event to get the selectedItem and selectedIndex values on the List control. All events belonging to the flash.events.Event package, such as the change event, generate an event object. The flash.events.Event class contains the information related to the event that occurred. Every time an event is dispatched, the flash.events.Event class automatically generates an event object, which has implicit properties referenced to the object that triggered the event.

The object to be used in the event handler must be sent as a parameter in the ActionScript function that handles the event:

```
<mx:List id="myList"
  dataProvider="{data}"
  labelField="name"
  width="50%"
  change="changeHandler(event)" />
```

In this way it is possible to access the properties that the event contains. Some of these properties are common to all of the objects; others depend on the type of event (and control) that has been released. (The event object was discussed in Solution 1-6.)

In the event handler of the solution you have used the currentTarget property contained in the event object to reference the List control properties selectedItem and selectedIndex:

```
var selectedItem:String = evt.currentTarget.selectedItem.toString();
var selectedIndex:String =
evt.currentTarget.selectedIndex.toString();
var myText:String = " You've selected: " + selectedItem;
myText += "\n" + "at the index: " + selectedIndex;
```

After being populated, the myText variable is sent to the show() method of the Alert class. Every time the user selects an item in the list, this variable will print the values relative to the selectedItem and selectedIndex in the alert window:

```
You've selected: <person>
  <name>Emanuele</name>
  <surname>Tatti</surname>
  <phone>5552341</phone>
  <age>23</age>
  </person>
at the index: 1
```

Note that the selectedItem contains the entire reference to the selected item in the data provider.

8. Save and run the application.

Initially the application displays values only in the List control; but when you select a name from the list, the other information on that person will appear in the Label controls, as shown in Figure 7-3.

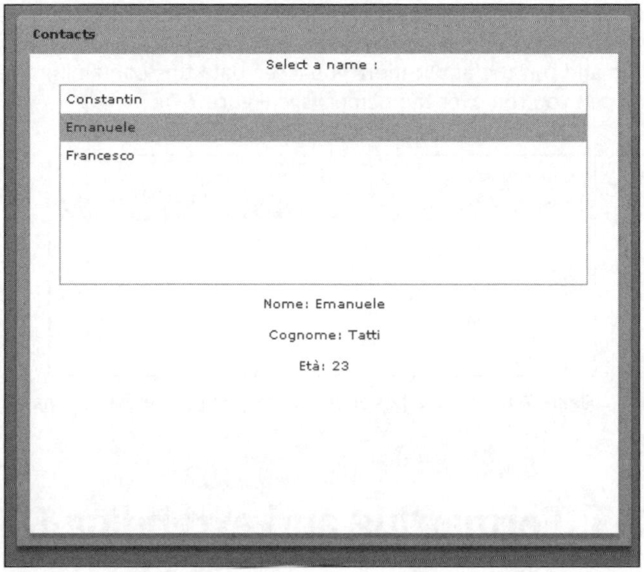

Figure 7-3. Once you select an item in the list, the other information is printed in the Label controls.

Expert tips

To give further information, list-based controls can be programmed to display data tips, or tool tips (text hints that appear when the mouse pointer hovers over an item) for rows in a List control. To use these data tips, simply set the value of the showDataTips property to true, and then set the text that you want to display in the data tip in the dataTipField property or the dataTipFunction.

Try changing the code highlighted as follows:

```
<mx:List id="myList"
  dataProvider="{data}"
  labelField="name"
  width="90%"
  change="changeHandler(event)"
  showDataTips="true"
  dataTipFunction ="myDataTip"/>
```

The value specified in the dataTipFunction property is an ActionScript function. Insert this function in the <mx:Script> block, as follows:

```
public function myDataTip(item:Object):String
{
  return item.surname + ", " + item.age;
}
```

The data tip function automatically takes an object reference to the item hovered over in the data provider as a parameter and returns the String to send to the data tip. If you now save the file and run the application, you'll see data tips containing the person's surname and age when you roll over the names (see Figure 7-4).

Figure 7-4. The data tips appear when you mouse over the names.

Solution 7-3: Formatting and extending DataGrid columns

Among all Flex controls, the DataGrid control is the most versatile for displaying complex data, including video, in rows and columns. The following features make it incredibly useful. You can do the following:

- Specify the order of the data and which data to render visible, defining the columns one by one using the <mx:DataGridColumn> tag.
- Resize and move the columns at runtime using drag and drop.
- Sort the data in ascending or descending order at runtime.
- Personalize column and row headers.
- Edit the text in the columns at runtime.
- Create a custom item renderer for customizing content inside columns.
- Add navigation to page through your data.
- Create locked rows and columns.

Every column in the DataGrid control is defined as an instance of the DataGridColumn object. The order in which DataGridColumn objects are declared determines the order in which they will appear in the DataGrid. There are also various ways to obtain this result; for example, by using the labelFunction() or extending the DataGridColumn class with ActionScript.

In this solution, you'll see how to personalize a DataGrid by modifying its columns.

What's involved

To collect data use XML data passed to the Flex application through an HTTPService request. The XML data structure looks like this:

```
<?xml version="1.0" encoding="utf-8"?>
<root>
  <person code="1">
  <name>Francesco</name>
  <surname>Rapana</surname>
  <phone>0039</phone>
  <age>23</age>
  </person>
</root>
```

You can find this XML file inside the assets folder of the Flex project.

Using the mx.formatters.PhoneFormatter class you'll apply a formatting to all the telephone numbers in a uniform way (refer to Chapter 4 for more about Flex formatters.)

You'll use the labelFunction property of the DataGridColumn to link to a callback function that personalizes the way in which the column will display the actual data. The function to assign to the property has to have the following definition:

```
labelFunction(item:Object, column:DataGridColumn):String
```

The method receives the item object of the dataProvider currently selected, and the column of the DataGrid control that is relevant to the function as parameters. It will output the same data formatted according to the criteria defined in the function. The labelFunction will take care of the formatting.

In this example, you'll use the Flex component PhoneFormatter, which enables you to define the string using a telephone number type format:

```
<mx:PhoneFormatter id="phoneFormatter" formatString="###-####" />
```

The format string ###-#### specifies that the numbers should be formatted as seven-figure numbers, distributed in a group of three, followed by a dash and then the other four figures.

The "Expert tips" section showed ActionScript extending the mx.controls.dataGridClasses.DataGridColumn class by creating an ActionScript class, as follows:

```
package com.flexsolutions.chapter7.controls.dataGridClasses
{
  import mx.controls.dataGridClasses.DataGridColumn;

  public class FormattedDataGridColumn extends DataGridColumn
  {
  }
}
```

In this custom class you'll define the behavior to apply to the custom column. In this solution you'll extend the DataGridColumn class to format the data in it through the labelFunction() by using the PhoneFormatter.

How to build it

The application will load the data from the XML file (data.xml in the assets folder of this Flex project) as in the previous solutions. The response data will be inserted in a collection variable, which will be bound to the DataGrid; the DataGrid defines a custom column containing the formatted telephone numbers among the DataGridColumn classes.

1. Create a new MXML application file by selecting File ➤ New ➤ MXML Application and name it Chapter_7_Flex_Sol_3.mxml.

2. Add an event handler for the creationComplete event of the <mx:Application> tag, as shown here:

```
<mx:Application xmlns:mx="http://www.adobe.com/2006/mxml"
  layout="vertical"
  creationComplete="onCreationComplete()">
```

This function will take care of launching the send() method for the remote call with the HTTPService.

3. Create the HTTPService object shown following, which will load the data from the XML file. Declare this code below the <mx:Application> tag:

```
<mx:HTTPService id="myHTTP"
  url="assets/data.xml"
  resultFormat="e4x"
  result="onResult(event)" />
```

This service will access to the specified XML file, using the E4X format to handle the response XML data and invoking the onResult() function on the result event after the data is returned.

4. Add an <mx:Script> block, as shown following. Here you manage the event handlers for the creationComplete event of the Application and the result event of the HTTPService. When the application launches the creationComplete event, the method will send the remote call to access the XML data. When response data are sent back, insert it in an XMLListCollection object, defined as Bindable, to be used as source data:

```
<mx:Script>
  <![CDATA[
    import mx.collections.XMLListCollection;
    import mx.controls.dataGridClasses.DataGridColumn;
    import mx.rpc.events.ResultEvent;

    [Bindable]
    private var xmlData:XMLListCollection = null;

     private function onCreationComplete():void
    {
      myHTTP.send();
    }
```

```
    private function onResult(event:ResultEvent):void
    {
      xmlData = new XMLListCollection(event.result.person);
    }

  ]]>
</mx:Script>

<mx:HTTPService id="myHTTP"
  url="assets/data.xml"
  resultFormat="e4x"
  result="onResult(event)" />
```

5. Define a Formatter class to format telephone numbers and add it to the MXML code, like so:

```
<mx:HTTPService id="myHTTP"
  url="assets/data.xml"
  resultFormat="e4x"
result="onResult(event)" />
<mx:PhoneFormatter id="phoneFormatter" formatString="###-####" />
```

The Formatter classes of Flex can be called by using MXML or ActionScript. In both cases, no formatting will be applied until the format() method of the class has been launched. This method accepts the value to be formatted as parameter and returns the String with the formatting applied.

6. Add the following MXML code below the PhoneFormatter tag, which is necessary to display the DataGrid. It takes data from the XML source, xmlData, and a Label control that will use the data binding to display the telephone numbers selected:

```
<mx:Panel title="Contact data" width="80%" layout="vertical"
horizontalAlign="center" >

  <mx:DataGrid id="myDG" width="80%" height="100%"
dataProvider="{xmlData}">
    <mx:columns>
      <mx:DataGridColumn headerText="Name" dataField="name" />
      <mx:DataGridColumn headerText="Surname" dataField="surname" />
      <mx:DataGridColumn headerText="Phone" dataField="phone"
        labelFunction="phoneColumnLabel" />
    </mx:columns>
  </mx:DataGrid>

  <mx:Label text="The phone number selected is:
    {(myDG.selectedIndex != -1) ? myDG.selectedItem.phone: '' } " />

</mx:Panel>
```

7

Between the opening and closing of the DataGrid control you have declared the columns for displaying the name, the last name, and the phone number fields taken from the XMLListCollection:

```
<mx:DataGrid id="myDG" width="80%" height="100%"
dataProvider="{xmlData}">
    <mx:columns>
      <mx:DataGridColumn headerText="Name" dataField="name" />
      <mx:DataGridColumn headerText="Surname" dataField="surname" />
      <mx:DataGridColumn headerText="Phone" dataField="phone"
        labelFunction="phoneColumnLabel" />
    </mx:columns>
  </mx:DataGrid>
```

Note that the third column (the one that displays the phone field) uses a labelFunction, which is associated to the phoneColumnLabel() function. The function specified to the labelFunction does not have brackets because the labelFunction waits to receive a function as a data type.

The Label component will display the telephone number linked to the selected item; the labelFunction changes only the display, not the data underneath:

```
<mx:Label text="The phone number selected is:
  {(myDG.selectedIndex != -1) ? myDG.selectedItem.phone: '' } " />
```

7. Add the following code inside the <mx:Script> tag you defined earlier—this is the labelFunction:

```
private function onResult(event:ResultEvent):void
    {
      xmlData = new XMLListCollection(event.result.person);
    }


private function phoneColumnLabel(item:Object,
column:DataGridColumn):String
{

  if (!item.hasOwnProperty("phone"))
  {
    return "";
  }
  else
  {
    return phoneFormatter.format(item.phone);
  }
}
```

The function will receive an item object that will contain an XML node of <person> type and will use the formatter previously defined to customize the way in which the column will display the data.

8. Save and run the application. You should see the result shown in Figure 7-5.

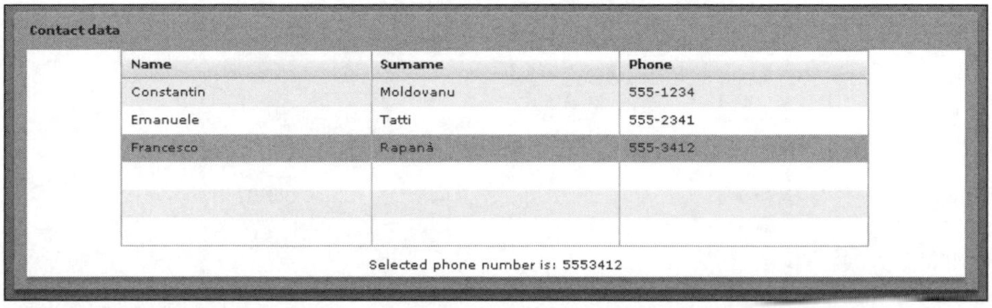

Figure 7-5. The phone column of the DataGrid displays the formatted values.

The DataGrid will display the telephone numbers in the third column, formatted in the way desired; if you select a row, the Label component will display the telephone number from that row, as it is in the underlying data structure.

Expert tips

In this solution you used the labelFunction property to change the format of a DataGridColumn, which is all well and good, but this approach is not exactly object-oriented. In fact, the code is embedded in the MXML file, making reusing the code difficult. For this reason, it is better to extend the DataGridColumn class of Flex to create a component that handles the actual formatting—you can then reuse this custom component in other projects whenever needed.

To extend the DataGridColumn, create an ActionScript class that uses the keyword extends to inherit all the features of the class to be extended.

1. Create the folder structure com/flexsolutions/chapter7/controls/ dataGridClasses by selecting File ➤ New ➤ Folder. Then create a new ActionScript class that extends the DataGridColumn class by selecting File ➤ New ➤ ActionScript class and then specifying the package of the class, its name, and the base class that you must extend (see Figure 7-6):

- Package: com.flexsolutions.chapter7.controls.dataGridClasses
- Name: FormattedDataGridColumns
- Superclass: mx.controls.dataGridClasses.DataGridColumn

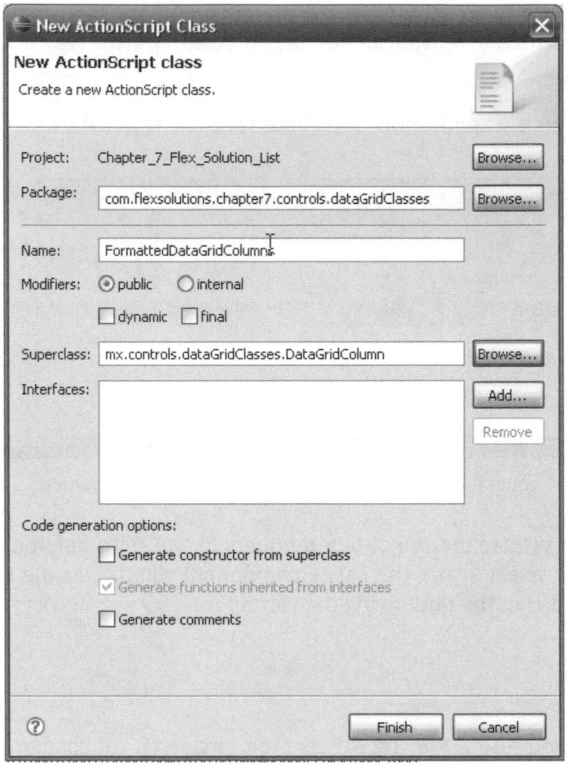

Figure 7-6. The ActionScript class window enables you to
create a class and specify the base class.

2. Call the FormattedDataGridColumn class (save it in the com/flexsolutions/
chapter7/controls/dataGridClasses folder) and extend the DataGridColumn
class, inserting the necessary ActionScript, as follows:

```
package com.flexsolutions.chapter7.controls.dataGridClasses
{
  import mx.controls.dataGridClasses.DataGridColumn;
  import mx.formatters.PhoneFormatter;

  public class FormattedDataGridColumn extends DataGridColumn
  {
  }
}
```

To be able to extend the DataGridColumn class, you have imported its package; you have
also imported the PhoneFormatter class.

3. Define two variables that you'll use in the class:

```
public class FormattedDataGridColumn extends DataGridColumn
{
  public static const PHONE:String = "phone";
  private var _phoneFormatter:PhoneFormatter = null;
```

The first variable is a static constant, while the second is a private variable.

4. Create the set method for the private variable _phoneFormatter:

```
public class FormattedDataGridColumn extends DataGridColumn
{
  public static const PHONE:String = "phone";
private var _phoneFormatter:PhoneFormatter = null;

  public function set formatterType(type:String):void
  {
    switch (type)
    {
      case PHONE:
      super.labelFunction = phoneFormatterFunction;
      break;
      default:
      //include error handling
    }
  }
}
```

The FormattedDataGridColumn custom class puts forward a read-only property: formatterType. Using this property it is possible to set a formatter for the column using a String in which you specify the type of formatter. In this specific custom class you have only the PhoneFormatter to play with, but it is easy to add other Formatter classes. For each additional formatter you have to create a static constant to identify the name in an unambiguous way and a private method that carries out the formatting operations.

The set method for the formatterType property does nothing more than assign the labelFunction to a phoneFormatterFunction method that you'll write in the next steps.

5. Below the set method, add the constructor of the class, as shown following. Here you'll invoke the super() and create the instance for the PhoneFormatter class:

```
public function FormattedDataGridColumn()
{
  super();
  _phoneFormatter = new PhoneFormatter();
  _phoneFormatter.formatString = "###-####";
}
```

The constructor is the first method invoked when an instance of the class is created. In this method you have invoked the constructor of the DataGridColumn with super() and defined an instance of the PhoneFormatter, specifying the formatString property with which the data will become formatted.

6. Finally, specify the method associated to the labelFunction in the constructor by adding the code shown following after the constructor declaration:

```
private function phoneFormatterFunction(item:Object,
column:DataGridColumn):String
{
```

335

```
      if (column != this)
      {
        return "";
      }
      if (!item.hasOwnProperty(super.dataField))
      {
        return "";
      }
      else
      {
        return _phoneFormatter.format(item[super.dataField]);
      }
    }
```

With this private method, you apply the formatting to the column containing the phone number.

The custom class has been created. This is the final code of the complete class:

```
package com.flexsolutions.chapter7.controls.dataGridClasses
{
import mx.controls.dataGridClasses.DataGridColumn;
import mx.formatters.PhoneFormatter;

public class FormattedDataGridColumn extends DataGridColumn
{
public static const PHONE:String = "phone";
private var _phoneFormatter:PhoneFormatter = null;

public function FormattedDataGridColumn()
{
super();
_phoneFormatter = new PhoneFormatter();
_phoneFormatter.formatString = "###-####";
}

public function set formatterType(type:String):void
{
switch (type)
{
case PHONE:
super.labelFunction = phoneFormatterFunction;
break;
default:
    //include error handling
}
}

private function phoneFormatterFunction(item:Object,
column:DataGridColumn):String
```

```
{
if (column != this)
return "";
if (!item.hasOwnProperty(super.dataField))
return "";
return _phoneFormatter.format(item[super.dataField]);
}
}
}
```

You can now go on and use it in the MXML file.

7. Open the Chapter_7_Flex_Sol_3.mxml file and insert the custom namespace in the <mx:Application> tag, as shown here:

```
<mx:Application xmlns:mx="http://www.adobe.com/2006/mxml"
xmlns:dataGridClasses=➡
"com.flexsolutions.chapter7.controls.dataGridClasses.*"
  layout="vertical"
  creationComplete="onCreationComplete()">
```

8. In the <mx:Script> block, import the package of the custom class just created by adding the following line at the beginning of the block:

```
<mx:Script>
<![CDATA[
import ➡
com.flexsolutions.chapter7.controls.dataGridClasses.*;
```

9. In the DataGrid, add the following column:

```
<mx:DataGrid id="myDG" width="80%" height="100%"➡
dataProvider="{xmlData}">
<mx:columns>
<mx:DataGridColumn headerText="Name"
dataField="name" />
<mx:DataGridColumn headerText="Surname"
dataField="surname" />
<mx:DataGridColumn headerText="Phone"
dataField="phone"
labelFunction="phoneColumnLabel" />

<dataGridClasses:FormattedDataGridColumn
headerText="Phone"
dataField="phone"
formatterType="{FormattedDataGridColumn.PHONE}" />

</mx:columns>
</mx:DataGrid>
```

You send the value of the read-only property formatterType to the custom class FormattedDataGridColumn by using the static constant FormattedDataGridColumn.

7

PHONE. The rest will automatically be performed by the class, and the data will be formatted. There is no need to specify the `labelFunction` in this node because it has been defined in the constructor of the same class.

10. Save and run the application.

Solution 7-4: Using item renderers and item editors

The default way in which Flex list-based controls display data is perfect for most situations. Sometimes, however, it's necessary to modify the way in which this data is displayed to the user; for example, if you want to display an icon or another Flex control inside a `DataGrid` column. To modify the appearance of data you can use custom item renderers and item editors. With these classes you can merge different data together in a single column, control how the data is displayed programmatically, and enable users to edit the data on the fly. To send the information from the list-based control to the item renderer or item editor, Flex uses the data property.

You can make data displayed in the list-based control as editable, so data can be modified by using `TextInput` controls. Once modified, the new values are stored in the item editor and can be passed back to other list-based controls. The item editors and item renderers are powerful features that enable developers to create complex displays of data in data-oriented applications.

What's involved

The `itemRenderer` property is defined in the `ListBase` class (http://livedocs.adobe.com/labs/flex3/langref/mx/controls/listClasses/ListBase.html). All the classes that extend it support the possibility of using a customized item renderer. The `itemEditor` property, on the other hand, is defined in the List class, which in turn extends `ListBase`.

The item renderer and item editor can be defined in different ways. First, you can directly link the class of the control you want to display in the list-based control to the `itemRenderer` or `itemEditor`:

```
<mx:DataGridColumn dataField="reorder"
  headerText="Values"
  itemRenderer="mx.controls.NumericStepper"
  editorDataField="value"
  rendererIsEditor="true"/>
```

This simple but powerful technique is called drop-in: the data to be linked to the control is sent to the `editorDataField` property, which links the property of the control to the data received by the data provider.

One thing you can't do with the drop-in approach is to specify single properties of a control. For example, you can't define the minimum and maximum property for the NumericStepper.

The second method, inline, overcomes this problem. It's applied by declaring the item renderer or item editor as nested tags of the list control:

```
<mx:DataGridColumn dataField="rating"
  headerText="Rating">

<mx:itemEditor>
  <mx:Component>
    <mx:NumericStepper minimum="0"
      maximum="100"/>
  </mx:Component>
</mx:itemEditor>


</mx:DataGridColumn>
```

The Flex component that you intend to use is specified inside the <mx:Component> tag, just as with a MXML tag. In this way, you can specify the single properties of the component, such as the minimum and maximum properties of the NumericStepper.

The third approach enables you to link an ActionScript class or an MXML component to an item renderer or item editor. This is the most powerful and versatile method in that it enables you to insert all the operations in one external file and reuse it wherever it is needed:

```
<mx:DataGrid id="myDG" itemRenderer="mypackage.MyRendererClass" />
```

The MyRendererClass must be a class that implements the interface IListItemRenderer; for example, Button, ComboBox, NumericStepper, or any type of Flex container. If you want to use the item renderer also as an itemEditor, you can set the rendererIsEditor property to true:

```
<mx:DataGrid id="myDG"
itemRenderer="path.to.the.package.MyRendererClass"
  editable="true" rendererIsEditor="true" editorDataField="value"/>
```

The editorDataField property indicates which properties of the renderer must be bound to the data provider. It is important that the property of the item renderer you have chosen, in this case value, has bindable setters and getters.

In this solution, you'll see how it is possible to use a ComboBox and CheckBox class as an item renderer and item editor.

How to build it

A DataGrid control will be used with two different item renderers in two different columns: one that extends the ComboBox class, and the other that extends the CheckBox class. The changes to the data will be displayed in a TextArea control.

1. Create a new MXML application file by selecting File ➤ New ➤ MXML Application and name it Chapter_7_Flex_Sol_4.mxml.

2. On the creationComplete event of the Application call the updateTextArea() event handler. Define this now, as follows:

```
<mx:Application xmlns:mx="http://www.adobe.com/2006/mxml"
 creationComplete="updateTextArea()">
```

3. Insert an <mx:Script> tag below the <mx:Application> tag, define the updateTextArea() event handler that will update the content of the TextArea control as follows:

```
<mx:Script>
  <![CDATA[
    import mx.controls.Alert;

    private function updateTextArea():void
    {
      myTA.text = myDG.dataProvider.toString();
    }

  ]]>
</mx:Script>
```

This function populates the TextArea with the dataProvider property used by the DataGrid control. Because the data provider is a complex object, you must use the toString() method to convert it into a String and render it correctly in a TextArea control.

4. Create the data source using the MXML <mx:XMLList> tag, as follows:

```
</mx:Script>
<mx:XMLList id="myDP" xmlns="">
  <article>
    <title>Flex 2 and EJB 3</title>
    <header>How to integrate Flex with
     J2EE and EJB 3 applications</header>
    <checked>false</checked>
    <rate>-1</rate>
  </article>

  <article>
    <title>AIR and the HTMLControl class</title>
    <header>Swf files and Javascript interaction in AIR</header>
    <checked>false</checked>
    <rate>-1</rate>
  </article>
```

```
<article>
  <title>Adobe LiveCycle PDFGenerator</title>
  <header>How to automate the generation
  of Adobe PDF documents</header>
  <checked>true</checked>
  <rate>4</rate>
</article>

</mx:XMLList>
```

The XMLList contains three <article> nodes in which other information is defined. This data source will be used as dataProvider of the DataGrid.

5. Define a Panel container below the closure of the </mx:XMLList> that will contain the DataGrid and the TextArea controls:

```
<mx:Panel title="Item renderer and editor example"
  width="500" height="400">
</mx:Panel>
```

6. In this Panel, you'll now insert the DataGrid for the visualization of the data, and a TextArea that will show how the data changes following the actions of the itemEditors. You'll use a Button to update the TextArea with the new modified data. Add the following now:

```
<mx:Panel title="Item renderer and editor example"
  width="500" height="400">

<mx:DataGrid id="myDG" editable="true"
  dataProvider="{myDP}"
  width="100%" height="50%">

  <mx:columns>
    <mx:DataGridColumn
      dataField="title"/>
    <mx:DataGridColumn
      dataField="header" />
    <mx:DataGridColumn
      dataField="checked" />
    <mx:DataGridColumn
      dataField="rate" />
  </mx:columns>
</mx:DataGrid>

<mx:TextArea id="myTA" width="100%" height="45%" />

<mx:Button label="Update" click="updateTextArea()" />
</mx:Panel>
```

Because the editable property has been set to true, you can now edit the data using the predefined TextInput controls. If you save and run the file, you can modify data in the

DataGrid columns and then apply these changes to the XML by clicking the Button. But there is still some more work to be done.

7. Modify the last two columns by inserting an `itemRenderer` that is used as an `itemEditor` drop-in, as previously explained:

```
<mx:DataGrid id="myDG" editable="true"
  dataProvider="{myDP}"
  width="100%" height="50%">

  <mx:columns>
    <mx:DataGridColumn
      dataField="title"/>
    <mx:DataGridColumn
      dataField="header" />

<mx:DataGridColumn width="20"
  rendererIsEditor="true"
  dataField="checked"
  sortable="false"
  headerText="">

  <mx:itemRenderer>
    <mx:Component>
      <mx:CheckBox creationComplete="init()">
      </mx:CheckBox>
    </mx:Component>
  </mx:itemRenderer>
</mx:DataGridColumn>
```

You have declared the itemRenderer with the inline approach, specifying the component as a nested MXML tag, and created an event handler in the creationComplete event of the CheckBox. When you work in the `<mx:Component>` tag, the scope for the functions and the variables is in that tag.

8. For this reason, you must specify the init() event handler with an `<mx:Script>` block in this declaration. You can create an `<mx:Script>` block within the inline itemRenderer declaration, like so:

```
<mx:DataGridColumn width="20"
  rendererIsEditor="true"
  dataField="checked"
  sortable="false"
  headerText="">

  <mx:itemRenderer>
    <mx:Component>
      <mx:CheckBox creationComplete="init()">

<mx:Script>
  <![CDATA[
```

```
        private var _data:Object;

        private function init():void
        {
          this.addEventListener(MouseEvent.CLICK, update);
        }

        [Bindable]
        override public function get data():Object
        {
          return _data;
        }

        override public function set data(o:Object):void
        {
          _data = o;
          if(o.checked == "true")
          {
            this.selected = true;
          }
          else
          {
            this.selected = false;
          }
        }

        private function update(event:MouseEvent):void
        {
          if(this.selected)
          {
            _data.checked = "true";
          }
          else
          {
            _data.checked = "false";
          }
        }

      ]]>
    </mx:Script>
      </mx:CheckBox>
        </mx:Component>
      </mx:itemRenderer>
    </mx:DataGridColumn>
```

To use the itemRenderer and make it work as an itemEditor, you had to override the setter and getter methods of the [Bindable] _data property:

```
[Bindable]
    override public function get data():Object
    {
      return _data;
    }

    override public function set data(o:Object):void
    {
      _data = o;
      if(o.checked == "true")
      {
        this.selected = true;
      }
      else
      {
        this.selected = false;
      }
    }
}
```

The update() function changes the value of the _data property when the user selects the CheckBox control. This function is registered with an addEventListener() in the init() event handler of the control's creationComplete event:

```
private function init():void
{
    this.addEventListener(MouseEvent.CLICK, update);
}
```

9. Modify the last column by inserting a ComboBox as itemRenderer, which will load an Array that you'll create on the creationComplete event of the component acting as data provider:

```
<mx:DataGridColumn
  dataField="rate"
  rendererIsEditor="true">
  <mx:itemRenderer>
    <mx:Component>
      <mx:ComboBox creationComplete="init()">
        <mx:Script>
          <![CDATA[
            import mx.controls.Alert;

            private var _data:Object;

            [Bindable]
            override public function set data(o:Object):void
            {
              _data = o;
              if(Number(o.rate) <= 0)
              {
```

```
                        this.selectedIndex = 0;
                    }
                    else
                    {
                        this.selectedIndex = Number(o.rate);
                    }
                }

                override public function get data():Object {
                return _data;
                }

                private function init():void
                {
                    this.dataProvider =  [ "Unrated",
                                             "Insufficient",
                                             "Sufficient",
                                             "Good",
                                             "Excellent" ];

                    this.addEventListener(MouseEvent.CLICK, update);
                }

                private function update(event:MouseEvent):void
                {

                    if(this.selectedIndex == 0)
                    {
                        _data.rate = "-1";
                    }
                    else
                    {
                        _data.rate = this.selectedIndex.toString();
                    }

                }
            ]]>
        </mx:Script>

      </mx:ComboBox>
    </mx:Component>
  </mx:itemRenderer>
</mx:DataGridColumn>
```

You have also created an event listener in both the itemRenderer and itemEditor to update the data from time to time on the click of the mouse. Without these event listeners the data would not be modified, so the itemEditor will not work.

10. Save and run the application.

Expert tips

Aside from personalizing the item renderer of DataGrid columns, it is also possible to personalize the headers of the columns using an item renderer. To define the class to use as headerRenderer, you specify the headerRenderer property of the DataGridColumn class.

Like the item renderers previously discussed, the header renderers must implement the IListItemRenderer interface. The headerRenderer property is predefined/set as DataGridItemRenderer.

1. To specify a headerRenderer, modify the MXML file created in this solution, adding the headerRenderer property and linking it to an external MXML component:

```
<mx:DataGridColumn
  editable="true"
  sortable="false"
  rendererIsEditor="true"
  editorDataField="data"
  dataField="checked"
  headerRenderer="Chapter_7_Flex_Sol_4_header">
```

2. Create an MXML component to use as headerRenderer. The component will have a Vbox container as a base container and a CheckBox and a Label control inside it. Create it by selecting File ➤ New ➤ MXML components, name it Chapter_7_ Flex_Sol_4_header, and insert the following MXML code into it, which will be displayed in the header of the DataGridColumn:

```
<?xml version="1.0" encoding="utf-8"?>
<mx:VBox xmlns:mx="http://www.adobe.com/2006/mxml"
  paddingLeft="0"
  horizontalAlign="center"
  clipContent="false">
  <mx:Canvas>
    <mx:CheckBox
      fontWeight="bold"
      x="6"
      buttonMode="true"
      useHandCursor="true"
      toolTip="This is a CheckBox" />

    <mx:Label id="lblFollowUp" text="Select All"
      width="100%" fontWeight="bold" x="23"
      toolTip="This is a CheckBox"/>

  </mx:Canvas>
</mx:VBox>
```

3. Save both files and run the application, and you'll see the CheckBox and the Label control displayed in the DataGridColumn, as shown in Figure 7-7.

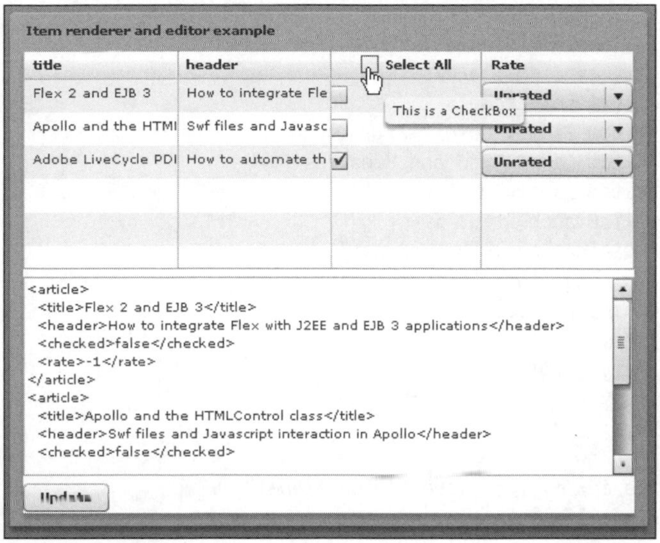

Figure 7-7. The MXML component becomes inserted as a renderer in the header of the DataGridColumn.

Solution 7-5: Displaying one-to-many data relationships

The classes discussed so far are perfect for displaying lists with just one level of depth, in which every element has a certain number of properties. Often, however, there are lists of elements with one-to-many relationships between them (for example, a list of employees with a telephone number and a list of companies with users, who all have their own telephone numbers and other attributes).

If you have the data organized hierarchically, you can use the Tree class to display it. Each item can be a branch or a leaf, and you can easily scroll through the data at different levels.

In this solution, you'll see how to represent data in a Tree control and enable the user to expand and collapse the data. This technique simulates a master/detail representation of data in that it creates a relationship based on two levels of information. The summary data for all items is shown, and you can expand individual items to show more detail on them.

What's involved

In this solution you'll use a Tree and a List control. The first will give a representation of the data hierarchy, while the second will display only the detailed information relative to each single data item. The Tree control is instanced using the <mx:Tree>tag that, as with all list-based controls, accepts the dataProvider property to be able to display the data:

```
<mx:XML format="e4x" id="myXML">
  <city label="Florence">
    <city label="Milan"/>
    <city label="Rome">
      <item label="Hotel" />
      <item label="Bed and Breakfast" />
      <item label="Dining"
        isBranch="true">
      <dining label="Restaurant" />
      <dining label="Pizzeria" />
      <dining label="Wine Bar" />
    </item>
    </city>
  </city>
</mx:XML>

<mx:Tree id="myTree" labelField="@label"
  showRoot="false"
  dataProvider="{myXML}"
  width="305" height="260"/>
```

The dataProvider of the Tree control can be an Array of objects or a String that contains a valid XML structure. In the example, you have created an XML structure using the `<mx:XML>` tag. The final result of the Tree is shown in Figure 7-8.

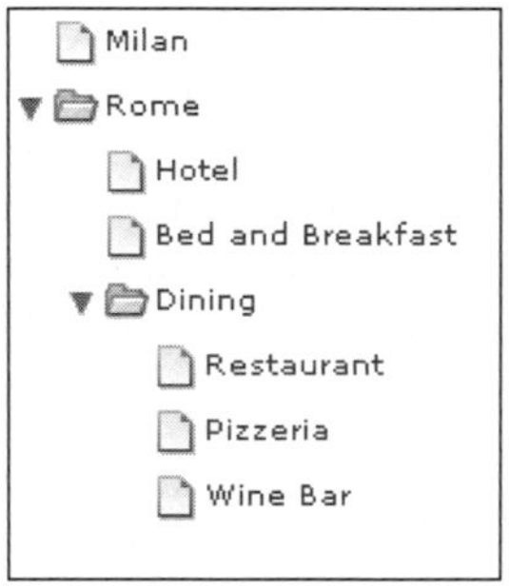

Figure 7-8. The Tree control visualizes the data in a hierarchical way.

The Tree control can read more than one root node or branch node.

In this solution you'll use a data source defined through an XMLList embedded in the code that will be used as the data provider of the Tree control.

How to build it

You'll start by creating the data model hierarchy.

1. Create a new MXML application file by selecting File ➤ New ➤ MXML Application and name it Chapter_7_Flex_Sol_5.mxml.

2. You create the data model with two levels of depth by using the <XMLList> tag. Add this code below the <mx:Application> tag:

```
<mx:XMLList id="myDP">
  <node>
    <node name="YouThru.com">
      <node name="Emanuele"
        surname="Tatti"
        age="23" wage="1200"/>
      <node name="Francesco"
        surname="Rapana" age="22" wage="1000"/>
      <node name="Constantin"
        surname="Moldovanu" age="23" wage="1200"/>
    </node>
    <node name="Acme spa">
      <node name="John"
        surname="Doe" age="32" wage="900"/>
      <node name="Max"
        surname="Power" age="28" wage="1500"/>
      <node name="Homer"
        surname="Simpsons" age="48" wage="200"/>
    </node>
    <node name="Comtaste Corp.">
      <node name="Marco"
        surname="Casario" age="29" wage="1500"/>
      <node name="Raffele"
        surname="Mannella" age="45" wage="1500"/>
      <node name="Liviu"
        surname="Stoica" age="25" wage="1300"/>
    </node>
  </node>
</mx:XMLList>
```

The data is composed of information on three companies; the names and other details of their employees are linked in. Each resource comprises a node for which the attributes name, surname, age, and wage have been declared:

```
<node name="Marco"
  surname="Casario" age="29" wage="1500"/>
```

3. Insert a Panel after the closure of the XMLList tag, as shown following. It will contain the two list-based classes:

```
<mx:Panel title="One to many relationship" width="500" height="400">

</mx:Panel>
```

4. Insert the Tree control in the Panel just created, as follows (note that you are link-ing the id of the XMLList used as the data provider):

```
<mx:Panel title="One to many relationship" width="500" height="400">

<mx:Tree id="myTree" width="250"
  height="100%"
  dataProvider="{myDP}"
  labelField="@name"
showRoot="false" />

</mx:Panel>
```

In the labelField property, you specified the element used as the root element in the Tree: labelField="@name".

Because the name of the companies is an attribute of the <node> tag, you have used the @name syntax. Save the file and run the application. At this point, three root elements will be created in the Tree control, in which the names of the people will be displayed (see Figure 7-9).

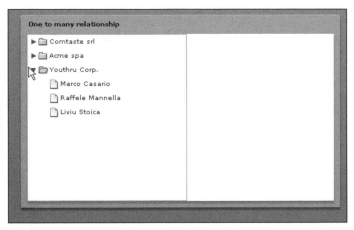

Figure 7-9. The Tree control displays data of the data model XMLList.

In this solution, you enable the user to click the name of an employee to display all the expanded details on that employee. To create the necessary data relationship, create a data binding between the Label controls and the selectedItem property of the Tree.

5. To do this, insert a Vbox container with four Label controls declared inside it as follows:

```
<mx:Panel title="One to many relationship" width="500" height="400">

<mx:Tree id="myTree" width="250"
  height="100%"
  dataProvider="{myDP}"
```

```
    labelField="@name"
  showRoot="false" />

<mx:VBox>
  <mx:Label text="Employee details" fontWeight="bold" />
  <mx:Label text="Name: {myTree.selectedItem.@surname}" />
  <mx:Label text="Age: {myTree.selectedItem.@age}" />
  <mx:Label text="Wage: {myTree.selectedItem.@wage}" />
</mx:VBox>

</mx:Panel>
```

The data binding accesses the details of the data in the XMLList data model through the selectedItem property and by directly accessing the name of the attribute using the wildcard @:

```
{myTree.selectedItem.@surname}
```

6. Save the file and run the application.

By selecting a node of the Tree and clicking a name, the detailed information will be displayed in the Label controls, as shown in Figure 7-10.

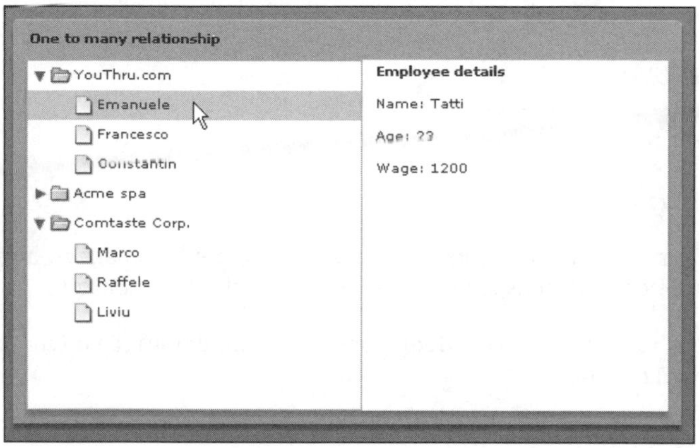

Figure 7-10. The detailed information is shown in the Label controls when they are selected by the user in the Tree.

Expert tips

Like all Flex controls, the Tree control can be customized in all its aspects. It provides properties for specifying icons: the folderOpenIcon, folderClosedIcon, and defaultLeafIcon properties. Then, with the use of the setItemIcon() method, you can specify the icon, or both the open and closed icons for the control's item. Therefore you associate a function to define icons by using its iconFunction property.

Now modify the solution created previously by adding customized icons on the Tree control. To use icon images you have to embed them in the MXML page. To import and embed an image in a Flex application, use the [Embed] metadata that you'll define in an <mx:Script> block via ActionScript.

> *I used Silk's set of icons (www.famfamfam.com/lab/icons/silk/) for the icon images. Silk is a free icon set with more than 700 icons that you can use for any of your web development or application development projects. These icons are licensed under a Creative Commons Attribution 2.5 License, so you can use them for any purpose and make any changes you like.*

1. Open the MXML file created in the solution and insert an <mx:Script> block below the <mx:Application> tag with the following code:

```
<mx:Script>
<![CDATA[

[Bindable]
[Embed(source="assets/one.png")]
private var icon1:Class;
[Bindable]
[Embed(source="assets/two.png")]
private var icon2:Class;
 [Bindable]
[Embed(source="assets/three.png")]
private var icon3:Class;
]]>
</mx:Script>
```

To make the [Embed] directive work, you have to associate the image to a variable typed as Class. The embedded icons are ready to be used in the Tree control.

2. Add the folderOpenIcon, folderClosedIcon, and defaultLeafIcon properties on the <mx:Tree> tag:

```
<mx:Tree id="myTree" width="250"
height="100%"
dataProvider="{myDP}"
labelField="@name"
showRoot="false"
folderOpenIcon="{icon1}"
folderClosedIcon="{icon2}"
defaultLeafIcon="{icon3}"/>
```

3. Save and run the application.

The icons will be used with each Tree leaf, as shown in Figure 7-11.

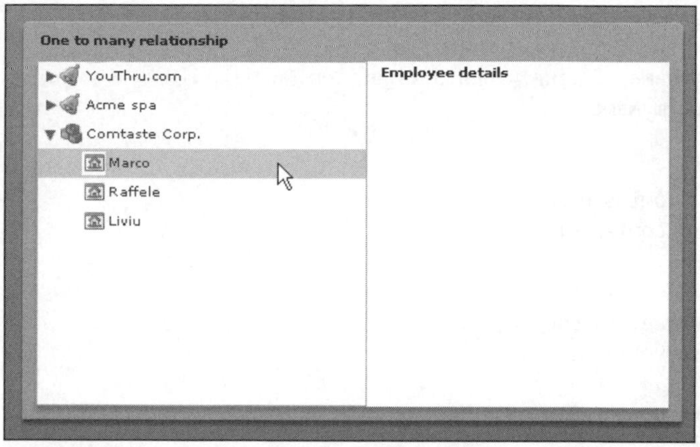

Figure 7-11. The embedded images are used as icons for the Tree elements.

Another powerful method to set icons in a Tree control is using the iconFunction property. It gives you total control on all icons for the control.

4. Insert the following code in the <mx:Tree> tag:

```
<mx:Tree id="myTree" width="250"
height="100%"
dataProvider="{myDP}"
labelField="@name"
showRoot="false"
folderOpenIcon="{icon1}"
folderClosedIcon="{icon2}"
defaultLeafIcon="{icon3}"
iconFunction="myIconFunction"/>
```

The Tree control iconFunction property specifies a function that sets all icons for the tree.

5. Add the function to the <mx:Script> block, in which you'll embed the icon images you need:

```
[Bindable]
[Embed(source="assets/comtaste.png")]
public var comtaste:Class;

 [Bindable]
[Embed(source="assets/youthru.png")]
public var youthru:Class;

 [Bindable]
[Embed(source="assets/youthru_close.png")]
public var youthruClosed:Class;
```

7

```
private function myIconFunction(item:Object): Class
{
var myName: String = new String(item.@name);
switch(myName)
{

case "Comtaste Corp.":
return comtaste;
break;
case "YouThru.com":
if(myTree.isItemOpen(item))
return youthru;
else
return youthruClosed;
break;

}
return null;
}
```

The myIconFunction() accepts an Object that contains the items of the dataProvider of the Tree control and returns a Class that is the embedded icon image to apply.

In the function you checked for the @name attribute of the XMLList (the dataProvider of the Tree) using a switch case. According to the @name value, you applied a different icon. Note that for the YouThru.com value, you created an if() condition to apply a different icon for the state of the Tree (open or closed):

```
case "YouThru.com":
if(myTree.isItemOpen(item))
return youthru;
else
return youthruClosed;
break;
```

6. Save the file and run the application.

The icons will be used with each Tree leaf, as shown in Figure 7-12.

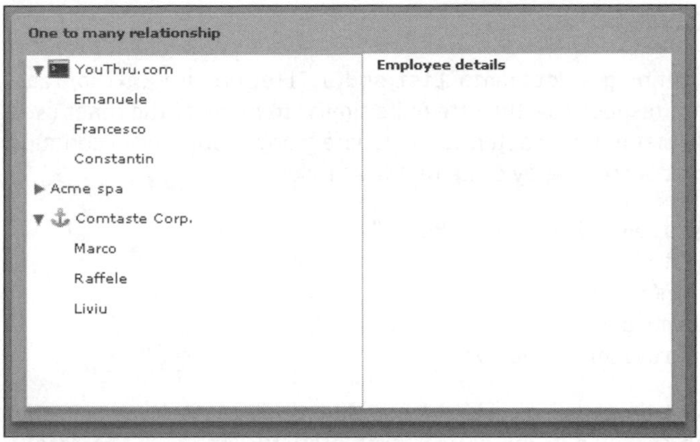

Figure 7-12. The Tree control iconFunction property specifies a function that sets all icons for the control.

Solution 7-6: The TileList and HorizontalList components

TileList and the HorizontalList are two Flex components that enable you to display the data in tabular form. HorizontalList displays items horizontally, while TileList displays the items in a table format made up of rows and columns of equal-sized tiles.

Every item is displayed as a cell of a table through the ItemRenderer defined for that object. For example, by modifying the default ItemRenderer, you can display a list of images on a line through the use of the HorizontalList or on lines and columns, just like in a table, by using the TileList.

You could get the same result by using the Tile or Hbox container and then inserting the data from the collection in them through the use of a Repeater container. The only substantial difference between the two approaches is memory management. When the containers are used, all the objects are instanced in memory when they're created, even if the instanced data is not visible to the user (which is pretty inefficient). When using the list-based controls, only the objects visible in that moment become instanced in memory, which cuts down on memory usage. (It could actually worsen the application performance if scrolling and changes to the display occur, however, because every time the display changes, new objects would have to be instanced.)

In this solution, you'll use both the TileList and HorizontalList controls to display data from an XML data model.

What's involved

The tags for defining a HorizontalList and a TileList are <mx:HorizontalList> and <mx:TileList>, respectively; they are quite similar to many of the other list-based controls you've already met in this chapter, so they share many properties in common with them. A HorizontalList is creating by using MXML as follows:

```
<mx:HorizontalList id="myHList"
  height="250"
  columnCount="3"
  columnWidth="125"
  dataProvider="myAC" />
```

The columnCount property indicates how many items will be displayed in the HorizontalList, with the width specified in the columnWidth property. As usual, the dataProvider property enables you to populate the component with the data to be displayed.

A TileList is created like this:

```
<mx:TileList id="myTList"
  height="500" width="500"
  maxColumns="5"
  rowHeight="150"
  columnWidth="100"
  dataProvider="myAC"/>
```

The maxColumns property of the TileList specifies the maximum numbers of columns that the component can have; it is possible to set the dimensions of the lines and columns with rowHeight and columnWidth.

In this solution you'll see how to use a HorizontalList to display a list of categories and a TileList to show the products contained in each of them.

How to build it

For this solution, the XML file (see the assets folder) contains categories and products. It has the following structure:

```
<?xml version="1.0" encoding="utf-8"?>
<dataroot>
  <category name="Flex Books" img="cat1.jpg">
    <product name="Flex Solutions" />
    <product name="Object Oriented ActionScript 3" />
    <product name="Essential Flex 2" />
  </category>
  <category name="Digital camera" img="cat2.jpg">
    <product name="Kodak EasyShare" />
    <product name="Minolta" />
  </category>
</dataroot>
```

1. Make sure that you created the assets folder in the Flex project. Copy and paste the products.xml file into this folder and refresh the project by right-clicking the Flex project in Navigator view and choosing the Refresh option from the context menu. You can also create the file on your own by selecting File ➤ New ➤ File and writing the XML structure shown previously.

2. Create a new MXML application file by selecting File ➤ New ➤ MXML Application and save it with the name Chapter_7_Flex_Sol_6.mxml.

3. Create an MXML data model to load the data from the products.xml file into the application and then convert it to an ArrayCollection:

```
<mx:Model id="myCategories" source="data/products.xml" />

<mx:ArrayCollection id="categoryAC" source="{myCategories.category}" />
```

The ArrayCollection is populated with the data loaded by the MXML model, which connects the source property of the ArrayCollection to the category property of the data model; in this case, it represents the repeating node of the XML file.

4. Insert the HorizontalList that will contain the list of the categories of the products, like so:

```
<mx:HorizontalList id="myHList"
    dataProvider="{categoryAC}"
    labelField="name"
    selectedIndex="0" width="200" />
```

You have set the ArrayCollection previously created from the XML file as the dataProvider of the HorizontalList, specifying which field of the category node has to be displayed in the labelField property (in this case, name).

By setting the selectedIndex property to 0, you automatically select the first object within the ArrayCollection (the ArrayCollection is zero-index-based) that will be shown in the HorizontalList at the startup; this property can be omitted if you do not want to display any products at application startup. You'll see why this happens in the next step.

5. Insert the TileList, which will contain the list of products. This time it is not appropriate to send the entire ArrayCollection to the component because you want only the products of the chosen category to appear:

```
<mx:TileList id="myTList"
    dataProvider="{categoryAC.getItemAt(myHList.selectedIndex).product}"
    labelField="name" width="200" />
```

The binding is between the dataProvider of the component and the item present in the ArrayCollection at the myHList.selectedIndex position. This value represents the item selected in the HorizontalList, which gives you the connection between the category selected and the relative products for that category. You must, however, remember to point at the product property of the XML file containing the products divided into categories, and display only the name field through the labelField property.

6. Save and run the application.

At the top, the categories appear, followed by the list of the products. As you select each category, the products in the TileList underneath will change.

In this example, you used HorizontalList and TileList with their default itemRenderer, displaying a simple Label. To improve the appearance of the display, you could add images for the categories and products with a simple custom itemRenderer. Modify the code of the solution like so:

```
<mx:HorizontalList
  id="myHList"
  dataProvider="{categoryAC}"
  selectedIndex="0"
  width="200"
  horizontalScrollPolicy="off">
  <mx:itemRenderer>
    <mx:Component>
      <mx:VBox
        horizontalAlign="center"
        width="100%" paddingRight="0"
        paddingLeft="0"  >
        <mx:Label text="{data.name}" />
        <mx:Image
          source="{'assets/'+data.img}"
          height="60" width="100"
          horizontalAlign="center"/>
      </mx:VBox>
    </mx:Component>
  </mx:itemRenderer>
</mx:HorizontalList>
```

The HorizontalList is the same as that seen previously, except that the horizontalScrollPolicy property is set to off, which enables you to not display the horizontal scrolling bar.

The ItemRenderer enables you to display a Label and an Image in a vertical layout, loading the data from the ArrayCollection at runtime. The images become loaded from the assets folder of the project, but this can be any folder of your choice in which you have inserted your images. The name of the image to be displayed for each category is present in the XML file (in the category nodes of the img field).

> Flash Player can't load JPG files saved as progressive JPEGs.

Expert tips

In both TileList and the HorizontalList, the allowMultipleSelection property enables you to select multiple items in the list by keeping the Ctrl/Cmd or Shift buttons pressed on the keyboard, as you'd expect in any desktop application.

To activate this feature, you just need to set the allowMultipleSelection property on the control to true:

```
<mx:TileList id="myTList" height="200" width="250"
    dataProvider="myAC"
    allowMultipleSelection="true" />
```

Unlike HorizontalList, in TileList it is possible to define the direction in which the items will be displayed. Possible values for the direction property are horizontal and vertical: in the horizontal display, the items will be inserted in a line until the entire width of the object has been filled; then it moves on the next line:

```
<mx:TileList
    id="myTList"
    dataProvider="{categoryAC.getItemAt(myHList.selectedIndex).product}"
    labelField="name" width="200"
    direction="vertical" />
```

If the lines displayed go off the screen, a vertical scroll bar will be shown.

In a HorizontalList, the items are displayed from right to left, with a possible horizontal bar if they go off the screen, and a vertical scrollbar will be visualized in the case of very tall cells.

7

Solution 7-7: Implementing drag-and-drop operations

Drag-and-drop functionality is a standard feature of most desktop applications, but is not as common or easy to achieve on web applications. However Flex brings this capability to web applications via the Drag and Drop Manager class, which enables you to drag and add an item from one list-based control to another component, for example. All Flex components can be drag-and-drop–enabled, and a few of them (DataGrid, List, Tree, HorizontalList, Menu, TileList, and PrintDataGrid) include built-in support for these operations through specific properties.

In this solution, you'll see how to add drag-and-drop functionality to list-based components.

What's involved

In list-based controls, all you need to do to implement drag and drop is correctly set the dragEnabled, dropEnabled, and dragMoveEnabled properties. With these properties set, Flex enables you to move items automatically from one control to another without manually specifying an event listener.

The properties and methods you can use in drag and drop are as follows:

- defaultDrop, IndicatorSkin: Indicates the graphic elements to use for the drop phase of the items (drop-insert indicator).

- dragEnabled: A Boolean value that determines whether the control is a drag initiator.

- dropEnabled: A Boolean value hat specifies whether the control can be a drop target.

- dragMoveEnabled: Specifies whether the items can be moved by the drag initiator to the drop target. It is a Boolean that adopts a true value when the dragEnabled property is set to true.

- calculateDropIndex: Items dropped in the drop target have an index value that identifies them, which is contained in this property.

- hideDropFeedback(): Removes the focus from the target and hides the drop feedback.

- showDropFeedback(): Performs the operations opposite to the preceding method. It shows the focus on the target and sets up the drop indicator in the correct position (where the drop operations should happen).

To enable a control to drag and drop, first set the dragEnabled property. By setting this property as true, if the user clicks an item in a component and keeps the button of the mouse pressed while moving, the drag is initiated.

At this point, Flex creates a DragSource object in memory that contains an items property, which contains a copy of the item or items selected on the component, and a source property, which contains the reference to the component from which the drag operation has been initiated (called **initiator**).

```
<mx:TileList id="myTile" width="200" height="300" dragEnabled="true" />
```

The dropEnabled property allows you to enable the component to receive the drop of the dragged item from another component. The item will be sent to the component on which it has been dropped (drop target) as long as it has the dropEnabled property set to true. The component can't accept the item and add it to the existing data or discard it if the format is not suitable.

```
<mx:HorizontalList id="myHList"
width="500" height="100" dropEnabled="true" />
```

Through the dragMoveEnabled properties it is possible to indicate whether the dropped item should be cancelled by the original component (initiator) once dropped on the destination component (target) or if a copy of the item should be made keeping it, therefore, on both components.

If this property is set to false, it is possible to simply copy the item from one component to another. Setting the property as true, the item will be moved to the new component; in this case, however, it is also possible to carry out the copy, instead of the move, if you keep the Control (Ctrl) key pressed while releasing the item. The value dragMoveEnabled will be considered only if the dragEnabled property of the component is also set to true.

```
<mx:Tree id="myTree" width="100" height="300" dragEnabled="true"
dragMoveEnabled="true" />
```

These properties are set to false by default, aside from the case of the dragMoveEnabled property of the Tree component, which is set by default as true.

How to build it

For this solution, you'll use two different components, both list-based controls. In one of the two objects you insert a collection to create items that you can subsequently drag onto the other object.

This first object will, therefore, have the dragEnabled property set to true, so that the component can behave like a drag initiator. In the second, you'll set the dropEnabled property to true, rendering it a possible drop target.

1. Create a new MXML application by selecting New ➤ File ➤ MXML Application and save it with the name Chapter_7_Flex_Sol_7.mxml.

2. Set the layout of the application as horizontal, like so:

```
<mx:Application xmlns:mx="http://www.adobe.com/2006/mxml"
  layout="horizontal">
```

3. Create an ArrayCollection, as follows, which will populate the first component:

```
<mx:ArrayCollection id="myAC">
  <mx:Object label="{new Date()}" data="{new Date()}"/>
  <mx:Object label="{new Date(2007,1,2)}" data="{new Date(2007,1,2)}"/>
  <mx:Object label="{new Date()}" data="{new Date()}"/>
</mx:ArrayCollection>
```

You have used the MXML ArrayCollection tag to define an Object, each of which possesses two properties, label and data. In these properties, a Date object is created.

4. Insert the first list-based control, as shown following. You use a DataGrid with a single column, set the ArrayCollection previously created as dataProvider, and enable the dragEnabled property:

```
<mx:ArrayCollection id="myAC">
  <mx:Object label="{new Date()}" data="{new Date()}"/>
  <mx:Object label="{new Date(2007,1,2)}" data="{new Date(2007,1,2)}"/>
  <mx:Object label="{new Date()}" data="{new Date()}"/>
</mx:ArrayCollection>

<mx:DataGrid dataProvider="{myAC}" width="200" dragEnabled="true">
  <mx:columns>
    <mx:DataGridColumn dataField="label" />
  </mx:columns>
</mx:DataGrid>
```

The dataField property of the DataGridColumn component contains the name of the property you want to show and that is present in every Object of the collection; in this case, it is the label property.

7

5. You add the component that will receive the drop and that will function as the drop target (in this case, a List) in which you'll enable the dropEnabled property:

```
<mx:List width="200" dropEnabled="true"/>
```

6. If the dragMoveEnabled is not enabled, the default operation is resorted to—the copy of the item stored in the List control is used. Now try to set the dragMoveEnabled property to true in the DataGrid:

```
<mx:DataGrid dataProvider="{myAC}" width="200"
  dragEnabled="true"
  dragMoveEnabled="true">
```

In this way, you have made the movement of the item from the first to the second control possible.

7. Save and run the application.

Try dragging an item from the first control. You'll see that a shadow appears, and you'll be able to drag it. When you pass over a component that is suitable for dropping the item onto, your cursor changes to a green circle with a + sign in it, as shown in Figure 7-13.

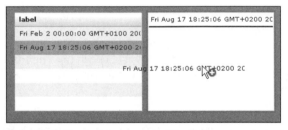

Figure 7-13. The built-in support of the list-based controls automatically handles drag-and-drop operations.

Expert tips

It is sometimes necessary to use the inverse function, enabling the dragging from the second object back to the first object. To do this you have to enable the dragEnabled and dropEnabled properties on both objects, like so:

```
<mx:DataGrid dataProvider="{myAC}" width="200"
  dragEnabled="true"
  dragMoveEnabled="true"
  dropEnabled="true">
```

and

```
<mx:List width="200"
  dragEnabled="true"
  dragMoveEnabled="true"
  dropEnabled="true"/>
```

In this scenario, when the user drags the item, a copy of it will be created. To prevent this situation you have to write ActionScript code and manage the drag-and-drop events.

Solution 7-8: Advanced drag and drop

It is very easy to implement the drag-and-drop operations using the built-in properties and methods in the list-based controls, but this is only the tip of the iceberg. You'll often want to customize and have more control over the data and components that you intend to drag.

Through the DragManager, DragSource, and DragEvent classes, Flex enables you to also create complex script to create and implement additional functions in the drag-and-drop operations classes:

- DragManager: Manages the drag-and-drop operations through public methods.
- DragSource. Specifies the data that will be dragged and enables you to manage and to register the listeners to run when determined events take place.
- DragEvent: Contains the drag-and-drop events to write event handlers when determined operations occur.

In this solution, you'll see how to use these classes to have more control over drag-and-drop operations. The solution will contain two List controls: the first functions as the container for the data to be dragged, and the second is the drop target onto which you can drag this data. Through the DragManager and DragEvent classes, you cancel the data in the List control when it's dropped onto the second List control.

What's involved

To manage the drag-and-drop operations and have control over the events released during the drag-and-drop phase, you can use ActionScript with the DragManager, DragSource, and DragEvent classes. Flex uses events to control and manage the drag-and-drop operations. For this reason you should have a good knowledge of the events that release during this phase.

In the following list, the events used during the drag-and-drop operations are laid out and described:

- dragEnter: Dispatched when the item is dragged over a component suitable to receive the drop; it is often used to change the aspect of the drop target component to give a clue to the user. The event is dispatched only at the moment of entering on the component.
- dragExit: Dispatched when the mouse exits from the drop target during the dragging phase; it can be used to restore aspects of the component modified by a preceding dragEnter event.
- dragOver: Occurs when the user moves the mouse into the area of the drop target during the dragging phase.

- dragDrop: Dispatched at the moment of the drop of the item on the drop target.
- dragComplete: Called immediately after the completion of the dragDrop event or when the drop takes place on a target that does not accept the drop.

These events are used directly in the list-based controls:

```
<mx:List id="myList" width="200"
  dataProvider="{myAC}"
  dragEnabled="true"
  dropEnabled="true"
  dragComplete="dragCompleteHandler(event)"/>
```

The dragCompleteHandler() event handler is released when the drag operation has been concluded and the data has been accepted or declined by the drop target. The dragComplete event is dispatched after the dragDrop event. Using ActionScript, specify the operations you want to apply to the release of this event:

```
private function dragCompleteHandler(evt:DragEvent):void {
  // whatever you want
}
```

In this solution, you'll apply the dragComplete event to drag the data from one List control to another. When the drop of the item has been successfully completed, the item is deleted from the data provider of the dragInitiator.

How to build it

You insert two List controls in the application: one containing the data and one to be the drop target. Under the latter, you'll insert a button to delete the data contained in it. Both List controls have to allow the drag, but in one way only—you don't want them to create copies of objects. The drag from the recycle bin to the first List control is necessary to be able to have a function of restoring data moved to the recycle bin.

1. Create a new MXML application by selecting New ➤ File ➤ MXML Application and save it with name Chapter_7_Flex_Sol_8.mxml.

2. Set the layout of the application as horizontal:

```
<mx:Application xmlns:mx="http://www.adobe.com/2006/mxml"
  layout="horizontal">
```

3. Add an ArrayCollection as shown here:

```
<mx:ArrayCollection id="myAC">
  <mx:Object objectID="1" label="First object" />
  <mx:Object objectID="2" label="Second object" />
  <mx:Object objectID="3" label="Third object" />
</mx:ArrayCollection>
```

The objects contained in the ArrayCollection contain three items typed as Object that define the data in their label and objectID properties.

4. Insert the List controls into the application, as follows:

```
</mx:ArrayCollection>
<mx:List id="myList" width="200" dataProvider="{myAC}" />
<mx:VBox horizontalAlign="center">
  <mx:List id="trash" width="200" />
  <mx:Button id="emptyTrash_Button" label="Empty Trash" />
</mx:VBox>
```

The first List control, myList, contains the data present in the ArrayCollection created in the preceding step. On its right, the second List control and the button to empty it display, centered vertical and horizontally. You have not enabled drag and drop at this point.

5. Enable the built-in drag and drop in the controls by adding the dragEnabled and dropEnabled properties:

```
<mx:List id="myList" width="200" dataProvider="{myAC}"
  dragEnabled="true"
  dropEnabled="true"/>

<mx:VBox horizontalAlign="center">
  <mx:List id="trash" width="200"
    dropEnabled="true"
    dragEnabled="true"/>
  <mx:Button id="emptyTrash_Button"
    label="Empty Trash" />
</mx:VBox>
```

By setting these properties to true, you can copy the items from one to the other. But the objective was to just move the items (not copy them), so you need to make a change.

6. Use the dragComplete event to obtain the desired behavior. Create an event handler that will be launched when this event is invoked. The event handler has to be specified on both List controls so that both are drop targets (their dropEnabled properties are set to true). Make the following changes now:

```
<mx:List id="myList" width="200" dataProvider="{myAC}"
  dragEnabled="true"
  dropEnabled="true"
  dragComplete="dragCompleteHandler(event)" />

<mx:VBox horizontalAlign="center">
  <mx:List id="trash" width="200"
    dropEnabled="true"
    dragEnabled="true"
    dragComplete="dragCompleteHandler(event)" />
  <mx:Button id="emptyTrash_Button" label="Empty Trash" />
</mx:VBox>
```

You now have to define the dragCompleteHandler() function to change the default behavior.

7

7. Next, you need to open an <mx:Script> tag and insert the function that will manage the dragComplete event into it. Insert the following at the beginning of the code, immediately before the ArrayCollection:

```
<mx:Application xmlns:mx="http://www.adobe.com/2006/mxml"
  layout="horizontal">
<mx:Script>
  <![CDATA[
    import mx.managers.DragManager;
    import mx.events.DragEvent;

    private function dragCompleteHandler(evt:DragEvent):void
    {
      if(evt.action != DragManager.NONE)
      {
        var listInitiator:List = List(evt.dragInitiator);
        var listAC:ArrayCollection = ➡
        ArrayCollection(listInitiator.dataProvider);
        var item:Object = evt.dragSource.dataForFormat("items")[0];
        for(var i:uint = 0; i < listAC.length; i++)
        {
          if(listAC.getItemAt(i).objectID == item.objectID)
          {
            listAC.removeItemAt(i);
            break;
          }
        }
      }
    }
  ]]>
</mx:Script>
```

Let's examine this code in detail. To use the DragSource and DragManager classes, it is necessary to import the relative libraries at the beginning of the <mx:Script> tag:

```
import mx.managers.DragManager;
import mx.events.DragEvent;
```

The dragCompleteHandler function receives the event object of DragEvent (in this case, evt), which contains all the data necessary for the management of the drag and drop (it takes type as a parameter).

The DragEvent class possesses three very important properties:

- action: String. The requested action.
- dragInitiator: IUIComponent. The component that initiated the drag.
- dragSource: DragSource. The DragSource object containing the data being dragged.

The event handler begins with a control. An if() condition checks that an action occurs at least. Use the NONE constant of the DragManager class:

```
if(evt.action != DragManager.NONE) {
  // code
}
```

If the event is linked to a valid drag-and-drop action, the condition is unverified. Take the dragInitiator property from the evt variable and copy the reference into a variable of List type because you know that the initiator of the drag is definitely a List control:

```
var listInitiator:List = List(evt.dragInitiator);
```

Insert the dataProvider from this variable into an ArrayCollection (it's necessary to carry out modifications relative to the drag movement):

```
var listAC:ArrayCollection = ➡
ArrayCollection(listInitiator.dataProvider);
```

You next declare a variable named item typed as Object that you populate with the value taken from the dragInitiator that is the item you have dragged. To do this, use the dataForFormat() method of the DragSource class, sending the items string as a parameter:

```
var item:Object = evt.dragSource.dataForFormat("items")[0];
```

The DragSource objects originating from the list-based controls always have items as the data format. The dataForFormat() method returns an array containing the data present in the dataProvider of the dragInitiator for the item selected. Therefore, you must select the first element of the array to obtain the Object relative to the dragged item.

At this point, to know which items have to be deleted, loop through the ArrayCollection, listAC, until you find the item that has been dragged. When you find it, remove it from that collection. The built-in drag-and-drop feature will have already copied the item into the dataProvider of the drop target:

```
for(var i:uint = 0; i < listAC.length; i++)
{
  if(listAC.getItemAt(i).objectID == item.objectID)
  {
    listAC.removeItemAt(i);
    break;
  }
}
```

8. Still in the <mx:Script> tag, you'll now create the function, enabling you to empty the second list. After the closing bracket of the event handler, dragCompleteHandler(), add the following function:

```
private function emptyTrash():void
{
  ArrayCollection(trash.dataProvider).removeAll();
}
```

Through the removeAll function of the ArrayCollection class, cancel all the elements present in the dataProvider of the second List control representing the recycle bin.

367

9. Execute the function on the click event of the Button control by adding the following code into the MXML:

```
<mx:Button id="emptyTrash_Button"
  label="Empty Trash"
  click="emptyTrash()" />
```

Now when the button is clicked, the emptyTrash() event handler is invoked.

10. Save and run the application.

It is now possible to drag items between the two List controls and then delete them from the second list, as shown in Figure 7-14.

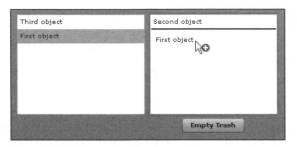

Figure 7-14. At the end of the drag-and-drop operations the data becomes cancelled from the dragInitiator.

Expert tips

The function of drag and drop can be extended by the list-based controls to all Flex components through the use of the DragManager class, which has a few static methods for managing the drag and drop (for example, the doDrag() function for initiating a drag operation) and acceptDragDrop() to signal that the drop target can accept the drop of an item when dragged over.

Solution 7-9: Using the AdvancedDataGrid with a Tree control

As you already know, the DataGrid a very powerful component at your disposal, and among the new features of Flex 3, there is the new AdvancedDataGrid component, which extends and enriches the functions of the DataGrid by adding new and very useful features, such as the following:

- Multicolumn sorting interface
- Cell-level formatting functions
- Tree view (hierarchical data and grouping data)

- Cell selection
- Custom rows
- Column grouping
- SummaryCollection
- PrintAdvancedDataGrid

In this solution, you'll see how to use the new AdvancedDataGrid control, applying some of these new characteristics.

What's involved

The new DataGrid is created using the AdvancedDataGrid tag:

```
<mx:AdvancedDataGrid
    id="myADG" / >
```

Being a list-based control, it accepts the dataProvider property, which specifies the data to be displayed in it. Just like the basic DataGrid, you can bind an ArrayCollection class to act as data provider. Consider the following XML structure, which you have already used more than once in this chapter:

```
<dataroot>
  <city><city>
    <id>1</id>
    <id_region>1</id_region>
    <region>PIEMONTE</region>
    <cityName>TORINO</cityName>
    <code>TO</code>
    <population>2236765</population>
    <male>1086745</male>
    <female>1150020</female>
    <family>886053</family>
  </city></city>
</dataroot>
```

You can load the XML data into an MXML data model and convert it into an ArrayCollection, like so:

```
<mx:Model id="myRegion" source="data/states.xml" />
<mx:ArrayCollection id="myAC" source="{myRegion.city}" />
```

You can now send the data to the AdvancedDataGrid and display it. To define which columns should be displayed in the AdvancedDataGrid, use the AdvancedDataGridColumn tag, for which you specify the dataField and headerText properties:

```
<mx:AdvancedDataGrid
    id="myADG"
    dataProvider="{myAC}"
```

7

```
width="550"
variableRowHeight="true"
wordWrap="true">

<mx:columns>
  <mx:AdvancedDataGridColumn headerText="ID"
    dataField="id"/>
  <mx:AdvancedDataGridColumn headerText="Region"
    dataField="region"/>
  <mx:AdvancedDataGridColumn headerText="Population"
    dataField="population" />
  <mx:AdvancedDataGridColumn headerText="City"
    dataField="cityName"/>
  <mx:AdvancedDataGridColumn headerText="Code"
    dataField="code"/>
  <mx:AdvancedDataGridColumn headerText="Family"
    dataField="family"/>
</mx:columns>

</mx:AdvancedDataGrid>
```

You don't see any difference in the tags used inside the control, compared to those used if you were using a standard DataGrid control. But there are immediate advantages of using an AdvancedDataGrid: You can now sort by multiple columns by holding down Ctrl/Cmd and clicking the desired headers. For example, Figure 7-15 shows the data sorted by population and also by the number of families.

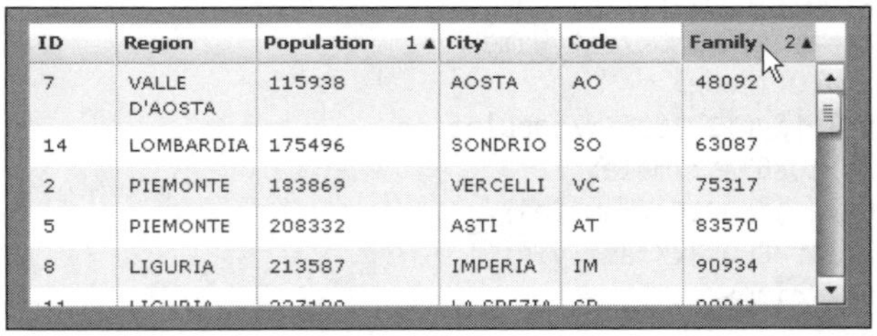

Figure 7-15. For multisorting, keep the Ctrl/Cmd key pressed while you select the header of a column.

In this solution, you'll see how to use a Tree control inside an AdvancedDataGrid to obtain a hierarchical representation of data.

How to build it

This solution works only with Flex 3 installed, so ensure that you have Flex Builder 3 installed (http://labs.adobe.com/technologies/flex/flexbuilder3/). One of the new features of Flex 3 is the capability to switch between the various versions of the SDK. This means that you can use the same integrated development environment (IDE) to develop

Flex applications on different versions (using the Flex 2 SDK or the Flex 3 SDK). Go to the properties of the project (select Project ➤ Properties), select the Flex Compiler category and select Flex 3 M3 (Beta 2), as shown in Figure 7-16.

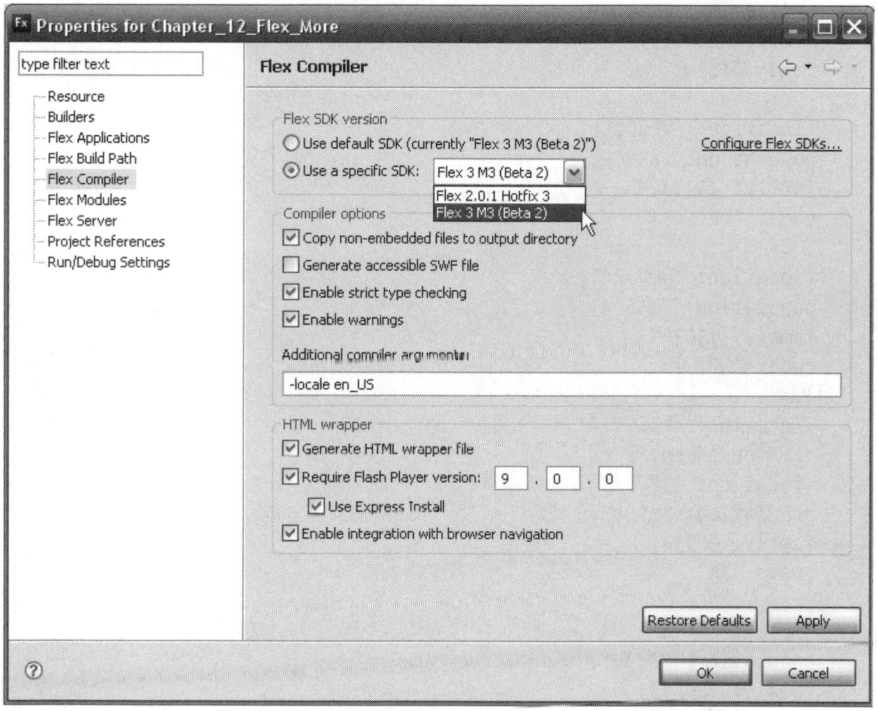

Figure 7-16. In Flex Builder 3 you can use different version of Flex SDK to compile applications.

> The code name of the Flex 3 beta is Moxie, so your Flex SDK could be named Flex Moxie.

You can download Flex Builder 3 and the Flex 3 SDK on the Adobe Labs site (http://labs.adobe.com/technologies/flex/flexbuilder3/).

1. Create a new MXML application by selecting New ➤ File ➤ MXML Application and name it Chapter_7_Flex_Sol_9.mxml.

2. Create an Array inside an <mx:Script> block, as shown following (it will function as the dataProvider for the DataGrid):

```
<mx:Application xmlns:mx="http://www.adobe.com/2006/mxml">

<mx:Script>
<![CDATA[
```

```
private var cities:Array = [
    { location: 'PIEMONTE',
        children: [
{ location: 'TORINO',
 population: 2236765,
 family: 886053,
 code: 'TO'
},
{ location: 'VERCELLI',
 population: 183869,
 family: 75317,
 code: 'VC'
},
{ location: 'NOVARA',
 population: 334614,
 family: 130363,
 code: 'NO' }
]},
{ location: 'LIGURIA',
        children: [
{ location: 'IMPERIA',
 population: 213587,
 family: 90934,
 code: 'IM'
},
{ location: 'SAVONA',
 population: 284647,
 family: 120883,
 code: 'SV'
},
 { location: 'GENOVA',
 population: 950849,
 family: 391796,
 code: 'GE'
}
]},
{ location: 'LOMBARDIA',
        children: [
{ location: 'VARESE',
 population: 797039,
 family: 289925,
 code: 'VA'
},
 { location: 'COMO',
 population: 522147,
 family: 188961,
 code: 'CO'
},
 { location: 'MILANO',
```

```
    population: 3738685,
    family: 1423856,
    code: 'MI'
   }
  ]
  }
];

]]>
</mx:Script>
```

The Array contains objects. Each object defines the location property on its first index. On the second index it creates a new Array, named children, formed from objects containing the properties location, population, family, and code:

```
{ location: 'PIEMONTE',
children: [
{ location: 'TORINO',
  population: 2236765,
  family: 886053,
  code: 'TO'
 }
```

Note that the location property is defined both in the first index of the Array and the first index of the nested children Array. This relationship will enable you to display the data in a hierarchical manner.

3. Add an AdvancedDataGrid control below the <mx:Script> block and define the AdvancedDataGridColumn inside it, as shown following. You use the cities Array as the dataProvider:

```
<mx:AdvancedDataGrid
  id="myADG"
  dataProvider="{cities}"
  width="90%"
  variableRowHeight="true"
  wordWrap="true">

  <mx:columns>
    <mx:AdvancedDataGridColumn headerText="Region"
      dataField="location"/>
    <mx:AdvancedDataGridColumn headerText="Population"
      dataField="population" />

    <mx:AdvancedDataGridColumn headerText="Code"
      dataField="code"/>
    <mx:AdvancedDataGridColumn headerText="Family"
      dataField="family"/>
  </mx:columns>
```

```
</mx:AdvancedDataGrid>

</mx:Application>
```

You have created four columns with the AdvancedDataGridColumn tag that display the location, population, code, and family data.

4. Save the file and run the application. You'll see a result like the one in Figure 7-17.

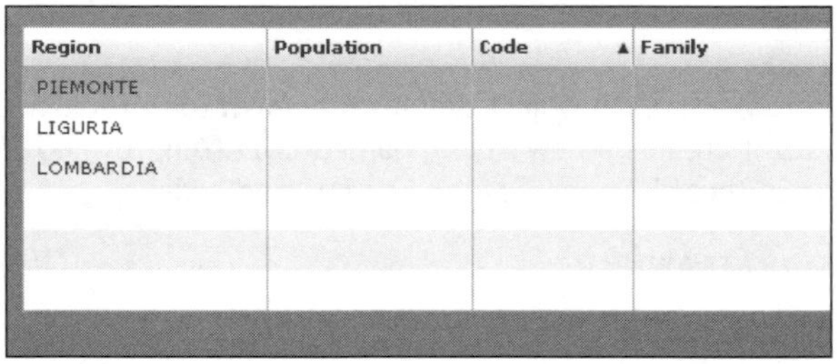

Figure 7-17. Only the first column is visualized with the values of the location property.

Only the location property is displayed onscreen because the other data is arranged hierarchically under the children property:

```
{ location: 'PIEMONTE',
children: [
{ location: 'TORINO',
 population: 2236765,
 family: 886053,
 code: 'TO'
}
```

To be able to visualize all the data, you must make a small modification to the application.

5. Modify the dataProvider of the AdvancedDataGrid like so:

```
<mx:AdvancedDataGrid
  id="myADG"
  dataProvider="{new HierarchicalData(cities)}"
  width="90%"
  variableRowHeight="true"
  wordWrap="true">
```

Here you have used the HierarchicalData class (http://livedocs.adobe.com/labs/flex3/langref/mx/collections/HierarchicalData.html), which is one of the new collection classes of Flex 3. HierarchicalData represents the data in a parent and child structure. It makes up part of the mx.collections package. You'll leave the rest of the MXML code unaltered and simply import the class using ActionScript.

6. Insert the HierarchicalData class in the block of <mx:Script> code before the cities Array:

```
<mx:Script>
 <![CDATA[
   import mx.collections.HierarchicalData;
```

7. Save the file and run the application again.

The AdvancedDataGrid will now display a Tree control in the first column. By expanding the node, all the data relative to that node in the other headers will be displayed, as shown in Figure 7-18.

Region	Population	Code	Family
▼ 🗁 PIEMONTE			
🗋 TORINO	2236765	TO	886053
🗋 VERCELLI	183869	VC	75317
🗋 NOVARA	334614	NO	130363
▶ 🗁 LIGURIA			
▶ 🗁 LOMBARDIA			

Figure 7-18. By clicking a node of the first column, all the data in the other headers will be displayed.

Expert tips

In this solution, you have used an Array created with ActionScript as data provider. Very often, however, you'll use data sent to you in response to a remote call. This data is not always structured in a hierarchical way, and it can be complicated to convert the original structure to hierarchical data. The Flex 3 SDK offers new classes that enable you to assign a GroupingCollection to a data provider instead of flat data (usually returned as response data).

To regroup the data in a grouping view, you must instance a Grouping object and specify the data to use for the regrouping through its fields property:

```
var myGroup:Grouping = new Grouping();
myGroup.fields = [new GroupingField("region")];
```

You can then create a GroupingCollection object and send the ArrayCollection to it—the flat data is contained in the source property:

```
var myGroupColl:GroupingCollection = new GroupingCollection();
myGroupColl.source = new ArrayCollection(myRegion.city);
```

Finally, link the Grouping object to the grouping property of the GroupingCollection object and create the collection class to send to the dataProvider of the AdvancedDataGrid:

```
myGroupColl.grouping = myGroup;
myGroupColl.refresh();
myADG.dataProvider = myGroupColl;
```

Let's walk through an example to explore this in more detail. You'll create a new application that uses an XML file loaded as an MXML data model and converted into flat

ArrayCollection data as a data provider. This ArrayCollection will be regrouped using the classes described previously; then the structured data will be displayed in an AdvancedDataGrid.

1. Open the file Chapter_7_Flex_Sol_9.mxml created in this solution and save a copy of it as Chapter_7_Flex_Sol_9_expert.mxml.

2. In the AdvancedDataGrid, remove the dataProvider property and insert an AdvancedDataGridColumn tag as the first column, as shown following. This uses the Region field as dataField:

```
<mx:AdvancedDataGrid
  id="myADG"
  width="90%"
  variableRowHeight="true"
  wordWrap="true">

  <mx:columns>
    <mx:AdvancedDataGridColumn headerText="Region"
      dataField="region"/>
    <mx:AdvancedDataGridColumn headerText="Population"
      dataField="population" />

    <mx:AdvancedDataGridColumn headerText="City"
      dataField="city"/>
    <mx:AdvancedDataGridColumn headerText="Family"
      dataField="family"/>
  </mx:columns>

</mx:AdvancedDataGrid>
```

3. Load the states.xml XML file, which is found in the data folder. You use an MXML data model that you insert immediately under the closing </mx:Script> tag:

```
</mx:Script>

<mx:Model id="myRegion"
  source="data/states.xml" />
```

4. Now convert the data contained in the data model into an ArrayCollection using the MXML tag ArrayCollection and its id and source properties. Add the following code:

```
<mx:Model id="myRegion" source="data/states.xml" />
<mx:ArrayCollection id="myAC"
  source="{myRegion.city}" />
```

The ArrayCollection points to the repeating node of the data model. The structure of the XML data is the following:

```
<dataroot>
<city>
    <cityName>
```

```
        <id>1</id>
        <id_region>1</id_region>
        <region>PIEMONTE</region>
        <city><cityName>TORINO</city></cityName>
          <code>TO</code>
          <population>2236765</population>
          <male>1086745</male>
          <female>1150020</female>
          <family>886053</family>
        </cityName >

<cityName >
..........
</cityName >

</city >

</dataroot>
```

This is the flat data, which you must now group to be able to use in the AdvancedDataGrid with a Tree control.

5. Insert an event listener on the creationComplete event of the <mx:Application> tag, as follows:

```
<mx:Application xmlns:mx="http://www.adobe.com/2006/mxml"
   creationComplete="init()">
```

6. In the <mx:Script> block created in the solution, you removed the cities Array and imported the necessary ActionScript classes. Then you defined the init() event handler, like so:

```
<mx:Script>
  <![CDATA[
    import mx.collections.HierarchicalData;
    import mx.collections.ArrayCollection;
    import mx.collections.Grouping;
    import mx.collections.GroupingCollection;
    import mx.collections.GroupingField;

    public function init():void
    {
      var myGroup:Grouping = new Grouping();
      myGroup.fields = [new GroupingField("region")];

      var myGroupColl:GroupingCollection = new GroupingCollection();
      myGroupColl.source = new ArrayCollection(myRegion.city);
      myGroupColl.grouping = myGroup;
      myGroupColl.refresh();
```

7

```
        myADG.dataProvider = myGroupColl;
    }
]]>
</mx:Script>
```

The init() function creates a Grouping object and a GroupingCollection. The Grouping class defines the fields used to group data, with the fields property specifying the field (or fields) to use to group the data. This property accepts an Array of the GroupingField object:

```
var myGroup:Grouping = new Grouping();
myGroup.fields = [new GroupingField("region")];
```

The GroupingCollection object enables you to create grouped data from flat data. With the source property you send the flat data to be grouped, while the grouping property specifies the Grouping instance applied to the source data:

```
var myGroupColl:GroupingCollection = new GroupingCollection();
myGroupColl.source = new ArrayCollection(myRegion.city);
myGroupColl.grouping = myGroup;
```

Before using the new object, you must launch the refresh() method of the collection class and then use it as dataProvider of the AdvancedDataGrid:

```
myGroupColl.refresh();
myADG.dataProvider = myGroupColl;
```

7. Save the file and run the application.

The result obtained is identical to the solution using an Array created with ActionScript, as shown in Figure 7-19.

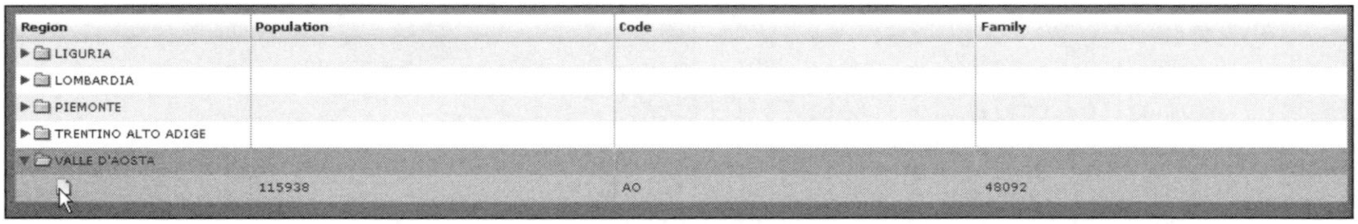

Figure 7-19. The flat files loaded by an MXML data model have been grouped using the Grouping and GroupingCollection classes.

Solution 7-10: Creating a custom column using item renderers

The AdvancedDataGrid improves and also adds new functions to item renderers. Item renderers and item editors were discussed in Solution 7-5; this solution looks at the new features offered by the new DataGrid.

With custom item renderers, it is possible to customize the appearance of the rows, columns, and cells of an AdvancedDataGrid. To apply an item renderer, the same process is used that you used for the DataGrid control, but the following new functions can be applied:

- Spanning multiple columns
- Using multiple renderers in the same column
- Customizing rows and columns with additional and calculated data not related to the data provider of the AdvancedDataGrid

In this solution you'll see how to create an item renderer contained in an external component, and how to apply it to an AdvancedDataGrid.

What's involved

To use the new features of the AdvancedDataGrid, you use a new property to apply and define an item renderer: AdvancedDataGrid.rendererProviders.

The rendererProviders property, unlike the itemRenderer property of the DataGrid, is not linked to a column of the DataGrid but is declared outside of the Array columns:

```
<mx:AdvancedDataGrid
  id="myADG"
  width="90%"
  variableRowHeight="true"
  wordWrap="true">

<mx:columns>
  <mx:AdvancedDataGridColumn headerText="Region"
    dataField="region"/>

  <mx:AdvancedDataGridColumn headerText="Population"
    dataField="population" />

  <mx:AdvancedDataGridColumn headerText="City"
    dataField="city"/>
  <mx:AdvancedDataGridColumn headerText="Family"
    dataField="family"/>
</mx:columns>

<mx:rendererProviders>
  <mx:AdvancedDataGridRendererProvider
    columnIndex="4"
    columnSpan="1"
    renderer="com.casario.myRendererComponent"/>
</mx:rendererProviders>

</mx:AdvancedDataGrid>
```

7

In this code, you created an item renderer (myRendererComponent) that spans a single column—the fourth column, in this case.

The rendererProviders property, like the columns property, contains an Array of AdvancedDataGridRendererProvider that defines the characteristics of an item renderer. This means that you can declare more than one AdvancedDataGridRendererProvider in the AdvancedDataGrid.

The use of the new rendererProviders property gives developers new capabilities to support item renderers, such as the following:

- Create summary rows columns with a renderer
- Create rows and columns that don't use data in the dataProvider of the AdvancedDataGrid
- Use more than one renderer in the same column

Instead of linking a numeric index to the columnIndex property, you can specify the id of a column to which the renderer will be linked. This gives you more control to reference the right column without forcing you to remember the exact index of it:

```
<mx:AdvancedDataGrid
  id="myADG"
  width="90%"
  variableRowHeight="true"
  wordWrap="true">

  <mx:columns>
    <mx:AdvancedDataGridColumn headerText="Region"
      dataField="region"/>

    <mx:AdvancedDataGridColumn headerText="Population"
      dataField="population" />

    <mx:AdvancedDataGridColumn headerText="City"
      dataField="city"/>
    <mx:AdvancedDataGridColumn headerText="Family"
      dataField="family"/>

    <mx:AdvancedDataGridColumn   id="renderCol"
      headerText="Total"
      dataField="total"/>

  </mx:columns>

  <mx:rendererProviders>
    <mx:AdvancedDataGridRendererProvider
      column="{renderCol}"
      columnSpan="1"
      renderer=➡
```

```
    "com.flexsolutions.chapter7.controls.myRendererComponent"/>
  </mx:rendererProviders>
```

```
</mx:AdvancedDataGrid>
```

You have defined another column defined in the Array of the columns property. The new column has an id property equal to renderCol. This value will be used in the column property of the AdvancedDataGridRendererProvider to link the item renderer to that column:

```
<mx:AdvancedDataGridRendererProvider
  column="{renderCol}"
..... />
```

Table 7-1 shows the item renderer properties that can be used with the AdvancedDataGridRendererProvider class:

Table 7-1. AdvancedDataGridRendererProvider properties

Property	Description
column	Contains the id of the column of the AdvancedDataGrid to use for the item renderer.
columnIndex	Contains the index of the column to use with the renderer (it is zero-based).
columnSpan	Specifies the number of columns that the renderer spans. To span all columns, the value is 0.
dataField	The data field used for the renderer. This is optional.
depth	Contains the depth in the tree to which the renderer will be applied. The topmost node of a tree has a depth of 1.
renderer	Contains the renderer.
rowSpan	Contains the number of rows spanned by the renderer.

In this solution you'll use an item renderer to create a column with a calculated value.

How to build it

For this solution you'll create a main application file in which you define an AdvancedDataGrid with an item renderer that will be an MXML component. Begin by creating the application.

> *This solution works only with Flex 3 installed, so ensure that you have Flex Builder 3 installed (http://labs.adobe.com/technologies/flex/flexbuilder3/).*

7

1. Create a new application file by selecting File ➤ New ➤ MXML Application, naming it Chapter_7_Flex_Sol_10.mxml.

2. As in the last solution, this file loads the states.xml XML file, which you import as an MXML data model and convert into an ArrayCollection. To display the data in hierarchical form, you must first convert it into a grouping object through the Grouping and GroupingCollection classes. In the preceding solution, you saw how to create grouped data: Add the following elements to create the user interface of the application:

```
<mx:Application xmlns:mx="http://www.adobe.com/2006/mxml"
  creationComplete="init()">

  <mx:Model id="myRegion" source="data/states.xml" />

  <mx:ArrayCollection id="myAC" source="{myRegion.city}" />

</mx:Application>
```

The application creates an init() event listener, in which you'll create the grouped data. With the <mx:Model> tag, you load the external XML file, states.xml, and convert it into an ArrayCollection.

3. Add the AdvancedDataGrid, as follows, for which you'll specify three AdvancedDataGridColumns to display selected data of the dataProvider:

```
<mx:AdvancedDataGrid
  id="myADG"
  width="90%"
  variableRowHeight="true"
  wordWrap="true">

  <mx:columns>
    <mx:AdvancedDataGridColumn headerText="Region"
      dataField="region"/>

    <mx:AdvancedDataGridColumn headerText="Population"
      dataField="population" />

    <mx:AdvancedDataGridColumn headerText="City"
      dataField="city"/>
    <mx:AdvancedDataGridColumn headerText="Family"
      dataField="family"/>
  </mx:columns>
</mx:AdvancedDataGrid>
```

The DataGrid doesn't have the dataProvider property. In fact, you'll set the value of this property via code in the init() function launched on the creationComplete of the <mx:Application> tag. The DataGrid shows four columns for which you have specified the headerText and dataField properties.

4. Insert the item renderer using the <mx:rendererProviders> tag and insert a column to display the rendered data, as shown following (note that the former is inserted outside of the <mx:columns> tag):

```
<mx:AdvancedDataGrid
  id="myADG"
  width="90%"
  variableRowHeight="true"
  wordWrap="true">

  <mx:columns>
    <mx:AdvancedDataGridColumn headerText="Region"
      dataField="region"/>

    <mx:AdvancedDataGridColumn headerText="Population"
      dataField="population" />

    <mx:AdvancedDataGridColumn headerText="City"
      dataField="city"/>
    <mx:AdvancedDataGridColumn headerText="Family"
      dataField="family"/>

    <mx:AdvancedDataGridColumn id="totalCol"
      headerText="Population Summary"/>
  </mx:columns>

  <mx:rendererProviders>
    <mx:AdvancedDataGridRendererProvider column="{totalCol}"
      depth="2"
      renderer="com.flexsolutions.chapter7.controls.totalRenderer"/>
  </mx:rendererProviders>

</mx:AdvancedDataGrid>
```

The column you added to the AdvancedDataGrid doesn't contain any reference to the dataProvider of the DataGrid. You have not specified its dataField property, as you did for the other columns, but instead used the id property to reference the rendered data:

```
<mx:AdvancedDataGridColumn id="totalCol"
  headerText="Population Summary"/>
```

The id property is used by the item renderer to link the data generated to the column. After the closure of the columns tag, you have inserted the item renderer through the rendererProviders property, which accepts an Array of the AdvancedDataGridRendererProvider object.

```
<mx:rendererProviders>
  <mx:AdvancedDataGridRendererProvider column="{totalCol}"
    depth="2"
renderer="com.flexsolutions.chapter7.controls.totalRenderer"/>
</mx:rendererProviders>
```

The depth property contains the depth in the Tree control in which the renderer will be applied. The specified renderer is located in the com.flexsolutions.chapter7.controls package and is called totalRenderer.mxml.

5. Before creating the custom item renderer, you must define the init() function, which releases on the creationComplete of the Application. To achieve this, insert the following <mx:Script> block under the <mx:Application> tag:

```
<mx:Script>
  <![CDATA[
    import mx.collections.HierarchicalData;
    import mx.collections.ArrayCollection;
    import mx.collections.Grouping;
    import mx.collections.GroupingCollection;
    import mx.collections.GroupingField;
    import mx.collections.ICollectionView;

    public function init():void
    {
      var myGroup:Grouping = new Grouping();
      myGroup.fields = [new GroupingField("region")];

      var myGroupColl:GroupingCollection = new GroupingCollection();
      myGroupColl.source = new ArrayCollection(myRegion.city);
      myGroupColl.grouping = myGroup;
      myGroupColl.refresh();

      myADG.dataProvider = myGroupColl;
    }
  ]]>
</mx:Script>
```

This function is the same as that created in the preceding solution. The myGroupColl collection class works as the dataProvider for the AdvancedDataGrid defined.

6. You now move on to the creation of the MXML component that will be used as item renderer. Create an MXML component in the com/flexsolutions/chapter7/controls folder by selecting File ➤ New ➤ MXML Component, basing it on a Label control and saving it as totalRenderer.mxml.

7. Insert an <mx:Script> block into your component as follows, in which you'll create the calculated data:

```
<?xml version="1.0" encoding="utf-8"?>
<mx:Label xmlns:mx="http://www.adobe.com/2006/mxml">
  <mx:Script>
    <![CDATA[

      override public function set data(value:Object):void
      {
        var tot:Number =
        Number(value["population"]) + Number(value["family"]);
```

```
            text = totalFormatter.format(tot);
            super.data = value;
         }
      ]]>
   </mx:Script>

   <mx:CurrencyFormatter id="totalFormatter" precision="0"
      currencySymbol=" people" decimalSeparatorFrom=","
      decimalSeparatorTo="," thousandsSeparatorFrom="."
      thousandsSeparatorTo="." useNegativeSign="true"
      useThousandsSeparator="true" alignSymbol="right"/>
   </mx:Label>
```

The renderer uses a CurrencyFormatter to format the data calculated by the function (Flex formatters were discussed in Solutions 4-8 and 4-9).

To be able to work on the calculated data, you must carry out an override of the data set-ter method of the Label class. This method accepts an Object as its parameter, which is the data provider of the AdvancedDataGrid:

```
override public function set data(value:Object):void
{

   var tot:Number =
   Number(value["population"]) + Number(value["family"]);

   text = totalFormatter.format(tot);
   super.data = value;

}
```

In the function you create a tot variable, which contains the sum of the population and family fields of the AdvancedDataGrid. To be able to intercept the values contained in the AdvancedDataGrid to perform the calculation, you use the Array value, specifying the dataField as its index.

The tot variable is then sent to the text property of the Label control and formatted by the CurrencyFormatter:

```
var tot:Number =➡
Number(value["population"]) + Number(value["family"]);

text = totalFormatter.format(tot);
```

8. Save the file and run the application. Try expanding the nodes of the tree in the AdvancedDataGrid. In the last column, Population Summary, the sum of the Family and Population data is displayed, as shown in Figure 7-20.

Region	Population	City	Family	Population Summary
▼ 🗀 LIGURIA				
🗋 LIGURIA	950849	GENOVA	391796	1.342.645 people
🗋 LIGURIA	227199	LA SPEZIA	90841	318.040 people
🗋 LIGURIA	213587	IMPERIA	90934	304.521 people
🗋 LIGURIA	284647	SAVONA	120883	405.530 people
▶ 🗀 LOMBARDIA				

Figure 7-20. The renderer is applied to the new column of the AdvancedDataGrid and shows the data calculated without any reference to the data provider.

Expert tips

You learned that you can render calculation fields using renderers in Flex 3, but you can go further, changing the styles of the data according to the value it assumes. For example, you could show different text labels according to the value that the data assumes or modify the styles to give extra emphasis to a particular value.

With a few modifications to the component that functions as renderer, totalRenderer. mxml, you can add an if() condition that checks to see whether the data exceeds a certain value. If it does, the text color and style change.

1. Open the totalRenderer.mxml file in the com/flexsolutions/chapter7/controls folder and modify the code by inserting the if() condition, as follows:

```
<mx:Label xmlns:mx="http://www.adobe.com/2006/mxml">
  <mx:Script>
    <![CDATA[

      override public function set data(value:Object):void
      {
        var tot:Number =➡
          Number(value["population"]) + Number(value["family"]);

        if (tot > 450000)
        {
          setStyle("color", "red");
          setStyle("fontWeight", "bold");
        text = totalFormatter.format(tot);
        }
        else
        {
          setStyle("color", "green");
          text = totalFormatter.format(tot);
        }

        super.data = value;
      }
    ]]>
  </mx:Script>
```

```
<mx:CurrencyFormatter id="totalFormatter" precision="0"
    currencySymbol=" people" decimalSeparatorFrom=","
    decimalSeparatorTo="," thousandsSeparatorFrom="."
    thousandsSeparatorTo="." useNegativeSign="true"
    useThousandsSeparator="true" alignSymbol="right"/>

</mx:Label>
```

In the set data() function, you have added an if() condition that carries out the check on the tot variable. If the variable is more than 450,000, the color of the text changes and it is put in bold, as shown in Figure 7-21.

2. Save the file and run Chapter_7_Flex_Sol_10.mxml.

Region	Population	City	Family	Population Summary
▼ 🗀 LIGURIA				
🗀 LIGURIA	950849	GENOVA	391796	1.342.645 people
🗀 LIGURIA	227199	LA SPEZIA	90841	318.040 people
🗀 LIGURIA	213587	IMPERIA	90934	304.521 people
🗀 LIGURIA	284647	SAVONA	120883	405.530 people
▶ 🗀 LOMBARDIA				

Figure 7-21. In the Population Summary column, the AdavancedDataGrid shows the data with a different color and style according to whether the sum returns a value that exceeds 450,000.

Solution 7-11: Using the SummaryCollection class with grouped data

In Flex 3 you can create a summary using the summaries property of the GroupingField class. The summary data can be visualized in a row of the AdvancedDataGrid.

In this solution you'll see how to do this.

What's involved

To create summary data, use the summaries property of the GroupingField class. This property accepts instances of the SummaryRow class, which makes up part of the mx. collections package. This class contains the fields property, which specifies an Array of one or more SummaryFields objects defining the data fields to create for the summary.

The SummaryFields class uses the dataField property to indicate the data to use for the summary, while its label property specifies the name of the data files containing the summary data. Finally, the operation property indicates the type of operation to carry out on the data. Table 7-2 specifies the numeric fields for this property.

Table 7-2. Values that can be sent to the operation property

Value	Description
SUM	Calculates the sum of the data specified in the dataField property
MIN	Returns the minimum value of the data specified in the dataField property
MAX	Returns the maximum value of the data specified in the dataField property
AVG	Calculates the average of the values specified in the dataField property
COUNT	Counts the data specified in the dataField property

Consider an ArrayCollection like that used in the preceding solution:

```
<mx:Model id="myRegion" source="data/states.xml" />
<mx:ArrayCollection id="myAC"
  source="{myRegion.city}" />
```

The ArrayCollection myAC has the same data structure seen in the city node of states.xml (the structure of this file was illustrated in Solutions 7-9 and 7-10). Therefore, to create a summary data you must first create grouped data:

```
<mx:GroupingCollection id="myGC" source="{myAC}">
<mx:Grouping>
<mx:GroupingField name="Region">
```

In the <mx:GroupingField> tag, specify the summaries property, which takes instances of the SummaryRow class:

```
<mx:summaries>
<mx:SummaryRow summaryPlacement="group">
```

For the SummaryRow class, specify the fields property, which defines the fields on which to carry out the summary operations. In this example, you create three different SummaryRow instances:

```
<mx:fields>

  <mx:SummaryField
    operation="SUM"
    dataField="population"
    label="total"/>

  <mx:SummaryField dataField="family"
    label="minFamily" operation="MIN"/>

  <mx:SummaryField dataField="population"
    label="maxPop" operation="MAX"/>
```

```
        </mx:fields>

      </mx:SummaryRow>
    </mx:summaries>
  </mx:GroupingField>
 </mx:Grouping>
</mx:GroupingCollection>
```

You have created three fields based on the population and family fields of the data provider myAC. The first `<mx:SummaryField>` calculates the sum of the population data of the ArrayCollection:

```
<mx:SummaryField
  operation="SUM"
  dataField="population"
  label="total"/>
```

The second `<mx:SummaryField>` (and the third) instead calculate the minimum value of the family data and the maximum value of the population data:

```
<mx:SummaryField dataField="family"
  label="minFamily" operation="MIN"/>

<mx:SummaryField dataField="population"
  label="maxPop" operation="MAX"/>
```

With these few steps, you have created SummaryField objects that are now ready to be inserted in an AdvancedDataGrid control.

In this solution you'll see how to display summary data in an existing column or as a single row of an AdvancedDataGrid.

How to build it

This solution uses two distinct files: the first is the main application file and the second is an MXML component that functions as renderer for the AdvancedDataGridRendererProvider class. To demonstrate both ways of creating grouped data, you'll use MXML to create the grouped data (you used ActionScript in the previous solution).

1. Create a new application file by selecting File ➤ New ➤ MXML Application and save it as Chapter_7_Flex_Sol_11.mxml. This file will use an XML file as data model, which you'll convert into an ArrayCollection before creating the GroupingCollection object.

2. Insert the following tag to create the source data to be grouped:

```
<?xml version="1.0" encoding="utf-8"?>
<mx:Application xmlns:mx="http://www.adobe.com/2006/mxml">
<mx:Model id="myRegion" source="data/states.xml" />
```

7

3. You can now declare the AdvancedDataGrid, for which you'll use a GroupingCollection class as dataProvider. Add the following code immediately under the <mx:ArrayCollection> tag. This class, which makes up part of the collection classes, enables you to convert flat data into group data, specifying a data source and declaring the GroupingField:

```
<mx:AdvancedDataGrid
  id="myADG"
  width="90%"
  variableRowHeight="true"
  wordWrap="true"
  initialize="gc.refresh();">

  <mx:dataProvider>
    <mx:GroupingCollection id="gc"
      source="{new mx.collections.ArrayCollection(myRegion.city)}">
      <mx:Grouping>
        <mx:GroupingField name="region">
```

The AdvancedDataGrid runs the refresh() method of the GroupingCollection class on the initialize event to make sure that the data is displayed in the DataGrid after it has been grouped. The dataProvider of the DataGrid is specified as a nested tag, and an <mx:GroupingCollection> tag is created. The GroupingCollection class accepts the source property to specify the flat data to use for the grouping.

The <mx:Grouping> tag declares a GroupingField Array to which the data to be used for the creation of the field is specified. This information is sent to it through the name property.

4. Add the summary data to the <mx:GroupingField> that you are creating by making the following addition to your code. The summary data you want to obtain returns the sum of the population field displayed in the AdvancedDataGrid to you:

```
<mx:AdvancedDataGrid
  id="myADG"
  width="90%"
  variableRowHeight="true"
  wordWrap="true"
  initialize="gc.refresh();">

  <mx:dataProvider>
    <mx:GroupingCollection id="gc"
      source="{new mx.collections.ArrayCollection(myRegion.city)}">
      <mx:Grouping>
        <mx:GroupingField name="region">
          <mx:SummaryRow summaryPlacement="last">
            <mx:fields>
              <mx:SummaryField
                operation="SUM"
                dataField="population"
```

```
          label="total"/>
        </mx:fields>
      </mx:SummaryRow>
    </mx:GroupingField>
  </mx:Grouping>
</mx:GroupingCollection>
</mx:dataProvider>
```

Among the `<mx:GroupingField>` tags, you have created the `<mx:SummaryRow>` tag. This tag accepts an `Array` of `SummaryField` for which you specify the data on which to run a type of operation and the label that will be used for the field:

```
<mx:SummaryRow summaryPlacement="last">
  <mx:fields>
    <mx:SummaryField
      operation="SUM"
      dataField="population"
      label="total"/>
  </mx:fields>
</mx:SummaryRow>
```

The summary field will return the sum obtained from the population field contained in the `GroupingCollection` object. The `summaryPlacement` property is specified to add the summary data to the grouped data.

5. You have created the summary data, so you can now insert the columns in which to display the data in the AdvancedDataGrid. Under the closure of the `</mx:dataProvider>` tag, add the columns element and the relevant AdvancedDataGridColumn tags, as follows:

```
</mx:dataProvider>
<mx:columns>
  <mx:AdvancedDataGridColumn headerText="Region"
    dataField="region"/>

  <mx:AdvancedDataGridColumn headerText="Population"
    dataField="population" />

  <mx:AdvancedDataGridColumn headerText="City"
    dataField="city"/>

  <mx:AdvancedDataGridColumn headerText="Family"
    dataField="family"/>

</mx:columns>
```

Here you have defined four columns, which will respectively contain the following data: region, population, city, and family. You can now add the summary data, having it written into a single row in the AdvancedDataGrid.

6. After the closing `</mx:columns>` tag, insert an `<mx:rendererProviders>` tag, as follows. This will use an external component as its renderer:

```
</mx:columns>
<mx:rendererProviders>
  <mx:AdvancedDataGridRendererProvider
     columnIndex="0"
     columnSpan="0"
     depth="2"
     dataField="total"

renderer="com.flexsolutions.chapter7.controls.summaryRenderer"/>
  </mx:rendererProviders>
 </mx:AdvancedDataGrid>
</mx:Application>
```

The item renderer summaryRenderer in the com.flexsolutions.chapter7.controls package spans an entire row. You have, in fact, specified its columnSpan and columnIndex properties at zero while the dataField property points to the label property of the SummaryField:

```
<mx:SummaryField
   operation="SUM"
   dataField="population"
   label="total"/>
<mx:AdvancedDataGridRendererProvider
   columnIndex="0"
   columnSpan="0"
   depth="2"
   dataField="total"
   renderer="com.flexsolutions.chapter7.controls.summaryRenderer"/>
```

7. Save the main application file. You'll now create the MXML component summaryRenderer, which will be used as a renderer.

8. In the com.flexsolutions.chapter7.controls folder, create a new MXML component by selecting File ➤ New ➤ MXML Component, named summaryRenderer.mxml and based on a Label. This component is very similar to that created in the preceding solution and consists of a Label that displays the total value returned from the summary data.

9. Add the following code to the component file:

```
<mx:Label xmlns:mx=http://www.adobe.com/2006/mxml
   textAlign="center">

<mx:Script>
 <![CDATA[

   override public function set data(value:Object):void
   {
     setStyle("color", "red");
```

```
        text = "This region has a population of: " +➡
          totalFormatter.format(Number(value["total"]));
        super.data = value;
      }
    ]]>
  </mx:Script>

  <mx:CurrencyFormatter id="totalFormatter" precision="0"
    currencySymbol=" people" decimalSeparatorFrom=","
    decimalSeparatorTo="," thousandsSeparatorFrom="."
    thousandsSeparatorTo="." useNegativeSign="true"
    useThousandsSeparator="true" alignSymbol="right"/>
  </mx:Label>
```

The text property of the Label is set by carrying out an override with the set data method and applying the format() method of the CurrencyFormatter to the total field:

```
        text = "This region has a population of: " +
          totalFormatter.format(Number(value["total"]));
```

10. Save the file and run Chapter_7_Flex_Sol_11.mxml. You'll see the final result. in which the summary data is visualized as an item renderer that spans an entire row (see Figure 7-22).

Region	Population	City	Family
▼ 📁 LIGURIA			
📄 LIGURIA	950849	GENOVA	391796
📄 LIGURIA	227199	LA SPEZIA	90841
📄 LIGURIA	213587	IMPERIA	90934
📄 LIGURIA	284647	SAVONA	120883
This region has a population of: 1.676.282 people			

Figure 7-22. The summary data created with the SummaryRow class is displayed as an item renderer that spans an entire row.

Expert tips

The Tree control used to represent data in the AdvancedDataGrid can be customized to display custom icons for leaf nodes. Table 7-3 shows the style properties you can edit and change for the Tree control.

Table 7-3. Tree control style properties

Property	Description
defaultLeafIcon	Edits the leaf icon
disclosureClosedIcon	Specifies the icon displayed next to a closed node

Continued

Table 7-3. Tree control style properties (continued)

Property	Description
disclosureOpenIcon	Specifies the icon displayed next to an open node
folderClosedIcon	Specifies the icon used for the closed folder of a node
folderOpenIcon	Specifies the icon used for the open folder of a node

You can edit these properties, changing their values within the AdvancedDataGrid control, using the setStyle() method or the <mx:Style> tag:

```
<mx:Style>
AdvancedDataGrid {
defaultLeafIcon:ClassReference(null);
folderOpenIcon:Embed(source=' assets/youthru.png');
folderClosedIcon:Embed(source=' assets/comtaste.png');
}
</mx:Style>
```

Summary

In this chapter you learned to use most of the Flex controls that enable you to display data. Flex provides a set of specific components for this type of operation, which facilitate the work of the developer to show data to the end user. These components are said to be list-based; through their dataProvider property, you populated them with the data to be shown. For example, the List control, which was created in Solution 7-1, enabled you to show a vertical list of items, while the Tree control represented hierarchical data under the form of an expandable tree.

The following controls make up part of the category of components defined as list-based:

- List
- HorizontalList
- DataGrid, AdvancedDataGrid
- Menu
- PrintDataGrid, AdvancedPrintDataGrid
- TileList
- Tree

Then you learned how to use the DataGrid and the new AdvancedDataGrid control in the application and how to use its powerful properties. These controls are the most versatile for displaying complex data, in rows and columns. The following features make it incredibly useful; you can do the following:

- Specify the order of the data and which data to render visible, defining the columns one by one using the `<mx:DataGridColumns>` tag
- Resize and move the columns at runtime using drag and drop
- Sort the data in ascending or descending order at runtime
- Personalize column and row headers
- Edit the text in the columns at runtime
- Create a custom item renderer for customizing content inside columns
- Add navigation to page through your data
- Create locked rows and columns

The solutions that used the new AdvancedDataGrid component showed its tremendous power. This control extends and enriches the functions of the DataGrid by adding new and very useful features you learned to use, such as the following:

- Multicolumn sorting interface
- Cell-level formatting functions
- Tree view (hierarchical data and grouping data)
- Cell selection
- Custom rows
- Column grouping
- SummaryCollection
- PrintAdvancedDataGrid

The chapter then discussed how to modify the way in which this data is displayed inside the list-based controls; for example, to display an icon or another Flex control inside a DataGrid column. To modify the appearance of data you used custom item renderers and item editors. With these classes, you merged different data together in a single column, controlled how the data was displayed programmatically, and enabled users to edit the data on the fly.

Drag-and-drop functionality is a standard feature of most desktop applications, but it is not as common or easy to achieve on web applications. However, Flex brings this capability to web applications via the Drag and Drop Manager class, which enables you to drag and add an item from one list-based control to another component, for example. A solution showed you how to implement the drag-and-drop features and how to take advantage of the built-in support for these operations through specific properties.

7

8 COMPILING AND DEPLOYING FLEX APPLICATIONS

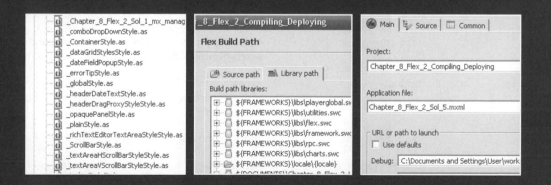

When compiling a Flex application you have to use Flex compiler, which can compile applications (SWF files created from MXML, from ActionScript, and from other assets) and component libraries (in SWC format.) In particular, it uses mxmlc.exe to compile applications and compc.exe to compile components.

The Flex Software Development Kit (SDK) is used for compilation whether you use Flex Builder (it's the Project ➤ Flex Compiler menu option) or the command-line compiler. It accepts options that enable you to enable or disable determined characteristics of the application. Table 8-1 shows some of the most common options that can be sent to the mxmlc.exe compiler:

> The mxmlc.exe *file is a Java jar file that you can find in the lib directory of Flex Builder.*

Table 8-1. Compiler options

Option	Description
accessible	Accepts true or false values and enables the accessibility features. It makes Flex components available to screen reader software.
debug	Accepts true or false values and specifies that a SWF file must be generated that includes line numbers and file names of all the source files. This option generates SWF files of large sizes.
default-background-color	Specifies the background color of the application.
default-frame-rate	Specifies the frame rate (24 fps is the default value).
incremental	Accepts true or false values to specify whether to enable incremental compilation. This value is true by default for Flex Builder.
load-config	Accepts the path of a personalized configuration file, which overrides the options defined in flex-config.xml.
optimize	Accepts true or false values and enables the optimization of the dimensions of the SWF file generated by the compiler.
output	Specifies the output path for the compiled files.
use-network	Accepts true or false values and enables you to disable the use of the network connection.

> *For a complete list of all the options that can be sent to the application compiler, see the Flex documentation ("About the application compiler").*

If you are using Flex Builder, you can specify these compiler options in the Additional Compiler Options box by selecting Project ➤ Properties ➤ Flex Compiler category.

On the other hand, if you are using the command-line compiler, specify these options as arguments in the command; for example:

```
mxmlc -use-network=false c:/workspace/myProj/myApp.mxml
```

Using a command-line compiler gives you total control over the compilation phase and enables you to create Flex applications without using the Flex Builder integrated development environment (IDE). It's free, too.

This command tells the compiler to compile the myApp.mxml file (located in the c:/workspace/myProj/ directory) and specifies the option of not using network services.

Yet another way to send options to the compiler is to write them into the flex-config.xml file located in Adobe\Flex Builder 3\sdks\3.0.0\frameworks (or if you use Flex Builder 2: Flex Builder 2 Plug-in\Flex SDK 2\frameworks).

If you open it you'll find elements that specify the different option values, fully commented. All you need to do is change the values inside the tags to change the compilation options. For example:

```
<!-- Turn on generation of debuggable swfs. ➡
False by default for mxmlc -->
<!-- but true by default for compc. -->
<debug>true</debug>
```

Another application compiler exists, which has been released by Adobe with the name Flex Compiler Shell. You can find it and download it on the Adobe Labs site (http://labs.adobe.com/wiki/index.php/Flex_Compiler_Shell). The Flex Compiler Shell is a utility that provides a shell environment to compile Flex applications, modules, and component libraries. As you'll see in Solution 8-2, this compiler uses a quicker compiling application because it eliminates the overhead of launching the JVM and loading the compiler classes.

The compc.exe component compiler similarly enables you to define the options to be included in a SWC file and all the necessary resources: classes, namespaces, and assets. This compiler can also be launched from Flex Builder or from the command line, and there are also options that can be set for this compiler. You can see a complete list of these options in the Flex documentation ("About the component compiler").

In this chapter you'll see how to use both the application and the component compiler to deploy and compile applications, including optimization techniques. This activity can be simple (one guy transfers the SWF and HTML files to the production server) or complicated (involving many different resources and team members).

8

The typical steps involved in the deployment phase of a Flex application are as follows:

- **Release phase:** The phase that prepares the system for the transfer of the application onto the production server. Before beginning this phase, a list is made of the necessary resources that must be transferred onto the server, connections to different domains, and any relevant proxy servers.
- **Install phase:** The phase in which the application is copied and configured.
- **Activate phase:** The startup phase of the application.

> *You might have other steps in your particular deployment process (for example, deactivate, adapt, uninstall, and retire).*

Solution 8-1: Using the mxmlc compiler

The Flex application compiler enables you to compile SWF files from MXML, ActionScript, SWC, and other resource files. Figure 8-1 shows the contents of the Flex SDK bin folder, in which the compilers are located.

Figure 8-1. The Flex compilers in the bin folder of Flex SDK.

The simplest way to compile an application is to drag the MXML file directly onto the mxmlc.exe file. In this way the compiled SWF file will be saved in the same directory as the MXML application.

If you want to have total control over the compilation procedure and send parameters to the compiler, you must call the mxmlc.exe file from the command line.

The mxmlc compiler is located within the Flex Builder installation folder: Adobe\Flex Builder 3\sdks\3.0.0\bin (if you're using Flex Builder version 2, the location is \Flex Builder 2 Plug-in\Flex SDK 2\bin folder). On a Mac system the folder is located in Applications\Adobe Flex Builder 3\sdks\3.0.0\bin.

To use it you have to use its full path: Adobe\Flex Builder 3\sdks\3.0.0\bin\mxmlc.exe. But if you create an environment variable that points to the compiler, you can launch the mxmlc compiler from anywhere, saving a lot of time. (You'll see how to create an environment variable later on.)

To launch the mxmlc.exe file, you must open the terminal/command prompt, navigate to the bin directory, and type the file name (Figure 8-2 shows this on Windows XP).

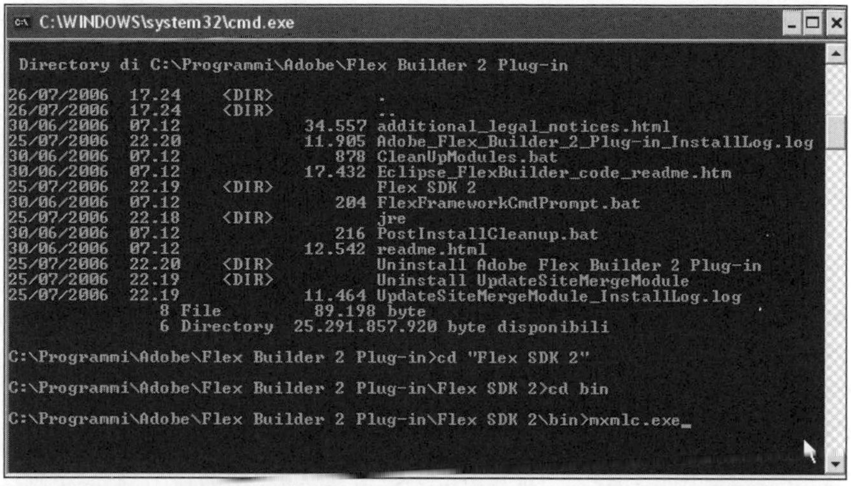

Figure 8-2. To launch the mxmlc compiler you must first enter it into the target directory

This is all well and good, but it can get tiresome typing in the full path to the file to be compiled every time. To get around this, you can create an environment variable.

To add environment variables in Windows, go to the System Properties dialog box in the Control Panel. Select Control Panel ➤ Performance and Maintenance ➤ System (or right-click My Computer and choose Properties). In the dialog box that opens, click the Advanced tab (see Figure 8-3).

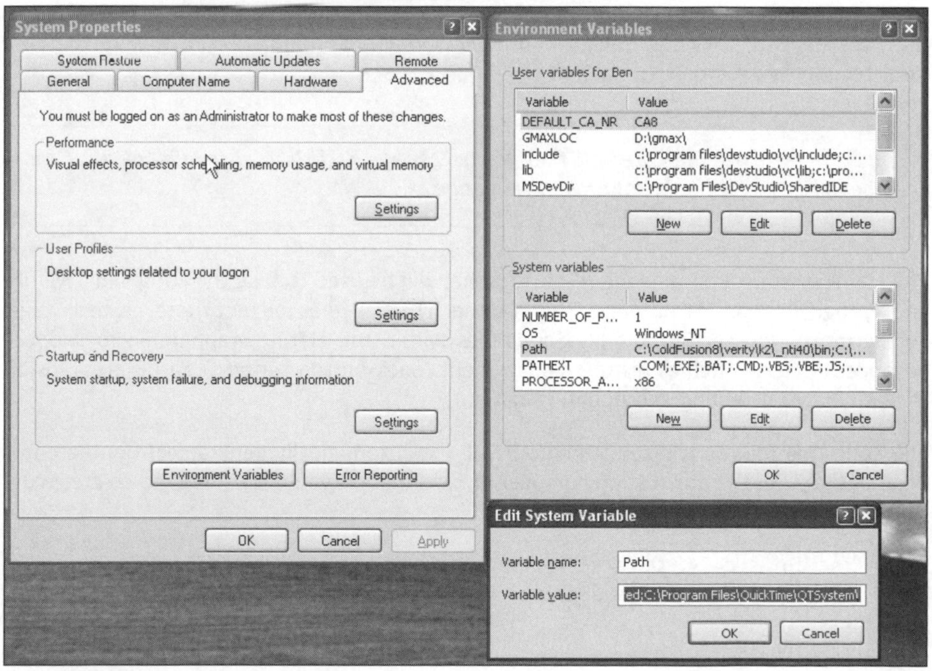

Figure 8-3. Adding enviroment variables

Next, click on the Environment Variables button. You'll see two types of variables: User and System variables. Choose a System variable, and click the New button.

In the new dialog box that opens, set the following values:

Variable name: mxmlc

Variable value: *yourDrive*:\\Adobe\Flex Builder 3 Plug-in\sdks\3.0.0\bin (if you use Flex Builder2, add this variable value to *yourDrive*: \Programs\Adobe\Flex Builder 2 Plug-in\Flex SDK 2\bin).

Click OK. At this point, having created an environment variable, you can launch the application compiler from the command line without needing to specify the full path to it every time.

What's involved

The mxmlc compiler is installed with the Flex SDK during the installation of Flex Builder or Livecycle Data Services (formerly Flex Data Services). The syntax to launch this compiler is the following:

```
mxmlc [options] myApp.mxml
```

With this syntax, the compiler automatically creates the myApp.swf file and puts it in the same directory in which the MXML file is found.

The mxmlc compiler does not generate the HTML page, only the SWF file. To deploy the application and see it in a common web browser you have to embed the SWF file into an HTML web page. You can create the HTML page on your own or use the HTML wrapper that comes with Flex (you can find HTML wrapper templates in the /resources/html-templates directory).

> The term **wrapper** indicates all the files necessary (XHTML and JavaScript files) for embedding the Flex application in a web page.

The HTML wrapper contains the HTML tags that will be used to take the compiled SWF file and embed it in an HTML page. This is done by using the <object> and <embed> tags. Furthermore, you can import JavaScript files within the HTML wrapper file to support advanced features such as history management (back button support) and Express Install (a Flash Player detecting and updating system).

The code that follows is taken from an HTML file automatically generated from the compilation that uses the application compiler of Flex Builder (you'll learn how to create a custom HTML wrapper in Solution 8-3):

```
<script src="AC_OETags.js" language="javascript"></script>
<script language="JavaScript" type="text/javascript">
<!--
// Globals
```

```
// Major version of Flash required
var requiredMajorVersion = 9;
// Minor version of Flash required
var requiredMinorVersion = 0;
// Minor version of Flash required
var requiredRevision = 0;
// -->
</script>
</head>
<script language="JavaScript"
type="text/javascript" src="history.js">
</script>
```

The mxmlc compiler uses the options and settings defined in the flex-config.xml file.

The Flex framework includes a configuration file named flex-config.xml, *which is used by default. This configuration file is a simple XML file that contains most of the default compiler settings for the application and component compilers. You'll see later on this chapter how to edit and customize it.*

These settings can be customized by changing their values in this file, or you can create a personalized configuration file and send it to the compiler with the load-config option.

You can see a list of all the options you can use and pass to the mxmlc compiler by using this command:

```
mxmlc -help list advanced
```

This is the output returned by the -help parameter:

```
C:\Documents and Settings\User>mxmlc -help list advanced
Adobe Flex Compiler (mxmlc)
Version 2.0.1 build 166910
Copyright (c) 2004-2006 Adobe Systems, Inc. All rights reserved

-benchmark
-compiler.accessible
-compiler.actionscript-file-encoding <string>
-compiler.allow-source-path-overlap
-compiler.as3
-compiler.context-root <context-path>
-compiler.debug
-compiler.defaults-css-url <string>
-compiler.es
-compiler.external-library-path [path-element] [...]
-compiler.fonts.flash-type
-compiler.fonts.languages.language-range <lang> <range>
-compiler.fonts.local-fonts-snapshot <string>
```

8

```
-compiler.fonts.managers [manager-class] [...]
-compiler.fonts.max-cached-fonts <string>
-compiler.fonts.max-glyphs-per-face <string>
-compiler.headless-server
-compiler.include-libraries [library] [...]
-compiler.incremental
-compiler.keep-all-type-selectors
-compiler.keep-as3-metadata [name] [...]
-compiler.keep-generated-actionscript
-compiler.library-path [path-element] [...]
-compiler.locale <string>
-compiler.namespaces.namespace <uri> <manifest>
-compiler.optimize
-compiler.services <filename>
-compiler.show-actionscript-warnings
-compiler.show-binding-warnings
-compiler.show-deprecation-warnings
-compiler.show-unused-type-selector-warnings
-compiler.source-path [path-element] [...]
-compiler.strict
-compiler.theme [filename] [...]
-compiler.use-resource-bundle-metadata
-compiler.verbose-stacktraces
-compiler.warn-array-tostring-changes
-compiler.warn-assignment-within-conditional
-compiler.warn-bad-array-cast
-compiler.warn-bad-bool-assignment
-compiler.warn-bad-date-cast
-compiler.warn-bad-es3-type-method
-compiler.warn-bad-es3-type-prop
-compiler.warn-bad-nan-comparison
-compiler.warn-bad-null-assignment
-compiler.warn-bad-null-comparison
-compiler.warn-bad-undefined-comparison
-compiler.warn-boolean-constructor-with-no-args
-compiler.warn-changes-in-resolve
-compiler.warn-class-is-sealed
-compiler.warn-const-not-initialized
-compiler.warn-constructor-returns-value
-compiler.warn-deprecated-event-handler-error
-compiler.warn-deprecated-function-error
-compiler.warn-deprecated-property-error
-compiler.warn-duplicate-argument-names
-compiler.warn-duplicate-variable-def
-compiler.warn-for-var-in-changes
-compiler.warn-import-hides-class
```

```
-compiler.warn-instance-of-changes
-compiler.warn-internal-error
-compiler.warn-level-not-supported
-compiler.warn-missing-namespace-decl
-compiler.warn-negative-uint-literal
-compiler.warn-no-constructor
-compiler.warn-no-explicit-super-call-in-constructor
-compiler.warn-no-type-decl
-compiler.warn-number-from-string-changes
-compiler.warn-scoping-change-in-this
-compiler.warn-slow-text-field-addition
-compiler.warn-unlikely-function-value
-compiler.warn-xml-class-has-changed
-debug-password <string>
-default-background-color <int>
-default-frame-rate <int>
-default-script-limits <max-recursion-depth> <max-execution-t
-default-size <width> <height>
-dump-config <filename>
-externs [symbol] [...]
-frames.frame [label] [classname] [...]
-help [keyword] [...]
-includes [symbol] [...]
-licenses.license <product> <serial-number>
-link-report <filename>
-load-config <filename>
-load-externs <filename>
-metadata.contributor <name>
-metadata.creator <name>
-metadata.date <text>
-metadata.description <text>
-metadata.language <code>
-metadata.localized-description <text> <lang>
-metadata.localized-title <title> <lang>
-metadata.publisher <name>
-metadata.title <text>
-output <filename>
-raw-metadata <text>
-resource-bundle-list <filename>
-runtime-shared-libraries [url] [...]
-use-network
-version
-warnings
```

In this solution you'll compile a Flex application using the Flex Builder compiler and the mxmlc utility tool.

How to build it

Begin by sending parameters to the Flex Builder compiler:

1. Open Flex Builder and create a new Flex project with the name Chapter_8_Flex_ Compiling_Deploying.

2. Create a new MXML application file by selecting File ➤ New ➤ MXML Application and name it Chapter_8_Flex_Sol_1.mxml.

3. In the file, insert a Label with text property equal to the string Hello World:

```
<mx:Application xmlns:mx="http://www.adobe.com/2006/mxml"➥
  layout="absolute">
  <mx:Label text="Hello World" />
</mx:Application>
```

4. Open the Flex Project Properties window by right/Ctrl-clicking with the mouse on the Flex project in Navigator view (or choose Project ➤ Properties from the menu). The Properties window displays a menu on the left, as seen in Figure 8-4.

5. Select the Flex Compiler option to access the advanced options that you can set in the Flex Builder compiler.

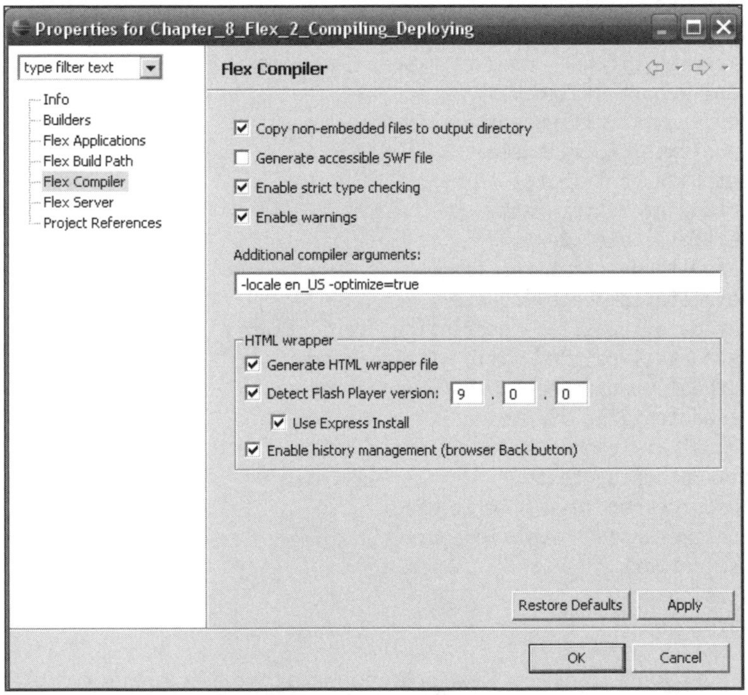

Figure 8-4. The Flex Compiler options in the Flex Project Properties window

The options that you can set on the compiler are as follows:

- Copy non-embedded files to output directory: Tells the compiler to copy the files that make up the application (but that have not been embedded in it) and puts them in the output folder.

- Generate accessible SWF file: Tells the compiler to create an accessible SWF file. The same result can be obtained by setting the additional argument accessible=true.

- Enable strict type checking: Specifies that the Flex project is compiled in Strict mode.

- Enable warnings: Enables you to see the warnings in Problems view at the bottom of the Flex Builder IDE.

- Generate HTML wrapper file: Tells the compiler to generate an HTML file in which the SWF application will be embedded.

- Detect Flash Player version: Specifies that a check will be carried out to detect the appropriate Flash Player version to run the application. If not, the user will be prompted to install it, and a mechanism to do so will be provided.

- Use Express Install: Provides support for Express Install.

- Enable history management (browser Back button): Provides support for history management (web browser Back button support).

Aside from the check boxes present in this window, there is also an Additional compiler arguments text field, which enables you to send further options to the compiler.

6. Keep the check boxes at their defaults and add the following options to the Additional compiler arguments text field:

```
-locale en_US  -optimize=true -keep-generated-actionscript
```

The optimize=true option reduces the file size of the SWF file that the compiler creates by optimizing the SWF file's bytecode, and the keep-generated-actionscript option prints all the ActionScript 3.0 classes that the compiler generates in the generated folder inside the bin folder of the Flex project, as shown in Figure 8-5.

> *Setting the keep-generated-actionscript option is a very useful setting for understanding what happens under the hood of Flex compilation. This is a great tool for learning the Flex framework and how it is based on just ActionScript 3.0 classes.*

7. Click OK and save the file.

8. In Navigator view, select the Flex project, right/Ctrl-click it, and select Refresh. You'll see a new folder appear: generated. On accessing it you'll see the list of all the classes involved in the compilation of the application (refer to Figure 8-4).

8

Figure 8-5. The generated folder contains all the ActionScript 3.0 classes involved in the compilation process.

The same compilation can be performed by launching the compiler directly from the command line (using `mxmlc.exe`). Provided that you set your environment variable (as explained earlier in the chapter), you can easily perform the compilation as follows:

9. Open your command prompt window, navigate to the folder containing your MXML file, and enter the following command:

```
mxmlc Chapter_8_Flex_Sol_1.mxml  -optimize=true➥
    -keep-generated-actionscript
```

At this point, the compiler will load all the options defined in `flex-config.xml`, the `Chapter_8_Flex_Sol_1.swf` file will be created in the same place as the `mxml` file—not in the bin folder, as it would be if you used the IDE for compilation (no HTML wrapper will be created, either).

If you check the contents of the Flex project folder you'll also now find two files: `Chapter_8_Flex_Sol_1.swf` and `Chapter_8_Flex_Sol_1.mxml`.

Expert tips

As discussed earlier, the `mxmlc` command-line compiler does not automatically generate a wrapper. It is necessary, therefore, to create the HTML file and all JavaScript files that will embed the SWF file by hand. This may sound complicated, but it's not so bad, really. The best way to do it is to use the six HTML template files (Flex 3 provides three additional template folders for AIR applications and for supporting the deep linking feature) in the \Adobe\Flex Builder 3 Plug-in\sdks\3.0.0\templates folder as a starting point. (If you are using Flex Builder 2 the location is under Flex SDK 2\resources\html-templates.) See Figure 8-6.

Figure 8-6. The HTML wrapper templates and the new Flex 3 wrapper for AIR applications

The HTML templates implement different features, which are as follows:

- client-side-detection folder: Contains functionality to detect Flash Player on the client. If the player is not found, it loads alternative content specified by the user. This information is specified in the HTML page within the JavaScript block code. It contains the index.template.html and AC_OETags.js files.

- client-side-detection-with-history folder: Provides the same addition as the previous template, and in addition supports history management in the history.js and history.swf files. It contains the index.template.html, AC_OETags.js, history.js, history.swf, and history.htm files.

- express-installation folder: Supports Express Install. It contains the index.template.html, AC_OETags.js, and playerProductInstall.swf files.

- express-installation-with-history folder: Contains the index.template.html, AC_OETags.js, history.js, history.swf, history.htm, and playerProductInstall.swf files. Besides supporting Express Install, it also adds history management.

- no-player-detection folder: Contains the index.template.html and AC_OETags.js files. This basic template gives you the option of importing an SWF file using an external JavaScript file and nothing else.

- no-player-detection-with-history folder: Contains the index.template.html, AC_OETags.js, history.js, history.swf, and history.htm files. It has the same functionality as the previous template, and in addition adds history management.

- client-side-detection-with-deeplinking folder: Adds the new deep linking feature to the client-side detection support. The term **deep linking** is used to describe support for URL-based navigation in applications that are not a traditional hierarchy of HTML pages (Ajax, Flash, Flex, and so on).

The choice of which template wrapper you use depends on the features that you want to give to your HTML web page.

These templates represent the starting point for creating a custom HTML wrapper for the Flex applications, and this is what you'll explore in detail in Solution 8-3.

8

Solution 8-2: Creating a custom configuration file

Flex contains a configuration file, flex-config.xml, located at Adobe\Flex Builder 3\ sdks\3.0.0\frameworks (if you're using Flex Builder 2, the location is \Flex SDK 2\ frameworks). This file is used in the compilation phase, and the options defined in it are read and applied by the application compiler.

You can modify this file to change the options sent to the compiler, or you can even create a completely separate custom config file and send it as a parameter to the compiler.

It should be emphasized that the Flex Builder compiler does not load the flex-config. xml file; it takes the options internally. It is, of course, possible to force the Flex Builder compiler to load a configuration file by inserting the load-config option as an additional argument. This same option is also used to load a custom configuration file—in this solution you'll see how to do this.

What's involved

To load a custom configuration file the load-config option is required, which accepts the path of the configuration file to be loaded as a value. This option is sent to the compiler and specifies the path and the name of the custom compiler file to use:

```
mxmlc -load-config = myCustomConfFile.xml
```

The compiler will use the myCustomConfFile.xml file instead of the flex-config.xml default file.

It is also possible to use the += operator to instruct the compiler to add the options declared in the custom file to the default configuration file:

```
mxmlc -load-config += myCustomConfFile.xml
```

The compiler will use the myCustomConfFile.xml file and the flex-config.xml default file.

There is also a third configuration file to consider: a local configuration file, which does not require you to point to it on the command line because the mxmlc compiler automatically searches for a local configuration file in the folder containing the MXML file. The file is named the same as the MXML application file, but with the -config.xml suffix appended to the end of the file name. For example, in the preceding solution, in which the name of the file was Chapter_8_Flex_Sol_1.mxml, the compiler will search for a local config file with the name Chapter_8_Flex_Sol_1-config.xml and use it together with flex-config.xml.

With three different config file types available to apply to your application, it is important to understand the order with which the compiler applies the options declared in these files.

The settings sent to the compiler via the command line with the load-config option have precedence over everything. They are, therefore, capable of overriding the settings of the other configuration files. The local config file has next-highest precedence and will still override the settings in the default flex-config.xml file (it has the lowest precedence of all).

This means that there will be an option precedence to consider:

- Options in the local configuration have precedence over options declared in the flex-config.xml file.
- Options set in a custom configuration file that the load-config option specifies have precedence over the local configuration file.
- Options set in the command line have precedence over all configuration file options.

Let's move on to the creation of a custom config file.

How to build it

Instead of trying to remember the correct syntax for creating a configuration file, the best thing to do is to open the flex-config.xml template in the Adobe\Flex Builder 3 folder Plug-in\sdks\3.0.0\frameworks (if you're using Flex Builder 2, the location is \Flex SDK 2\frameworks) and then copy it.

1. Open this file now—it will look like the following:

```
<flex-config>
<compiler>
<!-- Turn on generatation of accessible swfs. -->
<accessible>false</accessible>
<!-- Specifies the locale for internationalization. -->
<!-- not set -->
<!--
<locale>en_US</locale>
-->
<!-- List of path elements that form the roots of ActionScript➥
   class hierarchies. -->
<!-- not set -->
<!--
<source-path>
<path-element>locale/{locale}</path-element>
<path-element>string</path-element>
</source-path>
-->
 ...... cut ......
</flex-config>
```

It is a simple well-formed XML file in which every node corresponds to a config option; for example:

```
<accessible>false</accessible>
```

This declaration specifies that the SWF file should not be compiled using the accessibility settings. However, when you write the custom configuration file, you must slightly modify the original declaration of the root tag by specifying the XML declaration tag and the namespace:

```
<?xml version="1.0"?>
<flex-config xmlns="http://www.adobe.com/2006/flex-config">
</flex-config>
```

The xmlns property in the root tag specifies the Flex XML namespace. You can insert any values in this property:

```
<?xml version="1.0"?>
<flex-config xmlns="http://www.comtaste.com/flex-config">
</flex-config>
```

2. Copy the contents of the file into a new file called custom-config.xml. Save the file in the Flex project folder and change the first two lines to look like this:

```
<?xml version="1.0"?>
<flex-config xmlns="http://www.adobe.com/2006/flex-config">
  <compiler>
  ...
  </compiler>
</flex-config>
```

3. Now you'll declare metadata in the file, which will eventually be inserted in the compiled SWF file. Add the following into your custom config file immediately after the opening <compiler> tag:

```
<metadata>
  <title>Flex solutions Book</title>
  <publisher>FriendsOfED</publisher>
  <creator>Marco Casario</creator>
  <date>22 October 2007</date>
</metadata>
```

The metadata enables you to add information to the SWF file. This information can be read by search engines, so the Flex applications can be indexed and obtain a better ranking.

The values that can be set as metadata in the configuration file are the following:

- contributor
- creator
- date
- description
- language
- localized-description

- localized-title
- publisher
- title

4. Another option you'll often set as true is `<incremental>`, which enables incremental compilation. Find this option in the file, and make sure that it is set as follows:

```
<incremental>true</incremental>
```

Incremental compilation can save a lot of time for large applications as well as reduce compile time on small applications. When this option is set as `true`, the compiler analyzes the code and determines whether there are portions of it that have immediately changed. In this case, it recompiles only the newest classes.

5. For these purposes, you don't need most of the information in the config file that was in the original config file that you copied from. It should contain the following code, so delete any excess:

```xml
<?xml version="1.0"?>
<flex-config xmlns="http://www.adobe.com/2006/flex-config">
  <compiler>
    <metadata>
      <title>Flex solution Book</title>
      <publisher>FriendsOfED</publisher>
      <creator>Marco Casario</creator>
      <date>29 August 2007</date>
    </metadata>
    <incremental>false</incremental>
  </compiler>
</flex-config>
```

6. Save the `custom-config.xml` file.

All you need to do now is apply this configuration file to the compilation phase. To send this file to the compiler you'll use the load-config option. Either specify it in the Additional compiler arguments text field (found in Flex Builder by selecting Project ➤ Properties ➤ Flex Compiler) or specify it on the command line:

```
mxmlc myApp.mxml -load-config+=custom-config.xml
```

7. Compile your application using either of these methods.

While the `mxmlc` tool will use the `flex-config.xml` file as well as the `custom config` file, the Flex Builder project compiler does not use the `flex-config.xml` configuration file; it instead uses internal settings in addition to the custom config file.

If you wanted to use this file as a local configuration file, change the name of the config file to Chapter_8_Flex_Sol_1-config.xml, and save it in the same folder as Chapter_8_Flex_Sol_1.mxml. The compiler automatically searches for a local config file with the same name as the MXML file apart from an additional -config suffix.

8

8. Launch the mxmlc compiler again without any additional parameters. You'll compile the application again, but this time use the local config file you just created. The command you need this time is a lot simpler; you do not have to specify any parameter, you just need to write the following:

mxmlc Chapter_8_Flex_Sol_1.mxml

9. The Chapter_8_Flex_Sol_1.swf file will be compiled in the same folder as Chapter_8_Flex_Sol_1.mxml. The SWF file generated by the compiler loaded the local configuration settings declared in the Chapter_8_Flex_Sol_1-config.xml local configuration file.

Expert tips

This section outlines a few useful tips to consider in the compilation phase of an application.

If you want to quickly create a configuration file that you can subsequently edit and customize, you can use the dump-config option:

mxmlc -dump-config Chapter_8_Flex_Sol_1-config.xml

This creates a default config file that can be used and customized for your Chapter_8_Flex_Sol_1 application.

Adobe has released the Flex Compiler Shell on Labs (http://labs.adobe.com/wiki/index.php/Flex_Compiler_Shell), which is a utility providing a shell environment to compile Flex applications, modules, and component libraries. It is worth knowing about because it enables much quicker application compiling because it eliminates the overhead of launching the JVM and loading the compiler classes. It keeps everything in memory, and the compilation results can be kept in memory for subsequent compilations. This utility is intended for developers who use the command-line compiler.

This shell is meant for Flex 2.0.1. The most up-to-date version is part of Flex 3.0 and can be found with the Flex 3.0 SDK.

If you use the Flex Builder compiler you don't need this utility because Flex Builder already uses these optimizations. But if you usually use the command line, you might want to check it out. To install this utility, follow these steps:

1. Download and extract the contents of the fcsh zipped file (http://download.macromedia.com/pub/labs/flex_compiler_shell/flex_compiler_shell_012307.zip) and view the license agreement (http://labs.adobe.com/wiki/index.php/Flex_Compiler_Shell:License).

2. Copy the contents of the zipped file's bin directory to the SDK bin directory and the contents of the zipped file's lib directory to the SDK lib directory.

3. To use the Flex Compiler Shell, navigate to Flex SDK/bin using your prompt and run the following command:

```
(fcsh) mxmlc c:/myFlexApp.mxml
```

Furthermore, the utility returns a target id, which you can use for the following compilation:

```
fcsh: Assigned 1 as the compile target id.
```

You use the target ids when using subsequent commands:

```
(fcsh) compile 1
```

These are the benchmark results Adobe obtained by launching the same compilation twice on the flexstore sample application—once with the normal mxmlc.exe, and once with the Flex Compiler Shell:

```
(fcsh) mxmlc -benchmark=true flexstore.mxml
 Total time: 8885ms
 Peak memory usage: 84 MB (Heap: 58, Non-Heap: 26)
```

Compiling the same application multiple times will improve the performance on-time compilation. In fact, when you launch the second full compilation of the application it is much faster:

```
(fcsh) mxmlc -benchmark=true flexstore.mxml
 Total time: 5140ms
 Peak memory usage: 84 MB (Heap: 57, Non-Heap: 27)
```

8

Solution 8-3: Writing a custom dynamic wrapper

Flex applications are viewed on the Web by embedding the SWF file into an HTML page using the <object> and <embed> elements; JavaScript is then used (inline or imported from an external .js file) to reference and load the SWF file. Together, the HTML code and JavaScript necessary to load the SWF files are known as wrappers.

The Flex Builder compiler automatically generates the wrappers in the compilation phase of the Flex application. In fact, if you open the bin folder of a Flex project, you'll note that both compiled SWF files and HTML and JavaScript files exist in it.

The MXMLC compiler (mxmlc.exe) does not generate the HTML wrapper; it compiles only the SWF file. It is necessary to create the wrapper by hand if you use the command-line compiler.

As discussed at the end of Solution 1, Flex provides base templates to use for the wrappers, located in the Flex SDK 2\resources\html-templates folder: the client-side-detection, client-side-detection-with-history, express-installation, express-installation-with-history, no-player-detection, and no-player-detection-with-history folders. You can use any of these wrappers as a base for your wrapper by choosing the features you want to support the HTML file, and then modifying it.

In this solution, you'll see how to create a custom dynamic wrapper using Java Server Pages (JSP) to load the compiled Flex application.

What's involved

The wrapper can be a simple HTML page or can also use any server-side language that generates HTML code (Coldfusion, JSP, PHP, ASP.NET, and so on). You just need to make sure that you upload all the files connected with displaying the SWF onto your web server when deploying your application, along with the SWF itself.

> *One exception to the rule is Flex applications that use Flex Data Services (or LiveCycle Data Services)—in this case, the client can point directly at the MXML page. It will be the web tier compiler that will compile in SWF and the HTML wrapper on the fly. You can read more about the wrapper generated by Flex Data Services here:* `http://livedocs.adobe.com/flex/201/html/wwhelp/wwhimpl/common/html/wwhelp.htm?context=LiveDocs_Book_Parts&file=wrapper_131_04.html`.

Among the settings of the Flex compiler (found under the Flex Compiler category at Project ➤ Properties—see Figure 8-7) there is the section dedicated to the HTML wrapper in which you can do the following:

- Generate HTML wrapper file: If unchecked, generates only the SWF file without the wrapper.
- Detect Flash Player version: If unchecked, the verification of the version of Flash Player on the client is not carried out. If it is selected, it enables you to also specify the version, which must be present on the client.
- Use Express Install: Supports the Express Install feature.
- Enable history management (browser Back button): Supports history management.

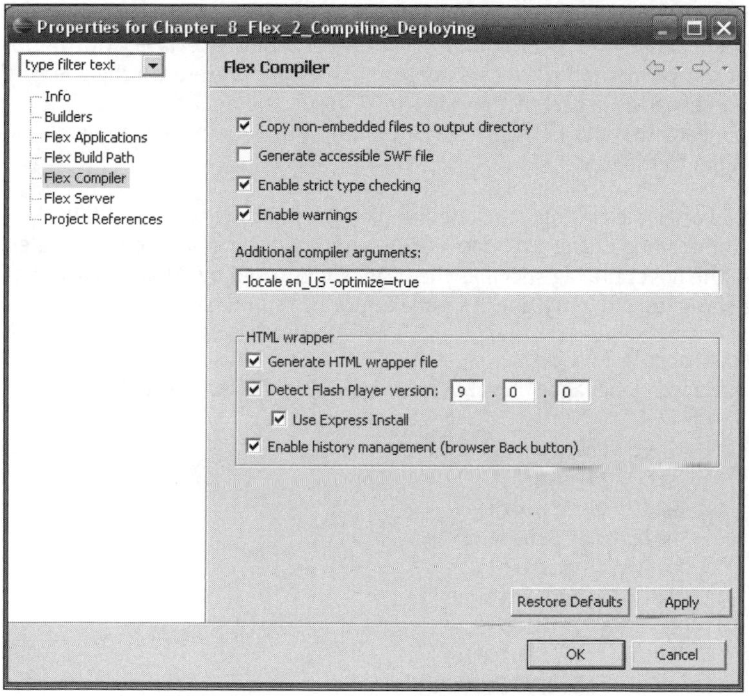

Figure 8-7. The Flex Properties options in the Flex Project Properties window

Let's open one of the six templates put at your disposal by Flex to see what the wrapper code looks like. If you chose the index.template.html file, located in the \Adobe\Flex Builder 3 Plug-in\sdks\3.0.0\templates\ no-player-detection folder (if you're using Flex Builder 2, the location is Flex SDK 2\resources\html-templates\no-player-detection), it would look like this (you'll go through the code in blocks to make it easier to understand):

```
<!-- saved from url=(0014)about:internet -->
<html lang="en">
  <head>
    <meta http-equiv="Content-Type" content=➡
"text/html; charset=utf-8" />
    <title>${title}</title>
    <script src="AC_OETags.js" language="javascript"></script>
    <style>
      body { margin: 0px; overflow:hidden }
    </style>
  </head>
```

Its internal code begins with a commented declaration, the so-called Mark of the Web (MOTW). This declaration is for Internet Explorer (IE) and is needed to run the contents of the page on the local machine because of the settings of the Local Machine Lockdown of Windows XP Service Pack 2.

Immediately after that you have the declaration of the <html> root tag and the meta information, page title, and script and style declarations. The JavaScript imported here carries out the verification of the version of Flash Player present on the client. The style declaration sets the margin of the body to 0 pixels and sets the overflow property to hidden. It means that the content that doesn't fit into the box is completely hidden and not accessible to the user.

Immediately after the closing head tag and the opening body tag, you'll find the JavaScript code for the loading of the SWF file. For browsers that have JavaScript disabled or don't support it, the noscript tag specifies the object tags (used by IE) and embed tags (used by Netscape Navigator) to carry out the same import if required:

```
<body scroll='no'>
  <script language="JavaScript" type="text/javascript">
  <!--
    AC_FL_RunContent(
    "src", "${swf}",
    "width", "${width}",
    "height", "${height}",
    "align", "middle",
    "id", "${application}",
    "quality", "high",
    "bgcolor", "${bgcolor}",
    "name", "${application}",
    "allowScriptAccess","sameDomain",
    "type", "application/x-shockwave-flash",
    "pluginspage", "http://www.adobe.com/go/getflashplayer"
    );
  // -->
</script>
<noscript>
  <object classid="clsid:D27CDB6E-AE6D-11cf-96B8-444553540000"➥
    id="${application}" width="${width}" height="${height}"➥
    codebase="http://fpdownload.macromedia.com/➥
                    get/flashplayer/current/swflash.cab">
    <param name="movie" value="${swf}.swf" />
    <param name="quality" value="high" />
    <param name="bgcolor" value="${bgcolor}" />
    <param name="allowScriptAccess" value="sameDomain" />
    <embed src="${swf}.swf" quality="high" bgcolor="${bgcolor}"➥
      width="${width}" height="${height}" name="${application}"➥
      align="middle"
      play="true"
      loop="false"
      quality="high"
      allowScriptAccess="sameDomain"
      type="application/x-shockwave-flash"
      pluginspage="http://www.adobe.com/go/getflashplayer">
    </embed>
```

```
        </object>
      </noscript>
    </body>
  </html>
```

The AC_FL_RunContent() JavaScript method (defined inside the AC_OETags.js file) was used to embed the SWF file contents (the Flex application) because Microsoft updated IE and changed how it displayed ActiveX content such as Adobe Flash Player, QuickTime players, Adobe Reader, Java, and other ActiveX controls.

To solve the problem don't use the <object> tag directly in the HTML page; replace the tag with a JavaScript file that writes the <object> tag from outside the actual HTML page.

If you open the AC_OETags.js external file you'll find the AC_FL_RunContent() JavaScript method with the following code:

```
var str = '';
    if (isIE && isWin && !isOpera)
    {
str += '<object ';
for (var i in objAttrs)
str += i + '="' + objAttrs[i] + '" ';
for (var i in params)
str += '><param name="' + i + '" value="' + params[i] + '" /> ';
str += '></object>';
    } else {
str += '<embed ';
for (var i in embedAttrs)
str += i + '="' + embedAttrs[i] + '" ';
str += '> </embed>';
    }

document.write(str);
```

This code writes the <object> tag from outside the actual HTML page and solves the problem of the active content issue on IE browser.

In this solution you'll see how to create a JSP wrapper to embed the Flex application.

How to build it

You want to create a JSP file that accepts parameters sent via the POST method and automatically generates the wrapper. When you develop Flex applications, there will be times when the default HTML wrapper generated by Flex Builder is not enough for the application's requirements. So you'll need to customize and generate a custom wrapper to host the Flex application.

In this solution you'll create a server-side page (using JSP, but you can write your page with your favorite server-side language) that helps generate a custom dynamic wrapper. You can reuse this small JSP application across different projects.

The parameters needed to define the wrapper are the following:

- **title**: Contains the title of the HTML page
- **id** and **name**: Contain the id of the application (Netscape uses the name parameter instead of id)
- **swf**: Specifies the SWF file to be embedded
- **width**: Contains the width of the application
- **height**: Contains the height of the application
- **bgcolor**: Specifies the background color of the page

The form you'll create in the JSP page will have form fields for each of these parameters. With these parameters the JSP file will create the wrapper necessary to load the compiled Flex application in the SWF file.

1. Create a new file in Flex Builder by selecting File ➤ New ➤ File and name it index.jsp. This file plays a double role: It enables the users to fill in a form of parameters through the simple text inputs, as well as generating the dynamic wrapper using the parameters inserted by the user in the form fields.

2. Start by adding the page declaration to the file, like so:

```
<%@ page language="java"
contentType="text/html; charset=utf-8"
pageEncoding="utf-8"
%>
```

This code specifies the language the page is using, the type of content of the file, the charset, and page encoding.

3. Declare the first block of HTML code to be generated, including the DOCTYPE, the MOTW, and the meta tag. Add this code at the bottom of the file:

```
<!DOCTYPE html PUBLIC "-//W3C//DTD XHTML 1.0 Transitional//EN"➥
  "http://www.w3.org/TR/xhtml1/DTD/xhtml1-transitional.dtd">
  <!-- saved from url=(0014)about:internet -->
<html xmlns="http://www.w3.org/1999/xhtml">
<head>
<meta http-equiv="Content-Type" content="text/html; charset=utf-8" />
```

The MOTW is a comment added to the HTML markup for a web page. This comment is used by IE to determine the security zone in which it should run the page. The MOTW is a feature of IE that enhances security by enabling the browser to force web pages to run in the security zone of the location the page was saved from instead of the Local Machine zone. You can learn more on the MSDN page: http://msdn2. microsoft.com/en-us/library/ms537628.aspx.

4. At this point you begin with the first parameter: the title of the page. This parameter contains the value to assign to the `<title>` element of the page. The JSP use the `getParameter()` method of the request object to intercept the parameters that are sent to it from the headings of the HTTP protocol. In this case you must define a variable that will contain the title value. Add this code to the bottom of the file:

```
<%
  String title = (String)request.getParameter("title");
%>
<title><%= (title != null) ? title: "Insert title" %></title>
```

Once intercepted, the `title` variable is sent to the `<title>` tag, if different from null.

> *The JSP request object gets the values that the client passes to the web server during an HTTP request. The object and its methods are used to take the value from the client's web browser and pass it to the server to process them.*

5. You'll now import the JavaScript file, `AC_OETags.js`, which carries out the client-side Flash Player detection (this file is located in the Flex SDK 2\resources\html-templates\client-side-detection folder.) You can also write a Cascading Style Sheet (CSS) style in the page in which you set the `overflow` property to `hidden` and reset the margins of the page to zero. The first definition (`overflow:hidden`) indicates that the content is clipped and that no scrolling user interface should be provided to view the content outside the clipping region. The second definition (`margin: 0px`) prevents any margin spaces between the application and the browser's margins.

6. Add the following code to the bottom of the file:

```
<script src="AC_OETags.js" language="javascript"></script>
<style>
  body {
    margin: 0px;
    overflow:hidden
  }
</style>
</head>
<body scroll="no">
```

7. Next, add the JSP to generate the other parameters that you need to successfully embed the SWF, as follows:

```
<%
  String swf = (String)request.getParameter("swf");
  String width = (String)request.getParameter("width");
  String height = (String)request.getParameter("height");
  String app = (String)request.getParameter("application");
  String bgcolor = (String)request.getParameter("bgcolor");
```

You have used the getParameter() method of the object request to get the parameters that were sent to the JSP page. Within the getParameter() method you have also specified the name of parameters to intercept: swf, width, height, application, and bgcolor. These parameters, as the title specifies in the second step, are taken from a form with those form fields declared.

8. You now insert a condition that checks whether the parameters have been sent to the file; otherwise, a form is added to the page to enable the user to fill in the parameters (title, id, name, swf, width, height, and bgcolor) if they are not provided. Add this code now:

```
if ((title == null) ||
   (swf == null) ||
   (width == null) ||
   (height == null) ||
   (app == null) ||
   (bgcolor == null) ||
   (title.length() == 0) ||
   (swf.length() == 0) ||
   (width.length() == 0) ||
   (height.length() == 0) ||
   (app.length() == 0) ||
   (bgcolor.length() == 0)
   ) {
%>
<form name="swfForm" method="post" action="index.jsp">
  <table border="0" cellpadding="5" width="80%" align="center">
    <tr><th colspan="2">SWF application parameters</th></tr>
    <tr><td>Page title</td>
    <td><input type="text" name="title" /></td>
    </tr>
    <tr><td>File name (without .swf extension)</td>
    <td><input type="text" name="swf" /></td>
    </tr>
    <tr><td>Width</td>
    <td><input type="text" name="width" /></td>
    </tr>
    <tr><td>Height</td>
    <td><input type="text" name="height" /></td>
    </tr>
    <tr><td>Application name (id)</td>
    <td><input type="text" name="application" /></td>
    </tr>
    <tr><td>Background color</td>
    <td><input type="text" name="bgcolor" /></td>
    </tr>
    <tr><td> </td>
    <td><input type="submit" name="ok" value="Submit" /></td>
    </tr>
  </table>
</form>
```

The form contains a text input that the user can use to insert the parameters that will generate the wrapper. Note that the name attribute of the text input corresponds to the names of the parameters passed to the getParameter() methods:

```
String swf = (String)request.getParameter("swf");
```

Therefore, when the user clicks the Submit button, the form will send the data to the same JSP page (index.jsp):

```
<form name="swfForm" method="post" action="index.jsp">
```

The page plays the double role to hold data filled in by the user in the form fields and generate the dynamic HTML wrapper according to the user's data received.

9. Next you create an else ... if structure that simply removes the .swf extension from the file name inserted by the user in the text input, if they do provide one. You need only the name of the file without the extension, which prevents any potential errors filled in by the users. Add this code to the bottom of the file:

```
<%
  } else {
    // remove extension from swf file name:
    int index = swf.indexOf(".swf");
    if (index >= 0) {
      swf = swf.substring(0, index);
    }
%>
```

10. Having collected all the parameters, now embed the SWF file. You do this by launching the AC_FL_RunContent() method contained in the external JavaScript file (AC_OETags.js). This method accepts the variables intercepted from the sending of the form as parameters. Add this code to the bottom of the file:

```
<script language="JavaScript" type="text/javascript">
  <!--
  AC_FL_RunContent(
    "src", "<%= swf %>",
    "width", "<%= width %>",
    "height", "<%= height %>",
    "align", "middle",
    "id", "<%= app %>",
    "quality", "high",
    "bgcolor", "<%= bgcolor %>",
    "name", "<%= app %>",
    "allowScriptAccess","sameDomain",
    "type", "application/x-shockwave-flash",
    "pluginspage", "http://www.adobe.com/go/getflashplayer"
    );
  // -->
</script>
```

8

The parameters sent to the JavaScript AC_FL_RunContent() function uses the JSP variable you have set with the getParameter() method.

11. The last block of code to add is the <noscript> element, which provides an alternative import method in case the client has JavaScript disabled. In this portion of code you use the HTML <object> and <embed> tags to carry out the importation of the SWF file, but you still send the intercepted parameters to the JSP. Add this final code block to the bottom of the JSP file:

```
<noscript>
  <object classid="clsid:D27CDB6E-AE6D-11cf-96B8-444553540000"➡
    id="<%= app %>" width="<%= width %>" height="<%= height %>"➡

codebase="http://fpdownload.macromedia.com/get/flashplayer/current/➡
    swflash.cab">
    <param name="movie" value="<%= swf %>.swf" />
      <param name="quality" value="high" />
      <param name="bgcolor" value="<%= bgcolor %>" />
      <param name="allowScriptAccess" value="sameDomain" />
      <embed src="<%= swf %>.swf" quality="high" bgcolor="➡
        <%= bgcolor %>"➡
        width="<%= width %>" height="<%= height %>" name="➡
        <%= app %>" align="middle"
        play="true"
        loop="false"
        quality="high"
        allowScriptAccess="sameDomain"
        type="application/x-shockwave-flash"
        pluginspage="http://www.adobe.com/go/getflashplayer">
      </embed>
    </object>
  </noscript>
<%
}
%>
</body>
</html>
```

The JSP file is complete. To be able to make this wrapper function, you must copy the JSP file onto an application server capable of running JSP (such as Tomcat, for example).

By launching the index.jsp page, you'll see the form appear with the text input. Insert the values in the text fields. By clicking the Submit button, you'll recall the same page, but the data that you have inserted in the text fields will be processed.

If you open the source of the page you have loaded you'll see that the result obtained is the actual HTML wrapper that you need to load your compiled Flex application!

In this solution you created a server-side page (you used JSP, but you can write your page with your favorite server-side language) that helps you to generate a custom dynamic wrapper. When you develop Flex applications, sometimes the default HTML wrapper generated by Flex Builder will not be enough.

Expert tips

Using the browser, it is possible to see the source code of the HTML file and of all the files that it uses, such as the JavaScript files, for example. You can use the View ➤ Source menu option for this purpose.

Other tools can be very useful in this regard; for example, the Firefox web developer toolbar (https://addons.mozilla.org/en-US/firefox/addon/60), which enables you to quickly obtain the source code of the HTML page and the JavaScript and CSS files.

For more information about the MOTW, see http://msdn.microsoft.com/workshop/author/dhtml/overview/motw.asp.

> *The MOTW can be easily inserted into an HTML page with Dreamweaver 8* (Command ➤ Insert Mark of the Web.)

Solution 8-4: Supporting the Express Install Flash Player feature

In Flash Player 6.0.65 a new feature was introduced to render the process of detecting and updating Flash Player even more simple and immediate.

This function loads a SWF file (Flash Player 6r65 or higher is required for it to run) that looks after the procedure of updating the Player by connecting directly to the Adobe site. The advantages of the use of Express Install are many, the most interesting of which is the possibility of contextualizing the update procedure.

Previously the update procedure forced the user to go to the Adobe site, meaning that users might lose reference to the sites they visit. With Express Install, the update procedure occurs in the same browser window, whereas the SWF file connects to the update page of the Adobe site invisibly.

The Express Install function requires that the browser have JavaScript enabled because JavaScript Flash Player detection is used to see whether the update is needed.

In this solution you'll see how to add support for Express Install to the wrapper you created in Solution 8-3.

What's involved

Express Install can launch an update process that installs the latest version of Flash Player. When the installation is complete, users are directed back to the web site to see the Flex application loaded.

To add the support for Express Install you must include the JavaScript file AC_OETags.js within the HTML wrapper. This file is located in the Flex SDK \resources folder and it contains the JavaScript functions that the HTML file calls to embed the Flex application's SWF file. You can import the AC_OETags.js using this syntax in the HTML page:

```
<script src="AC_OETags.js" language="javascript"></script>
```

In addition to the AC_OETags.js file, you have to add within your HTML wrapper a `<script>` block that is declared in the index.template.html file in the /resources/html-templates/express-installation/ folder:

```
<script language="JavaScript" type="text/javascript">
  <!--
    // Version check for the Flash Player that has the ability to start
    // Player Product Install (6.0r65)
    var hasProductInstall = DetectFlashVer(6, 0, 65);

    // Version check based upon the values defined in globals
    var hasRequestedVersion = DetectFlashVer(requiredMajorVersion,➡
      requiredMinorVersion, requiredRevision);

    // Check to see if a player with Flash Product Install is available
    // and the version does not meet the requirements for playback
    if ( hasProductInstall && !hasRequestedVersion )
    {
      // MMdoctitle is the stored document.title value used by the
      // installation process to close the window that started the
      // process. This is necessary in order to close browser
      // windows that are still utilizing the older version of the
      // player after installation has completed
      // DO NOT MODIFY THE FOLLOWING FOUR LINES
      // Location visited after installation is complete if
      // installation is required
      var MMPlayerType = (isIE == true) ? "ActiveX": "PlugIn";
      var MMredirectURL = window.location;
      document.title = document.title.slice(0, 47) + " - Flash Player➡
        Installation";
      var MMdoctitle = document.title;

      AC_FL_RunContent(
      "src", "playerProductInstall",
      "FlashVars", "MMredirectURL="+MMredirectURL+➡
```

```
        '&MMplayerType='+MMPlayerType+'&MMdoctitle='+MMdoctitle+"",
            "width", "${width}",
            "height", "${height}",
            "align", "middle",
            "id", "${application}",
            "quality", "high",
            "bgcolor", "${bgcolor}",
            "name", "${application}",
            "allowScriptAccess","sameDomain",
            "type", "application/x-shockwave-flash",
            "pluginspage", "http://www.adobe.com/go/getflashplayer"
            ) ;
        } else if (hasRequestedVersion)
        {
            // if we've detected an acceptable version
            // embed the Flash Content SWF when all tests are passed
            AC_FL_RunContent(
            "src", "${swf}",
            "width", "${width}",
            "height", "${height}",
            "align", "middle",
            "id", "${application}",
            "quality", "high",
            "bgcolor", "${bgcolor}",
            "name", "${application}",
            "allowScriptAccess","sameDomain",
            "type", "application/x-shockwave-flash",
            "pluginspage", "http://www.adobe.com/go/getflashplayer"
            );
        } else
        {// flash is too old or we can't detect the plugin
            var alternateContent = 'Alternate HTML content should be➡
placed here. '
            + 'This content requires the Adobe Flash Player. '
            + '<a href=http://www.adobe.com/go/getflash/>Get Flash</a>';
            document.write(alternateContent);// insert non-flash content
        }
    // -->
    </script>
```

This file is well commented and easy to understand; the initial checks include detection of the type of client-side browser that is loading the SWF file.

Then it moves on to the detection of the installed Flash Player version. To use the Express Install feature, the client needs at least Flash Player 6.0.65. If the detection fails (the user has an older version of Flash Player) you can either display alternate HTML content, redirect the user to the Adobe download page, or launch another type of Flash Player upgrade system such as the following:

- Macromedia Flash Player Detection Kit: www.adobe.com/products/flashplayer/download/detection_kit/
- SWFObject: Can detect minor versions and revision versions of Flash Player by passing the string value of the version you want: blog.deconcept.com/swfobject/
- Unobtrusive Flash Objects (UFO): A DOM script that detects the Flash plug-in and embeds Flash objects (files with the .swf extension): www.bobbyvandersluis.com/ufo/

Furthermore, it is necessary to add Global sections to the <script> block, in which you specify the minimum version of Flash Player that the user must have installed on the client for the application to run:

```
// -------------------------------------------------------------------
// Globals
// Major version of Flash required
var requiredMajorVersion = ${version_major};
// Minor version of Flash required
var requiredMinorVersion = ${version_minor};
// Minor version of Flash required
var requiredRevision = ${version_revision};
// -------------------------------------------------------------------
```

In addition to using the AC_OETags.js file, you must also deploy the playerProductInstall.swf file in the same location of your application (HTML and SWF) files.

In this solution you'll see how to add Express Install support to the HTML file generated in the previous solution.

How to build it

With just a few steps, it is possible to extend the features of Express Install to the HTML wrapper.

1. Obtain the HTML code generated by the JSP wrapper created in the preceding solution, either by viewing the source on the page as it appears in your browser when you run the JSP or in another way.
2. Copy the code into a new file called index.express.html.
3. Just before the closing </head> tag, add the Global section, which enables you to specify the minimum version required by Flash Player to load the Flex application:

```
<script language="JavaScript" type="text/javascript">
  <!--
    // -------------------------------------------------------------
    // Globals
    // Major version of Flash required
    var requiredMajorVersion = 9;
    // Minor version of Flash required
```

```
    var requiredMinorVersion = 0;
    // Minor version of Flash required
    var requiredRevision = 0;
    // -------------------------------------------------------------
  // -->
</script>
```

With this code, you have specified that at least version 9.0.0 of Flash Player needs to be installed before the user can run the Flex application. You can change this to other versions if you like, but it is not advisable.

4. You must now edit the portion of JavaScript code that launches the AC_FL_RunContent() method. In particular, you must insert other conditions that verify the value of the variables. These variables are hasProductInstall, which contains the minimum version of Flash Player required to make the Express Install work (the 6r65), and hasRequestedVersion, which contains the value of the version of Flash Player that must be present to load the Flex application. Add the following code now:

```
<script language="JavaScript" type="text/javascript">
  <!--
    // Version check for the Flash Player that has the ability to start
    //Player Product Install (6.0r65)
    var hasProductInstall = DetectFlashVer(6, 0, 65);

    // Version check based upon the values defined in globals
    var hasRequestedVersion = DetectFlashVer(requiredMajorVersion,➡
      requiredMinorVersion, requiredRevision);
```

5. Insert a conditional that verifies whether the Flash Player installed supports the Express Install feature, and whether it is a high enough version to run the Flex application. Add this now:

```
    // Check to see if a player with Flash Product Install is available
    // and the version does not meet the requirements for playback
    if ( hasProductInstall && !hasRequestedVersion ) {
      // MMdoctitle is the stored document.title value used by the
      // installation process to close the window that started
      // the process
      // This is necessary in order to close browser windows that are
      // still utilizing the older version of the player after
      // installation has completed
      // DO NOT MODIFY THE FOLLOWING FOUR LINES
      // Location visited after installation is complete if
      // installation is required
      var MMPlayerType = (isIE == true) ? "ActiveX": "PlugIn";
      var MMredirectURL = window.location;
      document.title = document.title.slice(0, 47) + " - Flash Player➡
        Installation";
      var MMdoctitle = document.title;
```

```
AC_FL_RunContent(
  "src", "playerProductInstall",
  "FlashVars", "MMredirectURL="+MMredirectURL+'&MMplayerType='+➡
MMPlayerType+'&MMdoctitle='+MMdoctitle+"",
  "width", "${width}",
  "height", "${height}",
  "align", "middle",
  "id", "${application}",
  "quality", "high",
  "bgcolor", "${bgcolor}",
  "name", "${application}",
  "allowScriptAccess","sameDomain",
  "type", "application/x-shockwave-flash",
  "pluginspage", "http://www.adobe.com/go/getflashplayer"
);
```

This condition runs the AC_FL_RunContent() method after having launched the procedure to update the player.

6. The last code section you need to add is an if ... else condition, which does nothing more than load the SWF file that embeds the Flex application. Add this to the bottom of your code:

```
} else if (hasRequestedVersion)
{
  // if we've detected an acceptable version
  // embed the Flash Content SWF when all tests are passed
  AC_FL_RunContent(
    "src", "${swf}",
    "width", "${width}",
    "height", "${height}",
    "align", "middle",
    "id", "${application}",
    "quality", "high",
    "bgcolor", "${bgcolor}",
    "name", "${application}",
    "allowScriptAccess","sameDomain",
    "type", "application/x-shockwave-flash",
    "pluginspage", "http://www.adobe.com/go/getflashplayer"
  );
} else
{  // flash is too old or we can't detect the plugin
  var alternateContent = 'Alternate HTML content should be placed➡
    here. '
  + 'This content requires the Adobe Flash Player. '
  + '<a href=http://www.adobe.com/go/getflash/>Get Flash</a>';
  document.write(alternateContent);  // insert non-flash content
}
// -->
</script>
```

This is the case in which the specified version of Flash Player is present, so the application is run. With these simple steps, you have added Express Install support to the base wrapper.

Expert tips

When you create alternate HTML content that will be displayed to users with old versions of Flash Player, one option is to redirect users to an Adobe page that lets them know the currently installed version of Flash Player on their computer.

On the Adobe site there is a very useful tool that shows you the specific version of the Adobe Flash Player currently installed and active in your browser: www.adobe.com/cfusion/knowledgebase/index.cfm?id=tn_15507. You can use this address to ascertain the installed version of the Flash Player on the client machine.

When creating custom wrappers, you might use different files (JavaScript, CSS, assets). In the deployment phase you must pay attention to the files to be transferred onto the production server. When using Express Install support, it is necessary to also copy the following files onto the server:

- AC_OETags.js
- playerProductInstall.swf

If history management support is used, the following files, which are located in the Flex SDK/resources/html-templates/ folder, must be transferred:

- history.js
- history.swf
- history.htm files

Adobe has created and freely distributed the Flash Player Detection Kit www.adobe.com/products/flashplayer/download/detection_kit/, which includes the documentation required to use the methods and the procedures for detecting and updating the end user's Flash Player version and the example files in JavaScript and ActionScript for client-side detection.

Solution 8-5: Compiling Flex components

Flex SDK enables you to use two different compilers: the application and component compilers. The application compiler enables you to compile the Flex applications in SWF format. In the preceding solutions you used the mxmlc compiler and the Flex Builder compiler.

The component compiler is used to generate files in SWC format, which is a compressed archive of Flex components and assets (Flex components were discussed in Chapter 2). The component compiler can be launched from Flex Builder, by defining a Library Project or by using the compc.exe command-line compiler. Both methods enable you to compile the following assets: component libraries, runtime shared libraries (RSLs), and themes.

The component compiler shares many of the options of the application compiler, but it also adds more:

- **directory**: Creates a SWC file in an open directory format. When you pass this option to the component compiler, it does not create a SWC file; it creates a directory that you'll use for RSLs. You can learn more about RSLs on the Adobe LiveDocs site: http://livedocs.adobe.com/flex/201/html/wwhelp/wwhimpl/common/html/wwhelp.htm?context=LiveDocs_Book_Parts&file=compiledeploy_142_02.html.

- **include-classes**: Specifies the classes that must be included in the compilation phase in the SWC file.

- **include-file**: Specifies the file to add to the SWC file.

- **include-namespaces**: Specifies the namespace to include in the library.

- **include-resource-bundles**: Specifies the resource bundles to insert in the SWC file.

- **include-sources**: Specifies the directories or the classes that must be sent to the SWC file.

In this solution you'll see how to use the component compiler to create a SWC file.

What's involved

To use the component compiler, you must first create the Flex components to compile. You'll create all these components inside a Flex Library project. These elements will be selected from the Flex Library Path window, which is opened by selecting Project ➤ Properties ➤ Flex Library Build Path. In this window, you add the elements to be compiled in the SWC file and set the output folder.

If you click OK, the SWC file that can be used in a Flex project is automatically compiled.

To import a SWC file, choose among the following:

- Add SWC: Adds the specified SWC file
- Add SWC Project: Adds an entire SWC Library project
- Add SWC Folder: Adds all SWC files present in the specified folder

By using one of these three options, you add the library to the Flex project. By opening the Component view in Design mode of Flex Builder, you see the component imported and ready to be dragged into the application.

How to build it

Create a simple Flex component, which you'll compile to a SWC file and then import into an MXML file.

1. Create a new Flex Library project by selecting File ➤ New ➤ Flex Library Project and give it the name Chapter_8_Flex_Library.

2. Create a new MXML component in this project, based on the ApplicationControlBar, and name it myAppControlBar.mxml.

3. Change some of the style properties of the ApplicationControlBar and insert a TextInput and a Button control. Change the component's code like so:

```
<mx:ApplicationControlBar
  xmlns:mx="http://www.adobe.com/2006/mxml"
  width="400" height="50"
  cornerRadius="3" >

  <mx:TextInput/>
  <mx:Button label="Search"
    cornerRadius="2"
    fontFamily="Arial"
    fontWeight="bold"/>
</mx:ApplicationControlBar>
```

4. To export this component as a SWC file, you must add it to the Flex Library Build Path, which you open by selecting Projects ➤ Properties ➤ Flex Library Build Path. This window, shown in Figure 8-8, displays different tabs that enable you to add different assets to the SWC compilation: classes, assets (components, images), and other library paths. In this case, you'll add the file myAppControlBar.mxml, which you add by simply ticking the check box. You can also set an output folder in which the SWC will be compiled. By default, this folder is the bin folder.

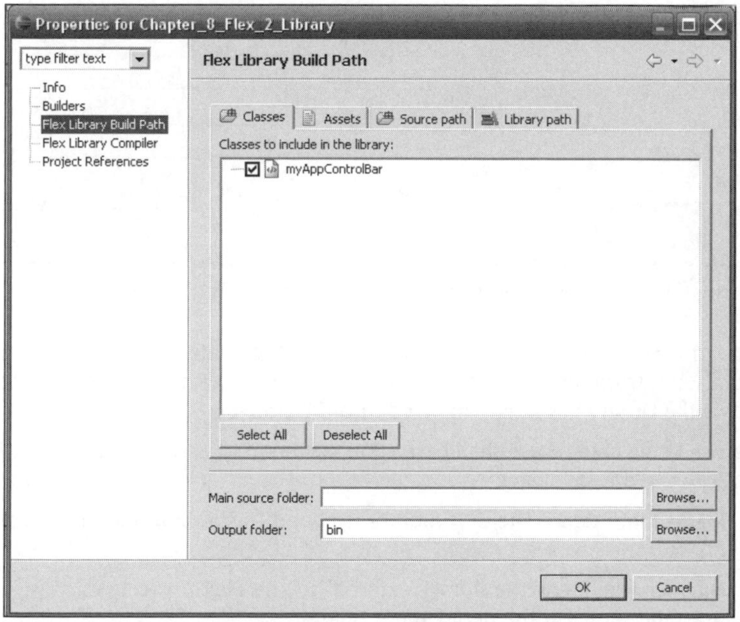

8

Figure 8-8. The Flex Library Build Path window enables you to import elements in the compilation of the SWC file.

After you click OK, Flex Builder automatically compiles the SWC file and inserts it in the bin folder. In these few steps, you have created a component and have used the Flex Builder component compiler to compile in the SWC file.

Next you'll import the SWC file into a Flex project by adding it into the Flex Build Path of the properties of the project.

5. Open the Flex project created for this chapter, Chapter_8_Flex_Compiling_Deploying, and launch the Project Properties by selecting Project ➤ Properties ➤ Flex Build Path. This screen (see Figure 8-9) displays two tabs: Source path and Library path. The latter enables you to import Flex libraries in the three different ways mentioned earlier (Add SWC, Add SWC Project, and Add SWC Folder).

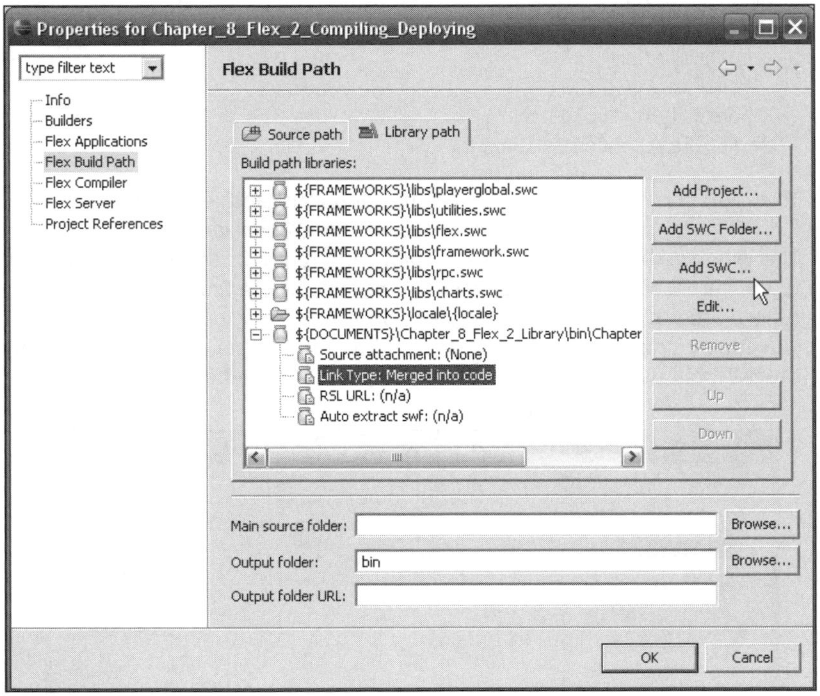

Figure 8-9. The SWC file has been added to the project of the Library Path.

6. Add the SWC file by clicking Add SWC and then select the file Chapter_8_Flex_Library.swc from the bin folder of the Flex Library project previously created. At this point the Library has been imported into the project.

7. Before being able to use the library, you still need to choose a Link Type. The three options are the following:

   - Merged into Code: The SWC library is added to the SWF file in the compilation phase.

   - External: Maintains the library external to the Flex project, so must be copied onto the server in the deployment phase.

   - Runtime Shared Library: The SWC file is used as an RSL.

8. Choose the first option, Merged into Code, as shown in Figure 8-10.

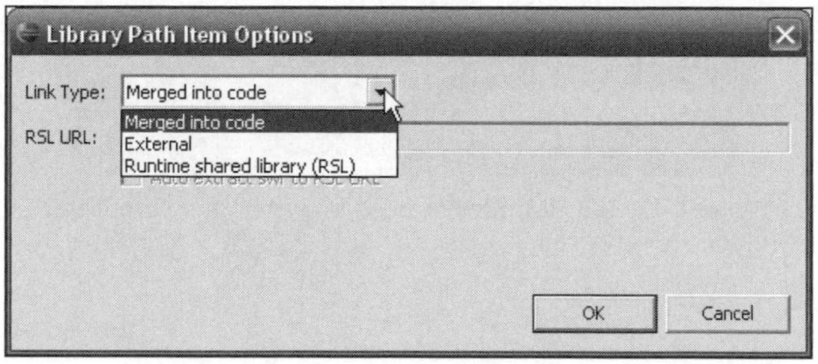

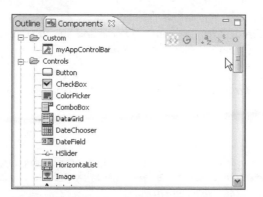

Figure 8-10. The Flex Library Path window enables you to import elements in the compilation of the SWC file.

9. Create a new MXML Application file named Chapter_8_Flex_Sol_4.mxml. Moving to Design mode, if you open the Component view, in the custom folder you can see the component (myAppControlBar) ready to be used, as shown in Figure 8-11.

Figure 8-11. The myAppControlBar library has been added to the Components view of FlexBuilder.

10. To test it, drag it into the file—you'll see the following MXML code:

```
<?xml version="1.0" encoding="utf-8"?>
<mx:Application xmlns:mx="http://www.adobe.com/2006/mxml"➥
  layout="vertical" xmlns:ns1="*">
  <ns1:myAppControlBar>
  </ns1:myAppControlBar>
</mx:Application>
```

As with any external Flex component, a custom namespace has been created in the application to import the SWC file and then the library has been recalled by referring to the name of the file myAppControlBar without the extension.

11. Save the file and run the application.

The SWC file will be compiled and added to the SWF file. The final result is shown in Figure 8-12.

Figure 8-12. The SWC file has been imported and compiled in the Flex application.

Expert tips

If you select the Runtime Shared Library option while importing the Library as Link Type property in the deployment phase, the SWC file has to be present on the deployment server. In this case, however, there is no need to bring anything with it because the SWC file is merged into the SWF file. The RSLs are useful when several files of an application use and share the same library.

In the main solution, you have used Flex Builder to compile the components. If you wanted to use the compc compiler from the command line to compile the component in SWC format, you would have written the following:

```
compc -source-path . -namespace http://www.comtaste.com➡
myAppControlBar.xml -include-namespaces http://www.comtaste.com -
output➡
myAppControlBar.swc
```

> As you did for the mxmlc compiler, to launch the compc compiler from every loca-
> tion you have to add it as an environment variable. Repeat the steps described in
> Solution 1-1 to create a environment variable.

The parameters sent to the compiler in the preceding command are as follows:

- **-source-path**: Specifies the path of the source files. You specify that the current directory should be used by setting . as a value.
- **-namespace**: Specifies a custom namespace.
- **myAppControlBar.xml**: The name of the manifest file.
- **-include-namespaces**: Includes the namespace in the library.
- **-output**: Specifies the name of the SWC file that will be compiled (myAppControlBar.swc).

The myAppControlBar.xml manifest file is a simple XML file that specifies the components and the assets to be added in the compilation phase of the SWC file. The importance of using a manifest file is that it enables you to declare references to any number of compo-nents in a namespace. So if you have many components to add to a SWF file and you want to point to a custom namespace in the MXML file, you can list them in a manifest file.

In this case, you use only an MXML component, so the file will contain only the following:

```
<?xml version="1.0"?>
<componentPackage>
  <component id=" myAppControlBar " class="myAppControlBar "/>
</componentPackage>
```

At this point, to import the file into the application, you can write the following code:

```
<?xml version="1.0" encoding="utf-8"?>
<mx:Application xmlns:mx="http://www.adobe.com/2006/mxml"
  layout="vertical"
  xmlns:mySWC=" http://www.comtaste.com">
  <mySWC:myAppControlBar />
</mx:Application>
```

Solution 8-6: Using the fdb command-line debugger

Because Flex Builder is based on Eclipse, it inherits several powerful features from it—such as the debugger perspective. Flex SDK offers a powerful utility to carry out the debugging of Flex applications: fdb. This debugger enables you to launch a debug session directly from the command line.

The fdb debugger is located in the bin folder of Flex SDK, and you can obtain a complete list of the options that can be sent to the compiler by typing the following:

```
fdb help
```

To launch a debug session with the compiler, it is necessary to have compiled a Flex application into a SWF file with the option -debug = true, which adds specific information to the SWF that is useful for debugging the application:

```
mxmlc -debug=true myApp.mxml
```

You also need to have a debugger version of Flash Player installed, which you'll find inside your Flex Builder directory (just in case, it can be downloaded from www.adobe.com/support/flashplayer/downloads.html).

Using the fdb compiler is quite easy. Open the Prompt window (Terminal in Mac OSX) and point to the Flex Builder or Flex SDK installation folder. Go to the bin directory and type fbd in the command line:

```
drive:/flex_inst/bin/fdb
```

The fdb prompt appears. Use the run command at the fdb prompt; the debug session is launched, and the fdb compiler automatically opens the SWF application in the window of the browser and connects to the debug version of Flash Player. This connection, which is in all effects a TCP/IP connection, transfers the information from the SWF file to the command line so that you can debug the application using proper debug features such as setting breakpoints and watching variables.

If the debugger version of Flash Player is not installed, an error is displayed, indicating that Flash Player does not support debugging sessions, as shown in Figure 8-13.

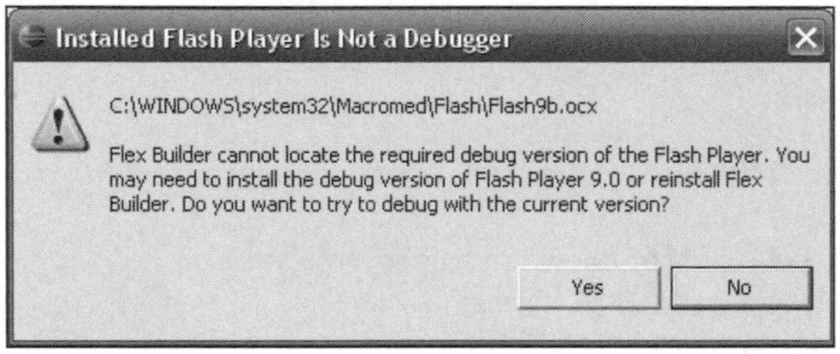

Figure 8-13. If you don't have the debug version of Flash Player, you'll see the following error message.

In this solution you'll see how to launch a debug session with the fdb command-line debugger.

What's involved

There are various ways to activate a debug session and launch the fdb debugger. But all methods begin from having compiled a SWF file with the debug option equal to true.

A debug session can be launched by using the stand-alone version of Flash Player. The stand-alone version is a version of Flash Player loaded outside of the browser and operates like an independent application. To carry out a session using the stand-alone Flash Player, do the following:

1. Navigate to the folder containing the SWF file you want to debug.

2. Launch the debugger by entering the following command-line command:

   fdb

3. After the fdb prompt has been run, launch the debugger session by entering the following command:

   run myApp.swf

When the debug session runs with the stand-alone version of Flash Player, it is not possible to perform any server requests (web services or HTTP requests) or carry out dynamic SWF loading. So it is preferable to use a debug session in a web browser.

To launch the web browser and carry out the debugging of a Flex application with the fdb tool, do the following:

1. Compile the application with the debug=true option specified; then create a HTML wrapper containing the SWF file. Transfer your application files to your web server.

2. Launch the debugger by entering the following into the command line:

fdb

3. Enter the run command and wait for Flash Player to connect. In the meantime, the text Waiting for Player to connect should appear.

4. Open the browser and load your application (you could also just enter the run myApp.html in fdb command).

In this solution you'll carry out a real debug test with the fdb by launching the session for a compiled SWF file.

How to build it

To simulate a debugging session, you'll launch the fdb debugger on the application Chapter_6_Flex_Sol_8.mxml in the Flex project Chapter_6_Flex_RPC. This file (which was created in Chapter 6) makes a remote call with the URKRequest object.

You'll launch a debugging session using the web browser.

1. Open a command prompt/terminal window and navigate to the folder containing the project and the compiled application.

2. Compile the application with the option debug=true:

mxmlc –debug=true Chapter_6_Flex_Sol_8.mxml

3. Launch fdb using the fdb command. The fdb prompt opens, as shown in Figure 8-14.

4. Enter the run command; the fdb debugger begins to open the connection to Flash Player.

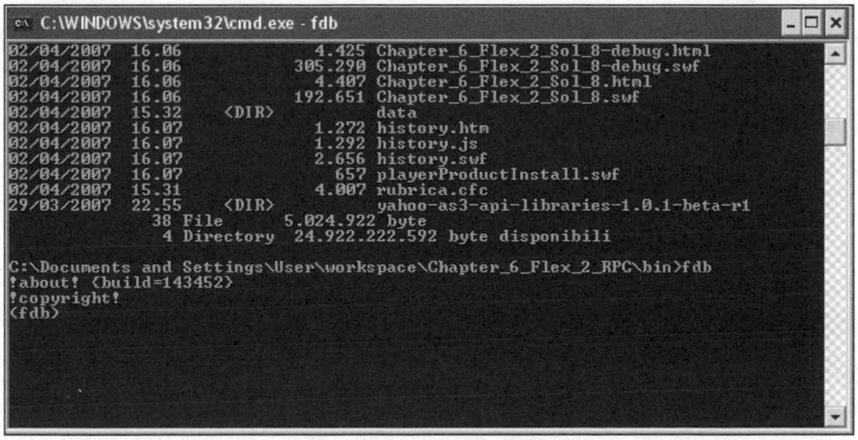

Figure 8-14. With the fdb prompt you can start the debugging session by typing run.

5. Make sure that your application files are uploaded to your web server and browse to the Chapter_6_Flex_Sol_8.html file in your web browser (created automatically during compilation if you used Flex Builder or created by you if you used the command line).

6. At this point the debugging session is open. You can use the following commands to perform various debug operations:

   - continue: Enables the debugger to proceed to the next phase of debugging.

   - file [file]: Enables you to carry out the debugging of an application without starting the application.

   - finish: Continues the session until you exit from the function.

   - next [N]: Moves forward one line of code. The argument N specifies the N times that the debugger will have to carry out this operation.

   - quit: Interrupts and exits from the debut session.

   - step [N]: Steps into the application as many times as specified in argument N.

To have a full list of operations and commands you can use to debug and navigate your Flex application, refer to the official documentation: http://livedocs.adobe.com/flex/2/docs/wwhelp/wwhimpl/common/html/wwhelp.htm?context=LiveDocs_Parts&file=00001542.html.

Expert tips

In a debugging session, an important aspect is that of being able to set breakpoints. Breakpoints can be set with the fdb debugger by using the break command, as follows:

```
(fdb) break completeHandler
```

In this case you have set a breakpoint on the completeHandler function. The break command accepts either a line number or a function name as subject; if no specific breakpoint is specified, the command sets a breakpoint at the current line of code.

You can also use the source command to load a list of commands from an external text file (a list of breakpoints, for example), which can save you a lot of time:

```
(fdb) source debugCommands.txt
```

Solution 8-7: Deploying Flex applications

The deployment of a Flex application can be a very simple operation or can become very complex, depending on the size of the project, its complexity, the number of team members involved, the project management process used, and many other factors. For projects that do not use LiveCycle Data Services (formerly Flex Data Services), the deployment activity can simply coincide with the transfer onto the production server of the files that you have compiled.

When you create a new project, Flex Builder creates the bin folder. This is where the compiled SWF file, HTML wrapper, and all the external assets of the project (images, CSS, RSLs, font, video, JavaScript files, and so on) are placed during compilation. This enables you to easily find everything that needs to be transferred to the production server during deployment.

Besides making sure that all the application files are transferred to the server, you must also make sure that the remote services continue to function on the production server. In fact, it might be necessary to change the settings and the security restrictions to avoid unforeseen errors during the access to remote data.

In this solution you'll see how to create a custom structure to deploy Flex applications.

What's involved

To be able to better understand exactly what is meant by carrying out the deployment of a Flex application, you must first understand the structure of a Flex project.

First, look at the structure of a Flex Builder project just after it's been newly created:

```
My Flex Project
|
|- bin
|- html-template
|- MyFlexProject.mxml
```

The bin folder contains the files compiled by the MXML compiler. The project's structure also contains the MXML application file (MyFlexProject.mxml) and the html-template folder that contains the HTML wrappers.

This structure works to begin with, but it can soon become unmanageable when you are dealing with a lot of different files and different types of assets. You need a directory structure that enables you to better manage the different resources used in the project, like so:

```
My Flex Project
|
|- bin
|- assets
|- images
|- data
|- video
|- fonts
|- rsl
|- html-template
|- MyFlexProject.swf
```

8

In this structure, the assets folder contains different folders to contain images, RSLs, video, fonts, and XML files. When this application is compiled with Flex Builder, the same structure, including all files, is replicated inside the bin folder:

```
My Flex Project
|
|- bin
  |- assets
  |- images
  |- data
  |- video
  |- fonts
  |- rsl
|- assets
|- images
|- data
|- video
|- fonts
|- rsl
|- html-template
|- MyFlexProject.swf
```

To carry out the deployment, you must copy the same directory structure onto the production server and transfer all the files, maintaining the same relative paths (see Table 8-2).

Table 8-2. Files to put onto the deployment server

Flex application	`myFlexApp.swf, myFlexApp.html`	Compiled Flex application and the HTML wrapper
External Assets	Folder and files used in the application	N/A
History manager	`history.swf, history.js`	To support history manager
Player detection	`playerProductInstall.swf, AC_OETags.js`	To support client detection of Flash Player

In this solution, you'll carry out the deployment of an application you created in Chapter 6, Chapter_6_Flex_Sol_6.mxml.

How to build it

For this example you'll use the file Chapter_6_Flex_Sol_6.mxml created in Solution 6-6. In this file you used a web service, using the WebService tag. You'll add an external image and an external CSS file to this file.

1. Open the file Chapter_6_Flex_Sol_6.mxml and save it as Chapter_8_Flex_Sol_6. mxml.

2. Create an assets folder inside the Flex project (select File ➤ New ➤ Folder) and in turn create two more directories inside this one: CSS and images.

3. Copy both the logo2.gif and backgrounds.swf images into the assets/images folder, which simply contains various graphic symbols. (They can be found in the code download files for this chapter.)

4. Create a new CSS file in the assets/CSS folder and call it myCSS.css (don't forget to also specify the extension of the file). Add the following CSS rules into this file:

```
Application {
  backgroundImage: Embed➥
    (source="../images/backgrounds.swf#greenstripe");
  backgroundGradientAlphas: 0.48, 0.45;
  themeColor: #009966;
  color: #000000;
}

ApplicationControlBar {
  highlightAlphas: 0.46, 0;
  fillAlphas: 0, 0;
  fillColors: #339999, #ffffff;
  backgroundAlpha: 1;
  cornerRadius: 3;
  dropShadowEnabled: true;
  shadowDistance: 3;
  shadowDirection: center;
  dropShadowColor: #666666;
}

Button {
  cornerRadius: 2;
  textIndent: 0;
  fontFamily: Arial;
  fontWeight: bold;
}

Panel {
  borderStyle: none;
  borderColor: #01b454;
  borderThicknessLeft: 4;
  borderThicknessTop: 0;
  borderThicknessBottom: 3;
  borderThicknessRight: 4;
  roundedBottomCorners: false;
  cornerRadius: 0;
  headerHeight: 21;
  backgroundAlpha: 0.87;
  highlightAlphas: 0.44, 0;
```

8

```
        headerColors: #003300, #999999;
        footerColors: #003300, #c7c7c7;
        dropShadowEnabled: true;
        shadowDistance: 0;
        titleStyleName: "mypanelTitle";
    }
    .mypanelTitle {
        letterSpacing: 0;
    }
```

You'll look at styles and CSS declarations in more detail (along with other techniques for modifying the look and feel of a Flex application) in Chapter 9. The most interesting property in the CSS is the specified definition for the Application tag on the backgroundImage property:

```
backgroundImage: Embed(source="../images/backgrounds.swf#greenstripe");
```

This property embeds the backgrounds.swf file into the main application SWF file upon compilation, so the background.swf file doesn't have to be present on the production server. Furthermore, only the symbol with the id equal to greenstripe becomes loaded, as specified by #greenstripe.

Pay attention also to the relative path that has been declared in the SWF file. With the CSS file being located in the assets/CSS folder, to be able to load the backgrounds.swf file (in the assets/images folder) you have to exit from that folder (with the double dots—double dots mean "go up one level in the directory tree") and position yourself in the images folder.

5. In the MXML file you import this CSS file using the Style tag and its source attribute, which enables you to specify an external CSS file. Add the following bold line to your code:

```
<mx:Application xmlns:mx="http://www.adobe.com/2006/mxml"➡
    layout="vertical"➡
    creationComplete="wsBlogAggr.getCategories.send()">

<mx:Style source="assets/CSS/myCSS.css" />
```

6. Add an Image tag to the right of the DataGrid and ComboBox controls, like so:

```
<mx:Panel x="10" y="10" width="475" height="400" layout="absolute"➡
    title="Solution 8-5: Deploy Flex Application">
<mx:Image width="126" source="assets/images/logo2.gif" x="0" y="10"/>
<mx:ComboBox x="134" y="24" id="categoryCbx"➡
    change="wsBlogAggr.getFeedsByCategory.send()"➡
    dataProvider="{wsBlogAggr.getCategories.lastResult}"➡
    labelField="categoryName">
</mx:ComboBox>
```

7. Compile the file and click the bin folder in Navigator view. You'll see that the directory structure has been replicated in this folder, and the external files have been copied (see Figure 8-15).

Figure 8-15. In the bin folder, the entire structure required by the application to run the SWF file will be replicated, including the external assets.

8. To carry out the deployment of this application take the contents of the bin directory and copy them onto the web server:

- Chapter_8_Flex_Sol_6.html
- Chapter_8_Flex_Sol_6.swf
- history.htm
- history.swf
- playerProductInstall.swf
- AC_OETags.js
- assets folder (contains the CSS and images folders)
- CSS folder
  - myCSS.css (inside the CSS folder)
- Images folder
  - logo2.gif (inside the images folder)

After the files are copied onto the production server, all that's left to do is test the application externally to verify that all the runtime data access functions correctly.

Expert tips

Using Flex Builder, it is possible to disable the automatic generation of the HTML wrapper in the HTML wrapper options of the Flex Compiler window (select Project ➤ Properties ➤ Flex Compiler), as shown in Figure 8-16.

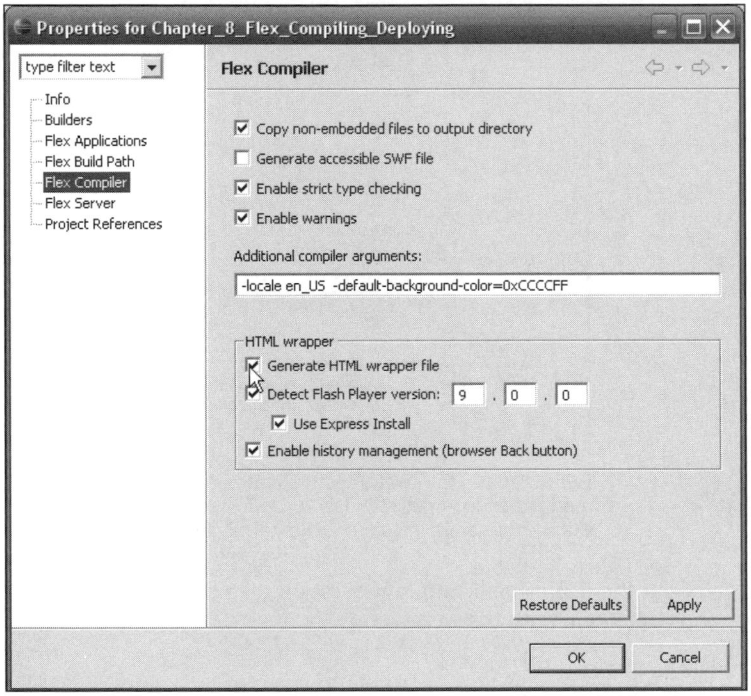

Figure 8-16. You can disable the generation of the HTML wrapper In the Flex Compiler option.

You can then specify which file templates to use for the wrapper file by creating a custom Run directive. By using the Run configuration panel (by selecting Run ➤ Run ➤ Flex Application) you can select the HTML wrapper files to be used by Flex Builder in the compilation phase. Uncheck Use defaults (shown in Figure 8-17 under the URL or path to launch box) and then specify the file templates to use both for the compilation phase and for the debug phase in the relevant file select boxes.

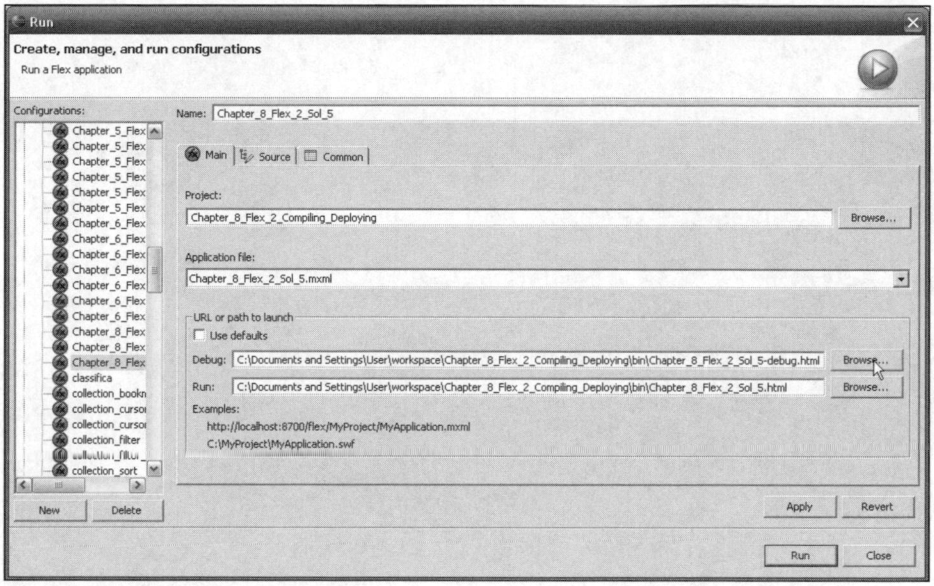

Figure 8-17. The Run configuration panel

Summary

The final steps that make your Flex application accessible to the users are the compilation and deployment phases. The Flex SDK offers two compilers for using Flex Builder or the command-line compiler. They accept options that enable you to enable or disable determined characteristics of the application.

Flex contains a configuration file (located at \Flex SDK 2\frameworks): flex-config.xml. It is used in the compilation phase and the options defined in it are read and applied by the application compiler.

In this chapter you learned how to compile an application using the mxmlc and the compc tools and how to create custom configuration files to be used by the compiler.

The wrapper term was introduced and you learned how Flex works to embed the SWF file into an HTML page using the <object> and <embed> elements.

The HTML code and JavaScript necessary to load the SWF file are known as wrappers, and Flex provides base templates to use for these wrappers, located in the Flex SDK 2\resources\html-templates folder.

The Flex Builder compiler automatically generates the wrappers in the compilation phase of the Flex application, but you can disable this option and create your own wrapper.

You also learned how to create and customize a dynamic wrapper using the JSP language.

The chapter concluded by showing you techniques to create custom structure to deploy Flex applications that can be used when deploying a Flex application.

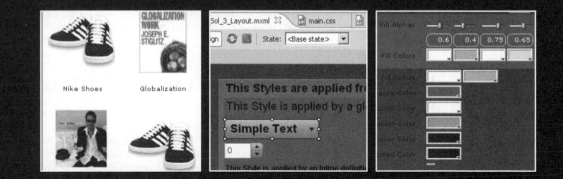

Flex allows developers and designers to create attractive and rich user interfaces and layouts for their Rich Internet Applications (RIAs). As noted in preceding chapters, defining the structure of the layout of an application in Flex is a very simple task. Unlike traditional web applications that use HTML and Cascading Style Sheets (CSS), with Flex you do not have to worry about writing lines of code exclusively for defining and formatting the elements of a page (or 100 lines of CSS code for positioning the elements).

The time required to test the web applications on different browsers and operating systems must also be added when working with HTML and CSS because the browser engines that interpret and render the elements of the page vary. Too often, this means having to perform bothersome "porting" of the application and creating specific custom CSS for a version of a particular browser, which requires extra time and costs.

RIAs developed with Flex run within the Flash Player installed on a common browser, and Flash Player renders the user interface elements of the page onscreen. This means that the web application is seen in the same way, independently of the operating system (Windows, Linux, Mac, Sun Solaris) and of the web browser.

This is a huge advantage that allows developers to save precious time and concentrate on functionality instead of the layout. And Flex and Flash Player add another level of user interface components that are not obtainable when using only the HTML elements available to standard browser-based web applications. This richer functionality can include anything that can be implemented in the Flash Player technology being used on the client side, including complex data visualization, native drag-and-drop operations, using a slider to change data, data binding, and so on.

Furthermore, Flex permits you to personalize and modify the look and feel of every single component that it puts forward. This means that the designer can change the appearance of a ComboBox or a DataGrid and mold it to particular graphic needs by modifying every single visual element of that control; define the CSS style to format components and elements of the entire applications; or use Flash, Fireworks, Photoshop, or Illustrator to create and expose user interface elements to be used in the Flex application.

This chapter shows how Flex works to position the elements in the application and how to personalize the look and feel of the controls. You will also use Flash and Fireworks to create user interface elements or entire user screens to import into a Flex application.

Solution 9-1: Designing the layout of a Flex application

Flex offers a series of components to help designers and developers manage application layout. These components, which are called **containers**, are elements defining rectangular regions of the screen that can contain controls or other containers. There are two types of containers:

- Layout containers: Allow you to define the sizing and the positioning of the elements contained in them. For example, VBox or Panel containers make up part of this category.

- Navigator containers: Allow you to define the user navigation in the other child containers. An example of this category of container is the TabNavigator or Accordion container.

Every container inherits properties and attributes that permit you to modify the layout, dimension, and positioning of the child elements.

There is one special layout container that will be discussed separately: the Application container. The <mx:Application> tag is the root container, which represents and contains the entire application. By modifying the rules of this container, you can modify the appearance of the entire application. If, in fact, you try to change the layout property of the <mx:Application> tag from absolute to vertical, all the elements of your application will be displayed vertically:

```
<mx:Application xmlns:mx="http://www.adobe.com/2006/mxml"
layout="vertical">
<mx:Panel title="My Panel">
<mx:Label text="Panel 1" />
</mx:Panel>

<mx:Panel title="My Panel 2">
 <mx:Label text="Panel 2" />
</mx:Panel>
</mx:Application>
```

The preceding code will create two Panel containers displayed vertically, as Figure 9-1 shows.

Even if the rules assigned to the <mx:Application> tag are inherited by all the elements of the page, this does not limit you from specifying different types of page positioning. You can, in fact, use the characteristics of the containers to change the position of the elements:

Figure 9-1. The layout property is set to vertical, so it sorts all the child elements in a vertical position.

```
<?xml version="1.0" encoding="utf-8"?>
<mx:Application xmlns:mx="http://www.adobe.com/2006/mxml"
layout="vertical">

<mx:Panel title="My Panel" width="100%">
<mx:Label text="Panel 1" />
</mx:Panel>

<mx:HBox width="100%">
<mx:Panel title="My Panel 2">
 <mx:Label text="Panel 2" />
</mx:Panel>
<mx:DataGrid>
<mx:columns>
<mx:DataGridColumn headerText="Column 1" dataField="col1"/>
<mx:DataGridColumn headerText="Column 2" dataField="col2"/>
```

```
<mx:DataGridColumn headerText="Column 3" dataField="col3"/>
</mx:columns>
</mx:DataGrid>
<mx:DateChooser/>
</mx:HBox>
</mx:Application>
```

This code sets the layout of the application as vertical, but an HBox container is inserted, which creates a horizontal positioning for all the elements specified in it, as shown in Figure 9-2.

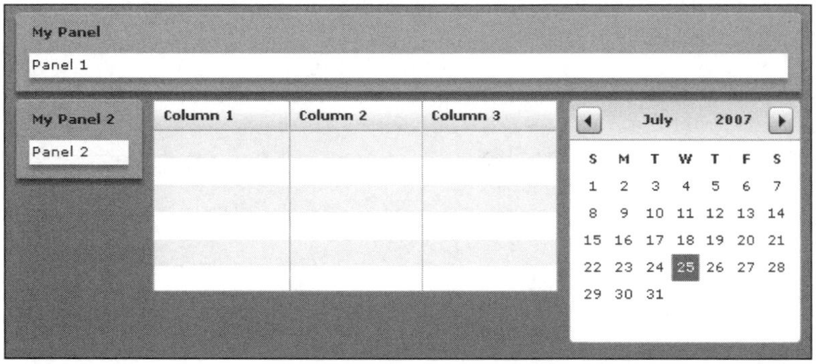

Figure 9-2. You can change the position of the elements by inserting other containers.

The layout property can assume three different values:

- Absolute: Default value assigned to the layout of the <mx:Application> tag that allows you to position the elements in an absolute way by specifying x and y
- Horizontal: Displays the elements horizontally
- Vertical: Displays the elements vertically

When creating the layout of a Flex application, you can follow different approaches. You can, in fact, let Flex determine the dimension and positioning of the elements without having to specify the width and height properties of every single component. Or you can specify these dimensions both in an absolute way (using dimensions in px) and a relative way (using values in percentages).

Finally, there is a third approach, discussed in the next solution, which allows you to control the dimension and the position by anchoring elements to locations in their container. This approach is known as **constraint-based layout**.

In this solution, you will create a layout of an application, mixing together some of the box-based containers (such as HBox, VBox, DividedBox, ControlBar, and ApplicationControlBar), the Canvas-based layout, and the hybrid layout containers (such as Application, Panel, and TitleWindow).

What's involved

Most of the containers and controls that you will deal with in this solution have already been used in the other chapters. In this solution you will concentrate mainly on creating a layout of a web application using the components that Flex makes available.

In this solution there is also a component that makes up part of the family of List-based controls: TileList. Like all the other List-based controls (DataGrid, HorizontalList, List, ComboBox, and Tree), it accepts the dataProvider property that specifies the data set to use to populate the control with data. In fact, this control displays a tiled list of items. Figure 9-3 shows a real TileList control application in the FlexStore application of Adobe (you can see it at the following address: http://examples.adobe.com/flex2/inproduct/ sdk/flexstore/flexstore.html).

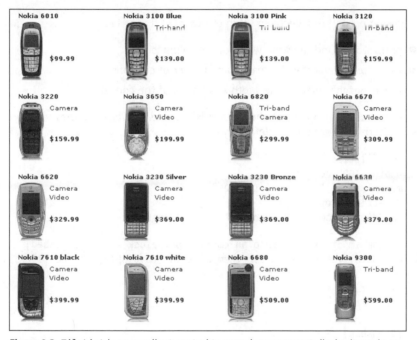

Figure 9-3. TileList is an excellent control to use when you must display items in an equal-sized layout.

The TileList control creates rows and columns of equal sized layout in a horizontal or vertical way. It is declared with the MXML tag <mx:TileList> and shares many of the properties, methods, and events of the List controls. The following code shows an example of a TileList container to which the dataProvider property declared as a nested tag is linked:

```
<mx:TileList
width="400" height="300"
maxColumns="3" columnWidth="125"
 paddingBottom="0" paddingLeft="0" paddingRight="0">
```

```
<mx:dataProvider>
 <mx:Array>
<mx:Object label="Nike Shoes"/>
<mx:Object label="Globalization""/>
<mx:Object label="iMac"/>
<mx:Object label="Mark Anthony"/>
<mx:Object label="Mark Anthony"/>
 </mx:Array>
</mx:dataProvider>
</mx:TileList>
```

The dataProvider of the TileList is populated with an Array of Objects that presents the label property. As for the List controls, the label property is automatically displayed onscreen.

The following properties have been set in the <mx:TileList> tag:

- columnWidth: Indicates the width of the columns
- maxColumns: Indicates the maximum number of columns
- width, height: Indicate the width and height of the control

Another very useful property of the control is direction, which enables you to display items in a horizontal or vertical (default) way:

```
<mx:TileList
width="400" height="300"
maxColumns="3" columnWidth="125"
direction="horizontal"
 paddingBottom="0" paddingLeft="0" paddingRight="0">
```

If you import images into an <mx:Script> block with the [Embed] metadata, you can then use them as icons to display in the TileList:

```
<mx:Script>
<![CDATA[

[Bindable]
 [Embed(source="/assets/product1.gif")]
 public var cam1:Class;
  ]]>
</mx:Script>

<mx:TileList
width="400" height="300"
maxColumns="3" columnWidth="125"
 paddingBottom="0" paddingLeft="0" paddingRight="0">

<mx:dataProvider>
<mx:Array>
<mx:Object label="Nike Shoes" icon="{cam1}"/>
```

```
<mx:Object label="Globalization" icon="{cam2}"/>
<mx:Object label="iMac" icon="{cam3}"/>
<mx:Object label="Mark Anthony" icon="{cam4}"/>
<mx:Object label="Mark Anthony" icon="{cam1}"/>
</mx:Array>
</mx:dataProvider>
</mx:TileList>
```

The properties of this control are many, and you can see them in the Adobe LiveDocs at the following address: http://livedocs.adobe.com/flex/2/langref/mx/controls/ TileList.html.

In this solution, you will create a layout that will also use a TileList control among the other controls.

How to build It

Begin by studying the layout that has been sent to you by your trusted designer. The graphic file, which is usually created with Photoshop (so it is in PSD or PNG format), shows your required objective. Figure 9-4 shows the final result that you will create step by step in this solution. You will then use this application to apply styles and to make the design more attractive. One of the disadvantages of Flex from the point of view of design is that by using all the standard components of the framework, the applications might all look similar. Instead, adding styles and skins to the page (discussed later in this chapter) changes the appearance of a Flex application.

9

Figure 9-4. The final result of the layout

For this project you will create an MXML application file and four external components. The graphics that you will use are located in the assets folder of the project, which you will create in Step 3. The MXML components will instead be inserted in the com.flexsolutions.chapter9.controls package.

1. Begin by creating a new Flex project that you will work on. Open Flex Builder and create a Flex project with the name Chapter_9_Flex_Layout. Step through, leaving everything else at their default values; then click Finish.

2. Create a new MXML application file by selecting File ➤ New ➤ MXML Application and name it Chapter_9_Flex_Sol_1_Layout.mxml.

3. Create the folders that will contain the images and the MXML components. Select File ➤ New ➤ Folder and create the assets folder. Then, still beginning from the root457of the project, create the following directory structure: com/flexsolutions/chapter9/controls.

4. Create the MXML components that will then be inserted in the main application file. In the com/flexsolutions/chapter9/controls folder create a new MXML component by selecting File ➤ New ➤ MXML Component and save it with the name TreeMenu. Base the component on a Tree control; this component will contain the navigation menu for navigating within the web application. To populate the Tree control, declare an <mx:XMLList> tag in which you will define the structure to be displayed:

```
<mx:Tree xmlns:mx="http://www.adobe.com/2006/mxml"
dataProvider="{treeData}"
labelField="@label"
showRoot="false"
 width="90%"
 height="100%">
<mx:XMLList id="treeData">

<mx:XMLList id="treeData">
<products label="Books">
<product label="Home and Garden"/>
<product label="Product Management"/>
<product label="Personal"/>
<product label="Computing"/>
<product label="Mind and Body"/>
<product label="Narrative"/>
<product label="Mind and Body"/>
<product label="Professional"/>
<product label="Personal"/>
</products>
<products label="Leather Goods">
<product label="Bags"/>
<product label="Sunglasses"/>
<product label="Footwear"/>
<product label="Travel"/>
</products>
<products label="Music">
```

```
<product label="CDs"/>
<product label="Dvds"/>
<product label="Instrumental"/>
<product label="Travel"/>
</products>
<products label="Consumer Electronics">
<product label="Audio and Video"/>
<product label="Camera and Photo"/>
<product label="Cell Phones and Service"/>
<product label="Video Games"/>
</products>
<products label="All Consumer Electronics" />
</mx:XMLList>

</mx:Tree>
```

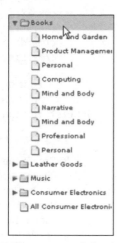

The structure of the <mx:XMLList> tag is represented by the Tree control to which it is linked through the dataProvider property (see Figure 9-5).

Figure 9-5. The structure defined in the <mx:XMLList> tag is displayed in the Tree control.

The control also uses the labelField property that specifies the label field to be displayed. In this example, the @label attribute is intercepted using the E4X syntax:

```
<mx:Tree xmlns:mx="http://www.adobe.com/2006/mxml"
dataProvider="{treeData}"
labelField="@label"
showRoot="false"
 width="90%"
 height="100%">
```

Finally, by setting the showRoot property as false, the Tree has been prevented from displaying the root node. This MXML component represents your menu, which will be inserted in a TabNavigator container (you'll add it in the main application file in Step 14).

5. Save the TreeMenu component.

6. Create a second MXML component, still in the same folder (com/flexsolutions/chapter9/controls), by selecting File ➤ New ➤ MXML Component and save it with the name TopList. Base the component on a List control. In fact, it will populate the second tab of the TabNavigator and show the most-sold products in your web application. You will now send a simple String item as a dataProvider to the List control, as the following code shows:

```
<mx:List xmlns:mx="http://www.adobe.com/2006/mxml"  width="90%"
        height="100%">
<mx:dataProvider>
<mx:String>1. iPhone</mx:String>
<mx:String>2. Flex Builder 3</mx:String>
<mx:String>3. Levi's Jeans</mx:String>
<mx:String>4. Stephen King</mx:String>
```

9

```
<mx:String>5. Levi's Jeans</mx:String>
<mx:String>6. Nokia N95</mx:String>
<mx:String>7. Nike</mx:String>
<mx:String>8. iPod</mx:String>
<mx:String>9. MacBook Pro</mx:String>
<mx:String>10. Flex Solutions</mx:String>
</mx:dataProvider>
</mx:List>
```

The List control is populated by the String item defined in the dataProvider that was declared as a nested tag of the List. You can see the final result in Figure 9-6.

Figure 9-6. The List control is used on the second tab of the TabNavigator.

7. Save the MXML component.

8. Create the third MXML component, still in the com/ flexsolutions/chapter9/controls folder, by selecting File ➤ New ➤ MXML Component. Save it as FilterProduct. Base the component on a VBox. This component (shown in Figure 9-4 on the right of the list of items) lets the user filter the products of the store according to certain criteria. The filters are applied through a ComboBox control that permits you to choose the category to display, an HSLider control to select the price as a filtering parameter, and two CheckBox controls to see the products that have the set characteristics. Using a TextInput you can carry out a product search in the store. The complete code of the MXML component is the following:

```
<mx:VBox xmlns:mx="http://www.adobe.com/2006/mxml"
width="320" height="300">

<mx:Label text="Find a Product by Name"/>
<mx:HBox width="300">
<mx:TextInput styleName="glass" width="196"/>
<mx:Button styleName="glass" label="Search" />
</mx:HBox>

<mx:Spacer height="5"/>

<mx:Label text="Filter by Category"/>

<mx:ComboBox id="series" width="140">
<mx:dataProvider>
<mx:Array>
<mx:String>All Categories</mx:String>
<mx:String>Books</mx:String>
<mx:String>Leather Goods</mx:String>
<mx:String>Music</mx:String>
<mx:String>Consumer Electronics</mx:String>
</mx:Array>
</mx:dataProvider>
</mx:ComboBox>
```

```
<mx:Spacer height="18"/>

<mx:Label text="Filter by Price"/>

<mx:HSlider id="priceSlider" minimum="0" maximum="2000"
tickInterval="50" snapInterval="10"
width="280"  values="[0,2000]" labels="[$0,$2000]"/>

<mx:Spacer height="18"/>

<mx:Label text="Required Features"/>

<mx:Spacer height="4"/>
<mx:HBox>
<mx:CheckBox label="Free Delivery"/>

<mx:Spacer height="4"/>
<mx:CheckBox  label="Best Buy"/>
</mx:HBox>

</mx:VBox>
```

In this code there are two interesting things to look at. One is the use of the `<mx:Spacer>` tag, which enables you to save a lot of time in the layout phase of the design. This tag allows you to simply space the elements out in a vertical or horizontal way. So when your designer tells you, "You have to move that element three pixels to the left and two pixels down!" you can respond in a fraction of a second.

The second interesting portion of code uses the HSlider control. This control, similar to VSlider, allows you to select a value by moving a slider thumb between the end points of the slider track. In your code you have to set the minimum and maximum intervals for the user to drag the slider thumb with the minimum and maximum properties. These properties set the allowed values on the slider. Furthermore, with the tickInterval property, you set the value that will be applied at each movement of the slider (50 units, in this case). The labels property adds labels and sets them at each tick mark, while the snapInterval property enables you to define the values between the minimum and maximum that the user can select:

```
<mx:HSlider id="priceSlider" minimum="0" maximum="2000"
tickInterval="50" snapInterval="10"
width="280"  values="[0,2000]" labels="[$0,$2000]"/>
```

> *For more information about the* HSlider *visit the Adobe LiveDocs documentation page:* www.adobeauthorizations.com/livedocs/flex/2/langref/mx/controls/ sliderClasses/Slider.html.

9

9. Create the fourth and last MXML component, still in the com/flexsolutions/chapter9/controls folder, by selecting File ➤ New ➤ MXML Component and saving it as MyTileList. This will be the component to contain the list of products to be displayed in the center of the page. You have already dealt with the TileList control in the "What's involved" section of this chapter, and have commented the properties that you will use for this component:

```
<mx:HBox xmlns:mx="http://www.adobe.com/2006/mxml"
width="400" height="300">
<mx:TileList
width="400" height="300"
maxColumns="3" columnWidth="125"
paddingBottom="0" paddingLeft="0" paddingRight="0"  >
<mx:Script>
<![CDATA[

[Bindable]
[Embed(source="/assets/product1.gif")]
private var cam1:Class;

[Bindable]
[Embed(source="/assets/product2.gif")]
private var cam2:Class;

[Bindable]
[Embed(source="/assets/product3.gif")]
private var cam3:Class;

[Bindable]
[Embed(source="/assets/product4.gif")]
private var cam4:Class;


]]>
</mx:Script>
<mx:dataProvider>
<mx:Array>
<mx:Object label="Nike Shoes" icon="{cam1}"/>
<mx:Object label="Globalization" icon="{cam2}"/>
<mx:Object label="iMac" icon="{cam3}"/>
<mx:Object label="Mark Anthony" icon="{cam4}"/>
<mx:Object label="Mark Anthony" icon="{cam1}"/>
</mx:Array>
</mx:dataProvider>
</mx:TileList>
</mx:HBox>
```

The TileList is populated by the dataProvider that is made up of an Array of objects. For each Object, the label and icon properties are defined. The first, label, is the label displayed for each item; the second, icon, is linked with a binding to the image imported in the <mx:Script> code block:

```
<mx:Script>
<![CDATA[

[Bindable]
[Embed(source="/assets/product1.gif")]
private var cam1:Class;

[Bindable]
[Embed(source="/assets/product2.gif")]
private var cam2:Class;

 [Bindable]
[Embed(source="/assets/product3.gif")]
private var cam3:Class;

 [Bindable]
[Embed(source="/assets/product4.gif")]
private var cam4:Class;


]]>
</mx:Script>
```

With the [Embed] metadata you can load the images from the assets folder. Each image corresponds to a product displayed in the TileList container. To be able to import the images, you must declare a variable typed as Class, and made [Bindable].

The TileList automatically loads these images because a binding exists between these variables and the icon property of the dataProvider:

```
<mx:dataProvider>
<mx:Array>
<mx:Object label="Nike Shoes" icon="{cam1}"/>
<mx:Object label="Globalization" icon="{cam2}"/>
<mx:Object label="iMac" icon="{cam3}"/>
<mx:Object label="Mark Anthony" icon="{cam4}"/>
<mx:Object label="Mark Anthony" icon="{cam1}"/>
</mx:Array>
</mx:dataProvider>
```

Now that you have created all four MXML components that are needed for your application, you can define the main application file created in Step 2 and import them.

10. Create the custom namespace on the <mx:Application> tag that will specify the package in which the MXML components are saved:

```
<mx:Application xmlns:mx="http://www.adobe.com/2006/mxml"
layout="vertical" paddingTop="0"
xmlns:com="com.flexsolutions.chapter9.controls.*" >
```

9

You have also declared the paddingTop property that you have set to 0. In this way, the space between the browser and the first element that you insert in the application will be removed.

11. Insert the image that contains the header of the application, below the `<mx:Application>` tag:

```
<mx:Image source="assets/header.jpg" id="idHeader"  />
```

You can already save the file and run the application. As shown in Figure 9-7, the image imported is immediately displayed onscreen, and no space exists between the border of the browser and the Flex application.

> The image has not been embedded into the application. This means that in the deployment phase of the application you must also copy the assets folder and the relative contents. Otherwise, the application will not load the image.

Figure 9-7. The header image is imported and displayed.

12. Insert an ApplicationControlBar container to contain a navigation menu made up of the LinkButton and TextInput controls that are needed to insert the login and password for the registered users. Insert the following code below the `<mx:Image>` tag:

```
<mx:ApplicationControlBar width="960" cornerRadius="0">
<mx:LinkButton label="What's New"/>
<mx:LinkButton label="Events"/>
<mx:LinkButton label="Special Offer"/>
<mx:Spacer width="90%" />
<mx:Label text="User"/>
<mx:TextInput width="81"/>
<mx:Label text="Password"/>
<mx:TextInput width="81"/>
<mx:Button label="Login" width="44"/>
</mx:ApplicationControlBar>
```

The ApplicationControlBar container has the same width as the header image imported in the preceding step. You have specified this value in the width property of the container. In this way, you ensure that its width is the same as that of the image. When you do not know what the width or height of an element that you want to link to the dimensions of another element will be, you can get help from the binding feature of Flex by writing the following:

```
<mx:ApplicationControlBar width="{idHeader.width}" cornerRadius="0">
```

In this way, the width of the `ApplicationControlBar` will take on the same dimensions as the width of the Image.

13. Add an `HDividedBox` after the closure of the `ApplicationControlBar`, which you will need to separate the menu on the left from the list of products in the part on the right of the page.

```
<mx:HDividedBox width="{idHeader.width}">
</mx:HDividedBox>
```

This container also has a width equal to the dimension of the image.

14. Look at the menu on the left side of the `DividedBox`. For this part, as you can see in Figure 9-4, there are two tabs that show two different menus. The first is the component with the Tree control (TreeMenu.mxml), while the second is the list of the most-sold products (TopList.mxml). Therefore, add a `TabNavigator` that will contain these two components:

```
<mx:HDividedBox width="{idHeader.width}">

<mx:TabNavigator width="170" height="100%">
<mx:VBox label="Category">
<com:TreeMenu id="myTree" width="98%" height="100%" />
</mx:VBox>
<mx:VBox label="Top Order">
<com:TopList id="topOrder" width="98%" height="100%" />
</mx:VBox>
</mx:TabNavigator>

</mx:HDividedBox>
```

The TabNavigator has an absolute width (170 pixels), but its height is expressed in terms of percentages. In particular, your TabNavigator will occupy the whole height of the space in which it has been inserted. The first tab is a VBox that invokes the TreeMenu component. The measurements of height and width expressed in percentages (width="98%" height="100%") have also been specified for this component.

The second tab invokes the component TopList in a VBox container.

15. Move on to building the central part of the page, in which you see the list of products and fields to set the research parameters and filters. These elements are always found declared in the `HDividedBox` and make up the second part of the container. Add the image, positioned in the middle of the page, and then import the components `MyTileList` and `FilterProduct`:

```
</mx:TabNavigator>

<mx:VBox>

<mx:Image source="assets/promo.jpg"/>

<mx:HBox>
```

9

```
<com:MyTileList id="myList" width="70%" height="100%" />

<com:FilterProduct id="filterComp" />

</mx:HBox>
</mx:VBox>

</mx:HDividedBox>
```

Box containers have been used to sort the elements in a horizontal or vertical position. The image, unlike the list and search fields, is positioned vertically. For this reason it has been declared in a VBox container. Instead, the list of products with the search fields and filters are positioned horizontally, as shown in Figure 9-8.

Figure 9-8. With the Box container the central elements of the page have been positioned.

16. Finish the creation of your layout by inserting the footer image of the page:

```
</mx:HDividedBox>

<mx:Image source="assets/footer.jpg"/>

</mx:Application>
```

17. Save the file and run the application.

The final result is what you saw at the beginning of the solution in Figure 9-4.

In this solution, you used a box and container layout by using the containers that Flex puts at your disposal. In the next solution you will apply another approach for the creation of the layout: the constraint-based layout.

Expert tips

Containers are a powerful means for creating complex layouts and for positioning elements in a precise way. But they can turn out to be problem because if used in an incorrect way, they can reduce the rendering performance of the application. To understand how to optimize the use of the containers for layout and the positioning/sizing of the elements, you must first understand how the rules that Flex applies to the components work.

Every container or control in Flex has default values. For example, the HBox container lays out its content in a horizontal row, while the Application container applies 24-pixel padding values, and so on.

This means that you must leave Flex to apply the default values and instead concentrate on the values that can be changed.

If, for example, the layout of an application must be mainly developed in a vertical way instead of inserting a VBox container immediately under the declaration of an <mx:Application> tag, it would be better to act on the layout property of the Application.

Instead of writing the following code:

```
<mx:Application xmlns:mx="http://www.adobe.com/2006/mxml">
<mx:VBox>
```

you can optimize the code and eliminate the nested VBox container by acting on the layout property of the Application:

```
<mx:Application xmlns:mx="http://www.adobe.com/2006/mxml"
layout="vertical" >
```

In fact, the rule to keep in mind and to apply when a container-based layout is applied is to try to reduce the number of containers used and, even more importantly, to limit the number of nesting Box containers inside a Panel or <mx:Application> tag. By avoiding nested containers, the Flash Player will render the Flex application more quickly onscreen.

Solution 9-2: Designing a constraint-based layout

The preceding solution created the layout of a Flex application, starting from the design that was provided by a hypothetical designer. You used the features of Flex to automatically position the containers and the controls, applying predefined rules to every element. You were careful to give width and height dimensions to the page elements, sometimes specifying them in pixels, other times in percentages.

However, another approach exists for positioning and laying out elements in a page: absolute positioning. This technique allows you to position user interface (UI) elements on the page with absolute precision. This means that for every element on the page, the x and y properties are specified. These properties define the exact positioning of that element onscreen. Not all containers, however, support this type of positioning. In fact, only the following three containers allow you to have children with absolute positioning:

9

- Application: Allows you to choose to apply an absolute positioning through the layout property
- Panel: Like the <mx:Application> tag, puts forward the same layout property that can be set as absolute
- Canvas: A container that accepts only the absolute positioning of the elements

The layout property accepts the following values that are static properties of the ContainerLayout class: ContainerLayout.VERTICAL, ContainerLayout.HORIZONTAL, and ContainerLayout.ABSOLUTE.

The Canvas container, like the other containers, specifies and draws an imaginary rectangular region in which it positions the child elements in an absolute way. With this container, you can, therefore, use only the layouts based on constraint or absolute positioning.

The following example illustrates the use of the Canvas container:

```
<mx:Canvas x="213" y="75" width="200" height="200">
<mx:DateField x="100" y="10"/>
<mx:Label x="6" y="13" text="Select a Date:"/>
<mx:Label x="8" y="55" text="Select a Quantity"/>
<mx:NumericStepper x="132" y="53"/>
<mx:HSlider x="10" y="127" width="180"/>
<mx:Label x="10" y="101" text="Filter by Price"/>
</mx:Canvas>
```

For each control inserted in the Canvas, you have specified the x and y property. The coordinates have the intersection of the Cartesian axis in the upper-left corner, as shown in Figure 9-9. In this way, you have positioned the element in the container in an absolute manner.

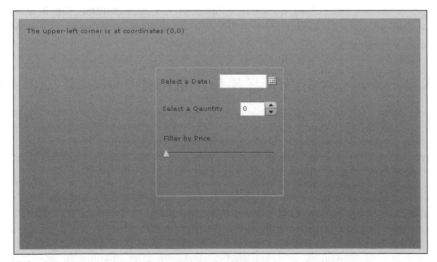

Figure 9-9. The Canvas container positions the elements in an absolute manner.

> *The x and y properties also accept negative values, so you can position an element outside of the visible area of the page and then change its position through ActionScript.*

The Canvas container does not have any particular default property for automatically distancing the elements by adding borders of padding. This means that when you create the layout, you must ensure that the elements are not overlapping. To make this operation simpler, you can switch Flex Builder to Design view.

You can create a constraint-based layout only if the containers you use support the absolute value for their layout property. The constraint-based approach forces the positioning of elements relative to the rectangular region of the parent container. In this way you anchor the child element to the edges of the container.

What you get is an element that changes its position based on the dimension and position of the container. The final result is that if the user resizes the application window (the browser window), the elements recalculate its new position.

Before beginning to apply a constraint-based layout, it is worthwhile to understand which benefits or disadvantages there are in the use of this approach for the application design. Certainly the performance of the application in the rendering phase of the layout will have benefits because Flash Player does not make the CPU work too hard to calculate the position of the elements of the page in an automatic way. The x and y positions are, in fact, specified. The disadvantage is that the position for every element must be specified, and the interface of the application does not redimension at the different resolutions or when the user scales the browser window size.

In this solution, you will see how to create a constraint-based layout using the Flex Builder integrated development environment (IDE).

What's involved

You have seen that to create a constraint-based layout, you must use containers that support absolute layout. Therefore, you must study the layout of your application so that the elements of the page will be contained in a Canvas container, or in the <mx:Application> tag or Panel, but with the property layout set to absolute.

Having considered this, you can use the constraint-based properties that any Flex component puts forward to specify the constraints:

- top, bottom, left, right: These properties represent the distance between the sides of the component and the container.

- horizontalCenter, verticalCenter: These properties represent the distance between the component's center point and the container's center point.

The following example applies constraints to the Canvas container and to a Label control that is located in the Application, whose layout property is set as absolute:

```
<mx:Application xmlns:mx=http://www.adobe.com/2006/mxml
 layout="absolute">

<mx:Canvas width="200" height="200"
horizontalCenter="0" verticalCenter="0">
<mx:DateField y="10"  x="100"/>
<mx:Label x="6" y="13" text="Select a Date:"/>
<mx:Label x="8" y="55" text="Select a Quantity"/>
<mx:NumericStepper x="132" y="53"/>
<mx:HSlider x="10" y="127" width="180"/>
<mx:Label x="10" y="101" text="Filter by Price"/>
</mx:Canvas>
<mx:Label text="The upper-left corner is at coordinates (0,0)"
left="20" top="20"/>

</mx:Application>
```

The Canvas has the properties horizontalCenter and verticalCenter set at 0. This enables you to always position it in the center of the page, with respect to the visible portion in the browser. Instead, the Label control is anchored at the left and top sides 20 pixels from its container's sides (in this case, the container is the Application itself).

In this solution you will create a constraint-based layout by using the Navigator container Accordion. This particular container enables you to define a sequence of collapsible containers that are rendered visible one at a time. The other panels can be opened only through the title bar.

This container allows you to notably improve the usability of the application and is useful in any application in which several screens are required to complete an operation. A classic use of an Accordion is to represent a registration form in which users have to fill in multiple form items. In this scenario, the user must usually insert a lot of information: personal data, shipping address, payment options, credit card information, preferences, and so on.

To declare an Accordion, the <mx:Accordion> tag is used; for every child you must specify the label property, which will be used as a title bar. The following example shows an Accordion container with three panels, shown in Figure 9-10:

```
<mx:Application xmlns:mx=http://www.adobe.com/2006/mxml
 layout="absolute">

<mx:Accordion width="400" height="250"
horizontalCenter="0" verticalCenter="0">

<mx:Canvas label="Step 1" width="100%" height="100%">
<mx:DateField y="10"  x="100"/>
<mx:Label x="6" y="13" text="Select a Date:"/>
<mx:Label x="8" y="55" text="Select a Quantity"/>
<mx:NumericStepper x="132" y="53"/>
<mx:HSlider x="10" y="127" width="180"/>
```

```
<mx:Label x="10" y="101" text="Filter by Price"/>
</mx:Canvas>

<mx:Form label="Step 2" width="100%" height="100%">
<mx:FormHeading label="Insert you personal information">
</mx:FormHeading>
<mx:FormItem label="Name">
<mx:TextInput>
</mx:TextInput>
</mx:FormItem>
<mx:FormItem label="Last Name">
<mx:TextInput>
</mx:TextInput>
</mx:FormItem>
<mx:FormItem label="Email">
<mx:TextInput>
</mx:TextInput>
</mx:FormItem>
</mx:Form>

<mx:Form label="Step 3" width="100%" height="100%">
<mx:FormHeading label="Payment Option">
</mx:FormHeading>
<mx:FormItem label="Name">
<mx:RadioButtonGroup id="myRB" />
<mx:RadioButton groupName="myRB" label="Credit Card" />
<mx:RadioButton groupName="myRB" label="Bank Account" />
<mx:RadioButton groupName="myRB" label="PayPal" />
</mx:FormItem>
</mx:Form>

</mx:Accordion>

</mx:Application>
```

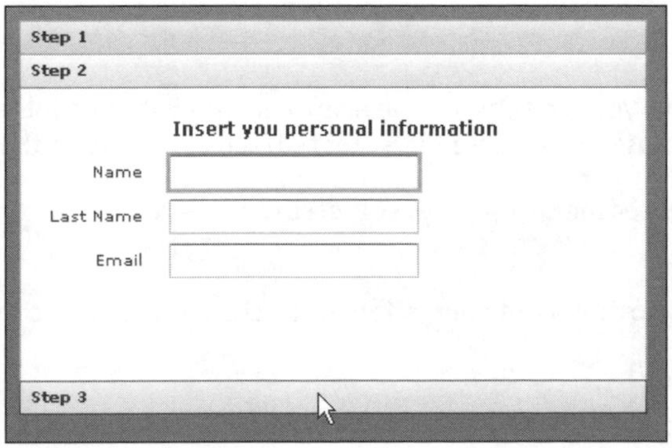

9

Figure 9-10. The Accordion container shows three child panels.

Your Accordion container creates a sequence of three child panels, but displays only one panel at a time. Each container declared in each child panel defines the label property that is used as a title for the child panel:

```
<mx:Canvas label="Step 1" width="100%" height="100%">

<mx:Form label="Step 2" width="100%" height="100%">

<mx:Form label="Step 3" width="100%" height="100%">
```

You can select another panel by clicking directly on the title bar or by modifying the following properties via ActionScript:

- selectedChild: Contains the identifier, id property, of the active child
- selectedIndex: The index of the active child
- numChildren: Contains the number of children defined in the Accordion

You can, therefore, easily add Button controls that enable you to move from one panel to another on the click event. Add the following code to the preceding example:

```
<mx:Application xmlns:mx="http://www.adobe.com/2006/mxml"
layout="absolute">

<mx:HBox horizontalCenter="10" verticalCenter="-150">
<mx:Label x="114" y="26" text="Navigate the Accordion's child"/>
<mx:Button  label="Previous"
click="myACC.selectedIndex = myACC.selectedIndex - 1;" x="306" y="24"/>
<mx:Button  label="Next"
click="myACC.selectedIndex = myACC.selectedIndex + 1;" x="390" y="24"/>
</mx:HBox>

<mx:Accordion width="400" height="250" id="myACC"
horizontalCenter="0" verticalCenter="0">

<! -- the same code of the example above -->

</mx:Accordion>
```

In an HBox container you have inserted a Label and two Button controls. The buttons on the click event increase or decrease the selectedIndex property of the Accordion:

```
myACC.selectedIndex = myACC.selectedIndex - 1
myACC.selectedIndex + 1
```

In this way, the Accordion container is forced to change the view of the child panel, as shown in Figure 9-11.

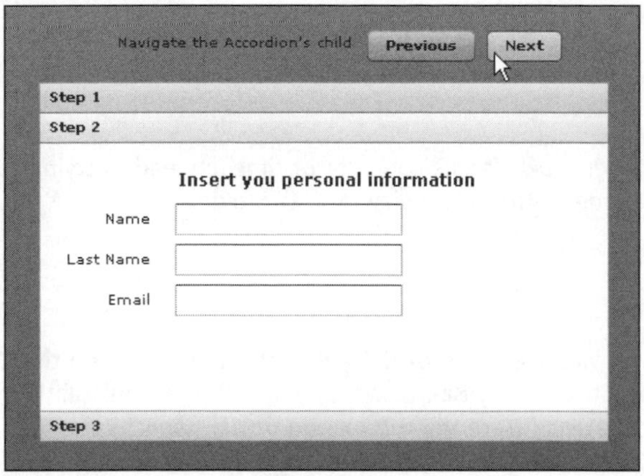

Figure 9-11. By clicking the Button controls, you can navigate through the Accordion container.

Even though it is simple to act on the properties left, top, bottom, and right by defining them via code, Flex Builder offers a powerful visual system to create these layout types. In fact, by moving on to Design mode and accessing the Flex Properties view under the Layout category, all the constraints properties can be set in a visual way.

Figure 9-12 shows the Constraints view and how to set the values for the various properties by acting on the check box that the interface puts forward.

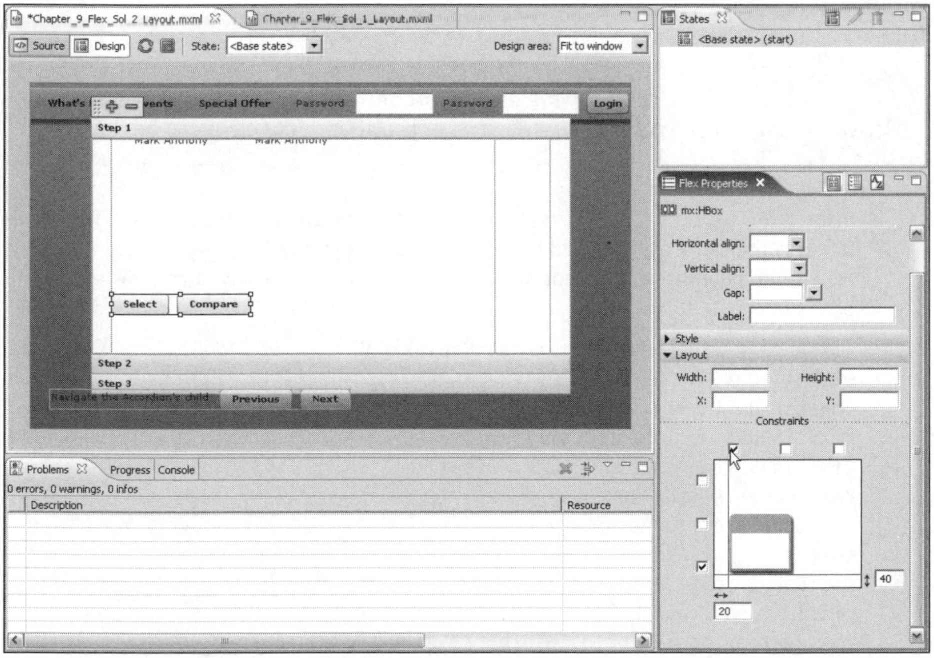

Figure 9-12. In the Flex Properties view under the layout category, constraint settings can be applied in a visual way.

In the example shown in Figure 9-12 you have set the bottom and left properties as follows:

```
<mx:HBox bottom="40" left="20">
```

Using this visual panel usually saves you a lot of time, instead of trying to write the values in the Code view mode of the Editor view of Flex Builder.

How to build it

In this solution, you will use some of the elements created in Solution 9-1. In particular, inserting the ApplicationControlBar, to which you will give constraints in order to always maintain a certain distance from the top margin of the application. Then, in the first child panel of the Accordion container, you will insert the MyTileList container saved in the com.flexsolutions.chapter9.controls package.

1. Create a new application file by selecting File ➤ New ➤ MXML Application and give it the name Chapter_9_Flex_Sol_2_Layout.mxml. To invoke the MXML component MyTileList, you must first create the custom namespace in the <mx:Application> tag:

```
<mx:Application xmlns:mx="http://www.adobe.com/2006/mxml"
layout="absolute"
xmlns:com="com.flexsolutions.chapter9.controls.*">
```

Be sure that the layout property of the <mx:Application> tag is set to absolute. This is a necessary move to be able to create a constraint-based layout.

> Note that the default value for the layout property is vertical. If you leave this property empty, the vertical value will be applied to its child elements by default.

2. Insert the ApplicationControlBar under the <mx:Application> tag. This container is the same as that used in Solution 9-1, but you will specify the top property, which will guarantee that that ApplicationControlBar always has a distance of 5 pixels from the top border:

```
<mx:ApplicationControlBar cornerRadius="0"
width="100%" x="0" top="5">
<mx:LinkButton label="What's New"/>
<mx:LinkButton label="Events"/>
<mx:LinkButton label="Special Offer"/>
<mx:Spacer width="90%" />
<mx:Label text="Password"/>
<mx:TextInput width="81"/>
<mx:Label text="Password"/>
<mx:TextInput width="81"/>
<mx:Button label="Login" width="44"/>
</mx:ApplicationControlBar>
```

Regarding dimensions of width, the container will occupy the entire portion of the screen, but will position itself always at 5 pixels from the top border of the <mx:Application> tag. Even if the user changes the window size, the container will recalculate its position to respect the value specified in the top property.

3. Insert the Accordion container below the ApplicationControlBar. This container will also have constraint properties that will force it to remain always positioned at the center of the page. To obtain this result, set the horizontalCenter and verticalCenter properties like so:

```
<mx:Accordion width="80%" height="80%" id="myACC"
horizontalCenter="0" verticalCenter="0">

</mx:Accordion>
```

To center an element, you must set the two horizontalCenter and verticalCenter properties to 0. Furthermore, you have given a height dimension as a percentage so that it will occupy 80 percent of the space of the window.

4. You can now insert the child panels in the Accordion. In this example, you will create three child panels. The first panel contains the component MyTileList, which you will declare in a Canvas container. This enables you to define values of constraints for the MXML component that will be relative to the edges of the Accordion container, not to the Application. Insert the first child panel with the following code below the opening <mx:Accordion> tag:

```
<mx:Accordion width="80%" height="80%" id="myACC"
horizontalCenter="0" verticalCenter="0">

<mx:Canvas label="Step 1"
width="100%" height="100%">

<com:MyTileList id="myList" width="459" height="80%"

 horizontalCenter="0" verticalCenter="0"/>

<mx:HBox bottom="10" left="10">
<mx:Button label="Select"/>
<mx:Button label="Compare"/>
</mx:HBox>

</mx:Canvas>
```

The MyTileList component is positioned at the center of the area occupied by the Canvas container in the Accordion. Given that you have assigned a value of 100% to the width and height of the Canvas, the MyTileList component will be positioned exactly at the center of the area that the Accordion will put at your disposal.

After the component, you have inserted an HBox container with two Button controls. The Box container is positioned 10 pixels from the bottom and left borders of the container. You can now save and compile the file. Try to change the dimension of the browser

9

window and watch how the positions of the elements change as a consequence. In particular, the MyTileList component will always position itself in the center while the two Button controls will position themselves at the bottom left, as shown in Figure 9-13.

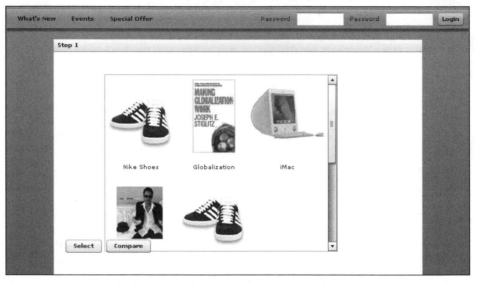

Figure 9-13. By resizing the browser window, the ApplicationControlBar and the elements in the Accordion will position themselves, respective to the values that you have given in the constraint properties.

5. Add the second child panel for the Accordion by inserting another Canvas with a Form in it. Insert the following code immediately under the closure of the previous Canvas container in the Accordion:

```
<mx:Canvas label="Step 2" width="100%" height="100%">
<mx:Form height="100%"
top="10"  left="40" right="20">
<mx:FormHeading label="Personal information">
</mx:FormHeading>
<mx:FormItem label="Name">
<mx:TextInput>

</mx:TextInput>
</mx:FormItem>
<mx:FormItem label="Last Name">
<mx:TextInput>

</mx:TextInput>
</mx:FormItem>
<mx:FormItem label="Email">
<mx:TextInput>
```

```
</mx:TextInput>
</mx:FormItem>
</mx:Form>
</mx:Canvas>
```

The Form sets the following constraint properties:

```
top="10"
left="40"
right="20"
```

This means having a distance from the upper border of the Canvas equal to 10 pixels, and of 40 and 20 pixels from the right and left borders of the Canvas.

This second child panel was also created following a constraints-based layout.

6. Insert the last child panel, which will be a simple Form without any declaration of constraint type. If you try to declare the top, left, bottom, or right properties for these Form containers you will see that nothing will happen because the Form is not contained in a container that supports absolute positioning. Immediately under the closure of the Canvas, insert the following code:

```
<mx:Form label="Step 3" width="100%" height="100%">
<mx:FormHeading label="Payment Option">
</mx:FormHeading>
<mx:FormItem label="Name">
<mx:RadioButtonGroup id="myRB" />
<mx:RadioButton groupName="myRB" label="Credit Card" />
<mx:RadioButton groupName="myRB" label="Bank Account" />
<mx:RadioButton groupName="myRB" label="PayPal" />
</mx:FormItem>

</mx:Form>

</mx:Accordion>
```

7. Finish the application by inserting two Button controls that will enable you to navigate the Accordion container by changing its selectedIndex property. Insert the following code underneath:

```
<mx:HBox bottom="20" height="22" left="20">
<mx:Label x="114" y="26" text="Navigate the Accordion's child"/>
<mx:Button  label="Previous"
click="myACC.selectedIndex = myACC.selectedIndex - 1;" />
<mx:Button  label="Next"
click="myACC.selectedIndex = myACC.selectedIndex + 1;""/>
</mx:HBox>
</mx:Application>
```

The HBox container has the constraint properties bottom and left set at 20 pixels.

8. Save the file and run the application.

9

If you resize the window of the browser, you will see how all the elements declared in the absolute container, and to which you have applied constraints, will be repositioned, as shown in Figure 9-13.

The advantages of using this approach of constraints-based layout include being able to position the objects in the page in a precise and reliable way. Therefore, if your graphics are formed of pixels and require absolute precision, this is without a doubt the technique that you should follow. These types of layout are, however, not ideal when it is necessary to dynamically change the size of items that do not all fit.

Expert tips

By adding simple effects on the resizing of the elements in the application, you can render the entire application more attractive with little effort. In fact, with Flex behavior you can add animation and motion to any object in response to an action (system- or user-based).

A **behavior** is a combination of a trigger paired with an effect. A **trigger** is an action, such as a mouse click on a component, a component getting focus, or a component becoming visible. An **effect** is a visible or audible change to the target component that occurs over a period of time, measured in milliseconds. Examples of effects are fading, resizing, and moving a component.

1. Change your application by simply adding a Fade effect. Insert the following code above the <mx:ApplicationControlBar> tag:

   ```
   <mx:Fade id="myFadeEffect" alphaFrom="0" alphaTo="1" />
   ```

For this effect, you have used the alphaFrom and alphaTo properties that create a Fade effect that goes from transparent to opaque. This effect has only been declared, and if you try to run the file, you will not see anything happen. You must first apply this effect to the object and at the event on which it should release.

2. The Accordion, as with all UIComponent classes, puts forward the resizeEffect property. This property releases when an event of resize type is run. In the example, a resize event releases every time the user carries out a resize of the browser window. The resizeEffect property accepts the identifier of the effect that you have declared in the preceding step as a value:

   ```
   <mx:Accordion width="80%" height="80%" id="myACC"
   horizontalCenter="0" verticalCenter="0" resizeEffect="{myFadeEffect}">
   ```

3. Save the file and run the application to see the Fade effect applied to the Accordion and its child panels.

Solution 9-3: Customizing Flex components using styles

Styles in Flex allow you to change the appearance of the application. The main risk of using the controls and containers that Flex offers is having usable and functional applications that have quite similar graphic interfaces because the Flex components have predefined properties that define their graphic aspect.

Using styles, it is possible to modify many of these properties and to give a more personal graphic touch to the application. In fact, styles enable you to change settings such as the color, the dimension of the font, the background, and so on, and they can be programmed and applied both at runtime and at compile time (see Solution 11-3).

To define the styles in Flex is really very simple in that you use CSS as the language. Therefore, in the same way in which you define the CSS for the elements of an XHTML page, in Flex you use the CSS to change the aspect of the elements that make up the Flex application.

To define a style in an MXML page, use the `<mx:Style>` tag, in which you can write CSS code to change and specify the properties that you intend to customize. The `<mx:Style>` tag also enables you to load an external CSS file. This technique is very useful in that it allows you to define a file that is external to the document that can be applied and reused across different projects.

There are different methods to apply and define the styles, and the use of an approach over another depends obviously on the result that you intend to obtain. The styles can be declared in the following ways:

- **Global styles definitions** are applied to the entire application; often used to declare a background color, a font type, or whatever settings must be applied at global level to the entire application. The global styles definition has the lowest precedence in that if one of the other definitions of style is used in the application, the global definition will be overridden.

- **Inline styles definitions** define styles in the tag on which you want to apply them. These settings will be applied only to the instances of a component.

- **Type selectors** help you apply a new style to an entire category of a specific component. Imagine having to apply the same styles to the ComboBox controls. Instead of applying this style for every instance of the ComboBox component, you can declare a type selector style directly on all types of ComboBox controls.

- **Class selectors** define the settings that can be recalled in a Flex component through the styleName property. In this way, all the definitions declared for that CSS class will be automatically inherited by the component that has recalled them. These style definitions also render reuse of the CSS in the project for every component you want.

- **External style definitions** let you declare a CSS file external to the application and to then recall and reuse its definitions in a Flex project. The external CSS file is created just like XHTML—by inserting CSS code in the file.

9

In this solution you will see how to change the styles of the application created in Solution 9-1.

> *Flex does not permit you to change all the properties of a component through styles, and not all CSS properties are supported. For example, Flex does not support the ID selector. Furthermore, the styles do not permit you to change the shape of a component. To obtain this result you must instead use the skins, or graphical elements (or ActionScript classes), which permit you to completely change the graphical aspect of a component.*

What's involved

Before moving on to the example that you will use for this solution, you will see how the different approaches for the declaration of Flex styles differ.

Begin with global style creation. This approach enables you to define styles that are applied at global level to the entire application and to all its components. You use the global selector in a CSS declaration:

```
<mx:Style>
global
{
font-family: Arial;
font-size: 18;
}
</mx:Style>

<mx:Label text="This Style is applied by a global selector" />

<mx:ComboBox>
<mx:String>Simple Text</mx:String>
<mx:String>Simple Text</mx:String>
<mx:String>Simple Text</mx:String>
</mx:ComboBox>
```

The text in the Label and the ComboBox control inherit the styles declared in the `<mx:Style>` block and in the global selector. Figure 9-14 shows how the styles are applied to the two controls.

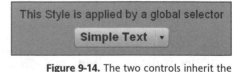

Figure 9-14. The two controls inherit the global styles.

Now apply the inline styles. These definitions are written directly in the tag to which you want to apply them. The following code is added to that created for the global style definition to help you to better understand the inheritance for the styles.

These are examples of inline styles definitions:

```
<mx:Style>
global
{
font-family: Arial;
font-size: 18;
}
</mx:Style>

<mx:Label text="This Style is applied by a global selector" />

<mx:ComboBox>
<mx:String>Simple Text</mx:String>
<mx:String>Simple Text</mx:String>
<mx:String>Simple Text</mx:String>
</mx:ComboBox>

<mx:NumericStepper id="numericStepper"
 color="#ff0080" disabledColor="#AAB3B3"/>
<mx:Label  text="This Style is applied by an Inline definition"
fontFamily="Arial" fontSize="12" fontWeight="bold"/>
```

In this code example, you defined the NumericStepper font color and the disabledColor, which is the color that will be applied when the component is disabled. Furthermore, the fontFamily and the fontSize have been specified like the Label control (declared immediately after).

As shown in Figure 9-15, the NumericStepper and the Label control underneath override the settings defined for the global selector and instead apply the style definitions applied inline.

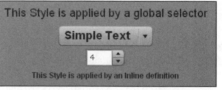

Figure 9-15. The two controls inherit the global styles.

The type style definitions enable you to define the styles that will be applied to an entire category of components. To declare a type selector, use the name of the component for which a style should be defined. The following code applies type selector styles to the <mx:Application> tag and to a Panel container:

```
<mx:Style>
global
{
font-family: Arial;
font-size: 18;
}

    Application
    {
    backgroundColor: #0066cc;
```

```
        backgroundGradientColors: #106a96, #0099ff;
        backgroundGradientAlphas: 1, 1;
        themeColor: #009dff;
        color: #0b333c;
    }


    Panel
    {
        corner-radius: 0;
        header-height: 27;
        background-color: #0099ff;
        color: #000000;
        border-thickness: 12;
        border-color: #cccccc;
        background-alpha:28;
        }


    </mx:Style>

    <mx:Panel layout="vertical"
    title="This Styles are applied from a Global selector"
     height="245">

    <mx:Label text="This Style is applied by a global selector" />
    <mx:ComboBox>
    <mx:String>Simple Text</mx:String>
    <mx:String>Simple Text</mx:String>
    <mx:String>Simple Text</mx:String>
    </mx:ComboBox>
    <mx:NumericStepper id="numericStepper"
     color="#ff0080" disabledColor="#AAB3B3"
     fontFamily="Verdana" fontSize="12"/>
     <mx:Label  text="This Style is applied by an Inline definition"
    fontFamily="Arial" fontSize="12" fontWeight="bold"/>
    </mx:Panel>
```

Applying a style to the <mx:Application> tag, which is the root tag of the Flex application, means changing the aspect of the entire project. In this code example, you have declared the color settings of the background and the font for the <mx:Application> tag:

```
    Application
    {
    backgroundColor: #0066cc;
    backgroundGradientColors: #106a96, #0099ff;
    backgroundGradientAlphas: 1, 1;
    color: #0b333c;
    }
```

For the Panel, you have changed physical aspects of the container. In fact, set the corner-radius property to 0 and you have eliminated the rounded borders of the classic Panel; and with the header-height property, you have changed the height of the header:

```
Panel
{
    corner-radius: 0;
    header-height: 27;
    background-color: #0099ff;
    color: #000000;
    border-thickness: 12;
    border-color: #cccccc;
    background-alpha:28;
    }
```

Figure 9-16 shows the final result with all the styles applied.

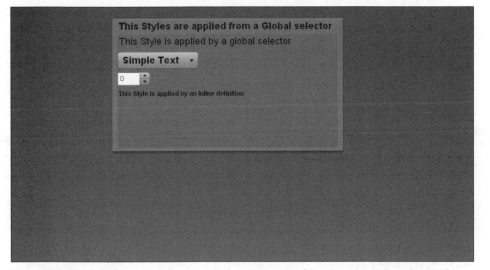

Figure 9-16. The type selector styles are applied on the <mx:Application> tag and on the Panel container.

Despite the fact that you have checked only a few styles of the application, it has already been notably changed.

The class selectors enable you to define style settings that are linked to a class. These definitions can be recalled by any component using the styleName property. Add two class selector definitions to the code that you will then apply to the ComboBox control and to a Button control that you will insert in the code:

```
<mx:Style>
global
{
font-family: Arial;
```

```
font-size: 18;
}

Panel
{
corner-radius: 0;
header-height: 27;
background-color: #0099ff;
color: #000000;
border-thickness: 12;
border-color: #cccccc;
background-alpha:28;
}

Application
{
backgroundColor: #0066cc;
backgroundGradientColors: #106a96, #0099ff;
backgroundGradientAlphas: 1, 1;
themeColor: #009dff;
color: #0b333c;
}

.myClass1
{
textSelectedColor:#2B333C;
textRollOverColor:#2B333C;
disabledColor:#AAB3B3;
color:#0B333C;
}

.myButtonClass
{
cornerRadius: 0;
textIndent: 0;
letterSpacing: 3;
highlightAlphas: 0, 0.62;
color: #0000ff;
fontFamily: Georgia;
fontSize: 12;
fontWeight: bold;
}

</mx:Style>

<mx:Panel layout="vertical"
title="This Style is applied from a Global selector"  height="245">
<mx:Label text="This Style is applied by a global selector" />
```

```
<mx:ComboBox styleName="myClass1">
<mx:String>Simple Text</mx:String>
<mx:String>Simple Text</mx:String>
<mx:String>Simple Text</mx:String>
</mx:ComboBox>

<mx:NumericStepper id="numericStepper"
 color="#ff0080" disabledColor="#AAB3B3"
 fontFamily="Verdana" fontSize="12"/>

<mx:Label  text="This Style is applied by an Inline definition"
fontFamily="Arial" fontSize="12" fontWeight="bold"/>

<mx:Button label="Button" styleName="myButtonClass"/>
</mx:Panel>
```

The two declarations of styles with the class selector are defined always using the dot in front of the name of the class. This is a rule that enables Flex to interpret the definitions that are not selector types, but are class selector types. The same standard is used by CSS for XHTML pages.

This example creates two class selectors for which the following property is defined:

```
.myClass1
{
textSelectedColor:#2B333C;
textRollOverColor:#2B333C;
disabledColor:#AAB3B3;
color:#0B333C;
}

.myButtonClass
{
cornerRadius: 0;
textIndent: 0;
letterSpacing: 3;
highlightAlphas: 0, 0.62;
color: #0000ff;
fontFamily: Georgia;
fontSize: 12;
fontWeight: bold;
}
```

These two style definitions were then applied to the ComboBox and to the Button controls through the styleName property. With CSS you have defined many classes, but it could turn out to be difficult to apply them via code and to remember the names. With Flex Builder, you can easily apply the style definitions class, visibly moving to Design mode in Editor view. In fact, by selecting the component to which you want to apply the class definition, from the Flex Explorer view under the Style category, there is a drop-down menu style. From this menu, you can apply the class to that component, as shown in Figure 9-17.

9

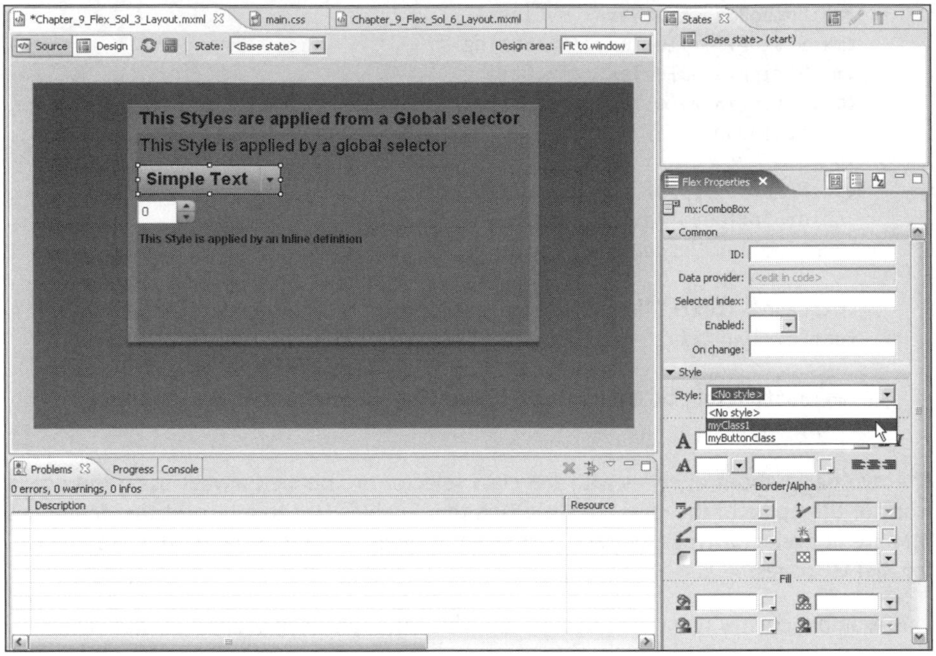

Figure 9-17. Applying the styleName property of the components, linking it to the class definition declared in the <mx:Style> block

```
<mx:ComboBox styleName="myClass1">
<mx:String>Simple Text</mx:String>
<mx:String>Simple Text</mx:String>
<mx:String>Simple Text</mx:String>
</mx:ComboBox>
<mx:Button label="Button" styleName="myButtonClass"/>
```

The two classes declared in the <mx:Style> tag have been applied to the ComboBox and to the Button by declaring the name of the class in the styleName property.

> *When the class selectors are recalled and applied to the* styleName *property, the dot in front of the name of the class is no longer used.*

The last approach in the style declaration uses an external CSS file to recall all the styles. To create an external page of styles, all you need to do is create a new CSS file from Flex Builder by selecting File ➤ New ➤ File CSS. The CSS file will contain the only CSS declarations contained in the <mx:Style> block. In your example, your external CSS file will contain the following code:

```
/* CSS file
/* Path: assets/
/* File Name: main.css
```

```
*/

global
{
font-family: Arial;
font-size: 18;
}

Panel
{
    corner-radius: 0;
    header-height: 27;
    background-color: #0099ff;
    color: #000000;
    border-thickness: 12;
    border-color: #cccccc;
    background-alpha:28;
    }

    Application
    {
    backgroundColor: #0066cc;
    backgroundGradientColors: #106a96, #0099ff;
    backgroundGradientAlphas: 1, 1;
    themeColor: #009dff;
    color: #0b333c;
}

.myClass1
{
textSelectedColor:#2B333C;
textRollOverColor:#2B333C;
disabledColor:#AAB3B3;
color:#0B333C;
}

.myButtonClass
{
    cornerRadius: 0;
    textIndent: 0;
    letterSpacing: 3;
    highlightAlphas: 0, 0.62;
    color: #0000ff;
    fontFamily: Georgia;
    fontSize: 12;
    fontWeight: bold;
}
```

This CSS file includes the only CSS declarations without any MXML code.

9

To recall the external CSS file you will use the source property of the `<mx:Style>` tag, in which you will specify the path and the name of the CSS file to import:

```
<mx:Style source="assets/main.css"/>
```

In this solution you will apply the styles by using the different declarations illustrated in the section on the application created in Solution 9-1.

How to build it

For this solution, begin from the layout that you have designed in Solution 9-1 and create the styles that you will need to change its appearance.

1. Open the file Chapter_9_Flex_Sol_1_Layout.mxml from the Flex project and save it as Chapter_9_Flex_Sol_3_Layout.mxml.

2. Create a new CSS file in which you will declare all your styles. The approach of the external CSS file is preferred in that it separates the MXML declarations from the CSS styles. It therefore renders the code more legible and enables you to easily use the same CSS for different projects. Select File ➤ New ➤ CSS file and create the main.css file that you will save in the assets folder. The file created by Flex Builder is automatically opened in the IDE and is empty except for the first line of comment:

```
/* CSS file
```

3. Even though there isn't any particular order for writing the CSS files, it is best practice to follow the logical and hierarchical order of the CSS that will be applied to the application: global, type selector, and class selector. You could also decide to order the CSS declarations by the type of control. In this way, you would have the type selector declared together with the class selector that is applied to these same controls. Finally, if you intend to follow the approach used to create the CSS for XHTML pages, you can write the CSS declarations and divide them according to the logical portion of the page: header, menu, content, footer, font style, and so on.

> If you want to learn more about best practices of well-formed CSS, there are a lot of resources on the Web. Or pick up a book on CSS; for example, CSS Mastery: Advanced Web Standards Solutions, by friends of ED (www.friendsofed.com/book.html?isbn=1590596145).

4. Begin by inserting the styles for the `<mx:Application>` tag. In particular, you will load an image to use for the background. The background image will be a SWF file for which you will specify a symbol name. Open the CSS and write the first declaration:

```
Application
{
    backgroundImage: Embed(source="backgrounds.swf#bluestripe");
    themeColor: #000066;
}
```

The backgroundImage property allows you to specify an image to use as background. For your solution you have loaded a SWF file (that you will find in the assets folder), in which different graphic symbols have been created. The graphic symbol that you want to use is specific, with the # symbol followed by the identifier of the symbol:

```
backgroundImage: Embed(source="backgrounds.swf#bluestripe");
```

The image is embedded in the page and merged into the compiled SWF file. The backgrounds.swf file embeds different graphic symbols that you can use as backgrounds for your application. To load a different graphic symbol, change the value after the # and assign one of the following values to it: greenstripe, redstripe, industrial, or tartan.

The themeColor property enables you to specify a value that will be used throughout the Flex application and on components. The values that accept this variable, aside from the hexadecimal ones, are the following:

- haloOrange
- haloBlue
- haloSilver
- haloGreen

These constants refer to the Halo theme supported by Flex (discussed later in this chapter).

5. Add the style declaration for the ApplicationControlBar to the CSS by inserting a type selector:

```
ApplicationControlBar
{
    backgroundColor: #ffffff;
    backgroundAlpha: 0;
    cornerRadius: 17;
    dropShadowEnabled: true;
    shadowDistance: 3;
    shadowDirection: center;
    dropShadowColor: #000099;
}
```

For this component, the background color, the alpha, the shadow settings, and the corner radius have changed. Figure 9-18 shows the result in the application.

Figure 9-18. The ApplicationControlBar inherits the styles defined in the CSS.

From the figure, you can also note how the background images have been applied to the application, having specified it in the <mx:Application> tag.

6. Change the appearance of the scrollbar that appears in the application. Create a type selector on the VScrollBar tag and act on its properties to change the color of the elements that make up the scrollbar:

```
VScrollBar
{
    cornerRadius: 0;
    fillAlphas: 0.25, 0.52, 1, 0.65;
    fillColors: #00ffff, #0000ff, #0033ff, #0066ff;
    trackColors: #0066ff, #00ffff;
    themeColor: #0000cc;
    borderColor: #000099;
}
```

7. Add other styles to change the appearance of the TextInput, Button, and ComboBox controls. Most of these controls are located in the right part of the application in the MXML component FilterProduct (<com:FilterProduct id="filterComp" />). By importing the CSS file into the Application file, all the external components will inherit the styles defined and imported in the main application. Add the following code in the main.css file immediately under the VScrollBar type selector:

```
TextInput
{
    borderStyle: solid;
    backgroundAlpha: 0.23;
    dropShadowEnabled: true;
}

Button
{
    cornerRadius: 0;
    highlightAlphas: 0.36, 0.61;
}

ComboBox
{
    cornerRadius: 0;
    backgroundAlpha: 0.18;
    dropDownStyleName: "myComboBoxDropDowns";
}

.myComboBoxDropDowns
{
    cornerRadius: 7;
    borderThickness: 5;
}
```

You have given a border style of solid type to the TextInput control, rendering its background color a little transparent, with the backgroundAlpha property. Finally, you have enabled a drop shadow effect.

For the Button and the ComboBox controls, you have removed the rounded borders, setting the cornerRadius property at 0. Furthermore, the ComboBox uses the dropDownStyleName property that enables you to link a class selector that will be applied to the drop-down list of the control. The myComboBoxDropDown class is declared immediately after the ComboBox type selector.

> *The* dropDownStyleName *property specifies the name of a* CSSStyleDeclaration *to be used by a* ComboBox. *In Flex 3,* dropDownStyleName *is a deprecated style. Use the new* dropdownStyleName *style instead.*

The final result of the style definitions created up until now is shown in Figure 9-19.

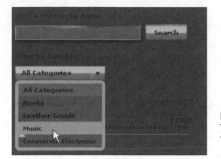

Figure 9-19.
The styles applied to the ComboBox, TextInput, and Button controls

8. Complete the styles for the section on the right of your application by creating a type selector for the HSlider control. Insert the following CSS code in the main.css file, immediately under the class selector .myComboBoxDropDown:

```
HSlider
{
    dataTipOffset: 10;
    tickLength: 4;
    tickThickness: 1;
    tickColor: #000099;
    showTrackHighlight: true;

}
```

An interesting property is showTrackHighlight, which marks the distance form the beginning of the HSlider to the position where the tick is dragged with a colored line (see Figure 9-20).

Figure 9-20.
The showTrackHighlight property mark with a colored line the distance from the dragged tick

9

9. Move on to the navigation menu of the application. On the left there is a TabNavigator that contains two child tabs to which two MXML components are linked. The first tag, Category, displays a Tree control with all the categories of products in the catalogue. The second tab, Top Order, displays a List control with the store's most-sold products. Insert styles to change the look and feel of the TabNavigator, just below the HSlider styles:

```
TabNavigator {
    tabHeight: 27;
    cornerRadius: 0;
    horizontalGap: 3;
    horizontalAlign: left;
    paddingLeft: 0;
    backgroundAlpha: 0.19;
    backgroundColor: #0099ff;
    borderStyle: inset;
    borderColor: #ffffff;
    dropShadowEnabled: true;
    tabStyleName: "myTabs";
    firstTabStyleName: "myTabs";
    lastTabStyleName: "myTabs";
    selectedTabTextStyleName: "mySelectedTabs";
}

.myTabs
{
    cornerRadius: 14;
    highlightAlphas: 0.36, 0;
    backgroundAlpha: 0.35;
    borderColor: #ffffff;
}
```

TabNavigator (similar to ComboBox) uses the selectedTabTextStyleName property that enables you to specify a class selector to use to define the style of the selected child tab. The myTabs class is specified immediately under it. This class changes the aspect of the Tab menu, whose rounded borders are rendered even more pronounced, and the background color is rendered more transparent.

10. Modify the aspect of the Tree control by inserting the following CSS code in the main.css file:

```
Tree
{
    backgroundAlpha: 0.21;
    backgroundColor: #0099cc;
    borderStyle: solid;
    borderThickness: 7;
    textIndent: 0;
    dropShadowEnabled: true;
```

```
    fontFamily: Arial;
    fontSize: 11;
    cornerRadius: 10;
}
```

You have added a background color, a solid border style, and a drop shadow effect to the control, and you have changed the font family and the font size.

Figure 9-21 shows the TabNavigator and Tree controls, modified in their aspects.

11. The second tab of the TabNavigator, Top Order, displays a List control with the most-requested products. Add the type selector for the List control in the CSS file:

```
List {
    backgroundAlpha: 0.4;
    borderThickness: 7;
    cornerRadius: 10;
}
```

Figure 9-22 shows the new appearance of the List control:

Figure 9-21. The TabNavigator and Tree controls with the new graphic appearance

12. Writing the CSS code in the main.css file is done. Now you must import it into your main application file. Open the file Chapter_9_Flex_Sol_3_Layout.mxml and insert the <mx:Style> tag immediately under the <mx:Application>:

```
<mx:Style source="assets/main.css" />
```

13. Insert a new <mx:Style> block and insert CSS code to change the formatting of the text used by the LinkButton control declared in the ApplicationControlBar:

```
<mx:Application xmlns:mx="http://www.adobe.com/
➥ 2006/mxml"
layout="vertical" xmlns:com="com.flexsolutions.
➥ chapter9.controls.*"
paddingTop="0">

<mx:Style source="assets/main.css" />

<mx:Style>
 LinkButton
{
  color: #ffffff;
  cornerRadius: 0;
  letterSpacing: 2;
  rollOverColor: #15a0f8;
  fontFamily: Arial;
```

Figure 9-22. The new appearance of the List control

9

```
        fontSize: 12;
        fontWeight: bold;
    }
    </mx:Style>

    <mx:Image source="assets/header.jpg" id="idHeader"/>

    <mx:ApplicationControlBar width="960" cornerRadius="0">
    <mx:LinkButton label="What's New"/>
    <mx:LinkButton label="Events"/>
    <mx:LinkButton label="Special Offer"/>

    <mx:Spacer width="90%" />
    <mx:Label text="Password"/>
    <mx:TextInput width="81"/>
    <mx:Label text="Password"/>
    <mx:TextInput width="81"/>
    <mx:Button label="Login" width="44"/>
    </mx:ApplicationControlBar>
```

This second <mx:Style> block demonstrates that it is possible to have an external CSS file applied in the application, but you can then create styles that act at the page level or at the level of the single component. The internal CSS style declarations will override the styles defined in the external CSS file.

14. Save and run the application.

With a few solutions, and by adding simple CSS code, you can transform your applications and render them much more attractive from a graphical point of view.

Figure 9-23 shows how the new application appears with Flex styles applied.

Figure 9-23. The new application with styles applied

Expert tips

Because the style inheritance can often create style problems in the application, it is necessary to understand how styles are applied. This classification sorts the priority with which Flex applies the styles:

1. Inline style

2. Class selector

3. Type selector

4. Global style

Suppose that you have the following situation of style declaration:

```
.myClass
{
    fontSize: 10;
}

Label
{
    fontSize: 12;
}
```

```
global
{
    fontSize: 14;
}
```

On the Label control you have the following definition:

```
<mx:Label  text="Text text text" id="myLabel"
fontSize="20" styleName="myClass"   />
```

When you run the application, your Label will assume 20 px as font size, or that defined as inline style.

> The setStyle() method allows you to change styles via ActionScript by accessing the instance name of components. Here is a simple example of setStyle() method usage:
>
> myLabel.setStyle("fontSize", 30);
>
> The styles that are defined using the setStyle() method of StyleManager have precedence over the styles defined using CSS code. Bear in mind, though, that the setStyle() method is one of the most expensive CPU calls for the client because all the children have to be notified about the new style object.

To work with styles in Flex, Adobe has developed a Flex application called Flex Style Explorer (see Figure 9-24) that enables you to apply all styles to all Flex controls without writing a line of code. The Flex Style Explorer application is located here: http://examples.adobe.com/flex2/consulting/styleexplorer/Flex2StyleExplorer.html.

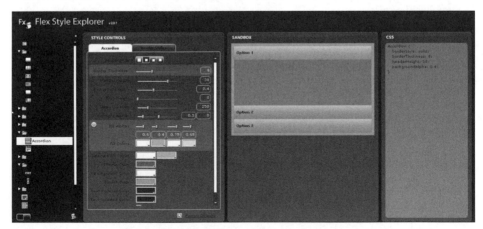

Figure 9-24. The Flex Style Explorer application

Solution 9-4: Applying graphical skins

Styles are a powerful tool for changing and personalizing the look and feel of a Flex application. But there are times when it is necessary to apply a design that completely changes the graphic nature of the components. It is no longer sufficient, therefore, to simply change the background color, the font, or the dimension of the characters.

In these cases, you must turn to skins. **Skinning** is the technique used to change the appearance of a component by modifying or extending its visual elements. Skins can be both graphic elements that use images and SWF files, and ActionScript classes that use the drawing API.

Each Flex component is composed of a series of graphic elements that, put together, give the component its appearance. For example, a Button is made up of elements that define the appearance of its up, over, and down states. These elements can be changed and personalized.

In this solution, you will see how to apply graphical skins to change the look and feel of some Flex components.

What's involved

Graphical skins consist of embedded images (PNG, JPG or GIF file types) or SWF files that are used as visual elements to substitute the classic graphic elements that make up the component. In a classic workflow, the designer sends you these elements and you then have to embed them into the Flex application. The choice of using input such as images or SWF files depends on the visual treatment, project requirements, and skill of the designer. But you should also consider that the use of bitmap images can turn out to be heavier in terms of file size because graphic elements must be embedded. Instead, by using vector images in SWF files, the weight of the file will be reduced and the graphic elements will not pixelate when scaled.

9

> The GIF and PNG 24 image types (as well as the vector SWF elements) support transparency.

Graphical skins can be applied using the following methods:

- **Inline skin**: The declaration that is made directly in the tag of the component to which you want to apply the skin. However, if you have to use embedded elements as graphical skins, use the @Embed tag directive within the declaration:

```
<mx:Button
label="Send"
upSkin="@Embed(source='assets/but_upSkin.png')"
downSkin="@Embed(source='assets/but_downSkin.png')"
/>
```

This code example uses two images, but_upSkin.png and but_downSkin.png, which substitute the graphic upSkin and downSkin elements used for a Button control.

- **CSS declaration**: With a CSS declaration, you can apply graphical skins. You can declare the CSS using a type selector or also a class selector. In this case, the elements must be embedded in the application. Use the Embed directive (without the @ symbol) to make Flex embed the graphic elements. The CSS can be declared in the document in the <mx:Style> tag or as external files and recalled using the source attribute of the <mx:Style> tag:

```
<mx:Style>
     Button
{
        overSkin: Embed("assets/but_overSkin.png");
        upSkin: Embed("assets/but_downSkin.png");
 }
   </mx:Style>
<mx:Button label="Send" />
```

In this code example, you have declared a type selector that applies the graphical skins for the overSkin and upSkin elements of a Button control.

You can also use a class selector as a skins declaration using CSS and then apply it to the Flex components using the styleName property (refer to Solution 9-3):

```
<mx:Style>
     .buttonSKin
{
        overSkin: Embed("assets/but_overSkin.png");
        upSkin: Embed("assets/but_downSkin.png");

}
   </mx:Style>
<mx:Button label="Send" styleName="buttonSKin" />
```

- setStyle(): Because skins are defined as style properties, you can use the setStyle() methods to apply the graphical skins at runtime. When you use the setStyle() method, you must create variables types as Class in an <mx:Script> block to embed the elements used:

```
<mx:Script>
<![CDATA[

        [Embed(source='assets/but_overSkin.png');]
        public var over:Class;

        [Embed(source='assets/but_downSkin.png')]
        public var up:Class;
```

```
        private function changeSkin():void {
            myBtn.setStyle("upSkin",up);
            myBtn.setStyle("overSkin",over);

        }
]]>
</mx:Script>

    <mx:Button label="Send" id="myBtn" click="changeSkin()"/>
```

At the click of the Button, the changeSkin() function will be called, and the skins embedded in the <mx:Script> block will be applied:

```
[Embed(source='assets/but_overSkin.png')]
public var over:Class;

[Embed(source='assets/but downSkin.png')]
public var up:Class;
```

In this solution you will apply graphical skins to the layout created in Solution 9-3.

How to build it

In this solution you will apply a graphical skin for the Button and the ComboBox components of the application created in Solution 9-3. Create three graphic elements in PNG format for the upSkin, overSkin, and downSkin of the Button by using Adobe Fireworks. You can download a free and completely functioning trial of the program directly from the Adobe site (www.adobe.com/go/devcenter_fw_try).

> You can choose to use any other graphical program that enables you to export PNG files at 32 bit.

1. Open the file Chapter_9_Flex_Sol_3_Layout.mxml and save it as Chapter_9_Flex_Sol_4_Layout.mxml. This will be the file on which you will work and apply the skin elements. You'll use the setStyle() method to declare and apply skins.

2. Open Adobe Fireworks and create a new document. Don't worry about giving it final dimensions immediately. For now, create a document of 250 × 250 pixels. Open the Common Library by selecting Window ➤ Common Library and go to the Buttons category, as shown in Figure 9-25. You can choose among many buttons that are found in this category or create your own personalized button. In this solution, the Buttons: 2 State Green Bevel Button was dragged onto the document.

Figure 9-25.
The 2 State Green Bevel Button is dragged onto the document.

9

3. The button has been imported as a symbol. For this solution, however, you must create three PNG files, one for each state of the button: overSkin, upSkin, and downSkin. You must, therefore, only take the state up from this symbol. To do this, double-click the symbol on the document and it will open in the appropriate window, as shown in Figure 9-26. From this window, you can select the elements on the upSkin state of the button. Carry out a multiple selection by dragging the mouse pointer while pressing down the mouse, as shown in Figure 9-26, and copy the elements.

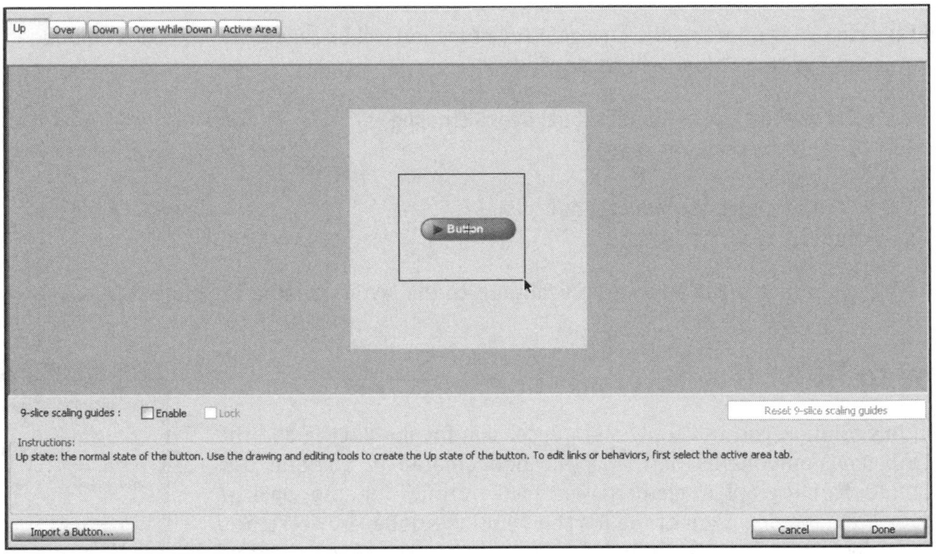

Figure 9-26. The symbol indow opens.

4. Click Done or Cancel in the symbol window and return to the document you have created. Delete the symbol and paste the graphical elements. At this point, on the area of the document there will no longer be the symbol; only the graphical elements you have copied appear (see Figure 9-27).

5. Before exporting your button that will be used for the upSkin of the Button, resize the image and render it transparent. Both operations are obtained from the Properties panel at the bottom of the document. Clicking outside of the canvas, go to the Properties panel and change the canvas color to be transparent and click the Fit to Canvas button, as shown in Figure 9-28. By doing so, you have rendered the document transparent and resized it to the exact size of the image.

Figure 9-27. Cancel the symbol and paste the graphical elements copied in the symbol window.

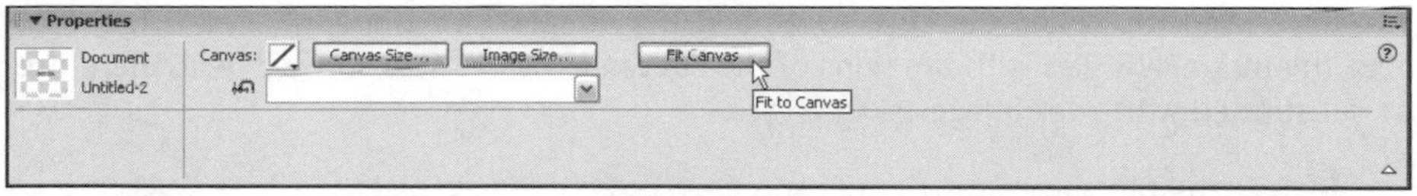

Figure 9-28. Change the canvas color to be transparent and click the Fit to Canvas button.

6. You are now ready to export the image. On the palette on the right, open Optimize and Align Panel. From the drop-down menu, select PNG32 as the format, as shown in Figure 9-29. In this way, you have set the settings that will be used to export the image. Select File ➤ Export and save the file as upSkinBut.png in the assets folder of the Flex project.

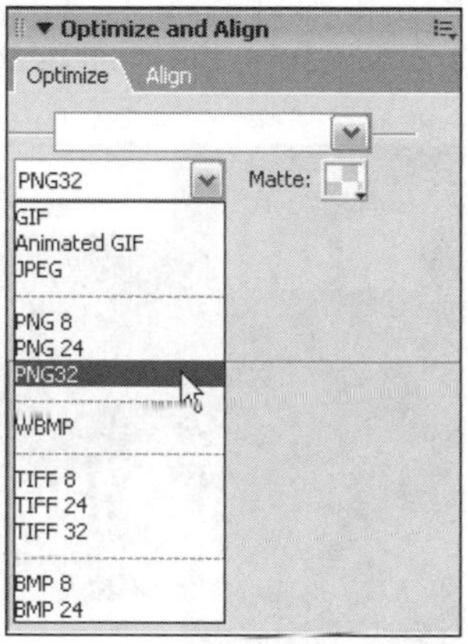

7. Repeat the same procedure from Step 3 to Step 6 by creating two other graphic elements that will be used as overSkin and downSkin. The only difference in these buttons is that you will copy the graphic elements onto the downSkin and overSkin states of the symbol (as you saw in Step 3). Export the elements as overSkinBut.png and downSkinBut.png in the assets folder.

Figure 9-29. Selecting the format

8. You can now return to Flex Builder and embed the images into the application to apply the skins. Open the file Chapter_9_Flex_Sol_4_Layout.mxml and insert a selector type for the Button in which you will set the graphical skins in the <mx:Style> block:

```
<mx:Style>
LinkButton
{
color: #ffffff;
   cornerRadius: 0;
   letterSpacing: 2;
   rollOverColor: #15a0f8;
   fontFamily: Arial;
   fontSize: 12;
   fontWeight: bold;
}
Button
{
overSkin: Embed("assets/overSkinBut.png");
upSkin: Embed("assets/upSkinBut_trans.png");
downSkin: Embed("assets/downSkinBut.png");

}
</mx:Style>
```

You have used the Embed directive to embed the images into the application. The code links the three PNG files with the skins of the Button control's states, which will, therefore, be substituted with your images.

9. Save the file and run the application.

Figure 9-30 shows the final result with the Button control to which the custom skins have been applied. Click the Button controls and you will see that only the upSkin, overSkin, and downSkin states will be loaded from the other custom skins.

Figure 9-30. The Button controls in the application have new graphical skins.

Having declared the graphical skins using a type selector, the skins will be applied to any Button control used in the application. If you want to apply the skins only to some instances of the component, you can declare the skins with a class selector in CSS and then link the CSS class with the styleName property.

The following code shows this example:

```
<mx:Style>
.buttonSkin
{
overSkin: Embed("assets/overSkinBut.png");
upSkin: Embed("assets/upSkinBut_trans.png");
downSkin: Embed("assets/downSkinBut.png");

}
</mx:Style>
```

To recall the class and apply it to the Button control, use an inline style definition on the <mx:Button> tag:

```
<mx:Button styleName="glass" label="Search"
width="110" styleName="buttonSkin " />
```

10. Continue your solution by creating skins for the ComboBox control. Instead of using images as graphical assets, you will use a SWF file in which various symbols are defined. You can create different graphic symbols in the file to use as skins of the Flex components. To load a symbol present in the same SWF file, use the symbol property on the Embed directive:

```
Embed(source="assets/style.swf", symbol="dropDown_Over");
```

In this way, you can optimize the management of the graphic elements used, having a single file in which all the necessary graphical assets have been created.

11. The SWF file that you will use has been created using Adobe Flash. In the solution, you used a SWF file for which the graphic symbols necessary for skinning a ComboBox control have already been created. You can, however, create your theme file and use it in Flex. To design Flex skins with Flash, you must first download the Flash skin template file (http://download.macromedia.com/pub/developer/flex_ skins_flash.zip) and unzip it to a folder on your computer. Inside the unzipped folder called flex_skins_flash, double-click the flex_skins.fla file. Flash will open, and you can edit and customize the existing artwork, or delete the existing artwork and draw your own.

> *For the* ComboBox *graphical assets I used a theme created by* ScaleNine.com: http:// scalenine.com/blog/2007/01/04/wmp-11-drop-down-skin/. *You can download the zip file and use it. ScaleNine is a great resource for learning about skinning Flex components.*

12. You can find the styles.swf file in the assets folder of the Flex project. This file contains the graphical skins to apply to the ComboBox control. You must, therefore, only embed the file and the symbols you need and apply the graphical skins. Open the file Chapter_9_Flex_Sol_4_Layout.mxml and insert a type selector for the ComboBox control in the <mx:Style> block:

```
<mx:Style>
LinkButton
{
color: #ffffff;
   cornerRadius: 0;
   letterSpacing: 2;
   rollOverColor: #15a0f8;
   fontFamily: Arial;
   fontSize: 12;
   fontWeight: bold;
}

Button
{
overSkin: Embed("assets/overSkinBut.png");
upSkin: Embed("assets/upSkinBut_trans.png");
downSkin: Embed("assets/downSkinBut.png");
```

9

```
        }

        ComboBox
        {
        upSkin: Embed(source="assets/style.swf", symbol="dropDown_Up");
        overSkin: Embed(source="assets/style.swf", symbol="dropDown_Over");
        downSkin: Embed(source="assets/style.swf", symbol="dropDown_Down");
        disabledSkin: Embed(source="assets/style.swf", symbol="dropDown_Up");
        color: #ffffff;
        dropDownStyleName:"dropMenu";
        paddingLeft:28;
        }

        .dropMenu {

        backgroundColor: #000000;
        backgroundAlpha: .5;
        borderColor: #231f20;
        cornerRadius: 5;
        color: #ffffff;
        textRollOverColor: #000000;
        textSelectedColor: #ffffff;
        disabledColor: #666666;
        selectionColor: #7BD3F7;
        paddingLeft:10;
        }

        </mx:Style>
```

The ComboBox uses the skin assets for the upSkin, overSkin, downSkin, and disabledSkin
states. For each of these states, a different graphical asset has been specified:

```
        upSkin: Embed(source="assets/style.swf", symbol="dropDown_Up");
        overSkin: Embed(source="assets/style.swf", symbol="dropDown_Over");
        downSkin: Embed(source="assets/style.swf", symbol="dropDown_Down");
        disabledSkin: Embed(source="assets/style.swf", symbol="dropDown_Up");
```

With the Embed directive you have embedded the style.swf file, but you also specified
the symbol name to use. This symbol has been created in Flash and it resides within the
compiled SWF file.

Furthermore, you have specified a class selector to use on the drop-down menu by sending it to the dropDownStyleName property:

```
        dropDownStyleName:"dropMenu";
```

The .dropMenu class has been declared immediately under the ComboBox type selector.

> *Even if you have already established styles for the* ComboBox *controls in the* main.css *file by declaring these new settings as local styles, these styles will have precedence and override the CSS styles in the external CSS file.*

13. Save the file and run the application.

The application will have all the Button controls and ComboBox controls loaded with the new graphical skins, as shown in Figure 9-31.

Figure 9-31. The Button and the ComboBox controls in the application have new graphical skins.

Skinning in Flex is another very powerful tool that, when linked with styles, is capable of completely changing the appearance of an application by modifying its appearance in a substantial way. You can create your set of skin assets, export them as SWC, and then import them to use them in your Flex applications.

Expert tips

As you have seen in this solution, the setStyle() method enables you to load styles and skins at runtime. However, the method does not allow you to apply skins to a whole category of controls. If, for example, you want to apply a defined skin to all the Button controls at runtime, you have to invoke the setStyle() method for every instance of that component, as shown in the following code:

```
<mx:Script>
<![CDATA[

    [Embed(source='assets/but_overSkin.png');]
    public var over:Class;

    [Embed(source='assets/but_downSkin.png')]
    public var up:Class;

    private function changeSkin():void {
    myBtn.setStyle("upSkin",up);
    myBtn.setStyle("overSkin",over);

    myBtn_2.setStyle("upSkin",up);
    myBtn_2.setStyle("overSkin",over);

    myBtn_3.setStyle("upSkin",up);
    myBtn_3.setStyle("overSkin",over);

    }
]]>
</mx:Script>

<mx:Button label="Send" id="myBtn" click="changeSkin()"/>
<mx:Button label="Send" id="myBtn_2" />
<mx:Button label="Send" id="myBtn_3" />
```

The changeSkin() applies the skins defined with the metadata [Embed] to every instance of the Button controls.

If you want the changeSkin() function to be applied to the same skins as all the Button controls, you have to use the StyleManager class. This class, created in the mx.managers class, manages all the CSS declarations that are converted into ActionScript code in the compilation phase. Through the getStyleDeclaration() method, the StyleManager class enables you to access type or class selectors that have been created with CSS and to apply them via code at runtime:

```
StyleManager.getStyleDeclaration("Button").setStyle("upSkin", up);
```

This line of code applies the skin for the upSkin state of any instance of a Button control.

> *The* getStyleDeclaration() *method returns the Selector object typed as CSSStyleDeclaration:*
>
> ```
> var mySelObj:CSSStyleDeclaration =
> StyleManager.getStyleDeclaration('.className');
> ```

Using the StyleManager class, you can also load an external CSS file at runtime using the loadStyleDeclarations() method that accepts the path and the name of the CSS file to be loaded as a parameter:

```
StyleManager.loadStyleDeclarations("assets/BasicStyles.swf")
```

With this method, you can create different CSS that you can load at runtime, depending on the choices made by the user.

Solution 9-5: Applying programmatic skins

With graphical skins you can create graphical elements and use them as skins for the Flex components. But Flex also offers another possibility that is more advanced and complex, but gives you total control over the skins. With the introduction of the drawing API in ActionScript contained in the flash.display.Graphics class, you can programmatically create skins for components. These techniques are called **programmatic skins** because they're applied only via ActionScript code instead of as graphical assets.

The use of programmatic skins, aside from furnishing total control over the skins, also results in smaller file size because there is no embedding of images in the application. Furthermore, programmatic skins can operate at runtime on any type of event; for example, a button click or component resizing.

In this solution, you will create an ActionScript class that with the drawing API will design a geometric form that will be used as a skin for the Button control.

What's involved

To create a programmatic skin, it is necessary to create a subclass of one of the following classes:

- ProgrammaticSkin: Used most often for the creation of skins. It is found in the mx.skins package and implements the IFlexDisplayObject, ILayoutClient, and IStyleable interfaces.

- Border: Extends the ProgrammaticSkin class. It adds support for the borderMetrics property for the skins that need a border and do not use a background image. It is found in the mx.skins package.

- RectangularBorder: A subclass of the Border that adds support to the backgroundImage property. It is found in the mx.skins package.

Therefore, the first step of creating a programmatic skin is to choose one of the three classes and extend it, creating a subclass.

After creating a subclass, you must override the method used to draw the visual elements of the class: the updateDisplayList(). This is a protected method and expects to receive two parameters that declare the width and the height of the skin. This method is recalled automatically every time the class must redraw the skin.

9

If you chose to use the RectBorder and Border classes to create the programmatic skin, in addition to overriding the updateDisplayList() method you must also override the setter/getter method of the borderMetrics property. In this way, the property will return your values to you instead of the default values.

The following code shows the skeleton of a subclass of the Border class:

```
package com.flexsolutions.chapter9.skins
{
import mx.skins.Border;
import mx.core.EdgeMetrics;

public class MySkin extends Border
{
public function MySkin() {}

override protected function updateDisplayList(
unscaledWidth:Number, unscaledHeight:Number):void
{
// code to define the skin
}

public function get borderMetrics():EdgeMetrics
{
 //return EdgeMetrics.EMPTY;
}
}
}
```

Once you have created the class and defined the skins in the updateDisplayList() function with the drawing API, you can apply the programmatic skin to the Flex component. To do this, use one of the techniques that you have already seen and used for the graphical skins:

- **Inline skins**: The declaration that is done directly in the tag of the component to which you want to apply the skin. However, having to use embedded elements as graphical skins, use the @Embed tag directive within the declaration.

- **CSS declarations**: Used to apply graphical skins. You can declare the CSS using a type selector or a class selector. Also in this case, the elements must be embedded in the application. Use the Embed directive (without the @ symbol) so that Flex embeds the graphic elements. The CSS can be declared in the document of the <mx:Style> or as an external file and recalled using the source attribute of the <mx:Style> tag.

- **setStyle() method**: Because the skins are defined as style properties, you can use the setStyle() method to apply the graphical skins at runtime. When you use the setStyle() method, you must create variables typed as Class to embed the elements used.

The only difference that you must consider when applying a programmatic skin is that you are not dealing with a graphical asset, but with an ActionScript class, so specify a reference to the class that the component should use:

```
<mx:Style>

Button
{
upSkin: ClassReference('com.flexsolutions.chapter9.skins.MySkin');
downSkin: ClassReference('com.flexsolutions.chapter9.skins.MySkin');
overSkin: ClassReference('com.flexsolutions.chapter9.skins.MySkin');
}
</mx:Style>
```

You have applied the programmatic skin using the CSS declaration. On the states of the Button control, you have specified the package and the ActionScript class that the control should use as skins with the ClassReference.

If you wanted to use the inline declaration to apply the skins instead, you would write the following:

```
<mx:Button label="Send"
upSkin="com.flexsolutions.chapter9.skins.MySkin"
downSkin="com.flexsolutions.chapter9.skins.MySkin"
overSkin="com.flexsolutions.chapter9.skins.MySkin" />
```

Therefore, you link the MySkin class to the skin properties upSkin, downSkin, and overSkin.

If you were using the setStyle() method to apply the programmatic skins, you would instead write everything in the <mx:Style> code block:

```
<?xml version="1.0" encoding="utf-8"?>
<mx:Application xmlns:mx="http://www.adobe.com/2006/mxml"
layout="absolute"
 creationComplete="applyProgrammaticSkin()">

<mx:Script>
<![CDATA[
import com.flexsolutions.chapter9.skins.MySkin

private function applyProgrammaticSkin():void
{
myBtn.setStyle("upSkin", MySkin);
myBtn.setStyle("overSkin", MySkin);
myBtn.setStyle("downSkin", MySkin);
}
]]>
</mx:Script>
```

9

```
<mx:Button label="Send" id="myBtn" />

</mx:Application>
```

For all three approaches you have always specified the same class for each state of the Button control. It is also possible to intercept, through the property name of the Border, ProgrammaticSkin, or RectangularBorder class, the property name that returns the name of the state on which to apply the skin. Therefore, by adding a simple switch() {} statement, you can apply different skins, defining them in the same class:

```
package com.flexsolutions.chapter9.skins
{
import mx.skins.Border;
import mx.core.EdgeMetrics;

public class MySkin extends Border
{
public function MySkin() {}

override protected function updateDisplayList(
unscaledWidth:Number, unscaledHeight:Number):void
{
// code to define the skin

switch (name)
{
case upSkin:
//your code for the upSkin
break;

case overSkin:
//your code for the overSkin
break;

case downSkin:
//your code for the downSkin
break;
}
}

override public function get borderMetrics():EdgeMetrics
    {
    return EdgeMetrics.EMPTY;
    }
}
}
```

The drawing API of ActionScript and its explanation is out of the scope of this book, but the methods that you will use are the following:

- beginFill()
- beginGradientFill()
- clear()
- curveTo()
- endFill()
- lineStyle()
- lineTo()
- moveTo()
- drawRoundRectComplex()

In this solution, you will create a custom programmatic skin that you will then apply to your Flex controls.

How to build it

Create two different ActionScript classes that you will use for the programmatic skins on two different Flex components: a Button control and a Canvas container. For the Button control, you will create a subclass of the ProgrammaticSkin class; for the container, you will create a subclass of the RectangularBorder class in which the latter accepts the borderSkin property.

1. Start by creating the skins folder in com/flexsolutions/chapter9/. In this folder you will save your two ActionScript classes.

2. Create the first class by selecting File ➤ New ➤ ActionScript Class and save it as MySkin.as in the package com.flexsolutions.chapter9.skins. Select the skins. ProgrammaticSkin class as a super class and select the check box Generate constructor from superclass. You can use the New ActionScript Class dialog box to set all these settings without writing code. The MySkin class is formed from the following code:

```
package com.flexsolutions.chapter9.skins
{
import mx.skins.ProgrammaticSkin;

public class MySkin extends ProgrammaticSkin {

public function MySkin() {}

}
}
```

3. Import the Graphics class from flash.display and create the variable _backgroundColor typed as uint that will contain the hexadecimal value to use as background for the states of the Button control:

```
package com.flexsolutions.chapter9.skins
{
import mx.skins.ProgrammaticSkin;
import flash.display.Graphics;

public class MySkin extends ProgrammaticSkin {

public function MySkin() {}

private var _backgroundColor:uint;

}
}
```

4. After creating the subclass, you must override the updateDisplayList() method to be able to create a programmatic skin. This method is called every time the skin of a component must be drawn or redrawn:

```
package com.flexsolutions.chapter9.skins
{
import mx.skins.ProgrammaticSkin;
import flash.display.Graphics;

public class MySkin extends ProgrammaticSkin {

public function MySkin() {}

private var _backgroundColor:uint;

override protected function updateDisplayList(
unscaledWidth:Number, unscaledHeight:Number ):void
{

switch( name )
{
case "upSkin":
_backgroundColor = 0xf046df;
break;
case "overSkin":
_backgroundColor = 0xf8a3ef;
break;
case "downSkin":
_backgroundColor = 0xac0d9c;
break;
case "disabledSkin":
_backgroundColor = 0x999999;
break;
}
}
}
}
```

The protected updateDisplayList() method accepts two parameters that correspond to the width and height to apply to the component. In the method, you have inserted a switch() statement that, according to the value that is sent to the name variable, sets the _backgroundColor variable to a different value:

```
switch( name )
{
case "upSkin":
_backgroundColor = 0xf046df;
break;
case "overSkin":
_backgroundColor = 0xf8a3ef;
break;
case "downSkin":
_backgroundColor = 0xac0d9c;
break;
case "disabledSkin":
_backgroundColor = 0x999999;
break;
}
```

The name variable is sent to the ProgrammaticSkin class and contains the name of the state of the skin. In the case of a Button, you have managed the skins for the states of upSkin, overSkin, downSkin, and disabledSkin.

5. Using the drawing API, draw the skin that will be substituted by the standard visual elements of the Button controls. Insert this code in the updateDisplayList() method:

```
override protected function updateDisplayList(
unscaledWidth:Number, unscaledHeight:Number ):void
{

switch( name ) {
case "upSkin":
_backgroundColor = 0xf046df;
break;
case "overSkin":
_backgroundColor = 0xf8a3ef;
break;
case "downSkin":
_backgroundColor = 0xac0d9c;
break;
case "disabledSkin":
_backgroundColor = 0x999999;
break;
}

var g:Graphics = graphics;
g.clear();
```

9

```
g.beginFill(_backgroundColor,1);
g.lineStyle(.8,0xff0080,.5);
g.drawRoundRectComplex(0,0,
unscaledWidth,unscaledHeight,
0,20,0,20);
g.endFill();
}
```

The `ProgrammaticSkin` class has the graphics property that contains an instance of the `flash.display.Graphics` class. It is, in fact, the `Graphics` class that contains the methods for the drawing API. After inserting the instance of the property graphics in the variable g, invoke the `clear()` method to remove the elements used by the current state:

```
g.clear();
```

At this point, you can start to design your element. With the `beginFill()` method, set the background color with the shape that will be filled and specify a style for the line used for the perimeter of the shape with the `lineStyle()` method:

```
g.beginFill(_backgroundColor,1);
g.lineStyle(.8,0xff0080,.5);
```

Use the `drawRoundRectComplex()` method to design a rounded rectangle to which to send the values that you want to apply to the rectangle:

```
g.drawRoundRectComplex(0,0,
unscaledWidth,unscaledHeight,
0,20,0,20);
```

The `drawRoundRectComplex()` static method draws a rounded rectangle and accepts the following parameters:

```
drawRoundRectComplex(graphics:Graphics,
                     x:Number, y:Number,
                     width:Number, height:Number,
                      topLeftRadius:Number,
                      topRightRadius:Number,
                      bottomLeftRadius:Number,
                      bottomRightRadius:Number)
```

For more information about this method, have a look at the Adobe LiveDocs: http://livedocs.adobe.com/flex/201/langref/mx/utils/GraphicsUtil.html.

The last line of code marks the end of the fill:

```
g.endFill();
```

6. Save the `MySkin` class. The programmatic skin is ready to be applied to the `Button` control. In the next step, you will create a main application file in which you will apply the skins using the `setStyle()` method.

7. Create a new MXML application file by selecting File ➤ New ➤ MXML Application and name it Chapter_9_Flex_Sol_5_Layout.mxml. Insert a Button control and assign it an id, as shown in the following code:

```
<?xml version="1.0" encoding="utf-8"?>
<mx:Application xmlns:mx="http://www.adobe.com/2006/mxml"
layout="absolute">
<mx:Button label="Send" id="myBtn"
x="134.5" y="104" />
</mx:Application>
```

8. Add an <mx:Script> block in the page in which you will define a function that applies the programmatic skin with the setStyle() method. Write the following code immediately under the <mx:Application> tag:

```
<mx:Script>
<![CDATA[
import com.flexsolutions.chapter9.skins *;
private function applyProgrammaticSkin():void
{
myBtn.setStyle("upSkin", MySkin);
myBtn.setStyle("overSkin", MySkin);
myBtn.setStyle("downSkin", MySkin);
myBtn.setStyle("disabledSkin", MySkin);
}
]]>
</mx:Script>
```

To apply the programmatic skin you must first import the ActionScript class that you intend to use as a skin. Then you can use the setStyle()method by invoking it from the id of the Button for which you want to apply the skin and link the MySkin class to every state:

```
myBtn.setStyle("upSkin", MySkin);
myBtn.setStyle("overSkin", MySkin);
myBtn.setStyle("downSkin", MySkin);
myBtn.setStyle("disabledSkin", MySkin);
```

If you run the application, you will not see any skin applied to the Button control. You must, in fact, launch the applyProgrammaticSkin() function on a system or user event. Use the creationComplete event of the Application.

9. Call the applyProgrammaticSkin() function on the creationComplete event of the <mx:Application> tag:

```
<mx:Application xmlns:mx="http://www.adobe.com/2006/mxml"
layout="absolute"
creationComplete="applyProgrammaticSkin()" >
```

10. Save and run the application.

9

As you can see in Figure 9-32, the Button will have a completely different shape from the standard one. You will now create a programmatic skin that you will apply to a Canvas container to see the differences for the skins between a container and a control.

Figure 9-32. With its custom shape, the Button draws with the drawing API.

11. Create a new ActionScript class by selecting File ➤ New ➤ ActionScript Class and save it as CanvasSkin.as in the package com.flexsolutions.chapter9.skins. Select the mx.skins.RectangularBorder class as a super class and select the check box Generate constructor from superclass. You can use the New ActionScript Class dialog box to set all these settings without writing code. For the Canvas container, you had to use the RectangularBorder class as a super class because the container has a border.

12. Similar to MySkin, import the Graphics class and override the updateDisplayList() method:

```
package com.flexsolutions.chapter9.skins
{

import mx.skins.RectangularBorder;
import flash.display.Graphics;

public class CanvasSkin extends RectangularBorder
{
public function CanvasSkin() {}

private var _backgroundColor:uint;
private var g:Graphics = graphics;

override protected function updateDisplayList
(unscaledWidth:Number, unscaledHeight:Number):void
{  }

}
}
```

You have declared two private variables: _backGroundColor (that will contain the hexadecimal value of the background color) and the g variable (that will contain the graphics property).

13. Insert the code to define the shape to use in place of the default elements of the Canvas container in updateDisplayList(). You have also used the drawRoundRectComplex() method in this class to create a geometrical rectangular shape with rounded borders:

```
override protected function updateDisplayList
(unscaledWidth:Number, unscaledHeight:Number):void
{
```

```
super.updateDisplayList(unscaledWidth, unscaledHeight);
_backgroundColor = getStyle("backgroundColor");
g.beginFill(_backgroundColor,1.0);
g.lineStyle(0,0,0);
g.drawRoundRectComplex(0,0,unscaledWidth,unscaledHeight,30,30,30,30);
g.endFill();
}
```

The first line in the method calls the super.updateDisplayList(unscaledWidth, unscaledHeight). This call is necessary when you create a subclass of the RectangularBorder class.

Use the getStyle() method to remove the value that was inserted by a determined property with the styles. In this case, you have removed the value of the backgroundColor specified as style in the main application file and have used it in the beginFill() method:

```
_backgroundColor = getStyle("backgroundColor");
g.beginFill(_backgroundColor,1.0);
```

> If you want to change the default background color of the Canvas container, insert this value in the constructor of the programmatic skin class:
>
> ```
> public function MyButtonSkin()
> {
> _backgroundColor = 0xFFBB00;
> }
> ```

This class will now be applied to a Canvas using the CSS and the ClassReference directive as a method to apply to the skins.

14. Open the main application file and insert an <mx:Style> block in which you will create a type selector for the Canvas container that will load the skins in the CanvasSkin class:

```
<mx:Application xmlns:mx="http://www.adobe.com/2006/mxml"
layout="absolute"
creationComplete="applyProgrammaticSkin()" >

<mx:Style>
Canvas
{
  borderSkin:
ClassReference('com.flexsolutions.chapter9.skins.CanvasSkin ');
}
</mx:Style>

<mx:Script>
<![CDATA[
import com.flexsolutions.chapter9.skins.*;
```

9

```
private function applyProgrammaticSkin():void
{
myBtn.setStyle("upSkin", MySkin);
myBtn.setStyle("overSkin", MySkin);
myBtn.setStyle("downSkin", MySkin);
myBtn.setStyle("disabledSkin", MySkin);
}
]]>
</mx:Script>
```

The ClassReference points at the ActionScript class.

15. Add the Canvas container into the application and specify the properties cornerRadius and backgroundColor. Position the container with a constraint rule to make it appear in the center of the page:

```
<mx:Canvas width="323" height="256"
backgroundAlpha="0.7"
cornerRadius="5"
horizontalCenter="0"
verticalCenter="0" backgroundColor="#c0c0c0">

<mx:Button label="Send" id="myBtn"
x="134.5" y="104" />

</mx:Canvas>
</mx:Application>
```

16. Save the file and run the application.

Figure 9-33 shows the final result with the Canvas container that inherits the shape that has been linked to it with the programmatic skin.

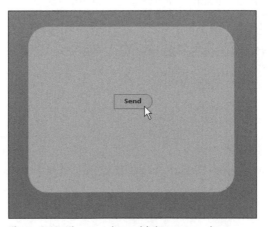

Figure 9-33. The container with its custom shape draws with the drawing API.

Expert tips

When you create your skin using ActionScript, you can also apply effects to the shape that you are drawing. Modify the MySkin class created in this solution, which is acted on the Button control, applying a drop shadow effect using the DropShadowFilter class.

1. Open the MySkin.as file. Import the DropShadowFilter class into the MySkin class:

```
package com.flexsolutions.chapter9.skins
{
import mx.skins.ProgrammaticSkin;
import flash.display.Graphics;

import flash.filters.DropShadowFilter;
```

2. Declare the dropShadow variable for which you will specify some of its properties:

```
public class MySkin extends ProgrammaticSkin {

public function MySkin() {}

private var _backgroundColor:uint;

private var dropShadow:DropShadowFilter = new DropShadowFilter();

override protected function updateDisplayList(
unscaledWidth:Number, unscaledHeight:Number ):void
{

switch( name ) {
case "upSkin":
_backgroundColor = 0xf046df;
break;
case "overSkin":
_backgroundColor = 0xf8a3ef;
break;
case "downSkin":
_backgroundColor = 0xac0d9c;
break;
case "disabledSkin":
_backgroundColor = 0x999999;
break;
}

var g:Graphics = graphics;
g.clear();
g.beginFill(_backgroundColor,1);
g.lineStyle(.8,0xff0080,.5);
g.drawRoundRectComplex(0,0,unscaledWidth,unscaledHeight,0,20,0,20)
g.endFill();
```

```
dropShadow.color = 0x000000;
dropShadow.blurX = 10;
dropShadow.blurY = 10;
dropShadow.angle = 0.5;
dropShadow.alpha = 0.5;
dropShadow.distance = 5;

filters = [dropShadow];
}
}
}
```

To apply the effect just created, use the property filters, to which you will send the dropShadow object that was just created, as the first index of an Array.

You can change the values in the dropShadow properties to see how your Button control changes as a consequence.

3. Save the file and run the main application file.

Figure 9-34 shows the final result with the Button control with the drop shadow effect applied.

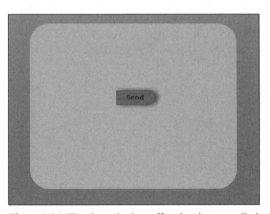

Figure 9-34. The drop shadow effect has been applied to the button.

Solution 9-6: Customizing the style of rows and columns of an AdvancedDataGrid control

The AdvancedDataGrid control is a new component added to Flex 3 that extends the DataGrid control, adding new functions for displaying complex data. In Chapter 7, you saw the more important features of this new and powerful control, creating solutions for the following:

- Multicolumn sorting
- Displaying tree view (hierarchical data and grouping data)
- Multiple cell selection
- Column grouping
- Applying a `SummaryCollection`
- Using `PrintAdvancedDataGrid`

There are, however, other new features that more directly regard the styles that can be applied to rows and columns of an `AdvancedDataGrid`.

In this solution you will see how to customize the style of rows and columns at runtime.

What's involved

For rows and columns, the styles are applied to the `AdvancedDataGrid` control using a callback function. This function is sent to the `styleFunction` property to format both rows and columns. The callback function accepts two parameters:

- data: An `Object` that contains the `dataProvider` used by the `AdvancedDataGrid`
- column: Typed as `AdvancedDataGridColumn` and contains the reference to the column of the `AdvancedDataGrid`

Furthermore, the callback function returns an `Object` that contains the values used to apply the styles. The values are specified with the style names, declaring them in the following form:

```
{ styleName: value, styleName: value }
```

Therefore, to launch the callback function and apply the styles to the rows, specify the styleFunction property on the AdvancedDataGrid tag:

```
<mx:AdvancedDataGrid
id="adg"
dataProvider="{myAC}"
width="90%"
variableRowHeight="true"
wordWrap="true"
styleFunction="styleCallback">

<mx:columns>
<mx:AdvancedDataGridColumn headerText="Region"
dataField="region"/>
<mx:AdvancedDataGridColumn headerText="Population"
dataField="population"  />
<mx:AdvancedDataGridColumn headerText="Code"
dataField="code"/>
<mx:AdvancedDataGridColumn headerText="Family"
```

9

```
                    dataField="family"/>
                    </mx:columns>

                    </mx:AdvancedDataGrid>
```

Then write the callback function styleCallback() in an <mx:Script> block and have it return the values of the styles that you want to apply to the row of the control to you:

```
public function styleCallback (data:Object, column:
AdvancedDataGridColumn):Object
{
    return {//styleName:value};
}
```

If you intend to apply the styles at runtime, you must understand how and when the callback function is called by the AdvancedDataGrid. The styleFunction is invoked when the control is first drawn and every time the invalidateList() method is invoked.

In fact, if you intend to apply the styles at runtime, you must invoke the invalidateList() method to refresh the display of all rows in the AdvancedDataGrid.

In this solution, you will see how to apply styles to rows based on the values that the user selects in a List control. In the "Expert tips" section you will also see how to apply the styles to columns of the AdvancedDataGrid control.

How to build it

In this solution, you will use the states.xml file already used in Chapters 6 and 7. You can open the Flex projects of those chapters and copy the file from the directory data. The structure of the file is very simple:

```
<dataroot>
<city>
<id>1</id>
<id_region>1</id_region>
<region>PIEMONTE</region>
<cityName>TORINO</ cityName >
<code>TO</code>
<population>2236765</population>
<male>1086745</male>
<female>1150020</female>
<family>886053</family>
</city>
<city>
..... other nodes ....
</city>
</dataroot>
```

The root tag is dataroot, while the repeating node is city. You will use an ArrayCollection as dataProvider for the AdvancedDataGrid.

> *This solution requires Flex Builder 3 and the Flex 3 SDK. You can download it from the Adobe Labs site:* http://labs.adobe.com/technologies/flex/.

1. Open Flex Builder 3, create a new main application file by selecting File ➤ New ➤ MXML Application, and save it as Chapter_9_Flex_Sol_6_Layout.mxml.

2. Create a new folder in the Flex project and call it data. In this folder copy the file states.xml that you created in Chapters 6 and 7 (or create the file from scratch and save it with that name).

3. Load the states.xml file using an <mx:Model> tag that you will then convert into an ArrayCollection. Insert the following code:

```
<?xml version="1.0" encoding="utf-8"?>
<mx:Application xmlns:mx="http://www.adobe.com/2006/mxml">
<mx:Model id="myRegion" source="data/states.xml" />
<mx:ArrayCollection id="myAC" source="{myRegion.city}" />
</mx:Application>
```

The ArrayCollection myAC points at the repeating node of the myRegion data model and will function as dataProvider for the AdvancedDataGrid.

4. Insert the AdvancedDataGrid for which you will specify four <mx:AdvancedDataGridColumn> tags that will display just some of the data loaded in the dataProvider:

```
<mx:ArrayCollection id="myAC" source="{myRegion.city}" />

<mx:AdvancedDataGrid
id="adg"
dataProvider="{myAC}"
width="90%"
variableRowHeight="true"
wordWrap="true">

<mx:columns>
<mx:AdvancedDataGridColumn headerText="Region"
dataField="region"/>

<mx:AdvancedDataGridColumn headerText="Population"
dataField="population"  />

<mx:AdvancedDataGridColumn headerText="Code"
dataField="code"/>

<mx:AdvancedDataGridColumn headerText="Family"
dataField="family"/>
</mx:columns>
</mx:AdvancedDataGrid>
</mx:Application>
```

9

The control displays the following data in the region, population, code, and family columns. This data is specified in the dataField property of the <mx:AdvancedDataGridColumn> tag. You can already save the file and run the application to see the data displayed in the control. Before applying the styles to the rows, insert a List control from which the user can select the city to which the styles will be applied.

5. Under the AdvancedDataGrid insert an HBox that contains a Label and a List control. The List control will use the same ArrayCollection as that used by the AdvancedDataGrid as dataProvider, but will display the city names:

```
<mx:HBox>
<mx:Label  text="Select the city to highlight" />

<mx:List id="myList" dataProvider="{myAC}"
  labelField="cityName" />
  </mx:HBox>
```

The List control specifies the data that you intend to display in the labelField property. It will be on the change event of this control that you will apply the styles to the row of the AdvancedDataGrid control.

6. Define the callback function through the styleFunction function of the <mx:AdvancedDataGrid> control. Insert the code in bold in the tag:

```
<mx:AdvancedDataGrid
id="adg"
dataProvider="{myAC}"
width="90%"
variableRowHeight="true"
wordWrap="true"
styleFunction="styleCallback">
```

The styleFunction is invoked when the control is first drawn and every time the invalidateList() method is invoked. Therefore, you must remember to invoke the invalidateList() method when the user uses a city name in the List control.

7. Insert an <mx:Script> block in which you will create a variable that will contain the value of the city name selected by the user in the List control and the styleCallback() callback function:

```
<mx:Application xmlns:mx="http://www.adobe.com/2006/mxml">
<mx:Script>
<![CDATA[

private var citySel:String;

private function styleCallback(data:Object,
column:AdvancedDataGridColumn):Object
{
 if (data["city"] == citySel)
    return {color:0xFF0000, fontWeight:'bold',fontStyle:'italic'};
```

```
    return null;
  }
]]>
</mx:Script>
```

The styleCallback() function returns an Object that contains the values that will be used to apply the styles. In the function, an if() condition verifies in which rows the following expression occurs (or when the city selected in the List control and conserved in the citySel variable is equal to the value of the city of the column of the AdvancedDataGrid control):

```
if (data["city"] == citySel)
```

When this expression occurs, the style is applied, and the object for which the style properties are specified is returned: color, fontWeight, and fontStyle:

```
return {color:0xFF0000, fontWeight:'bold',fontStyle:'italic'};
```

The styleCallback() function instead returns a null if the expression has not occurred.

8. All you need to do is add two simple ActionScript instructions on the event change of the List control:

```
<mx:HBox>
<mx:Label  text="Select the city to highlight" />
 <mx:List id="myList" dataProvider="{myAC}"
labelField="cityName"
change="citySel=myList.selectedItem.cityName;
adg.invalidateList();" />
</mx:HBox>
```

On the event change, the citySel variable is set to the value selected by the user in the List control: myList.selectedItem.cityName. This value will then be used in the expression of the if() cycle in the styleCallback() function. To update and apply the style in the line, invoke the method on the invalidateList() AdvancedDataGrid control.

9. Save the file and run the application.

After a city is selected in the List control, the corresponding row relative to that city will change style in the AdvancedDataGrid control, as shown in Figure 9-35.

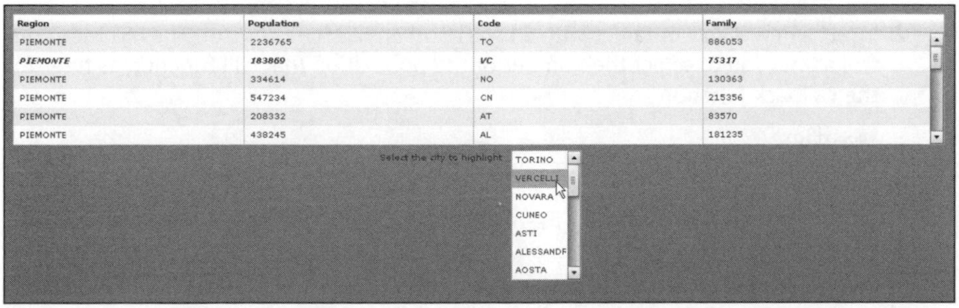

Figure 9-35. The style will be applied to the row of the AdvancedDataGrid control.

Expert tips

To apply styles to a column of the AdvancedDataGrid control, use the same styleFunction property, but declare it on the AdvancedDataGridColumn:

```
<mx:AdvancedDataGridColumn headerText="Population"
dataField="population" styleFunction="ColStyleCallback"/>
```

In this way, the callback function will act exclusively on the column, not on the entire set of rows.

Modify the code created in this solution by inserting an HSlider that will function as a filter on the number of the population. In fact, you will apply a style to the whole column of the population that has a higher value than that selected on the HSlider control.

1. On the column that contains the value of the population, specify the callback function on the styleFunction property:

```
<mx:AdvancedDataGrid
  id="adg"
  dataProvider="{myAC}"
  width="90%"
  variableRowHeight="true"
  wordWrap="true"
  styleFunction="styleCallback">

<mx:columns>
<mx:AdvancedDataGridColumn headerText="Region"
dataField="region"/>


<mx:AdvancedDataGridColumn headerText="Population"
dataField="population" styleFunction="ColStyleCallback"/>

<mx:AdvancedDataGridColumn headerText="Code"
dataField="code"/>
<mx:AdvancedDataGridColumn headerText="Family"
dataField="family"/>
</mx:columns>
</mx:AdvancedDataGrid>
```

2. Insert a new HBox container with a Label and an HSlider control. The HSlider control allows you to select the number of the population that will function as filter for the callback function:

```
<mx:HBox>
<mx:Label  text="Select a city of the Region to highlight" />

  <mx:List id="myList" dataProvider="{myAC}"
labelField="cityName"
change="citySel=myList.selectedItem.region;
```

```
adg.invalidateList();" />
</mx:HBox>

<mx:HBox>
 <mx:Label  text="Select the population" />
 <mx:HSlider id="mySlider"
 minimum="100000" tickInterval="500000"
 maximum="4000000"
 snapInterval="50000" labels="[100 K,4 Mln]"
 change="popValue=mySlider.value;
 adg.invalidateList();" width="256"/>
 </mx:HBox>
```

On the change event of the HSlider, assign the value that the user has selected on the control to the popValue variable. You will create this variable in the next step in the <mx:Script> block. Furthermore, you have set the values for some of the properties of the HSlider (see Figure 9-36).

Figure 9-36. The HSlider control enables you to select the number of the population that will function as a filter for the callback function.

3. You can now add the popValue variable and the style function in the <mx:Script> block.

```
<mx:Script>
<![CDATA[

private var citySel:String;

private var popValue:int;


private function styleCallback(data:Object,
  col:AdvancedDataGridColumn):Object
{
  if (data["region"] == citySel)
  return {color:0x0009bd,backgroundColor:0xFFF552,
  fontWeight:'bold',fontStyle:'italic'};

  return null;
}


private function ColStyleCallback(data:Object,
  col:AdvancedDataGridColumn):Object
{
```

9

```
if(data["population"] <= popValue)
return {color:0x0009bd,  textAlign:'center',
            fontFamily:'Verdana', fontSize: 12};

return null;
}

]]>
</mx:Script>
```

The ColStyleCallback() function checks the popValue variable. This value is that which the user has selected from the HSlider control. If the expression is verified, the Object is returned with the values color, textAlign, fontFamily, and fontSize:

```
private function ColStyleCallback(data:Object,
  col:AdvancedDataGridColumn):Object
{
if(data["population"] <= popValue)
return {color:0x00FF00,  textAlign:'center',
            fontFamily:'Verdana', fontSize: 12};

return null;
}
```

4. Save the file and run the application.

By moving the tick of the HSlider you will see how the styles are applied to the population column of the AdvancedDataGrid according to the value selected by the user (see Figure 9-37).

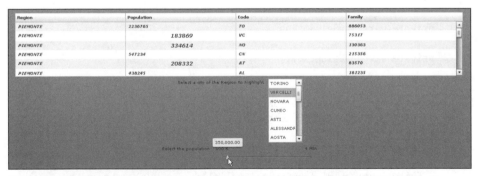

Figure 9-37. The HSlider control enables you to select the number of the population that will function as a filter for the callback function.

Solution 9-7: Using and embedding fonts in Flex applications

Flex manages the fonts by classifying them according to the following typology:

- **System fonts**: Fonts that are installed on the operating system of the user. They can be used by the Flex application with no additional file size because the fonts are not compiled into the SWF file.

- **Device fonts**: Fonts that refer to the generic fonts category and are interpreted differently by different operating systems or user settings. Device fonts are classified in _sans (sans-serif), _serif (serif), and _typewriter (monospace) typefaces that are commonly interpreted by the operating systems in the following system fonts: Helvetica/Arial, Times New Roman, and Courier. The great advantage of using these fonts is that users do not need to have the exact font installed on their system. But Flash Player will try to locate a similar font and make the best guess.

- **Embedded fonts**: Fonts that are embedded in the application and compiled in the SWF file, resulting in an increase in the file size of the SWF that is directly proportional to the complexity of the font face glyphs. In Flex, any TrueType fonts (TTFs) can be embedded. The advantage is that any user will see the text that uses the embedded font formatted in the same way, without the font having to be installed on his computer.

The use of system or device fonts is what limits the size of the SWF file because it does not request the embedding of the font in the compilation phase. Classic fonts can be used that are installed on most operating systems, such as, Arial, Verdana, or Times New Roman. An advantage of using the device fonts is the localization of the application for multiple languages. In this scenario, the client machine is responsible for choosing the right font for the application according to the language of the operating system.

The disadvantages of using these font types depend on the graphical choice of your application. For example, device fonts cause display problems when the text is rotated, when the alpha is modified, or when animations are applied. Furthermore, it is not possible to change the anti-aliasing on the font because it is applied automatically.

> *Anti-aliasing* is the technique of minimizing the distortion artifacts known as aliasing when representing a high-resolution signal at a lower resolution. Font and font rasterization involve some anti-aliasing to onscreen text to make it smoother and easier to read.

Figure 9-38 shows two texts to which an enlargement has been applied. The text on the left shows aliased text, while the text on the right shows the smoothest anti-aliased text:

9

Figure 9-38. The left figure shows a font without antialiasing; the right one shows anti-aliased text.

In this solution, you will see how to apply all three types of fonts that Flex allows you to use.

What's involved

Specifying the use of a system or device font in Flex is very easy. It is, in fact, sufficient to change the name of the font to use by specifying it in the font-family or fontFamily property if you use it as inline property of an MXML tag style property.

You can set this style by directly adding the MXML tag to the inline property:

```
<mx:Label text="This is a sample text"
 fontFamily="Verdana" />
```

Or you can use the CSS declarations by setting the font-family style in an <mx:Style> block:

```
<mx:Style>
Label
{
font-family: "Arial";
}

</mx:Style>

<mx:Label text="This is a sample text"  />
```

The same applies to device fonts, except that you can use one of the three font categories available to you:

```
<mx:Style>
Label
{
font-family: "_sans";
}

</mx:Style>

<mx:Label text="This is a sample text"  />
```

When used by the client, the application will then choose a font installed on the system that makes up part of that font category.

To use the embedded fonts, you can follow two different routes: use the [Embed] meta-data within ActionScript, or use the CSS and the @font-face property.

The [Embed] metadata sets the path of the font using the source attribute, and (with the fontName attribute) specifies the name of the font that you can use to apply the embed-ded font. The metadata alone does not permit the application to reference the font; to make it work, it is necessary to declare a variable immediately under the metadata typed as Class:

```
<mx:Script>
<![CDATA[

[Embed(source="C://WINDOWS/Fonts/BROADW.TTF",
               fontName="Broadway")]
private var _myEmbeddedFont:Class;

]]>
</mx:Script>

<mx:Label text="This is a sample text"
fontFamily="Broadway"  />
```

You can also embed a font using CSS with the @font-face directive. The use of the [Embed] metadata or CSS depends on how you intend to manage styles in your application. If, for example, you have an external CSS that contains the declarations of style of the elements of the application, it is probably preferable to embed the font inside the CSS.

Let's see an example that uses the @font-face directive to embed a font:

```
<mx:Style>
@font-face
{
src: url("C://WINDOWS/Fonts/comic.TTF");
fontFamily: Comic;
}
</mx:Style>

<mx:Label text="This is a sample text"
fontFamily="Comic"  />
```

The @font-face directive uses the src attribute to specify the path of the font that must be declared in url(), and defines the name of the font imported through the fontFamily property.

When you embed a font, only one weight of the font outline is embedded. So if you want to use that font by applying the bold style to it, you must import the font class with the bold style applied:

```
<mx:Style>
@font-face
{
```

9

```
    src: url("C://WINDOWS/Fonts/comic.TTF");
    fontFamily: Comic;
}

@font-face
{
src: url("C://WINDOWS/Fonts/comicbd.TTF");
fontFamily: ComicBold;
}

</mx:Style>

<mx:Label text="This is a sample text"
fontFamily="ComicBold"  />
```

In this solution, you will see how to apply and use the three types of fonts used by Flex.

How to build it

The application will be formatted by two Panel containers that will contain the same elements: a ComboBox, a TextArea, and a Button control. You will apply different fonts to these controls, using both system, device, and embedded fonts.

1. Create the application file in Flex Builder by selecting File ➤ New ➤ MXML Application and naming it Chapter_9_Flex_Sol_7_Layout.mxml.

2. Insert two Panel containers that will contain the controls. The first Panel will contain the components to which you will apply different fonts, but using only system and device fonts. The second Panel will contain the same elements, but will use embedded fonts. Insert the following code:

```
<mx:Application xmlns:mx="http://www.adobe.com/2006/mxml"
layout="horizontal">

<mx:Panel width="250" height="200" layout="absolute"
title="System/Device fonts">

<mx:TextArea x="10" y="45" height="61">
<mx:text>Lorem ipsum dolor sit amet,
consectetur adipisicing elit,
sed do eiusmod tempor incididunt ut
labore et dolore magna aliqua.
</mx:text>
</mx:TextArea>

<mx:ComboBox x="10" y="10" >
<mx:String>First Value</mx:String>
<mx:String>Second Value</mx:String>
</mx:ComboBox>
```

```
<mx:Button x="10" y="114" label="Button" />

<mx:ControlBar>
</mx:ControlBar>
</mx:Panel>

<mx:Panel width="250" height="200" layout="absolute"
 title="Embedded Fonts">

<mx:TextArea x="10" y="42"
height="64">
<mx:text>Lorem ipsum dolor sit amet,
consectetur adipisicing elit,
sed do eiusmod tempor incididunt ut
labore et dolore magna aliqua.
</mx:text>
</mx:TextArea>

<mx:ComboBox x="10" y="10" >
<mx:String>First Value</mx:String>
<mx:String>Second Value</mx:String>
</mx:ComboBox>

<mx:Button x="10" y="114" label="Button"/>
<mx:ControlBar>
</mx:ControlBar>

</mx:Panel>
```

You have differentiated the two Panel containers by assigning different titles to them. Their layout property is set to absolute, which forces you to specify absolute positioning for the child elements in the Panel by specifying the properties x and y. The two ComboBox controls are populated by defining two simple strings with the <mx:String> tag:

```
<mx:ComboBox x="10" y="10" >
<mx:String>First Value</mx:String>
<mx:String>Second Value</mx:String>
</mx:ComboBox>
```

Notice that the TextArea controls have dummy text. You have inserted the classic Latin text Lorem ipsum … in the text property declared as a nested tag:

```
<mx:TextArea x="10" y="42"
height="64">
<mx:text>Lorem ipsum dolor sit amet,
consectetur adipisicing elit,
sed do eiusmod tempor incididunt ut
labore et dolore magna aliqua.
</mx:text>
</mx:TextArea>
```

9

Before closing the Panels, a ControlBar was inserted.

3. Insert an <mx:Style> block immediately under the <mx:Application> tag, in which you will declare a CSS class. To create a CSS class you can use any name, but it must begin with a period (.myClassName). In this way, Flex will recognize those settings as a CSS class and can apply them to the text elements:

```
<mx:Style>
.simpleText
{
font-family: "_serif";
font-size: 14;
}
</mx:Style>
```

The simpleText class uses the device font _serif by using the font-family directive. The Times New Roman font is usually applied to this font category (Macintosh systems use Times font). The font is also set to 14 px with the font-size directive. To apply a CSS class to a text, use the styleName property in the next step.

4. Define the fonts to use for the controls in the first Panel by acting on the fontFamily property. You can set this property by manually inserting code or by making use of the Flex Properties view that you access from the Design mode of the Flex Builder Code Editor, as shown in Figure 9-39.

```
<mx:Panel width="250" height="200"
➥ layout="absolute"
title="System/Device fonts">

<mx:TextArea x="10" y="45" height="61"
styleName="simpleText">
<mx:text>Lorem ipsu dolor sit amet,
consectetur adipisicing elit,
sed do eiusmod tempor incididunt ut
labore et dolore magna aliqua.
</mx:text>
</mx:TextArea>

<mx:ComboBox x="10" y="10"
fontFamily="Times New Roman"
fontWeight="bold" fontSize="14">
<mx:String>First Value</mx:String>
<mx:String>Second Value</mx:String>
</mx:ComboBox>

<mx:Button x="10" y="114" label="Button"
fontFamily="Courier New" fontSize="12"/>
```

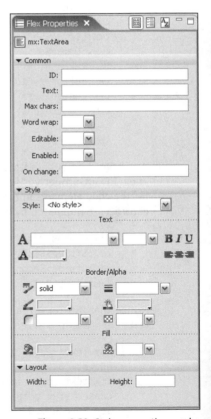

Figure 9-39. Style properties can be declared visually by the Flex Properties view.

```
<mx:ControlBar>
</mx:ControlBar>
</mx:Panel>
```

You have changed the font used by the application for the three controls. For the TextArea control you have linked the CSS class that you created in the preceding step to the styleName property:

```
<mx:TextArea x="10" y="45" height="61"
➥ styleName="simpleText">
```

Instead, for the ComboBox you have used the inline fontFamily property to use the Times New Roman system font for which you have specified a bold fontWeight and a text dimension equal to 14 pixels (fontSize property):

```
<mx:ComboBox x="10" y="10"
fontFamily="Times New Roman"
fontWeight="bold" fontSize="14">
```

Also for the Button control, you have specified the use of a system font (Courier New) by using the same inline properties:

```
<mx:Button x="10" y="114" label="Button"
fontFamily="Courier New" fontSize="12"/>
```

You can already see how the fonts for these three controls will be displayed by running the application or by moving to the Design mode in the Code Editor of Flex Builder. The result is shown in Figure 9-40.

5. Look at the second Panel (that is, its controls). You will use the embedded fonts by importing them with two techniques: by using the [Embed] metadata and the @font-face directive in CSS. Add an <mx:Script> block and declare the [Embed] metadata that will import the Broadway font installed on the system with the name BROADW.TTF:

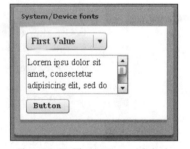

Figure 9-40. The system and device fonts are applied to the text used in the controls.

```
<mx:Application xmlns:mx="http://www.adobe.com/
➥ 2006/mxml"
layout="horizontal">

<mx:Script>
<![CDATA[
[Embed(source="C://WINDOWS/Fonts/BROADW.TTF",
        fontName="Broadway")]
private var _myEmbeddedFont:Class;
]]>
</mx:Script>

<mx:Style>
```

On Windows systems, the fonts folder is located in the following path: C:/WINDOWS/Fonts/. All the fonts installed in the system are located in this folder.

Mac OS X has multiple Fonts folders. It uses four or more Fonts folders, depending on the software installation and the number of users:

Table 9-1. Standard Fonts folders

Font type	Folder
User	/Library/Fonts/
Local	/Library/Fonts/
Network	/Network/Library/Fonts/
System	/System/Library/Fonts/
Classic	/System Folder/Fonts/

The [Embed] metadata uses the source attribute to specify the absolute path of the font to embed and links a name to this font to be able to reference it in the application. To import the font, you must declare a variable typed as Class immediately under the metadata.

6. Use the second method to embed the font. In the <mx:Style> block, import the font by using the @font-face directive:

```
<mx:Style>

@font-face
{
src: url("C://WINDOWS/Fonts/comic.TTF");
font-family: Comic;
}

@font-face
{
src: url("C://WINDOWS/Fonts/comicbd.TTF");
fontFamily: ComicBold;
}

.simpleText
{
font-family: "_serif";
font-size: 14;
}
</mx:Style>
```

The @font-face rule is the same as that used in the XHTML pages to define a font descriptor (www.w3.org/TR/REC-CSS2/fonts.html#font-descriptions) because Flex supports the W3C CSS standard.

The following example shows how a font is imported in an XHTML page and how the font is applied to an H1 heading (note that Flex uses a similar format in its declaration):

```
<!DOCTYPE html PUBLIC "-//W3C//DTD XHTML 1.0 Strict//EN"
"http://www.w3.org/TR/xhtml1/DTD/xhtml1-strict.dtd"><HTML>
  <HEAD>
    <TITLE>Font test</TITLE>
    <STYLE TYPE="text/css" MEDIA="screen, print">
      @font-face {
        font-family: "Robson Celtic";
        src: url("http://www.mydomain.com/fonts/rob-celt")
      }
      H1 { font-family: "Robson Celtic", serif }
    </STYLE>
  </HEAD>
  <BODY>
    <H1> This heading is displayed using an embedded font</H1>
  </BODY>
</HTML>
```

To use the embedded fonts, use the same properties used for the system and device fonts: fontFamily.

7. Specify the fontFamily property in the controls contained in the second Panel, as shown in bold:

```
<mx:Panel width="250" height="200" layout="absolute"
 title="Embedded Fonts">

<mx:TextArea x="10" y="42"
fontFamily="Comic" fontSize="12"
height="64">
<mx:text>Lorem ipsum dolor sit amet,
consectetur adipisicing elit,
sed do eiusmod tempor incididunt ut
labore et dolore magna aliqua.
</mx:text>
</mx:TextArea>

<mx:ComboBox x="10" y="10"
fontFamily="Broadway" fontSize="12">
<mx:String>First Value</mx:String>
<mx:String>Second Value</mx:String>
</mx:ComboBox>
```

9

```
<mx:Button x="10" y="114"
label="Button" fontFamily="ComicBold"/>

<mx:ControlBar>
</mx:ControlBar>
</mx:Panel>
```

The TextArea control uses the fontFamily Comic font, which was embedded in the <mx:Style> block with the @font-face rule. The Button control also uses the second font embedded in the <mx:Style> block. Instead, the ComboBox uses the fontFamily Broadway font, imported using the [Embed] metadata in ActionScript.

8. Save and run the application.

As shown in Figure 9-41, the specified fonts are applied to all the controls.

To carry out a test and see the real benefits of the use of the embedded fonts, publish the application and see it on a client who has not installed the font. You will see that the text is formatted with that font because the font is merged into the SWF file.

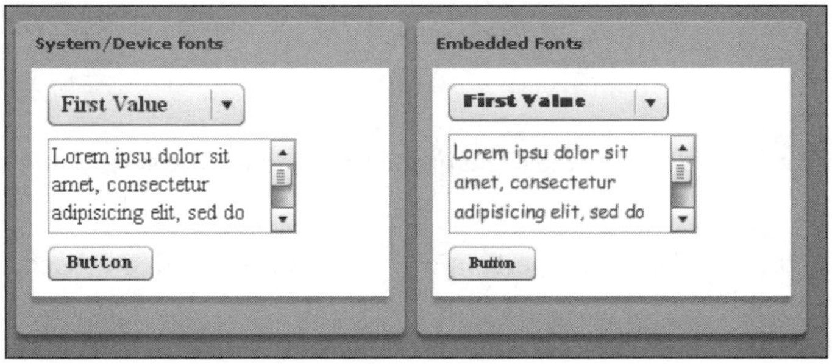

Figure 9-41. The system and device fonts are applied to the text used in the controls.

Expert tips

When you use an embedded font you can import it by using its name instead of pointing at the TTF file. In fact, the operating system links a name to every font, and this name can be used both by the [Embed] tag and the @font-face directive.

1. Modify the <mx:Script> block of the file created in this solution by adding a new font but using its system name:

```
<mx:Script>
<![CDATA[
[Embed(source="C://WINDOWS/Fonts/BROADW.TTF", fontName="Broadway")]
private var _myEmbeddedFont:Class;

[Embed(systemFont="Papyrus",
fontName="Pap",
```

```
fontWeight="bold",
mimeType="application/x-font-truetype")]
private var _myEmbeddedFontName:Class;

]]>
</mx:Script>
```

Instead of using the attribute source of the [Embed] metadata, use the systemFont property that you link to the name of the font recognized by the system. Furthermore, you must also add the MIME type through the mimeType attribute that assumes the value application/x-font or application/x-font-truetype to import a font.

> *Multipurpose Internet Mail Extensions (MIME) is an Internet standard that extends the format of e-mail to support text in character sets other than US-ASCII, nontext attachments, multipart message bodies, and header information in non-ASCII character sets.*

2. Apply the same procedure to font embedding using its system name by specifying it in CSS. Add the following code to the <mx:Style> block:

```
<mx:Style>

@font-face
{
src: local("Lucida Sans");
font-family: Lucida;
}

@font-face
{
src: url("C://WINDOWS/Fonts/comic.TTF");
font-family: Comic;
}
.simpleText
{
font-family: "_serif";
font-size: 14;
}
</mx:Style>
```

Using the CSS @font-face directive changes; instead of using the src attribute, use local, in which you specify the system name of the font.

3. You can now apply these new embedded fonts to the text by modifying the fontFamily properties of the controls in the second Panel of your application:

```
<mx:Panel width="250" height="200" layout="absolute" title="Embedded
Fonts">

<mx:TextArea x="10" y="42"
fontFamily="Pap" fontSize="12" height="64">
```

```
<mx:text>Lorem ipsu dolor sit amet,
consectetur adipisicing elit,
sed do eiusmod tempor incididunt ut labore
et dolore magna aliqua.</mx:text>
</mx:TextArea>

<mx:ComboBox x="10" y="10"
 fontFamily="Lucida" fontSize="12">
<mx:String>First Value</mx:String>
<mx:String>Second Value</mx:String>
</mx:ComboBox>
<mx:Button x="10" y="114"
➥ label="Button" fontFamily="Comic"/>
<mx:ControlBar>
</mx:ControlBar>
</mx:Panel>
```

4. Save and run the application.

Figure 9-42 shows the final result with the new fonts used for the ComboBox and the TextArea control.

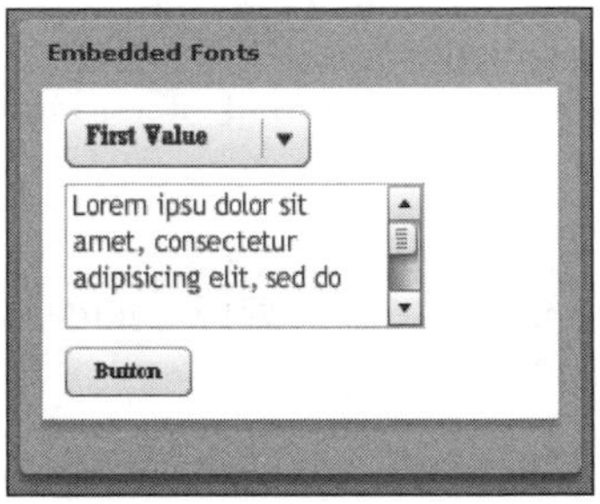

Figure 9-42. System and device fonts are applied to the text used in the controls.

Solution 9-8: Importing Flash CS3 assets into Flex

Although Flex is an ideal tool for quickly creating RIAs, there are times when Flash still proves to be the best tool; for example, during animation creation using the Timeline. The concept of the Timeline is missing in Flex (I would say that this is a huge advantage), in which everything is programmed in a single screen.

Adobe Flash CS3 compiles applications in SWF files that are compatible with Flash Player 9, just like Flex. It is, therefore, easy to believe that between the two products there can be a strong integration. (Adobe has worked a lot in this area, giving the capability to Flash developers to create Flex controls, containers, skins, and assets that can then be imported and used in Flex.) Aside from loading and interacting with SWF files, which is native for Flex with the SWFLoader, you can use a command in Flash CS3 to directly create a Flex component starting from a Flash file. To use this function you must use the Flex Component Kit for Flash CS3.

The Flex Component Kit for Flash CS3 is a free extension that you can download with the Adobe Extension Manager tool (www.adobe.com/exchange/em_download/) and install it in Flash CS3. With this extension you can save a Flash asset as a Flex component in SWC format. This format (discussed in Chapter 2) can be imported into the Flex project as a Library; you can then use it like any other component.

In this solution you will create a Flex component from Adobe Flash CS3 that you will export using the Flex Component Kit.

What's involved

To install and use the Flex Component Kit, you need to have the following software (as well as having Flex 2.0.1 or better installed):

- **Flash CS3 Professional**: Download a trial version here: http://www.adobe.com/go/flash.
- **Adobe Extension Manager**: This software is included with all the CS3 suites and the Adobe Master Collection, or you can download it here: www.adobe.com/exchange/em_download/.

After installing these two programs, you can proceed to installing the extension Flex Component Kit file for Flash CS3 that must be downloaded here: http://download.macromedia.com/pub/labs/flex_flash_integrationkit/flex_component_kit_042307.mxp.

> The MXP format stands for Macromedia (now Adobe) Extension Package File.

Double-click the downloaded MXP file and follow the instructions in the Extension Manager that will automatically open, as shown in Figure 9-43.

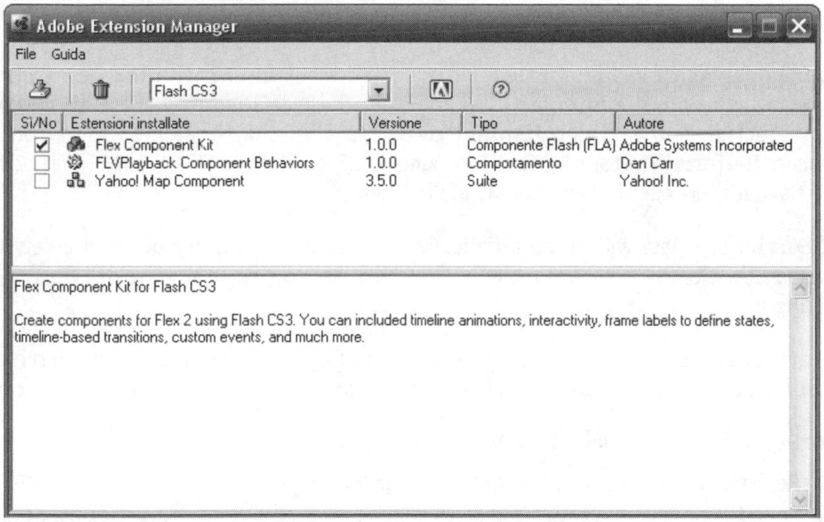

Figure 9-43. Follow the instructions in the Extension Manager to install the Flex Component Kit file.

Once you have installed the extension, you can open Adobe Flash CS3 and check that the installation has been successful by selecting Make Flex Component from the Commands menu (see Figure 9-44).

Figure 9-44. The new Make Flex Component command

This new command enables you to import Flash assets such as SWC files into Flex applications.

The components that will be created and exported by Flash CS3 with this new command are subclasses of the UIMovieClip class found in the mx.flash package. This class is, in turn, a subclass of the flash.display.MovieClip class that implements the following interfaces: IDeferredInstantiationUIComponent, IToolTipManagerClient, IStateClient, IFocusManagerComponent, and IconstraintClient.

The UIMovieClip class will be automatically inserted in the Library of Flash assets when the Make Flex Component command is launched, so you do not have to worry about importing it.

There are no particular constraints in the creation of a Flash content that will then have to be exported as a Flex component. Follow this advice to guarantee a successful export:

- Exported content must be a MovieClip symbol.
- Registration point should be in the upper-left corner.
- Frame rate should be 24 to match Flex's default frame rate (this operation will be automatically performed when you execute the Make Flex Component command).
- The symbol name in the Library should be a valid ActionScript class name.

The use of Flash to create components that will then be used in Flex is handy, especially when you want to use functions that only Flash has (for example, using the Timeline to create animation or using components of Flash to skin the Flex components).

In this solution you will create a Flash file that will use the new FLVPlaybackCaptioning components. The captioning component (FLVPLaybackCaptioning) is a new component that has been added to Flash CS3 (see Figure 9-45) that works with the FLVPlayBack component to add captioning functions. The text that is displayed is loaded and synchronized by an XML file.

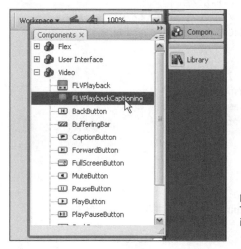

Figure 9-45.
The new FLVPlaybackCaptioning option in the Components panel of Flash CS3

The FLVPlaybackCaptioning component loads captions in the FLVPlayback component through the use of a Timed-Text XML document. This is a W3C standard (www.w3.org/AudioVideo/TT/).

The Timed-Text specification (www.w3.org/AudioVideo/TT/) should cover all necessary aspects of Timed Text on the Web. Typical applications of Timed Text include real-time subtitling of foreign-language movies on the Web, captioning for people lacking audio devices or who have hearing impairments, karaoke, scrolling news items, and teleprompter applications.

In this solution you will create a file in Flash that you will then export with the Flex Component Kit and use in a Flex application.

How to build it

This solution will be composed of more files. Create a file with Adobe Flash CS3 using FLVPlaybackCaptioning and FLVPlayback components, which you will export with the Flex Component Kit. Once the component is generated, an SWC file will then be imported in the Flex project and used in a new main application file. Create an XML file that will be used by the Flash file to read the captioning to synchronize to video. This solution uses an FLV file recorded with a digital camera, but you can use any video in FLV format.

9

1. Create the file that will be used to create the captioning. This file is a simple XML file that can be created with any text editor. You can also use Flex Builder and create a new file by selecting File ➤ New ➤ File and saving it as captions.xml in the same folder in which you will create the Flash file. In this example, a folder named fla was created. Insert the following code into this XML file:

```
<?xml version="1.0" encoding="UTF-8"?>
<tt xml:lang="en" xmlns="http://www.w3.org/2006/04/ttaf1"
xmlns:tts="http://www.w3.org/2006/04/ttaf1#styling">
<head>
<styling>
<style id="1" tts:textAlign="right"/>
<style id="2" tts:color="transparent"/>
<style id="3" style="2" tts:backgroundColor="white"/>
<style id="4" style="2 3" tts:fontSize="20"/>
</styling>
</head>
<body>
 <div xml:lang="en">
<p begin="00:00:00.25" dur="00:00:15.00">
Exhibition at Palacavicchi Club - Rome, Italy, July 2007
</p>
<p begin="00:00:15.10"dur="00:00:16.00">AbsoluteMambo members:</p>
<p begin="00:00:16.10" dur="00:00:18.00" >Sabrina Ranucci</p>
<p begin="00:00:18.10" dur="00:00:20.00">Martina di Cesare</p>
 <p begin="00:00:20.10" dur="00:00:23.00">Katia Madonna</p>
 <p begin="00:00:22.10" dur="00:02:25.00">
Visit website http://www.absolutemambo.it to see the upcoming
exhibition!
</p>
</div>
</body>
  </tt>
```

The timings to use for your video have been inserted in the captions.xml file. You have defined six different timings for which the starting and finishing times have been specified (begin and dur attributes).

To take the exact timings for your video, you can use the time code in the FLV Encoder. Adobe Flash CS3 FLV Video Encoder is a stand-alone, video-encoding application that lets you encode video in FLV format. As an alternative, you can use the Preview parameter in the FLVPlayback component. Otherwise, you can use QuickTime or Windows Media Player interfaces. For more information, go to http://livedocs.adobe.com/flash/9.0/flvencoder/FLV_27.html.

If you want to look in more detail at captioning in Flash 8 and Flash CS3, read Flash 8 Video, *by Tom Green and Jordan L Chilcott (friends of ED:* www.friendsofed. com/book.html?isbn=159059651X). *You can also read these two useful tutorials, also by Tom Green:* www.digital-web.com/articles/captions_flash_video/ *and* www. digital-web.com/articles/captions_flash_video_2.

2. Open Flash CS3 and create a new Flash file that you will save as videoCaption.fla. In this file, immediately create a new MovieClip symbol by selecting Insert ➤ New Symbol, as shown in Figure 9-46. The Create New Symbol dialog box opens. Name this MovieClip symbol videoCaption and leave MovieClip as Type. Click OK. The symbol has been created and inserted in the Flash Library (you will find this panel on the right side of the working area). You will create the entire interface of the component in this MovieClip that you will export.

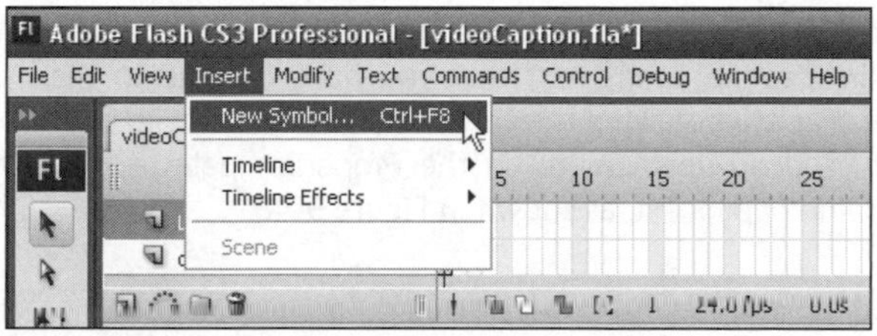

Figure 9-46. Inserting a new symbol

3. Make sure that you have opened the videoCaption MovieClip (you can open it by double-clicking it in the Library). From the Components panel on the right side of the working area, select Window ➤ Components and then drag an FLVPlayback component and an FLVPlaybackCaptioning component onto the Stage (see Figure 9-47). While the first component should be positioned and dimensioned, the second (FLVPlaybackCaptioning), will not be visible at runtime, so you can put it wherever you prefer.

Figure 9-47.
Dragging an FLVPlayback component and an FLVPlaybackCaptioning component to the Stage

9

4. Select the FLVPlayback component and click the Parameters tab in the Property Inspector. The Parameters tab allows you to specify properties for the selected components. Immediately assign the FLV video that you want to load to the source property of the component. For this example, you will use the salsa.flv video that you will find in the fla folder of the Flex project. If you want, you can link a skin to the FLVPlayback by clicking from the Parameters panel on the Skin property. The Select Skin dialog box will be opened, and you can select one of the skins from the drop-down menu.

5. Create a dynamic text field using the Text tool from the Tool palette. This text field will contain the captioning text that you have defined in the captions.xml file. Make sure that after clicking the Text field, the Dynamic Text option is selected from the Text type drop-down menu in the Properties palette. Give the text field the instance name captionTxt, as shown in Figure 9-48.

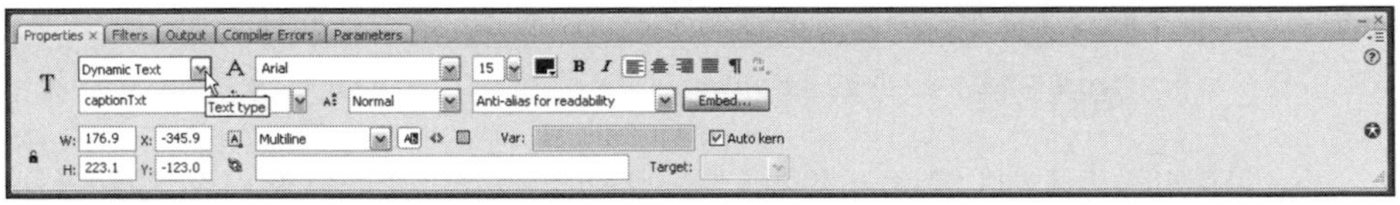

Figure 9-48. The settings of the dynamic Text field in the Properties palette

6. Select the FLVPlaybackCaptioning component and from the Parameters palette specify the following parameters:

- autoLayout: false
- captionTargetName: captionTxt
- flvPlaybackName: auto
- showCaptions: true
- simpleFormatting: false
- source: captions.xml

Figure 9-49 shows how the Parameters palette of the FLVPlaybackCaptioning component should look:

Figure 9-49. The settings in the Parameters palette

Through the source property FLVPlaybackCaptioning component, load the text that should be used as subtitles for the video and automatically link the timing of the text to the video.

7. Save the file. If you want to see a preview, you have to drag the MovieClip from the Library onto the Stage of the main Timeline and select Publish the Flash File (File ➤ Publish). You can see the final result in Figure 9-50.

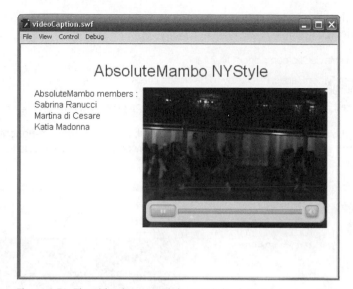

Figure 9-50. The video is run, and the text is loaded and synchronized.

8. All that is left is to export the MovieClip as a Flex component using the kit you installed. Open the Library and select the videoCaption MovieClip. When you export a Flex component from Flash, the command can be performed only on MovieClips in the Library. Go to the Commands menu and select the Make Flex Component command, as shown in Figure 9-51.

> *Make sure that you have installed the extension Flex Component Kit file for Flash CS3* (http://download.macromedia.com/pub/labs/flex_flash_integrationkit/ flex_component_kit_042307.mxp).

9

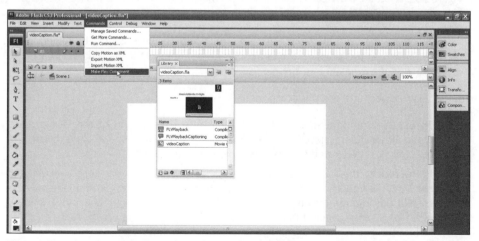

Figure 9-51. Select the MovieClip in the Library and then select the Make Flex Component command.

After launching the Make Flex Component command, Flash lays out the setting for using the Flex component, carrying out the following two operations:

- Imported UIMovieClip component to library.
- Component "videoCaption" is ready to be used in Flex.

This text is inserted in the Output panel in the Properties palette, as shown in Figure 9-52.

Furthermore, in the Library, the UIMovieClip class is added, in that all the components that will be created and exported from Flash CS3 with this new command are subclasses of the UIMovieClip class.

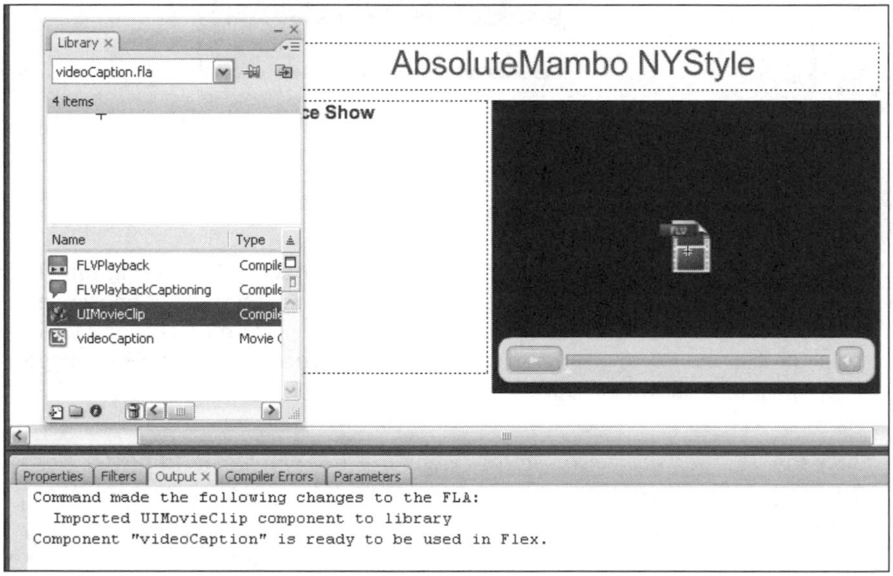

Figure 9-52. Select the MovieClip in the Library from the Commands menu and select the Make Flex Components command.

9. To create the SWC file from Flash, you must publish the Flash file by selecting File ➤ Publish. At this point, in the same folder that contains the Flash file on which you are working, you will find the file videoCaption.swc.

You can now import and use this component in Flex.

10. To use the component, you must add it to the Library path of the Flex project. Open Flex Builder, select Project ➤ Properties ➤ Flex Build Path ➤ Library Path, and add the SWC generated by Flash, as shown in Figure 9-53.

11. In the root of the Flex project, copy the salsa.flv file, the captions.xml file, and the SWF file you chose as a graphic skin for the FLVPlayback component (in the case of the solution created in Flash, it is the SkinUnderAllNoVolNoCaptionNoFull. swf file). Create a new MXML application file by selecting File ➤ New ➤ MXML Application and name it Chapter_9_Flex_Sol_8_Layout.mxml.

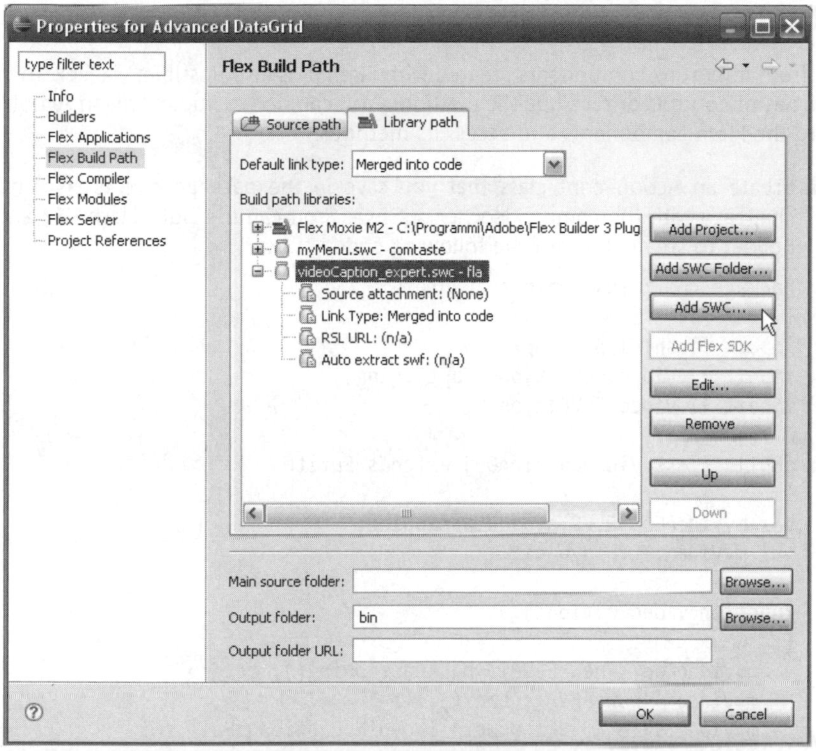

Figure 9-53. Add the SWC file to the Library path of the Flex project.

12. Add the custom namespace to import the component in your application. On the `<mx:Application>` tag, insert the following code:

```
<mx:Application xmlns:mx="http://www.adobe.com/2006/mxml"
layout="vertical" xmlns:comp="*">
```

13. You can now use the custom namespace to invoke the component created by Flash. To do this, insert the reference to the name of the SWC file imported in the namespace comp:

```
<mx:Application xmlns:mx="http://www.adobe.com/2006/mxml"
   layout="vertical" xmlns:comp="*">

<comp:videoCaption id="myFlashVideo" />

</mx:Application>
```

14. Save the file and run the application to see the Flash component imported and used by the Flex application.

Expert tips

Aside from importing components created with Flash, it is also possible, via Flex, to invoke properties of controls or recall public methods. You can, for example, link an ActionScript class to the Flash components and access its methods.

1. Create an ActionScript class that you save in the package com.flexsolutions. chapter9 with the name VideoCaptionObj.as. You can use both Flash CS3 and Flex Builder to create it. Insert the following code:

```
package com.flexsolutions.chapter9
{
import flash.display.Sprite
import fl.video.FLVPlaybackCaptioning;
import fl.video.FLVPlayback;

public class VideoCaptionObj extends Sprite
{
var myVideoCap:FLVPlaybackCaptioning;
var myVideo:FLVPlayback;

function videoCaption()
{
   myVideoCap = new FLVPlaybackCaptioning();
   myVideo = new FLVPlayback();
   myVideo.skin = "SkinUnderAllNoVolNoCaptionNoFull.swf ";
   myVideo.setSize(320,240);
   addChild(myVideoCap);
   addChild(myVideo);
}

public function setSources(xmlSource:String,
flvSource:String):void
{

   myVideoCap.source = xmlSource;
   myVideo.play(flvSource);
}

}

}
```

The class creates an instance of the FLVPlaybackCaptioning component and the FLVPlayback component and adds them on the Stage with the addChild() method. It then gives a dimension to the FLVPlayback component and applies a graphic skin for the video controller. Finally the public method setSources() has been declared that accepts, as a parameter, the path of the FLV file and the XML file that contains the text to use for the captioning.

This class will enable you to create a completely empty MovieClip in Flash that will be created in a completely dynamic way via ActionScript 3.

2. Create a new file in Flash CS3 and repeat the same steps that you carried out to export an SWC component to use in Flex. However, the MovieClip that you will create will be empty. Make sure to drag the FLVPlaybackCaptioning and the FLVPlayback components that will be instanced via code into the Flash Library (not onto the Stage). Insert the following code as frame script on the first frame of the MovieClip Timeline:

```
import com.flexsolutions.chapter9.videoCaptionObj

var myCap:VideoCaptionObj = new VideoCaptionObj();
addChild(myCap);
```

This code imports the class that you have created and creates the instance of the VideoCaptionObj object.

3. Run the Make Flex Component command and publish the file.

4. Import the new SWC file into Flex by selecting Project ➤ Properties ➤ Flex Build Path ➤ Library Path and add the SWC file generated by Flash.

5. Create a new MXML application file by selecting File ➤ New ➤ MXML Application, name it Chapter_9_Flex_Sol_8_expert_Layout.mxml, and insert the following code:

```
<mx:Application xmlns:mx="http://www.adobe.com/2006/mxml"
layout="vertical" xmlns:comp="*">

  <mx:Script>
  <![CDATA[

private function createVideo():void
{
myFlashVideo.setUpVideo('captions.xml','salsa.flv');
}
  ]]>
  </mx:Script>

  <comp:videoCaption id="myFlashVideo" initialize="createVideo()" />

</mx:Application>
```

You have imported the videoCaption component and given it an identifier: myFlashVideo. On the initialize event of the component, call the function createVideo() that will in turn recall the public method setUpVideo() of the ActionScript class used by the Flash component.

6. Save the file and run the application.

The video salsa.flv is loaded, and the caption text is synchronized.

Summary

Flex allows developers and designers to create attractive and rich user interfaces and layouts for their RIAs. In this chapter you learned about techniques for changing the look and feel of applications and the appearance of Flex components.

You created a basic layout in Flex using containers and controls, starting from a PNG layout provided by a designer. You used the features of Flex to automatically position the containers and controls, applying predefined rules to every element. You gave width and height dimensions to the page elements, sometimes specifying in pixels and other times in percentages.

You used the constraint-based layout approach for positioning and laying out elements in a page with absolute positioning. This technique allows you to position user interface elements of the page with absolute rule. This means that for every element of the page, you specify its x and y properties, which define its exact positioning onscreen.

To give a more personal graphical touch to the application, you learned how to use styles in Flex. Styles allow you to change settings such as the color, the dimension of the font, the background, alphas, and more. They can be programmed and applied at both runtime and compile time.

The chapter then discussed skinning the Flex application to change the appearance of components by editing their visual elements or by creating new ones. You learned the programmatic skins technique to write ActionScript classes that use the drawing API of Flash Player.

At the end of the chapter you discovered one of the new features of Flash CS3: the Flex Component Kit. Adobe has worked to give Flash developers the capability to create Flex controls, containers, skins, and assets that can then be imported and used in Flex. Besides being able to load and interact with SWF files, you can use a command in Flash CS3 to directly create a Flex component starting from a Flash file. To use this function, you must also use the Flex Component Kit for Flash CS3.

10 FLEX SECURITY

Security is a fundamental aspect in the development of an application, and different levels of security can be guaranteed to each project—taking into consideration the interaction with data and remote calls.

Flex applications are SWF files that are loaded from Flash Player. The SWF file, usually contained in an HTML page, is deployed on the server and used on the client. The content of an SWF file consists of ActionScript instructions in binary format, which means that a large part of the levels of security is managed by Flash Player or from the remote server that hosts the application.

Flash Player runs inside a security sandbox that protects the client from possible damaging attacks. A **sandbox** is a security mechanism for safely running programs. The Flex framework also provides security mechanisms that guarantee security when you access a remote call with web services, HTTP services, and remote objects.

Flex applications have two types of security: declarative and programmatic. **Declarative** security operates at server level and uses configuration, authentication, and authorization to protect the server and the application hosted by it from undesired visits. This type of level of security does not act on a single application; it defines the general rules applied at server level. **Programmatic security**, on the other hand, gives the developer more granular and precise control over a single application and over the various external resources used by it.

The advantage of one method over another is evaluated case by case. It is easy to guess that declarative security renders the application independent and more reusable because no settings or code are applied at that level.

At the client level, the Flex application consists of an SWF file that contains all the calls to external resources. Because this SWF file is loaded on the client's machine by Flash Player, the level of security at this level depends exclusively on Flash Player.

The security sandbox of Flash Player enables an SWF file deployed on the domain `www.mydomain.com` to load resources and data from that domain. Therefore, if the SWF application is that of Flex, if you try to recall an external resource from a different domain (such as `www.myotherdomain.com`), the security sandbox of Flash Player will block your attempt.

In fact, Flash Player creates different security sandboxes for each domain. The following domain examples are all considered individual domains by Flash Player:

- `http://comtaste.com`
- `www.comtaste.com`
- `http://194.242.61.188`
- `http://blog.comtaste.com`
- `https://casario.blogs.com`

In this chapter you'll look at problems that can occur when you apply security levels to a Flex application.

Solution 10-1: Using a cross-domain policy file to load data on a different domain

Flash Player does not allow an application to receive data from any type of domain different from the one in which the SWF is loaded. In fact, when the Flex application is downloaded onto the client from Flash Player, a security sandbox is applied that limits the exchange of data to only the domain from which the SWF file has been downloaded.

Although this may seem inconvenient, it guarantees a very effective level of security. In fact, it enables you to avoid improper and potentially damaging use with respect to the capacity of the player that Adobe offers. The JavaScript language offers a security model that is very similar.

Fortunately Flash Player provides the capability of loading data from different domains with these three methods:

- Use a cross-domain policy file that specifies the names of the domains that can be accessed and external data.
- Create a proxy on the server that access the data.
- Use the Security.allowDomain() method to grant the access.

You'll use each of these methods in the solutions in this chapter.

The cross-domain file is an XML file in which you can specify the valid domains to which the server can permit the exchange of and access to data from calls originating from the SWF files outside of that domain. This file must be positioned on the principle root of the web server that the Flex application is contacting and permit access to the following external resources:

- Video and file audio
- Images (PNG, JPG, GIF and SVG formats)
- Data in XML text files
- Socket server and XML socket connections
- SWF files

In this solution you'll see how to create a cross-domain file.

What's involved

The cross-domain file is an XML-based file that must be saved with the name crossdomain.xml. Being a valid XML file, it inherits all the rules of this language. The file, in fact, begins with an xml declaration and with the <cross-domain-policy> root tag:

```
<?xml version="1.0"?>
<cross-domain-policy>

</cross-domain-policy>
```

10

In the root tag you can declare the domains that the server will deem valid to establish a connection and exchange data:

```
<?xml version="1.0"?>
<cross-domain-policy>
  <allow-access-from domain="www.comtaste.com" />
</cross-domain-policy>
```

You can specify as many child nodes as you want to authorize to make calls:

```
<?xml version="1.0"?>
<cross-domain-policy>
  <allow-access-from domain="www.comtaste.com" />
  <allow-access-from domain="www.youthru.com" />
  <allow-access-from domain="www.mobymobile.com" />
</cross-domain-policy>
```

When the SWF file tries to make a request to the external domain (to a different domain from that on which the SWF is loaded) Flash Player sees whether a cross-domain policy file exists on that domain. So it searches for the presence of the crossdomain.xml file on the web root of that server. After it is found, Flash Player reads the contents of the XML file. If specified, it allows the SWF file that made the request to complete the operation.

The crossdomain.xml file can have an effect only on the domain in which it is copied. Imagine having transferred the crossdomain.xml file onto the domain www.comtaste.com. In the policy file you have specified that all the calls from the server www.augitaly.com are allowed:

```
<?xml version="1.0"?>
<cross-domain-policy>
  <allow-access-from domain="www.augitaly.com" />
</cross-domain-policy>
```

When a SWF file executed from the domain www.augitaly.com attempts to access resources on the www.comtaste.com domain, Flash Player automatically loads the crossdomain.xml file from that domain (www.comtaste.com) to check whether that call is allowed. If it is allowed, as shown previously, the resources on the www.comtaste.com domain are accessible to the SWF file.

Every <allow-access-from> node contains the domain attribute, which accepts the following values:

- IP address
- Domain name
- Use of a domain wildcard

The following child nodes are, therefore, all valid:

```
<?xml version="1.0"?>
<cross-domain-policy>
  <allow-access-from domain="88.149.156.198" />
  <allow-access-from domain="www.augitaly.com" />
  <allow-access-from domain="*" />
</cross-domain-policy>
```

The `<allow-access-from domain="88.149.156.198" />` node specifies the IP address of the `www.mobymobile.com` domain, whereas the `<allow-access-from domain="*" />` node uses the * wildcard to declare that any domain can load data from this server.

> *Pay attention when you use the * wildcard in the `<allow-access-from>` tag because you'll give the access to resources from any domain.*

There are some limitations of the declaration in the domain attributes:

- Wildcards can't be used when the IP domain is specified.
- Flash Player does not carry the DNS resolution. So if you specify an IP address, access is granted only to SWF files loaded from that IP address, not those loaded with domain-name syntax.

The `<allow-access-from>` node also accepts the secure attribute, which is set by default as true, but enables you to limit the connections that come from non-HTTPS protocol:

```
<allow-access-from domain="www.augitaly.com" secure="false" />
```

If you set the secure attribute to false you allow SWF files on a non-HTTPS server to load data from the HTTPS server.

> *Adobe advises against the use of this attribute because it exposes the server to snooping and spoofing attacks.*

In this solution you'll create a cross-domain policy file to load XML data from a server different from the one on which the Flex application resides.

How to build it

As with every new chapter, you begin by creating a new Flex project.

1. Open Flex Builder and create a Flex project using File ➤ New ➤ Flex Project with the name Chapter_10_Flex_Security. Click the Finish button.

2. Create a new XML file that will contain the domain settings by selecting File ➤ New ➤ File and assigning the name crossdomain.xml. Write the following XML code in that file:

10

```
<?xml version="1.0"?>
<cross-domain-policy>
  <allow-access-from domain="www.youthru.com" />
</cross-domain-policy>
```

This file specifies the domain for which a Flex application published on the domain www.comtaste.com can access data on another domain (in the solution you used the www.youthru.com domain, but you can replace it with your own).

This file must be transferred onto the web root of the server on which the call of the Flex application will be made. In this case you transferred the crossdomain.xml file onto the www.youthru.com web root.

3. From the data folder of the project created in Chapter 6, copy the XML file regions.xml and move it into a folder for the new project. Create a folder called data in the Chapter_10_Flex_Security project by selecting File ➤ New ➤ Folder. Copy the file into this folder.

The regions.xml file is a simple XML file that contains the regions of Italy:

```
<dataroot>
  <region>
    <id>1</id>
    <region>PIEMONTE</region>
  </region>
  <region>
    <id>3</id>
    <region>LOMBARDIA</region>
  </region>
</dataroot>
```

The root tag <dataroot> contains the repeating node <region>. In the application file (created in the next step) you'll use this XML file, which you'll position on a different domain.

4. Copy the regions.xml file onto the server on which you have copied the crossdomain.xml file (in this case it's the www.youthru.com domain).

5. You can now create the application file in Flex Builder. Create a new MXML application file by selecting File ➤ New ➤ MXML Application and name it Chapter_10_Flex_Sol_1.mxml.

6. This application will use the URLLoader class to load the external XML file published on a different domain. (Refer to in Solution 6-8 in Chapter 6 for a refresher on this class.) Insert the following ActionScript code into the file:

```
<mx:Script>
  <![CDATA[

    private var myURLService:URLLoader;

    private var myURL:URLRequest =  new➡
    URLRequest("http://www.youthru.com/flexsolutions/regions.xml");
```

```
    [Bindable]
    private var myData:XMLList;

    private function init(event:Event):void
    {
       myURLService = new URLLoader();
       myURLService.addEventListener(Event.COMPLETE, completeHandler);
       XML.ignoreWhitespace = true;
    }

    private function completeHandler(event:Event):void
    {
       myData = new XMLList(myURLService.data);
       myList.dataProvider = myData.region.region;
    }
  ]]>
</mx:Script>
```

It is practically the same code as the one defined in Solution 6-8. The myURL variable contains the absolute URL into which you have copied the XML file. You are trying to load the data into the Flex application from a domain different from the one on which the application resides.

Create an instance of the URLLoader class in the init() function and register the completeHandler() event handler on the COMPLETE event. This function links the dataProvider property to a List control with the values returned from the call to the file www.youthru.com/flexsolutions/regions.xml.

7. Now add a List control and a Button control. The latter will take care of launching the remote call by invoking the load() method of the URLLoader class to which the myURL variable that contains the instance of the URLRequest class will be sent:

```
</mx:Script>

<mx:List id="myList"  />

<mx:Button label="Send Remote Call"
click="myURLService.load(myURL);"/>

</mx:Application>
```

If you run the application without first copying the crossdomain.xml file onto the web root of the www.youthru.com domain, you'll get a security error and a sandbox violation (error #2044 and #2048 of Flash Player):

Error #2044: Unhandled SecurityErrorEvent:. text=Error #2048: Security sandbox violation

8. Save the file and run the application. Before running it, the application must be copied onto the www.comtaste.com domain or your own domain.

10

By clicking the button, the load() method of the URLLoader class is invoked and the HTTP call to the XML file is carried out. When the Flex application makes the call to a different domain, the Flash Player searches for the presence of a policy file on that server. When it finds the file, it verifies whether the domain from which the call originates is specified in one of the <allow-access-from> nodes. If the outcome of the search is positive, the data is loaded, as shown in Figure 10-1.

Figure 10-1.
The XML file is loaded and its data is inserted in the List control.

Expert tips

The URLLoader class enables you to load data from a URL as text, binary data, or URL-encoded variables. In this solution you downloaded an XML file. Even if you use only the complete event, the class also puts forward other events, which are very useful for tracking the progress of the call to the remote data:

- httpStatus: Released when the load() method of the URLLoader tries to address data through the HTTP protocol.
- ioError: Released if a fatal error in connection occurs, so the download of the data is terminated.
- open: Released when the load() method establishes the connection and causes the download of data to begin.
- progress: Tracks the progress of the download of data. It also puts forward properties that enable you to know the total number of bytes downloaded (bytesLoaded) and those to be downloaded (bytesTotal).
- securityError: Released if an error in the security sandbox of Flash Player occurs.

You could have extended the code by managing other event handlers like so:

```
myURLService.addEventListener(Event.OPEN, openHandler);
myURLService.addEventListener(ProgressEvent.PROGRESS, progressHandler);

private function openHandler(event:Event):void
{
  mx.controls.Alert.show("openHandler: " + event.type);
}
```

```
private function progressHandler(event:ProgressEvent):void
{
mx.controls.Alert.show("progressHandler loaded:" +➥
  event.bytesLoaded➥
    + " total: " + event.bytesTotal);
}
```

With the addEventListener() method you registered two event handlers that will be executed when Event.OPEN and ProgressEvent.PROGRESS are dispatched. The two event handlers will raise two alert boxes, as shown in Figure 10-2.

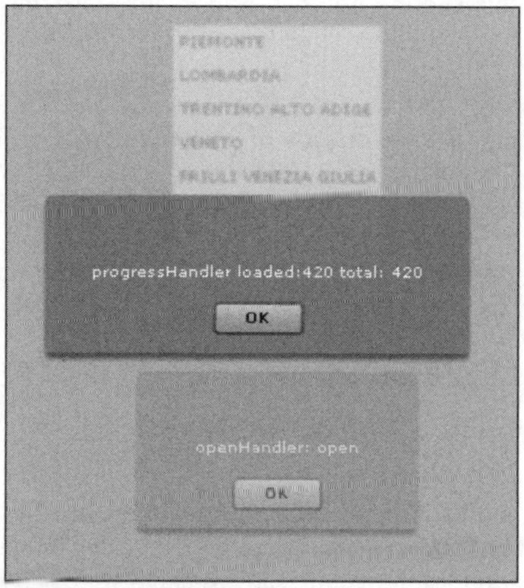

Figure 10-2. The window that appears when the events are released.

You have seen how it is possible to specify valid domains from which remote calls can be received by loading a cross-domain file onto the web root of the server. With the Security class contained in the flash.system package, you can specify a different name or an alternate directory in which Flash Player will look for the policy file.

By default, cross-domain files must be named crossdomain.xml and must reside in the root directory of the server. But if you use the Security.loadPolicyFile() method, you can force the SWF file to check for a different name or check in a different directory location.

With the Security.loadPolicyFile() method you can specify a remote path that points directly at the policy file:

```
Security.loadPolicyFile(➥
"http://www.youthru.com/flexsolutions/mypolicyfile.xml");
```

Although a cross-domain file published on the web root of the server operates at a global level for the whole server, a policy file loaded with the loadPolicyFile()method from a subdirectory applies its settings only to that directory and its subdirectories.

Solution 10-2: Loading SWF files into a Flex application with allowDomain()

You have already seen the constraints that the sandbox security of Flash Player imposes for loading assets external to the application (that is, residing on a different domain.)

With the SWFLoader control you can load an SWF file or an image in various formats (GIF, JPG, PNG, and SVG) in a Flex application. The source property of the SWFLoader enables you to specify content to load by sending its relative or absolute URL.

If the SWF file to be loaded is found on another domain, Flash Player does not permit it to be loaded.

However, there is a way around this. The Security class has the allowDomain() method, which gives you access to a SWF file outside of your domain. If, in fact, the Flex application that is calling the SWF file resides on a different domain, the SWF file must be able to grant access to it with the Security.allowDomain() method.

This technique is called **cross-domain scripting**. In this solution you'll see how to use the allowDomain() method to load a SWF file in a Flex application that resides on a different domain.

What's involved

The SWFLoader control, similar to the Image control you used in past solutions, enables you to load external images and SWF files. The control can reduce or increase the dimensions or scale of the loaded content, but can't receive the focus. Obviously the content loaded in the SWFLoader control maintains its interactivity and enables the user to interact with it.

To create a SWFLoader control you can use the MXML tag <mx:SWFLoader> or do it through ActionScript using the SWFLoader class inside the mx.controls package. The source property of the control enables you to specify the content to be loaded:

```
<mx:SWFLoader id="mySWF" width="300"
    source="myFile.swf" />
```

With ActionScript:

```
var mySWFL:mx.controls.SWFLoader = ➡
new mx.controls.SWFLoader()
mySWFL.source = 'myFile.swf';
```

You can also specify an absolute path and create an event handler to manage any eventual errors:

```
<mx:SWFLoader id="mySWF" width="300"
    source="http://www.youthru.com/flexsolutions/Chapter_10➡
    _Flex_Sol_2_allowDomain.swf"
    securityError="errorHandler(event)"/>
```

Having specified a different domain, if you try to run the file you get an error because of the Flash Player security sandbox that impedes data loading.

To be able to load and script the contents of the SWF you can use the `allowDomain()` method of the Security class:

```
Security.allowDomain("www.youthru.com")
```

This method can be used in an asymmetrical manner (specifying the `allowDomain()` method only on the SWF file that is being accessed—the accessing party) and in a symmetrical manner (by declaring the method in both files). In this way, you can carry out cross-domain scripting on both files. Figure 10-3 shows the scenario in which the `allowDomain()` method can help.

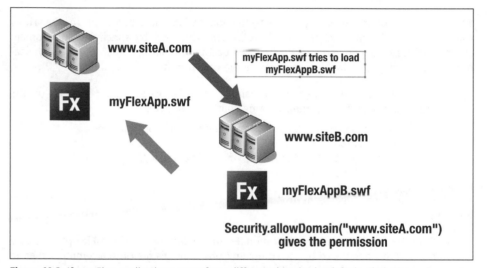

Figure 10-3. If two Flex applications come from different domains by default, Flash Player does not allow `myFlexApp.swf` to script `myFlexAppB.swf` nor `myFlexAppB.swf` to script `myFlexApp.swf`. The `Security.allowDomain()` method gives permission to SWF files for cross-scripting.

In this solution you'll see how to use the `allowDomain()` method to load a SWF file from a different domain to the one on which the Flex application is deployed.

How to build it

For this solution you'll create two SWF files: the same file created in Solution 10-1, which will function as the SWF file to be loaded; and the Flex application that uses `SWFLoader` to load. You'll specify the `allowDomain()` method on both files to create a symmetrical access for both files.

1. Open the `Chapter_10_Flex_Sol_1.mxml` file and save a copy of it with the name Chapter_10_Flex_Sol_2_allowDomain.mxml. This application loads a remote XML file by using the `URLRequest()` class. You'll use this application as the SWF file to load in another application that will act as the container.

10

2. You add only the allowDomain() method to this file. Create an <mx:Script> block below the Application tag:

```
<mx:Script>
  <![CDATA[

import flash.system.Security;

private function initDomain():void
{
  Security.allowDomain("www.mobymobile.com/flexsolutions/");
}
  ]]>
</mx:Script>
```

You have imported the Security class into the application and created the initDomain() function in which you declare the allowDomain() method by specifying the domain www.mobymobile.com/flexsolutions. This will be the domain on which the Flex application will be deployed; it will also try to make the call from here.

3. Create the initDomain() event handler on the preinitialize event of the Application by making the following change to the code:

```
<mx:Application xmlns:mx=http://www.adobe.com/2006/mxml➥
  layout="vertical"
  creationComplete="init(event);" preinitialize="initDomain()"
  height="300" width="300">
```

You have also given dimensions to this file, setting the width and height properties at 300 pixels.

4. Save the file and run the application. From the bin folder of the Flex project take the SWF file generated by the compiler. Copy only this file onto a remote server. In this case, it will be transferred onto the www.youthru.com/flexsolutions/domain.

5. You can now move on to creating the file that will load this file. Start by creating a new MXML file by selecting File ➤ New ➤ MXML Application; name it Chapter_10_Flex_Sol_2.mxml.

6. Declare the SWFLoader control in the application by adding the following code:

```
<mx:Application xmlns:mx="http://www.adobe.com/2006/mxml" >
<mx:Script>
  <![CDATA[
    import flash.system.Security;
  ]]>
</mx:Script>

<mx:SWFLoader id="mySWF" width="300"
  source="http://www.youthru.com/flexsolutions/Chapter_10➥
    _Flex_Sol_2_allowDomain.swf"/>
</mx:Application>
```

The SWFLoader control loads the SWF file created and published in the preceding steps on the www.youthru.com domain. Add the allowDomain() method to this file for the symmetrical cross-domain scripting and add an event handler on the securityError event of the SWFLoader control. This event releases when a security error occurs in the phase of the call.

7. Insert the method of the Security class on the preinitialize event of the Application and create an event handler on the securityError event. Add the following to your Application file:

```
<mx:Application xmlns:mx="http://www.adobe.com/2006/mxml"
  preinitialize="Security.allowDomain(
                         'www.youthru.com/flexsolutions/');">


<mx:Script>
  <![CDATA[
    import mx.controls.Alert;
    import flash.system.Security;

    private function errorHandler(evt:Event):void
    {
      mx.controls.Alert.show('Error ' + evt.type);
    }
  ]]>
</mx:Script>

<mx:SWFLoader id="mySWF" width="300"
  source="http://www.youthru.com/flexsolutions/➥
  Chapter_10_Flex_Sol_2_allowDomain.swf"
  securityError="errorHandler(event)"/>

</mx:Application>
```

At this point, you have created the application that carries out the loading. There is nothing left to do but copy this application onto the domain that you have specified in the allowDomain() method of the SWF file that is loaded (Chapter_10_Flex_Sol_2_ allowDomain.swf).

In this case, you transfer this file onto the www.mobymobile.com/flexsolutions/ domain.

8. Save the file and run the application. Copy the SWF application file onto the domain.

So at the end you have this scenario:

- Chapter_10_Flex_Sol_2_allowDomain.swf is uploaded to www.youthru.com/ flexsolutions/, which has the following allowDomain() declaration:

  Security.allowDomain("www.mobymobile.com/flexsolutions/");

- Chapter_10_Flex_Sol_2 is uploaded to www.mobymobile.com/flexsolutions/ that has the following allowDomain() declaration:

  Security.allowDomain('www.youthru.com/flexsolutions/');

10

Expert tips

When you use the SWFLoader control, the object loaded remains external to the application. It is, however, possible to embed the content in a page using the Embed statement:

```
<mx:SWFLoader id="mySWF" width="300"
source="@Embed(source=myFile.swf)" />
```

The use of the Flex SWFLoader control works well with imported SWF files created in Adobe Flash that add graphics or animations to an application, but are not intended to have a large amount of user interaction. If you import SWF files that require a large amount of user interaction, you should build them as custom Flex components. (See Solutions 2-1, 2-2, and 2-3).

Solution 10-3: Storing persistent data

Flex applications become completely loaded on the client of the user. While the user interacts with the application, the information is stored in memory and is cancelled only when the SWF file is closed.

In other programming languages information about users is collected by using **cookies**, which are text files stored on the client that contain information linked to a particular domain. They are a mechanism of persisting data from a session on a web application.

For example, in Java Server Pages (JSPs), to set a cookie and save values in it, a code such as the following is used:

```
Cookie myCookie = new Cookie ("name", "Marco");
myCookie.setPath("/");
response.addCookie(myCookie)
```

In ActionScript, shared objects enable Flash Player to save data on the client—they are basically cookies for Flash. The shared objects in ActionScript are of two types: local (saved on the client machine) and remote (stored on the server). Remote shared objects (RSOs) require Flash Media Server or Flash Remoting. In Flex applications, you can use local shared objects (LSOs), but to take advantages of RSOs you need Flash Media Server or Flash Remoting installed on the web server.

The SharedObject class is responsible for creating, manipulating, and deleting shared objects. The class puts forward the following methods and properties:

- clear(): Deletes all the data of the shared object and deletes the shared object file from the computer of the user.
- flush(): Forces the writing of a shared object on the client.
- getLocal(): Returns the shared object present on the client. If the object is not found, it creates a new one.

- getSize(): Returns the dimension in bytes of the shared object. The default value is 100KB, which can be increased by the settings of the Flash Player client side. (The Flash Player Settings Manager is located here: www.macromedia.com/support/documentation/en/flashplayer/help/settings_manager.html.)

- data: The property that stores the attributes that the shared object contains.

- onStatus: The event handler that is released in the moment in which an error or a warning occurs.

In this solution you'll see how to use the SharedObject class to store persistent data in a Flex application.

What's involved

Shared objects provide the developer with the possibility of storing the information relative to that user on the client. Aside from storing information, the shared objects can also contain ActionScript data types or entire objects, such as the value object (refer to Chapter 3).

Even if the default setting that Flash Player assigns on the client is only 100KB, you can increase this value by opening the window of the Settings Manager. Doing this enables you to manage global privacy settings, storage settings, security settings, and automatic notification settings. By entering in the option from the Global Storage Settings panel menu (see Figure 10-4), you can decide to assign the default storage settings up to an unlimited value.

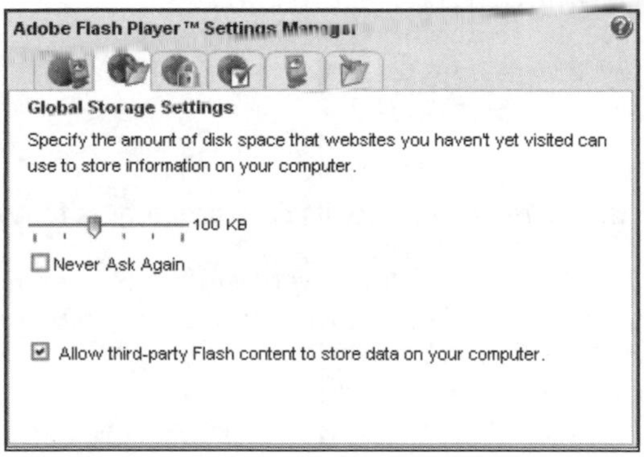

Figure 10-4. The Global Storage Settings panel enables you to set the size of the LSOs.

Shared objects are saved on the client, in the sol format, in the following locations:

- PC: C:\DocumentsandSettings\[Username]\ApplicationData\Macromedia\ FlashPlayer\[domain]\[pathToApplication]\[ApplicationName]\ sharedObject.sol directory

- Mac: app data/Macromedia/Flash Player/#SharedObjects

- Linux: ~/.macromedia/Flash_Player/#SharedObjects

Depending on the access that Flash Player has on the client's machine, the path in which the shared objects are stored could change.

To create and open a shared object, the getLocal() method is used, which searches to see whether the shared object you specified already exists on the client. If the method finds it, it loads it. If the result of the search is negative, the method creates an empty one and assigns it the name that you have sent as the parameter:

```
private var myLSO:SharedObject = SharedObject.getLocal("userData");
```

It is also possible to send a second parameter to the getLocal() method that specifies a location for the shared object:

```
private var myLSO:SharedObject = SharedObject.getLocal("userData",
"/");
```

In the "Expert tips" section of this solution you'll see how to use the pathname parameter for sharing data between Flex applications.

To add data to a shared object you can use the data property, which is an object that stores information in the file. Take, for example, an MXML data model in Flex that stores the values that the user has inserted in the TextInput controls:

```
<mx:Model id="myModel">
  <rootTag>
    <firstName>{myComp.nameTxt.text}</firstName>
    <surname>{myComp.surnameTxt.text}</surname>
    <email>{myComp.emailTxt.text}</email>
    <check>{myComp.remindChk.selected}</check>
    <radio>{myComp.newsletter.selectedValue}</radio>
  </rootTag>
</mx:Model>
```

To save properties in the shared object, use its data property as follows:

```
myLSO.data.firstName = myModel.firstName;
myLSO.data.surname =  myModel.surname;
myLSO.data.email = myModel.email;
myLSO.data.check = myModel.check;
myLSO.data.radio = myModel.radio;
```

This example demonstrates the power of the shared objects as containers of even complex information. In fact, you could store an Array or a complex Object in the shared object. Unfortunately, what you can't do is insert any type of visual controls in it (such as a ComboBox or a DataGrid).

Although Flash Player writes the values to the shared object file when the user quits the application, you can use the flush() method to guarantee the writing on disk of the file immediately. This method can accept the dimension in bytes as a parameter, which must be used when the file is saved:

```
private var flushResult:String = myLSO.flush();
```

As you can guess, the flush() method returns a String that contains the result of the writing. An error might occur if the Global Storage Settings (www.macromedia.com/ support/documentation/en/flashplayer/help/settings_manager.html) of the user do not allow the rescue of the LSO or if it is trying to save more data than that which the user has set in the Global Storage Settings.

If the operation of writing on the disk was positive instead, the method returns the String SharedObjectFlushStatus.FLUSHED.

In this solution you'll see how to save an ActionScript value object in a shared object.

How to build it

Shared objects can also store ActionScript instances. From the point of view of a Flex application this means that there is the possibility of creating a shared object that contains an ActionScript data model or a value object (discussed in Chapter 3)

In this solution you'll first create an ActionScript class that acts as a value object that will contain two properties: firstName and surname.

1. Create a new folder structure in the Flex project by selecting File ➤ New ➤ Folder called com/flexsolutions/chapter10. The chapter10 folder will contain the ActionScript class.

2. In this folder, create a new ActionScript Class by selecting File ➤ New ➤ ActionScript class and name it DataVO.as. This class represents the value object. Add the following lines of code:

```
package com.flexsolutions.chapter10
{
  public class DataVO
  {
  private var _firstName:String;
  private var _surname:String;

    public function DataVO(firstName:String, surname:String)
  {
     this._firstName = firstName;
     this._surname = surname;
  }
  }
}
```

In the DataVO constructor, the class defines the two private variables: _firstName and _surname. The DataVO constructor will be invoked when the class will be first instanced, and the two properties will have to be sent to it.

> *The **constructor** is a special method that uses the same name of the class. It never has an explicit return type, it is not inherited, and it is called when an object is created.*

10

3. Now you'll create an ActionScript class that takes care of creating and removing the shared object, sending it the ActionScript value object as information. Create an ActionScript class by selecting File ➤ New ➤ ActionScript class, call it WriteData.as, and save it in the com/flexsolutions/chapter10 folder.

4. In this class you'll first import the SharedObject classes of the ActionScript value object and registerClassAlias (which will be discussed shortly). Add the following code to the class now:

```
package com.flexsolutions.chapter10
{
  import flash.net.registerClassAlias;
  import flash.net.SharedObject;
  import com.flexsolutions.chapter10.DataVO;
  import mx.controls.Alert;
```

The registerClassAlias() method enables you to register an instance of an ActionScript class in an LSO, which uses the Action Message Format AMF3 to encode information.

AMF is a proprietary data format created by Adobe (formerly Macromedia). It's a binary format for data serialization/deserialization and remote method invocation, and it's used by Flash Remoting, NetConnection, NetStream, LocalConnection, and SharedObject. AMF3 in Flex is used with the RemoteObject components.

When you save an instance of a class in the data property of the LSO, the instance can't be read when you remove that information because it has not been encoded with type information.

5. Specify the constructor of the class; inside it launch the registerClassAlias() method—add the following to the class:

```
package com.flexsolutions.chapter10
{
  import flash.net.registerClassAlias;
  import flash.net.SharedObject;
  import com.flexsolutions.chapter10.DataVO;
  import mx.controls.Alert;

  public class WriteData
  {
    public function WriteData( )
    {
      registerClassAlias( "com.flexsolutions.chapter10.DataVO", DataVO
);
```

This method accepts two parameters: the first is the package of the class; the second is the reference to the class that you want to map. In this case, you have registered the ActionScript value object as a class. By doing so, the LSO can correctly encode the instance of the class.

6. You now create a shared object using the getLocal() method. This method performs a double function: It carries out a search to see whether a shared project already exists on the client machine. If it does not, the method creates an empty one:

```
public class WriteData
{
  public function WriteData( )
  {
    registerClassAlias( "com.flexsolutions.chapter10.DataVO", DataVO
);
    var myLSO:SharedObject = ➡
    SharedObject.getLocal( "userData" );
```

7. Because the getLocal("userData") method will search for the existence of a shared object with the name userData, you must insert an if() condition to perform the different operations according to whether the shared object has been created or is not yet present on the client. Add this now:

```
public class WriteData
{
  public function WriteData( )
  {
    registerClassAlias( "com.flexsolutions.chapter10.DataVO", DataVO
);
var myLSO:SharedObject = ➡
 SharedObject.getLocal( "userData" );
    if ( myLSO.data.user == undefined )
    {
      var myVO:DataVO = new DataVO("Marco", "Casario");
      myLSO.data.user = myVO;
      myLSO.flush();
      mx.controls.Alert.show("The LSO has been created");
    }
    else {
      mx.controls.Alert.show( "Welcome" + ➡
    myLSO.data.user._firstName);
    }
  }
}
}
```

8. If the shared object has not yet been created so its properties result as undefined, create an instance of the ActionScript value object to which you'll directly send the two properties _firstName and _surname:

```
var myVO:DataVO = new DataVO("Marco", "Casario");
```

9. Then put this instance of this class in the data property of the shared object myLSO:

```
myLSO.data.user = myVO;
```

10. Finally, write the shared object on disk using the flush() method.

11. If the shared object has been already created, make an Alert.show() display by writing the property _firstName contained in the instance of the ActionScript value object:

```
mx.controls.Alert.show( "Welcome " + myLSO.data.user._firstName);
```

12. Now you need an MXML main application file to invoke the ActionScript class that creates the shared object. Create a new MXML file by selecting File ➤ New ➤ MXML Application and call it Chapter_10_Flex_Sol_3.mxml. The application has to import the WriteData class and create an instance of it:

```
<mx:Application
xmlns:mx="http://www.adobe.com/2006/mxml"
layout="vertical" xmlns:com="com.flexsolutions.chapter10.*">

<mx:Script>
<![CDATA[
import mx.controls.Alert;
import com.flexsolutions.chapter10.WriteData;
private var myLSO:WriteData;

]]>
</mx:Script>
<mx:Panel width="458" height="269" layout="absolute"
title="Solution 10-3: Using Local Shared Object">

<mx:Button label="Create LSO"
click="myLSO = new WriteData()"
x="149" y="24"/>

</mx:Panel>
</mx:Application>
```

The <mx:Script> block imports the WriteData class from the com.flexsolutions.chapter10 package and creates a myLSO variable typed as WriteData. When you click the Button control the WriteData() will be invoked and the shared object will be created:

```
click="myLSO = new WriteData()"
```

13. Save the MXML file and run the application. Click the button and you'll see the SharedObject created on your local system (search for the userData.lso file).

Expert tips

A shared object can also be destroyed by using the clear() method. For example, you can add a public method to the class WriteData.as:

```
public function destroySharedObject():void
{
  mySO.clear();
}
```

The clear() method deletes only the file, but not the directory structure created to save it. If you want to simply empty the shared object of its properties instead, use delete:

```
delete example.data.user;
```

It might also be useful to check the amount of disk space used by a shared object. To check this value you can use the showSettings() method that shows the Security Settings panel in Flash Player. This method accepts a value of the SecurityPanel class as a parameter, which in the case of the dimension of a shared object is equivalent to SecurityPanel.LOCAL_STORAGE.

You can then add another public method to the WriteData.as class:

```
private function getSize():void {
  Security.showSettings(SecurityPanel.LOCAL_STORAGE);
}
```

A Flex application can create multiple shared objects. To do this it is sufficient to assign different instance names to the getLocal() method:

```
public var myLSO:SharedObject = SharedObject.getLocal("user");
public var myLSO1:SharedObject = SharedObject.getLocal("shoppingCart");
```

Solution 10-4: Mashup applications using the LocalConnection and the Yahoo! Maps API

10

When you used the SWFLoader control, you learned how to import an external SWF file into a Flex application. Flash Player enables you to make the two SWF applications interact through its application programming interface (API), both if the applications have been loaded on the same domain and if they are found on different domains.

With the LocalConnection class it is possible to invoke defined methods in another LocalConnection object on the same client computer. The LocalConnection can communicate with files created in ActionScript 3.0, but also with objects created in ActionScript 1.0 or 2.0. Flash Player takes care of automatically managing the connection between these objects.

In the communication between two different SWF files, the LocalConnection objects act as sending objects on one side and as receiving objects on the other. In a SWF file, the methods to be invoked will be declared, whereas these methods will be used in the other.

The send() and connect() methods of the LocalConnection class are necessary to enable the communication between the sending and receiving of SWF files.

The send() method invokes the name of the method specified between its parameters using an open connection with the connect() method on the other SWF file:

```
myLocalConnectionObj.send(➡
                'myConnection', 'myMethod');
```

This is the syntax of the send() method in the scenario in which the two SWF files that are interacting are found in the same domain. If the files are on different domains instead, you must precede the parameter connectionName with the domain name that is invoking the method:

```
myLocalConenctionObj.send(➡
'www.comtaste.com:myConnection', 'myMethod');
```

This method communicates to Flash Player that the two LocalConnection objects are not found on the same domain. The myConnection parameter is the LocalConnection object's domain name and corresponds to the name of the domain that contains the call to the connect() method:

```
receivingLocalConn.allowDomain('www.siteB.com');
receivingLocalConn.connect('myConnection');
```

The connect() method enables you to establish a connection with the LocalConnection object and receive commands from the send() method:

```
myLocalConnectionObj.connect('myConnection');
```

Also in this scenario, the questions related to the security of the Flex applications and of Flash Player play a fundamental role. In fact, there are two main possibilities for the LocalConnection objects:

- **SWF files on the same domain:** The communication between LocalConnection objects doesn't have to deal with any security sandbox problem because Flash Player enables communication between SWF files on the same domain.
- **SWF files on different domains:** The security sandbox that Flash Player is subject to does not permit communication between two SWF files that are located on different domains. To break this sandbox rule and enable this communication, it is necessary to use the allowDomain() method of the Security class.

For the latter, you must add the allowDomain() method in the code of the SWF file that makes the connection with the connect() method:

```
myLocalConnectionObj.allowDomain('www.mobymobile.com');
myLocalConnectionObj.connect('myConnection');
```

In this solution you'll see how to use LocalConnection to communicate with an SWF file created with Flash using the Yahoo! Maps API.

What's involved

The first step of creating a connection between two SWF files is to create an instance of the LocalConnection class found in the flash.net package. Then, through the send() and connect() methods, you can invoke the functions and create the connection between the two SWF files.

In this solution you'll create a Flex application that integrates the API of Yahoo! Maps. You must first obtain an ID and the AS-Flash API component.

To be able to use the Yahoo! API, you need to do some preliminary work before you even start the example. Follow these steps:

1. First, it is necessary to register in the section of Yahoo! Developer Network at https://developer.yahoo.com/wsregapp/index.php. In the registration form you must insert a domain in the Web Application URL field. This is the domain onto which you transfer the Flex application. In this example, the www.comtaste.com/flexsolutions/ domain was inserted.

2. At the end of the registration you'll be redirected to a page containing your App ID (make note of this because you'll need it later).

3. Aside from obtaining the ID, it is necessary to download and install the AS-Flash API, which can be downloaded for free at http://developer.yahoo.com/maps/. Here you'll find a link to the AS-Flash API (as shown in Figure 10-5), which enables you to create a Flash application displaying Yahoo! Maps via ActionScript. Download the Yahoo! Maps MXP (Macromedia eXtensions Package) from this page: http://developer.yahoo.com/maps/flash/componentEULA.html. Accept the terms of agreement and unzip the file.

The Yahoo! Maps Developer APIs

Select from among our comprehensive set of Maps APIs to make your web site or application come alive with the rich content and dynamic user interaction of Yahoo! Maps. Integrate a store locator with a few lines of code, view highway traffic patterns, or create custom routes — whatever you can dream of, Yahoo! Maps Web Services make it easy to build Yahoo! Maps based applications. Yahoo! Maps' built-in Geocoder enables you to specify an address or latitude/longitude coordinates: no need to call an additional service or write special code.

- **Yahoo! Maps Simple API**
  Lets you easily overlay your map data using the Yahoo! Maps web site to display your maps. No programming is necessary.

- **Yahoo! Maps Flash APIs**
  Embed maps in your web site or application using the free Macromedia Flash player for a rich user experience.

  AS-Flash API - Create a Flash application that displays Yahoo! Maps using ActionScript®.

  JS-Flash API - Create great applications quickly with our scriptable Flash maps and JavaScript™. No Flash programming is required!

  Flex™ API - Flex developers can use the Flex API with Macromedia's Presentation Server Technology to create powerful applications.

- **Yahoo! Maps AJAX API**
  Use the power of DHTML and JavaScript to host your own maps. We provide the JavaScript functions to make map-making a breeze.

Figure 10-5. Download the AS-Flash API from the Developer Network section of Yahoo!.

4. Now double-click the file YahooMap.mxp, and the Extension Manager will be automatically opened. You must have Adobe Flash integrated development environment (IDE) 8 or CS3 installed, as shown in Figure 10-6.

5. Follow the automatic procedure for the installation of the component and open Flash IDE.

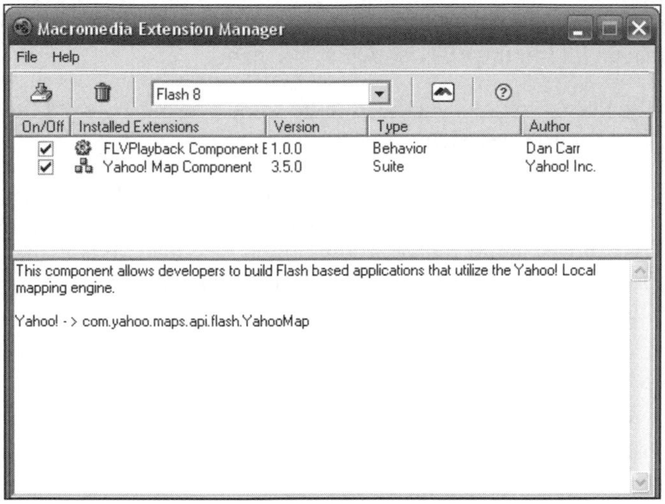

Figure 10-6. By clicking the YahooMap.mxp file, the Extension Manager opens, which will install the component in the Flash IDE.

At this point you can start to create the file using the Flash IDE and then communicating this SWF file to the Flex application.

How to build it

In this solution you'll create a simple mashup application that will use the Yahoo! Maps API. The application is made up of two parts: a SWF file created in Flash 8 (or Flash CS3) that embeds and displays the Yahoo! Maps API, and the other SWF file developed in Flex that gives the possibility to view the map in one of the following three states: Map, Hybrid, and Satellite.

1. In Flash, select File ➤ New to create a new Flash Document; save the file with the name map.fla.

2. Add the component by going to the Components panel and opening the Yahoo category, as shown in Figure 10.7. Drag the component onto the Stage.

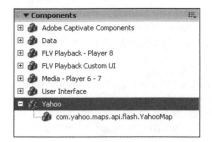

Figure 10-7.
In the Components panel the new component for Yahoo! Maps has been added.

The Components panel should already be open in the IDE of Flash; otherwise you'll find it under the menu option Windows ➤ Components.

3. Assign yahoo as instance name to the yahoo component. The instance name of an object in Flash is set from the input name of the Properties panel at the bottom of the screen (or from the menu Windows ➤ Properties). By doing so, you can access the component via ActionScript by referring to its name.

4. Select the first frame on the Timeline panel and open the Actions panel (Windows ➤ Actions). Insert the following ActionScript code as the frame script:

```
import com.yahoo.maps.tools.PanTool;
var myLC_S:LocalConnection = new LocalConnection();
yahoo.addEventListener(com.yahoo.maps.api.flash.YahooMap.➥
  EVENT_INITIALIZE, init);

function init(event)
{
  yahoo.addTool(new PanTool(),true);
  myLC_S.send("flexApp", "initMap");
}

myLC_S.setMapType = function (myData:Object):Void
{
  yahoo.setMapViewType(myData.type);
}

myLC_S.connect("flashApp");
```

The ActionScript code is quite simple. First, you imported the PanTool class into the com.yahoo.maps.tools package. Then you created an instance of the LocalConnection class. In this way you have a LocalConnection object that can make the connection between this file and the Flex application, as well as send events that occur in the part of the Flash application. Furthermore, this object is listening to events that can be released in the Flex application.

To be able to complete the operations on the Yahoo! Map, the yahoo component must be initialized. Using the addEventListener() method, register an event handler on the EVENT_INITIALIZE event of the yahoo component. The following are the three lines of code illustrated until now:

```
import com.yahoo.maps.tools.PanTool;
var myLC_S:LocalConnection = new LocalConnection();
yahoo.addEventListener(com.yahoo.maps.api.flash.YahooMap.↦
    EVENT_INITIALIZE, init);
```

The init() function does nothing more than add a tool to the map that has just been initialized: the PanTool. This tool enables you to move inside the map using the mouse. The second line of ActionScript code of the init() function sends an event to the Flex application through the LocalConnection object and specifies the name of a function() that becomes launched—initMap():

```
function init(event)
{
  yahoo.addTool(new PanTool(),true);
  myLC_S.send("flexApp", "initMap");
}
```

Finally, you created a function for the LocalConnection object that will be launched by the Flex application. This function takes an Object as parameter, myData, which is used to specify which state of map must be loaded and displayed. The Yahoo! Map enables you to load maps in three different states: Map, Satellite, and Hybrid:

```
myLC_S.setMapType = function (myData:Object):Void
{
  yahoo.setMapViewType(myData.type);
}
```

The myData Object has a property named type that contains the state of the map to display. This parameter is sent to the setMapViewType() method.

In the last line of code the connection with the Flash application is created by using the connect() method of the LocalConnection object:

```
myLC_S.connect("flashApp");
```

5. Publish the Flash file and then copy the resulting SWF file into the Flex project folder created in this chapter.

Now turn your attention to Flex. You'll create a new ActionScript class that extends the LocalConnection class and that will be used by the application to communicate with the Flash file.

6. Open Flex Builder and create an ActionScript class in the com\flexsolutions\ chapter10 folder of the Flex project.

7. Call this class MapLocalConnection.as and specify the LocalConnection class as its superclass. In this way, the procedure will create an ActionScript class that extends the LocalConnection class:

```
package com.flexsolutions.chapter10
{
  import flash.net.LocalConnection;
```

```
    public class MapLocalConnection extends LocalConnection
    {

    }
}
```

This class will take care of creating the connection with the LocalConnection class defined in the Flash file.

8. Specify a Boolean variable in the class that will be set as true in the moment in which the map in the Flash file will be initialized. Make the connection to the LocalConnection object with the connect() method; then define a method to invoke the function setMapType defined in the Flash file. Add the following code to the bottom of the new file:

```
public class MapLocalConnection extends LocalConnection
{
  private var isInit:Boolean;

  public function MapLocalConnection(server:String = "flexApp")
  {
    connect(server);
    super();
  }

  public function initMap():void
  {
    isInit = true;
  }

  public function setMapType(type:String):void
  {
    if (isInit)
    {
      send("flashApp", "setMapType", {type:type});
    }
  }
}
```

The last method, setMapType(), accepts a parameter, type, typed as String that is sent using the send() method of the LocalConnection object to the setMapType() function defined in the Flash application. This value will communicate to the map object to load a certain type of visualization instead of another.

9. Create a new MXML file by selecting File ➤ New ➤ MXML Application and call it Chapter_10_Flex_Sol_4.mxml. This file will load the SWF file created using Flash (Flash applications are published and compiled in an SWF file) with the SWFLoader control and invoking the ActionScript class MapLocalConnection.

10. Define an <mx:Script> block in which you'll create an instance of the class; add the following to the Application file:

```
<?xml version="1.0" encoding="utf-8"?>
<mx:Application xmlns:mx="http://www.adobe.com/2006/mxml"
  layout="vertical">

<mx:Script>
  <![CDATA[
    import com.flexsolutions.chapter10.MapLocalConnection;

    private var map_LS:MapLocalConnection = ➥
                    new MapLocalConnection();
  ]]>
</mx:Script>
```

11. Insert a ComboBox control containing the three options you'll send to the LocalConnection object. Doing this enables you to select the type of display of the map in the Flash application—you'll save the selection in the shared object, thereby allowing the application to remember the user's preferences:

```
<mx:ComboBox id="myCbx" change="setMap(event)">
  <mx:dataProvider>
    <mx:Array>
      <mx:Object label="Map" />
      <mx:Object label="Satellite" />
      <mx:Object label="Hybrid" />
    </mx:Array>
  </mx:dataProvider>
</mx:ComboBox>
```

Run the setMap() event handler on the change event of the ComboBox, which brings with it the event object. This function invokes the setMapType() method defined in the LocalConnection object of the Flash file.

12. Add the setMap() event handler into the <mx:Script> block:

```
    private var map_LS:MapLocalConnection = ➥
                    new MapLocalConnection();

private function setMap(event:Event):void
{
map_LS.setMapType(ComboBox(➥
                event.currentTarget).selectedItem.label);
}
```

In this function you launch the setMapType() method defined in the LocalConnection object, to which you send the item selected by the user in the ComboBox as value.

13. The last step is to recall the Flash map.swf file with the SWFLoader control. Add the SWFLoader tag to the top of your Application file, as shown here:

```
  </mx:ComboBox>

  <mx:SWFLoader id="yahoo"
    autoLoad="true"
      source="map.swf" />
  </mx:Application>
```

14. Save the file. Copy the SWF file and the relative HTML wrapper generated by the Flex Builder compiler onto your web server and run the application.

The Flex application loads the SWF file created in Adobe Flash. It embeds Yahoo! Maps; with the ComboBox control the user can select the type of map displayed in the Flash application (see Figure 10-8).

Figure 10-8.
The new component for Yahoo! Maps has been added.

Expert tips

Besides accepting a valid domain name to make calls and access data, the allowDomain() method also enables unpredictable domain names to be specified. In fact, there are times when the domain name from which the call originates is not known or the LocalConnection object needs to receive calls from different domains.

If you precede the connection name of the send() method with an underscore (_) you indicate that the receiving and sending LocalConnection objects are in different domains. And if you use the symbol * in the allowDomain() method, communication between the two domains is allowed. For example:

```
// This is the receiving local object
myLC_receiving.allowDomain('*');
myLC_receiving.connect('_flexApp');

// This is the sending local object
myLC_sending.send('_flexApp, 'methodName');
```

Use this technique when you want Flash Player to know that the LocalConnection objects (receiving and sending) are not found on the same domain.

The Yahoo! Maps API understands many libraries that expose many features. Useful libraries that create complex applications, called **widgets**, are user interfaces that enable you to add tools that interact with the user.

You can easily add widgets (such as the NavigatorWidget, ToolBarWidget, or SatelliteControlWidget) and tools (such as the PanTool or a CustomSWFTool) to your Flash/Flex application that embeds Yahoo! Maps to help users navigate and better use the map.

To add a widget, you use the addWidget() method, which has the following syntax:

```
yahoo.addWidget(myWidget:Object);
```

To add the NavigatorWidget, which offers support to many map-navigation functions, write the following:

```
import com.yahoo.maps.widgets.NavigatorWidget;

function init(event)
{
  yahoo.addTool(new PanTool(),true);

  var myWidget:NavigatorWidget("open");
  yahoo.addWidget(myWidget);

  myLC_S.send("flexApp", "initMap");
}
```

Solution 10-5: Creating a proxy server-side service for Flash Player cross-domain security

As discussed, the Flash Player security sandbox stops SWF files from loading data or external resources from domains other than that in which they are published. In Solution 10-1, you saw how to create a cross-domain file to enable the SWF to access data on other domains (the cross-domain file is published onto the root directory of any domains that you want the SWF to access).

Sometimes you won't be able to put a cross-domain file on the destination server. To solve this problem you can use a server-side proxy file that consists of a script published on the server (in any server-side language: PHP, JSP, Coldfusion, ASP.NET, and so on), which acts as a bridge between the Flex application and the remote data to load. Instead of directly accessing external resources on different domains, Flex will access this proxy service, which looks after accessing the resources on the specified domains.

In this solution you'll create a proxy file to use with an HTTPService call, which loads a Really Simple Syndication (RSS) feed published on a different domain to the one in which the Flex application is published.

What's involved

The server-side proxy file (created using PHP language) is published onto the web server on which the Flex application is deployed. From here, the Flex application invokes the proxy server file instead of pointing directly at the data on another domain.

This file will take care of making the call and receiving the data on the different domain, and in turn will return it to the Flex application.

The Remote Procedure Call (RPC), which is made with an HTTPService call, will call the proxy method and will send it the URL of the RSS feed to load as parameter in GET or POST:

```
<mx:HTTPService id="myHS" url="http://localhost:8080/proxy.php"
  method="GET" result="myAS = myHS.lastResult.rss.channel.item➡
  as  ArrayCollection">
<mx:request xmlns="">
  <url>http://www.corriere.it/rss/homepage.xml</url>
</mx:request>
</mx:HTTPService>
```

Instead of an HTTPService class, you can also use one of the other RPC classes: WebService or RemoteObject. This will change the server-side script to be used.

The PHP file will receive the parameter of the remote RSS feed to load and will return a variable that contains the XML of the feed as result data of the call. The proxy method returns the value of the request in a variable it sends to the application using the lastResult property of the HTTPService instead of printing it directly to the screen:

```
curl_setopt($ch, CURLOPT_RETURNTRANSFER, 1);
```

You'll see in this solution how to create the proxy file in both PHP and JSP.

How to build it

Begin by creating the proxy server method in PHP.

1. In Flex Builder create a new file by selecting File ➤ New ➤ File and save it with the name proxyMethod.php.

2. Add the following PHP code to your new file:

```
<?php
  set_time_limit(0);
  $url = $_GET['url'];
  $ch = curl_init($url);
  curl_setopt($ch, CURLOPT_RETURNTRANSFER, 1);
  curl_setopt($ch, CURLOPT_TIMEOUT, 100);
```

10

```
        $response = curl_exec($ch);

        if (curl_errno($ch)) {
          print curl_error($ch);
        } else
        {
          curl_close($ch);
          header("Content-type: text/xml");
          header("Content-length:", strlen($response));
          print $response;
        }
      ?>
```

The PHP file receives the url parameter in GET ($url = $_GET['url'];) and inserts the RSS values of the page in a $response variable. This variable will contain the exact XML content of the RSS file sent to it.

In this case, the remote proxy proxyMethod.php file has been published at the following address: http://88.149.156.198/develop/xmloutput.

3. Now create the Flex application. Create a new MXML file by selecting File ➤ New ➤ MXML Application and save it as Chapter_10_Flex_Sol_5.mxml.

4. Write an <mx:Script> block in which you declare two private variables. The first will contain the response data of the HTTPService call, whereas the second variable will contain the URL of the RSS feed. Add this code to your file:

```
<mx:Script>
  <![CDATA[
    import mx.collections.ArrayCollection;

[Bindable]
private var myAS:ArrayCollection = new ArrayCollection();

[Bindable]
private var myURL:String = ➡
    'http://www.corriere.it/rss/homepage.xml';
  ]]>
</mx:Script>
```

5. Insert the HTTPService call that invokes the PHP remote proxy and sends the URL specified in the <mx:Script> block as its parameter. Add the following below the <mx:Script> block:

```
<mx:HTTPService id="myHS"➡
  url="http://88.149.156.198/develop/xmloutput/getrssurl.php"
  method="GET"➡
  result="myAS = myHS.lastResult.rss.channel.item as  ArrayCollection">
  <mx:request xmlns="">
    <url>{myURL}</url>
  </mx:request>
</mx:HTTPService>
```

The HTTPService invokes the PHP file to which it sends the url parameter, creating a binding with the myURL variable. On the result event the myAS variable is set using the lastResult property of the HTTPService.

6. Complete the file by adding a DataGrid control to display the response data and by calling the RPC service invoking the send() method on the creationComplete of the Application. Add the following to the bottom of your file:

```
<mx:Application xmlns:mx="http://www.adobe.com/2006/mxml"
layout="vertical" creationComplete="myHS.send()">

<mx:HTTPService id="myHS"➥
  url="http://88.149.156.198/develop/xmloutput/getrssurl.php"
  method="GET"➥
  result="myAS = myHS.lastResult.rss.channel.item as  ArrayCollection">
  <mx:request xmlns="">
    <url>{myURL}</url>
  </mx:request>
</mx:HTTPService>


  <mx:DataGrid id="myDG" dataProvider="{myAS}">
    <mx:columns>
      <mx:DataGridColumn dataField="category"
        headerText="Category" />
      <mx:DataGridColumn dataField="title"
        headerText="Description" />
      <mx:DataGridColumn dataField="pubDate"
        headerText="Date" />
    </mx:columns>
  </mx:DataGrid>
</mx:Application>
```

7. Save the file and compile it. Then copy the SWF file with the HTML Wrapper and the PHP file onto a web server.

8. Run the application. You should see the RSS feed displayed in the Flex application. Neat, huh?

This solution looked at an alternative to using cross-domain to enable Flex applications to access data on other domains. In many contexts, this is the only practical alternative—you'll often have to use data on a domain other than yours.

Expert tips

The same proxy method can also be created by using JSP as server-side language. Create a new file from Flex Builder by selecting File ➤ New ➤ File and save it with the name proxy.jsp. All you need to do is convert what is written in PHP into JSP code. The script then becomes the following:

10

```jsp
<%@ page language="java" contentType="text/html; charset=utf-8"
  pageEncoding="utf-8"
  import="java.io.BufferedReader,
  java.io.InputStreamReader,
  java.io.IOException,
  java.io.InputStream,
  java.net.MalformedURLException,
  java.net.URL,
  java.net.URLConnection"
%>
<%!
  private String contentURL;
  public static final String CONTENT_URL_NAME = "contentURL";
%>
<%
  // get the url through the request:
  If (contentURL == null) {
    contentURL = (String)request.getAttribute(CONTENT_URL_NAME);
    if (contentURL == null)
      contentURL = (String)request.getParameter(CONTENT_URL_NAME);
  }
  if (contentURL == null)
    throw new ServletException("A content URL must be provided, as a ➡
    '" + CONTENT_URL_NAME +➡
    "' request attribute or request parameter.");

  URL url = null;
  try {
    // get a connection to the content:
    url = new URL(contentURL);
    URLConnection urlConn = url.openConnection();

    // show the client the content type:
    String contentType = urlConn.getContentType();
    response.setContentType(contentType);

    // get the input stream
    InputStream in = urlConn.getInputStream();
    BufferedReader br = new BufferedReader(new InputStreamReader(in));
    char[] buffer = new char[1024];
    String contentString = "";
    String tmp = br.readLine();
    do
    {
      contentString += tmp + "\n";
      tmp = br.readLine();
    }
    while (tmp != null);
```

```
      out.flush();
      out.close();
    }
    catch (MalformedURLException me) {
      // on new URL:
      throw new ServletException(➥
                      "URL: '" + contentURL + "' is malformed.");
    }
    catch (IOException ioe) {
      // on opne connection:
      throw new ServletException("Exception while opening '" +➥
      contentURL + "': " + ioe.getMessage());
    }
    catch (Exception e) {
      // on reading input:
      throw new ServletException("Exception during proxy request: " ➥
              + e.getMessage());
    }
  %>
```

Save this file as getrssurl.jsp and transfer it onto the web server.

On the Flex side the only thing you have to change is the address defined within the url property of the HTTPService tag. The url has to point to the JSP file:

```
<mx:Application xmlns:mx="http://www.adobe.com/2006/mxml"
layout="vertical" creationComplete="myHS.send()">

<mx:HTTPService id="myHS"➥
  url="http://88.149.156.198/develop/xmloutput/getrssurl.jsp"
  method="GET"➥
  result="myAS = myHS.lastResult.rss.channel.item as  ArrayCollection">
  <mx:request xmlns="">
    <url>{myURL}</url>
  </mx:request>
</mx:HTTPService>

  <mx:DataGrid id="myDG" dataProvider="{myAS}">
    <mx:columns>
      <mx:DataGridColumn dataField="category" headerText="Category" />
      <mx:DataGridColumn dataField="title" headerText="Description" />
      <mx:DataGridColumn dataField="pubDate" headerText="Date" />
    </mx:columns>
  </mx:DataGrid>
</mx:Application>
```

Save the file, run the application, and then copy the SWF file with the HTML Wrapper and the JSP file onto a web server. Load the application to see the RSS feed displayed in the Flex application.

10

> *Adobe Technotes are published here:* www.adobe.com/cfusion/knowledgebase/ index.cfm?id=tn_16520. *You can download proxy methods in the following languages: ColdFusion, ASP, and Java Servlet.*

Solution 10-6: Authenticating users in Flex

User authentication, which is a fundamental aspect of many web applications, prevents access to undesired users and makes an application more secure. Many applications also modify their user interfaces depending on user preferences or permission levels.

The process of authentication consists of collecting information, called **user credentials** (usually a username and password), from users to verify their identity. To be verified, the information to check against must reside in a repository such as a database, Lightweight Directory Access Protocol (LDAP), or XML file. The user credentials can be verified in client-side mode (without making remote calls to services or databases, which isn't a common or secure practice) or in server-side mode.

After the user credentials are verified, the state of the user must be maintained during the life cycle of the application. This also can be done on the client side, in which all the information resides in memory (via a session or shared object, for example) or at the server level (which requires the interrogation of the credentials through an RPC service: HTTPServices, WebServices, or RemoteObject).

In this solution you'll see how to apply an authentication system that keeps the state of the user during the entire life cycle of the application. It will also modify the application based on the user permission level.

What's involved

Carry out the verification of user credentials by accessing an XML file with the HTTPService and create a User class to contain all the information on the state of the user accessing the application. This class will reside on the client and maintain the information in the application's memory.

The XML file will contain the username and password data to verify the authentication of the user, and the role attribute to specify the role of the user who is entering the application. This information establishes how the application should behave, and which features to activate or deactivate according to the role type.

This is the structure of the XML file:

```
<users>
  <user role="admin">
    <username>admin</username>
    <password>admin</password>
```

```
      </user>
      <user role="visitor">
        <username>marco</username>
        <password>casario</password>
      </user>
   </users>
```

An HTTPService service invokes a JSP file that will collect the values of this XML file. Based on the information users insert in the text inputs, it will verify whether they can access the application (and which role they can use).

Based on the type of role that is returned from the HTTP call, a function will be invoked. In particular you'll make a DataGrid control editable according to the role of users. This authentication method is known as **role-based authentication**, and all users who access the application have one role (or more).

So the value of the editable property of the DataGrid depends on whether the user who is accessing has a visitor role or an administrator role.

To obtain this result create a data binding on the editable property with a Boolean variable declared in the User class:

```
<mx:DataGrid x="10" y="10" width="352"
editable="{userApp.isAdmin}">
```

The process of authentication will use one of the great features of Flex: states. States enable you to declare different states in the same application that are displayed when the user carries out certain operations in the application.

A state in Flex is created with the <mx:State> tag declared as a child node of the <mx:states> tag:

```
<mx:states>
<mx:State name="logged">
```

In the state you can remove elements present in the page or add new ones:

```
<mx:RemoveChild target="{button1}"/>
<mx:AddChild relativeTo="{panel1}" position="lastChild">
  <mx:DataGrid x="10" y="10" width="352" >
</mx:AddChild>
```

With these lines of code you have removed a Button control with the id equal to button1 and you have added a DataGrid control to the new state. In this example, you'll use states to change the user interface when the user has logged in to the application. Using states you'll also manage successful and failed login attempts. States can be created both through MXML or ActionScript code by using the Design mode of Flex Builder, which enables you to define a state through the States view (see Figure 10-9).

10

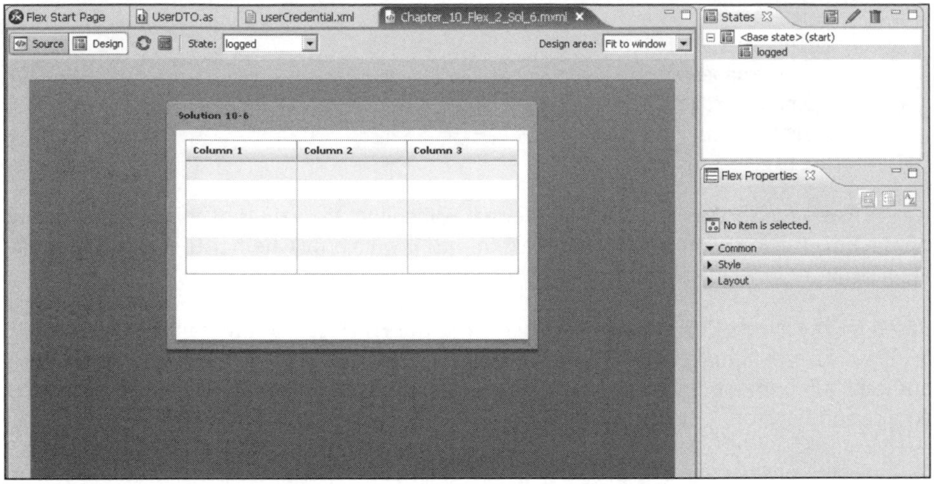

Figure 10-9. The States view enables you to create and work very quickly with the states.

How to build it

In this solution you'll use four different files:

- A JSP file for the remote call that will read and verify the credentials of the user from an XML file
- The XML file itself, containing the user credentials
- The Flex application with three states declared in it
- An ActionScript class containing all the information regarding the state of the user

Let's go to work.

1. Open Flex Builder and create a new file by selecting File ➤ New ➤ File menu and save it as userCredential.xml in the data folder. This file contains the information relative to the authorization and to the roles that will be used in the authentication phase.

2. Add the following code to the file:

```xml
<?xml version="1.0" encoding="UTF-8"?>
  <users>
    <user role="admin">
    <username>admin</username>
    <password>admin</password>
  </user>
  <user role="visitor">
    <username>marco</username>
    <password>casario</password>
  </user>
  <user role="visitor">
```

```
        <username>user</username>
        <password>user</password>
</users>
```

The code shows three users that will be accepted and authenticated by the application: an administrator and two visiting users. The role is defined in the role attribute of the user node.

3. The XML file is used by a JSP file that will be called by an HTTPService. The JSP file accepts the two parameters (username and password) that it will use to verify with the access data defined in the XML file.

3a. Create a JSP file in Flex Builder by selecting File ➤ New ➤ File menu and save it as login.jsp. Add the following code:

```
<?xml version="1.0" encoding="UTF-8" ?>
<%@ page language="java" contentType="text/html; charset=UTF-8"
    pageEncoding="UTF-8"
import="java.io.File,
javax.xml.parsers.DocumentBuilder,
javax.xml.parsers.DocumentBuilderFactory,
org.w3c.dom.Document,
org.w3c.dom.Element,
org.w3c.dom.Node,
org.w3c.dom.NodeList"

%><%
// get request parameters:
String username = (String)request.getParameter("username");
String password = (String)request.getParameter("password");

// user role:
String role = "";
boolean loggedIn = false;

if ((username != null) && (password != null)) {
// parse the credentials file:
DocumentBuilderFactory factory = DocumentBuilderFactory.newInstance();
try {
DocumentBuilder builder = factory.newDocumentBuilder();
// path to the credentials file;
// DocumentBuilder.parse() accepts as input an InputStream instance,
// therefore it is possible to store the credentials file on a web site
// and access it through HTTP, instead of storing it locally:
Document document = builder.parse(new File("C:\\userCredential.xml"));

// get all 'user' tags:
NodeList users = document.getElementsByTagName("user");
Node user = null;
Element userElem = null;
```

10

```
// loop  through each 'user' node in xml file and for each 'user'
// check if login suceeds; if one 'user' can authenticate
// the request username and password, stop:
for (int i = 0; i < users.getLength() && (!loggedIn); i++) {
user = users.item(i);

// 'user' nodes are all elements, in the credentials file:
if (user.getNodeType() == Node.ELEMENT_NODE) {
userElem = (Element)user;

// get 'username' and 'password' children from 'user' element;
Node userNode = userElem.getElementsByTagName("username").item(0);
Node passNode = userElem.getElementsByTagName("password").item(0);
if ((userNode != null) && (passNode != null)) {
// check request username and password against credential data:
if (username.equals(userNode.getFirstChild().getNodeValue()) &&
password.equals(passNode.getFirstChild().getNodeValue())) {
// get the associated 'role' attribute if login suceeded:
role = userElem.getAttribute("role");
loggedIn = true;
}
}
}
}
} catch (Exception e) {
// includes parsing errors, IO errors:
e.printStackTrace();
}
}

// build xml response:
String replyMessage = "<users>\n" +
"<user>\n" +
"<isLogged>" + loggedIn + "</isLogged>\n" +
"<isAdmin>" + role.equals("admin") + "</isAdmin>\n" +
"<userName>" + username + "</userName>\n" +
"</user>\n" +
"</users>\n";

out.println(replyMessage);
%>
```

The JSP file is put on the web server, transferred to the following address: www.comtaste.com/flexsolutions/login.jsp.

You can now move on to the creation of the Flex application. Create the ActionScript UserDTO class, which will contain three properties:

- isLogged: A Boolean that specifies whether the user is authenticated and logged in
- isAdmin: A Boolean that contains the role of the user who is connected
- userName: A String that contains the username of the user

Create a logOut() method that sets the properties isLogged and isAdmin to false. This is the situation in which the user should no longer be logged in to the application.

4. Create a new ActionScript class by selecting File ➤ New ➤ ActionScript Class and save it in the com\flexsolutions\chapter10 folder with the name UserDTO. Enter the following lines of code into it:

```
package com.flexsolutions.chapter10
{
  public class UserDTO
  {
    private var _isLogged:Boolean;
    private var _isAdmin:Boolean;
    private var _userName:String;

    public function UserDTO()
    {
    }

    public function set isLogged(admin:Boolean):void
    {
      this._isAdmin = admin;
    }

    public function get isLogged():Boolean
    {
      return _isLogged;
    }

    public function set isAdmin(logged:Boolean):void
    {
      this._isLogged = logged;
    }

    public function get isAdmin():Boolean
    {
      return _isAdmin;
    }

    public function set userName(user:String):void
    {
      this._userName = user;
    }
```

```
public function get userName():String
{
  return _userName;
}

public function logOut():void
{
  this.isLogged = false;
  this.isAdmin = false;
}

}
}
```

The class uses the getter/setter methods for the properties that have been declared as private. Finally, on the logout() method that will be invoked in the moment in which the user wants to log out, the two Boolean properties, isLogged and isAdmin, will be set to false.

5. Move on to the creation of the MXML file. Select File ➤ New ➤ MXML Application and create the file Chapter_10_Flex_Sol_6.mxml.

6. Define a Panel that contains the form to insert the username and the password. Add the following to the file:

```
<mx:Panel title="Solution 10-6" layout="absolute" width="392"➥
  height="260" id="panel1">
<mx:Form x="10" y="10" width="352"
        height="162" id="form1">
    <mx:FormHeading label="Insert data"/>
    <mx:FormItem label="User">
      <mx:TextInput id="userTxt" />
    </mx:FormItem>
    <mx:FormItem label="Pass">
      <mx:TextInput displayAsPassword="true"
              id="passTxt" />
    </mx:FormItem>
  </mx:Form>
<mx:Button x="296" y="180"
label="Submit"
click="myHS.send()"
 id="button1"/>
</mx:Panel>
```

On the click of the button, the send() method of a HTTPService, which you'll now declare, is invoked.

7. Insert a HTTPService into the file, which will be responsible for making the remote call to the JSP file that you created in Step 2.

```
<mx:HTTPService id="myHS"
  url="http://www.comtaste.com/flexsolutions/login.jsp"
 result="resultHandler(event)"
 fault="faultHandler(event)">
 <mx:request xmlns="">
   <username>{userTxt.text}</username>
   <password>{passTxt.text}</password>
 </mx:request>
</mx:HTTPService>
```

The remote service accepts two parameters, the username and the password, that the user inserts in the text input controls. Furthermore, you have created two event handlers to manage the release of the event: result and fault.

8. Add an <mx:Script> block to the MXML below the Application tag and above the HTTPService tag, in which you declare an instance of the UserDTO ActionScript class. The properties of this class will be set in the resultHandler() function that will be called when the result event of the HTTPService fired. Add the following to the MXML file:

```
<mx:Script>
  <![CDATA[
    import mx.rpc.events.FaultEvent;
    import mx.rpc.events.ResultEvent;
    import mx.collections.ArrayCollection;

    import com.flexsolutions.chapter10.UserDTO;
    [Bindable]
     private var userApp:UserDTO = new UserDTO();
    [Bindable]
     private var myDP:ArrayCollection;

    private function init():void
    {
        myDP = new ArrayCollection (➡
        [{author:"Marco Casario", title:"Flex  Solutions"},➡
        {author:"Raffaele Mannella", title:"Flex Solutions"}]➡
        );
    }

    private function resultHandler(event:ResultEvent):void
    {
    }
    private function faultHandler(event:FaultEvent):void
    {
    }

  ]]>
</mx:Script>
```

10

The myDP property represents the data provider you'll link to the DataGrid. The init() function will be launched on creationComplete so the ArrayCollection becomes populated:

```
<mx:Application xmlns:mx=http://www.adobe.com/2006/mxml➥
    layout="vertical"
    creationComplete="init()">
```

The two handler functions are currently empty. You'll get to them later, but you must first define the states in the application before you declare the operations in those functions.

The application will react differently depending on the result returned to it by the JSP file when it has checked the login information supplied by the user. The user interface of the application will be different depending on whether the user logs in successfully or not, and the application will display different features depending on whether the user is a visitor or an administrator.

Use states to manage these scenarios in Flex. To create a state in Flex you can use the States view, which is visible in Design mode (you saw this in Figure 10-9).

9. Click New State to add a new state to the application (see Figure 10-10).

Figure 10-10.
The New State option enables you to add a new state to the page.

The New State dialog box opens and enables you to define the name of the new state (Name field), to specify what state the child should be (the Based on field) and whether it should be the starting state (the Set as start state check box).

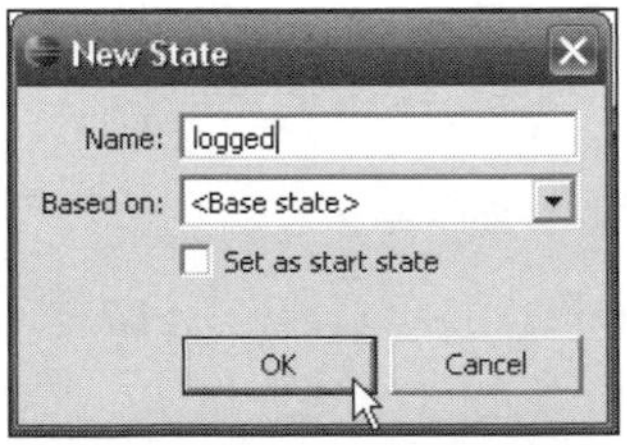

Figure 10-11.
The New State dialog box enables you to define a name for the state that you are creating.

10. Call the first state logged (refer to Figure 10-11) and leave the other options as they are. Click OK. This state will represent the situation for the user to correctly log in.

By default, this state, being the child of the base state, will contain the same user interface elements: a Panel, a Form container, two TextInput controls, and a Button.

Be sure that the logged state is selected in States view.

11. Remove the Form, the TextInput controls, and the Button. Add a Label and a DataGrid using Design mode, dragging the controls from the Components view.

12. In the Text property of the Label (accessed from the Flex Properties view,) set the following value:

Welcome {userApp.userName}

13. If you return to Code mode of Flex Builder you can see the code that the IDE has written. You need to make a few small modifications to the code by adding the DataGrid, the dataProvider, and editable property:

```
<mx:State name="logged">
  <mx:RemoveChild target="{form1}"/>
  <mx:RemoveChild target="{button1}"/>
  <mx:AddChild relativeTo="{panel1}" position="lastChild">
    <mx:Label x="10" y="10" text="Welcome {userApp.userName}"➦
      width="248" fontWeight="bold"/>
  </mx:AddChild>
  <mx:AddChild relativeTo="{panel1}" position="lastChild">
    <mx:DataGrid x="10" y="36" height="149" id="myDG"
      dataProvider="{myDP}" editable="{userApp.isAdmin}">
    </mx:DataGrid>
  </mx:AddChild>
</mx:State>
```

While the RemoveChild property specifies the tags to remove for this state, the AddChild property inserts a Label and a DataGrid. The DataGrid has a data binding with the property myDP (which contains the data to be displayed in it) and the isAdmin property of the userApp object. This property contains the roles of the authenticated user.

The finished first state should look like Figure 10-12.

14. Create another state called notLogged. Position yourself in States view and click the New State button. Assign the name notLogged to the state and choose Base state as parent in the Based on field.

15. In this state, leave Form, TextInput and Button as they are, and just add one Label to the interface.

16. Give the Label the following properties using the Flex Properties view:

- Text: UserName and Password are wrong. Try again!
- Width: 352
- fontWeight: bold
- color: #ff0000

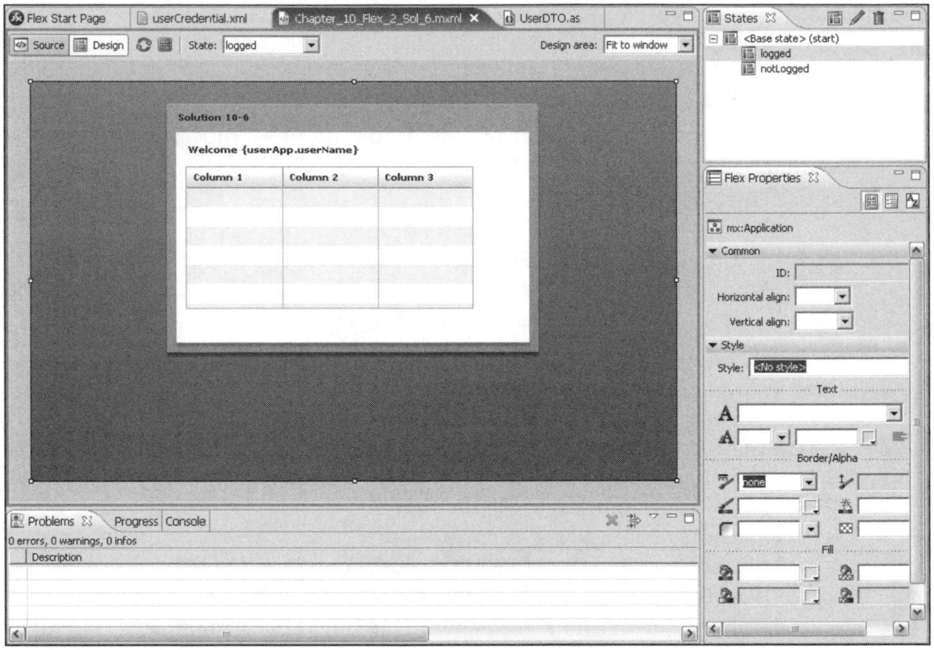

Figure 10-12. The first state has been created.

The notLogged state will be displayed in the case in which the user is not authorized by the HTTPService call, which in this case returns the isLogged variable with a false value.

17. You can now take care of the event handlers. The resultHandler() function should populate the properties of the userApp class with the values that are returned to it from the JSP. According to these values the application will switch from the current state to a new state. Populate the event handler with the following code:

```
private function init():void
  {
    myDP = new ArrayCollection([➡
      {author:"Marco Casario", title:"Flex  Solutions"},➡
      {author:"Raffaele Mannella", title:"Flex  Solutions"}]➡
      );
  }

private function resultHandler(event:ResultEvent):void
{
  userApp.isAdmin = event.result.users.user.isAdmin;
  userApp.isLogged = event.result.users.user.isLogged;
  userApp.userName = event.result.users.user.userName;

  if (userApp.isLogged)
  {
    currentState = "logged";
```

```
    }
    else
    {
      currentState = "notLogged";
    }
```

After populating the properties of the userApp object with an if() condition, see whether users have the rights required for accessing the application (see Figure 10-13). If they can get access and the isLogged property is true, change the States view to the logged state.

18. The faultHandler() handles potential error situations by writing error messages in a temporary variable, which will then be used in an Alert box:

```
private function faultHandler(event:FaultEvent):void
{
  var errorTxt:String = event.fault.faultCode;
  errorTxt += event.fault.faultDetail;
  errorTxt += event.fault.faultString;

  mx.controls.Alert.show(errorTxt);
}
```

19. Save and run the application.

By inserting the username and password in the field of the forms, you can see how the application behaves. If you insert admin/admin as values and click the Submit key, you'll be authenticated by the system and will enter as an administrator in the application. The DataGrid that displays the data is editable, demonstrating that the role with which the system has recognized you is that of administrator.

You can also perform other tests by accessing as normal visitors or inserting an incorrect login and password.

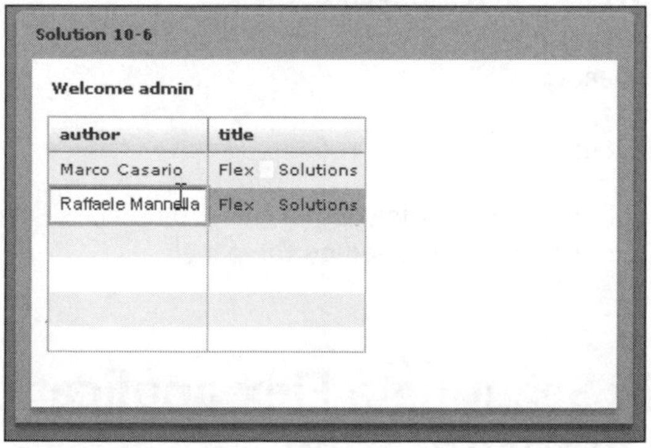

Figure 10-13. The authentication system of the application loads a state of the application according to the rights of the user.

Expert tips

You'll now improve the user experience by adding a pleasant effect for the transition between the states. Flex provides the Transition class in the mx.states package that defines a set of effects that can be applied during the various changes of state that occur in an application.

To specify which changes of state you want to apply the transitions to, use the fromState and toState properties. Furthermore, by using the Parallel or Sequence effects you can define the Transition with multiple effects:

```
<mx:Transition id="toDefault" fromState="*" toState="*">
  <mx:Sequence target="{panel1}">
    Your Effect here
  </mx:Sequence>
</mx:Transition>
```

In the application you'll insert a transition with a Blur type effect, which will release when a change of state occurs. This effect will be applied on the internal Panel and therefore, on all its content.

Add the following block of code in the main application file, immediately under the declaration of the Application tag:

```
<mx:transitions>
  <mx:Transition id="toDefault" fromState="*" toState="*">
    <mx:Sequence target="{panel1}">

      <mx:Blur id="blurImage" duration="500"
        blurXFrom="0.0" blurXTo="10.0"
        blurYFrom="0.0" blurYTo="10.0"/>
      <mx:Blur id="unblurImage" duration="500"
        blurXFrom="10.0" blurXTo="0.0"
        blurYFrom="10.0" blurYTo="0.0"/>
    </mx:Sequence>
  </mx:Transition>
</mx:transitions>
```

Save and run the application and try logging in. When you click Submit and the state is changed, a transition effect will be released on the panel.

Solution 10-7: Securing a Flex application using server-based authentication

In the preceding solution you used a role-based authentication technique that operated on the client. This type of approach enables you to work on a single application and transfer all aspects of security onto the client. This is all well and good, but there is a big drawback to this approach—there isn't any security on the server side, which means that anyone could enter the application. Using web server authentication has the advantage that all users are already set up in a web server system in which you can control all the aspects, rights, and roles of each of them.

There are situations in which it is preferable or is requested to authenticate on the server, which requires a web site that stores and updates information relative to the users of that domain. This authenticates user credentials and defines their roles in the application. You can implement this in one of the following ways:

- JDBC Login Module
- LDAP Login Module
- Windows Login Module
- Custom JAAS Login Module

In this solution you'll see how to apply a basic authentication system onto a JRun application server.

> JRun is also the application server installed by default during the process of installation of Flex Data Services (see Chapter 14 for more on FDS).

What's involved

The processes and operations you'll develop on JRun can be replicated on other J2EE-compliant application servers. Java 2 Enterprise Edition (J2EE) has a set of standards published by Sun that constitutes the basis for numerous application servers in business. JRun, Tomcat, BEA WebLogic, JBoss, and IBM WebSphere include some of the application servers that follow the specifications of the J2EE standards.

Flex applications or FDS are usually deployed on Java application servers, such as the ones described here. The security model defined by the J2EE standards is based on a roles model. Users and roles are defined by a many-to-many relationship.

Even though all the compatible servers are based on J2EE standards, each one manages users and roles in a different way—by using graphical user interfaces (GUIs) or directly editing the XML configuration files. The definitions in these XML files are inherited and shared by all the applications that operate under a particular instance of the application server and are, therefore, fundamental for the whole cycle of existence of your applications.

Another important consideration of J2EE application authentication is that it can be integrated with other methods, such as LDAP, which is a standard protocol for integrating and modifying directory services.

The security construction of J2EE is part of the Java Servlet 2.2 API specifics. The J2EE framework provides tools for implementing and maintaining the security of the applications.

10

In this solution you'll use JRun as the application server. The JRun security implementation includes the following components:

- XMLLoginModule: Uses the JRunUserManager service to access user and role data from an XML-based file that contains the users and roles.

- JRunUserManager service: Puts forward the authentication methods for authenticating; authorizing; and dynamically adding, modifying, and deleting users and roles.

- User store: This is the file containing the information relative to authentication and authorization. The file is located in the SERVER-INF/jrun-users.xml server and has the following format:

  - **jrun-users**: The root element that contains all the information

  - **encryption**: Specifies whether passwords are encrypted

  - **user**: Specifies the user's credentials; username and password

  - role: Defines a role and all the users that are associated to that role, role name, and username

- auth.config: Specifies the user store and the login modules that the server uses for authentication and authorization.

In this solution you'll see how to configure the mechanism of the user store by default by modifying the XML SERVER-INF/jrun-users.xml file.

> *The procedures demonstrated for the JRun application server can also be applied to other J2EE-compliant servers.*

How to build it

Note that this solution assumes that you already have JRun installed. To get it installed, either install Livecycle Data Services (which installs it by default) or check out the official documentation of Livecycle Data Services: http://casario.blogs.com/mmworld/2007/06/livecycle_data_.html.

1. Open the jrun-users.xml file in the SERVER-INF/ folder. This file contains the list of users with their authorization and associates them with their roles. The default security mechanism's user store is based on XML-format that includes elements for user and role definitions:

   - jrun-users: the root element

   - encryption: uses encrypted passwords

   - User: contains user definition that specifies with the subelements; username and password

   - Role: contains a role name and the list of users assigned to the role; role name and username

2. Insert the following XML code to create users and passwords to authenticate the access of these users:

```
<?xml version="1.0" encoding="UTF-8"?>
<!DOCTYPE jrun-users PUBLIC "-//Macromedia Inc.//DTD jrun-users
4.0//EN"➡
  "http://jrun.macromedia.com/dtds/jrun-users.dtd">
<jrun-users>
  <encryption>false</encryption>
  <user>
    <username>admin</username>
    <password>admin</password>
  </user>
  <user>
    <username>Marco</username>
    <password>CasarioPass</password>
  </user>
```

3. After the users are specified, create the roles by adding the <role> nodes. Remember that each role is associated to a user. Add the following to the bottom of the file:

```
  <role>
    <rolename>flexadmin</rolename>
    <username>admin</username>
  </role>
  <role>
    <rolename>visitor</rolename>
    <username>Marco</username>
  </role>
</jrun-users>
```

If you observe the structure of the XML file, each user is defined with a node and an element:

```
<user>
  <user-name>Marco Casario</user-name>
  <password>casario</password>
</user>
```

Each role element is defined with a node. It is possible to define more users to link to a single role, however:

```
<role>
  <role-name>flexuser</role-name>
  <user-name>admin</user-name>
  <user-name>guest</user-name>
  <user-name>flex</user-name>
</role>
```

10

4. After all the modifications have been carried out manually on the `jrun-users.xml` file, the JRun server must be restarted to be sure that the new security information is available. Do this now.

Basic server authentication uses the HTTP protocol (with minimal encryption) to pass the user's information to and from the browser. You can use the HTTPS protocol to ensure an additional encrypted level.

In this solution when the browser tries to load a Flex application that is secured by constraints in the `jrun-users.xml` file, the user is forced to enter a username and password in a pop-up box that the browser creates.

Expert tips

JRun also offers an administration console to develop some operations relative to security. Among other things, this console enables you to modify users and roles in the XML file by using a GUI: the JRun Administration Console (JMC), which is a web-based administration console that enables you to manage and control the security level of the application server.

This console is usable only with the full version of JRun, not with the one installed with FDS. Log on to the JMC at `http://localhost:8000`, click the server that you want to use, go to the Services option, and then choose Security, which shows you a form from which you can add and modify users and roles.

To add a user, simply click Edit Users under the User Manager option and then choose Add New User. The same procedure is used to add a user to a role that already exists. Assign a name, a password, and a role to the user. JRun enables you to assign one or more roles to users through two handy windows.

To create or edit a role using the JRun security panel, all you need to do is click Edit Roles under the Role Manager option. From here it is possible to add or edit a role. If an already existing role is selected from the Role Settings dialog box, you can see all the users to which it is linked and add or remove others. This information is contained in the server root of JRun in the SERVER-INF folder in the `jrun-users.xml` file.

If you intend to give access to a user with the role of administrator to the Administration console, you must declare the node as role for this user:

```
<role>
  <rolename>jmcadmin</rolename>
  <username>admin</username>
</role>
```

Summary

The developer's goal is to create an effective and rich Flex application, but also a robust and secure one. So security is a fundamental aspect of application development.

Flex applications are SWF files loaded from Flash Player. This means that many levels of security are managed by Flash Player or from the remote server that hosts the application.

This chapter discussed Flash Player security, and you learned that Flash Player runs inside a security sandbox that protects the client from possible damaging attacks. Flash Player does not allow an application to receive data from any domain different from the one in which the SWF is loaded.

Fortunately, Flash Player provides the possibility of loading data from different domains to that in which the application is contained, with three methods illustrated in the chapter's solutions:

- Use a cross-domain policy file that specifies the names of the domains that can be accessed and external data.
- Create a proxy on the server that recalls the data.
- Use the Security.allowDomain() method to grant the access.

The LocalConnection class was used to enable communication between two different SWF files and to invoke defined methods in another LocalConnection object on the same client computer.

User authentication is a fundamental aspect of many web applications. It prevents access to unwanted users and helps make an application more secure. The process of authentication consists of collecting information from the user (user credentials) to verify their identity. You used two different approaches: a client-side form-based authentication and a role-based authentication.

10

11 ADVANCED FLEX BUILDER TECHNIQUES

One of the reasons why Flex Builder is so powerful is that it is based on the core engine of Eclipse, the well-known programming environment given to the community of developers by IBM.

Eclipse (www.eclipse.org) is an open-source application, written in Java, which originally gained great popularity in the Java development community. Besides having built-in Java support, the application is also becoming popular in other development communities thanks to the wide variety of plug-ins and modules that have been developed to enable it to support other well-known languages such as XHTML, Cascading Style Sheets (CSS), PHP, and JavaScript for Ajax development.

Flex Builder is based on Eclipse, so it inherits a lot of its strengths (it can even be installed as an Eclipse plug-in, as well as the stand-alone version). This chapter shows you how you can put a lot of those strengths to work to improve your Flex development. You'll look at how to use the integrated development environment (IDE) of Flex Builder at its best, how to make complete use of its functions, and how to increase the efficiency of the environment to make it even more productive.

Solution 11-1: Improving Flex Builder performance

Flex projects can use many files and can import other projects to share and use libraries or components realized in the past. These possibilities might result in a very large workspace/directory structure, so you need to work carefully to optimize your workspace. Eclipse and Flex Builder are environments that require a lot of system memory to work at their best and they could start to slow down if the Flex project grows more and more. The bigger your project and your workspace, the more memory is needed for working in a fast and productive way.

In addition, a feature that Flex Builder has enabled by default is **Build Automatically**, which automatically carries out a build of the entire workspace (and returns any errors it finds) every time a file inside the project is rescued or modified. This option can be a big help to you at compile time, when you're trying to track down troublesome errors and do final checks before publication, but it also really slows down development time if you have it turned on all the time. In fact, the build operation could take several minutes if you have many Flex projects defined in the workspace, so it's a good idea to have this feature turned off unless you really need it.

This solution explores some practical solutions to optimize the performance of Flex Builder and reduce the waiting time in the phase of development of a Flex project.

What's involved

Applications created with Flex Builder can range from simple web applications, such as an image gallery, to sophisticated Rich Internet Applications (RIAs) with the complexity of desktop applications. And the more complicated they get, the more of a performance hit

Flex Builder takes. You can often arrive at a point in which Flex Builder requests a few minutes to open or ten seconds to build and compile the entire project. It can be really frustrating—nobody likes twiddling thumbs for several seconds, waiting to start a program or to test code that has just been written.

There are many solutions that you can apply to the Flex Builder environment to optimize its use and reduce the waiting time. Let's get to them now.

How to build it

One simple rule to follow, dictated by common sense, is that you should limit the number of projects open at the same time on the workspace of Flex Builder (the workspace has to open each project separately, and it is easy to forget about a project and leave it open, even when you aren't working on it). You have the option of keeping a project in the workspace, but in a closed state. In the startup and build phases of the program, all the projects that are closed are ignored.

Let's look at how to do this now.

1. Among the other panels, Flex Builder displays Navigator view on the right of Editor view. This panel contains all the projects defined in the workspace you are working in (see Figure 11-1). If this view is not already open, open it by selecting Window ➤ Show View ➤ Navigator.

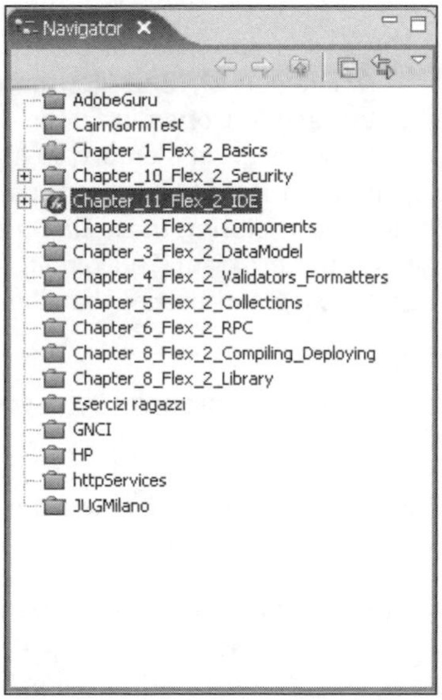

Figure 11-1.
The Navigator view shows all the projects defined in the workspace of Flex Builder.

2. To close a project, you must right-click the project folder you want to close and select the Close Project option from the context menu, as shown in Figure 11-2. Closing a project does not mean removing it from Navigator view. The icon of the folder will change, and you can't open it in that folder to select files from within it. When you need to use it again, you can simply reopen the project by right-clicking the project folder and selecting Open Folder from the menu.

Figure 11-2.
You can access the option to close the project from the context menu of the project folder.

Closing the projects you're not using reduces the memory required by Flex Builder to manage the entire workspace (and also the waiting time for startup and carrying out a build). In fact, the closed projects aren't used by the compiler when the application file runs or is saved.

Another thing that can affect the performance of the IDE is when too many files are open in Editor view. You'll often have to work with many files simultaneously, and files that are no longer needed and could be closed are forgotten about and left open in Editor view. Flex Builder maintains every project that has a file open in Editor view in memory, so if you have ten files open you can take up hundreds of megabytes of RAM. Aside from paying more attention to the number of files open in Flex Builder and closing those that aren't required, you can help yourself by using a useful option of the program. You can, in fact, limit the number of files that you can keep open in Editor view and ensure that the IDE automatically closes them.

3. To access these settings, go the Preferences dialog box of the program by selecting Window ➤ Preferences ➤ General ➤ Editors (see Figure 11-3).

When selected, the Close editors automatically check box enables you to choose from the following options:

- Number of opened editors before closing: Defines the maximum number of files that can be opened at the same time in the Editor.

- When all editors are dirty or pinned: Enables you to choose to open a new editor or prompt to save and reuse.

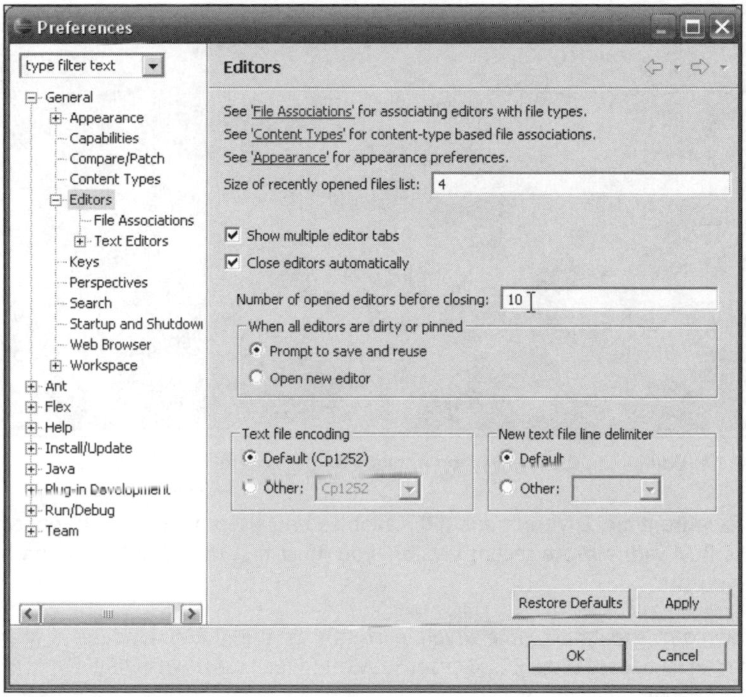

Figure 11-3. You can access Editor options from the Preferences dialog box of Flex Builder.

The maximum number of opened editors before closing depends mainly on the configuration of your machine. If you have a large quantity of free RAM available, you can keep more open comfortably.

If you have installed Flex Builder in stand-alone mode, the Java Virtual Machine (JVM) installed will be an older version—using a more recent version could improve the general performance of the environment. This problem might not exist if Flex Builder has been installed as a plug-in of Eclipse; in this case you are more likely to have kept your JVM updated to the latest stable version. Let's look now at how you can make sure the JVM is current.

4. To find out which version of the JVM you have installed, run the following from the command line (or from a Terminal window under the Applications ➤ Utilities folder on a Mac):

```
FlexBuilder installation folder\jre\bin>java -version
```

This will provide you with the current version installed and functioning on your system, as you can see in Figure 11-4.

11

Figure 11-4. Confirming the JVM version installed on the system

The J2SE Java Runtime Environment (JRE) enables end users to run Java applications. To update the JVM with a more recent version, you must first download a version of the JRE from the Sun site.

5. Download the latest JRE, which currently is the JRE 6 Update 1 at https:// sdlc5e.sun.com/ECom/EComActionServlet;jsessionid=3EEC9F9DE992E616CD345E 43DFFC9D0E.

6. To update Flex Builder to use the new JRE, you must copy the jre folder in the package you just downloaded to the installation folder of Flex Builder, overwriting the one that's already there. (Make sure that you back up the old jre folder somewhere else before overwriting it, just in case anything goes wrong!) Copy the folder of the JRE 6 Update 1 into the jre folder of Flex Builder and start the program.

> *The JVM is the engine used to execute Java bytecodes. The difference between JVM and JRE is that the JRE is a specific implementation of the JVM, including the core libraries.*

Another way to improve the performance of the development environment is to increase the quantity of RAM it can use by updating settings inside the FlexBuilder.ini file, found in the root of the Flex Builder folder. This file enables you to set arguments that will be sent to the JVM and is present only when Flex Builder is installed in stand-alone mode.

7. Find this file, open it, and find the following two parameters, which specify the amount of RAM used by the program. Before editing the file, make sure to back it up.

- Xms: Specifies the minimum amount of RAM used. The default value is 128MB.

- Xmx: Specifies the maximum amount of RAM used. The default value is 512MB.

8. Depending on how much RAM you have available, increase these values. If, for example, you have 2GB of RAM, the following values would be quite comfortable:

- Xms: 512MB
- Xmx: 1024MB

The best advice is to always use values that are multiples of 8.

If you have installed the Flex Builder as a plug-in of Eclipse instead, you can directly act on the values that regulate the Eclipse environment, and the benefits will be automatically inherited by Flex Builder.

9. If you have Eclipse installed, the equivalent file, `eclipse.ini`, can be found in the Eclipse folder. The equivalent arguments within this file are as follows:

- -vmargs
- -Xms40m
- -Xmx256m

The `vmargs` option is used to customize the operation of the JVM to run Eclipse.

As a general rule, the more memory assigned to the JVM, the better the IDE performance will be. You can, therefore, use these settings according to the configuration that you have on your system.

For systems with 512MB of RAM, the following settings in the `eclipse.ini` file would be suitable, even if they don't take into consideration that the system might need to manage other open programs besides Eclipse:

- -vmargs
- -Xms256m
- -Xmx256m
- -XX:PermSize=128m
- -XX:MaxPermSize=128m

For systems with 1024MB of RAM, the following settings work well:

- -vmargs
- -Xms512m
- -Xmx512m
- -XX:PermSize=256m
- -XX:MaxPermSize=256m

For systems with 2048MB of RAM, the following settings are suitable:

- -vmargs
- -Xms1024m
- -Xmx1024m

11

- -XX:PermSize=512m
- -XX:MaxPermSize=512m

In this configuration, there is no difference between the Xms and Xmx values, and between the minimum and maximum memory used. The benefit of such a configuration is to have faster startup for applications that use almost all the provided memory so that the JVM doesn't have to waste time by asking for more memory from the operating system at runtime (it's all done once at startup).

To help keep the resources that Eclipse uses under control, it is recommended that you use two excellent tools produced by Kyrsoft (www.kyrsoft.com): the memory monitor plug-in and the Status Monitor plug-in.

These two plug-ins enable you to carry out a dynamic inspection of the Workbench memory consumption, the automatic and manual forced execution of garbage collection, the visualization of a settable warn memory indication, and much more. It makes it much easier to see whether there is an issue with your memory consumption that needs to be acted on.

Expert tips

In this solution, you have seen how to check the version of the JRE installed on the system: launching the java -version command on the command line. You can also find this information in Flex Builder by selecting Menu ➤ About Eclipse SDK and then selecting Configuration Details from the resulting dialog box, as shown in Figure 11-5.

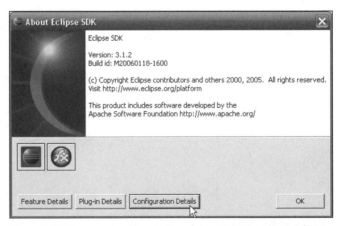

Figure 11-5. You can view the version of the JRE in the About Eclipse SDK dialog box.

If you scroll through the list that appears, you'll find the following lines that report the version of the JRE installed:

java.runtime.name=Java(TM) 2 Runtime Environment, Standard Edition

java.runtime.version=1.4.2_12-b03

To install a new plug-in such as those produced by Kyrsoft select Help ➤ Software Update ➤ Find and Install.

Search for a plug-in to install in the Updates dialog box, and the work will automatically be carried out by Flex Builder, as shown in Figure 11-6.

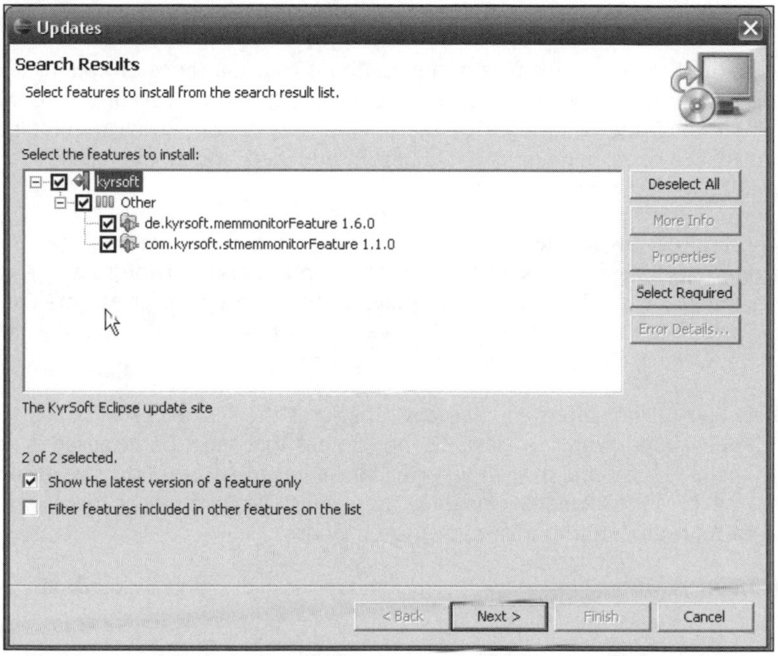

Figure 11-6. The plug-ins will be automatically downloaded and installed.

Another technique to optimize the performance of an application is that of working on different workspaces and switching from one workspace to another.

In this way, instead of concentrating all projects in a single workspace that becomes over-loaded, you can subdivide in a logical way and load just the projects you need to work on immediately.

To change a workspace in Flex Builder, select File ➤ Switch Workspace.

Another way to switch workspaces is to create shortcuts (or aliases on the Mac) that make Eclipse run with the workspace on which you want to work. To obtain this result, you can create a system shortcut on Windows or an alias on the Mac (right-click the desktop and choose New ➤ Shortcut) and use the data argument in the command line when you launch Eclipse (this works only for Flex Builder installed as an Eclipse plug-in):

"C:\Program Files\eclipse\eclipse.exe" -data C:\myWorkspace\myFlexProjects\ FlexSolutions

Solution 11-2: Localized applications using the resource bundle

It often happens that the project on which you're working must be multilingual. Developers must find solutions to provide a localized application for users of different nationalities.

A classic method to create this type of application is to use a series of XML files, each of which contains content relative to a different language. In this way, according to the user's choice or the language being used by the operating system in which the application is being loaded, the corresponding XML file becomes loaded, and all the information in the project will be in the correct language.

Even if this approach is simple and efficient, it does have many disadvantages. You must manage multiple XML files, each of which can contain a lot of information—a single change in the content will require several files to be updated, which is time-consuming and error-prone. Loading such information can also be very slow, increasing the user's waiting time in the initial phase of loading the application.

Fortunately Flex Builder offers an alternative that uses the ResourceBundle API to create localized applications. With this class, all the content that must be localized is removed from the main application, and the information is linked to property files through the metadata tag [ResourceBundle] variable. These files will, in turn, be organized into a structure of folders according to the language they use.

In this solution you'll see how to use this technique through the ResourceBundle API.

What's involved

To create a localized application, first remove all the content to be localized from the MXML file. The content will be accessed by using the ResourceBundle class defined as metadata in ActionScript or with the @resource directive in MXML.

If ActionScript is used, the [ResourceBundle] metadata will be declared above the variable:

```
[ResourceBundle("helloWorld")]
private static var MYRB:ResourceBundle;
```

> *You can't use the new keyword to instance a* ResourceBundle *variable.*

The MYRB value will change according to the language to be used, and you can access keys defined in the resource bundle with the getString() method.

Instead, if you use the @Resource directive in MXML, you specify a resource bundle name and a key that corresponds to the name of the properties file that contains the key:

```
<mx:Button id="sendBtn"
label="@Resource(bundle='myResources',
key='btnLabel')" />
```

The following example demonstrates the use of both options:

```
<?xml version="1.0" encoding="utf-8"?>
<mx:Application xmlns:mx="http://www.adobe.com/2006/mxml"
layout="vertical">
<mx:Script>
<![CDATA[
 import mx.resources.ResourceBundle;
 [ResourceBundle("helloWorld")]

 private static var MYRB:ResourceBundle;

 private function getLocalizedText(key:String):String{
 return MYRB.getString(key);
 }
]]>
</mx:Script>
<mx:Button  label="@Resource(key='hello', bundle='helloWorld')" />
<mx:Label  text="{getLocalizedText ('welcome')}" />
</mx:Application>
```

To use the ResourceBundle class in ActionScript, it is first necessary to import the mx.resources.ResourceBundle class, after which it is possible to declare the static variable that will contain the actual resource bundle:

```
[ResourceBundle("helloWorld")]
private static var MYRB:ResourceBundle;
```

This variable will be linked to a string that will contain the text in the language chosen through the getString() method. You have invoked this method in the getLocalizedText() function, which accepts the key to be associated as a parameter:

```
private function getLocalizedText(key:String):String{
return MYRB.getString(key);
}
```

This function will be invoked in the object, which will visualize the text (in this example, it is contained in a Label control):

```
<mx:Label text="{getLocalizedText ('welcome')}" />
```

Instead, as far as the use of the @Resource directive used in MXML is concerned, you have linked the bundle and the key directly in the label property of a Button control:

```
<mx:Button label="@Resource(key='label_btn', bundle='helloWorld')" />
```

11

In this way, you can localize a value without needing to declare either a variable or a function. The syntax of the @Resource directive is the following:

```
@Resource(bundle="bundle", key="key")
```

For now, you have defined only the entities that will be localized and inserted them in the exact point in which they should appear. It is obviously not sufficient to be able to make the localized application function—the localized strings also require a container. This container is a simple properties file created in a user-created local directory. The properties file is a text file that must contain strings that are Latin-1– or UTF-8–encoded and follows the same format of the Java properties file: key = value (and saved in a simple text format that stores keys and values).

In the example, the properties file should contain the following information in the following format:

```
welcome = Hello World
label_btn = Hello World
```

After creating the first properties file, you then create another properties file to localize the strings in the Italian language:

```
welcome = Ciao Mondo
label_btn = Ciao Mondo
```

These two files must be inserted in different folders for each locale. You'll create subdirectories for each language in which you plan to have resource bundles. The subdirectory names should match the locale names you plan to use.

For English, the properties file will be inserted in the folder en_EN (or en_UK); for Italian, it is inserted in the folder it_IT:

```
\locale\en_EN
\locale\it_IT
```

How does the application understand which properties file it should load?

In the compilation phase, the compiler creates a SWF file that will load the properties file in one folder instead of another. In fact, you must create a SWF file for every locale (language) folder.

To create a localized SWF file for the en_EN language, add the following parameters to the compiler in Flex Builder:

```
-locale en_EN -source-path locale/{locale}
```

You'll compile the application by using the properties file in the en_EN locale. To have the application localized in Italian, compile again but change the parameters of the compiler:

```
-locale it_IT -source-path locale/{locale}
```

You can also use the command-line mxmlc compiler to compile the application outside of the Flex Builder by using the same syntax:

```
mxmlc -locale en_EN -sp locale/{locale} -o myAPP_en.swf main.mxml
```

For the version of the application that is localized in Italian, launch the compiler with the following syntax:

```
mxmlc -locale it_IT -sp locale/{locale} -o myAPP_en.swf main.mxml
```

In this solution you'll see how to apply the ResourceBundle API in a real context. You'll change the labels of the header of the columns of a DataGrid according to the language that the user selects from a series of radio buttons.

How to build it

Before moving on to the creation of the MXML application, create the properties files that will be needed to contain the localized strings. These files will be put in a custom folder within the project. Inside this folder there will be a subfolder that will contain the properties files.

1. Open Flex Builder and create a Flex Project with the name Chapter_11_Flex_IDE. Click the Finish button. Create a locales folder in the Flex project. Select File ➤ New ➤ Folder, create the locales folder, and then create a lang folder inside it. This last folder will contain all the properties files. The project will have the structure shown in Figure 11-7.

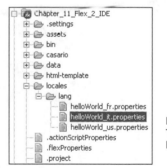

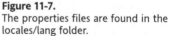

Figure 11-7.
The properties files are found in the locales/lang folder.

2. Inside the lang folder, create three properties files: rb_us.properties, rb_it.properties, and rb_fr.properties. They will localize the application in English, Italian, and French, respectively.

The three files each contain three keys and their values. For example, the file to localize the application in English contains the following text:

```
col1 = Regions
col2 = Cities
col3 = Population
myLbl = Choose a Language
```

3. Add the preceding lines to the rb_us.properties file.

4. Add the following to the rb_it.properties file. It contains the same key as the previous file, but the values are now changed into Italian:

```
col1 = Regioni
col2 = Citta
col3 = Provincie
myLbl = Scegli la lingua
```

5. Open the rb_fr.properties file and insert the following text:

```
col1 = Régions
col2 = Villes
col3 = Population
myLbl = Recherche langues
```

You have created three files that will function as resource bundles to localize the application. You can now move on to creating the MXML file, inserting into it the variables that will be associated with these files.

6. Create a new MXML file by selecting File ➤ New ➤ MXML Application and call it Chapter_11_Flex_Sol_2.mxml.

7. The example application used for this solution will contain a DataGrid control that will load the data from an external XML file. This XML file is the same one used in Chapter 6, so you can copy the data folder from the old Flex project to the new one. To copy a folder in Flex Builder, you can simply copy and paste. The XML file that you'll load is states.xml, which contains the following XML data structure:

```xml
<?xml version="1.0" encoding="UTF-8"?>
<dataroot>
<city>
<id>1</id>
<id_region>1</id_region>
<region>PIEMONTE</region>
<city>TORINO</city>
<code>TO</code>
<population>2236765</population>
<male>1086745</male>
<female>1150020</female>
<family>886053</family>
</city>
</dataroot>
```

8. Insert the DataGrid and load the data in the external XML file using an HTTPService, as follows:

```
<mx:HTTPService id="myHS" url="data/states.xml"
result="myAC = myHS.lastResult.dataroot.city as ArrayCollection"
showBusyCursor="true"/>
```

```
<mx:DataGrid id="myDG"
dataProvider="{myAC}" x="92" y="49">
<mx:columns>
<mx:DataGridColumn headerText="" dataField="region" />
<mx:DataGridColumn headerText="" dataField="city" />
<mx:DataGridColumn headerText="" dataField="population" />
</mx:columns>
</mx:DataGrid>
```

The HTTP call loads the states.xml file in the local data folder. On the result event of the call, you populate the myAC variables that you'll create in the next step. This variable, typed as ArrayCollection, points directly at the repeating node of the content of the XML file through the lastResult property.

The DataGrid used creates a data binding with the myAC variable linking it as data provider.

Please note that the headerText property of the DataGridColumn tags have intentionally been left empty. This property will be populated by aiming at the values of the resource bundles.

9. Insert an <mx:Script> block, as shown following. Here you define the ArrayCollection variable myAC and create the references with the ResourceBundle class, using the metadata [ResourceBundle].

```
<mx:Script>
<![CDATA[
import mx.resources.ResourceBundle;
import mx.collections.ArrayCollection;
[Bindable]
private var myAC:ArrayCollection;

 [ResourceBundle("rb_it")]
 private var myRB_it:ResourceBundle;
 [ResourceBundle("rb_us")]
 private var myRB_us:ResourceBundle;
 [ResourceBundle("rb_fr")]
 private var myRB_fr:ResourceBundle;

]]>
</mx:Script>
```

After importing the ResourceBundle class of the mx.resources package, you define three variables of the ResourceBundle: myRB_it, myRB_us, and myRB_fr. The bundle property, which contains the name of the file with the localized strings, will be sent as a parameter to the metadata [ResourceBundle] declared previously for each of these variables.

These variables alone can't load the data in the bundle. This operation is rendered possible from the getString() method of the ResourceBundle class. You'll recall this method in a function that is run when the user selects the type of language to be loaded from a set of radio buttons.

11

10. Insert the group of radio buttons, along with a Label control. This control will contain content originating from the resource bundle in its text property:

```
<mx:Label text="" />
<mx:VBox>
  <mx:RadioButtonGroup id="languageGroup"
    change="changeLang()" />
  <mx:RadioButton label="it" groupName="languageGroup"
    selected="true" />
  <mx:RadioButton label="us" groupName="languageGroup"/>
  <mx:RadioButton label="fr" groupName="languageGroup"/>
</mx:VBox>
```

A VBox was inserted because the Application has the layout property set at horizontal.

The RadioButtonGroup launches the event handler changeLang() on the event change. This function will have the sole job of creating a custom event, which will be bound to a second function that uses the getString() method to load the values in the properties files.

11. Create a changeLang() event handler and the localizeLang() function to which the custom event will be associated. Insert the following code within the <mx:Script> block:

```
private function changeLang():void{
var e:Event = new Event("langChanged");
this.dispatchEvent(e);
}

[Bindable(event="langChanged")]
 private function localizeLang(key:String):String{
return this["myRB_"+languageGroup.selectedValue].getString(key);
}
```

Let's run through this section of code piece by piece. You have already dealt with custom events in Chapter 2. To create a custom event, use the Event class to which you send the name of the new event as a parameter. This event will automatically generate an event object, which in turn is sent to the dispatchEvent() method:

```
var e:Event = new Event("langChanged");
this.dispatchEvent(e);
```

The custom event is created and launched in the moment in which the changeLang() function is performed. This happens on the event change of the RadioButtonGroup.

When the langChanged custom event is dispatched, the localizeLang() function is performed. This mechanism is rendered automatic by having created a binding between the custom event and the function itself through the use of the [Bindable] metadata:

```
[Bindable(event="langChanged")]
```

The localizeLang() function accepts a String as parameter and returns the actual value defined in the properties file as value and correspondingly to the parameter key that it has been sent:

```
[Bindable(event="langChanged")]
private function localizeLang(key:String):String
{
   return this["myRB_"+languageGroup.selectedValue].getString(key);
}
```

The ResourceBundle that is loaded is dynamic and varies according to the value that the user has selected in the radioButtonGroup:

```
return this["myRB_"+languageGroup.selectedValue].getString(key);
```

Depending on which radio button is selected, the value languageGroup.selectedValue assumes one of the three following values: it, us, and fr. This mechanism loads the properties file containing the values in the language chosen by the user.

12. To see the values loaded in the application, you must associate the localized values with the controls. In the solution, the values that change are the headers of the DataGridColumns and the text of the Label that therefore must launch the localizeLang() function to send the corresponding key value to. Add the following code:

```
<mx:Label text="{localizeLang('myLbl')}" />

<mx:VBox>


<mx:RadioButtonGroup id="languageGroup"
change="changeLang()" />
<mx:RadioButton label="it"  groupName="languageGroup"
selected="true" />
<mx:RadioButton label="us"  groupName="languageGroup"/>
  <mx:RadioButton label="fr"  groupName="languageGroup"/>
 </mx:VBox>

<mx:DataGrid id="myDG"
  dataProvider="{myAC}" x="92" y="49">
  <mx:columns>
    <mx:DataGridColumn headerText="{localizeLang('col1')}"
      dataField="region" />
    <mx:DataGridColumn headerText="{localizeLang('col2')}"
      dataField="city" />
    <mx:DataGridColumn headerText="{localizeLang('col3')}"
      dataField="population" />
  </mx:columns>
</mx:DataGrid>
```

11

13. Before compiling the application, you must launch the send() method of the HTTPService so that the remote call is carried out and run the localizeLang() function at the startup of the application. This is done by adding the following creationComplete property to the <mx:Application> tag:

```
<mx:Application xmlns:mx="http://www.adobe.com/2006/mxml"
layout="horizontal"
creationComplete="changeLang();myHS.send()">
```

14. Add a parameter to the compiler of Flex Builder (by selecting Project ➤ Properties ➤ Flex Compiler), as shown in Figure 11-8.

```
-source-path locales/lang
```

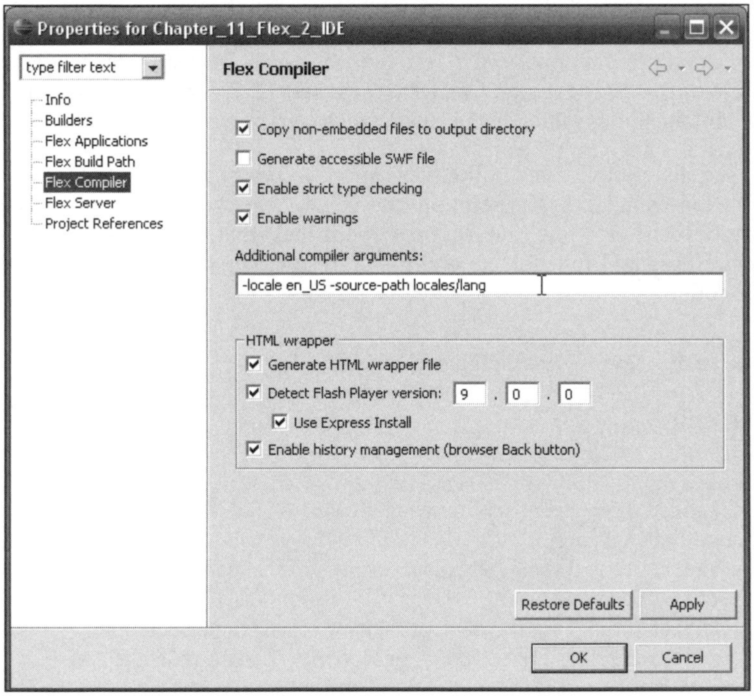

Figure 11-8. Communicating the existence of the properties files in the locale folder to the compiler.

15. You're now ready to save and run the application.

The final result is shown in Figure 11-9.

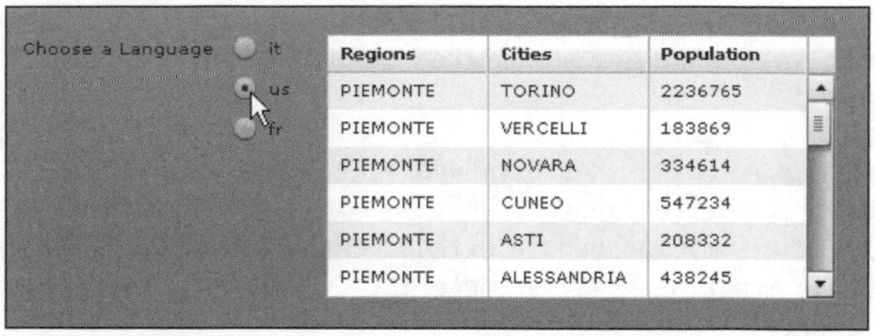

Figure 11-9. The final application that dynamically changes the resource bundle according to the choice of the user.

> *For some languages, you need the required glyph installed on your system (for example, to see accented French).*

Expert tips

In the process of localization, Flex also enables you to use an ActionScript class as a localized resource. In a project that requires the use of different languages to be used by different users worldwide, the developer also has to confront problems related to cultural and economic differences. It thus becomes useful and often essential to have different models and functions according to the locale.

The most classic example is that of an e-commerce application that in the checkout phase must calculate the final cost, taking different postage costs and currency into account—depending on the country the user comes from.

In this case, having the possibility of loading different ActionScript classes that change their behavior and their methods based on the locale is very useful.

To use the localized classes, the steps are very similar to those used in the main example of this solution. The [ResourceBundle] metadata is used to define a new class that references all the classes in the resource bundle. But instead of using the getString() method, the getObject() method will be used:

```
import mx.resources.ResourceBundle;

[ResourceBundle("myClassBundle")]
 private var myRB:ResourceBundle;

private function localizeClass():String{
var myRC:Object = myRB.getObject("myClass");
 myLabel.text  = myRC.getString();
}
```

The [ResourceBundle] metadata specifies the name of the ActionScript class used to embed the localized classes as parameter.

To create a bundle class, it is necessary to extend the ResourceBundle class and save it in the locale folder. An example of a bundle class is the following:

```
package {
  import mx.resources.ResourceBundle;
  import myLocalizedClass;
  public class myClassBundle extends ResourceBundle {
    public function myClassBundle() {
      super();
    }

    override protected function getContent():Object {
      var myClassRef:Object = new Object();
      myClassRef ["myLocalizedClass"] = myLocalizedClass;

      return myClassRef;
    }
  }
}
```

In the bundle class, you have overridden the getContent() method that creates a reference for all the classes necessary to the ResourceBundle. In the example, the myLocalizedClass class was declared with the following code:

```
myClassRef ["myLocalizedClass"] = myLocalizedClass;
```

The localized myLocalizedClass class defines the getString() method, which is recalled by the application and has the sole job of returning the localized string of text:

```
package {
  public class myLocalizedClass {

    public function myLocalizedClass () {
    }
    public function getString():String {
      return "Ciao";
    }
  }
}
```

You can also use a class to load embedded assets in resource bundles. Remember that to use embedded assets in resource bundles, it is necessary to create a class for every asset to be loaded:

```
package {
  import mx.core.BitmapAsset;
  [Embed(source='logo.gif')]
  public class myLocalizedClassAsset extends BitmapAsset {
```

```
      public function myLocalizedClassAsset() {
      }
    }
  }
```

You can then add the reference to the bundle class:

```
package {
  import mx.resources.ResourceBundle;
  import myLocalizedClass;
  public class myClassBundle extends ResourceBundle {
    public function myClassBundle() {
      super();
    }

    override protected function getContent():Object {
      var myClassRef:Object = new Object();
      myClassRef ["myLocalizedClass"] = myLocalizedClass;
      myClassRef ["myLocalizedClassAsset"] = myLocalizedClass;

      return myClassRef;
    }
  }
}
```

Solution 11-3: Customizing the look and feel of applications at runtime by loading CSS

As discussed before, CSS styles in Flex enable you to change the look and feel of an application by applying style rules to individual components—the background of a form or the text inside a single text field (or at a global level, for example, "all the text in the application needs to be bold and green").

A new addition in the release of Flex 2.0.1 is the possibility of loading the styles at runtime by using the StyleManager class to load the SWF files that contain the different CSS declarations. The CSS files created will be compiled in SWF files by Flex Builder using the new Compile CSS option (accessed from the context menu by right-clicking the CSS file in Navigator view).

With this new feature, you can create applications that enable the user to choose from a variety of themes as they work in your application, for example.

You should also consider loading *all* your CSS at runtime. An advantage of loading your CSS at runtime is that the CSS styles are located outside of your application files, which reduces loading times and promotes reusability.

FLEX SOLUTIONS: ESSENTIAL TECHNIQUES FOR FLEX 2 AND 3 DEVELOPERS

Loading a CSS at runtime involves three steps:

1. Write the CSS to be applied.
2. Compile the CSS in a SWF file using the mxmlc compiler.
3. Execute the loadStyleDeclarations() method of the StyleManager class to load the SWF files in the application.

In this solution you'll see how to load different style sheets to change the styling of the application at runtime.

What's involved

To load CSS declarations in Flex, the StyleManager class is used. This class, which makes up part of the mx.styles package, enables you to access the classes and type selectors through the ActionScript programming language.

Through the getStyleDeclaration() method, you can apply a style, defining it both as a selector type as well as a class selector:

```
mx.styles.StyleManager.getStyleDeclaration(➡
style_name).setStyle("property", value);
```

Therefore, you can write this to apply a style to a DataGrid:

```
import mx.styles.StyleManager;
StyleManager.getStyleDeclaration("DataGrid").setStyle("cornerRadius",5)
;
```

The getStyleDeclaration() enables you to apply styles to a single control. If you want to apply the fontSize property to a Label and a DataGrid, you should define this property separately for each of them, specifying two declarations of the getStyleDeclaration() method:

```
import mx.styles.StyleManager;
StyleManager.getStyleDeclaration("Label").setStyle("fontSize",12);
StyleManager.getStyleDeclaration("DataGrid").setStyle("fontSize ",12);
```

You can use the global keyword for the getStyleDeclaration() method to apply styles to the entire application. But there is another method you can use to create global CSS style declarations: use the CSSStyleDeclaration class, which enables you to create and modify style sheets at runtime and apply the CSS classes to the application. To define the CSS settings on a CSSStyleDeclaration object, the setStyle() method is used:

```
var myCSS:CSSStyleDeclaration = new CSSStyleDeclaration ("myclass");
myCSS.setStyle('fontSize', '12');
myCSS.setStyle('fontFamily', 'Arial');
```

In this code example, you have created a myCSS object data typed as CSSStyleDeclaration, to which you have declared two properties, fontSize and fontFamily, with the setStyle() method.

To apply these styles as selectors to a component, use the setStyleDeclaration method:

```
StyleManager.setStyleDeclaration("DataGrid",myCSS,true);
```

If, instead, you want to apply the CSS declarations as a CSS class to apply to the components through the styleName property, write the following:

```
StyleManager.setStyleDeclaration(".myClass",myCSS,true);
```

To apply the CSS declarations, you find the component you want to apply it to and specify the name of the class in its styleName property, as follows:

```
<mx:DataGrid id="myDG" styleName="myClass"/>
```

To remove a CSS style, there exists a clearStyleDeclaration() method that cancels the style that has been sent to it as parameter:

```
StyleManager.clearStyleDeclaration(".myClass", true);
```

With the new release of Flex Builder 2.0.1 and Flex Builder 3 (www.adobe.com/products/flex/flexbuilder), the StyleManager class puts forward another two methods: loadStyleDeclarations() and unloadStyleDeclarations().

To be able to create a SWF file starting from a CSS file, use a new feature of Flex Builder: Compile CSS. This function can be accessed from the context menu by right-clicking the CSS file in Navigator view.

After having compiled the CSS file to a SWF to load the style declarations container in this file at runtime, write the following:

```
StyleManager.loadStyleDeclarations("myCSSdeclaration.swf")
```

How to build it

As with every new chapter, you'll begin with the creation of a Flex project.

1. Open Flex Builder and point to the Flex project created for this chapter: Chapter_11_Flex_IDE.
2. Create an assets folder inside the project and create two CSS files inside it. Call them myCSS1.css and myCSS2.css.
3. Insert the following CSS rules into myCSS1.css:

```
Datagrid{
  borderColor: #FF8000;
  borderStyle:solid;
  color:#C0C0C0;
  cornerRadius:5;
  fontSize:9;
  fontFamily:Arial;
  rollOverColor:#FF80FF;
}
```

11

```
Button {
  color: #FF9933;
  fontSize: 9;
  fontFamily:Arial
}
```

You have created two type selectors. The first acts on the DataGrid control, while the second acts on the Button. Every Button or DataGrid in the Flex application inherits those styles because they have been specified with type selectors.

4. Insert the following styles into myCSS2.css:

```
Datagrid{
  borderColor:#FF8000;
  borderStyle:solid;
  color:#C0C0C0;
  cornerRadius:5;
  fontSize:12;
  fontFamily:Verdana;
  rollOverColor:#FF80FF;
}

Button
{
  fontSize:12;
  color: #FF9933;
   fontFamily:Verdana
}
```

These two files will be loaded at runtime into the Flex application, and you'll add the capability for the user to dynamically switch between them.

5. Before being able to load these files, you have to compile them in SWF format. To do this, you can use the Flex Builder component compiler. Right-click each one and select the option Compile CSS to SWF from the context menu. The CSS files will be compiled as SWFs and inserted in the bin folder of the Flex project.

6. At this point you can create the Flex application that will be styled with the CSS SWFs. Create an MXML file by selecting File ➤ New ➤ MXML Application and save it with the name Chapter_11_Flex_Sol_4.mxml.

7. Insert the following user interface elements into the application:

```
<mx:Button id="first" label="Load the first CSS"
click="applyRuntimeStyleSheet(event)"/>
<mx:Button id="second" label="Load the second CSS"
click="applyRuntimeStyleSheet(event)" />

<mx:Label text="This is my Label"/>
<mx:DataGrid>
  <mx:columns>
    <mx:DataGridColumn headerText="Column 1" dataField="col1"/>
```

```
        <mx:DataGridColumn headerText="Column 2" dataField="col2"/>
        <mx:DataGridColumn headerText="Column 3" dataField="col3"/>
    </mx:columns>
</mx:DataGrid>
```

Each Button launches the applyRuntimeStyleSheet() function, to which the event object is sent as parameter. This function will have the job of loading the CSS files with the loadStyleDeclarations() method when the user clicks the buttons.

8. Insert an <mx:Script> block, in which you declare the event handler applyRuntimeStyleSheet():

```
<mx:Script>
  <![CDATA[
    import mx.styles.StyleManager;
    public function applyRuntimeStyleSheet(evt:Event):void
    {
      if (evt.target.id == "first")
      {
        StyleManager.loadStyleDeclarations("assets/myCSS1.swf")
      }
      else if (evt.target.id == "second")
      {
        StyleManager.loadStyleDeclarations("assets/myCSS2.swf")
      }
    }
  ]]>
</mx:Script>
```

The applyRuntimeStyleSheet() event handler checks the property target id containing the id of the component that has fired the event with an if() cycle. If this property is equal to the value first, the first CSS file will be loaded with the loadStyleDeclarations() method of the StyleManager(StyleManager. loadStyleDeclarations("myCSS1.swf")) class; otherwise, it will instead load the myCSS2.swf file.

9. Save the file and run the application.

Try clicking the two buttons; you'll see how the formatting of the elements dynamically changes according to whether the first .swf or the second .swf becomes loaded. The loadStyleDeclarations() method returns an instance of the IEventDispatcher class, which you can use to trace the loading of the CSS file that has taken place.

You can, in fact, access the StyleEvent.PROGRESS, StyleEvent.COMPLETE, and StyleEvent.ERROR events, to which you can assign an event listener (a function for managing the event) with the addEventListener() method:

```
var myStyle:IEventDispatcher =➥
 StyleManager.loadStyleDeclarations("myCSS1.swf");
myStyle.addEventListener(➥
mx.events.StyleEvent.COMPLETE, handleComplete);
```

11

With this code, you register the `mx.events.StyleEvent.COMPLETE` event to the `handleComplete()` function in that you can communicate to the user the loading of style sheets that has taken place or apply the same to my Flex application.

Expert tips

In this solution you used the Flex Builder compiler to compile the CSS files into SWF files, but you can also use the command-line component compiler to do this. To compile a CSS file, use the compiler on the command line with the following syntax:

- mxmlc myCSS1.css
- mxmlc myCSS2.css

When you load CSS at runtime and switch from one to another, the style declarations might overlap. To prevent this, it's a best practice to unload the CSS before loading and applying a new one.

To carry out the unloading of a CSS file and its declarations, use the `unloadStyleDeclarations()` method, to which you send the name of the CSS file and a Boolean value that represents the update parameter:

```
StyleManager.unloadStyleDeclarations( 'myCSS1.swf', true );
```

Solution 11-4: Documenting the application with the ASDoc tool

Little by little, as the application grows, and more and more files become involved, it becomes necessary to create decent documentation. Simple code commenting is often not enough, and having reference documentation available that you can quickly access can save you precious time in the development phase, particularly when you work in a team.

The Adobe Flex Language Reference (see http://livedocs.adobe.com/flex/2/ langref/) was created with a command-line tool called **ASDoc**, which generates reference documentation of the actual ActionScript classes or MXML components by going through and reading the comments in the code. The good news is that you can use this tool to create your own application documentation.

This tool is located in the bin folder of the Flex SDK directory in the Flex installation directory. Simply launching the tool generates a directory structure containing HTML files that correspond exactly to the packages of the ActionScript classes and MXML components in your application.

Because the ASDoc tool generates documentation by reading your code comments, you need to use a specific syntax in your comments so that ASDoc can correctly interpret and format the information. In this solution you'll see how to generate an API Language Reference for a small Flex project.

What's involved

Before you launch the ASDoc tool and send it the relevant parameters, you must understand how to use the correct syntax in the comments.

To define an ASDoc comment in ActionScript, use the characters /** to define the beginning of the comment and */ for the end. In the comment you can add formatting to the text and define new paragraphs using HTML <p> elements:

```
/**
* AsDoc Comment
*
* <p>Author: Marco Casario</p>
* <p>Date: 01/01/2007</p>
*/
```

You can also use the <code> element to specify a different formatting for the text included in this tag (it is usually used when code is used in the middle of simple description text) and many more. A complete list of the HTML tags you can use in ASDoc documentation can be found at http://livedocs.adobe.com/flex/201/html/asdoc_127_8.html#186379.

ASDoc comments are generally used to comment a class, a function, an interface, or any other element that requires a description. These comments must be positioned immediately above the declaration that you intend to document. Other comments in the body of the code will be ignored by the ASDoc tool.

You can differentiate comments to be linked to the parameters that the method accepts and the values it returns. The ASDoc syntax enables you to define these special comments with @param and @return tags. The first, @param, defines a description for every parameter accepted by the method. The second, @return, describes the value returned by the method:

```
/**
* This is a comment to describe the <code>applyContact()</code> method.
*
* @param name This is the name of the user selected.
* @param id This is the email of the user selected.
*
* @return Returns an ArrayCollection.
*
* @see createUser()
*/
public function applyContact(name:String, id:Number):ArrayCollection {}
```

Instead, the @see tag creates a reference to a class that in some way is linked to it.

11

Other useful tags include the following:

- @default: Specifies the default values for a property
- @private: Prevents the ASDoc tool from generating documentation for the elements

You can also use the ASDoc tool to document MXML files, although this documentation will still need to be inserted inside the ActionScript code in the <mx:Script> tags because comments inserted between the MXML tags will not be interpreted.

In this solution you'll document Solution 2-8, created in Chapter 2.

How to build it

In Solution 2-8 you extended the Event class to be able to pass data when the event is released. This data was transported from the event object and sent as a parameter to the dispatchEvent method.

1. Create a structure of folders inside the Flex project: com/flexsolutions/chapter11.

2. Open the Flex project created in Chapter 2 (Chapter_2_Flex_Components) and copy the following files into the directory that you have just created:

   Chapter_2_Sol_8_app.mxml

   com/flexsolutions/chapter2/Chapter_2_Sol_8_CB.mxml

   com/flexsolutions/chapter2/Chapter_2_Sol_8_DG.mxml

   com/flexsolutions/chapter2/Chapter_2_Sol_8.as

Figure 11-10 shows how the files must be distributed in the folder structure.

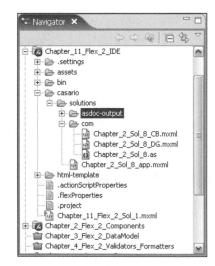

Figure 11-10.
The directory structure that you just created

3. You'll now begin to comment the classes and the components ready for the ASDoc tool to create the reference documentation. Start with the ActionScript class, which extends the Event class. Add the ASDoc comment seen as follows to describe the class:

```
package com.flexsolutions.chapter11
{
    import flash.events.Event;

/**
 * The <code>Chapter_2_Sol_8</code> class extends the
 * <code>Event</code> class to support
 * the propagation of complex data through the event model
 *
 * @see flash.events.Event
 */
    public class Chapter_2_Sol_8 extends Event
    {
```

In this first block of code, you created a comment to describe why you need this class. In the descriptive text, you also used an HTML tag, <code>, every time you referred to an item in the code. With the @see tag, you created a connection to the flash.events.Event class that you are extending.

A common error that should therefore be avoided is to begin the block of comments immediately above the import statement. By doing so, you'll obtain a comment on that code, not on the entire class.

4. Proceeding with the code of the custom event class, you find the declaration of two properties. Add a comment for each of these two properties, as seen following:

```
/**
 *   <code>evProp</code> property typed as String contains
 *   the name of the event specified by the Event metadata
 *
 * @default null
 *
 */
    public var evProp:String;

/**
 *
 *   <code>BLOG_CHANGED</code>
 *   is the static constant used to refer to the event
 *   @default changeBlog
 */
    // best practise: define the type property as static constants
    public static const BLOG_CHANGED:String = "changeBlog";
```

11

In the second comment block, you used the @default tag, which specifies the default value of the property. Notice also that when you create the documentation with the ASDoc tool, the comment immediately above the property BLOG_CHANGED, declared with the symbol //, is ignored by the tool. Only the comments that are included between the symbols /** */ will be interpreted.

5. The class continues, declaring the constructor. You also add the comment to this code:

```
/**
* Constructor.
*
*  @param evParam Reference to the event name
*
*  @param type Reference to the type of the event
*/
public function Chapter_2_Sol_8(evParam:String,type:String)
{
  super(type);
  this.evProp = evParam;
}
```

The constructor accepts two parameters—to document it you have used the @param tag to specify and describe the values that the constructor expects to receive.

6. Finally, you comment the only method of the custom class that carries out the override of the clone() method of the parent class:

```
/**
*    This method overrides the clone() method of the
*    Event class to guarantee the bubbling of the event model
*
*  @return An instance of the <code>Chapter_2_Sol_8</code> class
*/
override public function clone():Event
{
  return new Chapter_2_Sol_8(evProp,type);
}
}
}
```

This method does not accept parameters; it returns the instance of the custom class. For this reason, inside the comment you have specified the value that you expect to be returned from this method in the code with the @return tag.

You have finished commenting the custom class and can now move on to the two MXML components. The ASDoc tool also enables you to comment the MXML file, but it will only recognize comments inside the <mx:Script> block.

7. Open the Chapter_2_Sol_8_CB file, which takes care of causing the event to release with the dispatchEvent method when the user selects a new value in the ComboBox control.

8. Add an ASDoc comment directly above the first event handler:

```
<mx:Script>
  <![CDATA[

    import com.flexsolutions.chapter11.Chapter_2_Sol_8;

    /**
    * The <code>changeHandler()</code> is an event handler
    * that triggers when the user change the value from the
    * <code>ComboBox</code>.
    * <p>It creates the instance of <code>Chapter_2_Sol_8</code> class
    * and dispatches the event passing it the event object.
    *
    */
    private function changeHandler():void
    {
      var eventObj:Chapter_2_Sol_8 = new Chapter_2_Sol_8(
      myCombo.value as  String,Chapter_2_Sol_8.BLOG_CHANGED);
      dispatchEvent(eventObj);
    }

  ]]>
</mx:Script>
```

9. The second component, Chapter_2_Sol_8_DG, has only one property declaration. Don't add a comment to this file; instead, insert blocks of comments in the Chapter_2_Sol_8_app.mxml application file in the casario folder. To enable ASDoc to ignore elements, use the ASDoc @private tag. It won't be visible to the ASDoc tool, so it doesn't generate any type of comment:

```
<mx:Script>
  <![CDATA[

    import com.flexsolutions.chapter11.Chapter_2_Sol_8;

    /**
    *  @private
    */
    [Bindable]
    private var selectedMenu:String=
    "http://weblogs.macromedia.com/mesh/index.xml";
    /**
    *  @private
    */
    private function eventFired(event:Chapter_2_Sol_8):void
    {
```

11

```
          selectedMenu = event.evProp;
          if (selectedMenu == "null")
          {
            mx.controls.Alert.show("Please Choose a valid Blog");
            return;
          };
          hs.send();
        }
      ]]>
    </mx:Script>
```

You can now launch the ASDoc tool and generate the documentation for the files.

> To launch the ASDoc utility from any location, you must add it to your environment variables (see Solution 8-1 in Chapter 8). The ASDoc utility is located in the Flex Builder folder \Flex SDK X\bin.

The ASDoc tool accepts some parameters. You can get a complete list of the parameters that can be sent to it by entering the following command:

```
asdoc –help
```

The -doc-sources parameter that you'll use most often makes the tool carry out a recursive search in a directory of all the files for which an output will be generated.

10. In the example, you want to generate reference documentation for all the files in the casario folder, so open the command prompt, navigate to the casario folder in the Flex project, and launch the tool with the following syntax:

```
asdoc -source-path. -doc-sources.
```

This command line specifies to the ASDoc tool to search all the files contained in the directory from which it is run. It will generate an output for these files.

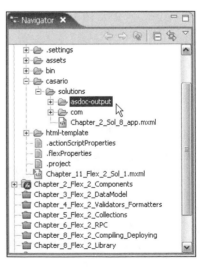

11. Go to Navigator view of the Flex Builder and carry out a Refresh (right-click the Flex project and select the Refresh option). You'll see that the folder asdoc-output has been created, as shown in Figure 11-11.

Figure 11-11.
The documentation files become generated in the asdoc-output folder.

This folder contains all the files that make up your reference documentation. Launch the index.html file to consult and read the comments. Figure 11-12 shows the results generated by the ASDoc tool, with the documentation created for the custom class.

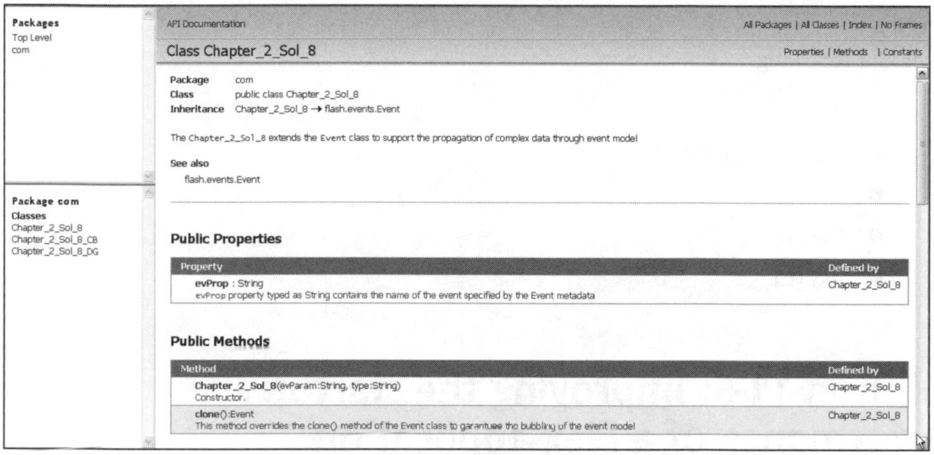

Figure 11-12. The documentation for the Chapter_2_Sol_8.as class

Expert tips

The ASDoc tool parses the blocks of comments and generates documentation from them. This process usually works fine, but if it encounters non–UTF-8 characters, the generation process of the references will be interrupted, and an error will be returned to you, indicating the number of lines in which the problem was noted.

If you want to use non–UTF-8 symbols (for example, > and <), you have to escape them by using the < and > entity references.

It is possible to specify a portion of text in a block of ASDoc comments that you don't want to be interpreted by the tool during generation. This situation is useful when you want to insert comments that are temporary or needed as internal communication for the development team.

To do this you can use a CSS class called hide, as seen following on the <span> tag:

```
/**
 * The <code>changeHandler()</code> is an event handler
 * that triggers when the user change the value from the
 * <code>ComboBox</code>.
 * <p>It creates the instance of <code>Chapter_2_Sol_8</code> class
 * and dispatches the event passing it the event object.
 *
 *<p class="hide">Hey Igor check this code out and test it on your
 *        Linux machine! Thanks, Marco. </p>
 *
 */
```

In this comment, the following block of text is not visible in the documentation:

```
*<p class="hide">Hey Igor check this code out and test it on your
*        Linux machine! Thanks, Marco. </p>
```

The ASDoc tool treats some metadata items as if they were properties or methods, including the following:

- [Bindable]
- [DefaultProperty]
- [Effect]
- [Event]
- [Style]

Solution 11-5: Improving the startup performance of a Flex application

As you well know, the deployment of a Flex application consists of compiling a project into one or more SWF files and associated assets, and placing those files onto a web server. Because only one main application file can exist for every Flex project, you'll always find yourself in the situation of having one main SWF file that will act as an entry point into the application, and will call all the other files.

This main file will be the first file loaded by the user when they access your web site; thus it becomes crucial to try to keep this file as small as possible so the user doesn't have to endure long initial waiting times.

There are many techniques to optimize the size of this file. One method is to organize its associated resources using a technique called **deferred creation**. To apply this technique, you must have a good understanding of how the objects defined in the application are loaded into Flash Player. By decreasing the number of components created when the application loads the SWF, it is possible to noticeably improve the startup performance.

The events are most commonly loaded in the following order:

1. preinitialize

2. initialize

3. creationComplete

4. updateComplete

5. applicationComplete

The order is not always the same—it depends on the type of containers or controls and the order in which they are defined in the application. For example, the navigator containers have a different creation order because only the children of the visible view are created.

After all the components have been loaded and drawn onscreen, the application launches the last event: applicationComplete. In the case of containers with multiple views (such as TabNavigator, ViewStack, and Accordion), there can be a bit of a performance hit because you are loading all the views into the application even before the user sees them in the application.

In these cases, however, you can use the creationPolicy property to force Flex to not load the nonvisible views until the user requests them (for example, the nonselected tabs in a TabNavigator container).

Deferred creation means that multiple-view containers give less initial weight to the application, loading its descendents' contents only when the user navigates within them.

In this solution, you'll see how to defer the creation of Flex objects by using the creationPolicy property.

What's involved

The creationPolicy property determines how a container creates its children (or descendents) when it is loaded. Furthermore, its value also changes according to the type of container: single view or multiple view.

The creationPolicy property accepts the values described in the following table.

Value	Description
All	Specifies that all the containers are created and that all the controls in their child views are loaded. This means that the startup of the application will be slower.
Auto	Specifies that all the navigator containers are created (the default), but Flex does not immediately load all their children. They will be created only if they are visible, which means that the application will start up faster, but users will have to wait the first time they navigate to a new view of the application.
None	Specifies that no controls are instanced in the container until it is instanced manually. To instance a container manually, the createComponentsFromDescriptors() method is used.
Queue	Specifies that Flex will load containers and then create the children of the queued containers. The order used is that in which they appear in the application. You can use the creationIndex property to change the loading order. This option is used to establish a creation order.

The following example sets the creationPolicy property to all on an Accordion container. In this way, the container will immediately instantiate all controls for every view contained in it:

11

```
<mx:Application xmlns:mx="http://www.adobe.com/2006/mxml">
  <mx:Accordion id="acc1" height="400"
    width="400"
    creationPolicy="all">

    <mx:VBox label="Panel 1">
      <mx:Label text="Panel 1"/>
      <mx:Button label="Click Me"/>
    </mx:VBox>
    <mx:Form label="Panel 2">
      <mx:FormItem label="First Name" height="100%">
        <mx:TextInput />
      </mx:FormItem>
    </mx:Form>

    <mx:VBox label="Panel 3">
      <mx:Label text="Panel 3 "/>
    </mx:VBox>

  </mx:Accordion>
</mx:Application>
```

This code increases the startup time of the application because every component in the Accordion will be loaded and instantiated as soon as the application is loaded. In the following section you'll see how to decrease the initial load time by creating a deferred component setting the creationPolicy property to none.

How to build it

When set to none, the creationPolicy property tells Flex to not load (and therefore not render) the container and all its contents. Not making the components available to the user at all would mean a very ineffective application, so you would manually instantiate these components by using the createComponentsFromDescriptors() method. Flex puts forward objects called **descriptors** that describe the components in an Array.

The syntax of this method is the following, where the recurse argument specifies whether Flex must recursively instantiate the children of the component:

baseContainer.createComponentsFromDescriptors(recurse:Boolean):Boolean

This parameter accepts a Boolean. Let's get to work and implement an application making use of the methods just discussed.

1. Create a new MXML application file by selecting File ➤ New ➤ MXML Application and call it Chapter_11_Flex_Sol_6.mxml.

2. Inside the application, insert an Accordion with three views, like so:

```
<mx:Accordion id="myAccordion" height="400"
  width="400"
  creationPolicy="none">
  <mx:VBox label="Panel 1" id="myVerticalBox">
    <mx:Label text="Panel 1" id="myLabel"/>
    <mx:Button label="Click Me" id="myBtn"/>
  </mx:VBox>
  <mx:Form label="Panel 2" id="myForm">
    <mx:FormItem label="First Name" height="100%">
      <mx:TextInput id="firstName" />
    </mx:FormItem>
  </mx:Form>
  <mx:VBox label="Panel 3" id="myVerticalBox3">
    <mx:Label text="Panel 3 " id="myLabel3"/>
  </mx:VBox>
</mx:Accordion>
```

The Accordion has the creationPolicy="none" property, which tells Flex not to load the container, its contents, or any of the navigator components' child views. When you launch the application, the container isn't visible; you have to explicitly call the instantiation methods with the createComponentsFromDescriptors() method.

3. Insert a TextArea and a Button. The TextArea will contain information relative to the objects contained in the Array of the descriptors. The Button enables you to launch a function that will use the createComponentsFromDescriptors() method to make the component visible.

```
<mx:Button label="Create Accordion" click="istComp();" />
<mx:TextArea id="myTxt" width="400" height="200" />
```

On the click of the Button the istComp() event handler is launched, which forces the Accordion container to be loaded.

4. Add an <mx:Script> block, as shown following. Here you'll define the istComp() function, which will follow the method and print the descriptors of the component in the TextArea:

```
<mx:Script>
  <![CDATA[
    import mx.core.ComponentDescriptor;
    private function istComp():void
    {
      myAccordion.createComponentsFromDescriptors();
      var numberDesc:int = myAccordion.childDescriptors.length;

      for (var i:int = 0; i < numberDesc; i++) {
        var compDesc:ComponentDescriptor = ➡
        myAccordion.childDescriptors[i];
        var propObj:Object = compDesc.properties;
```

```
                    myTxt.text += compDesc.id + " is a " + compDesc.type + "\n";

                    for (var value:String in propObj) {
                      myTxt.text += "Property: " + value + ➥
                       ": " + propObj[value] + "\n";
                    }
                  }
                }
              ]]>
           </mx:Script>
```

The `mx.core.ComponentDescriptor` class must be imported, which is done in the first line of code.

The `istComp()` function starts with the execution of the `createComponentsFromDescriptors()` method to create the instance of the container:

```
    myAccordion.createComponentsFromDescriptors();
```

The information contained in the descriptors is found in the `childDescriptors` Array. A `for()` loop will read all the data contained in this Array using the length of the `childDescriptors`:

```
    var numberDesc:int = myAccordion.childDescriptors.length;
    for (var i:int = 0; i < numberDesc; i++) {
```

The code in the `for()` loop merely cycles all the properties in the Array of the descriptors and prints them in the TextArea control:

```
    for (var i:int = 0; i < numberDesc; i++) {
    var compDesc:ComponentDescriptor = myAccordion.childDescriptors[i];
    var propObj:Object = compDesc.properties;

    myTxt.text += compDesc.id + " is a " + compDesc.type + "\n";

    for (var value:String in propObj) {
    myTxt.text += "Property: " + value + ": " + propObj[value] + "\n";
    }
    }
```

5. Save and run the application to see the result.

The deferred creation techniques you used in this solution can reduce the overall application startup time to make it appear as short as possible to the user.

When you click the Button, the Accordion container will be loaded and rendered visible, as shown in Figure 11-13, and the following text will be printed into the TextArea control:

myVerticalBox is a [class VBox]

Property: label: Panel 1

myForm is a [class Form]

Property: label: Panel 2

myVerticalBox3 is a [class VBox]

Property: label: Panel 3

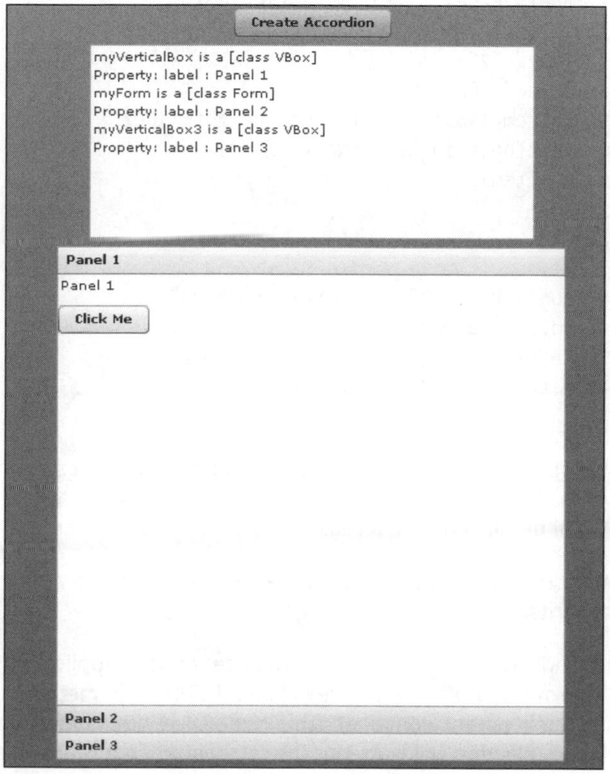

Figure 11-13. The Accordion container appears at the click of the button.

Expert tips

Another technique for notably improving the startup performance is that of order creation. The creationPolicy property accepts the value queue as parameter, which tells Flex to load the components in a particular order (which can be specified using the creationIndex property). This property indicates the order with which the component will be instantiated.

The following example shows the use of the creationPolicy when set to the queue value and how to specify the creationIndex property:

```
<mx:VBox label="Panel 1" id="myVerticalBox"
  creationPolicy="queued"
  creationIndex="3">
  <mx:Label text="Panel 1" id="myLabel"/>
  <mx:Button label="Click Me" id="myBtn"/>
</mx:VBox>

<mx:VBox label="Panel 2" id="myVerticalBox2"
  creationPolicy="queued"
  creationIndex="2">
  <mx:Form  id="myForm">
    <mx:FormItem label="First Name" height="100%">
      <mx:TextInput id="firstName" />
    </mx:FormItem>
  </mx:Form>
</mx:VBox>

<mx:VBox label="Panel 3" id="myVerticalBox3"
  creationPolicy="queued"
  creationIndex="1">
  <mx:Label text="Panel 3 " id="myLabel3"/>
</mx:VBox>
```

The creationIndex property specifies the order of loading; in this case, it is the complete reverse of how the Vbox container was declared. The last Vbox, with the id equal to myVerticalBox3, will be loaded first because its creationIndex is set at 1.

Note also that the creationPolicy property was declared for every VBox container. This property is not inheritable.

Another way to improve the general performance of the application is to use the removeChild(), removeChildAt(), and removeAllChildren() methods to detach the components from their parent container. This removal is not immediate, however; the Flash Player garbage collection will carry out the removal when it is possible for it to do so.

Solution 11-6: Building modular applications with modules

Chapter 2 discussed the importance of subdividing the application into logical parts to be able to render the code more usable (with better encapsulation) and maintainable. The runtime shared libraries (RSLs) are classic examples of this modular approach for Flex applications, but are statically linked at compile time.

Flex makes the `mx.modules` package available to you, which provides you with classes to create modular applications loaded at runtime that optimize the loading time of the application.

The modules are SWF files that are loaded by the application and can be shared across different projects. These files are not loaded at application startup, but only when the user requests them. Furthermore, in the development phase, the development team can work on a single SWF file or module and does not have to recompile the entire application to see and test any modifications made.

Every module extends the `ModuleBase` class and is loaded from the shell corresponding to the main application when it is requested. In this solution you'll see how to create a modular application.

What's involved

To create a modular application, you must first create the main file that will load the external module files. This file, which is called shell, consists of an `Application` that uses the `<mx:ModuleLoader>` tag to load the single modules:

```
<mx:Application xmlns:mx="http://www.adobe.com/2006/mxml">
<mx:ModuleLoader id="myModule" url="myModule.swf" />
```

The `myModule.swf` module is a compiled MXML file that extends the `ModuleBase` class in ActionScript or the Module class in MXML:

```
<?xml version="1.0" encoding="utf-8"?>
<mx:Module
  xmlns:mx="http://www.adobe.com/2006/mxml"
  layout="horizontal">
  <mx:Label text="This is my module" />
</mx:Module>
```

As is the case when you create an MXML component, it is necessary to put the namespace attribute in the `<mx:Module>` tag. It is also possible to recall other modules in a module using the same syntax declared in the shell:

```
<mx:ModuleLoader id="myOtherModule" url="myOtherModule.swf" />
```

To compile a module, you can use the internal compiler of Flex Builder or the command-line mxmlc compiler. When you use Flex Builder to compile the module, it is necessary to add it to the project as an Application. To do this, select Project ➤ Properties ➤ Flex Applications, click Add, and add the modules by selecting the MXML files, as shown in Figure 11-14.

11

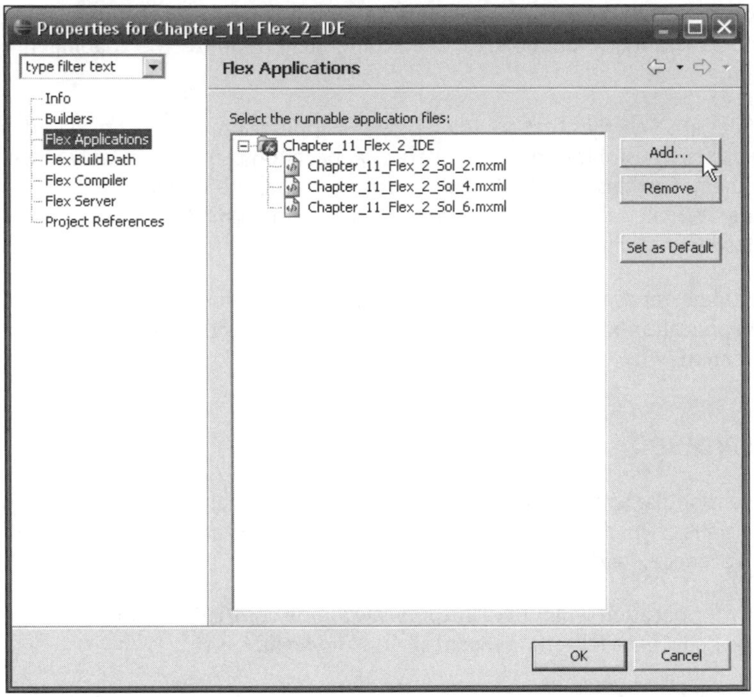

Figure 11-14. To compile a module from Flex Builder, you must add it to the project as an Application.

How to build it

To create a modular application, first create the file that will load the modules. This file, which is called shell, corresponds to the main application file.

1. Create a new application file by selecting File ➤ New ➤ MXML Application and save it as Chapter_11_Flex_Sol_7.mxml.

2. In this file, create a Panel with the ControlBar and a ToggleButtonBar navigator container. This check enables you to create a series of buttons that have the toggle function built in:

```
<mx:Panel width="400" height="250"
  layout="vertical"
  title="Choose a Form to fill"
horizontalAlign="center">

  <mx:ControlBar>

    <mx:ToggleButtonBar
      id="myTB"
```

```
          borderStyle="solid"
          horizontalGap="1"
          itemClick="clickHandler(event);">

          <mx:dataProvider>
            <mx:String>Individual</mx:String>
            <mx:String>Company</mx:String>
          </mx:dataProvider>
        </mx:ToggleButtonBar>
      </mx:ControlBar>
    </mx:Panel>
```

The MXML <mx:dataProvider> was used to define the series of buttons in the ToggleButtonBar control. In the tag, the String objects have been declared using MXML. Each String corresponds to a Button; in this case, the buttons are individual and company, as shown in Figure 11-15.

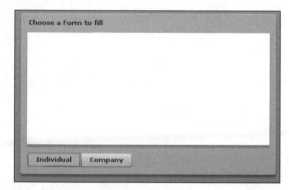

Figure 11-15. The two button controls load two modules.

The buttons will load two different modules containing two different forms for the user to complete, according to whether it involves a physical person or a company. To be able to load the modules, it is necessary to declare the <mx:ModuleLoader> tag.

3. Insert the <mx:ModuleLoader> tag in the Panel to which you set an id:

```
<mx:Panel width="400" height="250"
  layout="vertical"
  title="Choose a Form to fill"
  horizontalAlign="center">

<mx:ModuleLoader id="myModule" />
```

If the <mx:ModuleLoader> tag is declared without the url attribute, no module will be loaded. Modules are loaded during the phase in which the buttons of the <mx:ToggleButtonBar> are clicked. To do this, you must manage the itemClick event of the navigator container and create the corresponding event handler.

11

4. Add an event handler on the itemClick event to the <mx:ToggleButtonBar> tag, as follows:

```
<mx:ToggleButtonBar
 id="myTB"
borderStyle="solid"
horizontalGap="1"
itemClick="clickHandler(event);">
```

This function will load the module according to the button that has been clicked by the user. To load a module via ActionScript, use the loadModule() method. This method does not accept parameters; it directly loads the module specified in the url property of myModule, the ModuleLoader object:

5. Create an <mx:Script> block, as shown following. Here you specify the clickHandler() event handler. To use the loadModule() method you must first import the mx.modules package and specify the url property:

```
<mx:Script>
  <![CDATA[
    import mx.events.ItemClickEvent;
    import mx.modules.*;

    private function clickHandler(event:ItemClickEvent):void {

      myModule.url = event.label + ".swf";
      myModule.loadModule();
    }
  ]]>
</mx:Script>
```

In the clickHandler() function you set the url property of the ModuleLoader object to the label defined as a String in the dataProvider of the ToggleButtonBar. To the label, add the SWF extension because the module is an external SWF file. The values to choose from in the application are Individual.swf and Company.swf. Before running the application you must create these two modules.

Creating a module in Flex Builder means creating an MXML file that has <mx:Module> as its root tag. You can create an MXML component and select that tag from the combo box Based On (shown in Figure 11-12). The module will be created and added to the project and therefore compiled in SWF.

6. Create the first module by selecting File ➤ New ➤ MXML Component, select the <mx:Module> tag as the tag for it to be based on, and call it Individual.mxml.

7. In this file, insert a simple Form container with three text inputs and a button, like so:

```
<?xml version="1.0" encoding="utf-8"?>
<mx:Module
  xmlns:mx="http://www.adobe.com/2006/mxml"
  layout="vertical">
```

```
<mx:Form width="100%">
  <mx:FormHeading label="Fill the Form for Individuals"/>
  <mx:FormItem label="Name">
    <mx:TextInput/>
  </mx:FormItem>
  <mx:FormItem label="Last Name">
    <mx:TextInput/>
  </mx:FormItem>
  <mx:FormItem label="Job">
   <mx:TextInput/>
  </mx:FormItem>
  <mx:FormItem>
    <mx:Button label="Button"/>
  </mx:FormItem>
</mx:Form>

</mx:Module>
```

The module is an MXML component, which starts with the declaration of the `<mx:Module>` tag. It is important to note that like almost all other MXML components, the namespace `xmlns:mx=http://www.adobe.com/2006/mxml` becomes specified on the root tag.

8. Now follow the same process to create the `Company.mxml` module by selecting File ➤ New ➤ MXML Component. Select the `<mx:Module>` tag as the tag for it to be based on, and call it Company.mxml.

9. In this file, insert a simple Form container with three text inputs and a button:

```
<?xml version="1.0" encoding="utf-8"?>
<mx:Module
  xmlns:mx="http://www.adobe.com/2006/mxml"
  layout="vertical">

  <mx:Form width="100%">
    <mx:FormHeading label="Fill the Form for Companies"/>
    <mx:FormItem label="Company">
      <mx:TextInput/>
    </mx:FormItem>
    <mx:FormItem label="Full name">
      <mx:TextInput/>
    </mx:FormItem>
    <mx:FormItem label="Role">
      <mx:TextInput/>
    </mx:FormItem>
    <mx:FormItem>
      <mx:Button label="Button"/>
    </mx:FormItem>
  </mx:Form>

</mx:Module>
```

11

These two modules differ only in the TextInput labels. If users choose to complete the form for an individual (Individual.mxml file), they have to fill in First Name, Last Name, and Job; whereas if they select the form for a company (Company.mxml file), they have to insert the name of the company, full name, and role in the company.

This simple example helps you understand how modules can be useful to break the application into logical pieces. These forms will not be loaded at the start of the application, only when the user clicks the ToggleButtonBar and explicitly requests them. This means that you'll have a smaller SWF and a reduced application startup time.

10. Save and run the main application.

Note that at the startup of the application, even though the button of the ToggleButtonBar is selected, no module is loaded. You could add the url attribute to the ModuleLoader to load the first module at startup:

```
<mx:ModuleLoader id="myModule" url="individual.swf" />
```

Expert tips

ToggleButtonBar is a navigator container that enables you to specify, through a data provider, the buttons that should be visualized. These buttons manage the state selected and deselected. In this solution you used simple String objects as dataProviders, but it is also possible to define objects to which you can associate a graphic icon to place next to the label of the button:

```
<mx:ToggleButtonBar
  borderStyle="solid"
  horizontalGap="5"
  itemClick="clickHandler(event);">
  <mx:dataProvider>
    <mx:Object label="Flash"
      icon="@Embed(source='assets/img1.gif')"/>
    <mx:Object label="Director"
      icon="@Embed(source='assets/ img2.gif')"/>
  </mx:dataProvider>
</mx:ToggleButtonBar>
```

The Object tag has two properties: label and icon. The icon attribute specifies an image to use as an icon for the button, whereas the label property defines the label that will appear next to the icon.

When you load modules deployed on a server different from that on which the application resides, you have to use the allowDomain() method. This technique (refer to Solution 10-2 in Chapter 10) enables cross-domain access to SWF files and data.

By specifying the target domain from which the module must be loaded, you guarantee that the application will be authorized to access that content. On the remote server in which the module is resident, it is necessary to copy the cross-domain file (refer to Solution 10-1), which will have syntax similar to the following:

```
<cross-domain-policy>
<allow-access-from domain="http://www.serverModuleHosted.com" />
</cross-domain-policy>
```

In the loaded module, insert the allowDomain() method on the preInitialize event to enable communication with the shell application:

```
public function init():void
{
 Security.allowDomain("http://www.myserver.com");
 Security.loadPolicyFile("http://www.myserver.com/crossdomain.xml");
 var myURL:URLRequest =
     new URLRequest("http://www.myremoteserver.com/crossdomain.xml");
 var loader:URLLoader = new URLLoader();
 loader.load(myURL);
}
```

Instead, in the loaded module, insert this code:

```
public function initMod():void
{
 Security.allowDomain("http://www.loaderServerName.com");
}
```

Using this approach, you can load modules published on different domains to that of the shell application.

Summary

Flex Builder is the tool for creating RIAs with Flex. It's a very powerful environment and it's based on the core engine of the well-known Eclipse. Further, you can customize and optimize the environment faster than you can work and develop your Flex applications.

This chapter explored techniques to improve your Flex development. It started by analyzing how to optimize the use of memory that Flex Builder uses by applying some simple rules, such as the following:

- Limit the number of projects open at the same time on the workspace of Flex Builder.

- Increase the quantity of RAM that it can use by updating settings inside the FlexBuilder.ini file, found in the root of the Flex Builder folder.

Then you learned about localized application in Flex. It often happens that the project on which you are working must use a different language. This solution used a Flex ResourceBundle API to create localized applications. With this class, all the content that must be localized is removed from the main application and the information is linked to property files through the metadata tag [ResourceBundle] variable.

11

A new addition to the release of Flex 2.0.1 was the possibility of loading the styles at runtime using the `StyleManager` class to load the SWF files that contain the different CSS declarations. The CSS files created will be compiled in SWF files by Flex Builder using the new Compile CSS option. You showed how to use this new feature to change the appearance of a Flex application at runtime.

Little by little, as the application grows, and more and more files become involved, it becomes necessary to create decent documentation. Simple code commenting is often not enough, and having reference documentation available that you can quickly access can save you precious time in the development phase (particularly when you work in a team). You learned how to use the ASDoc tool to generate reference documentation of the actual ActionScript classes or MXML components of the Flex applications.

The end of the chapter discussed a technique to improve the startup performance of a Flex application: deferred creation. By decreasing the number of components created when the application loads the SWF, it is possible to noticeably improve startup performance.

And speaking of startup performance, Flex modules provide you with classes to create modular applications loaded at runtime that optimize the loading time of the application.

The modules are SWF files that are loaded by the application and can be shared across different projects. These files are not loaded at application startup, but only when the user requests them. Furthermore, in the development phase, the development team can work on a single SWF file or module; it doesn't have to recompile the entire application to see and test any modifications made.

12 MORE FLEX FRAMEWORK LIBRARIES AND UTILITIES

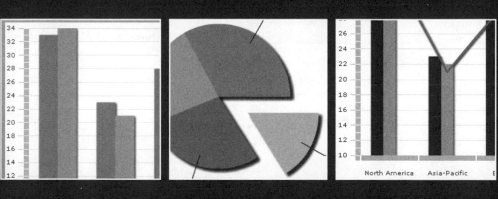

Flex is a huge framework that offers a great number of utilities and components for developers of Rich Internet Applications (RIAs). For example, one additional package of libraries is that of Flex charting components, which allows you to show data in one of the many charts included with this set of libraries.

The charting components, even if they must be bought separately, integrate into the Flex framework and are programmed like the core components of Flex. With MXML tags and ActionScript code, you can choose among more than 10 different graphs to represent the data. You can also add user interaction or transition effects to make the chart even more attractive.

In this chapter, you'll see how to use some Flex libraries that offer advanced functions to make your applications even more useful.

Solution 12-1: Displaying data in a chart

Charts are a powerful way to communicate and visualize interpretations of data in an immediate and efficient way to the user. In the preceding solutions (refer to Chapter 6 and Chapter 7) you learned how to display data in list-based controls in the form of a DataGrid, List, or Tree. Flex gives you charting components (www.adobe.com/products/flex/charting/) as additional tools that you can install on your copy of Flex Builder that allow you to create charts (bar charts, line charts, bubble charts, pie charts, and so on). Furthermore, by using ActionScript, it is possible to program user interaction and to create animation.

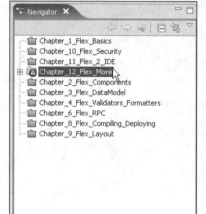

Figure 12-1.
The Navigator view shows all the projects defined in the Flex Builder workspace.

Displaying data in a graph gives a quick overview of the relationships that exist between the data. Figure 12-1 shows how a single data series becomes visualized through a column chart:

Table 12-1 shows a list of the supported chart types that can be used:

Table 12-1. Supported chart types

Chart type	Chart control class
Area	AreaChart
Bar	BarChart
Bubble	BubbleChart
Candlestick	CandlestickChart
Column	ColumnChart

Chart type	Chart control class
HighLowOpenClose	HLOCChart
Line	LineChart
Pie	PieChart
Plot	PlotChart

All chart components are subclasses of the Cartesian chart class, except for PieChart, which is a subclass of the PieChart class. Although the Cartesian charts represent a set of data points in rectangular shapes, the PieChart class is a subclass of the PolarChart class and it represents data in circular space.

In this solution you'll see how to represent data through the use of charts and graphs.

What's involved

Flex charting components give RIA developers a set of components to use to create many different chart types. Furthermore, they allow control of the look and feel of the chart and to add interaction with the user.

You can see charting components in action by connecting to the Flex Component Explorer at the following address: http://examples.adobe.com/flex2/inproduct/sdk/explorer/ explorer.html.

Here, under the Charts section, you'll find all the charting components that you can use. The Flex Component Explorer is also an excellent didactic instrument in that it shows all the components of the Flex Software Development Kit (SDK) with the relative code to use.

Even though there are many chart types, the instructions to program them are similar. In fact, each chart declaration begins with the opening of the tag relative to the chart type that you intend to use, the declaration of the series of data to use, the declaration of the axes, the style, and other elements such as grid lines:

```
<mx:ColumnChart id="column" dataProvider="{medalsAC}">
<mx:series>
    <mx:ColumnSeries xField="Country"
      yField="Gold" displayName="Gold"/>
    <mx:ColumnSeries xField="Country"
      yField="Silver" displayName="Silver"/>
    <mx:ColumnSeries xField="Country"
      yField="Bronze" displayName="Bronze"/>
</mx:series>
```

12

```
<mx:horizontalAxis>
<mx:CategoryAxis categoryField="Country"/>
</mx:horizontalAxis>
</mx:ColumnChart>
```

This code used the ColumnChart type. An array of ColumnSeries specifies the data to visualize in a chart.

The <mx:horizontalAxis> tag specifies which data should be visualized in the horizontal axis. To specify the data to visualize in the vertical axis, use the <mx:verticalAxis> tag.

The Flex 3 SDK also adds new functions to the charting controls, such as the possibility to program highlighting, thresholding, and data labels.

How to build it

In this solution, you'll create an application that will use two chart types: a pie chart and a column chart. The two charts use an ArrayCollection as dataProvider that contains the values of IT world market shares (real) in 2001 and 2004. The column chart shows a diagram for each geographic zone, while the pie chart shows the global cover in a year. Through the MenuBar navigator container (the Navigator container is discussed in Solution 13-1), you'll load the data of 2001 or 2004 shown in the PieChart.

> This solution requires Flex 3 SDK. To complete the solution you must install Flex Builder 3 (http://labs.adobe.com/technologies/flex/flexbuilder3/).

1. You'll create the project that will contain all the solutions of Chapter 12. Select File ➤ New ➤ Flex Project to create a project with the name Chapter_12_Flex_More.

2. Create the application file from File ➤ New ➤ MXML Application and save it with the name Chapter_12_Flex_Sol_1_More.mxml. Insert the first elements of the user interface:

```
<mx:Application xmlns:mx="http://www.adobe.com/2006/mxml"
layout="horizontal" verticalAlign="top">

<mx:ApplicationControlBar width="100%" dock="true">
<mx:MenuBar id="myMenu"
labelField="@label">

<mx:XMLList>
    <menuitem label="Choose the Year" >
    <menuitem label="2001"/>
    <menuitem label="2004"/>
    </menuitem>
</mx:XMLList>

</mx:MenuBar>
</mx:ApplicationControlBar>
```

The ApplicationControlBar container has its property dock set at true and its width at 100%. In this container, a MenuBar component was inserted. To populate the MenuBar, you have declared the XMLList as a nested tag, which creates an XML list of items.

Through the <menuitem> nodes, you'll create the menu items that will be visualized from the MenuBar. The menu is displayed onscreen, as shown in Figure 12-2, and uses the labelField property to link the label to the attribute label of the <menuitem>:

```
<mx:MenuBar id="myMenu"
labelField="@label">
<mx:XMLList>
<menuitem label="Choose the Year" >
<menuitem label="2001"/>
 <menuitem label="2004"/>
</menuitem>
```

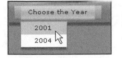

Figure 12-2.
The MenuBar component creates a menu bar that is used to navigate within an application.

3. Before creating the two chart components, you must declare the variable that will function as dataProvider and permit the chart components to represent the data. Open an <mx:Script> block to import the classes necessary to this solution and to declare the variable typed as ArrayCollection:

```
<mx:Script>
<![CDATA[
import mx.events.MenuEvent;
import mx.collections.ArrayCollection;

[Bindable]
public var market:ArrayCollection = new ArrayCollection([
{area:"North America", year2001:"33", year2004:"34"},
{area:"Asia-Pacific", year2001:"23", year2004:"21"},
{area:"Europe", year2001:"28", year2004:"30"},
{area:"Rest of the world", year2001:"16", year2004:"15"}
]);

[Bindable]
private var currentYear:String = "2001";
]]>
</mx:Script>
```

You have imported the MenuEvent class because you'll manage the event object created by this class when a value is selected from the MenuBar component.

The market variable is an ArrayCollection that contains the data of the market in percentages divided by year and region. This is the variable used to represent the data in the charts. The <mx:Script> block concludes with the declaration of the currentYear variable that will contain a String to use as binding with the title of a Panel.

12

4. Create the first chart component with a ColumnChart control that represents the data for each geographic zone through columns. You insert this chart in a Panel container. Immediately after the ApplicationControlBar closes, write the following code:

```
</mx:ApplicationControlBar>

<mx:Panel title="Information Technology world market">

<mx:ColumnChart id="columnChart"
dataProvider="{market}" showDataTips="true">
<mx:horizontalAxis>
<mx:CategoryAxis
dataProvider="{market}"
categoryField="area" />
</mx:horizontalAxis>
<mx:series>
<mx:ColumnSeries xField="area"
yField="year2001"
displayName="2001" />
<mx:ColumnSeries xField="area"
yField="year2004"
displayName="2004" />
</mx:series>
</mx:ColumnChart>
</mx:Panel>
```

The ColumnChart uses the ArrayCollection variable market, defined in the <mx:Script> block as dataProvider. Specify the data that you want to represent on the horizontal axis of the graph as </mx:horizontalAxis>. Using this <mx:CategoryAxis> tag, you can specify which data to visualize by taking it from the ArrayCollection that is linked as dataProvider to the ColumnChart. In the solution, on the horizontal axis (y axis), you'll show the data contained in the property area of the variable market, sending it to the categoryField property:

```
<mx:ColumnChart id="columnChart"
dataProvider="{market}" showDataTips="true">
<mx:horizontalAxis>
<mx:CategoryAxis
dataProvider="{market}"
categoryField="area" />
</mx:horizontalAxis>
```

In the solution, you want to compare the values (in percentages) of the IT market in 2001 and 2004 in the ColumnChart, as shown in Figure 12-3. You must, therefore, specify that a series of data, not just one single data point, is shown on the x axis. To declare a data series for the ColumnChart component, use the ColumnSeries chart to which you sent the attributes:

- xField: Specifies the data to show on the x axis
- yField: Specifies the data that determines the y axis of the top of a column
- displayName: Specifies the label to show in the data tips (data tips are discussed in the "Expert tips" section of this solution)

To obtain the result shown in Figure 12-3 (save the file and run the application), insert two declarations in the <mx:ColumnSeries> tag, one for the values of 2001 and another for the values of 2004:

```
<mx:series>
<mx:ColumnSeries xField="area"
yField="year2001"
displayName="2001" />
<mx:ColumnSeries xField="area"
yField="year2004"
displayName="2004" />
</mx:series>
```

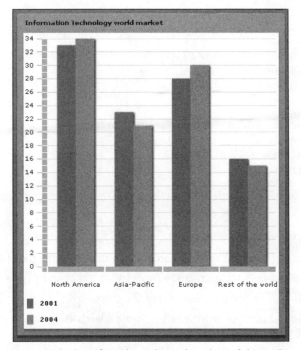

Figure 12-3. The ColumnChart shows the values of the market divided by region in the years 2001 and 2004.

5. Add the second chart that represents the data with a pie chart. This graph allows you to have a quick overview and to compare the data. In the solution, the pie chart shows the values (in percentages) of the market in the various regions. Insert this code immediately after the closure of the Panel that contains the ColumnChart:

```
</mx:Panel>

<mx:VBox>
<mx:Panel title="Information Technology world market in {currentYear}">
<mx:PieChart id="pieChart"
dataProvider="{market}" >
<mx:series>
<mx:PieSeries id="pieSeries" field="year2001"
nameField="area"
labelPosition="callout"/>
</mx:series>
</mx:PieChart>
</mx:Panel>

</mx:VBox>
```

The pie chart uses the same ArrayCollection as dataProvider and shows only a single series of data at a time. With the use of the <mx:pieSeries> tag, you specify that the data of year 2001 is represented (in the field property):

```
<mx:series>
<mx:PieSeries id="pieSeries" field="year2001"
nameField="area"
labelPosition="callout"/>
</mx:series>
```

The labelPosition property specifies how to visualize the labels. It accepts the following values:

- none: No labels will be visualized.
- outside: The labels will be drawn around the border of the pie chart.
- callout: The labels are specified in two vertical stacks on the side of the pie chart.
- inside: The labels are visualized inside the chart.
- insideWithCallout: Draws the labels inside the chart. It also draws the labels to call out if it shrinks below a certain size.

Figure 12-4 shows the pie chart and the labels drawn using vertical stacks on the side of the pie chart (save and run the file to compile the application).

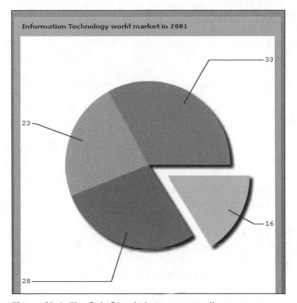

Figure 12-4. The labelPosition property allows you to specify how to visualize the labels of the pie chart. In this example, its values have been set as callouts.

This solution lacks the possibility of showing the values for 2004 in the PieChart control. The MenuBar must be used to show a different year and change the values represented in the pie chart.

6. Add an event listener to the itemClick event in the MenuBar to launch the function that will change the data visualized in the pie chart:

```
<mx:MenuBar id="myMenu" labelField="@label"
itemClick="changePieChart(event)">
```

7. In the <mx:Script> block add the event handler changePieChart() that sets the property field of the pie chart to the year 2001 or 2004, according to the item selected in the MenuBar:

```
 [Bindable]
private var currentYear:String = "2001";

private function changePieChart(event:MenuEvent):void
{
var itemLabel:String = event.item.@label;

switch( itemLabel )
{
case "2004":
pieSeries.field = "year2004";
currentYear = "2004";
break;
```

12

```
case "2001":
pieSeries.field = "year2001";
currentYear = "2001";
break;
}
}
]]>
</mx:Script>
```

The MenuBar creates a MenuEvent event object type that contains the information relative to the item selected in the MenuBar by the user. With an if() condition, you check whether the user has selected the value 2004 or 2001. This information is contained in the event.item.@label property. This syntax uses the E4X specification (refer to Solution 6-4) to read the value of the label attribute of the XMLList specified in the MenuBar:

```
<mx:MenuBar id="myMenu" labelField="@label"
        itemClick="changePieChart(event)">
        <mx:XMLList>
            <menuitem label="Choose the Year" >
                <menuitem label="2001" />
                <menuitem label="2004"/>
            </menuitem>

        </mx:XMLList>
    </mx:MenuBar>
```

By getting the value selected by the user, you can change the field property of the PieSeries, making it automatically change the representation of the data in the pie chart:

```
var itemLabel:String = event.item.@label;
switch( itemLabel )
{
case "2004":
pieSeries.field = "year2004";
currentYear = "2004";
break;

case "2001":
pieSeries.field = "year2001";
currentYear = "2001";
break;
}
```

8. Save the file and run the application.

At application startup, the data relative to 2001 is shown in the pie chart. But if you select a different year in the MenuBar, the data will change, and the pie chart will be automatically redrawn as shown in Figure 12-5.

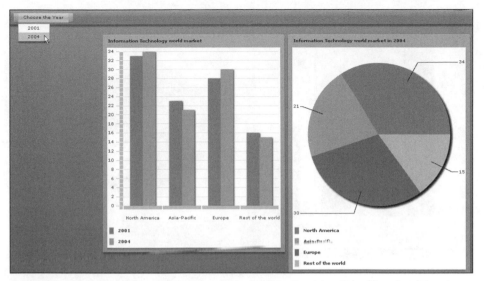

Figure 12-5. When you select a different year in the MenuBar, the data will be filtered and the pie chart will be automatically redesigned to show the new data.

Expert tips

The chart components also allow you to represent complex data in a form that is easy and immediately understandable. However, it is often useful to provide a legend that informs the user about the data that is laid out in the charts. For example, in the ColumnChart, you have inserted two data series that show two columns of different colors (refer to Figure 12-5): one with the data for 2001 and another with the data for 2004. In this scenario it becomes very useful to explain what a column represents with a legend.

To add legends to charts in Flex, you just need to use the <mx:Legend> tag, which accepts the following parameters:

- dataProvider: Contains the id of the chart for which it must create the legend
- labelPlacement: Indicates the position of the labels: left, top, right, or bottom
- direction: Specifies whether the visualization must be vertical or horizontal

1. In the example, you add the legends for the two charts by adding the following code immediately under the closure of the tag:

```
</mx:ColumnChart>
<mx:Legend dataProvider="{columnChart}"/>

</mx:PieChart>
<mx:Legend dataProvider="{pieChart}" direction="horizontal"/>
```

12

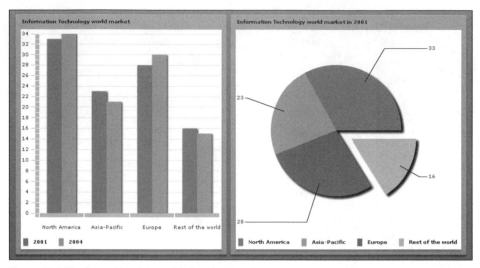

Figure 12-6. The legend has been added to the two charts.

The PieChart component provides exploding wedges to highlight and represent particular data. There are three properties supported by the PieSeries to obtain this effect:

- explodeRadius: Contains the percentage of the pie radian to apply when exploding the wedges. Accepts values from 0 to 1.

- perWedgeExplodeRadius: Contains an array whose values are added to the value of explodeRadius to determine the percentage of the pie radian amount of each individual wedge of the pie. It is an array of values that varies from 0 to 1.

- reserveExplodeRadius: Contains an amount of the available pie radian to reserve for animating an exploding wedge.

2. Explode a wedge by inserting an Array on the perWedgeExplodeRadius property:

```
<mx:series>
<mx:PieSeries id="pieSeries" field="year2001"
nameField="area"
labelPosition="callout"
perWedgeExplodeRadius="[0,0,0,.3,0,0]" />
</mx:series>
```

3. Save and run the application to see the final result shown in Figure 12-7.

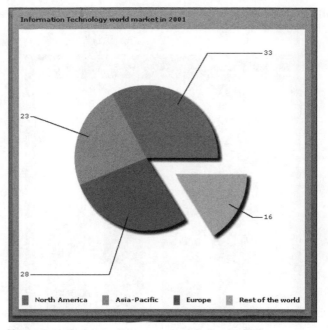

Figure 12-7. The PieSeries supports exploding wedges.

A chart type that is very similar to the ColumnChart is the BarChart control, which allows you to represent data as a series of vertical bars. The declaration of this type of chart is very similar to the ColumnChart; only the tags for specifying the data series and the representations of the axes change. With these slight differences, you can exchange the ColumnChart created in this solution with a bar chart:

```
<mx:Panel title="Information Technology world market in a Bar Chart">
<mx:BarChart id="barChart"
dataProvider="{market}"
showDataTips="true">
<mx:verticalAxis>
<mx:CategoryAxis
categoryField="area" />
</mx:verticalAxis>
<mx:series>
<mx:BarSeries yField="area"
xField="year2001"
displayName="2001" />
<mx:BarSeries yField="area"
xField="year2004"
displayName="2004" />
</mx:series>
</mx:BarChart>
<mx:Legend dataProvider="{barChart}"/>
</mx:Panel>
```

12

4. Save and run the application to see the BarChart graph drawn in the application, as shown in Figure 12-8.

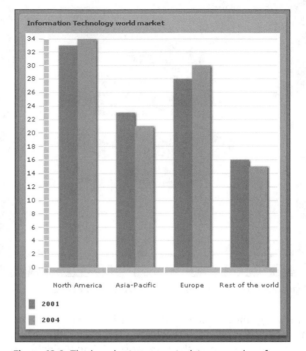

Figure 12-8. The bar chart represents data as a series of vertical bars.

Solution 12-2: Working with events and effects with chart components

Aside from being able to represent graphic data in different ways, the chart components allow the user to interact with them. A click on a slice of a pie chart and a mouse hovering over a column of a column chart are examples of interaction between the user and the chart. The chart components inherit all the events of the UIComponent class and therefore the mouseMove, mouseOver, mouseDown, and mouseUp events (from the MouseEvent class), furthermore adding other events based on the ChartBase class:

- itemClick: Releases when the user clicks a data point

- itemDoubleClick: Intercepts the double-click of the user on a data point

- itemMouseDown: Releases when the mouse is clicked on and kept pressed (and not yet released) on a data point

- itemMouseUp: Releases when the user releases the button of the mouse on a data point

- itemMouseMove: Releases when the user moves the mouse onto a data point
- itemRollOut: Intercepts the exit of the mouse from a data point
- itemRollOver: Releases when the user moves the mouse over a data point

> *When referring to charts, a data point is the intersection of two coordinates.*

All these events release when the user interacts with a data point and are all of ChartItemEvent class type, contained in the mx.charts.events package. The ChartItemEvent class creates an event object that carries the hitData property. This property, which is an instance of the HitData class, contains the information relative to the data point on which the user has made the event release in an object.

The chart components support some particular effects that can be applied to the data visualized in the graph: SeriesInterpolate, SeriesSlide, and SeriesZoom. These effects are applied to the graph with the standard effect triggers such as showEffect, hideEffect, showDataEffect, and hideDataEffect. These effects act at chart level, so they are applied to all the data involved in the representation.

In this solution you'll see how to manage events on the data points of a graph and in particular how to apply effects to render the representation of the data even more readable.

What's involved

To manage the interaction of the user with the charts, you must decide which event to link to the function. The event handler can be registered using the addEventListener method launched on an initialization function:

```
chart.addEventListener(ChartItemEvent.ITEM_ CLICK, detailHandler);
```

It can also be launched directly by using the event as an attribute of the tag that defines the chart:

```
<mx:LineChart id="myChart"
    dataProvider="{market}"
    showDataTips="true"
itemClick="detailHandler(event)" >
```

Both examples obtain the same result—the itemClick event is dispatched when the user clicks a data point, and the event handler detailHandler() is called. The ChartItemEvent class generates an event object that contains the hitData property. This property, an instance of the HitData class, contains the information relative to the data point on which the user has clicked.

You can, for example, make the event handler detailHandler() return all the values contained in the hitData property to you by running a for .. in cycle:

12

```
private function detailHandler(evt:ChartItemEvent):void
{
var props:String = new String();

for (var prop:String in evt.hitData.item)
{
props += evt.hitData.item[prop] + "\n";
}
mx.controls.Alert.show(props,"Show the hitData object values");
}
```

You'll see this example applied to the solution.

There are three effects that are supported only by charting: SeriesInterpolate, SeriesSlide, and SeriesZoom. These effects are used and linked to a data series and are applied when data changes. To create effects on the data series, first define the type of effect you want to use:

```
<mx:SeriesSlide
  id="myEffectShow"
  duration="500"
  direction="up"
/>
```

In this case, you have chosen to create a SeriesSlide effect to which you have set the duration property (which represents the duration time of the effect in milliseconds and its direction).

You can now apply this effect to one or more data series in the chart:

```
<mx:series>
<mx:ColumnSeries id="firstColumn"
xField="area"
yField="year2001"
displayName="2001"
  showDataEffect="myEffectShow" />
```

With this code, you have created an effect of SeriesSlide type that is applied to the ColumnSeries with the id equal to firstColumn when the data is displayed. The effect is not applied when the chart is drawn; only when data changes.

In this solution, you'll see how to apply effects and events to the charting to render the user experience even more attractive.

How to build it

1. Create a new file by selecting File ➤ New ➤ MXML Application and save it as Chapter_12_Flex_Sol_2_More.mxml. You create an event listener on the creationComplete of the application:

```
<mx:Application xmlns:mx="http://www.adobe.com/2006/mxml"
layout="horizontal" verticalAlign="top"
creationComplete="init()">
```

2. You insert an `<mx:Script>` block immediately under the `<mx:Application>` tag, into which you'll import the classes necessary for the example and define the ArrayCollection that will be used as dataProvider for the charting:

```
<mx:Script>
<![CDATA[
import mx.charts.events.ChartItemEvent;
import mx.charts.HitData;
import mx.controls.Alert;
import mx.events.MenuEvent;
import mx.collections.ArrayCollection;
import mx.controls.Menu;

[Bindable]
public var market:ArrayCollection = new ArrayCollection([
{area:"North America", year2001:"33",year2002:"34", year2004:"35"},
{area:"Asia-Pacific", year2001:"23", year2002:"22",year2004:"21"},
{area:"Europe", year2001:"28", year2002:"29",year2004:"30"},
{area:"Rest of the world", year2001:"16",year2002:"18", year2004:"15"}
]);

[Bindable]
private var currentYear:String = "2001";
]]>
</mx:Script>
```

Considering that you'll create events on the chart, you have to import the ChartItemEvent and HitData classes.

The variable market contains an Array of objects with the following properties: area, year2001, year2002, and year2004. This variable will be used as dataProvider for the charting, and its values will be represented graphically. The variable currentYear contains a String that represents the year for which it has been chosen to view the data.

3. Insert the user interface elements into the application, giving the user the ability to choose the year for which to display the data in the graph:

```
</mx:Script>
<mx:ApplicationControlBar width="100%" dock="true">
<mx:MenuBar id="myMenu" labelField="@label"
  itemClick="changeChartData(event)">

<mx:XMLList>
 <menuitem label="Choose the Year" >
 <menuitem label="2001" />
 <menuitem label="2002"/>
 <menuitem label="2004"/>
```

12

```
    </menuitem>

  </mx:XMLList>
 </mx:MenuBar>
</mx:ApplicationControlBar>
```

The MenuBar, which is the same as that in Solution 12-1, manages the event handler changeChartData() on the itemClick that will change the data filtering it by year. The MenuBar becomes populated using an XMLList as dataProvider and the label attribute as data to visualize (labelField="@label").

> **4.** Add the first of the two graphs, the ColumnChart, to which you add a new data series in line chart format. The charting can, in fact, understand multiple data series, also using a different visualization, as shown in Figure 12-9. You insert the following code immediately after the closure of the <mx:ApplicationControlBar> tag:

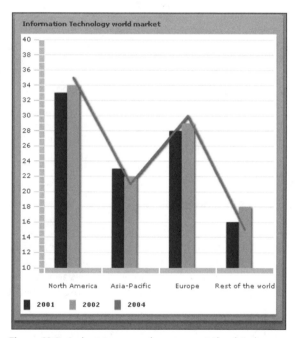

Figure 12-9. A chart type can also represent the data in other forms using different data series.

```
<mx:Panel title="Information Technology world market">
<mx:ColumnChart id="columnChart"
dataProvider="{market}"
showDataTips="true"
dataTipFunction="customTip">
<mx:horizontalAxis>
<mx:CategoryAxis
```

```
categoryField="area" />
</mx:horizontalAxis>
<mx:verticalAxis>
<mx:LinearAxis minimum="10" maximum="40"/>
</mx:verticalAxis>
<mx:series>
<mx:ColumnSeries xField="area"
yField="year2001"
displayName="2001" />
<mx:ColumnSeries xField="area"
yField="year2002"
displayName="2002" />
 <mx:LineSeries
xField="area"
yField="year2004"
displayName="2004">
</mx:LineSeries>
</mx:series>
</mx:ColumnChart>
<mx:Legend dataProvider="{columnChart}" direction="horizontal"/>
</mx:Panel>
```

The <mx:ColumnChart> tag specifies two properties that provide visual clues to the user: showDataTips and dataTipFunction. The showDataTips property, when set as true, allows you to enable the visualization of the tips on every single series of data, as shown in Figure 12-10. By default all the data contained in the dataProvider of the chart will be displayed, but through the dataTipFunction property you can specify a function in which you can specify the data to visualize in the tip:

```
<mx:ColumnChart id="columnChart"
dataProvider="{market}"
showDataTips="true"
dataTipFunction="customTip">
```

Aside from having specified the horizontal axis of the graph for which you have defined a categoryField, you have also added a vertical axis. This addition allows you to define a different type of representation of data to superimpose on the vertical axis of the ColumnChart. In this case, you have added a LinearAxis that specifies its maximum and minimum value:

```
<mx:horizontalAxis>
<mx:CategoryAxis
categoryField="area" />
</mx:horizontalAxis>
<mx:verticalAxis>
<mx:LinearAxis minimum="10" maximum="40"/>
</mx:verticalAxis>
```

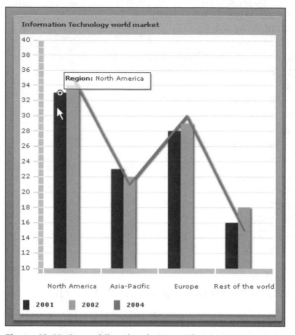

Figure 12-10. By enabling the showDataTips property, you can specify which data to show in the tool tip by setting a function of the dataTipFunction property.

Then, with respect to Solution 12-1, a series of LineSeries type has been added in the data series of the charting, for which you have specified the properties xField and yField (or the data to use for the x and y axes to draw the graph). The LineSeries provides the classic line graph (refer to Figure 12-9):

```
<mx:series>
<mx:ColumnSeries xField="area"
yField="year2001"
displayName="2001"
 />
<mx:ColumnSeries xField="area"
yField="year2002"
displayName="2002" />
  <mx:LineSeries
xField="area"
yField="year2004"
displayName="2004">
</mx:LineSeries>
</mx:series>
```

5. Add a second graph that will represent the data based on the year selected in the MenuBar. The chart type that you'll use is the LineChart control, for which you'll specify only one data series—the graph will represent the values divided by region, one year at a time. On this chart, you'll manage an event that will release when the

user clicks a data point. Add the following code under the closure of the Panel created in the preceding step:

```
<mx:Panel title="Information Technology world market in {currentYear}">
<mx:LineChart id="myChart"
dataProvider="{market}"
showDataTips="true"
itemClick="detailHandler(event)" >
<mx:horizontalAxis>
 <mx:CategoryAxis
categoryField="area"
/>
</mx:horizontalAxis>
<mx:series>
<mx:LineSeries id="myLineSeries"
yField="year2001"
displayName="2001"
showDataEffect="interpolate">
</mx:LineSeries>
</mx:series>
</mx:LineChart>
<mx:Legend dataProvider="{myChart}" direction="horizontal"/>
   </mx:Panel>
```

The LineChart uses the same dataProvider as the ColumnChart. Enable the tool tip display by setting the showDataTips property as true, and create the event listener on the itemClick event:

```
<mx:LineChart id="myChart"
dataProvider="{market}"
showDataTips="true"
itemClick="detailHandler(event)" >
```

After specifying the horizontal axis and the categoryField to use on that axis, insert an </mx:LineSeries> element. The tag uses the yField property to show the values for 2001 and uses the showDataEffect property to specify an effect when the data changes. This LineChart, in fact, loads and represents different data according to the choice of the user on the MenuBar, and at every change, applies the effect declared in the showDataEffect="interpolate" property:

```
<mx:horizontalAxis>
<mx:CategoryAxis
categoryField="area"/>
</mx:horizontalAxis>
<mx:series>
<mx:LineSeries id="myLineSeries"
yField="year2001"
displayName="2001"
showDataEffect="interpolate">
</mx:LineSeries>
</mx:series>
```

12

6. You must add the effect that will be applied on the LineChart. So add the `<mx:SeriesInterpolate>` tag to create the effect. You add the following code immediately under the closure of the `</mx:Script>` tag:

```
</mx:Script>

<mx:SeriesInterpolate id="interpolate" elementOffset="15" />

<mx:ApplicationControlBar width="100%" dock="true">
```

The `SeriesInterpolate` effect moves the graph with the existing data in a series to the new point. Instead of clearing the chart and then repopulating it, this effect keeps the data on the screen at all times. This type of effect can be used only with a `showDataEffect` trigger. In this case, you have set the `elementOffset` property specifying the amount of time that Flex delays the start of the effect on each element in the series. The property `duration` specifies the duration of the effect. Both of these values are expressed in milliseconds.

7. You must now add some event listeners for the events that you have created for some elements of the application. Begin with the `init()` function that releases on the `creationComplete` of the application. In the `<mx:Script>` block, under the declaration of the `currentYear` variable, add the following function:

```
[Bindable]
private var currentYear:String = "2001";

private function init():void
{
myMenu.addEventListener(MenuEvent.ITEM_CLICK, changeChartData);
}
```

This function does nothing more than invoke the `changeChartData()` function when the user chooses an item in the `MenuBar`.

8. Write the `changeChartData()` function, which you add immediately under the `init()` function:

```
private function changeChartData (event:MenuEvent):void
{
var itemLabel:String = event.item.@label;
switch( itemLabel )
{
case "2004":
myLineSeries.yField = "year2004"
currentYear = "2004";
break;
case "2002":
myLineSeries.yField = "year2002"
currentYear = "2002";
break;
case "2001":
myLineSeries.yField = "year2001"
```

```
currentYear = "2001";
break;
}
}
```

This function, according to the item chosen by the user in the MenuBar and contained in the event object event.item.@label, changes the values of the yField property of the myLineSeries and the currentYear variable:

```
if (event.item.@label == "2004") {

myLineSeries.yField = "year2004"
currentYear = "2004"; }
```

9. Create the customTip() event handler that is invoked by the dataTipFunction property of the ColumnChart and allows you to format the data to display in the tool tip. Add the following function to changeChartData:

```
private function customTip(obj:HitData):String
{
return "<b>Region:</b> "+ obj.item.area;
}
```

The dataTipFunction returns a String that represents the value to be displayed in the tool tip. The function accepts a HitData object, which contains the information on the data of every single data point as a parameter. In this case, you simply used the value obj.item.area to print the region in the tool tip. In the dataTipFunction, you can also use one of the Formatter classes to format the data:

10. The last event handler is the one that is invoked when the user clicks with the mouse on a data point of the line chart (itemClick="detailHandler(event)"). In the function, you have created a for .. in loop to make all the values contained in the event object of the ChartItemEvent class be returned to you in an alert box:

```
private function detailHandler(evt:ChartItemEvent):void
{
var props:String = new String();
var hitDataItem:Object = evt.hitData.item;
for each(var prop:String in hitDataItem)
{
props += prop + "\n";
}
mx.controls.Alert.show(props,"Show the hitData object values");
}
]]>
</mx:Script>
```

Figure 12-11 shows the alert box with the values contained in the hitData.item of the event object:

12

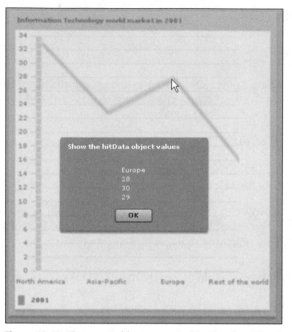

Figure 12-11. The event object generated by the ChartItemEvent class contains all the items of the data point on which the user has clicked in the hitData property.

11. Save and run the application.

Try to select a different year in the MenuBar and you'll see the SeriesInterpolate effect applied to the LineChart. Instead, by clicking on a data point of the LineChart, the alert box will open with the values contained in that data point.

Expert tips

Other than adding effects to the data displayed in the graph, you can also control the fill color for each series in the chart. The fill lets you specify how Flex draws the chart element.

There are two fill classes you can use to declare a gradient fill: the LinearGradient class and the RadialGradient class. Moreover, with the GradientEntry class you can define objects that control the gradient transition using these properties:

- color: A color value
- alpha: The transparency value
- ratio: The percentage where the transition will start in the graph to the next color

Modify the solution that you previously created to apply a GradientEntry pattern to the <mx:ColumnSeries> tag:

```
<mx:series>
<mx:ColumnSeries xField="area"
yField="year2001"
displayName="2001" >
 <mx:fill>
<mx:LinearGradient>
<mx:entries>
<mx:GradientEntry color="#0000FF" ratio="0" alpha="1" />
<mx:GradientEntry color="#0000DD" ratio=".1" alpha="1" />
<mx:GradientEntry color="#000022" ratio=".9" alpha="1" />
<mx:GradientEntry color="#000000" ratio="1" alpha="1" />
</mx:entries>
</mx:LinearGradient>
 </mx:fill>
 </mx:ColumnSeries>
```

1. Open the file created in this solution and edit the code declared in the Panel:

```
<mx:ColumnChart id="columnChart"
dataProvider="{market}"
showDataTips="true"
dataTipFunction="customTip">
<mx:horizontalAxis>
<mx:CategoryAxis

categoryField="area" />
</mx:horizontalAxis>
<mx:verticalAxis>
<mx:LinearAxis minimum="10" maximum="40"/>
</mx:verticalAxis>
<mx:series>
<mx:ColumnSeries xField="area"
yField="year2001"
displayName="2001" >
 <mx:fill>
<mx:LinearGradient>
<mx:entries>
<mx:GradientEntry color="#0000FF"
  ratio="0" alpha="1" />
<mx:GradientEntry color="#0000DD"
  ratio=".1" alpha="1" />
<mx:GradientEntry color="#000022"
  ratio=".9" alpha="1" />
<mx:GradientEntry color="#000000"
  ratio="1" alpha="1" />
</mx:entries>
</mx:LinearGradient>
 </mx:fill>
 </mx:ColumnSeries>
<mx:ColumnSeries xField="area"
```

12

```
        yField="year2002"
        displayName="2002" />
         <mx:LineSeries
           dataProvider="{market}"
             xField="area"
             yField="year2004"
             displayName="2004">
           </mx:LineSeries>
        </mx:series>
        </mx:ColumnChart>

        <mx:LineChart id="myChart"
        dataProvider="{market}"
        showDataTips="true"
        itemClick="detailHandler(event)" >
        <mx:horizontalAxis>
        <mx:CategoryAxis
        dataProvider="{market}"
        categoryField="area"
         />
        </mx:horizontalAxis>
        <mx:series>
        <mx:LineSeries id="lineSeries"
        yField="year2001"
        displayName="2001"
        showDataEffect="interpolate">
        <mx:lineStroke>
        <mx:Stroke
        color="0x0099FF"
        weight="5"
        alpha=".2"
        />
        </mx:lineStroke>
        </mx:LineSeries>

        </mx:series>
        </mx:LineChart>
```

The GradientEntry class defines the objects that control a transition as part of a gradient fill.

2. Save and run the application.

Solution 12-3: Adding video contents within Flex

Flash Player allows you to use a lot of different media in applications. It is possible to load images (GIF, JPG, PNG, and SVG), SWF files, audio in MP3, and FLV video files into Flash

Player. Because Flex applications are run within Flash Player, you can also take advantage of these media types in Flex.

You can add media to a Flex application by loading it as an external object or embedding it. The support for the FLV files is Flash Video, which can use three different video codecs: VP6 by On2, Spark by sorenson, or Screen.

Flex allows you to embed Flash Video and also use FLV, either through the ready-to-use VideoDisplay component or creating instances of the NetConnection and NetStream classes.

> *The NetConnection class allows you to play streaming Flash Video (FLV) files from either an HTTP address or a local drive. A NetStream object is the channel that can publish videos. See the Flex Livedocs for these two classes:* http://livedocs.adobe.com/flex/2/langref/flash/net/NetConnection.html *and* http://livedocs.adobe.com/flex/2/langref/flash/net/NetStream.html.

The VideoDisplay component does not have a graphic interface; it is only a container of the file video. Therefore, if you intend to provide a controller to put the video in pause, to go forward, or to go backward, you must create these functions.

In this solution, you'll see how to load an FLV video file into the application by interacting with its events.

What's involved

The VideoDisplay component is the container of the FLV video file. Through the source property of the component, set the video to load in it:

```
<mx:VideoDisplay id="myVideo" source="video.flv" />
```

Other than relative paths that point to Flash video, the source property also accepts URLs:

```
<mx:VideoDisplay id="myVideo"
source="http://www.myserver.com/video.flv"/>
```

The video will be downloaded progressively instead of streamed. To stream FLV files, it is necessary to have the Flash Media Server 2 installed on the web server (or to have an ISP that offers this service).

> *In this solution you don't use the Flash Media Server 2, but you'll load and publish Flash video files using the progressive download feature of Flash Player. If you want to understand the difference between progressive download and streaming video, read this article by Chris Hock:* www.adobe.com/devnet/flash/articles/flv_download.html.

12

To set the size of the video component, as for images, use width, height, and maintainAspectRatio properties. If the width and height properties are omitted, the VideoDisplay uses the original dimensions of the video. The maintainAspectRatio property is a Boolean; when set to false, the size of the media does not maintain its aspect ratio.

The VideoDisplay doesn't provide any graphic interface or video controller to carry out the classic operations of play, pause, stop, and volume. However, through the use of a few methods that provide these functions, they can easily be added:

- load()
- pause()
- stop()
- close()

The playheadTime property contains the current position of the playhead and returns the time as the playback of the video progresses. Instead, the volume property allows you to set the volume for the media and accepts values that vary from 0.0 to 1.00.

One of the characteristics of the FLV format is that these files can contain and conserve **cue points**, which are bookmarks in the video that trigger events when the playback reaches them. To create cue points, use the cuePointManagerClass property in the mx.controls.videoClasses.CuePointManager package and create an Array that contains an object with two properties: name and time:

```
<mx:VideoDisplay source="video.flv"
cuePointManagerClass="mx.controls.videoClasses.CuePointManager">
<mx:cuePoints>
<mx:Array>
<mx:Object name="myCuePoint1" time="30"/>
<mx:Object name="myCuePoint2" time="90"/>
<mx:Object name="myCuePoint3" time="120"/>

<mx:Object name="myCuePoint4" time="180"/>
</mx:Array>
</mx:cuePoints>
</mx:VideoDisplay>
```

The <mx:cuePoints> tag allows you to create an Array of objects and to create cue points in the video by linking a name and time for each point. In the code, you created four cue points at 30, 90, 120, and 180 seconds, respectively. Through the cuePoint event of the VideoDisplay, you can intercept when the playhead passes over a determined cue point:

```
<mx:VideoDisplay source="video.flv"
cuePointManagerClass="mx.controls.videoClasses.CuePointManager"
cuePoint="cuePointHandler(event);">

<mx:Script>
<![CDATA[
```

```
import mx.events.CuePointEvent;

private function cuePointHandler(event:CuePointEvent):void {
mx.controls.Alert.show("Cue Point: " +➥
 event.cuePointName + " reached at " + ➥
 String(event.cuePointTime) + "seconds");
}
]]>
</mx:Script>
```

The event handler cuePointHandler() is invoked when the playhead moves over one of the set cue points. The event object generated by the CuePointEvent class transports the information relative to the name and the time of the cue point that is intercepted in that moment.

In this solution you'll see how to create a small video player.

How to build it

In this solution you'll use three FLV files to load in a VideoDisplay. The videos will be selectable from a List control and will reside locally. You can use the FLV videos from the assets folder of the Flex project or use your own video files in FLV format. You can download many other videos from the Internet.

1. Create the file on which you'll work by selecting File ➤ New ➤ MXML Application and save it as Chapter_12_Flex_Sol_3_More.mxml. Create a new folder in the project by selecting File ➤ New ➤ Folder and call it assets. In this directory you'll insert the FLV video files (the FLV video files used for the solution are called show.flv, show_2.flv, and ipod.flv).

2. Add the List control to the file that lists the videos are available to choose from and load in the VideoDisplay component:

```
<mx:Application xmlns:mx="http://www.adobe.com/2006/mxml"
layout="vertical">
<mx:Panel  width="450" height="340"
layout="horizontal" title="TSVP - The Smallest Video Player">

<mx:List id="myList" width="100" height="240" >
<mx:dataProvider>
<mx:Object label="Salsa Show" data="assets/show.flv" />
<mx:Object label="Salsa LaShow" data="assets/show_2.flv" />
<mx:Object label="iPod Parody" data="assets/ipod.flv" />
</mx:dataProvider>
</mx:List>
</mx:Panel>
```

Inside a Panel, you have inserted a List control for which you have specified the dataProvider as a nested tag. The dataProvider is an Array of objects for which two properties have been defined: label and data. The label property will be automatically

12

used by the List control as the label to visualize in it, while the data property contains the path relative to the FLV file:

```
<mx:dataProvider>
<mx:Object label="Salsa Show" data="assets/show.flv" />
<mx:Object label="Salsa LaShow" data="assets/show_2.flv" />
<mx:Object label="iPod Parody" data="assets/ipod.flv" />
</mx:dataProvider>
```

When the user selects an item in the list, the data property will be sent to the source property of the VideoDisplay that will load and reproduce the video.

3. Immediately under the closure of the List control, add a VideoDisplay control:

```
<mx:VideoDisplay id="myVideo"
width="320"
height="240"
source="{myList.selectedItem.data}"
/>
```

The VideoDisplay control on the source property accepts the data property contained in the selectedItem object of the List control, which contains the relative path and the name of the FLV file to load as a value:

```
source="{myList.selectedItem.data}"
```

The file is ready to be run. However, you should add a simple controller to the VideoDisplay to pause the film, change the volume, and show the playback timing.

4. Add a ControlBar container. The ControlBar container is used together with, and is declared in, a Panel and creates a footer in which to insert controls or other containers. Put the video controller in the ControlBar:

```
<mx:VideoDisplay id="myVideo"
width="320"
height="240"
source="{myList.selectedItem.data}" />

<mx:ControlBar>
</mx:ControlBar>

</mx:Panel>
```

5. In the ControlBar container, insert two Button components to control the play and pause status of the video, a TextInput control that will contain the playback timing, and an HSlider control to change the volume of the video:

```
<mx:ControlBar>
<mx:Button label="Play" click="myVideo.play()" />
<mx:Button label="Pause" click="myVideo.pause()" />
```

```
<mx:TextInput editable="false"
text="Time: {myVideo.playheadTime.toPrecision(2)}"
 width="89"/>

<mx:Label text="Volume: " />
<mx:HSlider id="myVolume" maximum="1" width="100"
 creationComplete="myVolume.value = 0.75"  />
</mx:ControlBar>
</mx:Application>
```

The two buttons use the play() and pause() methods of the VideoDisplay control. The TextInput, instead, uses the playheadTime property that contains the current position of the playhead and returns the time as the playback of the video progresses. The value shown by this property is rounded off by the toPrecision() method to two values:

```
<mx:TextInput editable="false"
text="Time: {myVideo.playheadTime.toPrecision(2)}"
 width="89"/>
```

The HSlider control lets the user adjust the volume of the VideoDisplay. The volume property accepts a range of values from 0 to 1.00. By default, it is set at 0.75, so set its value to 0.75 on the creationComplete of the control.

```
<mx:HSlider id="myVolume" maximum="1" width="100"
 creationComplete="myVolume.value = 0.75"  />
```

6. To ensure that the setting of the volume acting on the HSlider control undergoes the modification on the VideoDisplay, you must create a binding between these two objects. Therefore, add the following code to the VideoDisplay control:

```
<mx:VideoDisplay id="myVideo"
width="320"
height="240"
source="{myList.selectedItem.data}"
volume="{myVolume.value}"/>
```

After you create the binding between the volume property of the DisplayList and the value property of the HSlider, every time the user changes the value on the slider, this new value is applied to the video.

7. Save and run the application.

Figure 12-12 shows the final result with the VideoDisplay and its controller.

12

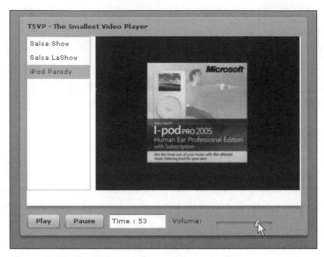

Figure 12-12. The VideoDisplay and its controller

Expert tips

Flash Player, through its Real Time Messaging Protocol (RTMP), supports the streaming of the FLV files by moving to the Flash Media Server. Using the VideoDisplay to carry out the streaming of a video is simple. The only thing that changes is the protocol that is used to access and load the FLV file:

```
<mx:VideoDisplay id="myVideo"
source="rtmp://www.myserver.com/video.flv" />
```

It is also possible to set the bufferTime property of the component to specify a buffer time before playing the video. In this way, you are sure that the first seconds of the video have been loaded, so you won't have interruptions in the initial reproduction:

```
<mx:VideoDisplay id="myVideo"
source="rtmp://www.myserver.com/video.flv"
bufferTime="5" />
```

The VideoDisplay has a method, attachCamera(), which allows you to use the webcam installed on the actual computer as audio and video stream. To use the VideoDisplay in this way, it is sufficient to create a Camera object in the flash.media package and invoke its static method getCamera(). The following code uses the webcam as audio and video stream to link to a VideoDisplay component:

```
<mx:Script>
<![CDATA[
import flash.media.Camera;

private var myCamera:Camera;
```

```
public function streamCamera ():void
{
myCamera = Camera.getCamera();
videoDisp.attachCamera(myCamera)
}
]]>
</mx:Script>

<mx:VideoDisplay id=" videoDisp " width="240" height="120"
creationComplete="streamCamera();"/>
```

Solution 12-4: Printing from a DataGrid

Web applications, through the use of CSS and media types, manage to create the appropriate formatting for the print version of the page or contents. You can indicate which objects to print, determine the size of the font, and apply complex formatting.

With SWF applications, however, printing has always been a problematic operation. But with Flex and ActionScript 3 (and thanks to the print features of Flash Player), things have changed, and now the developer can create containers and controls that will print exactly what the user expects to print. In fact, you can control the printed output by setting what to print.

The classes that are used to implement the functions of printing are the FlexPrintJob and the PrintDataGrid class.

The FlexPrintJob class, which is a wrapper of the PrintJob API of Flash Player, allows you to print one or more Flex components. With this class you can subdivide the output to be able to scale to fit the page or manage multiple pages.

Instead, the PrintDataGrid is a subclass of the DataGrid. This class visualizes the data contained in the DataGrid in a table with line borders optimized specifically to be able to print.

In this solution you'll see how to print the contents of a three-column DataGrid format.

What's involved

To manage the functions of printing, it is necessary to generally instance the FlexPrintJob class, invoking its start() method, adding one or more objects to print with the addObject() method and sending, and starting the print process with the send() method.

Therefore, the steps required to create a print process are few:

```
var myPrintJob:FlexPrintJob = new FlexPrintJob();
```

12

You first instantiate a FlexPrintJob object. On this object you can invoke the methods necessary to create the print operation:

```
myPrintJob.start();
```

The start() method initializes the FlexPrintJob object and forces the operating system to open the Print Dialog window.

With these two lines of code you have not yet specified what must be printed. With the addObject() method you indicate the objects that must be included and sent as output for the print operation:

```
printJob.addObject(myPanel, FlexPrintJobScaleType.MATCH_WIDTH);
printJob.addObject(myDataGrid);
```

You have added a Panel and a DataGrid as objects to print. All the contents of the Panel will be printed. Each object declared in the addObject() method starts on a new page.

On the invocation of the addObject() for the Panel, you have sent the constant FlexPrintJobScaleType.MATCH_WIDTH as a second parameter to the method. The second parameter of the addObject() method is the scaleType that determines how to scale the output. The FlexPrintJobScaleType class contains the following static properties:

- MATCH_WIDTH: The default value if nothing is specified. Scales the object to fill the page width. If the object exceeds the page height, the excessive part will be printed on another page.
- MATCH_HEIGHT: Scales the object to fill the page height. If the object exceeds the page width, the excessive part will be printed on another page.
- SHOW_ALL: Scales the object so it is printed on a single page.
- FILL_PAGE: Scales the object to fill at least one page
- NONE: Does not apply any scaling to the object.

Finally, you must invoke the send() method to send the object or the objects to print to the printer:

```
printJob.send();
```

With these few lines of code, you have created a print process to which you have sent two objects: a Panel (and its contents) and a DataGrid.

There will, however, be scenarios in which it will be necessary to create a print-specific format. In this case you would have to externally create an object that contains the print layout, as you do for web applications, when you define a CSS for the print operation. To create a separate object for the print layout, you have to create a Flex component through MXML or ActionScript. This external component will then be sent to the addObject() method.

In Flex, the DataGrid is the most powerful control for the representation of even complex data. For this reason it operates in a much more controlled way as far as printing is concerned. The PrintDataGrid control is a subclass of the DataGrid created for optimizing printing operations, which permits you to print all the rows and columns, even if they are not visible in the DataGrid and do not have a specified height.

In this solution you'll see how to print the contents of a DataGrid using the PrintDataGrid control and the FlexPrintJob class.

How to build it

In this solution you'll see two different ways to create and manage the printing operation. In the first method you'll use a single file, while in the "Expert tips" section of this solution you'll see how to create an MXML component that will function as a print-specific layout.

1. You create the main application file by selecting File ➤ New ➤ MXML Application and save the file as Chapter_12_Flex_Sol_4_More.mxml. This file will contain a DataGrid that will display a screen of data. On the click of the button, this data will be printed. You define an event listener on the creationComplete event:

```
<?xml version="1.0"?>
<mx:Application xmlns:mx="http://www.adobe.com/2006/mxml"
creationComplete="onCreationComplete()">
```

The onCreationComplete() method will populate the collection variable that will be used as dataProvider for the DataGrid.

2. Insert the user interface of the application. You add a Panel, under the <mx:Application> tag, in which you declare a DataGrid, a TextInput, a ControlBar container, and a Button:

```
<mx:Panel title="Product list" height="75%" width="75%">
<mx:DataGrid id="dataGrid" dataProvider="{productAC}">
<mx:columns>

<mx:DataGridColumn
headerText="Product name" dataField="product" />
<mx:DataGridColumn
headerText="Product quantity" dataField="quantity" />
<mx:DataGridColumn
headerText="Product price" dataField="price" />
</mx:columns>
</mx:DataGrid>

<mx:Text id="countText"
text="Total number of products:
{productAC.length.toString()}." />

<mx:ControlBar>
<mx:Button id="printButton" label="Print" click="myPrintJob()" />
</mx:ControlBar>
</mx:Panel>
```

12

The DataGrid uses the productAC variable as dataProvider. This variable will be created in the <mx:Script> block in the successive steps but as structure, it will have an Array of objects with the product, quantity, and price properties.

For each property, a column is created in the DataGrid with the DataGridColumn tag, for which the properties headerText, which is the label of the header of the column, and dataField, which is the property of the dataProvider to load in the column, become defined:

```
<mx:DataGrid id="dataGrid" dataProvider="{productAC}">
<mx:columns>
<mx:DataGridColumn
headerText="Product name" dataField="product" />
<mx:DataGridColumn
headerText="Product quantity" dataField="quantity" />
<mx:DataGridColumn
headerText="Product price" dataField="price" />
</mx:columns>
</mx:DataGrid>
```

The TexInput control shows the length of the ArrayCollection that converts into a String with the toString() method. The Button in the ControlBar container launches the event handler myPrintJob() when it is clicked. It is this function that will have the task of printing the contents of the DataGrid and creating the instances of the FlexPrintJob and PrintDataGrid:

```
<mx:Text id="countText"
text="Total number of products:
{productAC.length.toString()}." />

<mx:ControlBar>
<mx:Button id="printButton" label="Print" click="myPrintJob()" />
</mx:ControlBar>
```

3. Insert an <mx:Script> block and begin by importing the classes necessary for the solution:

```
<mx:Script>
<![CDATA[
import mx.printing.FlexPrintJobScaleType;
import mx.printing.PrintDataGrid;
import mx.printing.FlexPrintJob;
import mx.controls.dataGridClasses.DataGridColumn;
import mx.collections.ArrayCollection;
]]>
</mx:Script>
```

4. Add the event handler onCreationComplete(), which has the job of creating and populating the productAC variable typed as ArrayCollection. Add the following code immediately under the class importing:

```
    [Bindable]
    private var productAC:ArrayCollection;

    public function onCreationComplete():void
    {
        productAC = new ArrayCollection();

        populateProducts(50);
    }
```

After having initialized the ArrayCollection, the onCreationComplete() function invokes the populateProducts() method, to which it sends the parameter 50. This method creates a for() loop and populates the variable with a number of elements equal to the number that has been sent as a parameter. In this case, you'll create an ArrayCollection of 50 elements.

5. Immediately under the populateProducts() function with which you'll add the values to the productAC variable, add the following:

```
    private function populateProducts(length:int):void
    {
    var obj:Object;
    for (var i:int; i < length; i++)
    {
    obj = new Object();
    obj.product = "Product " + (i + 1).toString();
    obj.quantity = Math.ceil(Math.random() * length);
    obj.price = Math.random() * length;

    productAC.addItem(obj);
    }
    }
```

The function launches a for() loop that adds the properties quantity and price to a variable typed as Object. The values that are inserted in this object are calculated in a random way using the Math.random() method. The output that is produced and inserted into the object is something similar to the following (quantity and price values might differ because they are generated randomly):

object property: Product 50

object quantity: 19

object price: 34.97734288685024

At the end of every cycle, the object is inserted in the ArrayCollection with the addItem() method:

```
    productAC.addItem(obj);
```

12

6. The last function to add to the <mx:Script> block is the myPrintJob(), which is launched by clicking the button on the ControlBar container. This function creates and initializes the FlexPrintJob object and PrintDataGrid control. The created PrintDataGrid is sent to the addChild() method of the FlexPrintJob. In the "Expert tips" section of this solution you'll also see how to use an external MXML component to link to the FlexPrintJob. You insert the following code, immediately under the closure of the preceding function:

```
public function myPrintJob():void
{
var printJob:FlexPrintJob = new FlexPrintJob();
if (printJob.start()) {
// create a PrintDataGrid
var printDataGrid:PrintDataGrid = new PrintDataGrid();
printDataGrid.visible = false;
printDataGrid.width = printJob.pageWidth;
printDataGrid.height = printJob.pageHeight;
printDataGrid.dataProvider = dataGrid.dataProvider;
// add it to the current application:
application.addChild(printDataGrid);

// column names in the PrintDataGrid match the properties of the
// object in the data proivider array;
// change column names to custom ones:
var col:DataGridColumn;

for (var i:int = 0; i < printDataGrid.columns.length; i++) {
col = printDataGrid.columns[i];
switch (col.headerText)
{
case "product":
col.headerText = "Product name";
break;

case "quantity":
col.headerText = "Product quantity";
break;

case "price":
col.headerText = "Product price";
break;
}
}
printDataGrid.validateNow();

// print the first page and call for the next pages, if any:
printJob.addObject(printDataGrid, FlexPrintJobScaleType.MATCH_WIDTH);
while (printDataGrid.validNextPage) {
printDataGrid.nextPage();
```

```
    printJob.addObject(printDataGrid, FlexPrintJobScaleType.MATCH_WIDTH);
    }

    // remove PrintDataGrid from current application:
    application.removeChild(printDataGrid);

    // add a status text, at the end:
    // note that the colored background is also printed; a custom
    // component can be provided,
    // to set the background color to #FFFFFF (white)
    printJob.addObject(countText, FlexPrintJobScaleType.NONE);
        }
        // start printing:
        printJob.send();
    }
```

The function begins with the creation of the FlexPrintJob object and PrintDataGrid control. The width and height properties are set, and the dataProvider, the same one used in the DataGrid, is sent to it. The PrintDataGrid is displayed and added to the application with the addChild() method:

```
    var printJob:FlexPrintJob = new FlexPrintJob();
    if (printJob.start()) {
    var printDataGrid:PrintDataGrid = new PrintDataGrid();
    printDataGrid.visible = false;
    printDataGrid.width = printJob.pageWidth;
    printDataGrid.height = printJob.pageHeight;
    printDataGrid.dataProvider = dataGrid.dataProvider;
    application.addChild(printDataGrid);
```

Once the PrintDataGrid object is instanced, the columns and links to the data that will have to be provided for the print method are created. To create the columns, add columns of the printDataGrid of the instances of the DataGridColumn classes to the Array:

```
    for (var i:int = 0; i < printDataGrid.columns.length; i++) {
    var col:DataGridColumn = printDataGrid.columns[i];

    switch (col.headerText) {
    case "product":
    col.headerText = "Product name";
    break;
    case "quantity":
    col.headerText = "Product quantity";
    break;
    case "price":
    col.headerText = "Product price";
    break;
    }
```

12

The FlexPrintJob operation customizes each page through the PrintDataGrid, so you must call the validateNow() method to update the page layout before you print each page:

```
printDataGrid.validateNow();
```

Finally, add the objects to the PrintDataGrid. Print the first page and call for the next pages, if any:

```
printJob.addObject(printDataGrid, FlexPrintJobScaleType.MATCH_WIDTH);
while (printDataGrid.validNextPage) {
printDataGrid.nextPage();
printJob.addObject(printDataGrid, FlexPrintJobScaleType.MATCH_WIDTH);
```

Finally, the function concludes with the removal of the PrintDataGrid control, adding the TextInput control to the printJob and sending the print with the send() method:

```
application.removeChild(printDataGrid);

printJob.addObject(countText, FlexPrintJobScaleType.NONE);
    }
printJob.send();
```

7. Save the file and run the application.

After clicking the Print button, the Print dialog box of the operating system will open (see Figure 12-13).

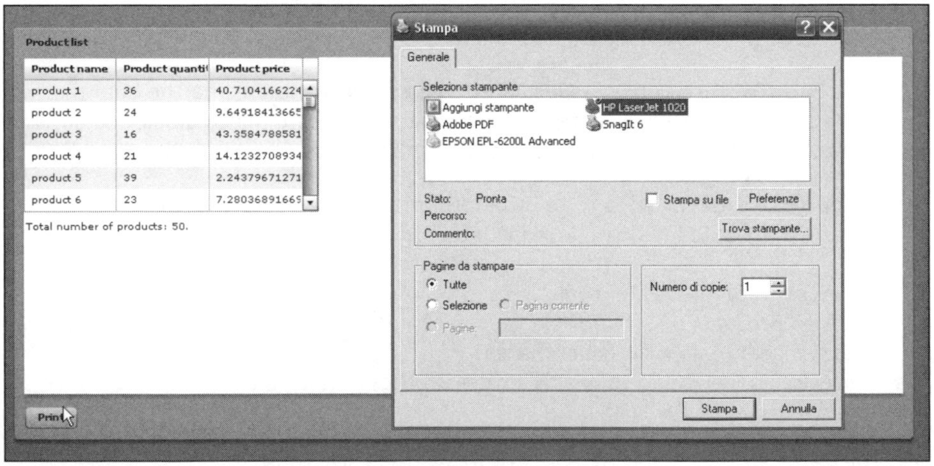

Figure 12-13. The Print dialog window appears.

If you request a print preview or use the PDF printer, you can see which data and in which format the information will be printed (see Figure 12-14).

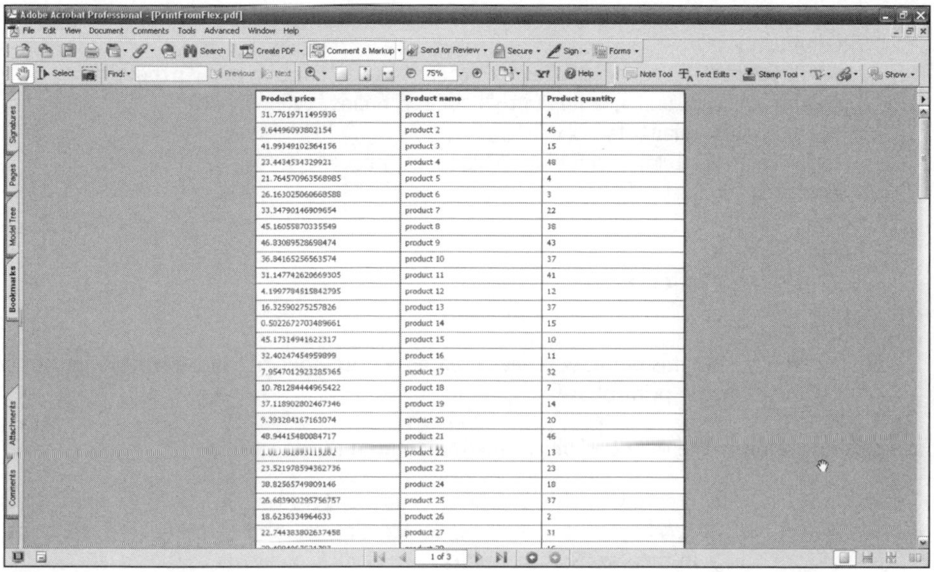

Figure 12-14. The result of the print

Expert tips

In this section, you'll see how to create an MXML component and use it for print layout. You'll use an external CSS file to have more control over the print layout and its data.

1. You created the folder structure that contains the component: com.flexsolutions. chapter12. Inside this folder create a new folder named print by selecting File ➤ New ➤ Folder. In this last folder, you insert the MXML component from File ➤ New ➤ MXML Component that you save as ProductDatagridPrintView.mxml and base on the VBox container. You insert an <mx:Script> block in which you create the dataProvider variable that you'll send from the application file to the component:

```
<mx:VBox xmlns:mx="http://www.adobe.com/2006/mxml" xmlns="*"
backgroundColor="white">
<mx:Script>
<![CDATA[
import mx.collections.ArrayCollection;
[Bindable]
public var dataProvider:ArrayCollection = null;
]]>
</mx:Script>
```

2. You can also define the PrintDataGrid and the columns that it should print. The PrintDataGrid is created and managed just like a DataGrid control:

```
<mx:PrintDataGrid id="productDataGrid"
dataProvider="{dataProvider}"
width="60%" height="100%" sizeToPage="true">
```

12

```
   <mx:columns>
   <mx:Array>
   <mx:DataGridColumn headerText="Product name" dataField="product" />
   <mx:DataGridColumn headerText="Product quantity"
     dataField="quantity" />
   <mx:DataGridColumn headerText="Product price"
     dataField="price" />
   </mx:Array>
   </mx:columns>
   </mx:PrintDataGrid>
   </mx:VBox>
```

3. Save the file. At this point, you have created a print-specific layout component that you'll use for the print phase.

You can now modify the myPrintJob() function created in the solution.

4. Open the file created in this solution, Chapter_12_Flex_Sol_4_More.mxml, and save it as Chapter_12_Flex_Sol_4_expert_More.mxml and modify the function myPrintJob() in the <mx:Script> block:

```
public function myPrintJob():void {
var printJob:FlexPrintJob = new FlexPrintJob();

if (printJob.start()) {
var printComp: ➡
com.flexsolutions.chapter12.print.ProductDatagridPrintView =➡
new com.flexsolutions.chapter12.print.ProductDatagridPrintView. ➡
ProductDatagridPrintView();
addChild(printComp);

printComp.width=printJob.pageWidth;
printComp.height=printJob.pageHeight;
printComp.productDataGrid.dataProvider = dataGrid.dataProvider;

if(!printComp.productDataGrid.validNextPage)
{
printJob.addObject(printComp);
}

else
{

printJob.addObject(printComp);

while(true)
{
printComp.productDataGrid.nextPage();
```

```
if(!printComp.productDataGrid.validNextPage)
{
printJob.addObject(printComp);
break;
}
else
{

printJob.addObject(printComp);

}
}
}
removeChild(printComp);
}

printJob.send();
}
```

The function creates an instance of the printComp component that adds to the page:

```
var printComp:➡
com.flexsolutions.chapter12.print.ProductDatagridPrintView = ➡
new com.flexsolutions.chapter12.print.ProductDatagridPrintView();
addChild(printComp);
```

The printComp component is sent to the addObject() method of the printJob object that propagates the information for the print phase:

```
printJob.addObject(printComp);
```

5. Save the file and run the application.

You created a separate component used for the printing operation. This approach is very useful when you want to create custom content and separate the code from the main application file.

Solution 12-5: Debugging applications with the Logging framework

Debugging an application represents an important and delicate phase of the workflow of any project. It is essential for every developer to have powerful instruments to carry out the debug. Flex Builder inherits a large part of these debug functions from Eclipse and the IDE on which it is based, but the Flex SDK contains extra functionality to increase the debugging capability.

The Flex Debugging perspective is launched from the Flex Builder environment when the application is run in Debug mode. Instead of performing the classic Run command, the

12

Debug mode is launched. The application is automatically launched, and the browser opens, but Flash Player starts in Debug mode, and Flex Builder switches to the Flex Debugging perspective. All operations of breakpoints, expressions, or traces of variables can be activated while the application is being used in the browser. Figure 12-15 shows the Flex Debugging perspective:

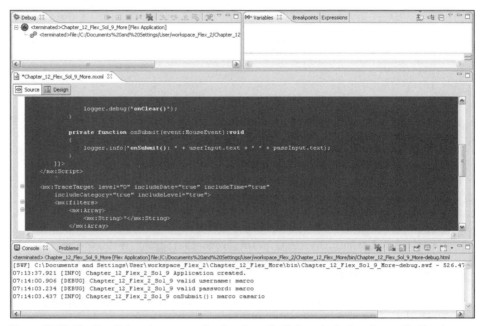

Figure 12-15. The Flex Debugging perspective is automatically launched when the application is run in Debug mode.

The Logging API of Flex SDK allows you to write and send messages to an output created by the developer. The Logging API consists of three principal components: the Logger object, the log target, and the destination.

The Logger sends the messages to the target through the methods of the Log class that implements the ILogger interface.

The log target defines where the messages should be written. Flex allows you to specify two different log targets: TraceTarget and MiniDebugTarget. The log target most used is the TraceTarget, which implements the ILoggerTarget interface, and sends messages through the trace() function.

The destination represents where the message should be written. Usually, the destination is a file, but it can also be an object in memory.

In this solution, you'll create a file that uses the Logging API to carry out a debug session.

What's involved

To be able to complete the solution, or to carry out the debug of the application and, therefore, launch Flex Debugging perspective of Flex Builder, the Debug version of Flash Player must be installed. You can download the Flash Player Debug from the Adobe site in the Flash Player Support Center section: www.adobe.com/support/flashplayer/downloads.html.

To use the Logging API and send the messages to the Flash Player Debug, you must first of all define the log target and add it to the Log object:

```
myLogTarget:TraceTarget = new TraceTarget();
Log.addTarget(myLogTarget);
```

The TraceTarget can also be defined in MXML using the <mx:TraceTarget> tag:

```
<mx:TraceTarget level="0" includeDate="true" includeTime="true"
includeCategory="true" includeLevel="true">
<mx:filters>
<mx:Array>
<mx:String>*</mx:String>
</mx:Array>
</mx:filters>
</mx:TraceTarget>
```

With the tag filters, you can restrict the logging system to only a few packages or classes. In this code example, you used the symbol * that specifies including the logging only for the file or the class in which it is created.

Then, using the getLogger() method of the Log object, you can send a message to the file that you intend to debug:

```
Log.getLogger("myMXMLfileOrClass").info("My message");
```

A log message can define two values: the message level and category. The latter is required to define the origin of the message and to decide what will be displayed by the logging system.

In this solution you'll see how to launch a debug session and send messages to the Flex Builder console.

How to build it

The simplest method for sending debugging messages to the Console of Flex Builder when in Debug mode is to use the trace() function. The limit of using this function is that it does not have the support to configure the target to send complex messages, to specify a message category, and to have different error levels.

12

To filter a message with the Log class, a category and a level are used. A **category** is used to filter messages sent from a logger. It's a simple String. A level provides filtering options for the message defining the constants on the LogEventLevel class.

The LogLevelEvent has six different levels of messages that are defined as constants, shown in Table 12-2.

Table 12-2. Levels of message

Logging level	Constant value	Description
ALL	0	Messages of all logging levels are logged
DEBUG	2	Includes the DEBUG, INFO, WARN, ERROR, and FATAL messages in log files
INFO	4	Includes INFO, WARN, ERROR, and FATAL messages in log files
WARN	6	Includes WARN, ERROR, and FATAL messages in log files
ERROR	8	Logs a critical and includes ERROR and FATAL messages in log files
FATAL	1000	Logs a fatal error and includes FATAL messages in log files

You'll see how to implement the Logging framework in a simple application.

1. You create a new main application file by selecting File ➤ New➤ MXML Application and save it as Chapter_12_Flex_Sol_5_More.mxml. You create an event listener on the creationComplete of the <mx:Application> tag:

```
<?xml version="1.0" encoding="utf-8"?>
<mx:Application xmlns:mx="http://www.adobe.com/2006/mxml"
  layout="vertical"
creationComplete="onCreationComplete()">
```

2. You begin by defining the user interface of the application, which will be formatted in a simple Form container with two text inputs and two buttons in it:

```
<mx:Form>
<mx:FormItem label="Username" required="true">
<mx:TextInput id="userInput" />
</mx:FormItem>
<mx:FormItem label="Password" required="true">
<mx:TextInput id="passInput" displayAsPassword="true" />
```

```
    </mx:FormItem>
    </mx:Form>
    <mx:ControlBar>
    <mx:Button id="resetButton" label="Reset" click="onClear(event)" />
    <mx:Button id="submitButton" label="Submit" click="onSubmit(event)" />
    </mx:ControlBar>
    </mx:Application>
```

The two buttons launch two methods. The Reset button will have the task of emptying the text input controls, while the Submit button will make the logging system release.

Furthermore, the solution will send messages to the target log, even if the user inserts a nonvalid value in the TextInput controls. To obtain this result, define two StringValidators in the file.

3. Above the Form container, insert two StringValidator tags, which will send a message to the log target on their valid and nonvalid events:

```
<mx:StringValidator id="userValidator" minLength="4"
source="{userInput}" property="text"
valid="{logger.debug('valid username: ' + userInput.text)}"
invalid="{logger.error('invalid username')}" />

<mx:StringValidator id="passValidator" minLength="4"
source="{passInput}" property="text"
valid="{logger.debug('valid password: ' + userInput.text)}"
invalid="{logger.error('invalid password')}" />
```

As you can see, a message using the logger.debug() and logger.error() methods has been sent. This is one of the advantages of using the Logging API of Flex, that of being able to assign a different category to the type of message that is sent. The ILogger interface defines a method for each log level: debug(), info(), warn(), error(), and fatal().

In the example, you send an error message when the invalid event releases, while you send a message of debug when the valid event of the validator releases.

4. Before adding the <mx:Script> block, specify the log target in MXML, declaring an <mx:TraceTarget> tag. You insert this tag between the <mx:Application> tag and the StringValidator:

```
<mx:TraceTarget level="0" includeDate="true" includeTime="true"
includeCategory="true" includeLevel="true">
<mx:filters>
<mx:Array>
<mx:String>*</mx:String>
</mx:Array>
</mx:filters>
</mx:TraceTarget>
```

12

5. You can insert the `<mx:Script>` block and create the code necessary to create the Log object:

```
<mx:Script>
<![CDATA[
import mx.logging.Log;
import mx.logging.ILogger;

private var logger:ILogger = null;

private function onCreationComplete():void
{
logger = Log.getLogger("Chapter_12_Flex_2_Sol_9");

logger.info("Application created.");
}

private function onClear(event:MouseEvent):void
{
userInput.text = "";
passInput.text = "";

logger.debug("onClear()");
}

private function onSubmit(event:MouseEvent):void
{
logger.info("onSubmit(): " + userInput.text + " " + passInput.text);
}
]]>
</mx:Script>
```

The code begins with the importing of the necessary classes and the creation of the logger variable typed as ILogger:

```
import mx.logging.Log;
import mx.logging.ILogger;

private var logger:ILogger = null;
```

Then, the event handler is created on the creationComplete event on the Application. In this function the getLogger() is invoked, to which the name of the MXML file is specified and a message is sent to the console using the info() method of the Log object:

```
private function onCreationComplete():void
{
logger = Log.getLogger("Chapter_12_Flex_2_Sol_9");

logger.info("Application created.");
}
```

When the button resets, the event handler onClear() is launched, which empties the text inputs and sends another message to the log target. Finally, the event handler onSubmit() dispatched on the click event of the Submit button, sends a message with the values inserted by the user in the TextInput controls:

```
private function onClear(event:MouseEvent):void
{
userInput.text = "";
passInput.text = "";

logger.debug("onClear()");
}

private function onSubmit(event:MouseEvent):void
{
logger.info("onSubmit(): " + userInput.text + " " + passInput.text);
}
]]>
</mx:Script>
```

6. Save the file and debug the application. Be sure that you don't launch the classic Run command from Flex Builder. To start the Debug mode of Flash Player, it is necessary to launch the application in Debug mode from by selecting Run ➤ Debug.

The application is launched in the browser, and Flex Builder switches the perspective to Flex Debugging in the background. You can now use the application and see the messages printed in the Console view of the Flex Builder, as shown in Figure 12-16.

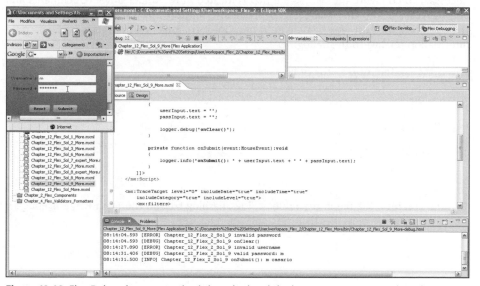

Figure 12-16. Flex Debugging perspective is launched and the logger messages are written in Console view.

In the solution you'll receive the following output:

08:13:29.328 [INFO] Chapter_12_Flex_2_Sol_9 Application created.

08:13:53.140 [ERROR] Chapter_12_Flex_2_Sol_9 invalid username

08:14:02.406 [DEBUG] Chapter_12_Flex_2_Sol_9 valid password: m

08:14:02.531 [INFO] Chapter_12_Flex_2_Sol_9 onSubmit(): m casario

08:14:04.593 [ERROR] Chapter_12_Flex_2_Sol_9 invalid username

08:14:04.593 [ERROR] Chapter_12_Flex_2_Sol_9 invalid password

08:14:04.593 [DEBUG] Chapter_12_Flex_2_Sol_9 onClear()

08:14:27.890 [ERROR] Chapter_12_Flex_2_Sol_9 invalid username

08:14:31.406 [DEBUG] Chapter_12_Flex_2_Sol_9 valid password: m

08:14:31.500 [INFO] Chapter_12_Flex_2_Sol_9 onSubmit(): m casario

As you can see, the various messages are visualized with a different log level according to the method used: debug(), info(), error().

Expert tips

By default, the debugger version of Flash Player does not permit trace logging. It is, in fact, necessary to configure the mm.cfg file that is located in the folder drive \Documents and Settings\user_name (for Mac OSX: /Application Support/Macromedia/Flash Player/). If this file does not exist, you can create it because it is a plain text file that contains some information relative to the debug:

This is the content of the mm.cfg file:

TraceOutputFileName=c:/logs/flashlog.txt

ErrorReportingEnable=1

TraceOutputFileEnable=1

MaxWarnings=0

This file creates a log file in the folder c:/logs/flashlog.txt and the Flash Player Debugger will write the trace messages that the application has sent to it in it.

Solution 12-6: Uploading files to the server

Uploading and downloading files from the client to the server are operations that are often indispensable in an application. Uploading files that reside on the client's computer is a feature on which many web applications have founded their success. Would YouTube or Flickr (two of the most well-known web applications) be as successful if they did not offer the possibility of uploading files from the user's computer to the web server?

Flex and Flash Player allow developers to create upload and download functions through the FileReference class. Each file that is selected by the user represents a FileReference object and contains the information relative to the file size, type, name, creation date, and modification date.

Chapter 10 discussed Flash Player sandbox security and the cross-domain file. For uploading and downloading files, the SWF application can access files only within its own domain or domains specified by the cross-domain policy file (refer to Solution 10-1).

The FileReference class allows you, through the browse() and download() methods, to select a file from the computer from the dialog window and to download a file from the server to the computer. Only one action can be invoked at a time.

To send the file from the client machine to the web server, a script written in any server-side language that expects the HTTP POST request with the following elements must be present:

- Content-Type: With a value typed as multipart/form-data.
- Content-Disposition: With a name attribute set to "Filedata" and a file name attribute set to the name of the original file. If you want to assign a custom name attribute, you can pass a value for the uploadDataFieldName parameter in the upload() method of the fileReference class.
- The binary contents of the file.

In this solution, you'll see how to create a Flex application to carry out a local file upload on the web server. You'll use a server-side script written in Java Server Pages (JSP).

What's involved

To create an instance of the FileReference class, you can use the new operator or directly launch the browse() method of the class that returns an array of FileReference objects:

```
var myFileReference:FileReference = new FileReference();
```

To carry out the upload of a file to a server, use the browse() method of the FileReference object. In this way, the user can select the file from the prompt dialog window, and the upload() method will carry out the transfer of the file to the server.

When the user selects a local file, the SELECT event releases; by managing this event, you can check that the file has been correctly selected and send it to the server:

```
private function uploadFile():void
{
var fileObj:FileReference = new FileReference ();
try
{
    var success:Boolean = fileObj.browse();
}
catch (error:Error)
{
    trace("Unable to open the dialog window.");
}

fileObj.addEventListener(Event.SELECT, selectHandler);
fileObj.addEventListener(Event.COMPLETE, completeHandler);
}
```

The uploadFile() function has activated the process of selecting the file with the browse() method. You have then created two event listeners on the SELECT event, which release when the user selects a file on its computer, and the COMPLETE event, which releases when users select a file on his computer, and the event that instead releases when the operation of upload has been successful:

```
function selectHandler(event:Event):void
{
var myServerScript:URLRequest =
new URLRequest("http://myDomain.com/uploadScript.jsp");

    try
    {
        fileObj.upload(myServerScript);
    }

    catch (error:Error)
    {
        trace("The file was not uploaded.");
    }
}
```

The event handler that releases on the SELECT event creates a URLRequest variable that contains the URL of the server-side script to which to send the file selected with the HTTP POST request. If no errors occur, which you check with a try...catch, the upload() method is invoked to which the URLRequest object is sent as a parameter:

```
function completeHandler(event:Event):void
{
    trace("File Uploaded !");
}
```

The completeHandler releases when the COMPLETE event has been dispatched and the file has therefore been uploaded to the server.

There are other events that are dispatched in the upload phase of the file:

- Event.OPEN: Starts when the upload procedure begins.

- ProgressEvent.PROGRESS: The event lasts for the entire upload phase until the COMPLETE event releases.

- HTTPStatusEvent.HTTP_STATUS: Occurs when there is an upload error due to the HTTP.

- IOErrorEvent.IO_ERROR: Occurs when there is an error in the upload due to the errors of authentication on the server (if any), to the transmission of the file on the part of Flash Player, or from the invalid protocol on the url parameter.

In this solution, you'll create a file upload operation using a server-side script written in JSP.

How to build it

To handle an upload operation, you need to create a server-side file that will put the file onto the server and the MXML application.

1. You create a new application file by selecting File ➤ New ➤ MXML Application and save it as Chapter_12_Flex_Sol_6_More.mxml. On the <mx:Application> tag, add a custom namespace to import the flash.net package and define an event listener for the creationComplete event:

```
<mx:Application xmlns:mx="http://www.adobe.com/2006/mxml"
layout="vertical"
horizontalAlign="left"
xmlns:net="flash.net.*"
creationComplete="onCreationComplete()">
```

2. Define a Form container immediately under the <mx:Application> tag, which will allow the user to insert the remote URL that will contain the server-side script on the server. The Flex application will run the script to upload the file on the domain from which the SWF file is loaded (refer to Solution 10-1 for the issues of Flash Player's sandbox security). Create a TextInput control that contains the name of the file that the user will select from his computer and a Text control that will contain the status of the upload operation to always give feedback to the user:

```
<mx:Form>
<mx:FormItem label="Remote URL">
<mx:TextInput id="urlInput" width="200" />
</mx:FormItem>
<mx:FormItem label="File name">
<mx:TextInput id="fileInput" editable="false" width="200" />
</mx:FormItem>
<mx:FormItem label="Status">
<mx:Text text="{status}" />
```

12

```
        </mx:FormItem>
        </mx:Form>
        </mx:Application>
```

3. Under the closure of the last FormItem, insert a ControlBar that displays two Button controls. One Button will permit you to select a file through the dialog window; the second will run the upload of the selected file:

```
<mx:Text text="{status}" />
</mx:FormItem>

<mx:ControlBar>
<mx:Button id="selectBut"
label="Select file" click="selectFile(event)" />
<mx:Button id="uploadBut" label="Upload file"
click="uploadFile(event)" enabled="{fileSelected}" />
</mx:ControlBar>

</mx:Form>
</mx:Application>
```

The upload operation is, therefore, divided into two steps. The first, defined by the event handler selectFile(), makes the user select the file. The selected file is contained in the instance of the FileReference object. The second step is that of carrying out the upload defined in the event handler uploadFile(). Note that the Button uploadBut is enabled only if the fileSelected variable is true. This Boolean variable is set as true only if the file has been correctly selected:

```
<mx:Button id="uploadBut" label="Upload file"
click="uploadFile(event)"
enabled="{fileSelected}" />
```

You now move on to writing the ActionScript code and all the functions for carrying out the upload operations of a file.

4. Insert a block of Script code between the <mx:Application> tag and the Form container. You begin with the declaration of the properties that will be used in the application and by defining the event handler onCreationComplete():

```
<mx:Application xmlns:mx="http://www.adobe.com/2006/mxml"
layout="vertical"
horizontalAlign="left"
xmlns:net="flash.net.*"
creationComplete="onCreationComplete()">

<mx:Script>
<![CDATA[
import mx.controls.Alert;
```

```
[Bindable]
private var fileRef:FileReference;
[Bindable]
private var fileSelected:Boolean = false;
[Bindable]
private var status:String = "Select file";

private function onCreationComplete():void
{
fileRef = new FileReference();
fileRef.addEventListener(Event.SELECT, onFileSelected);
fileRef.addEventListener(Event.COMPLETE, onUploadComplete);
fileRef.addEventListener(ProgressEvent.PROGRESS,
                                      onUploadProgress);
fileRef.addEventListener(IOErrorEvent.IO_ERROR, onUploadError);
fileRef.addEventListener(
SecurityErrorEvent.SECURITY_ERROR, onUploadError);
}
]]>
</mx:Script>
```

The fileRef variable contains the instance of the FileReference object. The fileSelected variable is a Boolean that specifies whether the file has been correctly selected and the upload method can, therefore, be invoked. The status variable advises the user when the upload process is terminated.

The creationComplete() function creates the FileReference object and, with the addEventListener method, manages the following events: Event.SELECT, Event.COMPLETE, ProgressEvent.PROGRESS, IOErrorEvent.IO_ERROR, and SecurityErrorEvent.SECURITY_ERROR.

You must, therefore define the event handlers for these events.

5. When the Select File button is clicked, the selectFile() function is invoked. This function must simply go and launch the browse() method for the FileReference object. You write the function under the closure of the function onCreationComplete():

```
private function selectFile(event:MouseEvent):void
{
fileRef.browse();
}
```

Once the browse() method is launched, the Event.SELECT event is dispatched.

6. After the closure of the selectFile() function, you add the first event handler that releases on the SELECT event, or more precisely when the user has selected a file from the dialog window:

12

```
private function selectFile(event:MouseEvent):void
{
fileRef.browse();
}

private function onFileSelected(event:Event):void
{
fileSelected = true;
fileInput.text = fileRef.name;
status = "Ready";
}
```

The function sets the fileSelected variable as true. This variable is linked with a binding to the enabled property of the Button that launches the upload. When it is true, the button becomes clickable for the user.

Then, the name of the selected file is inserted in the TextInput fileInput, taking the name property of the object FileReference, and finally the "Ready" string is assigned to the status variable.

7. The Upload File button launches the uploadFile() function on the click event. This function invokes the upload() method of the FileReference object. You add the function after the closure of the event handler onFileSelected():

```
private function onFileSelected(event:Event):void
{
fileSelected = true;
fileInput.text = fileRef.name;
status = "Ready";
}

private function uploadFile(event:MouseEvent):void
{
if (!fileSelected || (urlInput.text.length == 0))
{
Alert.show("Insert a URL and select a file.");
return;
}

fileRef.upload(new URLRequest(urlInput.text));
}
```

The function checks that a URL address has been inserted by the user in the urlInput text input. If this input is empty, an alert box appears and communicates to the user to insert it. If it already exists, the upload() method is launched, to which a URLRequest object is sent as value:

```
fileRef.upload(new URLRequest(urlInput.text));
```

When the upload() method is invoked, the COMPLETE event is dispatched together with the ProgressEvent.PROGRESS and all other events of eventual error, IOErrorEvent. IO_ERROR, and SecurityErrorEvent.SECURITY_ERROR.

8. After the closure of the uploadFile() function, add the event handlers that are invoked if an error occurs in the upload phase of the file:

```
private function uploadFile(event:MouseEvent):void
{
if (!fileSelected || (urlInput.text.length == 0))
{
Alert.show("Insert a URL and select a file.");
return;
}

fileRef.upload(new URLRequest(urlInput.text));
}
private function onUploadProgress(event:ProgressEvent):void
{
status = ((event.bytesLoaded * 100) / event.bytesTotal).toString();
}

private function onUploadComplete(event:DataEvent):void
{
status = "Complete";
}

private function onUploadError(event:Event):void
{
if (event is IOErrorEvent)
{
Alert.show((event as IOErrorEvent).text.toString());
}
else if (event is SecurityErrorEvent)
{
Alert.show((event as SecurityErrorEvent).text.toString());
}
}
]]>
</mx:Script>
```

The onUploadProgress() function releases on the ProgressEvent.PROGRESS event that lasts for all of the upload phase until the COMPLETE event is released. In the event handler, you simply insert the value of total bytes loaded in the upload phase using the bytesLoaded property of the event object of the PROGRESS class.

The onUploadComplete() function sets the status variable on the Complete string, while the event handler onUploadError() shows the error that has occurred, if any, in an alert box.

> *Flash Player is not capable of attempting to send a test upload. Therefore, it cannot establish if the server or the file will be uploaded. You can, however, send the value of* true *as the third parameter to the* upload() *method to force a test on the connection to the server.*

There is nothing left but to create the server-side script to put on the web server and that will receive the file to upload to the server.

9. You create a file by selecting File ➤ New ➤ File and save it as upload.jsp. This JSP file uses the FileUpload class (which you can download from http://jakarta. apache.org/commons/fileupload/) copied onto the web server and performs the upload of the file on the web server:

```
<%@ page language="java" contentType="text/html;
charset=UTF-8" pageEncoding="UTF-8"
import=➡
"java.io.File,java.util.List,java.util.Iterator,org.apache.commons.file
upload.*"
%>
<!DOCTYPE html PUBLIC "-//W3C//DTD XHTML 1.0 Transitional//EN"➡
"http://www.w3.org/TR/xhtml1/DTD/xhtml1-transitional.dtd">
<html xmlns="http://www.w3.org/1999/xhtml">
<head>
<meta http-equiv="Content-Type" content="text/html; charset=UTF-8" />
<title>Upload handler</title>
</head>
<body>
<%
// requires:
// http://jakarta.apache.org/commons/fileupload/
if (FileUpload.isMultipartContent(request)) {
DiskFileUpload upload = new DiskFileUpload();
List items = upload.parseRequest(request);
Iterator it = items.iterator();

while(it.hasNext()) {
FileItem item = (FileItem)it.next();

if(!item.isFormField()) {
File fileRef  = new File(item.getName());
File savedFile = new File(getServletContext().getRealPath("/"),
fileRef.getName());
item.write(savedFile);
}
}
}
%>
</body>
</html>
```

This file is put on your web server, and the file will be recalled by the upload() method of the Flex application. The path of the server-side script is inserted into the urlInput field that you had created in the Form container:

```
<mx:FormItem label="Remote URL">
<mx:TextInput id="urlInput" width="200" />
</mx:FormItem>
```

10. Save the file and run the application.

To be able to test the application you must publish the SWF file on the same domain in which the server-side script upload.jsp resides.

In the text input urlInput, insert the remote address of the JSP file and then click the Select file button. The Open dialog window opens, as shown in Figure 12-17. Select a file from your computer and click the Upload file button. The file is sent to the remote script and is uploaded to the server.

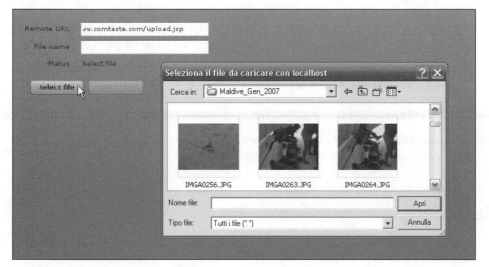

Figure 12-17. By clicking the Select file button, you can select a file on your own PC and then send it.

Expert tips

By using ColdFusion as the server-side script for the upload of the file onto the server, the code to write is very simple. The CFFILE tag is used, which manages the transfer of the file from the Flex application to the server by going and specifying the attributes action, filefield, destination, and nameconflict:

```
<cffile action="upload" filefield="Filedata"
destination="#ExpandPath('./')#"
nameconflict="OVERWRITE" />
```

12

Furthermore, the `FileReference` class allows you to filter the type of file that must be selected by restricting the choice of file format. Through the `FileFilter` class, you can communicate to the dialog window to show or to ensure that only files with specific extensions are selected:

```
var imageFilter:FileFilter =
new FileFilter("Only Image formats (*.jpg, *.jpeg, *.gif, *.png)",
"*.jpg; *.jpeg; *.gif; *.png");
```

In this way, the Open dialog window will show only the files that have a specific format in the `FileFilter` object.

To create a download operation and download a file from the server onto the local computer, you instead use the `download()` method. This method accepts two parameters:

- `request`: A `URLRequest` object that contains the URL of the file to download
- `defaultFileName`: Specifies a default file name that appears in the download dialog window

The path of a file that is downloaded from the server is relative to the SWF file of the application. The following code downloads an XML file that is found in the same data directory as the SWF document:

```
var fileRef:FileReference = new FileReference();
var myUrl:URLRequest = new URLRequest("data/file.xml");
fileRef.download(myURL, "fileFromServer.xml");
```

With these few lines of code, you have saved the `file.xml` file on the local computer, to which you have given the default name `fileFromServer.xml`.

Summary

The Flex framework offers a great number of classes and utilities to the developers of RIAs. In this chapter you explored some of the additional features of the Flex framework such as the Flex charting components, the `VideoDisplay` component, the `PrintJob` class, and the Logging API.

In the first solution, you took advantage of the Flex charting components that allow you to show data in one of the many charts in this set of libraries.

Charting components (www.adobe.com/products/flex/charting/) are an additional tool you can install on your existing copy of Flex Builder that allows you to use built-in charts.

You also looked at the way video can be used with Flex through the Flash Player's built-in capabilities. It is possible to add media to a Flex application by loading it as an external object or embedding it. You used the `VideoDisplay` component to load an external FLV video into an application.

Another interesting Flex library is the PrintJob API that allows developers to create containers and controls that will print exactly that which the user expects to print. You used the PrintJob classes to implement the functions of printing: the FlexPrintJob and the PrintDataGrid class. Then you created a custom Flex component that acted as content for the printing activities.

The chapter concluded by discussing the second perspective that Flex Builder supports (the Flex Debugging perspective) and the FileReference API. You created a file that used the Logging API to carry out a debug session.

Flex and the Flash Player allow developers to create the function of upload and download through the FileReference class. Each file that is selected by the user represents a FileReference object and contains the information relative to the file's size, type, name, creation date, and modification date.

The next chapter will be dedicated to the user navigation in Flex applications. You'll learn how the Navigator containers work and how to use the more common navigation containers to be able to provide the user with the possibility of navigating and moving around inside a Flex application.

12

13 USER NAVIGATION IN FLEX APPLICATIONS

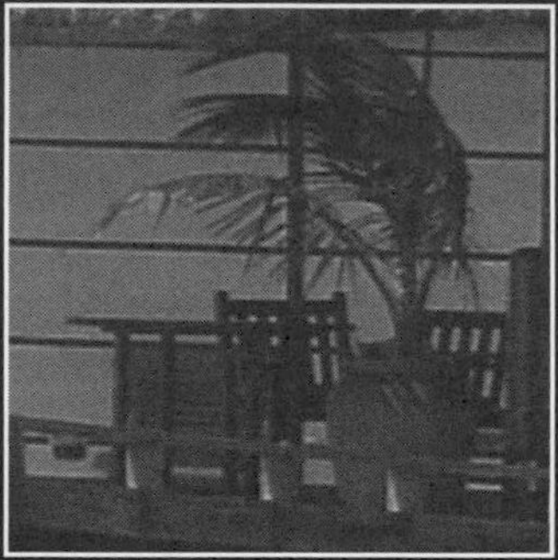

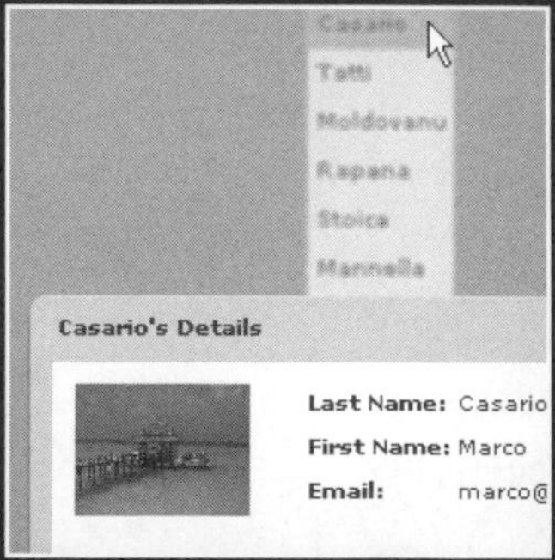

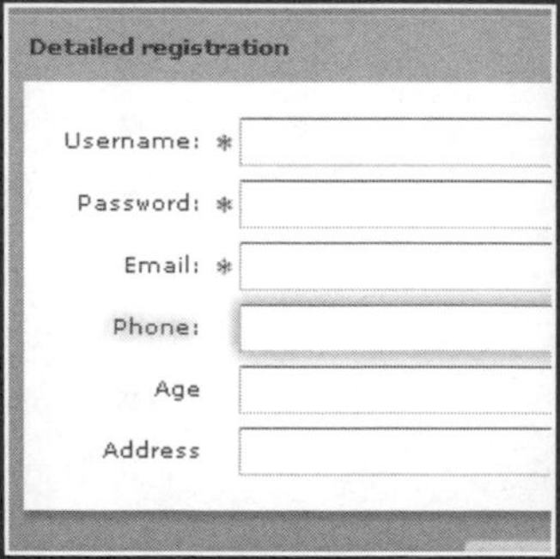

Flex framework gives developers the ability to create complex application and user interaction using containers and controls to reduce programming complexity. Flex applications and web applications can be made up of many objects that users can interact with and use to navigate through applications. The difference between a Flex application and a web application is that the former uses a one-page approach, while the latter uses a multipage approach (except for a web application developed with technologies such as Ajax, Lazlo, and SilverLight). It means that the user moves within the same page and can choose where to go. It's obvious that in this scenario it is very important to provide a good navigation system in Flex.

Aside from the simple containers such as Panels, VBox, and HBox, Flex offers powerful Navigator containers to create and manage objects, which allow you to move around in the application, loading different pages and objects.

When it is necessary to manage different views of the application, view states come into play. States allow you to manage different views of the same application in the same file. Through simple properties, it is possible to switch between one view and another, rendering portions of the page visible or invisible.

This solution shows you how Navigator containers work and how to program a navigation system for the Flex applications.

Solution 13-1: Moving through the application with Navigator containers

A subclass of Flex containers is represented by the Navigator container. This type of container allows you to navigate and move around in the application, showing the different elements of the user interface according to the path that the user chooses.

The following lists some of the Navigator containers:

- ViewStack
- Accordion
- ButtonBar
- LinkBar
- MenuBar
- TabBar
- TabBarNavigator
- ToggleButtonBar

Furthermore, these containers allow you to control the interactions that the user makes in the application and to program the components of the application in response to these movements.

In this solution, you will see how to use the more common Navigator containers to help users navigate and move around inside a Flex application.

What's involved

A Navigator container allows you to navigate in a group of child containers. This means that a Navigator container provides the possibility of containing other containers and of specifying which should be visible and which should not.

The ViewStack Navigator container, which is the core of the Navigator containers, allows you to specify a selection of child containers that are arranged one on top of the other. Only the container that has the focus is visible; the others remain nonactive, so the user can't interact with them. The ViewStack container is linked to other Navigator components, which allow you to switch from one child to another.

Figure 13-1 shows the contents of a ViewStack and its child containers.

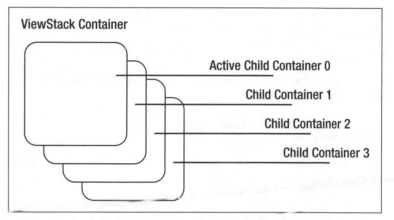

Figure 13-1. The stacked child containers inside a ViewStack container

To create a ViewStack, use the MXML tag <mx:ViewStack>. In this tag, you declare the child containers with the controls. Each container corresponds to a child. The following code shows a ViewStack with three children of Canvas type:

```
<mx:ViewStack id="myVS"
borderStyle="solid"
width="100%" height="80%">

<mx:Canvas id="Consulting"
label="Consulting" width="100%"
height="100%">
<mx:Label text="Consulting"
color="#000000"/>
</mx:Canvas>

<mx:Canvas id="Training"

label="Training"
width="100%" height="100%">
```

```
    <mx:Label text="Training" color="#000000"/>
</mx:Canvas>

<mx:Canvas id="Development"
label="Development" width="100%" height="100%">
<mx:Label text="Development" color="#000000"/>
</mx:Canvas>
</mx:ViewStack>
```

The ViewStack does not have built-in functions to change the display of one of its children. To carry out these operations, you must either write the code to manage the switch of the code in ActionScript or use one of the following controls:

- LinkBar
- TabBar
- ButtonBar
- ToggleButtonBar

To link the children of the ViewStack to one of these controls and navigate them, use the dataProvider property:

```
<mx:LinkBar fontWeight="bold"
dataProvider="{myVS}"/>
```

These controls have built-in functions that allow you to navigate and to change between the various child containers of the ViewStack, as shown in Figure 13-2.

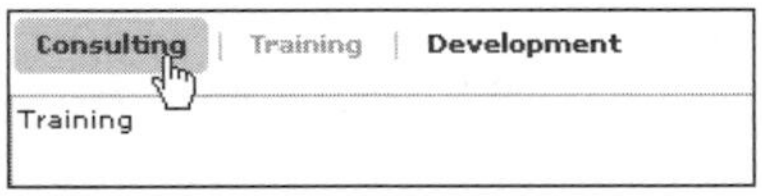

Figure 13-2. The LinkBar control allows you to navigate the ViewStack.

The ViewStack puts forward the following properties to control its child container:

- selectedIndex: Contains the index of the container that is active. The ViewStack has a zero-based index, so the value of the selectedIndex property varies from 0 to n-1. By setting this property, the child in the ViewStack is rendered active:

```
myVs.selectedIndex = 1;
```

- selectedChild: Specifies the name of the active child. In the previous ViewStack example, you defined the children with an id:

```
<mx:ViewStack id="myVS"
borderStyle="solid"
width="100%" height="80%">
```

```
<mx:Canvas id="Consulting"
label="Consulting" width="100%"
height="100%">
<mx:Label text="Consulting"
color="#000000"/>
</mx:Canvas>
```

- To switch to the child container named Consulting and make it visible, write the following:

```
myVs.selectedChild  = Consulting;
```

- numChildren: Contains the number of children defined in the ViewStack.

In this solution, you will use some of the Navigator containers, enabling the user to navigate inside the contents.

How to build it

In Flex applications, the Navigator containers let users navigate and change the display of the application according to the choices they make. The application can have different levels of navigation that can also be nested among them. Imagine the navigation tree for a Flex application (see Figure 13-3).

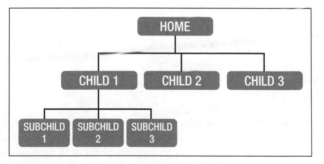

Figure 13-3. The navigation of a Flex application

The navigation is made up of three levels, and the solution produces this scenario using the Navigator containers.

1. Create the project that will contain all the solutions of Chapter 13. Select File ➤ New ➤ Flex Project to create a basic project with the name Charter_13_Flex_ Navigation. Create a new MXML file by selecting File ➤ New ➤ MXML Application and save it as Chapter_13_Flex_Sol_1_Navigation.mxml. Begin by inserting a Panel that functions as a container for all the other elements:

```
<mx:Application xmlns:mx="http://www.adobe.com/2006/mxml">
<mx:Panel title="Navigation Containers"
height="90%" width="90%" >
</mx:Panel>
</mx:Application>
```

13

2. Insert a TabNavigator within the Panel, which allows you to manage a set of tabs to navigate in it. This container will let you navigate in the second level of the structure of the page (see Figure 13-3). The TabNavigator acts in turn as container for other containers and creates a tab button for each container specified in it:

```
<mx:TabNavigator id="myTN"
width="100%" height="100%">
</mx:TabNavigator>
```

If you run the application with the following code you will not see anything appear as the interface of the application. Until you insert containers in the TabNavigator, it will create the tab buttons. Furthermore, only one child container at a time is displayed.

3. Insert the child containers in the TabNavigator. In this example, you will use VBox containers in which you will specify the label property. This property will be used by the TabNavigator as the label field for the tab button:

```
<mx:TabNavigator id="myTN"
width="100%" height="100%">

<mx:VBox label="Services">
<mx:Label text="Child container 1"/>
</mx:VBox>

<mx:VBox label="About">
<mx:Label text="Child container 2"/>
</mx:VBox>

<mx:VBox label="Contact">
<mx:Label text="Child container 3"/>
</mx:VBox>
</mx:TabNavigator>
```

The TabNavigator will create three tabs, as shown in Figure 13-4, in which it will insert Label controls. The TabNavigator Navigator container provides built-in functions that allow the user to click one of the tabs and change the content to be displayed. If you save and run the application, you can already move around and display all three labels in the container.

Figure 13-4. Three tabs defined in the TabNavigator container

4. Referring to the navigation structure of Figure 13-3, you must create another navigation level on the first child container. To do this, change the content of the VBox with the label equal to Services and insert a ViewStack in it. Because the ViewStack does not provide visual elements, to be able to move from one child to another, you will link a LinkBar to this component. Insert the following code in the first VBox declared in the TabNavigator:

```
<mx:VBox label="Services">

<mx:LinkBar fontWeight="bold"
dataProvider="{myVS}" />

<mx:ViewStack id="myVS"
borderStyle="solid"
width="100%" height="80%">

<mx:Canvas id="Consulting"
label="Consulting" width="100%"
height="100%">
<mx:Label text="Consulting"
color="#000000"/>
</mx:Canvas>

<mx:Canvas id="Training"

label="Training"
width="100%" height="100%">
<mx:Label text="Training" color="#000000"/>
</mx:Canvas>
```

13

```
<mx:Canvas id="Development"
label="Development" width="100%" height="100%">
<mx:Label text="Development" color="#000000"/>
</mx:Canvas>
</mx:ViewStack>

</mx:VBox>
```

The LinkBar uses a data binding with the ViewStack defined underneath as dataProvider property. In this way, the LinkBar creates as many link buttons as there are children in the ViewStack. This operation is automatic and renders the ViewStack navigable to the user. In the solution, the LinkBar will create three link buttons: Consulting, Training, and Development:

```
<mx:LinkBar fontWeight="bold"
dataProvider="{myVS}"
/>
```

In the ViewStack, Canvas containers have been declared with a Label control:

```
<mx:Canvas id="Consulting"
label="Consulting" width="100%"
height="100%">
<mx:Label text="Consulting"
color="#000000"/>
</mx:Canvas>
```

Also for the LinkBar: the label property of the child container is used as label field for the button.

5. The LinkBar provides the itemClick event, which releases when the user selects a link button. This event creates the event object that you can use to obtain information relative to the ViewStack. Insert an event handler for the itemClick event in the LinkBar tag:

```
<mx:LinkBar fontWeight="bold"
dataProvider="{myVS}"
itemClick="clickHandler(event);"/>
```

6. At the beginning of the code, immediately under the <mx:Application> tag, insert an <mx:Script> block in which to write the event handler clickHandler():

```
<mx:Script>
<![CDATA[
import mx.events.ItemClickEvent;
  private function clickHandler(event:ItemClickEvent):void {

mx.controls.Alert.show("You have selcted the button with the index:"
+ String(event.index) + "\n" + " and the label: " + event.label);
}
]]>
</mx:Script>
```

The event handler clickHandler() will print the values of the properties event.label and event.index, which contain (respectively) the label of the link button selected and the index of the link button selected in an alert box.

7. Save and run the application.

You have reproduced the structure of navigation at two levels by creating a nested Navigator container. When you run the application, you move to the second level of navigation by clicking the TabNavigator; you move to the third level (see Figure 13-5) by clicking the LinkBar. Furthermore, every LinkBar button produces an opening of the alert box.

Figure 13-5. Both the TabNavigator and the LinkBar allow you to navigate in the child containers.

Expert tips

By using the selectedIndex and selectedChild properties, you can program which container to make visible. This allows you to control the content to render it visible by linking it to a user or system event.

1. Add the following <mx:Hbox> at the end of the code created in the preceding solution (insert it after the closure of the <mx:TabNavigator> tag):

```
<mx:HBox>
<mx:Button label="Move to Tab 1" click="myTN.selectedIndex=0"/>
<mx:Button label=" Move to Tab 2" click="myTN.selectedIndex=1"/>
<mx:Button label=" Move to Tab 3" click="myTN.selectedIndex=2"/>
</mx:HBox>
```

2. Save and run the file.

By clicking the buttons, the content displayed in the TabNavigator will change, rendering the child containers that are linked to the visible tab buttons.

13

You could also use the selectedIndex property on a system event such as, for example, the creationComplete. This allows you to select application indexes of the Navigator container to render visible in the startup phase:

```
<mx:Application xmlns:mx="http://www.adobe.com/2006/mxml"
  creationComplete="myTN.selectedIndex=0">
```

3. Save and run the file again.

Solution 13-2: Creating and removing pop-up windows

The use of pop-up windows in web applications is useful for error or notification messages, login or advertisement procedures, and so on. Even if the tendency in these last few years is to try to keep the number of pop-up windows to a minimum, the latest release of Internet browsers such as Firefox and Explorer automatically block pop-ups. Moreover, most of the browser toolbars that have pop-up blockers (Google Toolbar, Yahoo Toolbar, Live Search, and so on) are now present on most users' computers.

In Flex, the concept of a pop-up is slightly different, in that the pop-up window that opens is found inside the application, so it is rendered to the screen by Flash Player. The pop-up of Flex is not, in fact, a new instance of a window of the browser, so it can bypass pop-up blockers.

Flex provides a built-in support for the pop-up, which allows you to also create complex windows to display articulated contents. You can, in fact, add Flex controls, images, external SWF files, videos, and audio files to the content of a Flex pop-up window. In Flex applications, pop-up windows are part of the application itself, not different instances of the browser window. Furthermore, you can create modal or nonmodal pop-ups.

> **Modal** pop-up windows are windows that, when displayed onscreen, prevent you from navigating and selecting any other content of the window.
>
> **Nonmodal** windows allow you to access and select other applications' contents onscreen.

The class that enables you to create pop-up windows is the PopUpManager in the mx. managers package. This class is a singleton that provides methods for the creation and removal of pop-up windows on top of the application user interface.

The **singleton** is one of the design patterns used to restrict instantiation of a class to one object. This is useful when exactly one object is needed to coordinate actions across the system. To look at this in more depth, read the definition of a singleton on Wikipedia: http://en.wikipedia.org/wiki/Singleton_pattern.

The createPopUp() method of the PopUpManager allows you to create a new pop-up window. This method accepts three parameters:

- The parent container for the pop-up
- The class from which to create the pop-up window
- A Boolean value that specifies whether the window must be modal or nonmodal

The createPopUp() returns an IFlexDisplayObject. Even if you can create a pop-up window based on any component, most of the time you will use the TitleWindow class.

In this solution, you will see how to create and remove a pop-up window.

What's involved

To manage a pop-up window, use the PopUpManager class and the TitleWindow container. The method that allows you to create and make a pop-up window visible is the createPopUp() method, which has the following syntax:

```
public static createPopUp(parent:DisplayObject, class:Class,
modal:Boolean = false): IFlexDisplayObject
```

You send the content that should be displayed in the page to the createPopUp() method. Most of the time you will use the TitleWindow container to define a custom MXML component to use as content for the pop-up window:

```
<mx:TitleWindow xmlns:mx="http://www.adobe.com/2006/mxml"
width="800" height="600"
title="Maldive">
</mx:TitleWindow>
```

You can insert any type of content that you create with Flex in this container. Once the content of this MXML component has been created, you can launch the createPopUp() method of the PopUpManager class and send it as a parameter:

```
<mx:Script>
<![CDATA[
import mx.managers.PopUpManager;
import mx.core.IFlexDisplayObject;
import myComponents.MyLoginForm;

private function createWin():void {

var MyPopUpWin:IFlexDisplayObject =
PopUpManager.createPopUp(this, myCustomTitleComp, false);
}
]]>
</mx:Script>
```

13

In this `<mx:Script>` you have created a nonmodal pop-up window to which you have sent the custom MXML component MyCustomTitleComp.mxml.

To launch the `createWin()` function and see the pop-up window, you can link it to a system or user event:

```
<mx:Button click="createWin();" label="Open PopUp"/>
```

The pop-up window will be created by clicking the button. After the new window is opened at a determined point, it has to be closed by the user before the application continues.

The `removePopUp()` method performs this task. Once a pop-up window is created, no close button will be shown to the user, and no event handler will be created. You must, therefore, first create a TitleWindow that provides the close button using its showCloseButton property:

```
<mx:TitleWindow xmlns:mx="http://www.adobe.com/2006/mxml"
showCloseButton="true"
width="240" height="120"
title="Maldive">
```

It subsequently programs the window closing at the click of the close button by creating an event listener on the close event:

```
this.addEventListener(Event.CLOSE,closeHandler)
private function closeHandler(evt:Event):void
{
    PopUpManager.removePopUp(this);
}
```

Figure 13-6 shows the close button created by the showCloseButton property of the TitleWindow.

Figure 13-6.
The TitleWindow adds the close button to the window
if its showCloseButton property is set as true.

To close a nonmodal window, you can also link the `removePopUp()` to a user event, such as the click of a button:

```
<mx:Button
label="Remove PopUp window"
click="PopUpManager.removePopUp(this);"/>
```

In this solution, you will see how to create and remove a pop-up window with the PopUpManager class.

How to build it

For this solution, you will create a simple application that opens a pop-up window to show a photo in its original dimensions. You will create a component-based custom MXML on the TitleWindow and you will send it to the createPopUp() method. The photo that you will use is located in the assets folder of the Flex project of this chapter, and it is a photo in JPG format (you can use any image you like).

1. Create the structure of the directory that will contain the MXML component. It is, in fact, a good rule to insert the MXML component and ActionScript class in a package, not in the root of the project. Select File ➤ New ➤ Folder and create the following folder structure: com\flexsolutions\chapter13\popup. The pop-up folder is the folder in which you'll save the MXML component.

2. Create an MXML component inside the pop-up folder you just created by selecting File > New > MXML Component based on the TitleWindow tag. Save it as MyPopUpWin.mxml. This component represents the content that will be displayed in the pop-up window created. Add the following properties to the TitleWindow tag:

```
<?xml version="1.0" encoding="utf-8"?>
<mx:TitleWindow xmlns:mx="http://www.adobe.com/2006/mxml"
creationComplete="init()"
showCloseButton="true"
width="800" height="600"
title="Maldive">
```

The TitleWindow container launches the event handler init() on creationComplete. This function will position the pop-up window in the center of the screen and register an event listener for the close button. The showCloseButton property is set as true. This renders the close button visible. Specify the dimensions of the window and its title.

3. You can add the event handler init() to the TitleWindow by adding an <mx:Script> block:

```
<mx:TitleWindow xmlns:mx="http://www.adobe.com/2006/mxml"
creationComplete="init()"
showCloseButton="true"
width="800" height="600" title="Maldive">

<mx:Script>
<![CDATA[
import mx.managers.PopUpManager;

private function init():void
{
PopUpManager.centerPopUp(this);
this.addEventListener(Event.CLOSE,closeHandler)

}
```

13

```
private function closeHandler(evt:Event):void
{
PopUpManager.removePopUp(this);
}
]]>
</mx:Script>
```

Before writing the init() function, the PopUpManager class is imported to be able to use its methods and events. Create the init() function, which uses the centerPopUp() method to center the window in the screen and register an event handler on the close button with the addEventListener() method.

The closeHandler() function does nothing more than make the pop-up window disappear with the removePopUp() method.

4. Finish the MXML component by inserting a VBox and an Image control, which will load the image in the assets folder in its original dimensions. Write the following code after the closure of the <mx:Script> tag:

```
</mx:Script>
<mx:VBox width="100%" verticalCenter="0">
<mx:Image source="@Embed('/assets/maldive.jpg')"/>
</mx:VBox>
</mx:TitleWindow>
```

The Image control in the source property embeds the image, which will be inserted in the SWF file in the compilation phase. The relative path that has been sent to the source property keeps note of the fact that the assets folder is found on the root of the project. Instead, the MXML component is saved in the com.flexsolutions.chapter13.popup folder of the project. For this reason, go back to the main root of the project with the "/assets/" key and enter the following into the assets folder:

```
<mx:Image source="@Embed('/assets/maldive.jpg')"/>
```

5. Save the MXML component.

6. Once you have finished writing the component to use as component for the pop-up window, create the application file that will launch and create this pop-up. Create an MXML application file by selecting File ➤ New ➤ MXML Application and save it as Chapter_13_Flex_Sol_2_Navigation.mxml. The file, as with all application files, must be saved on the root of the Flex project.

7. Insert some properties on the <mx:Application> tag and insert the user interface elements of the application:

```
<mx:Application xmlns:mx="http://www.adobe.com/2006/mxml"
layout="absolute"
paddingLeft="0" paddingRight="0">

<mx:Label x="191" y="46" text="Click on the image"/>

<mx:Canvas width="340" height="250" x="191" y="81">
<mx:Image id="Image1"
```

```
source="@Embed('assets/maldive.jpg')"
 width="320" height="240"
click="zoomPopUp(event)"/>

</mx:Canvas>
</mx:Application>
```

In a Canvas container, which enables you to position the controls in absolute mode, you have inserted an Image control that loads the image in the assets folder. On the click event of the Image you have launched the zoomPopUp() function, which has the job of creating and opening the pop-up with the image in its original dimensions.

8. Insert an <mx:Script> block immediately under the <mx:Application> tag and create the pop-up window in the ZoomPopUp() event handler:

```
<mx:Application xmlns:mx="http://www.adobe.com/2006/mxml"
layout="absolute"
paddingLeft="0" paddingRight="0">
<mx:Script>
<![CDATA[
import com.flexsolutions.chapter13.popup.MyPopUpWin;
import mx.managers.PopUpManager;

public function zoomPopUp(event:MouseEvent):void
{
PopUpManager.createPopUp(this, MyPopUpWin, false);
}
]]>
</mx:Script>
```

To be able to send the custom MXML component MyPopUpWin to the createPopUp(), you must first import it. The first link of this <mx:Script> block begins with this:

```
import com.flexsolutions.chapter13.popup.MyPopUpWin;
import mx.managers.PopUpManager;
```

The zoomPopUp() function does nothing more than use the createPopUp() method of the PopUpManager to which it sends the custom component as a class:

```
public function zoomPopUp(event:MouseEvent):void
{
PopUpManager.createPopUp(this, MyPopUpWin, false);
}
```

The pop-up window created is of the nonmodal type; the third parameter of the createPopUp() method is false.

9. Save and run the application.

Clicking the image displays a pop-up, as shown in Figure 13-7.

13

Figure 13-7. The TitleWindow opens with a click on the image.

To close the pop-up, click the close button in the top-right corner of the pop-up window. Clicking the button releases the removePopUp() method.

Expert tips

The pop-up window that you created in the solution is a nonmodal window. The difference between a modal and nonmodal window is that in the first type (modal) the user cannot interact or select any other content outside of the open window. You can, for example, keep clicking the image and more and more windows will open.

These types of windows are helpful when you want to focus the attention of the user on a single content, and the user cannot be distracted by other objects until the window has been closed.

The createPopUp() method accepts three parameters, the third of which specifies whether to create a modal or nonmodal window:

```
public static createPopUp(parent:DisplayObject, class:Class,
modal:Boolean = false): IFlexDisplayObject
```

By setting the value of the modal property as true, you create a modal window. You change the zoomPopUp() method in the application file, substituting the value of the last parameter from false to true:

```
public function zoomPopUp(event:MouseEvent):void
{
PopUpManager.createPopUp(this, MyPopUpWin, true);
}
```

If you save the file and run the application, you will see that everything behind the window becomes disabled by clicking the image and launching the pop-up, and you can't interact with any element until the window has been closed (see Figure 13-8).

Figure 13-8. When you create a modal pop-up window, you can't interact with the content of the application until that window has been closed.

Solution 13-3: Sending data to a pop-up window

After creating a pop-up window, you have to exchange data between the new window and the application. As with a custom component (refer to Chapter 2), to be able to send the data to a pop-up window, it is necessary to declare the variables that this will be able to receive.

In this solution, you see how to make a pop-up window communicate with the application by sending an ActionScript value object as data (refer to Solution 3-3).

What's involved

13

To make a pop-up window able to receive data from the application, the variable is declared in the pop-up. Therefore, in the TitleWindow, insert all the variables that window expects to receive in the <mx:Script> block:

```
<mx:TitleWindow
xmlns:mx="http://www.adobe.com/2006/mxml"
width="320" height="240"
>
```

```
<mx:Script>
<![CDATA[
[Bindable]
public var myVar1:String;
[Bindable]
public var myVar2:String;
]]>
</mx:Script>
```

In this example of code, you have declared two public variables: myVar1 and myVar2 as String. To send these two variables from the Application, you must cast the pop-up and type it as the custom MXML component and send the value to that component to the pop-up window.

In the Application, write the following:

```
var myPopUp:MyTitleWindowComponent = ➡
PopUpManager.createPopUp (this, MyTitleWindowComponent, true) as ➡
MyTitleWindowComponent;
myPopUp.myVar1 = "Hello";
myPopUp.myVar2 = "World";
```

The myPopUp variable is data typed as MyTitleWindowComponent, which corresponds to the custom component that defines the TitleWindow. In fact, in the parameters of the createPopUP() method you again send the MyTitleWindowComponent component.

Another method is that of using a variable of IFlexDisplayObject type:

```
var myPopUp:IFlexDisplayObject = ➡
PopUpManager.createPopUp (this, MyTitleWindowComponent, true);
MyTitleWindowComponent (myPopUp).myVar1 = "Hello";
MyTitleWindowComponent (myPopUp).myVar2 = "World";
```

The final result, which does not change, sends the data to the pop-up window.

> One of the powers of Flex is that you have multiple ways to do the same thing, so developers can choose the solution that best fits their needs. The IFlexDisplayObject *interface defines the interface for skin elements, so in this example you create the* myPopUp *variable that contains the* IFlexDisplayObject *returned by the* createPopUp *method:*
>
> ```
> public static createPopUp(parent:DisplayObject, class:Class
> modal:Boolean = false): IFlexDisplayObject
> ```

In this solution you will see how to send the values from a List control defined in an application to a pop-up window.

How to build it

You must create the custom component that will be sent to the pop-up to display the content of the window.

1. In the com\flexsolutions\chapter13\popup folder from the preceding solution, create an MXML component by selecting File > New > MXML Component and saving this file as DetailPopUp.mxml. The component will be based on a TitleWindow container.

2. Change some of the properties of the root tag TitleWindow and create an event listener on the creationComplete event:

```
<?xml version="1.0" encoding="utf-8"?>
<mx:TitleWindow
xmlns:mx="http://www.adobe.com/2006/mxml"
layout="absolute"
width="320" height="240"
showCloseButton="true"
borderAlpha="1.0"
 title="{firstname}'s Details"
creationComplete="init()"
>
```

You have specified the TitleWindow to display the close button on the top right of the window, setting the showCloseButton property as true. The init() function, which you launch at creationComplete, will be needed to register an event handler for the window closure.

The title of the TitleWindow is made up of a data binding on a firstname variable and of simple text:

```
title="{firstname}'s Details"
```

You will declare this and other variables in the <mx:Script> block.

3. Insert an <mx:Script> block under the <mx:TitleWindow> tag and import the classes necessary to the pop-up by declaring the variables that the window will be able to receive from the Application:

```
<mx:Script>
<![CDATA[
import mx.managers.PopUpManager;
import mx.events.CloseEvent;
[Bindable]
public var firstname:String;
[Bindable]
public var lastname:String;
[Bindable]
public var email:String;
```

13

You have declared three public variables, which will be those that will be sent by the Application to the pop-up window. The three variables are set as Bindable.

4. Write the init() function, which has the single task of registering an event listener when the close button of the pop-up window is clicked:

```
[Bindable]
public var firstname:String;
[Bindable]
public var lastname:String;
[Bindable]
public var email:String;

private function init():void
{
this.addEventListener( CloseEvent.CLOSE, closeMe );
}
```

5. Write the closeMe event handler that invokes the removePopUp() method immediately under the init() function:

```
private function closeMe( event:CloseEvent ):void
{
PopUpManager.removePopUp( this );
}
]]>
</mx:Script>
```

The removePopUp() method removes the window by closing it.

6. You can now take care of the user interface part of the application. Immediately after the closure of the <mx:Script> tag, add some elements, such as an Image control and Label controls:

```
<mx:Image width="80" height="80" x="10" y="10"
source="@Embed('/assets/maldive.jpg')"/>

<mx:Label x="114" y="10" text="Last Name:" fontWeight="bold"/>
<mx:Label x="114" y="30" text="First Name:" fontWeight="bold"/>
<mx:Label x="114" y="50" text="Email:" fontWeight="bold"/>
```

The Image control loads the image used in the preceding solution (you can import any image you prefer).

All the controls are positioned in absolute mode, specifying their x and y properties.

7. You insert another three Label controls, which this time will display the values of the variables sent to the Application:

```
<mx:Label x="183" y="10" text="{firstname}" />
<mx:Label x="183" y="30" text="{lastname}" />
<mx:Label x="183" y="50" text="{email}" />
</mx:TitleWindow>
```

The three Label controls create a binding with three variables defined in the <mx:Script>block.

You can now close the TitleWindow component and move on to creating the Application file.

8. Create an MXML file by selecting File ➤ New ➤ MXML Application and save it as Chapter_13_Flex_Sol_3_Navigation.mxml. This file will load the data from an XML file through an HTTPService and will display it in a List control. When the user clicks an item of the List control, the additional information on that item will be sent to the pop-up window and will be displayed in it.

9. Declare the HTTPService and invoke its send() method on creationComplete of the Application:

```
<?xml version="1.0" encoding="utf-8"?>
<mx:Application xmlns:mx="http://www.adobe.com/2006/mxml"
layout="vertical"
creationComplete="myHS.send();init()">

<mx:HTTPService id="myHS" url="data/users.xml"
 result="myAC = myHS.lastResult.users.user as ArrayCollection"
showBusyCursor="true"/>
```

The HTTPService service loads the data in the users.xml file, which you will create in the next step. On the result event, it populates a variable of ArrayCollection type with the response data.

On the creationComplete of the application, the service with the send() method is launched, and an init() function is called.

10. The users.xml file must be created in the data folder. Select File ➤ New ➤ File to create an XML file and save it as users.xml. This file should be saved in the data folder and will have the following structure:

```
<?xml version="1.0" standalone="yes"?>
<users>
<user>
<lastname>Marco</lastname>
<firstname>Casario</firstname>
<address>marco@email.com</address>
</user>
<user>
<lastname>Emanuele</lastname>
<firstname>Tatti</firstname>
<address>ema@email.com</address>
</user>
<user>
<lastname>Constantin</lastname>
<firstname>Moldovanu</firstname>
<address>constantin@email.com</address>
</user>
```

13

```
<user>
<lastname>Francesco</lastname>
<firstname>Rapana</firstname>
<address>francesco@email.com</address>
</user>
<user>
<lastname>Liviu</lastname>
<firstname>Stoica</firstname>
<address>liviu@email.com</address>
</user>
<user>
<lastname>Raffaele</lastname>
<firstname>Mannella</firstname>
<address>raffaele@email.com</address>
</user>
</users>
```

11. Under the HTTPService, insert the two elements of user interface: a Label and a List control:

```
<mx:Label text="Select a name on the List to view more info: " />
<mx:List id="myList" labelField="firstname"
dataProvider="{myAC}" />
</mx:Application>
```

The List control uses the variable myAC as dataProvider, the ArrayCollection populated by the response data from the HTTPService.

However, from the ArrayCollection only the labelField firstname is displayed. The values of lastname and address are not displayed.

12. You can add the <mx:Script> block and import the classes necessary to the file, declare the variable myAC, and write the init() function launched from the creationComplete of the application:

```
<mx:HTTPService id="myHS" url="data/users.xml"
 result="myAC = myHS.lastResult.users.user as ArrayCollection"
 showBusyCursor="true"/>

<mx:Script>
<![CDATA[
import mx.collections.ArrayCollection;
import mx.managers.PopUpManager;

import mx.core.IFlexDisplayObject;
import com.flexsolutions.chapter13.popup.DetailPopUp;

[Bindable]
private var myAC:ArrayCollection = new ArrayCollection();
```

```
private function init():void
{
myList.addEventListener( MouseEvent.CLICK, clickHandler );
}
```

Among the importation of the classes, there is also the custom component DetailPopUp, which contains the TitleWindow component that you created earlier. This component was, in fact, created in the package com.flexsolutions.chapter13.popup.

The init() function registers the click on an item on the List control with the addEventListener() method, linking it to the clickHandler() function. It is this function that will send the data to the pop-up window and provide the other details on the item selected by the user.

13. Immediately under the init() function, create the event handler clickHandler():

```
private function clickHandler( event:MouseEvent ):void
{
var myPopUp:IFlexDisplayObject = ➡
PupUpManager.createPopUp (this, DetailPopUp, true);
var myDetalPopUp:DetailPopUp = myPopUp as DetailPopUp;
var myTargetList:List = event.currentTarget as List;
var mySelectedListItem:Object = myTargetList.selectedItem;

myDetalPopUp.email = mySelectedListItem.address;
myDetalPopUp.firstname = mySelectedListItem.firstname;
myDetalPopUp.lastname = mySelectedListItem.lastname;

PopUpManager.centerPopUp( myPopUp );
}
]]>
</mx:Script>
```

The function begins by creating the myPopUp variable IFlexDisplayObject as type. The IFlexDisplayObject interface defines the interface for skin elements. The createPopUp method returns an IFlexDisplayObject as type:

```
createPopUp(parent:DisplayObject, 01
className:Class,
modal:Boolean = false,
childList:String = null):IFlexDisplayObject
```

Therefore, the myPopUp variable will contain the reference to the pop-up window. After creating it, use this variable to send the values corresponding to the item selected by the user to the three public variables defined in the pop-up:

```
DetailPopUp( myPopUp ).email =➡
List( event.currentTarget ).selectedItem.address;
DetailPopUp( myPopUp ).firstname =➡
List( event.currentTarget ).selectedItem.firstname;
DetailPopUp( myPopUp ).lastname =➡
List( event.currentTarget ).selectedItem.lastname;
```

13

In this way you send the data from the Application to the pop-up window.

The function concludes with the launch of the centerPopUp() method to center the window.

14. Save the file and run the application.

The data will be displayed in the List control. By selecting an item, the clickHandler function releases the pop-up window, to which the detailed data from the Application will be sent. Figure 13-9 shows the pop-up window opened with the information that has been sent to it from the List control in the application:

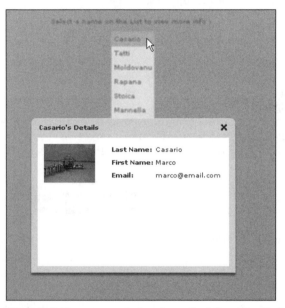

Figure 13-9. The pop-up window shows the information that has been sent to it by the selectedItem of the List control.

Expert tips

The PopUpManager class provides the addPopUp() method, which allows you to create pop-up windows with ActionScript without having to create MXML components. The addPopUp() method accepts the instance of the class that you intend to use as the content of the pop-up window as a parameter:

```
PopUpManager.addPopUp(myClassInstance, this, true);
```

Here is an example of a pop-up window created with the addPopUp() method. It is a simple window that contains a TextArea with Terms and Agreement, and a Button that permits the open window to be closed.

1. Create a new MXML application file by selecting File ➤ New ➤ MXML Application named Chapter_13_Flex_Sol_3_expert_Navigation.mxml. Immediately insert an `<mx:Script>` block, in which you will import the classes necessary to the example:

```
<mx:Application xmlns:mx="http://www.adobe.com/2006/mxml">
<mx:Script>
<![CDATA[
import mx.containers.TitleWindow;
iimport mx.controls.TextArea;
import flash.events.*;
import mx.managers.PopUpManager;
import mx.controls.Button;
import mx.core.IFlexDisplayObject;
```

2. Immediately under the importation of the classes, add the variable that will contain the instance of the TitleWindow, which will function as container for the elements of the pop-up:

```
private var myTitleContainer:TitleWindow = new TitleWindow();
```

3. Create the function that will be invoked when the button to open the window is pressed. The function must completely initialize and create all the contents of the pop-up window via ActionScript. When you create the components with ActionScript, you must assign the properties of width and height and use the addChild() method to add the component to the display list. Under the declaration of the variable myTitleContainer, add this event handler:

```
private function openWindow(event:MouseEvent):void {
myTitleContainer = new TitleWindow();
myTitleContainer.title = "Terms and Agreement";
myTitleContainer.width= 250;
myTitleContainer.height= 120;

var myTextArea:TextArea = new TextArea();
var myBtn:Button = new Button();

myBtn.label="close";
myTextArea.text = "You agree not to distribute the Website,
including but not limited to User Submissions without xxxxx's
 prior written authorization. You agree not to alter or modify
any part of the Website, including but not limited to xxxxx'
or any of its related technologies.";

myTitleContainer.addChild(myBtn);
myTitleContainer.addChild(myTextArea);

myBtn.addEventListener(MouseEvent.CLICK, closeHandler);

PopUpManager.addPopUp(myTitleContainer, this, true);
}
```

13

The width and height of the pop-up window are declared, and the title of the TitleWindow is specified. You then create a TextArea and a Button. The TextArea contains some simple text in its text property, while the button is needed to close the pop-up window.

The components are added in the TitleWindow with the addChild() method, and the addPopUp() method of the PopUpManager class is invoked. An event listener is created with the click of the button.

4. Under the closure of the openWindow() function, write the event handler closeHandler() that closes the window with the removePopUp() method:

```
private function closeHandler(event:MouseEvent):void
{
    PopUpManager.removePopUp(
                            event.currentTarget.parent);
}
        ]]>
</mx:Script>
```

5. The ActionScript code necessary to create the pop-up window is finished. You can now create the two elements of the user interface of the application:

```
<mx:Label text="Read and accept the Terms and Agreements window"/>
<mx:Button label="Open window" click="openWindow(event);"/>
</mx:Application>
```

6. Save and run the application.

In this "Expert tips" section, you saw how to use the addPopUp() method to create pop-ups at runtime. In fact, the PopUpManager class provides the addPopUp() method that allows you to create pop-up windows through ActionScript without having to create MXML components. This can be useful when you want to create dynamic contents to be shown in the window.

Solution 13-4: States and transitions using MXML and ActionScript

All Flex applications have at least one state, and the default state contains all of the contents used by the application. Flex allows you to nest content in states in a hierarchical structure.

States (or **view states**, as they are called by Flex) allow you to manage different views of the application in the same file. Through simple properties, it is possible to switch between one view and another, rendering portions of the page visible and invisible.

Furthermore, by using transitions, it is possible to add effects that will be applied in the changeover phase from one state to another. Besides adding pleasing visual effects, transitions allow you to provide a visual clue to the user and to concentrate attention on the part of the page that is undergoing the change.

In this solution, you will create a view state and apply a transition.

What's involved

To create a state in Flex, you can use Design mode of Flex Builder or define the new state via code (MXML or ActionScript).

With Design mode of Flex Builder, creating a state is very simple. From State view (on the top left, as shown in Figure 13-10), click the New State button to create a new state in the file.

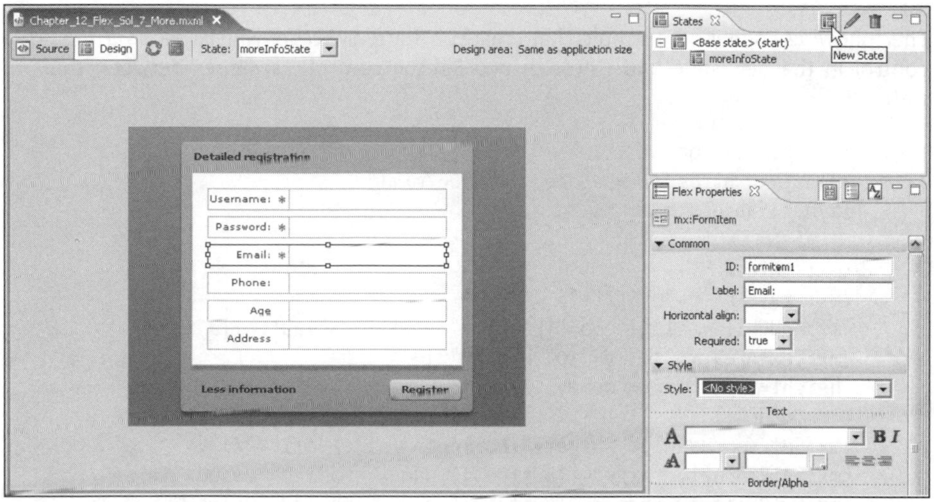

Figure 13-10. Use the New State button to create a new state.

Multiple states can be created in the page, but only one state can be displayed at a time (with the exception of Flex components defined in the default base state, which are always visible). To create a new state via MXML code, the <mx:State> tag is defined, to which a name is linked. To add elements in this state, the <mx:AddChild> tag is used, and you create the components to be added as nested tags. With the currentState property you specify the name of the state to render it visible.

A state uses the following elements to define the set of changes that must be applied:

- AddChild: Allows you to add new elements (controls and containers) to the state:

```
<mx:AddChild relativeTo="{panel1}" position="lastChild">
<mx:TextArea x="10" y="10" width="210"
 height="104" text="dummy text"/>
</mx:AddChild>
```

- RemoveChild: Allows you to remove elements in the passage from the old state to the new one.

- SetProperty: Allows you to act on the properties of the controls defined in the state:

```
<mx:SetProperty target="{button1}"
name="enabled" value="false"/>
```

- SetStyle: Allows you to modify the style for the elements present in the state:

```
<mx:SetStyle name="color" value="0xAAAAAA"/>
```

- SetEventHandler: Allows you to create and manage event handlers:

```
<mx:SetEventHandler target="{button2}"
name="click" handler="currentState=''"/>
```

The following code is an example that creates a state, myState, which inserts a TextArea control in the new state and (through two Button controls) switches between the two states:

```
<mx:Application
xmlns:mx="http://www.adobe.com/2006/mxml"
layout="absolute">

<mx:states>
<mx:State name="myState">
<mx:AddChild relativeTo="{panel1}" position="lastChild">
<mx:TextArea x="10" y="10" width="210"
 height="104" text="dummy text"/>
</mx:AddChild>
<mx:SetEventHandler target="{button1}" name="click"/>
<mx:SetProperty target="{button1}" name="enabled" value="false"/>
<mx:SetProperty target="{button2}" name="enabled" value="true"/>
<mx:SetEventHandler target="{button2}"
  name="click" handler="currentState=''"/>
</mx:State>
</mx:states>

<mx:Panel x="171" y="65" width="250" height="200"
layout="absolute" title="View States" id="panel1">

<mx:ControlBar id="controlbar1">
<mx:Button label="Show State" id="button1"
click="currentState='myState'"/>
<mx:Button label="Back" enabled="false" id="button2"/>
</mx:ControlBar>

</mx:Panel>

</mx:Application>
```

All these containers and controls are housed by the base state, so they will be visible across the child states.

The new state has been created with the <mx:State> tag, to which the name myState has been assigned. You have added a TextArea control with the <mx:AddChild> tag, and you have changed some of the properties of the elements that were contained in the first state. To act on and edit the properties and the events of controls in the states, use the <mx:SetEventHandler> and <mx:SetProperty> tags. In particular, the click of the Button control events is changed and properties enabled:

```
<mx:State name="myState">
<mx:AddChild relativeTo="{panel1}" position="lastChild">
<mx:TextArea x="10" y="10" width="210" height="104" text="dummy text"/>
</mx:AddChild>
<mx:SetEventHandler target="{button1}" name="click"/>
<mx:SetProperty target="{button1}" name="enabled" value="false"/>
```

To change and render the new state visible, use the currentState property on the click of the button:

```
<mx:Button label="Show State" id="button1"
  click="currentState='myState'"/>
```

To return to the first state, called the base state, all you need to do is set the currentState property to an empty value. This operation must be carried out by the second Button that (with the Back label and the event) must release when you find yourself on the myState state. For this reason, the event has been managed on the button with the <mx:SetEventHandler> tag in the definition of the state:

```
<mx:SetEventHandler target="{button2}"
name="click" handler="currentState=''"/>
```

Figure 13-11 shows the final result of the example.

Figure 13-11.
In the base state, the Back button is disabled, while it is possible to switch to the new state by clicking the Show State button.

The transitions allow you to define and specify effects applied to the changing of the view states. To create a transition, use the effect classes that can also be grouped together to apply complex transitions. To define a transition, use the <mx:Transition> tag; to create multiple transitions, you must specify every single effect in the <mx:Transitions> tag. Furthermore, for every transition, you must specify the following properties:

- fromState: Specifies the starting state that is changing. The default value is *, which means that any state is specified as starting state.

- toState: Specifies the state to which it is changing. The default value is *, which means that any state is specified as arrival state.

- effect: Represents the Effect object to run when the transition is applied.

To apply multiple transitions (known as composite effects), you can use the Sequence and Parallel tags. Parallel effect means that the effects play at the same time, while Sequence effect means that one effect has to stop before the new one is loaded.

The code in bold adds a transition effect, applied as a sequence of Blur effects on the Panel and Button elements:

```
<mx:Application xmlns:mx="http://www.adobe.com/2006/mxml"
  layout="absolute">
<mx:states>
<mx:State name="myState">
<mx:AddChild relativeTo="{panel1}" position="lastChild">
<mx:TextArea x="10" y="10" width="210"
 height="104" text="dummy text"/>
</mx:AddChild>
<mx:SetEventHandler target="{button1}" name="click"/>
<mx:SetProperty target="{button1}" name="enabled" value="false"/>
<mx:SetProperty target="{button2}" name="enabled" value="true"/>
<mx:SetEventHandler target="{button2}"
  name="click" handler="currentState=''"/>
</mx:State>
</mx:states>
<mx:transitions>
<mx:Transition id="myTransition" fromState="*" toState="*">
<mx:Sequence id="t1" targets="{[panel1,button1,button2]}">
 <mx:Blur duration="100"
blurXFrom="0.0" blurXTo="10.0" blurYFrom="0.0" blurYTo="10.0"/>
<mx:Blur duration="100"
blurXFrom="10.0" blurXTo="0.0" blurYFrom="10.0" blurYTo="0.0"/>
</mx:Sequence>
</mx:Transition>
</mx:transitions>

<mx:Panel x="171" y="65" width="250" height="200"
layout="absolute" title="View States" id="panel1">
<mx:ControlBar id="controlbar1">
<mx:Button label="Show State" id="button1"
  click="currentState='myState'"/>
<mx:Button label="Back" enabled="false" id="button2"/>
</mx:ControlBar>
</mx:Panel>
</mx:Application>
```

In this solution you will see how to use the states and the transition to provide a different procedure of registration according to the type of user who is using the application.

How to build it

The application is made up of a registration form that offers the possibility of two levels of data insertion. The first level prompts users to insert their username, password, and e-mail address. By clicking a button, it is possible to also provide phone number, age, and city. This second level of data insertion is managed through a state to which transition effects are also applied.

1. Create a new file by selecting File ➤ New ➤ MXML Application and save it as Chapter_13_Flex_Sol_4_Navigation.mxml. Insert a Panel in the file:

```
<?xml version="1.0" encoding="utf-8"?>
<mx:Application xmlns:mx="http://www.adobe.com/2006/mxml"
verticalAlign="middle" width="400" height="300">

<mx:Panel title="Registration" id="registrationPanel">
</mx:Panel>
```

2. Insert a ControlBar container in the Panel and define a LinkButton control and a Button in it. On the click of the first button, the new state that you will create using the currentState property will be loaded:

```
<mx:Panel title="Registration" id="registrationPanel">

<mx:ControlBar>
<mx:LinkButton label="Add more information" id="moreInfoLink"
click="currentState='moreInfoState'" />

<mx:Spacer width="100%" id="spacer"/>

<mx:Button label="Register" id="registerButton"/>
</mx:ControlBar>

</mx:Panel>
```

At the click, the LinkButton loads and switches from the base state to the state with the name equal to moreInfoState. This new state will contain other TextInput controls for inserting information.

The <mxSpacer> tag is needed to insert a horizontal space between the two buttons inserted in the ControlBar.

3. Insert a Form container in the Panel container with three TextInput controls:

```
<mx:Form id="registrationForm">
<mx:FormItem label="Username:" required="true">
<mx:TextInput />
</mx:FormItem>
```

```
<mx:FormItem label="Password:" required="true">
    <mx:TextInput displayAsPassword="true" />
</mx:FormItem>
<mx:FormItem label="EMail:" required="true" id="formitem1">
<mx:TextInput />
</mx:FormItem>
</mx:Form>
```

4. You can now create the new state. Use Design mode of Flex Builder, which you can access by clicking the Design button in Editor view, as shown in Figure 13-12.

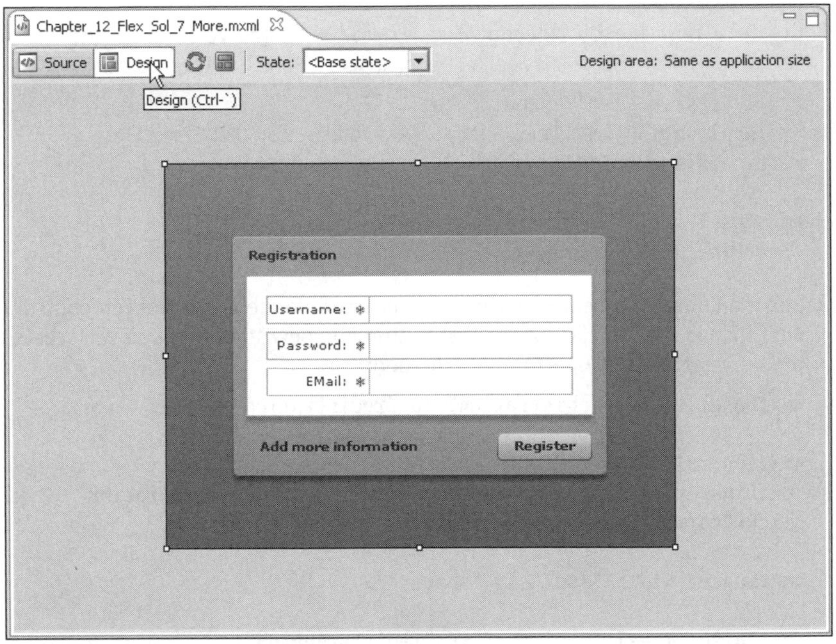

![Screenshot of Flex Builder Design mode showing a Registration form with Username, Password, and EMail fields, an "Add more information" link and a Register button.]

Figure 13-12. To move to Design mode, click the Design button in Editor view.

5. Having moved on to Design mode, you can access the State view on the top left and click the New State icon. The New State window opens, as shown in Figure 13-13. Insert the moreInfoState value in the Name field and click OK.

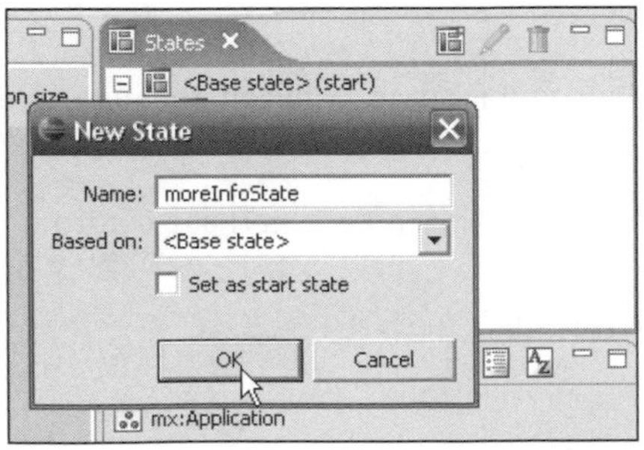

Figure 13-13.
The State view allows you to create a new state in a Flex application.

You have now created a new state.

6. After selecting `moreInfoState` in State view, add three `TextInput` controls within the `Form` container defined in the base state. Remaining in Design mode, you can drag them from the Component view directly onto the state. Follow successive operations directly from `Design` view:

> Change the title of the `Panel` container, inserting Detailed registration as its value.
>
> Remove the `LinkButton` on this state (you don't want to use the `LinkButton` inserted in the base state) and drag a new one by inserting the value Less information in the label. At the click event of the new `LinkButton`, reload the base state, sending an empty value to the `currentState` property.

If you now click Code mode to display the code that Flex Builder has written, you should see the following code for the creation of the state:

```
<mx:states>
<mx:State name="moreInfoState">
<mx:AddChild relativeTo="{registrationForm}"
position="lastChild" creationPolicy="all">
<mx:FormItem id="phoneItem" label="Phone:" required="false">
<mx:TextInput />
</mx:FormItem>
</mx:AddChild>

<mx:SetProperty target="{registrationPanel}" name="title"
value="Detailed registration"/>

<mx:RemoveChild target="{moreInfoLink}" />
<mx:AddChild relativeTo="{spacer}" position="before">
<mx:LinkButton label="Less information" click="currentState=''" />
</mx:AddChild>
<mx:AddChild relativeTo="{registrationForm}" position="lastChild">
<mx:FormItem label="Age">
    <mx:TextInput/>
</mx:FormItem>
</mx:AddChild>
<mx:AddChild relativeTo="{registrationForm}" position="lastChild">
<mx:FormItem label="Address">
    <mx:TextInput/>
</mx:FormItem>
</mx:AddChild>
<mx:SetProperty target="{formitem1}" name="label" value="Email:"/>
</mx:State>
</mx:states>
```

If you note any difference, you can simply make changes by hand in the code itself.

The new state is created and should show the elements like those shown in Figure 13-14.

13

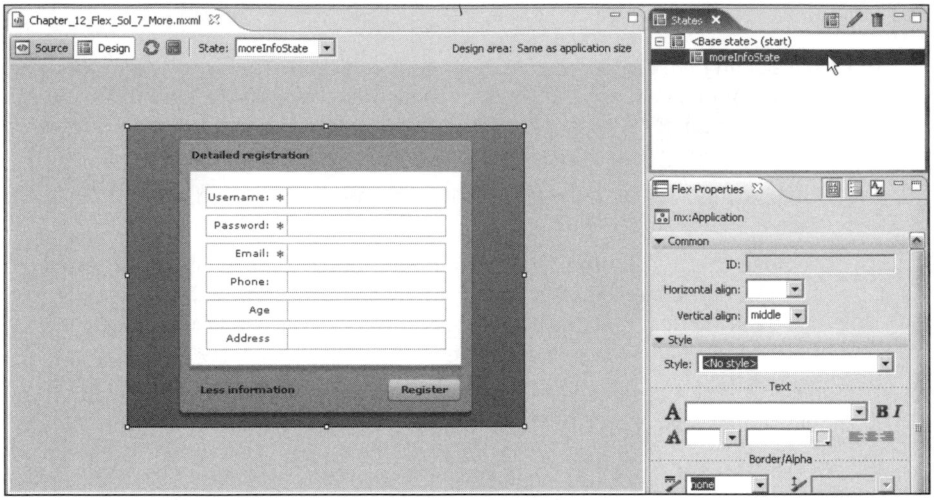

Figure 13-14. The new Flex controls are visible in the new state.

If you run the file by clicking the LinkButton in the ControlBar container with the label equal to Add more information, the state is loaded because you have already written the change on the currentState property on the click of the button:

```
<mx:ControlBar>
<mx:LinkButton label="Add more information" id="moreInfoLink"
click="currentState='moreInfoState'" />
```

7. Add a transition on the switch. The effect will have the task of creating a pleasing movement on the Panel and of making the TextInput controls visible. You will, therefore, use multiple transitions with a Parallel effect of Resize type and a Sequence on the Dissolve and Glow effects. Immediately after the closure of the </mx:states> tag, insert the transition:

```
</mx:states>

<mx:transitions>
<mx:Transition fromState="*" toState="*">
<!-- parallel effects -->
<mx:Parallel targets="➡
{[registrationPanel, moreInfoLink, registerButton, phoneItem]}">
<mx:Resize duration="500" easingFunction="Bounce.easeOut"/>
<!-- sequence effects on the added form item -->
<mx:Sequence target="{phoneItem}">
<mx:Dissolve duration="1000" alphaFrom="0.0" alphaTo="1.0" />
<mx:Glow duration="1000"
```

```
    alphaFrom="1.0" alphaTo="0.0"
    blurXFrom="30" blurXTo="0"
    blurYFrom="30" blurYTo="0" />
    </mx:Sequence>
    </mx:Parallel>
    </mx:Transition>
    </mx:transitions>
    </mx:Application>
```

The transition is applied when one state changes to another. In fact, the fromState and toState properties have been set with the value *:

```
    <mx:Transition fromState="*" toState="*">
```

The Resize effect is applied to the Panel control, to the LinkButton, to the register Button, and to the TextInput phoneItem through the Parallel tag, which allows you to specify different components to which to apply the same effect:

```
    <mx:Parallel targets="{[registrationPanel,
                                moreInfoLink,
                                registerButton,
                                phoneItem]}">

    <mx:Resize duration="500"
    easingFunction="Bounce.easeOut"/>
```

In the easingFunction property, you have used the Bounce class to apply an easeOut effect. The class will be imported in ActionScript in the next step.

In the <mx:Parallel> tag, an <mx:Sequence> tag has been inserted that is applied to the phoneItem control. Apply a Dissolve and Glow effect to this TextInput control, which will focus the attention of the user on the new information to be inserted:

```
    <mx:Sequence target="{phoneItem}">
    <mx:Dissolve duration="1000"
    alphaFrom="0.0" alphaTo="1.0" />
    <mx:Glow duration="1000"
    alphaFrom="1.0" alphaTo="0.0"
    blurXFrom="30" blurXTo="0"
    blurYFrom="30" blurYTo="0" />
    </mx:Sequence>
    </mx:Parallel>
```

Figure 13-15 shows the effect that is applied to the TextInput control.

13

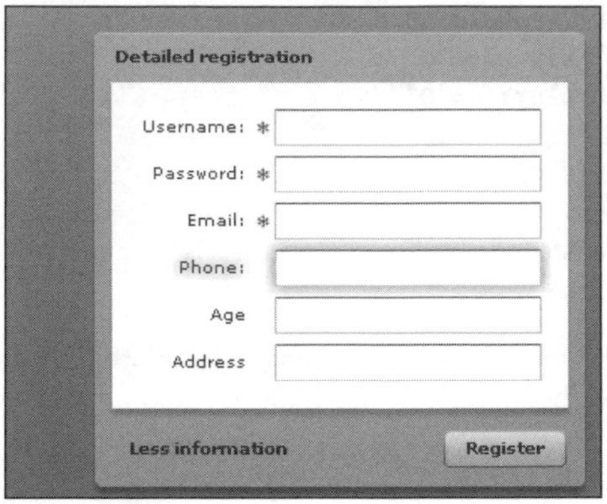

Figure 13-15. The elements are visible in the new state.

Before running the application, you must import the Bounce class that is used by the Resize effect.

8. Insert an `<mx:Script>` block immediately under the Application, in which you will simply import the Bounce class from the package `mx.effects.easing`:

```
<mx:Script>
<![CDATA[
import mx.effects.easing.Bounce;
]]>
</mx:Script>
```

9. You can now save the file and run the application.

After the link button is clicked, the Panel opens with an effect showing the TextInput controls contained in the new state.

Expert tips

View states and transitions can also be applied and used by way of ActionScript. The choice of using MXML or ActionScript obviously depends on the project, but brings about the same result.

Write the same solution as before, but create the states and the transition effects using only ActionScript code.

1. Create a new MXML file by selecting File ➤ New ➤ MXML Application and save it as Chapter_13_Flex_Sol_4_expert_Navigation.mxml. Add an event listener to the creationComplete event of the Application:

```
<?xml version="1.0" encoding="utf-8"?>
<mx:Application xmlns:mx="http://www.adobe.com/2006/mxml"
layout="vertical" creationComplete="onCreationComplete(event)">
```

2. Add an <mx:Script> block to import all the classes that you need. Because you have to manage both the states and the transitions, there are many classes that you have to import. Add the following code immediately under the <mx:Application> tag:

```
<mx:Script>
<![CDATA[
import mx.effects.Sequence;
import mx.effects.Glow;
import mx.effects.Dissolve;
import mx.effects.Resize;
import mx.effects.Parallel;
import mx.containers.FormItem;
import mx.states.Transition;
import mx.states.RemoveChild;
import mx.states.SetProperty;
import mx.controls.TextInput;
import mx.states.AddChild;
import mx.states.State;
import mx.events.FlexEvent;
import mx.effects.easing.Bounce;
```

Considering that you have to define the controls via ActionScript, it is also necessary to import the classes of the Flex controls and containers that you will create: TextInput and FormItem classes.

3. Immediately under the importation of the classes, add a variable typed as FormItem, which you set as null and will be the container for the TextInput control:

```
private var _phoneItem:FormItem = null;
```

You can now create the event handler onCreationComplete(). This function takes the event object created from the FlexEvent class as parameter and has the task of creating the view state.

4. Add the event handler onCreationComplete() under the declaration of the variable _phoneItem:

```
 private function onCreationComplete(event:FlexEvent):void
{
super.states = new Array();
super.states.push(createMoreInfoState());

super.transitions = new Array();
super.transitions.push(createMoreInfoTransition());
}
```

The function creates an Array of states and one of the transitions to which, using the push method, it adds the result of the functions createMoreInfoState() and createMoreInfoTransition():

```
super.states.push(createMoreInfoState());
super.transitions.push(createMoreInfoTransition());
```

13

5. Add the createMoreInfoState() function that adds a State object to the Array state that represents the view state:

```
private function createMoreInfoState():State
{
var myState:State = new State();
myState.name = "moreInfoState";
myState.overrides = new Array();// array of IOverride

// create phone form item:
_phoneItem = new FormItem();
_phoneItem.label = "Phone:";
_phoneItem.required = false;
_phoneItem.addChild(new TextInput());

// create a link button:
var linkButton:LinkButton = new LinkButton();
linkButton.label = "Less information";
linkButton.addEventListener(MouseEvent.CLICK, linkButtonHandler);

// define state:
myState.overrides.push(new AddChild(➥
registrationForm, _phoneItem, "lastChild"));
myState.overrides.push(new SetProperty(➥
registrationPanel, "label", "Detailed Registration"));
myState.overrides.push(new RemoveChild(moreInfoLink));
myState.overrides.push(new AddChild(spacer, linkButton, "before"));

return myState;
}
```

The function returns a State object. After creating the state, you have to assign it a name using the name property: state.name = "moreInfoState". You then create an Array of overrides. The view states are override objects that implement the IOverride interface. All entries in the State class overrides property array must implement this interface:

```
var state:State = new State();
state.name = "moreInfoState";
state.overrides = new Array();
```

The TextInput is then created, which is added with the addchild() method in the FormItem object, and a LinkButton is created. This latter, with the addEventListener() method, creates an event listener on the click event:

```
_phoneItem = new FormItem();
_phoneItem.label = "Phone:";
_phoneItem.required = false;
_phoneItem.addChild(new TextInput());
```

```
var linkButton:LinkButton = new LinkButton();
linkButton.label = "Less information";
linkButton.addEventListener(MouseEvent.CLICK, linkButtonHandler);
```

Finally, the function concludes with the creation of the state that is returned as a value to the function:

```
state.overrides.push(new AddChild(➥
registrationForm, _phoneItem, "lastChild"));
state.overrides.push(new SetProperty(➥
registrationPanel, "label", "Detailed Registration"));
state.overrides.push(new RemoveChild(moreInfoLink));
state.overrides.push(new AddChild(spacer, linkButton, "before"));
return state;
```

6. After the closure of the createMoreInfoState() function, create the event handler linked to the click event of the LinkButton. This function has the sole task of retuning to the initial state, setting the currentState property with an empty value:

```
private function linkButtonHandler(event:MouseEvent):void
{
this.currentState = "";
}
```

7. You have concluded the code relative to the creation of the new state. You can now move on to the function that will take care of applying the transition when the state changes. Add the createMoreInfoTransition() function under the linkButtonHandler() function:

```
private function createMoreInfoTransition():Transition
{
var t:Transition = new Transition();
t.fromState = "*";
t.toState = "*";

// create resize effect:
var resize:Resize = new Resize();
resize.duration = 500;
resize.easingFunction = Bounce.easeOut;

// create dissolve effect:
var dissolve:Dissolve = new Dissolve();
dissolve.duration = 1000;
dissolve.alphaFrom = 0.0;
dissolve.alphaTo = 1.0;

// create glow effect:
var glow:Glow = new Glow();
glow.duration = 1000;
glow.alphaFrom = 0.8;
```

13

```
        glow.alphaTo = 0.0;
        glow.blurXFrom = 10;
        glow.blurXTo = 0;
        glow.blurYFrom = 10;
        glow.blurYTo = 0;

        // create parallel effect:
        var parallel:Parallel = new Parallel();
        parallel.targets =➡
        [registrationPanel, moreInfoLink, registerButton, _phoneItem];

        // create sequence effect:
        var sequence:Sequence = new Sequence(_phoneItem);

        // mix together all the effects:
        sequence.addChild(dissolve);
        sequence.addChild(glow);
        parallel.addChild(resize);
        parallel.addChild(sequence);

        // add the combined effect to the transition:
        t.effect = parallel;

        return t;
        }
        ]]>
        </mx:Script>
```

The function returns a Transition object. Similar to when you created the transition effect in MXML, you must define the type of effect (also in ActionScript); an instance of the Parallel class, parallel, to create multiple transitions; an instance of the Sequence class, sequence, to create the Sequence effect; and then apply the effects with the addChild() method as if they were components.

The <mx:Script> block is finished. You have written all the ActionScript code necessary to create, define, and apply a transition effect to the states.

8. The MXML part is the same as in the previous solution. Add the following MXML code that defines the base state:

```
<mx:Panel title="Registration" id="registrationPanel">
<mx:Form id="registrationForm">
<mx:FormItem label="Username:" required="true">
<mx:TextInput />
</mx:FormItem>
<mx:FormItem label="Password:" required="true">
<mx:TextInput displayAsPassword="true" />
</mx:FormItem>
<mx:FormItem label="EMail:" required="true">
<mx:TextInput />
```

```
        </mx:FormItem>
        </mx:Form>

        <mx:ControlBar>
        <mx:LinkButton label="Add more information" id="moreInfoLink"
        click="currentState='moreInfoState'" />

        <mx:Spacer width="100%" id="spacer"/>
        <mx:Button label="Register" id="registerButton"/>
        </mx:ControlBar>
        </mx:Panel>
        </mx:Application>
```

9. Save the file and run the application.

The final result is the same as that obtained with the solution written in MXML, but this time you have declared state and transition effects using ActionScript language.

Solution 13-5: Moving within a Tree control using E4X

Chapter 7 discussed the Tree control and about how it is used to view hierarchical data. Imagine using a Tree control to represent the hierarchical tree of the people who make up a company. The people are arranged in groups that are located in a node of the tree, according to their area. In this kind of scenario, it becomes very useful to be able to search for particular nodes in the Tree control.

The Tree represents a data descriptor to parse and manipulate the data. You can create the following types of data descriptor to represent data in the Tree:

- XML: a valid string containing XML code (<mx:XML> or <mx:XMLList>)
- Objects: Array, an Array of objects or Object that contain an Array of items whose children are within an item named children
- Collections: Any object that implements the interface IcollectionView: ArrayCollection or XMLListCollection

Through the use of the E4X standard (refer to Solution 6-4), you can now parse the data represented in the Tree control by applying search criteria.

In this solution, you will see how to search for names of the resources represented in the Tree control by inserting the search parameters in a TextInput control.

What's involved

To populate a Tree control, you can use various data descriptors. In this solution you will use an XMLList format from the following elements:

```
<mx:XMLList id="data">
<node>
<node name="YouThru.com">
<node name="Emanuele"
surname="Tatti" age="23" wage="1200"/>
<node name="Francesco"
surname="Rapana " age="22" wage="1000"/>
<node name="Constantin"
 surname="Moldovanu" age="23" wage="1200"/>
 <node name="Marco"
surname="Casario" age="29" wage="1500"/>
</node>
<node name="Acme spa">
<node name="John"
surname="Doe" age="32" wage="900"/>
<node name="Max"
surname="Power" age="28" wage="1500"/>
<node name="Homer"
surname="Simpsons" age="48" wage="200"/>
</node>
<node name="Comtaste Corp.">
<node name="Marco"
surname="Casario" age="29" wage="1500"/>
<node name="Raffaele"
surname="Mannella" age="45" wage="1500"/>
<node name="Liviu"
surname="Stoica" age="25" wage="1300"/>
</node>
</node>
</mx:XMLList>
```

The XMLList defines a valid XML made up of element nodes and the @name attributes sur-name and age. This XMLList will be sent to the Tree through its dataProvider property and by specifying the labelField to link the data to be displayed in the control:

```
<mx:Tree id="tree" width="100%" height="100%"
showRoot="false"
dataProvider="{data}" labelField="@name" />
```

Figure 13-16 shows the Tree control populated by data. As you can see, the values con-tained in the @name attribute of the XMLList are displayed as labels.

To carry out a search in the Tree control, use the E4X standard that allows simplified access with respect to the XML Object class of ActionScript for parsing the XML data.

Referring to the XMLList object defined previously, you can use the following code to remove all the values of the @name attributes in the node tags:

```
var myItems:XMLList = data.node.node.@name;
```

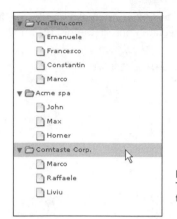

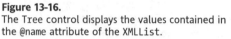

Figure 13-16.
The Tree control displays the values contained in
the @name attribute of the XMLList.

This code, instead, returns only the nodes that have the string Comtaste Corp as a value in
the @name attribute:

```
var searchStr:String = "Comtaste Corp";
var itemNames:XMLList =
data.node.node.(@name == searchStr);
```

With these few lines you have managed to apply a little search function to the content of
the XMLList.

However, once the value is found in the Tree control, you must expand the node that has
returned the search. In this way, you render the result of the search visible to the user,
highlighting the node found.

To carry out operations of opening and closing items in a Tree, you can use the following
methods:

- expandChildrenOf(item:Object, open:Boolean):void: This method is used to
  open or close all the items in a tree below the specified item.

- expandItem(item:Object, open:Boolean, animate:Boolean = false,
  dispatchEvent:Boolean = false, cause:Event = null):void: This method is
  used to open or close a branch item.

- isItemOpen(item:Object):Boolean: This method is used to return the Boolean
  true if the item branch specified is open.

In this solution you will see how to use the text inserted in a TextInput control to search
for that item in a Tree control.

How to build it

To manage the print function, it is necessary to instance the FlexPrintJob class, adding a
content to be printed and invoking its start() method.

1. Create a new file by selecting File ➤ New ➤ MXML Application and save it as Chapter_13_Flex_Sol_5_Navigation.mxml. Immediately insert the XMLList tag with the following structure:

```
<mx:Application xmlns:mx="http://www.adobe.com/2006/mxml"
layout="vertical" verticalAlign="middle">

<mx:XMLList id="data">
<node>
<node name="YouThru.com">
<node name="Emanuele"
surname="Tatti" age="23" wage="1200"/>
<node name="Francesco"
surname="Rapana " age="22" wage="1000"/>
<node name="Constantin"
 surname="Moldovanu" age="23" wage="1200"/>
 <node name="Marco"
surname="Casario" age="29" wage="1500"/>
</node>
<node name="Acme spa">
<node name="John"
surname="Doe" age="32" wage="900"/>
<node name="Max"
surname="Power" age="28" wage="1500"/>
<node name="Homer"
surname="Simpsons" age="48" wage="200"/>
</node>
<node name="Comtaste Corp.">
<node name="Marco"
surname="Casario" age="29" wage="1500"/>
<node name="Raffaele"
surname="Mannella" age="45" wage="1500"/>
<node name="Liviu"
surname="Stoica" age="25" wage="1300"/>
</node>
</node>
</mx:XMLList>
```

2. Under the closure of the <mx:XMLList> tag, insert a Panel and the Tree control in which you link the XML list to the dataProvider:

```
<mx:Panel title="Tree Search" height="100%" width="100%">
<mx:Tree id="tree" width="100%" height="100%"
showRoot="false" dataProvider="{data}" labelField="@name" />
</mx:Panel>
```

The Tree control uses the labelField property to specify the @name attribute that it uses as a label for the nodes to be displayed.

3. In the Panel, add an HBox container with the TextInput control and a Button:

```
<mx:Panel title="Tree Search" height="100%" width="100%">
<mx:HBox width="100%">
<mx:TextInput id="searchNameInput" />
<mx:Button label="Search by name" click="findByName(event)" />
</mx:HBox>
<mx:Tree id="tree" width="100%" height="100%"
showRoot="false" dataProvider="{data}" labelField="@name" />
</mx:Panel>
```

The TextInput control will be needed by the user to insert the search string, while the Button will launch the findByName() function that carries out the search for that string in the Tree control.

4. Insert the <mx:Script> block immediately under the <mx:Application> tag to create the findByName() function. This function will use E4X standard to search for the string inserted by the user in the TextInput and will expand the Tree on the node that is returned by the search:

```
<mx:Application xmlns:mx="http://www.adobe.com/2006/mxml"
layout="vertical" verticalAlign="middle">

<mx:Script>
<![CDATA[
import mx.controls.Alert;
 import mx.collections.XMLListCollection;

 [Bindable]
private var searchResult:XMLList;
private var searchResultIndex:uint = 0;

private function findByName(event:MouseEvent):void
{
var searchStr:String = searchNameInput.text;

if (searchStr.length == 0) {
Alert.show("Provide a search string.");
return;
}

tree.expandChildrenOf(data[0], false);

searchResult = data.node.node.(
   @name.toLowerCase().search(
   searchStr.toLowerCase()) > -1);
searchResultIndex = 0;

if (searchResult[searchResultIndex] != undefined)
expandNode(searchResult[searchResultIndex]);
}
```

13

The function takes the text value inserted in the TextInput and uses it to carry out the search in the XMLList, which is the dataProvider of the Tree control.

Using E4X, search inside the nodes of the XMLList and insert the result of the search in a variable:

```
searchResult = data.node.node.(@name.toLowerCase().search(

searchStr.toLowerCase()) > -1);
searchResultIndex = 0;
```

If the search returns a value and is, therefore, different from undefined, at least one result has been found, and the expandNode() function is invoked:

```
if (searchResult[searchResultIndex] != undefined)
{
expandNode(searchResult[searchResultIndex]);
}
}
```

The expandNode() function that you will add in the next step expands the Tree control on the node returned by the search.

5. Add the expandNode() function after the closure of the findByName() function:

```
private function expandNode(xmlNode:XML):void
{
while (xmlNode.parent() != null) {
xmlNode = xmlNode.parent();
tree.expandItem(xmlNode, true, false);
tree.selectedItem = searchResult[searchResultIndex];
}
}
]]>
</mx:Script>
```

This function accepts node items of the XMLList as value and creates a loop until it finds the value of the node:

```
while (xmlNode.parent() != null) {
```

In this loop it enters into the values of the Tree control, expands the item, and selects the node:

```
tree.expandItem(xmlNode, true, false);
tree.selectedItem = searchResult[searchResultIndex];
```

6. Save the file and run the application.

Insert a value in the TextInput control (be sure that it is present in the Tree control) and click the button. If the value is found in the Tree control, it will be opened and selected, as shown in Figure 13-17.

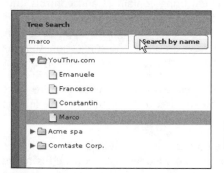

Figure 13-17.
If the outcome result is positive in a search, the Tree control is opened and the node is selected.

Expert tips

With a few small changes, you can create a function that searches for all entries in the Tree control that match some rules. For example, you can filter the data using two strings and expand the nodes of the Tree that match the criteria.

Have a look at the following code:

```
var filterBy:String = "name";
var filterValue:String = "Wii";

var items:XMLList = data.item.(attribute(filterBy) == filterValue);
```

The two variables, filterBy and filterValue, set the two criteria to apply to the data. The items variable, typed as XMLList, contains the result items that match the filters applied. You used the E4X standard to apply the filter to the data.

Now you can add the findNext() function in the ActionScript code to expand the next node that matches the criteria:

```
private function findNext(event:MouseEvent):void
{
// collapse tree:
tree.expandChildrenOf(data[searchResultIndex], false);
// search forward:
searchResultIndex += 1;

if (searchResult[searchResultIndex] != undefined)
expandNode(searchResult[searchResultIndex]);
}
```

13

Summary

User navigation is a crucial aspect of application design. The Flex framework gives developers the ability to create complex user interaction using containers and controls, thus reducing programming complexity. Flex applications and web applications can be made up of many objects that the user can interact with to navigate through the application. The Navigator container allows users to navigate and move around in the application, showing the different elements of the user interface according to the path that the user has chosen.

In this chapter, you learned how Navigator containers work and how to use the more common Navigator containers to be able to enable the user to navigate and move around inside a Flex application.

You then used the PopUpManager class to create pop-up windows in applications. In Flex, the concept of **pop-up** is slightly different: the pop-up window that is opened is found inside the application and is therefore rendered to the screen by Flash Player. A pop-up in Flex is not a new instance of a window of the browser, like a traditional pop-up, so it will bypass browser pop-up blockers.

You also looked at states and transitions. All Flex applications have at least one state. The default state contains all the contents used by the application. Flex allows you to nest contents in a hierarchy structure. View states, as they are called in Flex, allow you to manage different views of the application in the same file. You learned that by setting simple properties it is possible to switch between a view state and another, rendering portions of the page visible and invisible.

Finally, you explored methods that allow you to search for names of the resources represented in a Tree control, by inserting the search parameters in a TextInput control.

In the next chapter you'll learn how to port Flex web applications to the desktop using the new Adobe AIR cross-platform desktop runtime.

14 MIGRATING FLEX APPLICATIONS ON THE DESKTOP WITH ADOBE AIR

One of the characteristics of Rich Internet Applications (RIAs) developed with Flex is that they actually act as client-side applications. In fact, an RIA, after having been requested by users by launching the URL on a common browser, is downloaded onto the client and resides on the client for its entire life cycle. The interfaces created for RIAs are very rich and user-friendly, and many of the operations you use for desktop applications can also be developed for this type of application. For example, in Solutions 7-6 and 7-7, you saw that the classic operations of drag and drop are simple and quick to manage. The difference between a client-side application and a desktop application is small. The main reason why an RIA cannot be considered a desktop application is that it is loaded and run within the Flash Player that is a plug-in of the browser. This difference prevents the developer from using some of the functions that are native to desktop applications and very useful for most projects. The access to the file system to load, save, and edit local files, and the possibility of changing the appearance of the windows of the operating system are impossible because of the nature of RIAs.

Flex Builder 3 permits you to export the applications in Adobe Integrated Runtime (AIR) format, the new format from Adobe for loading RIAs outside of the browser and launching them as desktop applications.

Adobe AIR is a system of runtime cross-platforms (independent of the operating system) that permits developers to bring their knowledge of creating RIAs for the Web (Flash, Flex, HTML, JavaScript, Ajax) onto the desktop. The Adobe AIR project has the objective of bringing web applications from the Web to the desktop in a way that merges the best characteristics of both development worlds.

Therefore, developers can migrate their applications created for the Web and render them usable offline, meaning they can also use functions such as access to the file system and support of system window programming. And all this is in a context that is completely independent of the operating system. Adobe AIR will, in fact, be available for Windows, Mac OS X, and Linux environments.

Developing and exporting a desktop application using Adobe AIR is very simple and does not require learning a new language or development environment. In fact, Adobe AIR can run software created using Flex, Flash, or XHTML/JavaScript technologies, enabling them to use all the features of a classic desktop application.

To produce an application with Adobe AIR, you can use one of the following methods:

- Create it exclusively in Flex (or Flash)
- Base it on Flash, but with some content in HTML
- Create it using the classic HTML plus CSS and JavaScript
- Create it in HTML with Flash content
- Create it in one of the previous ways, but use the support of PDF

Adobe AIR runtime also includes an HTML and JavaScript engine: WebKit. This allows it to load entire HTML pages, also with complex JavaScript features.

WebKit is an open source web browser engine used by Safari for Mac OS X, and it adheres strongly to the web standards proposed by the Worldwide Web Consortium (W3C), such as CSS, XHTML, and JavaScript.

One strong point is the reduced size at runtime, thanks to its optimized code and without being affected much by the final weight of the application. It means that future AIR applications could be ported onto mobile devices because the WebKit engine itself has already been ported onto such devices.

Adobe's choice of basing it on an already existing engine instead of creating its own was because of the value of being able to exploit the work of a wide community of developers and companies (such as Apple) that keep their products updated. From Adobe's side, it can concentrate exclusively on the possible bugs of its platform and contribute to the improvement of the WebKit itself through the feedback of its users.

In this chapter, you will concentrate on creating AIR applications using the Flex Builder environment to be able to export an application in AIR format and launch it from a common desktop.

To run any Adobe AIR application, the AIR runtime is required to be installed on the client's machine. The runtime is totally free and it can be downloaded from Adobe's site: http://adobe.com/products/air.

You will see how to customize the OS windows, how to read and write a local file housed on the client, how to develop occasionally connected software detecting network connectivity, and how to keep the application updated.

Solution 14-1: Exporting a Flex application for the desktop

The Adobe AIR runtime lets developers use Flex technology to build applications that deploy to the desktop. Using your existing Flex 3 skills and the Flex Builder 3 tool, you'll be able to take advantage of the desktop capabilities of Adobe AIR to deploy the application to the desktop.

To create AIR applications you can use Flex Builder 3 and the Flex 3 SDK with the AIR APIs that the desktop runtime provides.

In this solution, you will use Flex Builder 3 and its integrated system to create and package Adobe AIR projects. Flex Builder 3, in fact, allows you to use a simple wizard to create an AIR project and an environment to test and debug AIR applications.

14

What's involved

Before creating an AIR application, you must have Flex 3 Software Development Kit (SDK) or Flex Builder 3 installed, and Adobe AIR installed at runtime.

At this point you can create your first AIR application, and Flex Builder 3 provides a wizard to create this type of project. There are a few differences, depending on whether Flex Builder 3 has been installed as a plug-in of Eclipse or in stand-alone mode. In the first case, to create an AIR project, the AIR Project option is found under the menu File ➤ New ➤ Other. From the window that opens, go to the Flex folder and choose AIR Project, as shown in Figure 14-1.

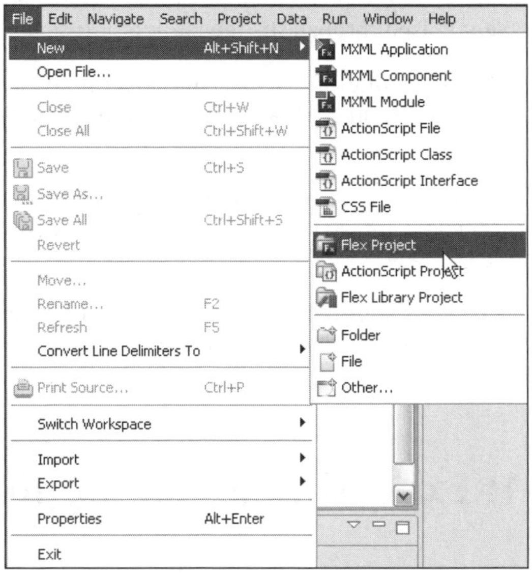

Figure 14-1. Creating an AIR project from Flex Builder in plug-in mode

In Flex Builder 3 in stand-alone mode, access the AIR Project option directly by selecting File ➤ New ➤ Flex Project and choosing Desktop Application as the Application type.

Then you can select the Server technology and the folder you want to use for compiled applications (the default folder is the bin folder). Figure 14-2 shows the first page of the wizard.

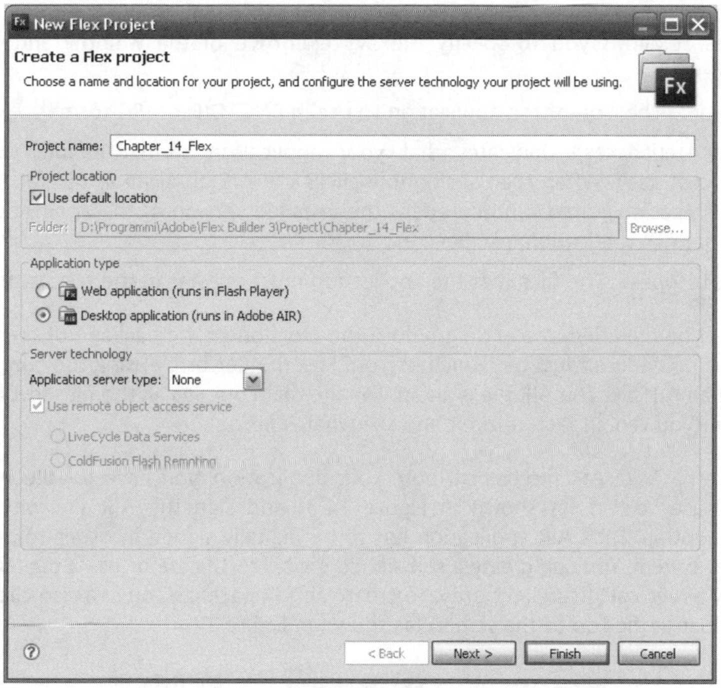

Figure 14-2. The first page of the wizard that defines an AIR project

An AIR application, unlike a Flex application, has the <mx:WindowedApplication> tag as root tag, in which the elements of the application become specified:

```
<mx:WindowedApplication
xmlns:mx="http://www.adobe.com/2006/mxml"
layout="absolute">

</mx:WindowedApplication>
```

Each application has an XML file linked to it, which specifies some properties of the application itself. This file, which is automatically created by Flex Builder and is in the same folder as the MXML file, is saved with the following name: nameOfMXMLFile-app.xml. It is an XML configuration file (AIR application descriptor file) that specifies parameters for identifying, installing, and launching AIR applications. If you open the file with Flex Builder (or any other text editor) and take a look at it, you can read useful comments that explain the content of the file. In the XML structure made up of nodes it is possible to specify the following:

- <name>: The name of the application that will be displayed by the operating system when the application is run on the desktop.

- <title>: The title of the application displayed in the AIR application installer.

- <description>: The description that will appear in the AIR application installer.

- <copyright>: The information on the copyright.

14

- `<rootContent>`: The name of the application file (HTML or SWF). Among the attributes, it allows you to specify the `systemChrome` of the window and the transparency.

- `<icon>`: The icon of the application to use in PNG, GIF, or JPG format.

- `<handleUpdates>`: Indicates that your application should handle the update process itself. When the user double-clicks the AIR application file for a new version, the integrated runtime opens the installed version of the application instead of the AIR application installer.

- `<fileTypes>`: The files that the application must register in the installation phase.

This file can be modified at any time before the creation of the package of the AIR application. This procedure must be launched from Flex Builder or by using the compilers that will create an AIR file. The AIR file is an archive file that contains all the files involved in the application (you can, in fact, unzip it and see what is inside).

To create a package AIR file to distribute your application, you have to select Project ➤ Export Release Version (as shown in Figure 14-3) and sign the AIR file with a Digital Certificate option. Each AIR application has to be digitally signed in order to be installed on another system. You can create a self signed digital certificate or use a digital signature granted by a root certificate authority. To create an AIR package you can also click the icon in the toolbar at the top of the screen (as shown in Figure 14-4).

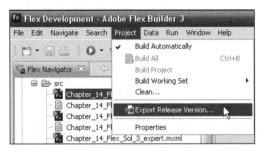

Figure 14-3. To export the AIR package, select the Adobe AIR folder

Figure 14-4. Click the icon on the toolbar to create an AIR package

Once the package of the application is created, it is ready to be distributed and deployed.

Because it is a desktop application, an AIR application must be directly installed on the computer of the final user. The distribution of a desktop application is different from that of a web application.

As a model of distribution for an AIR application, you can download the file to install from the web site, sending it via e-mail as an attachment or distributing it on a device such as a pen drive, CD-ROM, or DVD.

In this solution, you will create the first desktop application with Adobe AIR using both Flex Builder and Flex SDK.

How to build it

This time you will not create a Flex project from Flex Builder; instead you will create an AIR project.

1. From Flex Builder 3, select File ➤ New ➤ Flex Project and choose Desktop Application as the Application type. Insert Chapter_14_Flex_AIR as the name of the project and do not select any server-side language for the remote calls. Click Next on the next two screens, leaving all the settings at their default values. The AIR Project creates three folders: bin-debug, libs, and src. The src folder is the one that contains your mxml files.

This information will be inserted in the AIR application descriptor file (the XML file) that will be automatically created at the end of the wizard procedure.

2. Click Finish in the wizard. The AIR project and the two files will be created: Chapter_14_Flex_Sol_1.mxml and Chapter_14_Flex_Sol_1-app.xml. The first is the file of the application in which you will insert the elements for the user interface; the second is the AIR application descriptor file.

3. Open the Chapter_14_Flex_Sol_1-app.xml and insert the following information for the ID, Name, Description, and Copyright nodes of the AIR application:

ID : com.flexsolutions.chapter14.helloWorld
Name : My First Application
Description : This is my first application
Copyright : Marco Casario

4. The file Chapter_14_Flex_Sol_1.mxml is already open in the Editor of Flex Builder. Take note that the code of the application is slightly different from that of a Flex application. In fact, the root tag is the following:

```
<?xml version="1.0" encoding="utf-8"?>
<mx:WindowedApplication
xmlns:mx=http://www.adobe.com/2006/mxml
layout="absolute">

</mx:WindowedApplication>
```

The `<mx:WindowedApplication>` tag creates a simple window that functions as a container for the application. This window also contains simple controls for managing the title bar and close button.

14

5. To complete this first example, insert some controls. Specifically, enter Design mode of Flex Builder and drag a DateChooser and an Image control. The latter will load an image that is found in the assets folder of the project. You can use any image you like. The code of the MXML file, therefore, becomes the following:

```
<?xml version="1.0" encoding="utf-8"?>
<mx:WindowedApplication xmlns:mx="http://www.adobe.com/2006/mxml"
layout="absolute"
title="My first AIR Application"
backgroundAlpha="0.7">


<mx:DateChooser x="189" y="10"/>
<mx:Image x="19" y="10" source="assets/logo2.gif"/>


</mx:WindowedApplication>
```

Creating an AIR application using Flex Builder does not change the development process much with respect to a Flex application. You can, in fact use the same components and program with the same ActionScript code. What will change will be in the exportation phase of the project, in that you will create a package file to launch directly from the desktop.

You have also added to the <mx:WindowedApplication> a value for its backgroundAlpha that determines the transparency and its title. Solution 14-2 discusses how to change the look and feel of the windows in AIR applications.

6. Save the file. You must now select Run As ➤ 1 AIR Application to run the application as an AIR project (see Figure 14-5). If you have installed Flex Builder 3 as stand-alone, your context menu might differ.

Figure 14-5.
To test the application, run it as an AIR application.

The application is not launched in the browser, but as a desktop application. Note the application bar of the operating system in Figure 14-6.

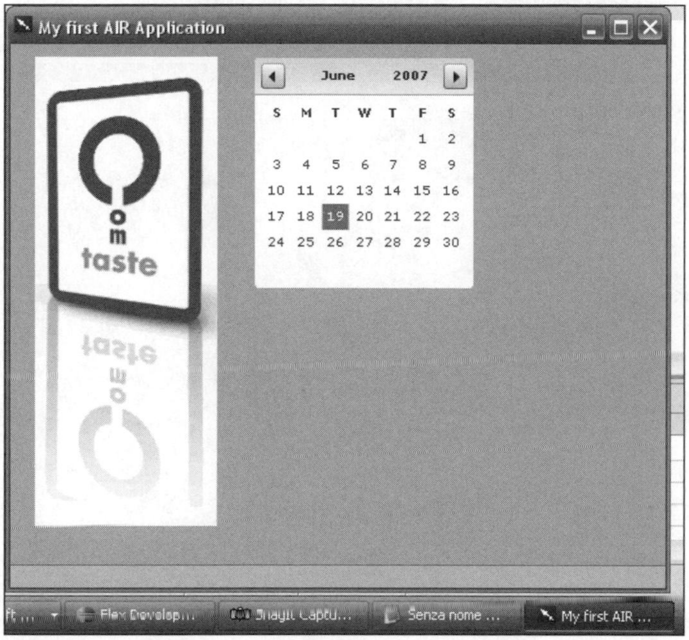

Figure 14-6. The AIR application is a desktop application.

To test the AIR application you must have AIR runtime installed (download it from http://www.adobe.com/go/air).

7. To distribute the application, you must now export and package your application selecting Project ➤ Export Release Version and sign the AIR file with a Digital Certificate option. The Export Release Version window opens, from which you can select the contents to insert in the AIR package (see Figure 14-7). Select which files to include (Include files) and where to save the AIR file, defining a path in the Save as field. Click Next and add a Digital Signature. You can leave all the default options and click Finish. You have now created the AIR package file.

You can now install and launch the application from the desktop by double-clicking the file Chapter_14_Flex_Sol_1.air, as shown in Figure 14-8.

14

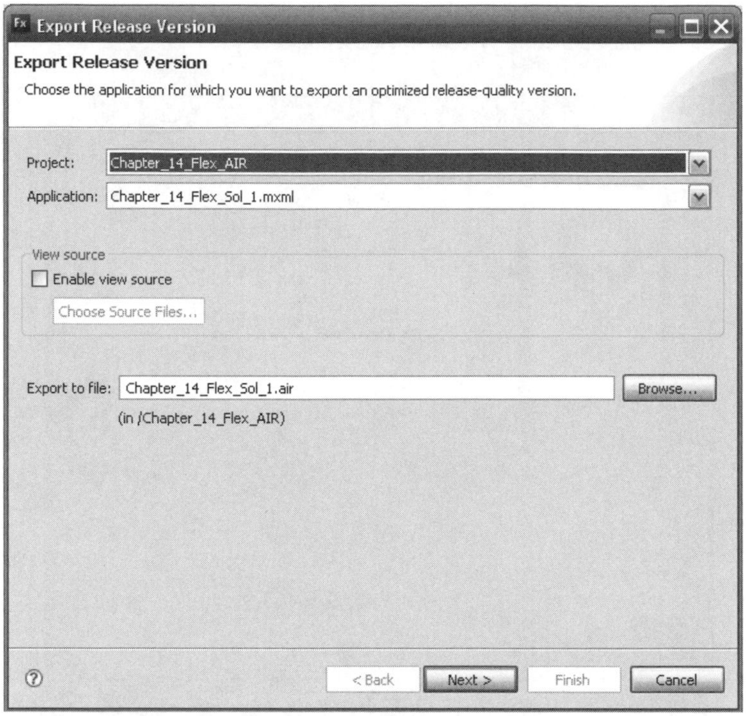

Figure 14-7. The application will be installed by launching the AIR file.

Figure 14-8. The installation of the AIR application

Expert tips

Even without using Flex Builder, it is possible to create AIR applications for the desktop. It is sufficient to have the Flex SDK installed.

The SDK for Adobe AIR puts two command-line compilers at your disposal that allow you to create AIR files without having the Flex Builder environment available, plus the following tools and libraries:

- Schema and template for the application.xml manifest file
- Default icons for Adobe AIR application
- Framework for Adobe AIR APIs
- Template for Adobe AIR application install badge
- Command line Adobe AIR Debug Launcher (ADL)
- Command-line Adobe AIR Developer Tool (ADT)

Every AIR application needs an AIR descriptor file—an XML configuration file that contains information about the application. If you use the Flex SDK, this file must be created manually.

1. To create an AIR descriptor file, use any text editor. Save the file as Chapter_14_ Flex_Sol_1-app.xml, paying attention to the extension. It must be an XML file.

2. Insert the following code in the file you just created:

```
<?xml version="1.0" encoding="UTF-8"?>
<application xmlns="http://ns.adobe.com/air/application/1.0.M4" ➥
appId="Chapter-15-Flex-Sol-1" version="1.0">

<name>Hello World Application</name>

<title>My first AIR Application</title>

<description>This is our first AIR application</description>

<copyright>Marco Casario - http://casario.blogs.com</copyright>

<rootContent systemChrome="standard" ➥
transparent="false" visible="true">[
SWF reference is generated]
</rootContent>

</application>
```

We will use the same code created in this solution.

3. Make sure you copy only the file Chapter_14_Flex_Sol_1.mxml and Chapter_14_ Flex_Sol_1-app.xml in the same folder. You can move on to compiling the application.

14

4. Compile the MXML file using the command-line compiler amxmlc. Open the command prompt and navigate in the folder of the AIR application (it should be in your Flex Builder workspace in the Flex project you're working on). Launch the following line:

```
amxmlc Chapter_14_Flex_Sol_1.mxml
```

> *To launch the* amxmlc *command-line compiler from any location, you have to add it as an environment variable (refer to Solution 8-1).*

5. To test the application, use the ADL compiler. Still working from the command prompt, insert the following line:

```
adl Chapter_14_Flex_Sol_1-app.xml
```

The compiler creates the application and launches automatically to allow the developer to test it.

6. To create the package of the AIR application, use the ADT compiler to which you send the parameter package and the files to insert in the package:

```
adt –package myApp.air ➡
Chapter_14_Flex_Sol_1-app.xml ➡
Chapter_14_Flex_Sol_1.swf
```

The package file myApp.air is created, which uses the information inserted in the AIR descriptor file, and the file Chapter_14_Flex_Sol_1.swf, which contains the application.

This AIR file can be distributed and installed on the desktop of any computer that has the AIR runtime installed.

Solution 14-2: Customizing OS windows using the AIR Window API

Creating and interacting with operating system windows has always been a dream for web developers. The browser has always set strict limits on the creation of pop-up windows, and pop-up blocker software has recently become necessary given the huge quantity of advertising messages that go around in these windows.

With Adobe AIR, the developer can finally access cross-platform APIs to create operating system windows using Flex (but also Flash or simple JavaScript). Furthermore, with AIR you can modify and completely personalize the look and feel of the window by changing the form and its transparency. This feature will render the desktop applications richer and more attractive for users.

In this solution, you will begin to use the AIR Window API and you will see how to create an operating system window, setting its properties and its content.

What's involved

An AIR application automatically creates the first window in which the application is inserted. This window is initialized with defined options in the AIR descriptor file, but if the root content is an SWF file, it is possible to access and modify the properties of this window through the stage.nativeWindow property. For example, to change the position in which the window should appear when the AIR application is launched, you can link it to the applicationComplete event (the corresponding event of creationComplete in Flex applications), an event handler that performs the following code:

```
var launchWindow:NativeWindow = this.stage.nativeWindow;
launchWindow.x = 400;
launchWindow.y = 400;
```

Instead, to create a new instance of the NativeWindow class, you must create an instance of the NativeWindowInitOptions object. In fact, the new NativeWindow becomes initialized by NativeWindowInitOptions:

```
var myWin:NativeWindowInitOptions =  new NativeWindowInitOptions();
```

From this object you can access the options to change the appearance of the window. There are three properties that determine a window style:

- type: Specifies the function of the window.
- systemChrome: Specifies whether to use the Chrome of the operating system. This property cannot be set to standard when transparent is true and/or type is lightweight.
- transparent: Specifies whether to activate the alpha blending for the window.

These properties are called by the instance of the NativeWindowInitOptions class. Therefore, the code that you write to be able to change these three options is the following:

```
var myWinOpt:NativeWindowInitOptions =  new NativeWindowInitOptions();
myWinOpt.transparent = false;
myWinOpt.systemChrome = NativeWindowSystemChrome.STANDARD;
var myWin:NativeWindow = new NativeWindow(myWinOpt);
myWin.visible = false;
```

The first line of code creates an instance of the NativeWindowInitOptions class, in which you will assign the values of the properties for the style of the window. In this code the transparent property is set as false, and the static constant is assigned as NativeWindowSystemChrome.STANDARD systemChrome. Finally, an instance of the NativeWindow class is created, to which you have sent a parameter to the constructor:

```
var myWin:NativeWindow = new NativeWindow(myWinOpt);
```

14

The parameter contains the properties that are defined in the NativeWindowInitOptions object.

Once the new window is created, you must declare an ActionScript constant to show contents in it. You can create objects in a dynamic way by programming them with ActionScript and adding them on the fly or by using the Loader class (contained in the flash.display package). You can insert an SWF file, an image, or an HTML page as a constant.

In this solution you will see how to work with windows in an AIR application and how to modify their appearance.

How to build it

Begin by creating an MXML application file from Flex Builder. Having defined the project as an AIR project in the first solution, Flex Builder automatically recognizes the type of project. When you create an MXML application file, it creates a file with the root WindowedApplication.

1. Create a new MXML file by selecting File ➤ New ➤ MXML Application file and save it as Chapter_14_Flex_Sol_2.mxml. Pay close attention to two things: in the AIR project the file Chapter_14_Flex_Sol_2-app.xml (AIR descriptor) has been created, and the MXML file begins with the following code:

   ```
   <mx:WindowedApplication
   xmlns:mx="http://www.adobe.com/2006/mxml"
   layout="absolute">
   ```

2. Add an event handler to the applicationComplete event that releases as the last event when the entire content of the application has been initialized and drawn onscreen. The applicationComplete event corresponds to the creationComplete in Flex. So write the event handler init() that is linked to this event:

   ```
   <mx:WindowedApplication
   xmlns:mx="http://www.adobe.com/2006/mxml"
   layout="absolute"
   applicationComplete="init();">
   ```

The init() function will do nothing more than modify some properties of the window (which acts on position and dimension) that becomes automatically created from AIR when the application is launched.

3. The application will be created from some Flex controls that will permit the user to create a new operating system window and change some of its properties. The user interface of the application is shown in Figure 14-9.

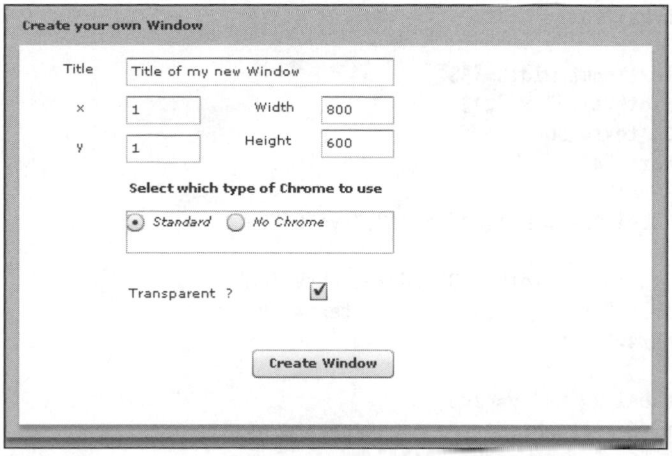

Figure 14-9. The AIR application with all its components

Begin by adding these components:

```
<mx:WindowedApplication
xmlns:mx="http://www.adobe.com/2006/mxml"
layout="absolute"
applicationComplete="init();">

<mx:Panel width="515"
layout="absolute" height="334"
title="Create your own Window">

<mx:Label text="Title" x="32" y="10"/>

<mx:TextInput id="titleString"
editable="true" x="83" y="10"
 width="210"
text="Title of my new Window"/>

<mx:Label text="x" x="42" y="40"/>

<mx:TextInput
width="58" id="xPosition"
 x="83" y="40"   text="1"
maxChars="4"/>

<mx:Label text="y"   x="42" y="70"/>

<mx:TextInput width="58"
id="yPosition"
x="83" y="70" text="1"
maxChars="4"/>
```

14

```
<mx:Label text="Width"  x="180" y="40"/>

<mx:TextInput width="58"
id="widthValue" x="235"
y="40" text="800"
maxChars="4"/>

<mx:Label text="Height" x="173" y="66"/>

<mx:TextInput width="58" id="heightValue"
editable="true" x="235" y="66" text="600"
maxChars="4"/>

<mx:Label x="83" y="103"
 text="Select which type of Chrome to use"
width="234" fontWeight="bold"/>

<mx:HBox height="33" width="210" x="83" y="129">

<mx:RadioButtonGroup id="Chrome"/>

<mx:RadioButton label="Standard"  value="standard"
groupName="Chrome" id="standardChrome"
selected="true" enabled="true" fontStyle="italic"
click="transparentOption.enabled = true" />

<mx:RadioButton label="No Chrome"
value="none" groupName="Chrome"
id="noChrome" fontStyle="italic"
click="transparentOption.selected = false;
          transparentOption.enabled = false" />

</mx:HBox>

<mx:Label x="83" y="184" text="Transparent  ?" width="106"/>

<mx:CheckBox id="transparentOption"
selected="true"  x="226" y="182"/>

<mx:Button label="Create Window" id="createWindowButton"
x="181" y="236"
/>


</mx:Panel>
</mx:WindowedApplication>
```

The user interface creates five text input controls contained in a Panel, editable by the user and allowing the setting of the following properties of the AIR window that will be created at runtime: the title, its position on the x- and y-axis, and its height and width. With two radio buttons inserted in an HBox container and making up part of the Chrome radio button group, it is possible to select the type of window to create by determining its systemChrome property.

Finally a check box will allow you to set the transparent property of the window.

Before the panel closes, the Create Window button will create the window. In fact, in the next step you will create an event handler that will be linked to the click of this button.

4. Insert the createNewWindow() event handler on the click of the Button event:

```
<mx:Button label="Create Window" id="createWindowButton"
x="181" y="236"
click="createNewWindow();"/>
```

The createNewWindow() function will take the values inserted by the user in the various Flex controls and create the relative window.

5. Add an <mx:Script> block immediately under the <mx:WindowedApplication> tag, in which you begin to define the init() event handler launched by the applicationComplete event:

```
<mx:Script>
<![CDATA[

private function init():void {
var launchWindow:NativeWindow = this.stage.nativeWindow;
launchWindow.x = 50;
launchWindow.y = 50;
launchWindow.width = 545;
launchWindow.height = 400;
 }

]]>
</mx:Script>
```

The init() function changes the value of some properties of the window when it is automatically created by AIR when the application is launched. To be able to access the properties and the methods of this window, an instance of the NativeWindow class is created, to which I send the reference of the window through the this.stage.nativeWindow property.

On this variable, launchWindow, I change the values of x,y position and height and width. That makes the window open at a distance of 50px from the corner on the top left of your video, and with a dimension of 545 × 400 pixels.

14

6. You must create an event handler createNewWindow() that executes on the click of the Button. In the <mx:Script> block, immediately under the closure of the init() function, you begin to declare the createNewWindow() function. You will analyze the code block by block, while you will go and write it. You begin with the creation of the instance of the NativeWindowInitOptions object for accessing the properties of the window that you will create:

```
public function createNewWindow():void {

var myWinOpt:NativeWindowInitOptions = new NativeWindowInitOptions();

myWinOpt.transparent = transparentOption.selected;
myWinOpt.systemChrome = Chrome.selectedValue.toString();

if(standardChrome.selected){
    myWinOpt.transparent = false;
}
```

The code of the function begins with the creation of the myWinOpt variable that contains the NativeWindowInitOptions object. Through this variable you can access the properties of the window. You therefore set the transparent property at the Boolean value that is sent back to you by the check box control (myWinOpt.transparent = transparentOption. selected). To the systemChrome, link the value selected by the user in the radio buttons (myWinOpt.systemChrome = Chrome.selectedValue.toString()). With an if() condition, check whether the transparent option is set to true. In this case, in fact, the systemChrome property cannot be set to standard when transparent.

7. Proceed in writing, adding the following ActionScript code, which will have the job of creating the NativeWindow window and its properties immediately under the closure of the if() condition:

```
var myNewWin:NativeWindow = new NativeWindow(myWinOpt);
myNewWin.visible = false;
myNewWin.title = titleString.text;
myNewWin.x = Number(xPosition.text);
myNewWin.y = Number(yPosition.text);
myNewWin.width = Number(widthValue.text);
myNewWin.height = Number(heightValue.text);

myNewWin.stage.align = "TL";
myNewWin.stage.scaleMode = "noScale";
```

The myNewWin variable contains an instance of the NativeWindow class. Send a parameter to the constructor new NativeWindow(myWinOpt). The myWinOpt parameter is the NativeWindowInitOptions object with the properties of the window. The visible property of the window is set to false.

You can then set the title, which you take from the input text control titleString, the x and y positions of the window that you take from the text fields xPosition and yPosition, and the width and height that you take from the text fields widthValue and heightValue.

The stage.align properties indicate the current alignment of the contents within the window that will assume the Top Left (TL) position. The stage.scaleMode property indicates current scaling of the contents within the window and will assume the value noScale.

You have defined and created the new window with its properties. But the window is not visible. In fact, you have sent false to the constructor as an option, rendering that window invisible. You have done this because you intend to create some content in it before rendering it visible.

8. In this step you will define a dynamic content by programming a simple field of text with ActionScript. Add the following code within the createNewWindow() method.

```
var myText:TextField=new TextField();
var formatText:TextFormat=new TextFormat();
var client:Sprite = new Sprite();

with(client.graphics){
    beginFill(0xFFAA00, 0.5);
    moveTo(0,0);
    lineTo(myNewWin.width, 0);
    lineTo(myNewWin.width, myNewWin.height);
    lineTo(0,myNewWin.height);
    lineTo(0,0);
    endFill();
}
with(formatText){
bold="true";
color=0x000000;
}
with(myText ){
x=myNewWin.width-(this.width/2);
y=myNewWin.height/2;
text="This is the New Window";
width=200;
setTextFormat(formatText);
}

myNewWin.stage.addChild(client);
myNewWin.stage.addChild(myText);
```

The TextField object is created and formatted from the property specified in the formatText object. You have also defined a third client object that is an instance of the Sprite() class that draws a rectangle on the screen in which the TextField will be displayed.

14

It is not enough to create the content to see it drawn in the window. You must, in fact, add it to the stage using the addChild() method of the stage of the window, to which you send the name of the two client and myText variables as parameters.

Before finishing this function, register an event that closes the created window.

9. Add the following code at the end:

```
client.doubleClickEnabled = true;
client.addEventListener(MouseEvent.DOUBLE_CLICK,
function(closeIt:MouseEvent):void
{
    closeIt.target.stage.nativeWindow.close();
});
myNewWin.visible = true;
 }
```

The addEventListener() method registers a function declared inline on the double-click event on the Sprite object. This function does nothing more than close the window using the code closeIt.target.stage.nativeWindow.close().

Finally, before closing the function, render the window visible by setting the relative property as true.

10. Save and run the application as an AIR application.

The final result is shown in Figure 14-10. You can change the values in the controls and generate your customized window.

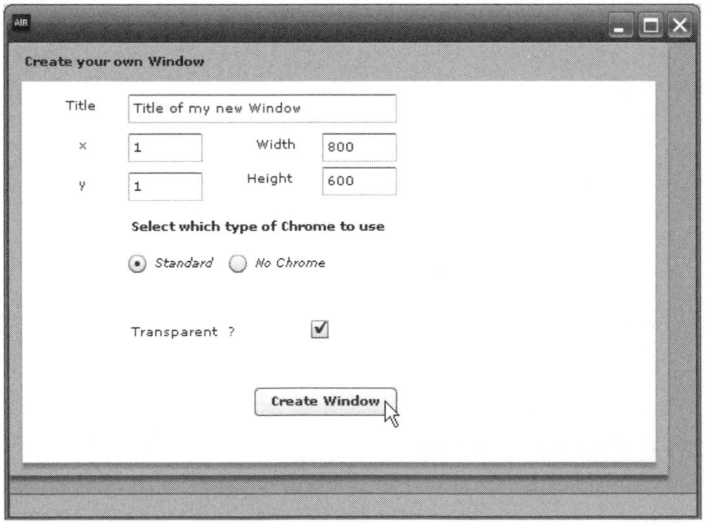

Figure 14-10. The AIR application

Expert tips

You learned how to use the transparent property of the NativeWindow class. If the Flex page uses the Cascading Style Sheet (CSS) properties background-image and background-color to customize the appearance of the application, the AIR window cannot be set to transparent. The same is true if the <mx:Application> tag uses a background color. This setting will override a transparent window mode.

So if you want to set the transparency of the application window, you can use these CSS-style declarations that override the appearance of background color and image in the application window:

```
<mx:Style>

Application
{
    background-image:"";
    background-color:"";
}
</mx:Style>
```

Another tip is that AIR has a property in the stage object that can put the window in full screen. The following code creates a full screen window setting the displayState property of the Stage to StageDisplayState.FULL_SCREEN:

```
stage.displayState = StageDisplayState.FULL_SCREEN;
```

To exit full-screen mode, the user presses the Escape key.

Solution 14-3: Accessing the file system

Flash Player has never given permission to developers to access the file system of the operating system. The only way Flex applications (and Flash) had the capability to work with persistent data was with the shared object—simple text files, very similar to the concept of cookies, which could be saved in a predefined folder of the computer and in which it was possible to save text. For a long time developers and users have dreamed about being able to access a determined directory to read and write and save a file.

Finally the wishes have been granted. With Adobe AIR, you can access, create, and work with the operating system's files and folders by using the classes contained in the flash.filesystem package:

- File: Represents a path to a file or directory
- FileStream: The object used to open, read, and write files
- FileMode: Specifies the string constants used in the open() and openAsync() methods of the FileStream class

14

The operations of the `File` class and the `FileStream` class can be both synchronous and asynchronous.

> *File system operations, such as writing, saving, and reading files, can be extremely slow compared with the classic processing of data on the Web. So the AIR SDK provides synchronous and asynchronous methods for performing these kinds of operations. A **synchronous** method starts and then waits for the operation to complete. While the method is in progress, the user cannot work on the application. The **asynchronous** method starts the operation and does not block the use of the application.*

This solution shows you how to work with the `File` and `FileStream` class to read the content of files and directories, starting from a directory specified by the user.

What's involved

In the `flash.filesystem` package there is the `File` class, which extends the `FileReference`. This class represents an object that creates a pointer to the file or to the directory in the file system. This class will be used in the desktop applications that you will develop with Adobe AIR for getting the path of a directory or a file, to copy or move files and directories, and to obtain a list of files or directories contained in a path.

Each `File` object possesses two properties that determine its path. The `nativePath` property specifies the path of a file according to the operative system; the `url` property uses the absolute path, using the URL scheme to point to a file (for example `file://c/documents/myfile.txt`).

Furthermore, the `File` object has properties for pointing to standard directories of the computer:

- `userDirectory`: Points to the user's home directory
- `desktopDirectory`: Points to the user's desktop directory
- `documentsDirectory`: Points to the user's document directory
- `applicationResourceDirectory`: Points to the unique AIR path associated to the application installed
- `applicationStorageDirectory`: Points to the path that defines the application storage directory

These properties can be used to open, read, or create a file. The ActionScript syntax for using the file object is the following:

```
var myFileObj:File = new File();
myFileObj.userDirectory.resolvePath("myData");
```

With this syntax, you have created a `File` object and you have made it point to the `myData` subdirectory found in the user's directory.

The path of these properties obviously changes according to the operative system. In fact, while the Windows systems use the syntax C:\Documents and Settings\userName\, Mac systems use /Users/marco/.

You can also access a determined directory using the url or nativePath property:

```
var myFileObj:File = new File();
myFileObj.url = "file://C:/AIR/"
file.nativePath = "C:/AIR/"
```

Instead, to permit the user to navigate in a directory, you can use the asynchronous method browseForDirectory():

```
myFile.browseForDirectory();
```

This method dispatches a SELECT event that returns the directory selected by the user. You can manage this event by registering it with an addEventListener() method:

```
myFile.addEventListener(Event.SELECT, selectHandler);
```

After pointing at a directory, you can access a file. The File object puts forward different methods to set the file to which it points:

- resolvePath(): Allows you to obtain a path relative to another given path: myFileObj.userDirectory.resolvePath("myFile.txt")
- getDirectoryListing(): Returns an array of all the files in a directory
- browseForOpen(): Presents the system dialog box from which you can select a file to open
- browseForSave(): Presents the system dialog box from which you can select a file to save
- browseForMultiple(): Presents the system dialog box from which you can select multiple files

In this solution, you will see how to read the content of a directory and differentiate the reading according to whether the object met is a directory or a file.

How to build it

Use the AIR project Chapter_14_Flex_AIR created in Solution 14-1.

1. Create a new file by selecting File ➤ New ➤ MXML Application and save it as Chapter_14_Flex_Sol_3.mxml. Because it is in an AIR project, the file will begin with the root tag WindowedApplication.

2. Define an event handler to associate to the applicationComplete event. This function will have the job of determining the dimensions of the window and its position:

14

```
<mx:WindowedApplication
xmlns:mx="http://www.adobe.com/2006/mxml"
layout="vertical"
applicationComplete="init();">
```

3. Insert an `<mx:Script>` tag in which you create the event handler init() and two variables that will be used in the application:

```
<mx:Script>
<![CDATA[

import mx.collections.ArrayCollection;
import flash.filesystem.File;

private var myFile:File = new File();

[Bindable]
private var resultData:ArrayCollection = new ArrayCollection();

private function init():void
{

stage.nativeWindow.width = ➥
        Math.min(500,Capabilities.screenResolutionX - 100);
stage.nativeWindow.height = ➥
        Math.min(300,Capabilities.screenResolutionY - 50);
stage.nativeWindow.x = 10;
stage.nativeWindow.y = 10;
stage.nativeWindow.visible = true;
}
]]>
</mx:Script>
```

The myFile variable is a File object that you will use to point to a directory. Instead, the resultData variable is an ArrayCollection that will contain the list of directories and files starting from a determined path. Furthermore, this variable will be used as data provider for a DataGrid, which will display that data returned by this reading.

The init() method assigns the dimensions of height and width to the window that contains the application. The dimensions are set by using the Math.min() method. This method, given two parameters, returns the smaller value. The parameters, which you have sent, are a static value and one that takes the resolution of the screen from the Capabilities property of Flash Player:

```
stage.nativeWindow.width = Math.min(500,Capabilities.screenResolutionX
- 100);
stage.nativeWindow.height = Math.min(300,Capabilities.screenResolutionY
- 50);
```

Therefore, the dimensions of the window vary according to the resolution on the client who performs the application.

The init() method concludes by positioning the window according to the x and y values 10 and rendering it visible.

4. Below the </mx:Script> code, you insert the elements of the user interface of the application: a TextInput control, a button, and a DataGrid. The last, the DataGrid, will contain the list of directories and files, the text input control will contain the path of the directory from which this list will be created, and the button will run the method that will open the system dialog box to permit the user to choose the path in which to begin:

```
<mx:HBox>
<mx:TextInput id="mypath" />
<mx:Button label="Select a Folder" click="openDir()" />
</mx:HBox>

<mx:DataGrid id="myDG" dataProvider="{resultData}"
wldth="80%" />
```

The DataGrid uses the ArrayCollection resultData as data provider, which becomes populated following the click of the Button and, therefore, from the execution of the openDir() method.

5. You can now add the openDir() method and work on some of the properties and methods of the File object. In the </mx:Script> block, after the init() method, you add the event handler that executes at the click of the Button:

```
private function openDir():void
{
myFile.addEventListener(Event.SELECT, selectHandler);
myFile.browseForDirectory("Choose a Directory");
}
```

The openDir() event handler uses the browseForDirectory() method to open the system dialog box and make the user select the directory to begin from (see Figure 14-11). Through the addEventListener() method, register the SELECT event that occurs in the moment when the user has selected a directory and has clicked the Open button of the dialog box. The next step is to create the event handler selectHandler().

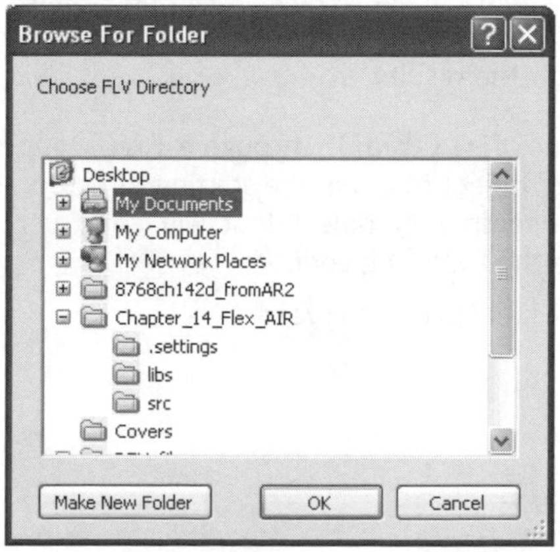

Figure 14-11.
The browseForDirectory() method opens the dialog box

14

6. Add the event handler selectHandler() immediately under the function that was just written. This function returns the name and path of the selected directory and then writes it in the TextInput control myFile. It also launches the listFile() function that will consequently populate the ArrayCollection:

```
private function selectHandler(e:Event):void
{
mypath.text = myFile.nativePath;
listFile();
}
```

The listFile() function will read the files contained in the directory selected by the user.

7. Insert the listFile() function under the selectHandler():

```
private function listFile():void
{
var dir:File = new File(mypath.text);
resultData.removeAll();
dir.addEventListener(FileListEvent.DIRECTORY_LISTING, dirListed);
dir.getDirectoryListingAsync();
}
```

The function begins by creating a File object to which it sends the path of the directory selected by the user as the value of the constructor:

```
var dir:File = new File(mypath.text);
```

In fact, the TextInput control mypath contains the path. Empty the resultData variable with the removeAll() method, the way it was previously populated. (If you do not do this operation, the values in the ArrayCollection will be added to those already inserted with every click of the button to select a new directory.)

In the listFile() function, launch the method of the File object getDirectoryListingAsync(), which launches an asynchronous operation that returns the content list of the directory sent to the File object. While the reading of the operation is being performed, the FileListEvent.DIRECTORY_LISTING event is dispatched. With an addEventListener, register an event handler, dirListed(), which will carry out the final controls. In particular, it checks for all content encountered that can be either a file or a directory. It will then populate the ArrayCollection that functions as data provider to the DataGrid that will, therefore, begin to show the results.

8. There is only one last function to define: dirListed(). Through a for() loop this event handler will check each and every object found in the starting directory. The results returned will be inserted in a temporary object that will construct the indexes of the ArrayCollection. Write the following code:

```
private function dirListed(event:FileListEvent):void
{
var node:File = new File();
var myType:String = new String();
var newData:Object = new Object();
var currentNodes:Array = new Array();
```

```
currentNodes = event.files;

for (var i:int = 0; i < currentNodes.length; i++)
{
node = currentNodes[i];
if (node.isDirectory)
{
myType = "Directory";
}
else
{
myType = "File";
}
newData = {name:node.name,
  path:node.nativePath,
  type:myType}
resultData.addItem(newData);
}
}
```

The function begins by creating the following variables:

- currentNodes: An array that contains all the elements in the directory in which the operation is being performed. These elements are contained in the event.files property created in the event object.

- node: A File object.

- myType: A string that contains the reference of the element found. It assumes the values File or Directory.

With a for() cycle, you loop in the elements of the directory taking the property currentNodes.length as extreme. An if() condition checks whether the element in question is a directory or a file. According to the case, it inserts a different string in the myType variable. Before exiting from the for() cycle, in a newData object you place the property name, path, and type that respectively contain the name of the directory or of the file, the path, and the type of element. This object will be added to the ArrayCollection with the addItem() method:

```
newData = {name:node.name,
  path:node.nativePath,
  type:myType}
resultData.addItem(newData);
```

At this point, the cycle moves on to the successive element contained in the currentNodes Array.

9. Save the file and run the AIR application.

With these few lines of code, you have created a directory listing application. Figure 14-12 shows the final result with the list of directories and files in the DataGrid.

14

795

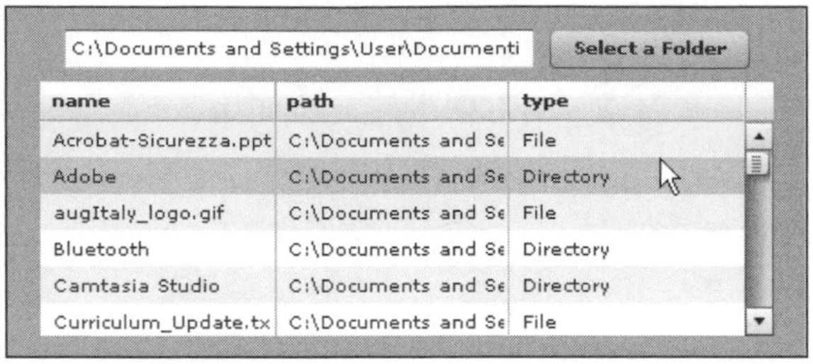

Figure 14-12. The browseForDirectory() method makes the dialog box appear.

Expert tips

In the solution you created, only the first level of the list of elements, files, or directories in a determined folder is returned to you. It is often useful to be able to add another navigation level, entering into subdirectories.

To obtain this result you just need to launch the function that delivers the list of the elements when it meets an element of directory type in a recursive way. By slightly modifying the MXML file, you can obtain this result, and you can display the content of the subdirectories you select in the same DataGrid.

1. Modify the listFile() function in the <mx:Script> block by simply adding a parameter that the function will accept:

```
private function listFile(startDir:String):void
{
var dir:File = new File(startDir);
resultData.removeAll();
dir.addEventListener(FileListEvent.DIRECTORY_LISTING, dirListed);
dir.getDirectoryListingAsync();
}
```

Because you have to provide the possibility of obtaining the list of objects contained in a directory that the user selects from the DataGrid (and to be able to use the function without rewriting it), I sent a string that represents the starting directory to which the list must be returned as parameter to the listFile().

I sent this parameter to the File object dir that is created: var dir:File = new File(startDir);

2. The listFile() function was recalled by the event handler selectHandler(). You must, therefore, modify this function and send it the requested parameter:

```
private function selectHandler(e:Event):void
{
mypath.text = myFile.nativePath;
listFile(myFile.nativePath);
}
```

The parameter that you send to it, which corresponds to the directory to which the list should be returned, is the nativePath.

The event handler selectHandler() was launched by the SELECT event of the browseForDirectory() method:

```
myFile.addEventListener(Event.SELECT, selectHandler);
```

If you save and launch the file, the application will function exactly like before. You can now add a button to the user interface that runs the listFile() function again, but this time sending it the directory selected by the user as parameter.

3. Immediately below the definition of the DataGrid, add the Button that when clicked will call the listFile() with the parameter of the new directory from which the list of elements is sent:

```
<mx:DataGrid id="myDG" dataProvider="{resultData}"
width="406" />

<mx:Button label="Select a Folder"
click="listFile(myDG.selectedItem.path)" />
```

The myDG.selectedItem.path parameter corresponds to the address selected by the user in the DataGrid. In fact, the resultData data provider contains objects with the following properties: name, path, and type.

4. Save the file and run the AIR application.

The Button now allows you to launch the listFile() function, even if a file is selected from the DataGrid, as shown in Figure 14-13. You must block the click when the object is not a directory.

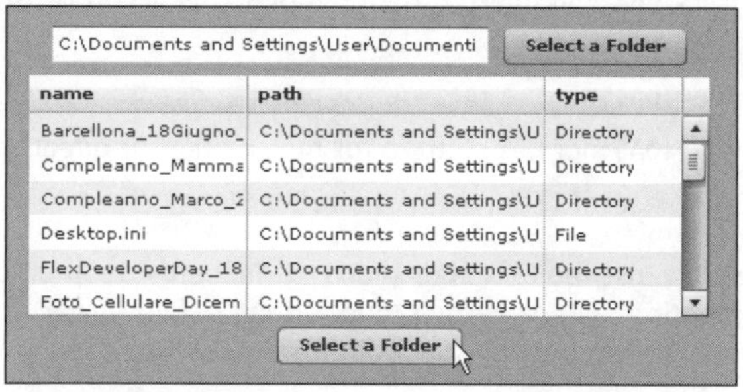

Figure 14-13. The new Button allows you to obtain the list of subdirectories selected in the DataGrid.

The Capabilities object has static properties that provide you with useful information on the file system when you create applications with AIR:

- Capabilities.hasIME: Contains a Boolean that specifies whether Flash Player is loaded by a system that has an input method editor installed
- Capabilities.language: Specifies the language used by the system

- Capabilities.os: Specifies the operating system
- Capabilities.screenResolutionY: Contains the resolution value of the y-axis (height)
- Capabilities.screenResolutionX: Contains the resolution value of the x-axis (width)

Solution 14-4: Reading and writing persistent data on local file system

In the previous solution, you saw how to interact with the local file system, reading the content of directories. With the flash.filesystem package, you can read and write files, as well as copy, move, and cancel them.

This gives you the ability to create desktop applications that can interact with the user's computer. To give you an idea of what you will be able to develop, look at some examples by downloading the AIR documentation. (Unzip the AIR documentation file in the air-flexsamples folder to find the AIR examples.)

The File class provides methods and properties for working with the file system. Those that are used most often include the following:

- name: Contains the name of the file
- exists: A Boolean that returns true or false according to whether the file or directory exists
- extension: Contains the extension of the file
- size: Specifies the dimension of the file in bytes
- isDirectory: A Boolean that returns true or false according to whether the element is a directory or not
- copyTo(), copyToAsync(): A method for copying directories or files
- moveTo(), moveToAsync(): A method for moving files or directories
- deleteFile(), deleteFileAsync(): Cancels a file

To open and close a file, use the FileStream class, which provides methods and properties for performing operations or for reading and writing a file. In particular, a file can be opened with the FileStream class by specifying the fileMode property with the following values:

- FileMode.READ: The file is opened for read-only mode.
- FileMode.WRITE: The file is opened for writing. If the file does not exist, it becomes automatically created. If data exist in the file, it becomes overwritten.
- FileMode.APPEND: The file is opened for appending. With this mode the data is added to the file, and the previously existing one does not become overwritten.
- FileMode.UPDATE: The file is opened in reading and writing mode. Depending on whether the file exists, it will be created or just opened.

In this solution, you will see how to read and write an XML file that will be saved in your local machine and contain the data inserted by the user in a form.

What's involved

To be able to interact with a file, you must first initialize a FileStream object. When a FileStream object is created, the mode in which the file will be opened is declared (reading or writing). To create a FileStream object you must send the reference of a File object to its open() method or openSync():

```
private var myFile:File;
private var stream:FileStream;

myFile = File.documentsDirectory;
myFile = myFile.resolvePath("userInfo.xml");
stream = new FileStream();
stream.open(myFile, FileMode.READ);
```

In this example of code, a File object is created that opens a file in the user's document directory.

> Having used the File.documentsDirectory *property, the* FileStream *object will search for the file in the document directory of the operating system. It doesn't matter whether the user is using a PC, Mac, or Linux system.*

The file that is opened is called userInfo.xml and is specified with the resolvePath() method of the File object. To open the file, use the open() method of the FileStream object to which you send two parameters: the File object reference and the fileMode. In the example written previously, the file opened in read-only mode. If you want to open the file to write data instead, declare the FileStream in the following way:

```
myFile = File.documentsDirectory;
myFile = myFile.resolvePath("userInfo.xml");

stream = new FileStream();
stream.open(myFile, FileMode.WRITE);
stream.writeUTFBytes(dataToWrite);
```

At the end of the file operations, you must close the FileStream using the close() method:

```
stream.close();
```

If you were to use the openAsync() method, the following events would be dispatched: Event.COMPLETE, Event.PROGRESS, and Event.IOError. Through the event listeners, you would have been able to manage the operation of opening and writing the file during all its phases, being able to also check for any errors that might have occurred.

14

In this solution you will begin to work with the files by reading and writing their content.

How to build it

In this solution, the user's document will be used as a directory of reading and writing of the file. Through the properties of the File object illustrated in Solution 14-1, you can change this path.

1. Create a new MXML file by selecting File ➤ New ➤ MXML Application and save it as Chapter_14_Flex_Sol_4.mxml. Define an event handler that releases on the applicationComplete of the root tag:

```
<mx:WindowedApplication
xmlns:mx="http://www.adobe.com/2006/mxml"
layout="absolute"
applicationComplete="init()">
```

Once the application is loaded, the init() function will search to see whether an XML file has already been created and written previously. In this case, it will read its contents and will load the data in the controls of the user interface.

2. Create the controls of the application. Insert a Form container and add TextInput controls. They are needed by users to insert their own data, perhaps to register for a service:

```
<mx:Form x="10" y="10" width="100%">
<mx:FormItem label="Name:">
<mx:TextInput id="nameTxt"/>
</mx:FormItem>
<mx:FormItem label="Last Name:">
<mx:TextInput id="lastTxt"/>
</mx:FormItem>
<mx:FormItem label="Email:">
<mx:TextInput id="emailTxt"/>
</mx:FormItem>
<mx:FormItem label="City:">

<mx:ComboBox id="cityCbx" >
<mx:dataProvider>
<mx:String>Rome</mx:String>
<mx:String>Milan</mx:String>
<mx:String>Florence</mx:String>
<mx:String>Venice</mx:String>
</mx:dataProvider>
</mx:ComboBox>
</mx:FormItem>
<mx:HBox>
<mx:Button label="Save Data" click="saveData()" />
<mx:Label id="dateTxt" />
</mx:HBox>
</mx:Form>
```

The Save Data button launches the saveData() function, which will be responsible for saving the data inserted by the user in the text fields and for writing them in the file.

You can now begin to add the ActionScript functions to the file.

3. Insert an <mx:Script> block. Begin by writing the init() function defined in the applicationComplete event and defining the variables that you will use in the code:

```
<mx:Script>
<![CDATA[
import flash.filesystem.*;

private var myFile:File;
private var stream:FileStream;
[Bindable]
private var xmlData.XML;

public function init():void
{

myFile = File.documentsDirectory;
myFile = myFile.resolvePath("userInfo.xml");
openXML();
}
```

You have declared three variables:

- myFile: Contains the File object
- stream: The FileStream object
- xmlData: Contains the data that will be written in the file created

The init() function uses the File object to point to the user document directory with the documentsDirectory property. Using the resolvePath() method, it specifies the XML file to point to (userInfo.xml) and performs the openXML() function. It is easy to guess that this function will open the XML file and will read its content.

4. Write the openXML function immediately under the closure of the init() function:

```
private function openXML():void
{
stream = new FileStream();
if (myFile.exists) {
stream.open(myFile, FileMode.READ);

xmlData = XML(stream.readUTFBytes(stream.bytesAvailable));
stream.close();
nameTxt.text = xmlData.userInfo.@name ;
lastTxt.text = xmlData.userInfo.@surname ;
emailTxt.text = xmlData.userInfo.@email ;
cityCbx.selectedItem = xmlData.userInfo.@city  ;
```

14

801

```
        dateTxt.text = xmlData.saveDate;
    }

    stage.nativeWindow.visible = true;
}
```

The function begins with the creation of the FileStream object. An if() condition checks whether the file to which the object File points to exists. If the file exists, it is opened with the open() method of the FileStream in read-only mode. If the file does not exist, it will be created and saved in the user's document directory:

```
stream.open(myFile, FileMode.READ);
```

The xmlData variable is populated with the values read in the XML file using the readUTFBytes() method, and the FileStream object is closed:

```
xmlData = XML(stream.readUTFBytes(stream.bytesAvailable));
stream.close();
```

When the xmlData variable is populated, a casting in XML is carried out. In this way, you can access the values of this variable using the E4X language.

The structure of the xmlData variable, which faithfully respects that of the XML file, is the following:

```
<?xml version="1.0" encoding="utf-8"?>
<user>
  <userInfo name="alessio"
    surname="casario"
    email="m.casario@comtaste.com"
    city="Rome"/>
<saveDate>Sat Jun 23 11:21:36 GMT+0200 2007
</saveDate>
</user>
```

The structure of this file becomes created from another method that you will write in the next steps.

Immediately under the FileStream closure, you wrote the values read by the XML file in the TextInput controls that define the user interface. This is the code that you wrote in the function and creates the binding with the data:

```
nameTxt.text = xmlData.userInfo.@name ;
lastTxt.text = xmlData.userInfo.@surname ;
emailTxt.text = xmlData.userInfo.@email ;
cityCbx.selectedItem = xmlData.userInfo.@city  ;
dateTxt.text = xmlData.saveDate;
```

The syntax that accesses the values of the XML nodes uses E4X standard that allows you to access attributes of the nodes using the keyword @.

The function closes, rendering the window of the application visible by accessing the property of the Window object: stage.nativeWindow.visible = true.

5. The button defined in the form launches the saveData() method. This method takes care of creating the XML structure of data by taking it from the TextInput controls and writing these values on the userInfo.xml file. Add this function in the <mx:Script> block:

```
private function saveData():void
{
xmlData = <user/>;
xmlData.userInfo.@name = nameTxt.text;
xmlData.userInfo.@surname = lastTxt.text;
xmlData.userInfo.@email = emailTxt.text;
xmlData.userInfo.@city = cityCbx.value;
xmlData.saveDate = new Date().toString();

var outputString:String = '<?xml version="1.0" encoding="utf-8"?>\n';
outputString += xmlData.toXMLString();
outputString = outputString.replace(/\n/g, File.lineEnding);

stream = new FileStream();
stream.open(myFile, FileMode.WRITE);
stream.writeUTFBytes(outputString);
stream.close();
}
]]>
</mx:Script>
```

The function starts by creating the structure of the xmlData variable. It specifies the <user> root tag, in which the userInfo tag will be created with the attributes @name, @surname, @email, and @city. The values of this attribute are taken from the TextInput controls:

```
xmlData = <user/>;
xmlData.userInfo.@name = nameTxt.text;
xmlData.userInfo.@surname = lastTxt.text;
xmlData.userInfo.@email = emailTxt.text;
xmlData.userInfo.@city = cityCbx.value;
```

One last node is specified, saveDate, which contains the data and the time of the last save:

```
xmlData.saveDate = new Date().toString();
```

The xmlData variable is inserted temporarily in a variable of String type, outputString, to which the declaration of the XML file and the line breaks are added:

```
var outputString:String = '<?xml version="1.0" encoding="utf-8"?>\n';
outputString += xmlData.toXMLString();
outputString = outputString.replace(/\n/g, File.lineEnding);
```

14

Finally, the FileStream object is created, which opens the file in write mode (FileMode.WRITE) and uses the writeUTFBytes() method to write the XML data in the file:

```
stream = new FileStream();
stream.open(myFile, FileMode.WRITE);
stream.writeUTFBytes(outputString);
```

The function ends with the closure of the FileStream.

6. Save the file and run the AIR application.

By inserting data in the TextInput controls and clicking the Save Data button, the data becomes saved in the file. You can close and reopen the application to see that the data previously saved is loaded in the form, as shown in Figure 14-14. If you open the user's document directory you will find the file userInfo.xml.

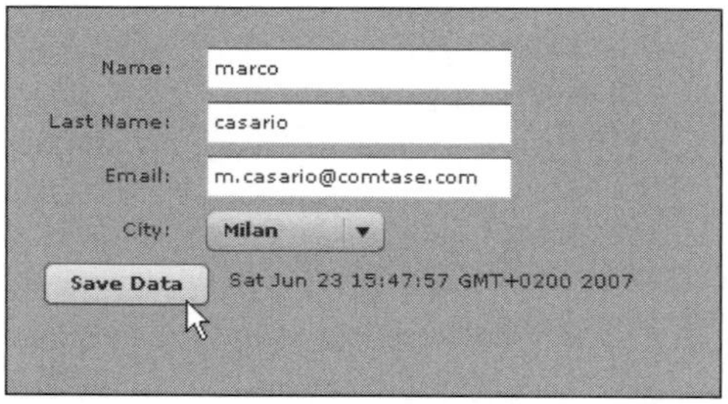

Figure 14-14. The data becomes loaded by the file userInfo.xml created in the user's document folder.

Expert tips

A large number of the methods of the FileStream class that operate with files can be declared as synchronous or asynchronous operations. The difference is that the asynchronous methods are run in the background and do not interrupt other operations. Therefore, the user can continue to interact with the application without having to wait until the results of reading or writing a file are completed. Flex also uses an asynchronous system in the remote procedure calls (RPCs) HTTPService, WebService, and RemoteObject.

To define the opening of a file as an asynchronous operation, use the openAsync() method that is declared the same way as the open() method: by sending the reference of the File object and the fileMode as a parameter.

Modify the previously created solution by working on part of the ActionScript code.

1. In the openXML() function, in the if() cycle, modify the code as follows:

```
private function openXML():void
{
stream = new FileStream();
if (myFile.exists) {
```

```
stream.openAsync(myFile, FileMode.READ);

stream.addEventListener(ProgressEvent.PROGRESS,progressHandler);
stream.addEventListener(Event.COMPLETE, completeHandler);

}
stage.nativeWindow.visible = true;
}
```

You have substituted the open() method with openAsync() and you have defined two event handlers for the PROGRESS and COMPLETE events. In fact, by loading the operations in the background, the openAsync() method allows you to monitor the process of opening the file. In this case you created an event handler for the phase in which the opening and reading of the file are performed (PROGRESS event) and an event handler for the completion phase of the operation (COMPLETE event).

2. Add the event handler progressHandler(), adding it immediately under the function openXML():

```
private function progressHandler(event:ProgressEvent):void
{
var str:String = "Byte total: " + ➡
        event.bytesTotal + "/n Bytes Loaded: " + ➡
        event.bytesLoaded;
asincTxt.text = str;
}
```

The first function, progressHandler(), creates a variable of temporary string type. This variable will contain the bytesTotal properties or the quantity of bytes loaded instead:

```
var str:String = "Byte total: " + event.bytesTotal + ➡
  "/n Bytes Loaded: "+ event.bytesLoaded;
```

These two properties are found in the event object generated by the ProgressEvent class.

The variable is then linked to a TextArea control that you will create in the next steps.

3. Immediately under the closure of the progressHandler(), function, add the second event handler that releases on the COMPLETE event of the openAsync() method:

```
private function completeHandler(event:Event):void
{
xmlData = XML(stream.readUTFBytes(stream.bytesAvailable));
stream.close();
nameTxt.text = xmlData.userInfo.@name ;
lastTxt.text = xmlData.userInfo.@surname ;
emailTxt.text = xmlData.userInfo.@email ;
cityCbx.selectedItem = xmlData.userInfo.@city  ;
dateTxt.text = xmlData.saveDate;

asincTxt.text = "The openAsin() method has completed" ;
}
```

14

When the file is opened (and the operation is completed) you can write the information in the file. In this function, you perform the same operations that you declared in the saveData( ) method of the synchronous method.

The function concludes with the writing of the following text in the TextArea control: "The openAsin() method has completed".

4. There is nothing left except inserting the TextArea control in the MXML code. Under the closure of the Form container, add a TextArea:

```
<mx:TextArea id="asincTxt"
x="26" y="184" width="248" height="96"/>
```

5. Save and run the AIR application.

This section showed how to use one of the asynchronous methods that the File and FileStream class provide.

Solution 14-5: Embedding HTML pages into desktop applications

Desktop runtime AIR incorporates the WebKit HTML engine. WebKit is an open source web browser engine and is well known across the Web because it's the engine used by Safari, Dashboard, Mail, and many other Mac OS X applications.

> *If you want to know more about the WebKit project (www.webkit.org), read the page dedicated to the engine on Wikipedia.*

For developers, having a runtime that can use an HTML engine means being able to incorporate applications, pages, or entire HTML sites. Furthermore, the HTML content loaded is an object that can be programmed and customized. In fact, by using the technique known as **script bridging**, any JavaScript code in the HTML page as with every single HTML component (through the Document Object Model [DOM]) can communicate using ActionScript and exchange information.

> *Script bridging enables ActionScript code in a Flex or AIR application to communicate and call methods in the JavaScript code declared in the HTML page and vice versa.*

In the classic Flex applications, obtaining this result was not possible. You could only create an IFRAME in HTML in which to load the SWF application and make it communicate with JavaScript using the ExternalInterface class or the Flex Ajax bridge.

In this solution, you will see how to read the content of an HTML file resident locally on the computer and how to interpret this code from the HTML control to obtain a preview of the HTML file.

What's involved

There are two methods used to load HTML content in an AIR application: the `<mx:HTML>` tag and the ActionScript `HTMLControl` class.

The MXML control tag, which extends the `UIComponent`, allows you to define a rectangular region in which to load the HTML code. As with any Flex control, it also provides properties and events that can be customized. An example of code to load an HTML page sending it an external URL as a parameter is the following:

```
<mx:HTML id="myHTML" width="100%" height="100%
   location="http://www.comtaste.com/"   />
```

The `location` property allows you to specify a remote or local URL that the HTML control will use to load the HTML content.

It is possible to assign an HTML document to the HTML control or also a portion of HTML code through the `htmlText` property:

```
<mx:HTML id="myHTML" width="100%" height="100%
   htmlText="<html><body>Hello World</body></html>"   />
```

Or through ActionScript:

```
var htmlCode:String = "<html><body>Hello World</body></html>";
myHTML.htmlText = htmlCode;
```

To enable the user to specify a file by selecting it from the actual hard disk, you can use the `browseForOpen()` method of the `File` object. This method opens the dialog box to navigate within the actual computer and choose the file. When the file is selected, the `FILE_CHOOSE` event is dispatched. By registering this event, you can create an event handler to perform operations with the file just selected (as seen in the previous solution):

```
fileToOpen.browseForOpen("Open");
fileToOpen.addEventListener(FileEvent.FILE_CHOOSE, openHandler);
private function openHandler(event:Event):void
{
var myFile:File = event.target as File;
// code
}
```

In this solution, you will create a small application that a HTML file specified by the user will read and will provide a preview of the HTML content using the HTML control.

How to build it

The application will have a TabBar navigation container as a user interface element, which will define two views for the application: one to display the code of the selected HTML file and another to obtain a preview of the file.

14

1. Begin by creating a new MXML file by selecting File ➤ New ➤ MXML Application and save it with the name Chapter_14_Flex_Sol_5.mxml. Modify the root tag by inserting a function on the applicationComplete event:

```
<mx:WindowedApplication
xmlns:mx="http://www.adobe.com/2006/mxml"
layout="absolute"
applicationComplete="init()">
```

The init() function has the job of giving the dimensions and the position to the window of the application. You also chose the absolute value for the layout property, which allows you to position the elements in the page in absolute mode; that is, specifying their x and y position.

2. You will write the init() function later. Now, you'll define another element of the user interface. You add an ApplicationControlBar, in which you insert a Label and a Button:

```
<mx:ApplicationControlBar width="100%" x="0" y="0" >
<mx:Label text="Choose an HTML File from your local drive >> " />
<mx:Button label="Open File" id="openBtn" click="openFile()"/>
</mx:ApplicationControlBar>
```

The ApplicationControlBar is positioned at the beginning of the application. In fact, its x and y properties are pointed at 0,0. In the ApplicationControlBar container, there is a label that provides a small textual aid to the user, explaining that a file must be selected. Instead, when clicked, the Button calls the openFile() function that will open the dialog box.

3. The application will provide two views, which are inserted and managed through a TabBar container. The TabBar control defines a horizontal or vertical row of tabs. In the solution, you populate the TabBar with two tabs, defined in the tabArray Array. This Array creates a data binding with the dataProvider property of the component:

```
<mx:TabBar id="myTB" itemClick="clickEvt(event);"
width="90%" dataProvider="{tabArray}"   x="37.5" y="65"/>
```

The tabArray Array will be subsequently created in an <mx:Script> block using the ActionScript syntax and will contain two labels: Code and Preview. Furthermore, on the itemClick event, which is dispatched when you click one of the tabs, the clickEvt() function is called. This function will render part of the interface visible or invisible.

4. Add an HBox with a TextArea immediately under the TabBar. The TextArea will display the content of the HTML file in it and the HTML code. As soon as the file is opened, it will have been read:

```
<mx:HBox id="codeBox" label="Code"
    width="90%" height="349" x="37.5" y="86">
<mx:TextArea id="codeTxt"
width="100%" height="100%" />
</mx:HBox>
```

This will be the first content to be shown when the application is loaded. Obviously, the TextArea control will be empty until a file will be selected by the user.

5. The second Hbox will instead have the <mx:HTML> tag that will wait to receive the focus to be able to display a preview of the HTML page chosen by the user:

```
<mx:HBox id="myBox" visible="false"
width="90%" height="344" x="37.5" y="86">
<mx:HTML id="myHTML" width="100%" height="100%" />
</mx:HBox>
```

The HBox container has its visible property set at false. In fact, at the activation of the application, its content will be hidden. It can be activated by clicking the Preview tab of the TabBar container.

You have created the interface of the application. You can now begin to create the functions and the event handlers necessary to perform the operations.

6. You insert an <mx:Script> block before the declaration of the ApplicationControlBar container, and you begin by importing the necessary classes and creating the private variables that you will use:

```
<mx:Script>
<![CDATA[
import flash.filesystem.*;
import mx.events.*;

private var myFile:File;
private var stream:FileStream = new FileStream();
private var fileToOpen:File = new File();
[Bindable]
private var tabArray:Array= [{label:"Code", data:"code"},
    {label:"Preview", data:"html"}];
```

The first three variables, myFile, Stream, and fileToOpen, will be used to open the file that should then be read. Instead, the tabArray is used as dataProvider for the TabBar container declared in the previous step:

```
<mx:TabBar id="myTB" itemClick="clickEvt(event);"
width="90%" dataProvider="{tabArray}"   x="37.5" y="65"/>
```

The tabArray variable contains two objects that specify the label and code property. These two objects define the number of tabs that will appear in the TabBar.

7. Immediately under the definition of the variables, create the first function that is launched on the applicationComplete of the root tag:

```
private function init():void
{
stage.nativeWindow.width = ➡
Math.min(800, Capabilities.screenResolutionX - 60);
stage.nativeWindow.height = Capabilities.screenResolutionY - 60;
```

14

```
stage.nativeWindow.x = 10;
stage.nativeWindow.y = 10;
stage.nativeWindow.visible = true;
}
```

The role of this function is that of defining the height and width of the window that will be created. These dimensions are calculated based on the screenResolutionY and screenResolutionX properties of the Capabilities class. After having assigned a dimension to the window, you position it by adding its x and y properties, and finally you render the window visible.

8. The user launches the openFile() method by clicking the button with id equal to openBtn. This method has the role of making the dialog box open, as shown in Figure 14-15, and of making the user select a file by navigating in the local file system. When a file is selected, the FILE_CHOOSE event is dispatched. You write this method immediately under the init() function:

```
private function openFile():void
{
fileToOpen.browseForOpen("Open");
fileToOpen.addEventListener(FileEvent.FILE_CHOOSE, openHandler);
}
```

Figure 14-15. The browseForOpen() method is called, and the dialog box is opened to navigate and select the file.

The browseForOpen() method allows users to navigate in a local file system. While with the addEventListener() method, the event handler openHandler for the FILE_CHOOSE event is registered. The FILE_CHOOSE event fires when the user selects a file in the Open dialog box.

9. You'll now write the code that will manage the reading of the file that was selected. The operation of reading is carried out by the FileStream object in asynchronous mode. This mode allows you to register event handlers to monitor the process of reading the file. Under the ActionScript code that you have written up to now, you add the event handler openHandler():

```
private function openHandler(event:Event):void
{
myFile = event.target as File;

stream = new FileStream();
stream.openAsync(myFile, FileMode.READ);

stream.addEventListener(Event.COMPLETE, readHandler);
stream.addEventListener(IOErrorEvent.IO_ERROR, errorHandler);

title = "You opened the  " + myFile.name;
myFile.removeEventListener(Event.FILE_CHOOSE, openHandler);
}
```

The function begins by creating a reference to the File object transported into the target property of the event object. This reference contains the path and the name of the file selected by the user:

```
myFile = event.target as File;
```

Then the FileStream object becomes initialized and its openAsync() method launched with the following parameters:

```
stream.openAsync(myFile, FileMode.READ);
```

The method will open the specified file in the myFile object in read-only mode. The operation is asynchronous, so it requires event listeners:

```
stream.addEventListener(Event.COMPLETE, readHandler);
stream.addEventListener(IOErrorEvent.IO_ERROR, errorHandler);
```

The COMPLETE event is dispatched when the operation of reading is concluded, while the IO_ERROR event is dispatched if errors have occurred in the phase of the reading of the file. In the next step you will define the two event handlers linked to these events.

The openHandler() function finishes by changing the title of the window of the application and removing the event listener on the FILE_CHOOSE event.

10. When the file is ready, the readHandler() function is invoked. This function reads the content of the file as UTF data with the readUTFBytes() method and inserts the results of the reading in the text field codeTxt:

```
private function readHandler(event:Event):void
{
var str:String;
var lineEndPattern:RegExp;
```

14

```
str  = stream.readUTFBytes(stream.bytesAvailable);
stream.close();

lineEndPattern = new RegExp(File.lineEnding, "g");
str = str.replace(lineEndPattern, "\n");

codeTxt.text = str;
}
```

Immediately after reading the file, the FileStream object closes the flow of reading by invoking the close() method. At that point, before inserting the data in the TextArea control, convert the system-specific line ending characters in the data to the "\n" character. To do this, use the replace() method of the String class:

```
str = str.replace(lineEndPattern, "\n");
```

11. The last event listener was invoked if an error occurred in the reading. In this case, write an error message in the TextArea. Add the following function in the <mx:Script> block:

```
private function errorHandler(event:Event):void
{
codeTxt.text  = "An error occurred. The file can't be opened!";
}
```

12. The last function to add to the <mx:Script> block by clicking the tab to change the view of the application. Figure 14-16 shows the two tabs defined by the TabBar container: Code and Preview. Code is opened by default at the startup of the application and displays the code of the opened HTML file. Preview displays the preview of the HTML file interpreted by the HTML engine of AIR runtime. To change views, an event listener is used on the itemClick event of the TabBar.

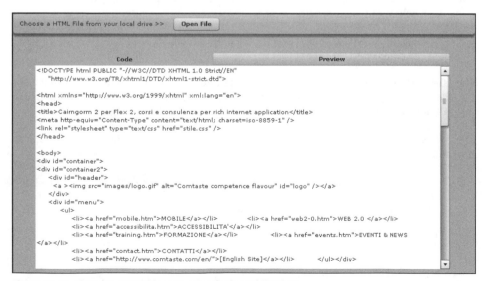

Figure 14-16. TheTabBar provides two tabs: Code and Preview.

Add the clickEvt() function with the following code before the closure of the <mx:Script> tag:

```
private function clickEvt(event:ItemClickEvent):void {

if (event.label == "Preview")
{
var htmlTxt:XML = XML(codeTxt.text);

codeBox.visible = false;
myHTML.htmlText = htmlTxt ;

myBox.visible = true;


} else if (event.label == "Code")
{
myBox.visible = false;
codeBox.visible = true;
}
}

]]>
</mx:Script>
```

This function simply checks which of the two tabs is pressed by accessing the event.label property of the event object. According to the tab pressed, the corresponding contents are rendered visible.

When the user clicks the Preview tab, you must display the preview of the html page loaded in the HTML control. To do this, all you need to do is to cast the code coming from the HTML file and show it in the codeTxt TextArea as an XML object. You then link this XML variable to the htmlText property of the HTML control, and the rest is done for you by the control.

13. Save and run the application.

If you select an HTML file in the local file system, you will see its HTML code represented in the TextArea. If you click the Preview tab, you will see the HTML page as if it were loaded in your Internet browser (see Figure 14-17).

14

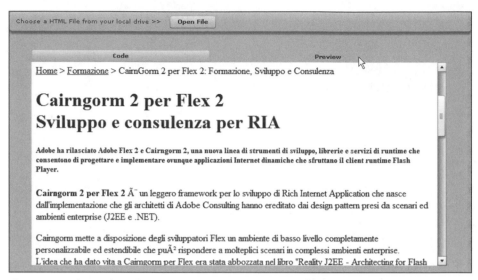

Figure 14-17. The Preview of the page renders the HTML code and shows the page as it would look in a normal web browser.

Expert tips

You can get the same result by using the HTMLControl class and adding HTML content with ActionScript code. To create an HTMLControl object and render it visible on the screen, you must create an instance of the HTMLControl class found in the flash.html package and add it to the window with the addChild() method:

```
import flash.html.HTMLControl
var myHTML:HTMLControl = new HTMLControl();

private function loadHTML(url:String):void
{
var myURL:URLRequest = new URLRequest(url);
myHTML.load(myURL);
myHTML.width = 400;
myHTML.height = 400;
stage.addChild(myHTML);
}
```

It is not possible to add an HTMLControl object as a child of a Flex container in that it does not extend the UIComponent. Therefore, either create a custom class that extends the UIComponent or add it directly to the window.

Solution 14-6: Creating occasionally connected applications

Desktop applications, unlike web applications, must consider and manage the situations in which there is an absence of connectivity. A desktop application must be able to permit the user to also work and interact in a scenario of uncertain and changing connectivity.

Adobe AIR provides an event that advises you when the network status changes: Event.NETWORK_CHANGE. This event is dispatched by the NativeApplication object contained in the flash.desktop.NativeApplication package and communicates to you the change that has occurred. But it does not notify you of the status: online, offline, virtual connection, and so on. Therefore, the only way to be sure whether you have a connection is to try.

To carry out tests of connectivity, Adobe AIR provides a monitoring framework service in the flash.desktop.NativeApplication. The servicemonitor.swc file is automatically included as a library and merged into the code by Flex Builder. An instance of the ServiceMonitor class will dispatch events at every status change of the connectivity. This allows you to check and test whether you are in an online situation. You can also decide to carry out checks at regular intervals by using a property of the ServiceMonitor class. These checks are useful in a situation of scarce or insecure connectivity.

In this solution, you will create a script that can be reused in every application that requires checking of connectivity status.

What's involved

The ServiceMonitor class provides the URLMonitor class that detects changes in connectivity for an HTTP call to a specific URL. Therefore, to test whether the application is in an online state, create an actual instance of the URLMonitor class and make it return the status of the test to you.

To use the URLMonitor class and related events, you must first import the necessary classes:

```
import flash.desktop.NativeApplication;
import flash.net.URLRequest;
import air.net.URLMonitor;
import flash.events.StatusEvent;
```

Create an instance of the URLMonitor class to which an URLRequest object will be sent. The URLMonitor class extends the ServiceMonitor class and has the role of detecting changes in HTTP connectivity for a specified URLRequest. Then you have to register the STATUS event of the StatusEvent class. This event returns the connectivity status of the application:

```
private var checkURL:URLMonitor;
checkURL = new URLMonitor(new URLRequest('http://www.comtaste.com'));
checkURL.addEventListener(StatusEvent.STATUS, statusHandler);
checkURL.start();
```

14

The STATUS event permits you to check whether the attempts to connect have been successful and whether the HTTP call to the URLRequest has been carried out. In this case, the application detects network activity.

In this solution you will create a function that returns the connectivity value and can be used to check the status of AIR applications.

How to build it

In this solution you will create an MXML application file, but you could also create a custom component to reuse across different projects.

1. Create a new MXML application file by selecting File ➤ New ➤ MXML Application and saving it as Chapter_14_Flex_Sol_6.mxml. Create an event listener for the applicationComplete event:

```
<mx:WindowedApplication
xmlns:mx="http://www.adobe.com/2006/mxml"
layout="absolute"
applicationComplete="init()">
```

The event handler init() has the job of assigning the dimensions and positions to the window and of checking the status of connection of the application. To do this, you have to use and import the following:

- The URLMonitor class, which extends the ServiceMonitor class in the air.net package, allows you to carry out an HTTP call and check the response to the status of the network activities

- The URLRequest class in the flash.net package that contains the test URL to use for the URLMonitor call

- The StatusEvent class in the flash.events package to register the event listener on the NETWORK_CHANGE event

- The NativeApplication class, found in the flash.desktop.NativeApplication package, allows an application to detect network change event whenever a network connection becomes available or unavailable.

2. Add an <mx:Script> block under the WindowedApplication tag and import the packages necessary to the application:

```
<mx:Script>
<![CDATA[
import mx.events.*;
import mx.controls.Alert;


import flash.desktop.NativeApplication;
import flash.net.URLRequest;
import air.net.URLMonitor;
import flash.events.StatusEvent;
```

3. Insert the declaration of the variables that you will use in the file under the import of the packages:

```
private var checkURL:URLMonitor;
 [Bindable]
private var isOnline:Boolean;
```

The checkURL variable is data typed as URLMonitor and is the variable that you will use to test the connectivity. The Boolean variable isOnline is returned by the control of the status and contains the true value if a presence of network activity has been found.

4. Insert the init() function immediately under the declaration of the variables. This function assigns dimensions and a position to the window and launches the checks for connectivity:

```
private function init():void
{

stage.nativeWindow.width = ➡
Math.min(800, Capabilities.screenResolutionX - 60);
stage.nativeWindow.height = Capabilities.screenResolutionY - 60;
stage.nativeWindow.x = 10;
stage.nativeWindow.y = 10;
stage.nativeWindow.visible = true;

checkHTTPCon("http://www.comtaste.com");
}
```

The last line of code of the init() function launches the checkHTTPCon() method, to which the string www.comtaste.com is sent as a parameter. The parameter is a valid URL that allows you to test the connection status.

5. Write the checkHTTPCon() function that will use the URLMonitor object to check the connectivity status. You'll break down the following code to comment what each part of the checkHTTPCon() function does:

```
private function checkHTTPCon(myurl:String):void
{
checkURL = new URLMonitor(new URLRequest(myurl));
checkURL.addEventListener(StatusEvent.STATUS, statusHandler)
checkURL.start();
}
```

Send an URLRequest object with the URL to which to connect as a parameter to the constructor of the URLMonitor class:

```
checkURL = new URLMonitor(new URLRequest(myurl));
```

You then register an event listener on the StatusEvent.STATUS event that occurs after the HTTP call has been performed from the URLMonitor and returns a value:

```
checkURL.addEventListener(StatusEvent.STATUS, statusHandler)
```

14

Carry out the remote call of the URLMonitor using the start() method:

```
checkURL.start();
```

The HTTP call is launched, and the STATUS event releases. You must, therefore, define the statusHandler() event handler.

6. The statusHandler() function does nothing more than check the property code of the event object generated by the StatusEvent class. This property contains the Service.available value if the connection is present, so the check was successful. At the end of the last function, close the <mx:Script> block:

```
private function statusHandler(evt:StatusEvent):void
{
if (evt.code == "Service.available")
{
isOnline = true;
} else
{
isOnline = false;
}
}

]]>
</mx:Script>
```

Depending on the response obtained by the property code, the if() condition sets the value of the Boolean variable isOnline as true or false. This variable will be used as data binding in the application and will furnish the information to the user.

7. After the <mx:Script> tag closes, add the only element of the user interface of the application. In an <mx:ApplicationControlBar> tag, insert a Label that communicates the status of the network returned by the check at application startup:

```
<mx:ApplicationControlBar width="100%" x="0" y="0" >
<mx:Label text="You're {isOnline ? 'Online': 'Offline'}"
 fontStyle="italic"  />
</mx:ApplicationControlBar>
</mx:WindowedApplication>
```

The Label control on the text property checks with an if() condition, written in contracted form, if the value of the Boolean variable is isOnline. If it is equal to true, it will write the text "Online". If the value is false instead, it will write "Offline":

```
<mx:Label text="You're {isOnline ? 'Online' : 'Offline'}"
fontStyle="italic"  />
```

8. Save and run the AIR application.

Once the application is opened, the check is performed, and the status is returned. This value appears in the Label of the ApplicationControlBar, as shown in Figure 14-18.

You're Online

Figure 14-18. The connectivity status of the application is displayed by the Label in the ApplicationControlBar.

Expert tips

In this solution, the status of the connection is checked at startup on the init() function, so it permits you to know only whether the startup status of the connection is active.

But what happens if the status of the network changes during the use of the application?

To be able to intercept connectivity changes during the life cycle, you can create an event listener linked to the NETWORK_CHANGE event and registered on the NativeApplication.

You see how to implement this function by slightly changing the solution.

1. Modify the init() function in the <mx:Script> block, adding an addEventListener() on the NativeApplication:

```
import flash.desktop.NativeApplication;
import flash.events.StatusEvent;

private function init():void
{

stage.nativeWindow.width = ➥
Math.min(800, Capabilities.screenResolutionX - 60);
stage.nativeWindow.height = Capabilities.screenResolutionY - 60;
stage.nativeWindow.x = 10;
stage.nativeWindow.y = 10;
stage.nativeWindow.visible = true;
checkHTTPCon("http://www.comtaste.com");
NativeApplication.nativeApplication.addEventListener Â
(Event.NETWORK_CHANGE, networkHandler);
}
```

To be able to create a reference to the NativeApplication you have to make sure to import the flash.desktop package.

The event listener will invoke the networkHandler() function when the Event.NETWORK_CHANGE event is dispatched. It happens when any connectivity changes occur during the application's life cycle.

14

2. There is nothing left to do but write the event handler networkHandler(); it will launch the checkHTTPCon function written in the solution:

```
private function networkHandler():void
{
checkHTTPCon("http://www.comtaste.com");
}
```

3. Save and run the AIR application.

Solution 14-7: Keeping the application updated

A classic web application that the browser loads from a remote server does not have particular problems related to its updating. It is enough to carry out the deployment of the new version of the application on the production server, and any user connecting to the URL of the application will load the new version.

However, this changes drastically for desktop applications. In fact, for desktop applications, managing the upgrade phase is a very delicate process that should be well planned. There are two ways to update the desktop application: furnish the user with an upgrade system that directly launches in the application itself and perhaps connects to the Web to download the updates, or distribute a new software module that contains the updates and install them locally. Many applications that you have installed on your computer use one or the other of these systems.

The AIR application is an application that is installed locally on the computer and is run within the AIR runtime. To update a new version of the application, you can follow two roads. The first and most popular is to create a new AIR file that contains an updated version of the application the user has installed. The second is to program the application so it searches for a new version to autoupdate. To update an AIR application programmatically, use the Updater class that (with the update() method) permits you to point to an AIR file on the user's computer and update it. The AIR file to which the update() method points must be located on the user's computer, but can be programmatically downloaded and saved from a remote server.

In this solution you will see how to use the Updater class to program the updating of an AIR application.

What's involved

The Updater class, contained in the flash.desktop package, allows you to use the update() method to install new versions of the application that is loading.

When the update() method is called, the runtime checks that the application ID specified in the AIR file corresponds to the application ID of the application that is calling the update() method and that the version strings correspond. The version string is a parameter that is sent to the update() method and is compared with the version string found in the application element specified in the AIR descriptor file.

The first tag of the AIR descriptor file is the <mx:Application> tag that specifies exactly how the version string is attributed:

```
<application xmlns="http://ns.adobe.com/air/application/1.0.M4"
appId="myAIRApp"
version="1.0 ">
```

This string can be declared in any valid string format. For example, this format:

version="Version #1"

Or this format:

version="1.0.0.1"

Or this format:

version="My 1 version"

To use the update() method, it is necessary to first create an instance of the Updater class:

```
private var myUpdater:Updater = new Updater();

private var appFile:File;

appFile = File.documentsDirectory;
appFile = appFile.resolvePath("myAIRapp.air");

myUpdater.update(appFile, "1.0.2");
```

The update() method accepts two parameters:

- airFile: A file object that contains the reference to the air file of the application
- version: The version string that will be compared with the version string of the application

In this solution, you will see how to implement a system of updating an application with the Updater class.

How to build it

The Updater class, contained in the flash.desktop package, allows you (by using the update() method) to install new versions of the application that is loading.

1. Create a new MXML application file by selecting File ➤ New ➤ MXML Application and save it as Chapter_14_Flex_Sol_7.mxml.

14

2. Add an <mx:Script> block and import the ActionScript classes you'll need for this solution:

```
<?xml version="1.0" encoding="utf-8"?>
<mx:WindowedApplication
xmlns:mx="http://www.adobe.com/2006/mxml"
layout="vertical">

<mx:Script>
<![CDATA[

import flash.filesystem.File;
import flash.filesystem.FileMode;
import flash.filesystem.FileStream;
import flash.net.URLRequest;
import flash.net.URLStream;
import flash.desktop.Updater;
```

The last class imported, the Updater class, is used with the update() method to update the application with a new version.

3. After importing the ActionScript classes, create an instance of the Updater class, a URLRequest object that contains the URL from which to load the updated AIR application and the class to read a file. Add the following code below the import statements:

```
private var myUpdater:Updater = new Updater();
private var appFile:File = new File();
private var myURL:URLRequest = ➡
new URLRequest("http://www.comtaste.com/myAIRApp_ver2.air");
private var myStream:URLStream = new URLStream();
private var fileByteArray:ByteArray = new ByteArray();
]]>

</mx:Script>
```

The URLRequest object contains the URL that points to an updated version of the AIR application. In the solution, the URL is www.comtaste.com/myAIRApp_ver2.air, but you can put the updated AIR application wherever you want.

4. The AIR application is made up of a simple Button control that invokes an event handler on its click event. The event handler will be responsible to start the updating process and check whether a newer version of the application exists. After the closure of the <mx:Script> block, add the following MXML code:

```
</mx:Script>


<mx:ApplicationControlBar width="100%" x="0" y="0" >
<mx:Label text="This is the Version 1.0 of my Application"
```

```
<mx:Button label="Check for Update" click="checkUpdate()" />

</mx:ApplicationControlBar>
</mx:WindowedApplication>
```

The checkUpdate() method will be invoked on the click event of the Button. This event handler will download the new application and notify it of the version being downloaded.

5. Add the checkUpdate() event handler in the <mx:Script> block below the instance declaration:

```
private var myStream:URLStream = new URLStream();
private var fileByteArray:ByteArray = new ByteArray();

private function checkUpdate():void
{

myStream.addEventListener(Event.COMPLETE, completeHandler);
myStream.load(myURL);

}
```

The checkUpdate() method loads the AIR application contained in the myURL variable. It uses the load() method of the URLStream class. Then an event handler is registered for the COMPLETE event. In the next step you'll write the completeHandler() method that will read the myAIRApp_saved_ver2.air and save it locally. In fact, to use the update() method, you must save the AIR file to the local machine.

6. Write the completeHandler() event handler below the checkUpdate() method:

```
private function completeHandler(evt:Event):void
{

myStream.readBytes(fileByteArray, 0, myStream.bytesAvailable);

writeFile();

}

private function writeFile():void
{
var tempFile:File = ➡
File.desktopDirectory.resolvePath("myAIRApp_saved_ver2.air");
var myStream:FileStream = new FileStream();

myStream.openAsync(tempFile,FileMode.WRITE);

myStream.writeBytes(fileByteArray,0,fileByteArray.length);
myStream.addEventListener(Event.CLOSE,writeComplete);
myStream.close();
}
```

14

```
private function writeComplete(evt:Event):void
{

appFile = File.desktopDirectory;
appFile = appFile.resolvePath("myAIRApp_saved_ver2.air");

myUpdater.update(appFile, "1.0");
}

]]>
</mx:Script>
```

After reading and locally saving the myAIRApp_saved_ver2.air application, the update() method is invoked within the writeComplete() method. The update() method accepts two arguments: the AIR application and the version string to compare. In the solution update() method checks whether the user has a version of the AIR file located on the desktop and compares the version string specified as the parameter of the update() method.

7. Save and run the application.

The code of the myAIRApp_saved_ver2.air application is very simple; it has a Label control with some text:

```
<?xml version="1.0" encoding="utf-8"?>
<mx:WindowedApplication
xmlns:mx="http://www.adobe.com/2006/mxml" layout="vertical">
<mx:ApplicationControlBar width="100%" x="0" y="0" >

<mx:Label text="This is the Version 2.0 of my Application"
 fontStyle="italic"  />

</mx:ApplicationControlBar>
</mx:WindowedApplication>
```

The update() method will check and match the version string defined in the AIR descriptor files of the two applications. If you open Chapter_14_Flex_Sol_7_ver2-app.xml, you'll see the version attribute declared on the first node:

```
<application
xmlns="http://ns.adobe.com/air/application/1.0.M4"
appId="Chapter-14-Flex-Sol-7-ver2"
version="2.0">
```

In Chapter_14_Flex_Sol_7-app.xml, the version attribute is as follows:

```
<application
xmlns="http://ns.adobe.com/air/application/1.0.M4"
appId="Chapter-14-Flex-Sol-7"
version="1.0">
```

Expert tips

When an AIR application is installed on the user's machine, AIR offers an installation window, as shown in Figure 14-19. The installation window is displayed the first time that the application is installed. For the updates, you can define a custom application user interface by specifying the handleUpdates element in the AIR descriptor file:

```
<!--
        If the handleUpdates element is present in the application
descriptor,
        then the AIR runtime will defer version updates to this
application.
-->
<!-- <handleUpdates/> -->
```

In this element, you can specify the graphic interface to be used as an alternative to the default Application Install window, shown in Figure 14-19.

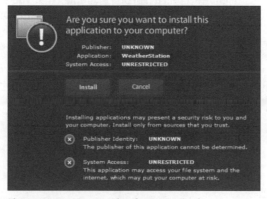

Figure 14-19. An example of a customized AIR Application Install window

When the handleUpdates element is used, and the user double-clicks the AIR file for a new version, the Adobe integrated runtime opens the installed version of the application instead of the default AIR application installer. So you can handle the update operations inside the AIR application.

Summary

Adobe AIR is a cross-platform runtime that permits the developer to port RIAs for the Web (using Flash, Flex, HTML, JavaScript, and Ajax) onto the desktop. The objective of the Adobe AIR project is to bring web applications from the Web to the desktop in a way that merges the best characteristics of both worlds for developers.

14

Flex Builder 3 permits you to export applications in Adobe AIR format. In this chapter you learned how to create an AIR project and take advantage of the features of AIR to do the following:

- Export Flex applications to the desktop
- Customize the window using the Window API
- Access the file system
- Read and write persistent data on the local file system
- Embed HTML pages in your application
- Develop occasionally connected applications
- Detect network connectivity
- Keep the application updated with the Updater class

You've now reached the end of the book. As you now understand, Adobe Flex is a huge framework that gives developers a lot of possibilities to create attractive RIAs. The aim of this book was to dive straight into practical code examples that you could build via step-by-step tutorials and plug straight in to your own code, saving you hours of development time.

Flex is changing the way RIAs are developed, and you are part of that change.

One last piece of advice: practice, practice, and experiment. It will make you a perfect Flex developer.

INDEX

Symbols

+= operator, 410
@ symbol, syntax of, 121

A

absolute positioning
    definition of, 465
    list of supporting containers, 465
acceptDragDrop(), 368
access modifiers, 61
access property, 290
accessible compiler option, 398
Accordion container
    adding Button controls for navigating panels, 470
    code example with three child panels, 468, 473
    defining a sequence of collapsible containers, 468
    defining the label properties used as titles, 470
    forcing positioning at the center of a page, 473
    inserting a Canvas container with a Form inside, 474
    <mx:Accordion>, 468
    numChildren property, 470
    resizeEffect property, 476
    selectedChild property, 470
    selectedIndex property, 470, 475
Action Message Format (AMF), 241
action property, 366
Actions panel, 577
ActionScript
    access modifiers, 61
    ActionScript 3.0 and the ECMA Script 262 standard, 2
    applying a drop shadow effect, 517
    applying a validation using validate(), 172
    applyProgrammaticSkin(), 513
    .as extension, 71
    beginFill(), 512, 515
    Book.as class, code example, 130
    CanvasSkin class, 515
    CanvasSkin.as, 514
    ClassReference, 515–516
    clear(), 512
    compiling ActionScript classes into SWF files, 2
    converting an MXML data model into an ActionScript object, 140
    converting an MXML data model using an ArrayCollection, 204
    creating a subclass of the ProgrammaticSkin class, 509
    creating an ActionScript class, 13, 41, 67, 83, 127, 181
    creating custom Event classes, 94
    creating programmatic skins, 509
    customizing error messages in, 161
    declaring the BindingUtils class, 23
    defining the ActionScript data model, 126, 129
    defining typed properties, 128

drawing a rounded rectangle, 512, 514
drawing a substitute skin, 511
drawing API, 505, 508, 511
drawRoundRectComplex(), 512, 514
DropShadowFilter class, 517
[Embed] metadata, 529
extending a class in, 68
extending Flex controls with, 12
flash.display.Graphics, 505, 512
flashPlayer ArrayCollection variable, 64–65
getStyle(), 515
Graphics class, 509, 514
importing and extending the ComboBox class, 14
inserting a TextInput for mobile telephone numbers, 161
instancing an ActionScript class, 128, 131
internal access modifier, 61
lineStyle(), 512
mapping a PHP value object to an ActionScript value object, 307
<mx:Script> block, 61–62, 64, 80, 91
MySkin.as, 509, 517
New ActionScript Class dialog, 14, 43, 509, 514
organizing files with .as extensions, 33
packages, 41, 127
private and public access modifiers, 61
procedure for declaring properties, 61
procedure for defining a method, 61
programmatic skins, definition of, 505
protected access modifier, 61
RectangularBorder class, 514
registering event handler functions with addEventListener(), 38
regular expressions, definition of, 179
static access modifier, 61
StyleManager class, 10
switch(), 508, 511
triggerEvent property, 164
updateDisplayList(), 510–511, 514
using to apply styles, 10
validating data using ActionScript 3.0, 160
var keyword, 61
See also Flex; Flex Builder
ActionScript components
    .as extension, 71
    comparing MXML and ActionScript components, 56, 67
    composite components, definition of, 82
    composite components, invoking, 87
    creating, 67
    creating an ActionScript class that extends a ComboBox class, 69
    creating an ActionScript class that extends a UIComponent class, 83
    developing a simple blog reader, 95